MAKING ORGANIZATIONS HUMANE AND PRODUCTIVE

MAKING ORGANIZATIONS HUMANE AND PRODUCTIVE: A HANDBOOK FOR PRACTITIONERS

Edited by

H. MELTZER
Washington University
Psychological Service Center
St. Louis, Missouri

WALTER R. NORD
Washington University
St. Louis, Missouri

A Wiley-Interscience Publication
JOHN WILEY & SONS
New York Chichester Brisbane Toronto

This publication is designed to provide accurate and authoritative information in regard to the subject matter covered. It is sold with the understanding that the publisher is not engaged in rendering legal, accounting, or other professional service. If legal advice or other expert assistance is required, the services of a competent professional person should be sought. *From a Declaration of Principles jointly adopted by a Committee of the American Bar Association and a Committee of Publishers.*

Library of Congress Cataloging in Publication Data:

Main entry under title:
Making organizations humane and productive.

"A Wiley-Interscience publication."
Includes index.
1. Organizational behavior—Handbooks, manuals, etc. 2. Personnel management—Handbooks, manuals, etc. 3. Organizational change—Handbooks, manuals, etc. I. Meltzer, Hyman, 1899- II. Nord, Walter R.
HD58.7.M34 658.4 81-7590
ISBN 0-471-07813-1 AACR2

Printed in the United States of America

10 9 8 7 6 5 4 3 2 1

If all good people were clever
And those that are clever were good,
This world would be nicer than ever,
We dream that it possibly could.

But it seems as though seldom, if ever,
Do the two hit it off as they should,
The good are so harsh to the clever,
The clever so rude to the good.

— Alfred North Whitehead's *Dialogues*

". . . to be not merchants of
dead yesterdays but guides
into untold tomorrows."

— Glenn Frank

CONTRIBUTORS

Clayton Alderfer, Ph.D.
Professor and Director of Advanced Management Studies
School of Organization and Management
Yale University
New Haven, Connecticut

Eugene Andrews, Ph.D.
Lieutenant Colonel, U.S. Army
Department of Behavioral Sciences and Leadership
U.S. Military Academy, West Point

Kenneth Ball, Ph.D.
President of Orchard Corporation of America
St. Louis, Missouri

Richard W. Beatty, Ph.D.
Professor of Organizational Behavior
University of Colorado
Boulder, Colorado

James W. Driscoll, Ph.D.
Assistant Professor
Sloan School of Management
Massachusetts Institute of Technology
Cambridge, Massachusetts

Raymond A. Ehrle, Ed.D.
Adjunct Professor
George Washington University
Washington, D.C.

Eli Ginzberg, Ph.D.
Director of the Conservation of Human Resources Project
Columbia University
New York, New York

Irwin L. Goldstein, Ph.D.
Professor and Director of Graduate Studies in Psychology
University of Maryland
College Park, Maryland

Gloria Gordon, Ph.D.
Division of Environmental Sciences
Columbia University
New York, New York

Donald L. Grant, Ph.D.
Professor of Psychology
University of Georgia
Athens, Georgia

Barbara Gray Gricar, Ph.D.
Assistant Professor of Organizational Behavior
Pennsylvania State University
University Park, Pennsylvania

J. Richard Hackman, Ph.D.
Professor of Organization and Management
Yale University
New Haven, Connecticut

Douglas T. Hall, Ph.D.
Professor of Organizational Behavior
Boston University
Boston, Massachusetts

Mary S. Henifin, M.P.H.
Division of Environmental Sciences
Columbia University
New York, New York

Madison W. Holloway, Ph.D.
Assistant Professor
University of Colorado
Boulder, Colorado

John M. Ivancevich, Ph.D.
Professor of Organizational Behavior
University of Houston
Houston, Texas

R. Stephen Jenks, Ph.D.
Adjunct Professor of Organizational Behavior
University of New Hampshire
Durham, New Hampshire

H. Russell Johnston, Ph.D.
Managing Director
Management Analysis Center
Caracas, Venezuela

Raymond A. Katzell, Ph.D
Professor of Psychology
New York University
New York, New York

Harry Levinson, Ph.D.
President of The Levinson Institute
Cambridge, Massachusetts

Ronald Lippitt, Ph.D.
Professor Emeritus of Psychology and Sociology
University of Michigan
Ann Arbor, Michigan

William H. Macey, Ph.D.
President of Personnel Research Associates, Inc.
Des Plaines, Illinois

H. Meltzer, Ph.D.
Professor of Organizational Psychology
Washington University
St. Louis, Missouri

Herbert H. Meyer, Ph.D.
Professor of Organizational Psychology
University of South Florida
Tampa, Florida

Henry Mintzberg, Ph.D.
Professor of Management Policy
McGill University
Montreal, Quebec

Walter R. Nord, Ph.D.
Professor of Organizational Behavior
Washington University
St. Louis, Missouri

Craig C. Pinder, Ph.D.
Associate Professor of Organizational Behavior
University of British Columbia
Vancouver, British Columbia

Patrick R. Pinto, Ph.D.
Associate Professor of Industrial Relations and Psychology
University of Minnesota
Minneapolis, Minnesota

David J. Pittman, Ph.D.
Chairman and Professor of Sociology
Washington University
St. Louis, Missouri

Erich P. Prien, Ph.D.
Professor of Organizational Psychology
Memphis State University
Memphis, Tennessee

Craig Eric Schneier, Ph.D.
Associate Professor of Organizational Behavior and Personnel Administration
University of Maryland
College Park, Maryland

Arthur Shulman, Ph.D.
Associate Professor of Social Psychology
Washington University
St. Louis, Missouri

Thomas E. Standing, Ph.D.

Manager of Management Resources
The Standard Oil Company (Ohio)
Cleveland, Ohio

Ronald N. Taylor, Ph.D.

Associate Professor of Organizational Behavior
University of British Columbia
Vancouver, British Columbia

Sharon Tucker, Ph.D.

Assistant Professor of Organizational Behavior
Washington University
St. Louis, Missouri

PREFACE

This book, as the title indicates, was designed to present organizational behavior knowledge for use by practitioners — executives, supervisors, and managers. The book should also be useful as a source book in graduate and advanced undergraduate courses dealing with human resources.

The book begins with a brief introductory chapter in which we attempt to set a context for considering the achievement of two sets of results — productivity and humaneness. The major topics in the book fall quite naturally into three parts. Each part contains papers by an authority on the topic and concludes with a response to the papers by a leading practitioner.

Part I is intended to provide an overview of knowledge on major managerial processes. Topics included are selection and appraisal; training for development; attitudes and motivation; communication and organizational dynamics; leadership and stress management; management and compensation; making supervision humane and productive; configurations of organizational structure; and planning and decision making in managing organizations. These papers were not designed to be comprehensive reviews of the literature. Rather the contributions consider the key concepts and research and concentrate on presenting this knowledge in a way that is useful to managers. All of the contributions in Part I are appraised by Dr. Russ Johnston.

Part II considers some of the many realities that confront organizations in the 1980s. Included are minorities, women, aging realities, opportunities for the handicapped, alcohol and other substance abuse, mobility and transfer, modernizing unions and union leadership, health, safety, shift time, and job stress. While these issues are often seen by managements as "problems," the contributors successfully show how these problem areas also contain opportunities to achieve productivity through humaneness. All of the contributions in Part II are appraised by Dr. Kenneth Ball, President of the Orchard Corporation of America.

Part III, "Innovation for Organization Development and Change," is devoted mostly to the consideration of how to make managing organizations humane and productive. Topics include organization diagnosis for development and change, work redesign, organizational development, career development, organizational collaboration, humanizing technology, effective settings for making organizations humane and productive, workers and work, some transatlantic perceptions, and humanizing planned change. Although these chapters are future oriented, some deal with topics that already are part of progressive management. All of the contributions in Part III are appraised by Thomas Standing from Standard Oil of Ohio.

The editors decided on the content of the book and which contributors to invite as a result of years of experience, including the chairing of symposia by the senior editor at the APA meetings sponsored by the Consulting Psychology Division and co-sponsored by the Industrial Organizational Division. Some of the symposia related to the present theme are Clinical Psychology in Industry: A Needed Revolution; Social Psychology in Industry: A Needed Revolution; Humanizing Organizational Behavior; Organizational Behavior in the New Economic Order; Vulgarizing, Popularizing, and Humanizing Organizational Behavior; and the Human Comedy in Managing Organizations. The actual writing of the book was instigated by Robert Lawless, at the time an editor for the Wiley-Interscience Division. After reading Meltzer's review of Seymour Saranson's book on *Work, Aging and Social Change,* he inquired about the possibilities of developing a book that would present knowledge in the field of organizational psychology in a more useful form to managers than other books. Lawless left Wiley-Interscience after the acceptance of our proposal and much of the development work was done with the help of his successor, Jerry Papke. Finally, the book was guided to completion by John Mahaney. We want to express our appreciation to all three of these men and particularly to Mr. Mahaney who had to see the book through to the end with us.

We have received much help from other people. We are indebted to the American Psychological Association for their permission to reprint large portions of several articles, which had appeared in a recent issue of *Professional Psychology,* co-edited by Dr. H. Meltzer and Dr. Ross Stagner. These articles reflect the keen editorial insights of Dr. Stagner. In addition we thank all our contributors whose hard work and prompt and thoughtful responses to our requests made this book possible. Also we thank Mrs. Ruth Sheetz for her special typing assistance. Finally, deserving of special appreciation is Ms. Beverly Swendsen for follow-up correspondence with the contributors and the publisher, and Wesley Gilliland, who is a graduate student at Washington University and assistant to Dr. Meltzer, for help in the preparation of the final manuscript.

H. MELTZER
WALTER NORD

St. Louis, Missouri
July 1981

CONTENTS

MAKING ORGANIZATIONS HUMANE AND PRODUCTIVE

—Introduction—

Skeptical Optimism and the Quest for Humane and Productive Organizations

Can organizations be made humane and productive? Some developments of the last several decades suggest that they can. For example, compared with conditions at the start of the 1950s:

1. More relevant knowledge is available for use and there are more trained professionals to contribute to knowledge in the making.
2. There are more knowledgeable consultants who are experienced in organization development and change, and many more are being trained.
3. A growing number of managers and executives are discovering that methods that seemed to work in the past are alienating the present generation of workers. Growth in the professionalization of management (through a variety of avenues such as training in schools of business) has prepared managers to draw on available knowledge. Confronted with the need for considering new approaches, these managers are willing to experiment and to acquire new knowledge, skills, and attitudes.
4. A growing number of procedures exists for translating knowledge into a form that can be applied by practitioners, and experience with these procedures has yielded many lessons and dispelled many myths about their implementation.
5. Some evidence suggests that Americans find their needs well met by their work the way it now is.

Consider each of these developments in a bit more depth.

Growth of Knowledge. The past few decades have witnessed the development of a new interdisciplinary field known as organizational behavior. Organizational behavior has drawn on a variety of academic fields. Beginning primarily with psychology and to a lesser degree sociology, the field now incorporates knowledge and methodologies from economics, political science, management, anthropology, and to a lesser extent history and philosophy. Seldom are these various approaches well integrated, but their relevance for understanding organizations is generally acknowledged.

The growth—both in scope and research, if not actual knowledge—of this field can be shown by examining the development and utilization of professional journals. In 1950 two major journals, *The Journal of Applied Psychology* and *Personnel Psychology*, accounted for 59 percent of the citations made in leading reviews of advances in knowledge. By 1970 these two journals accounted for only 12 percent of such citations. A number of new journals had been founded, and scholars were both publishing in and drawing on previously established journals. While traditional topics such as motivation, selection, training, and supervision continued to be central concerns, matters such as organization structure, technology, and organizational environment came to receive greater attention. Moreover, older concerns began to be considered under new headings such as job enrichment, organization development, and quality of work life.

Increased Numbers of Consultants and Teachers. Beginning in the late 1950s and 1960s business schools hired large numbers of behavioral scientists. Traditional personnel, human relations, and management courses came to include far more psychology and sociology than they had in the past. A new group of doctorally trained people, usually called organizational behaviorists, were being turned out. These people, in combination with the flow of applied social scientists (psychologists in particular), became the source of a large supply of professionals to train managers and to help organizations deal with the variety of problems they were facing, including motivation and control, communication, and employment of a culturally diverse work force.

Management Awareness of Needs for New Methods. A number of factors seem to have contributed to managers developing an awareness of the need for new methods for managing human resources. Several early developments played a part, and by 1950 organizations were quite different than they had been earlier in the century when classical management theory had developed. The 1920s had witnessed a great consolidation of organizations. Dominant firms were now larger and more complex than they had been in the past. Professional managers were gradually replacing the captains of industry. The work force had become more disciplined to formal organizations, better educated, and more unionized. In addition to these general trends, three people from the academic community provided the foundation on which the developments in human resources management would rest. The first of these was the work of Elton Mayo (1), which emphasized the need for displacing an attitude of futile planlessness, and the need for replacing what he called "the seamy side of human progress" with human understanding. In the 1920s and early 1930s psychology had little to contribute; psychologists were busy studying employment tests, fatigue, and vision. It was Mayo who came into the field of human relations in industry, with a background of knowledge of Freud for understanding maldeveloped people and Piaget for understanding undeveloped people. This was his way of contributing to what he referred to as the human problems in industrial civilization. His pioneering work included the well-known Western Electric studies of Roethlisberger and Dickson (2). Mayo's discovery of work groups merged in the group dynamics started by Kurt-Lewin, to produce new training and techniques and new ways of analyzing human relations in offices and factories. Lewin's work itself constituted another major development. Out of his theoretical and empirical work grew a series of developments including participative leadership, group dynamics (and T-groups), and strategies for introducing change.

The third person to contribute to human resources management was Douglas McGregor. McGregor published the *Human Side of Enterprise* (3) in 1960. His exposition of the traditional Theory X view of management and the more humanistically oriented Theory Y approach provided a simple set of labels that were useful in sensitizing managers to the assumptions about human beings that were involved in different management strategies. Moreover, by linking Theory Y assumptions to specific things managers could do (e.g., MBO, job enlargement, the Scanlon Plan) McGregor was able to communicate the implications of his philosophy in concrete terms.

By focusing on the work of Mayo, Lewin, and McGregor, we have omitted the contributions of a number of other important people. Writers such as Drucker, Argyris, Likert, Herzberg, and many others all were instrumental in providing a set of concepts that were presented to managers and to students. They have developed a common theme—that productivity and humaneness were mutually supportive and that in fact management based on humane processes was often more productive than management based on more traditional, authoritarian assumptions.

These newer approaches received impetus from a variety of perceived changes in the environment. As educational levels increased, organizations were assumed to require greater flexibility to deal with rapidly changing environments, and affluence made it appear that "lower level" human needs were satisfied and hence less useful as levers for motivating workers. Managers appeared to have much to gain from the newer approaches.

Growth in Procedures for Making Knowledge Useful. In the previous section several sets of procedures for introducing the new humane approach were noted. Through time this list has grown. While MBO has been the most widely employed, a number of others have attracted considerable attention. Job enrichment, the managerial grid, System 4, team building, and quality of work life are but a few of these programs. Although each of these terms is an umbrella for a wide variety of actions, they are all knowledge-based alternatives that modern organization behavior offers to managers for designing organizations that are simultaneously humane and productive.

In addition to these somewhat special procedures, we also have a great deal of knowledge about more traditional functions such as selecting, training, communicating, and compensating, which suggests other ways of combining productivity and humaneness. Much of this book is addressed to these more traditional functions, which receive less attention in the popular media but which provide considerable opportunity for achieving these objectives together.

Life and Work Satisfaction. We believe that much can be done to improve the quality of life, at work as well as outside the work place. However, there is considerable evidence that a large segment of the population feels that they are reasonably well off. Based on extensive interviews with 2200 adults Flanagan (4) concluded "that most of the adults in this country report that their needs and wants are well met in the areas most important to their quality of life" (p. 142). One of these areas was work, in which about 75 percent of adults at all ages reported that their needs were well met. In another extensive study, conducted in 1977, Quinn and Staines (5) asked individuals to say whether they were "very satisfied," "somewhat satisfied," "not too satisfied," or "not at all satisfied" with their job. Of those surveyed, 46.7 percent said they were very satisfied; another 41.7 percent said they were somewhat satisfied. When asked to rate their general life satisfaction 26.6 percent said they were very happy and 64.7 percent said they were fairly happy. Similarly, 14.7 percent said they found their life completely satisfying, and 74.6 percent said they found their life fairly satisfying. Although these data are subject to a number of alternative interpretations, they do suggest that many people feel their central needs are being met at work and elsewhere.

These five developments give us good reason to be optimistic about the possibility for combining humaneness and productivity. We have considerable knowledge. Much of this knowledge has been translated for use, and a large pool of talent is devoted to making more knowledge and translating it for use. However, this optimism must be tempered when other factors are considered. In particular when we examine the concepts of humaneness and productivity, as we do below, and consider how ineffective human beings often are in applying knowledge, pessimism seems more realistic than does optimism. The challenge is to improve application by having managers more adequately trained.

THE CONCEPTS OF HUMANENESS AND PRODUCTIVITY

The dictionary suggests that humaneness involves kindness, benevolence, and the moral qualities of human beings. Productivity involves being effective in bringing things about, particularly in abundance. To what degree can organizations possess both sets of qualities simultaneously? To what degree do the two imply conflicting objectives?

Answers to these questions are more complex than they often seem. For example, the question of "humane for whom?" is seldom raised. Results or processes that are humane for one group may not be humane for others. Similarly, we could ask, humane when? Now? In the long run? In the hereafter? Similar questions can be raised about productivity: When does abundance occur? When, to whom, and by what process are the fruits of abundance distributed? Who pays the costs and by what process are these costs allocated? We are not prepared to answer these questions in any abstract way. Our purpose in raising them is to point out the need to examine the terms humane and productive in more depth.

These two concepts share some basic similarities. First, they both appear to be desirable outcomes; most people would say more of each is better than less. Second, it appears that greater knowledge about all aspects of human existence should be useful in helping us achieve both sets of outcomes. Thus science and other forms of inquiry for advancing knowledge can be justified by appeal to either or to both sets of goals. Third, the terms are vague in the sense that they are more like "packages" than "concepts" (6). Although productivity is more precise and less dependent on value judgments than humaneness, as we will show below, even the term productive can include a variety of possible states. (For example, consider the inevitable tradeoff between quality and quantity.) Fourth, the above three characteristics of these terms mean that they are often used as political tools. Since they connote desirable yet vague results, and since paths to achieve each can be supported by creditable knowledge, they can be employed as "motherhood" phrases, to garner support for a wide variety of interests and agendas. As with other motherhood phrases, the terms come to obscure meaningful analysis; they invoke emotional support for a particular course of action and counter opposition. In short, a major similarity between the two terms is their vulnerability to becoming hollow.

Despite these important similarities there is a key difference between these two concepts, which, at least in our society, seems to result in a bias towards opting for productivity over humaneness when decisions are made. Generally productivity refers to results that are often tangible and measurable and that are apparent in the short run. In contrast, humaneness refers more to processes—to how things are done. Usually process considerations involve variables that are intangible and difficult to measure, and whose consequences are observable only over time, if they are observable at all. Since decision makers often attach greater weight to variables whose effects are easily measurable and quantifiable and opt for short run over long run benefits, productivity often appears to win out when increased humaneness would require decreased productivity.

Fortunately, the two objectives are not always in conflict with each other. Their relationship is much more complex. This complexity can be portrayed by considering two levels of outcomes—micro and macro.

At the micro level, the level of the individual firm, productivity and humaneness are often mutually supportive. Clealy productivity is a necessary condition for humaneness. If the firm is not productive enough to survive, its humaneness ceases to be a relevant issue. Moreover, since many efforts to foster humaneness involve direct costs, productivity is necessary to achieve slack resources, which can be allocated to achieving the humane outcomes. On the other hand, it often seems that productivity can be increased by inhumane processes (e.g., sweatshop conditions or coercion). In a free society if any labor is needed, it is clear that some humaneness is necessary for productivity, yet the relationship of the two goals above this minimum is far from clear. Although there is considerable evidence—much of which is discussed by the authors of the chapters in this volume—that above this minimal level increments of humaneness can lead to increased productivity, the "humaneness is a necessary condition for productivity" argument is as difficult to support convincingly as the "productivity is a necessary condition for humaneness" argument. Consequently productivity often is seen to be the logically prior and practically more important. Moreover, as suggested above, given the measurability of productivity and the fact that organization participants are often more apt to be rewarded for achieving fairly short-term rather than long-term goals, when the achievement of humaneness involves substantial risks in productivity, it is unlikely that the risky path will be taken. Thus, despite some mutualities of the two goals at the microlevel, decision makers are apt to consider productivity first.

At the macrolevel, the level of society as a whole, one can see similar mutualities but also see the need for tradeoffs and for a bias towards productivity. Again productivity is a necessary condition for humaneness; some degree of efficiency in the transformation of resources into goods and services is necessary for satisfying human needs. However, beyond this simple level, the interrelationships are more difficult to unravel. For one thing, it is not clear that all products are equally humane. Some products may be harmful to the users and even to nonusers. Similarly, some production processes have more costly "externalities" (e.g., pollution) than others. Finally, productivity by itself does not solve the distribution problem. While productivity has the humane benefit of making it easier to solve competing needs simultaneously, increases in productivity may be distributed in ways that, depending on one's values, may be more or less humane. Finally, as at the microlevel, actions designed to increase productivity may be experienced as nonhumane by those whose lives are directly affected by the changes. For example, improvements in productivity through technological change may require what economists call "short run" dislocations in the labor market. Almost without exception the people who are dislocated do not experience the process as a humane one. Investments in productivity make it possible for the society of the future to be more humane. However, those who make or are forced to make the investment often experience far less enjoyment and humaneness than they would have if such investments had not been made.

In sum, humaneness and productivity are related to each other in a complex way. Sometimes the two objectives are mutually supportive; at other times they are mutually exclusive. Answers to the question "can organizations be both humane and productive?" must always specify the domain over which they apply in terms of who benefits, who pays, when do the consequences occur, and what processes are used to determine these choices. Discussions of these issues may be beneficial if the protagonists keep in mind one key difference between productivity and humaneness, that productivity can often be measured as a rather concrete set of results, whereas humaneness is much more likely to be a characteristic of a process that, at least given current technology, is very difficult to define precisely, much less measure as validly as we can measure productivity.

In short, humaneness and productivity can be achieved simultaneously, but only under favorable circumstances. Consequently, just as it seemed reasonable to be optimistic, it also seems reasonable to be skeptical about the chances for designing organizations that are both humane and productive.

WISDOM LAG IN APPLYING KNOWLEDGE

There is yet another reason for being skeptical about the likelihood of having organizations that are humane and productive. There is a long lag between invention or discovery and the acceptance and actual utilization of knowledge. For example, the heart pacemaker was first conceptualized in 1928; it was first used in 1960. Similarly, input-output economic analysis was conceived in 1936; it was first applied in 1964. Likewise, it took 25 years to turn hybrid corn from concept into realization, and 19 years to do the same for hybrid small grains (7). Numerous other examples could be cited, to make the point that knowledge by itself does not ensure intelligent action. Although a great deal of effort has been devoted to explaining this lag, it is only imperfectly understood. What we seem to be lacking as a society is an intangible quality that some leading thinkers have termed "wisdom."

Knowledge about the impact of the cultural lag in organizations and in human behavior in general has been available ever since Ogburn considered the concept in his book *Social Change* (8). More recently, a number of people including Ogburn have talked about the wisdom lag as even more dangerous than the cultural lag as a barrier to healthy growth in organizations or human behavior. In their conclusions, they call our attention to the important fact too often not considered, that knowledge is not wisdom if not implemented in action.

An outstanding illustration of a wisdom lag is one related to the energy crisis that we are experiencing and have been hearing so much about. In 1952 President Truman appointed a commission of scientists to study the problem; the results were published in five volumes called *The Resources For Freedom* (9). For our present purpose, it is enough to give a brief quote from Truman's transmittal letter, which is included in each volume:

> In more than 70 specific recommendations the Commission points out the actions which, in its judgment, will best assure the mounting supplies of materials and energy which our economic progress and security will require in the next quarter century. It is my hope that this report and the actions which may be taken as a result of it will contribute significantly to the improvement of this nation's materials position and to the strengthening of the free world's economic security, both of which are the continuing objectives of the United States policy.

No actions were taken and no results followed of any consequence in the direction indicated in the report. We are now called to answer for our failure to apply knowledge on time instead of being confronted with the crisis years later.

Such lags have been explained by some writers as the result of the fact that our economy operates on rules developed in the days before the present concentration of economic power and global interdependence. Erwin Chargaff, for example, in an article called "Knowledge Without Wisdom" (10), notes a decline of scholarship in the use and institutionalization of specialists; his conclusion is that where expertise prevails, wisdom vanishes. According to Chargaff, modern phases of science and scholarship began with the rise of bourgeoisie: "Exploring and exploiting became synonymous, the collection of knowledge, another form of the accumulating of capital. Knowledge was not just power, but power infinitely augmentable; there were no limits, as there were to accumulating money." He refers to this condition as "intellectual inflation," because his notion is that knowledge produced on the assembly line is actually worthless. Similarly, Ritchie Calder (11) observed:

> Science is knowledge. Knowledge is not wisdom. Wisdom is knowledge tempered by judgment. What we need is a collective wisdom which can evaluate the trends in science and the inventory of technological achievement. (p.74)

What all this suggests is that, at best, this book can only be a beginning. In a sense, although we and our contributors have worked hard, the really hard task has to be left to the practitioners who we hope will read this volume. It is you who will have to do the implementation and provide the judgment that will transform the knowledge our contributors have provided into wise action.

Of course we are not comfortable with our inability to give the reader more specific guidance. In some ways we obviously have just "passed the buck." However, we can offer one further set of ideas that might be helpful to the practitioner who attempts to achieve productivity through humane processes.

A NEW LOOK AT THE OUTLOOK FOR MAKING ORGANIZATIONS HUMANE AND PRODUCTIVE

Over time different images about what constitutes effective management behavior exist. In many ways managers in the 1950s and before werre pressure experts, serving as kinds of human thermostats, to turn the best on and off the people below them. The climate of the 1960s set the stage for the development of the manager of the future, the manager of situations. Perceived this way, effective managers are people who:

1. Make things happen.
2. Are organizers.
3. Are judged by what his or her followers do.
4. Are oriented towards results and responsibility.
5. Pay attention to the competitive situation.
6. Move their organizations towards growth fields.
7. Hire new good men and women and move the best old ones to growth lines.

These guidelines were useful for the 1960s and 1970s but are less useful for today.

It is too early to tell what images will dominate the 1980s. However, a few likely candidates are apparent, although they are not all consistent with each other. One set of images stresses the "on–stage" behavior of managers—how they "come across." This perspective deemphasizes the technical aspects of management relative to their ability to play their roles well. The roles they must play well include not only those involving inspirational and figurehead functions within the organization but their appearance before the public. Many organizations are training their executives in how to respond effectively to newspaper reporters and to come across well in front of the television camera and the radio microphone. Informed observers are predicting that increasingly, chief executives will be used in television and radio advertisements. As we began the 1980s many experts agreed that a decisive part of the presidential campaign was the Carter-Reagan debate, during which Reagan was able to dispel people's fears about him by acting like a president. Another set of images also stresses appearances but has more to do with managing contexts in which others perform. Maccoby's concept of the gamesman is of this sort. The effective gamesman uses himself or herself as a stimulus to draw behavior from others and as a designer of situations in which others are motivated or enabled to do what is required. High levels of personal energy, interpersonal attractiveness and sensitivity (not to be confused with concern), and the desire to win seem to be important attributes. A third set of images stresses the rational-technical aspects of management. In this view the manager employs advanced analytical methods to make better decisions. As a result of advances in information processing technology, managers may be able to recentralize decision making, and their success will depend heavily upon their ability to use advanced analytical procedures and decision tools. Finally, there is what Ray Miles has called the human resource oriented manager. In this view the successful manager utilizes people effectively because he or she believes that by delegating, getting viewpoints from their subordinates, and providing for the development of human potentialities, better decisions are made and the organization is better prepared to confront the dynamic, turbulent aspects of its environment. Probably all of these as well as other images will play a role in characterizing the successful manager of the 1980s. However, we would like to suggest a fifth view, which is necessary if organizations are to be humane and productive. This view, which we believe is potentially compatible with all of the other images, stresses the role of vision and asks the manager to be a "skeptical optimist."

Work organizations today are not merely economic organizations. The roles they play are so pervasive and influential that some political scientists have argued that they are "private governments." Models from the past will not by themselves provide adequate guidelines. History shows that the most successful efforts at stabilization by fixation and compulsion do not offer anything but a long period of hibernation. The American economic scene today needs a fresh look at the realities of organizations in the setting of the world as it really is. Neither naive optimism nor the suspicion of pessimism will do. What is needed is some hybrid of the two, as postulated by Dobzansky's (12) concept of "evolutionary optimism." Dobzansky wrote:

> Optimists believe that ours is the best of all possible worlds and pessimists are those who fear that the optimists are right. This is a flippant but valid statement of truth. Optimism is often the result of ignorance of cold and unwelcome realities. There is, however, another kind of optimism which is pessimism surmounted. The world is far from perfect but it is not unalterable. I am tempted to call this evolutionary optimism. (p. 489)

Max Lerner's concept of "possibilists" expresses a similar thought.

In our view skeptical optimists and possibilists share some central traits. They are not blinded to the realities of the present and the potential of the future by views of the world that were useful in dealing with yesterday but have become obsolete today. Second, they are not so committed to a set of ideals or goals or ideologies that they are unable to take small steps towards those ends when only small are possible. Third, they have vision. They have images of desirable future states and of the realities that are apt to shape the future. Somehow they are able to incorporate these images (which are often difficult to document, support, or measure) into current decisions. They are able to resist some of the pressures that force other decision makers to assign too great a weight to tangible, measurable, short-run outcomes. Likewise, the "irrational" is viewed as being as *real* (not necessarily as desirable) as the rational. Finally, they are process oriented. They realize that the future may be shaped as much by *how* something is done as by *what* is done. Planning, system design, work design, political and economic activity, decision making procedures, and other aspects of social structures are important for what they achieve and also for the residual effects they have on the actors in the system and the characteristics they institutionalize in a social system.

At this point one may well ask, "What would an evolutionary optimist in management look like?" While it is always risky to make operational such an abstract concept through one example, particularly by relying on secondary sources, we feel that Robert Guest's (13) account of the quality of work life (QWL) program at the Tarrytown plant of General Motors captures much of what we mean.

According to Guest, in the late 1960s and early 1970s the plant was experiencing serious difficulties. Union-management relations were poor and absenteeism and turnover were high. Operating costs too were high. In short, it was one of the poorest of GM's plants. The QWL effort was "born out of frustration and desperation" (p. 76).

Guest described the details of the program, and we will highlight only a few. A major goal of the effort was to develop a process for generating worker involvement. This attempt was successful and the productivity and climate of the plant improved substantially. All this was accomplished despite the intervention of economic downturns, which necessitated layoffs.

What accounted for the success? Guest pointed out some likely reasons. For one thing, there was a commitment to a process for making work more meaningful, not for achievement of gains on some immediate objective measure. Second, there was a general goal, but no detailed master plan. The plan started out on a limited scale and people were able to respond flexibly to changing conditions. Third, there was sustained commitment. There was the realization that change itself was continuous and the QWL program had to be ongoing. Fourth, conflicts, no matter how minor they might appear, were dealt with; failure to do so could have altered the development of a crucial part of the process—trust. Fifth, management was willing and able to invest substantial resources without a clear picture of what would happen. As Guest put it, a plant manager of one of our largest corporations wanted "to spend over $1.6 million on a program that has no guarantee of any return in greater efficiency, higher productivity, or lower costs" (p. 76). Sixth, the union was seen as a partner in the process. Finally, the program was only a first step. While it created substantial changes, it did not attempt to do everything. For example, the assembly-line technology was virtually unchanged.

It is our view that individuals are key components in any such change process. Prepackaged programs will seldom be satisfactory in this area. We may do well to keep in mind what Lewis Mumford says: "We can all learn from John Glenn's experience." Glenn's life was endangered by the malfunctioning of his automatic controls operated from a remote center. After Glenn saved his own life by personal intervention, he emerged from his space capsule with the ringing words "Now, let man take over." The attitudes of the skeptical optimist seem to us to be useful tools in supporting men and women as they "take over" social processes for making organizations humane and productive.

An obvious question is, "Are we ourselves naive or are we being possibilists in resting our view of social change on the existence of a large enough corps of skeptical optimists?" Quite frankly, we do not know. However, to those skeptical optimists that do exist in the ranks of management, we offer the knowledge contributed by the authors in this volume.

SCOPE OF THIS HANDBOOK

This book is directed toward organizing existing knowledge to help practitioners achieve humaneness and productivity simultaneously, where possible. It is also intended to help people recognize where opportunities for this achievement are possible and to recognize where tradeoffs between the two are necessary. In this book we have not sought to redefine or reorient the field; even the innovations discussed in the final part of the book assume that the basic elements of our political-economic system will remain in their current form. We have not attempted to incorporate all the alternatives; for example, we ignore such concepts as widespread "worker ownership" and the "small is beautiful" argument as unlikely to be actualized on any significant scale during this period. It is within this context that we treat the central question of this book: Can organizations be humane and productive?

REFERENCES

1. Mayo, E. *The Human Problems of an Industrialized Civilization.* New York: Macmillan, 1933.
2. Roethlisberger, F. & Dickson, J. *Management and the Worker.* Cambridge: Harvard University Press, 1941.
3. McGregor, D. *Human Side of Enterprise.* New York: McGraw-Hill, 1960.
4. Flanagan, J. C. A research approach to improving the quality of life. *American Psychologist,* March 1978, 138–147.
5. Quin n, R. P. & Staines, G. L. *1977 Quality of Employment Survey.* Survey Research Center, Institute for Social Research. Ann Arbor, University of Michigan Press, 1979.
6. Kahn, R. L. Organizational development: Some problems and proposals. *Journal of Applied Behavioral Science,* 1974, **10**(4), 485–502.

7. *Battelle Columbus Laboratories.* National Science Foundation, 1973.
8. Ogburn, W. F. *Social Change With Respect to Culture and Original Nature.* New York, B. W. Heubsch, 1922.
9. U. S. President's Materials Policy Commission. *The Resources for Freedom.* Washington, D.C.: U. S. Government Printing Office, 1952.
10. Chargoff, E. Knowledge without wisdom. *Harpers,* May 1980, 41–48.
11. Lord Ritchie-Calder. A global science policy. *The Center,* 1974, **74**(5), 74.
12. Dobzansky, T. Changing man. *Science,* 1967, **155,** 409–414.
13. Guest, R. H. Quality of work life—Learning from Tarrytown. *Harvard Business Review, 1979,* **57**, 76–87.

— I —

MANAGERIAL PROCESSES FOR ACTION

It is human beings, managers as well as managers of managers, who make things happen. Only in recent years has a body of knowledge emerged that can serve as a foundation for management in action, and that gives due attention to human considerations as well as production—knowledge that is humane as well as productive. In Part I we attempt to review the managers; the section includes concepts and techniques as well as actual processes through which managers make things happen.

The contributors to Part I were chosen because of their knowledge of the concepts and techniques and their experience in helping managers to use this information. Since selection, training, compensation, and motivation for performance are all obviously fundamental concerns of managers, we begin with them. Also included is attention to the actual processes that make it possible not only to select, train, and develop individuals, but to keep the organization open and flexible. In particular we focus on communication, organizational dynamics, leadership in relationship to power and stress, making supervision humane and productive, configurations of organizational structure, and planning and decision making in managing organizations. Thus we have included what might be considered both microdimensions of management and macro ones. Although the emphasis is on topics that ordinarily are considered micro in nature, the contributors have attempted to link their specific areas to the larger whole. In this sense Part I presents micro in the light of macro. However, the most detailed attention to macromatters is in the final part of the book.

In the first chapter Grant organizes current knowledge about selecting people and appraising their performance in a manner that practitioners will find relevant and significant for their use. To obtain their objectives says he, "organizations need people who are able to learn and perform a wide variety of jobs, who will remain with the organization, who will come to work every day, who will readily adapt to changing organizational requirements, who will cooperate with their co-workers, who are motivated to perform up to the limits of their abilities, and who will present favorable views of the organization to their families, friends, and representatives of other organizations." Anyone connected with the running of an organization knows that without keeping track of performance there is no way of knowing the direction and growth of the company. Hence the need for monitoring or appraising. Grant considers the foregoing topics in a very practical fashion, presenting knowledge for use to people in a position to use that knowledge.

Unfortunately, a great deal of money is wasted on training because managers buy "canned" programs. In Chapter 2 on training for development, Irwin Goldstein, William Macey, and Erich Prien draw heavily on the efforts to develop methods of assessment of needs and emphasize the importance of beginning to establish techniques that help determine what behaviors are necessary for job performance before training. Practitioners will find a general consideration of these matters useful in making decisions about how to determine their needs before they set up a program or employ a consultant to set it up for them.

From the late 1960s on there has been a growing body of knowledge made available for use. One of the topics that received much of the attention was motivation, particularly its relationship to performance. Of particular interest to managers were McGregor's Theory X-Theory Y, Maslow's hierarchy of needs, and Herzberg's two-factor theory of satisfaction. In Chapter 3, Katzell reviews our knowledge about motivation in relation to performance in a very practical, realistic manner. He considers the interaction of individual and situational elements in influencing motivation and performance. He takes an important step beyond the work place to relate off-the-job adjustments with work adjustments, in line with present interest in quality of work life.

Pay has often been described in psychology books as not a significant factor in motivation. This concept of pay seemed to be supported by Herzberg's classification of pay as a maintenance and not a motivational factor. In his chapter, Ivancevich treats the whole problem of compensation with a much more thoroughgoing and realistic attitude. He also presents facts and expresses attitudes that can be of use in setting up reward systems. Ivancevich examines salaries, wages, bonuses, and benefits and considers the consequences that noncompensation rewards can have on an employee's sense of achievement and personal growth. Methods for determining the worth of a job, for appraising performance, and for tying pay to performance are approached as central elements in motivating employees. Ivancevich's chapter makes an important contribution towards stimulating awareness that sound management of a compensation plan requires an understanding of statistics, economics, behavioral sciences, and the law.

Of all the managerial processes involved in organizational dynamics, perhaps the most important is communication. Who communicates to whom? In what way? For what purpose? With what result? Hall and Andrews begin their chapter on communication with another question: "How does a person talk to an organization?" The authors pay a good deal of attention to the often ignored topic of individual-organization communication, and to consideration of what is a healthy communicator and what is communication competence. Too often the phrase "communication problem" obscures other social processes that are basic to the difficulties. Hall and Andrews point to the need to consider the role of mutual positive motivation, balancing the power of both parties, and synchronizing confrontation efforts and attitudes, if communication is to be understood. The last portion of the chapter presents a guide to humanizing organizational communication.

Although leadership has long been a popular topic in the growing knowledge of organizational behavior, power has not been. Levinson has constantly reminded us of the need to emphasize leadership as well as power. His treatment of these topics spans a variety of topics. His psychoanalytic background leads him to introduce such topics as self-esteem, power, stress management, and the role of aggression and its corollary, the management of dependency in addressing leadership. While he considers workers at all levels and the whole problem of worker alienation as well as worker collaboration, his focus remains on the leader as the instrument of fulfillment of the psychological contract with the organization.

In Chapter 7 Meyer begins his treatment of "Making Supervision Humane and Productive" by stating that "The supervisor undoubtedly has more influence on the productivity and morale of a work group than any other single factor." He lists and comprehensively considers eight factors that can facilitate the making of humane and productive organizations. He focuses on some of the "nitty-gritty" aspects of supervising: goal setting, giving feedback, using praise and recognition, criticizing, allowing employees to participate in decision making, combining consideration with emphasis on production. Much has been said and written about these matters, but Meyer's clear and direct treatment of them avoids the type of abstraction that so often gets in between sound theory and action.

Management theory has moved away from the "one best way" approach toward the "it all depends" approach, often known as contingency theory. Often, however, contingency approaches are so vague that they give little guidance to action. In Chapter 8 Mintzberg adds a much needed concreteness to the contingency perspective. He presents some of the important factors that influence the design of appropriate organizations and then integrates these thoughts to develop five basic structural configurations. The major advantages of Mintzberg's perspective over typical "it all depends" perspectives include the graphic nature of his presentation and its ability to capture the necessary complexities without becoming so cumbersome as to be of little value to managers.

In the last chapter of Part I, "Planning and Decision Making in Managing Organizations," Taylor starts with a quotation from Herbert Simon to the effect that "We do not need organizations so much as we need new decision processes." Taylor reviews research and practices related to the problem of decision making in managing organizations. He highlights (a) the emergence of decision analysis, (b) attention to goals in organizational decisions, (c) applications of multiattribute and utility theory (MAUT), (d) awareness of human cognitive limitations in information processing in decision making, and (e) awareness of the organizational context of managerial decision making. From Taylor's paper it is clear that sophisticated techniques for aiding the decision maker are developing rapidly and have given managers useful tools for improved decisions. However, he calls our attention to the fact that these tools are not panaceas. They will be applied by fallible humans subject to sharply limited ability to handle information and make judgments; they will be used in highly complex organizational contexts replete with social and political forces. Consequently the consequences of mechanistic models, no matter how sophisticated they may be, depend on the nature of the human system that attempts to use them.

Part I concludes with a perceptive paper by Russell Johnston of Monsanto Corporation. Johnston argues that often practitioners do not benefit from available knowledge because academics fail to present their work in a way that captures the process of management. He examines the papers of the contributors to Part I from this perspective and concludes by showing how one of the papers—Herbert Meyer's—can be used as a model for closing this gap.

—1—

Selecting People and Appraising Their Performance

Donald L. Grant

Organizations were invented by people to meet human needs for products and services. Quite obviously they are also staffed by people, ideally by people who are appropriate to the objectives of the organization. If all people were alike, the staffing problem would be simple; people could be plugged into the organization randomly. People, however, differ in terms of their abilities, educational backgrounds, work experience, interests, motives, and temperaments. With the possible exception of identical twins, each of us is unique.

To meet their objectives, organizations need people who are able to learn and perform a wide variety of jobs, who will remain with the organization, who will come to work every day, who will readily adapt to changing organizational requirements, who will cooperate with their co-workers, who are motivated to perform up to the limits of their abilities, and who will present favorable views of the organization to their families, friends, and representatives of other organizations. Because organizations also vary in their requirements, each organization must select people who will adapt to its particular specifications.

Regardless of its output, whether product(s), service, or some combination thereof, each organization must keep track of its performance. No organization is guaranteed success. To meet and to continue to meet its objectives, therefore, an organization must monitor the performance of its components and of each individual within each component. The monitoring process for individuals is referred to as performance appraisal.

Selecting people and appraising their performances poses many problems. The technologies for both are of relatively recent vintage and are far from fully developed. Methods for making selection decisions and for appraising performance are available, but seldom furnish all the information an organization may need.

Selection of people by most organizations must be based on relatively indirect methods. Furthermore, direct observations of job performance can seldom be made. Appraisal methods must depend largely on judgments of people who draw many inferences from information that is seldom accurate or complete. Yet selection decisions and appraisals of performance must be made.

SELECTION

Selection involves making decisions about people. Whether or not to hire, promote, transfer, demote, lay off, or terminate are decisions made daily in most organizations. Because errors in making selection decisions can be costly, relevant information on which to base such decisions is sought.

Human Resources Planning

Prior to seeking information about individuals, the organization must determine the numbers and kinds of people required and where they are to be placed. Because organizations must adapt to changing conditions (such as growth, new technology, and market variations), human resources planning is a continuing operation. As Schneider (1) observes, three kinds of analyses are required, namely organizational, staff, and job.

Organizational analysis provides information on the environment in which the organization exists. As the environment changes, so must the organization. Changes in organizational structure, in jobs, and even in organizational goals may be a consequence. In turn, the kinds of people necessary to accomplishing organizational objectives can be affected. The impact of automation on many organizations is an example.

Jobs are organizational entities. They must be designed to facilitate accomplishing organizational goals. The responsibilities and duties of each job, which are reflected in the tasks performed, determine the knowledge, skills, and abilities people must bring to a job in order to accomplish its objectives. Thus analyses of jobs are essential to determining an organization's personnel requirements.

Jobs are not static; they must adapt to changing organizational requirements. Furthermore, as will be discussed in Part III, there is no one best way to design jobs. A job designed to meet technological requirements, for example, may not fulfill human requirements. Consequently, human resources planning must consider the needs of people as well as organizational needs.

Finally, staff analysis is essential. An organization must have current information on its own people. A comprehensive personnel records system accompanied by analyses of the data available from the system can yield information pertinent to many selection decisions, especially those involving promotions, transfers, demotions, and terminations. Furthermore, deficiencies in the human resources of an organization can be identified, as well as how to correct such deficiencies through training programs, recruitment from outside the organization, and other possible means.

Recruitment

Filling vacancies in an organization, whether arising from its growth, changes in structure and function, or turnover of personnel, requires searching for people who can meet the requirements of the vacant positions. The sources for people are both internal and external. The nature of the positions to be filled along with the policies and practices of the organization will determine which of the sources is the more appropriate for a given position. Thus one aspect of a selection decision is involved in the decision of where to recruit. For entry jobs, recruiting from external sources is generally viewed as appropriate. For higher level jobs, the nature of the vacant position may determine whether it can be filled internally or whether external sources should be designated. Jobs requiring people trained in various specialties, for example, may require searching externally.

Recruitment has not been subject to as much extended study as the making of selection decisions. Recently, however, psychologists have produced a number of studies bearing on recruiting from external sources, which have many implications for recruitment practices. Following a review of such studies Wanous (2) has formulated a distinction between "traditional" and "realistic" recruiting.

Recruitment following the traditional model focuses on locating people who have the abilities to perform the jobs for which they are sought. That such jobs may not meet the needs of people hired for them is given little if any consideration. Once employed, such people may become dissatisfied and leave the organization, frequently after very short service. This is costly to the organization, especially if extensive training is involved.

In contrast, realistic recruiting seeks to give the prospective employee information concerning both the favorable and unfavorable aspects of the position for which an offer of employment is to be made. The prospective employee then has the option of deciding whether or not the position is acceptable. Studies of realistic recruiting have produced results beneficial to a number of organizations applying the approach. Wanous (2) has summarized the results of studies on realistic recruiting, which in general indicate that early losses of people can be reduced, though not eliminated, by application of this approach.

Selection Methods

Because direct observations of performance usually cannot be made in advance of making selection decisions, a number of methods for indirectly obtaining relevant information have been devised. Some of the methods provide very specific information about a person, a typing test for example, while others provide much more comprehensive information. Included are face-to-face interviews, references, psychological tests, biographical information, projective techniques, individual assessments, assessment centers, and appraisals of performance and potential.

Interviewing

The face-to-face interview probably is the most widely used method for obtaining information about people, especially for making hiring decisions. In practice the interview serves multiple purposes, not only for obtaining information but also for furnishing information to a job applicant. The interviewer supplies information about the organization and about the job or jobs for which an applicant is being considered. In so doing, as Wanous (2) notes, it is common practice for the interviewer to present a favorable picture of both the organization and the job. Rather than offering both positive and negative features of both, the interviewer tends to omit or even distort the negative aspects. As previously noted, ensuing disillusionment can contribute to losing people early in their organizational careers.

In obtaining information about prospective employees, interviewers seek to determine whether an applicant meets job requirements. An applicant, for example, may be lacking in the training considered essential, may be overqualified for available jobs, may have irrelevant work experience, may expect a salary above that being offered, may not want to live in the geographic area specified, or may have a work history that suggests he or she would be a poor risk for the organization. In addition to such information obtained from reviewing an application form and by questioning the applicant, the interviewer will seek to obtain information about the applicant as a person. By observing the applicant during the interview, by listening to his or her voice, and by noting how the applicant handles questions, the interviewer may seek to judge whether the prospective employee has the kind of personality desired for a particular job.

The subjective elements in interviewing have raised questions concerning its suitability for making or contributing to selection decisons. Many books and articles have been written on how to interview. In addition, workshops to train interviewers are held, both within and outside employing organizations, and many studies of the interviewing process have been conducted.

The conclusions from studies on interviewing as a selection method have not been very encouraging. From a review of such research, Schmitt (3) concludes, "There is not much in the research of the last half dozen years to bolster the confidence of a personnel interviewer concerned with the reliability and validity of his decisions." Yet Schmitt (3) and other psychologists involved in selection research believe that efforts to improve interviewing as a selection method and research on the process should be continued. These psychologists apparently recognize that organizations will continue to use the interview as an integral part of the selection process no matter what studies of interviewing indicate. Furthermore, many psychologists believe, despite much evidence to the contrary, that interviewing for selection purposes can be improved.

Reference Checks

Along with interviews, reference checks are universally used as part of the selection process. They may be obtained by letter, phone, or face-to-face conversation. Most organizations depend on them when hiring specialists or managerial personnel from outside their organizations. Within an organization, of course, the views of current supervisors concerning employees under consideration for promotion or transfer are frequently sought. In both instances, from without or within the organization, it is assumed that observations of current and past performance are pertinent to predicting future performance.

Though the assumption is logical, the practice leaves much to be desired. The information obtained may be distorted by bias or by concern of the person furnishing the information over what is to be done with it. Furthermore, the information may be irrelevant to the selection decision under consideration. Finding out that "Joe is a great guy" adds only noise to the selection process. Reference checks can be useful when they add specific information to that already obtained.

Psychological Tests

In contrast to interviews and reference checks, psychological tests have had relatively limited use, especially in smaller organizations, for making selection decisions. They unquestionably are and have been subject to much controversy, however. Much of the legal debate concerning selection has centered around the use of tests.

Many of the tests used for selection purposes are measures of ability, such as tests of knowledge, aptitude, and skill. Licensing examinations for auto drivers and for such professional fields as law and medicine usually include tests of knowledge. Demonstration of skill in driving an auto also is required of persons desiring licenses to drive. Another test of skill is the typing test, which many organizations require of applicants for jobs requiring the ability to type.

For selection purposes, however, many of the tests used are aptitude tests. Such tests are designed to measure potential for an occupation. A large variety of such tests have been developed and are available from test publishers. The aptitudes measured have many names and include verbal comprehension, mechanical comprehension, arithmetic reasoning, clerical speed, abstract reasoning, finger dexterity, and visualization. Descriptions and examples of such tests can be found in Schneider (1).

Tests of skill like a typing test are also referred to as "work sample" tests because they are designed to directly measure skills required on a job. They are frequently expensive to develop and administer, and many are designed for particular jobs. Some involve physical manipulation, such as tracing a complex mechanical circuit or operating a sewing machine, while others involve coping with people-oriented or language-oriented problems, such as participating in a group discussion, making a sales presentation, or deciding on actions presented by memos, reports, letters, and other items a manager might find in his or her in basket. Such tests have the advantage of being directly job related.

Other tests have been designed to measure such aspects of personality as temperament, interests, and values. Most of these tests are in reality questionnaires. Whereas ability tests require demonstrating competence in solving problems, performing a skill, exhibiting knowledge, or some combination of those, tests designed to elicit aspects of personality permit the respondent to answer questions that describe his or her preferences or behavior. Such answers are therefore under the control of the respondent, and consequently the tests are often referred to as "self-report" tests. Schneider (1) also describes a number of such tests.

Psychological tests have the advantage over interviews and reference checks of being standardized and objective. People taking such tests answer the same questions, solve the same problems, or perform the same skills. The tests are scored by trained scorers using keys to the correct answers. The only exception to such objective scoring are those work sample tests that require trained observers who rate performance observed on standardized rating scales. Many tests use paper-and-pencil question and answer sheets. The costs of the materials, administration, and scoring of the tests are low. They thus offer an economical means for gathering pertinent information on people being considered for job openings.

Many studies have been made of psychological tests as instruments in making selection decisions. Reviews of such research have been published by Ghiselli (4) and by Asher and Sciarrino (5). The results indicate that tests, especially aptitude and work sample tests, are predictive of performance in training, on the job, or both. The fact that they are not problem-free, however, will be discussed later on in this chapter.

Biodata

Whereas psychological tests focus on the current behavior of the individual, questionnaires designed to elicit biographical information are oriented toward a person's past. As Owens (6) observes, the use of such information in making selection decisions is based on the concept that a person's past behavior is predictive of his or her future behavior. Biographical information questionnaires are designed like tests and are scored objectively. The questions, however, pertain to a person's life experiences at home, in school, in college, at work, and at leisure.

In contrast to many psychological tests, biographical information questionnaires are not readily available for purchase. They must be designed for use by a particular organization, for an occupation, or for a specific job. The tailoring of such questionnaires is necessary because the answers to the questions must be keyed to measures of performance. A good example is provided by Thayer (7), who describes the research conducted over a 50-year period in the life insurance industry on a questionnaire designed for use in selecting salespersons. Modifications in the questionnaire arising from changes in the industry and in the backgrounds of applicants for sales positions are described by Thayer (7), thereby indicating that the tailoring process must also be a continuing one.

The costs involved in developing and maintaining biographical information questionnaires have limited the extent of their use as instruments in making selection decisions. Studies show, however, that they are not as subject to faking and the other biasing effects characteristic of self-report questionnaires. Reviews of such studies by Owens (6) and by Dunnette and Borman (8) disclose that biographical information questionnaires are indicative of success in a variety of industrial and other occupations. For a brief description of such questionnaires and the results of research on their use, the reader is referred to Schneider (1).

Projective Tests

The use of projectives, also briefly described by Schneider (1), in making selection decisions has been even more limited than that of biographical information questionnaires. Projectives are methods that require a person to respond to ambiguous stimuli, such as ink blots, drawings, or incomplete sentences. For example, a sentence starting "I am ______" is to be completed with whatever the person deems appropriate. A series of such sentences, all starting with different words or phrases, are completed and evaluated by a psychologist trained to interpret them.

The method is used by clinical psychologists in diagnosing clients seeking help with their personal problems. It also has been used in research on achievement motivation and in the selection of managers. Miner (9), for example, developed the *Miner Sentence Completion Scale* to assess the motivation to manage. He reports studies of its use that indicate that performance on the instrument is predictive of managerial success.

The obvious limitation on the use of projectives in making selection decisions arises from the need to have a trained psychologist interpret results obtained with them. The instrumentation itself is not very costly, but accompanying fees of trained psychologists may make the expense of large-scale use prohibitive. Their use as part of a broader assessment of individuals, however, is relatively common.

Individual Assessment

Historically, assessment of individuals has been an integral part of the practice of clinical and counseling psychologists in making diagnoses. Its application to making selection and other personnel decisions evolved after World War II and has become relatively widespread. Many consultants to industrial and other organizations specialize in making such assessments.

In application, the instrument is the psychologist. Using whatever methods are personally preferred, the psychologist evaluates the person to be assessed. For example, the psychologist may interview the individual at great length, two to three hours, and then formulate judgments about him or her from the information thus obtained. Or the psychologist may have the person take a number of psychological tests, complete a biographical information questionnaire, respond to one or more projectives, and then interview him or her. All of the information obtained from the tests, questionnaire, projectives, and interview is considered in making judgments about the individual.

The value of such assessments lies in the skill of the psychologist conducting them. The client organization pays for the skill regardless of the methods used by the psychologist in making the assessment. Because there is no agreement among psychologists concerning which are the more appropriate methods, those used vary greatly.

Once the assessment is concluded, the psychologist reports his or her conclusions and recommendations about the person assessed to the client organization. Decisions with respect to the person assessed are the responsibility of the organization.

Evaluations of individual assessments as aids in making selection decisions have seldom been made. Despite their costs, which are high, organizations retaining psychologists for this purpose tend to accept their value to the organization without challenge, much as a patient accepts the advice of his or her physician unquestionably. Needless to say, the high cost of such assessments tends to restrict their use to higher-level personnel in organizations. For information about the methods and processes involved, the interested reader is referred to Sundberg (10).

Assessment Center

The assessment center method is another and quite different approach to assessing people. An assessment center is a process in which trained assessors apply a variety of methods to evaluating people for selection or development purposes. The people assessed may be job applicants, candidates for promotion within an organization, or high-potential persons concerning whom higher-level management seeks information that can be used for further development. The assessors may be psychologists, though more likely they are managers trained in assessment center methods. The methods used may include psychological tests, projectives, and interviews, but most certainly include exercises that permit the assessors to observe those being assessed perform in situations that directly reflect job requirements.

The exercises have much in common with work-sample tests, some even being used as such, and are referred to as "simulations" because they simulate situations comparable to those found in work settings. An example is the previously noted in-basket exercise, which consists of messages, memos, letters, reports, and so forth that are characteristic of materials a manager finds in his or her in basket. The task is to organize the materials, assign priorities, make decisions, and communicate with subordinates, peers, superiors, customers, public officials, and others. Another example is the leaderless group discussion in which a group of persons being assessed meet as peers to resolve a problem. A third example consists of a sales presentation, which requires a prospective salesperson to prepare a sales pitch and present it to "customers" role-played by assessors.

The assessors observe performance in the exercises and prepare reports on their observations. After all of the exercises have been completed, the assessors meet as a group and evaluate each candidate on several dimensions that job analysis indicates are important to successful performance of the job for which the candidates are under consideration. The dimensions include such behaviors as leadership, decision making, organizing and planning, oral communications, desire to advance, and tolerance of uncertainty. Once the ratings for a candidate have been made and discussed, the assessors then judge the suitability of the candidate for the job involved. After all candidates have been evaluated, recommendations for each are made to line management, which uses the information in making its decisions with respect to selection or development. When the candidates assessed are members of the organization, a frequent practice is to provide them and their supervisors with complete feedback on performance at the assessment center.

The assessment center method is a judgmental process. It has the advantage over individual assessment, however, of combining the judgments of several assessors, usually four or more, and of being standardized for each candidate. Thorough training of assessors assures objectivity in observing and evaluating candidates. The practice of using organizational members, usually managers, as assessors lends credibility to the process.

Since its introduction to American industry in 1956 (see Bray, Campbell, and Grant [11]), the growth of the assessment center method, initially slow, has been phenomenal. Used at first by American firms to assess management potential, the assessment center method has become internationalized and is being applied to many occupations (sales, engineering, and foreign service officers, for example) in a variety of organizations, public as well as private.

Many studies of the assessment center method, which show that the method is predictive of subsequent success, have been conducted and their results published. A book edited by Moses and Byham (12) offers much information about the method, including applications of it and research involving it.

Though frequently used in making promotional decisions, appraisals of performance on a job may provide inadequate information. In the first place, as will be discussed at length further on in this chapter, they may be inaccurate. Even when accurate, however, the requirements of the job to which promotions are to be made may differ in crucial ways from those of the jobs held by candidates being considered. Effective performance as a technician, for example, does not qualify a person to become a supervisor, even of technicians doing the work with which the person is familiar. The interpersonal and administrative skills required may be lacking. For another example, an effective computer operator may not become an effective programmer. Again the skill requirements differ. The principle involved, though frequently ignored, is obvious; a candidate for promotion should have or should be able to develop the knowledge, skills, and abilities essential to success in the higher-level position. Assessment in advance of the promotional decision is indicated.

The reader, however, should not assume that assessment centers are required for making all promotional decisions. Many of the methods previously discussed may provide appropriate information without entailing the costs involved in applying the assessment center method. Furthermore, as will be discussed subsequently, appraisals for potential may provide the essential information.

Staffing the Selection System

Human resource planning, recruiting, and applying appropriate selection methods are all part of a system leading to selection decisions. It requires people to make such a system operate effectively. Larger organizations can afford to employ psychologists and other qualified people to design and implement the selection system. Furthermore, costs involved in improving and maintaining the system (for example, training interviewers, test administrators, and assessors) can be justified by the need to make high-quality selection decisions.

Smaller organizations may be more limited in providing personnel responsible for designing and implementing their selection systems. They can, however, make use of consultants to assist them with making selection decisions, especially the more crucial ones. Careful selection of consultants is of course necessary. Their credentials should be examined and the experiences of other organizations using their services should be sought. In addition, records of consulting services should be kept that permit evaluations of the effectiveness of the services. No organization is required to support consultants who fail to provide the kind and quality of service needed.

Line management should also have an important role in a selection system. Delegating all selection decisions to staff groups with no involvement of line management can be a poor practice. Where possible, line management should directly participate in making selection decisions, especially those, such as promotions, that are internal to the organization. When selection decisions must be delegated to staff groups (hiring decisions in larger organizations, for example), the selection system should be designed to provide feedback to the staff organization on the subsequent performance of the people thus selected. By this means corrections in the practices of staff personnel can be made.

Selection policies are of course crucial to the effectiveness of any organization. Higher management must take the responsibility for seeing to it that selection policies are appropriate and are implemented effectively. Data on terminations, absences, accidents, and job performance should be periodically reviewed. Though selection practices are certainly not fully responsible for the people problems of an organization, they can contribute to them and should be periodically audited.

Problems in Selection

No matter how well designed a selection system may be, errors in making selection decisions will be made. One source of error is that of selecting people who subsequently fail in performing their work. Employing organizations seek of course to minimize the number of failures arising from selection errors. Overlooked in this concern may be another source of error in making selection decisions, namely rejecting people who could succeed if selected. From the individual applicant's or employee's viewpoint, the second source of error is the more serious of the two.

Success or failure for individuals in organizations are consequences of complex interactions between characteristics of the individual and the work environment. Training, supervision, peer group relations, the reward system, opportunities for advancement, and many other factors in the work environment can facilitate or inhibit successful individual performance. Bray et al. (11), for example, report the effects of many work environment factors on the advancement of young managers in a large organization. Futhermore, measuring performance, as will be discussed, poses many problems and makes ascertaining levels of performance very difficult. Despite these caveats, however, research evidence accumulated over seventy years clearly demonstrates that people do vary in their job performances, and that the selection methods discussed can identify characteristics of people that relate to measures of performance.

Because of the complexities discussed and the limitations of selection methods, psychologists insist that selection methods must be validated. The objective is to reduce selection errors and to provide organizations with information pertinent to proper implementation of the selection methods. Validation procedures, as discussed by Guion (13) and by Schneider (1), are technically complex, and frequently difficult to implement. Miner and Miner (14) report that as a consequence many organizations have abandoned the use of psychological tests rather than undertake the validation process.

Regardless of the selection method used, organizations have recognized the need for probationary periods prior to committing themselves to retaining recently hired people in the employ of the organization. Unfortunately, this practice has not been universally applied within the organization to people promoted or transferred to jobs that may or may not be suitable for them. Living with error is a questionable practice, both for the individual involved and for the organization. A probationary period accompanied by an appropriate appraisal procedure and provisions for demotion could benefit all parties.

Use of probationary periods does not of course relieve an organization from making selection decisions nor from validating selection procedures. Subsequent to the passage of the Civil Rights Act of 1964 and the U.S. Supreme Court decision in *Griggs et al. v. Duke Power Company,* validation of selection criteria is legally required when minorities and other protected groups are adversely affected by their application. Miner and Miner (14) review the legal history and its implications for employing organizations. The current Uniform Guidelines on Employee Selection Procedures (15) specify the validation procedures that employing organizations are required to follow.

Related to issues raised by the need to validate selection procedures is one concerning the fairness of selection decisions. Psychological tests have been accused of being culturally biased with respect to minority groups, implying that for minorities scores on psychological tests are not relevant to subsequent job performance. Considerable research on the use of tests in making selection decisions does not support this contention, but the issue of fairness remains. The literature pertaining to the issue has become both voluminous and technically complex. For a recent summary, the reader is referred to Dunnette and Borman (8). Though the focus has been on psychological tests, any selection method is subject to challenge on the grounds of fairness to groups or individuals.

By now the reader is aware that making selection decisions poses many problems for an organization. The need for professional advice and assistance should be apparent. Yet organizations continue to be influenced by fads and to be fair game for purveyors of bogus selection methods. The history of psychological testing is strewn with examples of tests advertised as solving the selection problems of an organization by purchasing a particular test or testing service. Currently assessment centers appear to be a popular item that inadequately trained persons find profitable to market.

The psychological profession has sought to counter the misuse of selection methods by preparing and issuing standards for their use. These include standards issued by the American Psychological Association (APA), discussed by Guion (13), those issued by the APA Division of Industrial-Organizational Psychology, reprinted in Miner and Miner (14), and standards for assessment centers prepared by the Task Force on Assessment Center Standards (16). The technology intrinsic to selection methods and their applications requires trained professionals to develop and evaluate their utility for an organization. The prospective user, therefore, should obtain professional assistance and verify that the professional employed or retained has at least minimal qualifications, namely, a Ph.D. degree in psychology and a license or certificate to practice psychology from the state in which he or she has established practice.

Humanizing Selection

Organizations seek people who can perform the jobs for which they are employed. In making selection decisions the focus is on identifying people who have the knowledge, skills, and abilities required by the jobs to be filled. Whether the job, the organizational unit in which it is located, or the entire organization provides the kinds of activities and the environment desired by an individual is given little or no consideration in making selection decisions. It is left up to the individual to prove his or her worth to the organization in return for pay and other benefits from the organization.

As a consequence, organizations tend to accept relatively high loss rates from their younger and newer employees as part of the cost of doing business. Little thought is given, except when the loss rates become excessive, as to how losses of personnel could be reduced. The next recession resolves the issue, at least temporarily.

The trend today, discussed in Part III, toward improving jobs and work environments is directed at making the quality of work life more satisfactory for people doing the work. Along with this general trend an active interest, discussed by both Schneider (1) and Wanous (2), toward taking into account the needs of the individual in making selection decisions has emerged.

The primary approach, described by Wanous (2) and previously discussed, is that of realistic job previews, which are designed to give people being considered for a job objective information about what the work is really like. In making his or her decision in response to a job offer, the individual is provided pertinent information on which to base a decision. The principle of course could be applied to promotional situations and transfers as well as to hiring people. The research with job previews is quite new and may only be a beginning to matching people with jobs and organizations. As career development, discussed in Part III, evolves, much more concern with both individual and organizational needs can be given due consideration.

The benefits from such a strategy should be greater satisfaction on the part of the individual and less disruption from losses of personnel, absences, grievances, and so forth for the organization. The individual would gain greater control over his or her own life without necessarily requiring the organization to sacrifice its objectives. A well-planned tradeoff of needs could benefit both the organization and its people.

APPRAISING PERFORMANCE

To track performance organizations develop measures or indices of accomplishment. Business organizations use return on investment, the "bottom line," as an overall measure of success, but also obtain direct measures of sales, production, customer complaints, number of grievances, and so forth on a periodic basis to track performance of organizational components. For individual employees, however, objective measures of performance are seldom available. Instead organizations use appraisals of performance, usually based on the judgments of supervisors, to monitor individual performance.

Purposes of Appraising Performance

Appraisals of performance serve administrative, research, and counseling purposes. Pay actions for individuals, especially managers and specialists, are frequently determined by their appraisals. Many compensation plans are designed to reward merit. In addition, as previously noted, decisions with respect to promotions, transfers, demotions, and terminations may be based on performance appraisals. For the individual, therefore, obtaining favorable appraisals are crucial to his or her success in the organization. Because of its importance in the reward system, moreover, the appraisal process serves the organization as a means for controlling its members.

Appraisals of performance can also be used for research purposes. In validating selection methods, for example, appraisals may be used as criteria for determining whether or not one or more selection instruments or procedures are related to job performance. Those that show a statistical relationship to performance can then be used in making selection decisions.

Supervisors may also use performance appraisals in counseling their subordinates. Through praise for satisfactory performance and suggestions for improving performance, a supervisor presumably can motivate a subordinate to perform more effectively. The pay increase that accompanies a favorable appraisal serves too as an additional reward for satisfactory performance.

Traditional Approaches to Appraising Performance

To insure comparability in making appraisals throughout an organization, the procedures are incorporated in an appraisal plan. It is a common practice for organizations to have their personnel departments formulate such plans. Historically, a wide variety of plans have been devised. Despite variations in content, the foci of appraisal plans are on the mechanics of making appraisals and using the results. Customarily some form of rating is incorporated in the plan, though narrative reports of employee performance may be required as an alternative to or supplement to a rating procedure. Henderson (17) describes the available rating methods, which include graphic rating scales, forced choice, critical incidents, ranking, paired comparisons, and behaviorally anchored rating scales.

Once an appraisal plan has been formulated and approved by higher management, information concerning the plan is disseminated to the people in the organization. Memoranda, meetings at which the plan is described and discussed, in-house newspapers, and other communication media are employed in disseminating the information.

Provision is customarily made in such plans for the timing of appraisals. They may be made annually, semiannually, or on each employee's service date. At the specified time, each supervisor rates his or her subordinates. The supervisor then meets with each subordinate to discuss the rating(s). The appraisal form is then forwarded, most likely through channels, to the personnel department, which is responsible for seeing that appropriate pay actions ensue. A copy of the appraisal form may be filed in the employee's personnel folder for future reference.

Clearly the role of the supervisor in the process described is a key one. Presumably, prior to rating each subordinate, the supervisor has observed the performance of the subordinate, retained what has been observed, recalled the information, interpreted it, and rated the subordinate on the basis of the information thus obtained and evaluated. The supervisor is thus judge and jury.

The process of rating is viewed, quite accurately, by those rated as highly subjective. It is not popular with them, nor for that matter with the supervisors who are required to make the ratings. Objections to perceived inequities may be raised, and dissatisfaction may be a consequence.

Errors in Rating Performance

Rating people on work performance is a complex process. It is implicitly assumed, though seldom recognized, that the rater has made accurate observations of performance and has observed representative samples of each subordinate's performance. In addition, memory of the observations is assumed to be accurate and interpreted correctly. The ensuing ratings are accepted as being valid.

In reality, favorable or unfavorable biases of a supervisor with respect to a subordinate may influence the entire process, from observing through rating. The observations of performance may be sporadic, incidental, and insufficient. Memory of the observations may be faulty; the supervisor, for example, may recall only the most striking incidents. No record or diary of observations may have been kept. Interpretation of information recalled may be incorrect; the supervisor may, for example, conclude that Mary is lazy, when in fact nobody has given Mary the information she needs to do her work. The supervisor's ratings of his or her subordinates, therefore, can be very inaccurate. It is quite likely too that the supervisor has never been trained in how to make accurate ratings.

In addition to the complexities of the rating process, many other factors can influence the output. Subordinates want favorable ratings, and may bring pressure on their supervisor to rate correspondingly. The supervisor, recognizing that the ratings are to be reviewed by his or her superiors, may want the group to appear as good performers in comparison to other work groups. Whatever the influences may be, studies reported by Landy and Farr (18) show that ratings for administrative purposes tend to be higher than when made for research purposes, where they are kept confidential.

An additional factor, frequently ignored, arises from turnover, both internal and external to the organization. Where supervisors and subordinates change frequently, a common occurrence in our dynamic society, obtaining accurate ratings may be impossible. Stable relationships appear to be an essential requirement of traditional rating practices.

Whatever the causal factors may be, and they are difficult to trace, studies of performance ratings indicate that many errors in making ratings are made. Both Henderson (17) and Landy and Farr (18) summarize the results of such studies and describe the many kinds of errors commonly made. As a consequence, appraisals for administrative purposes are of questionable value. Improvements in the procedures employed are essential if "merit" in work performance is to be accorded more than lip service.

Using Appraisals for Counseling

The use of appraisals for counseling purposes is a common practice. A supervisor meets with his or her subordinates individually and discusses their performance ratings with them. Such appraisal interviews provide feedback to the subordinate and, it is hoped, motivates him or her to improve job performance.

In a series of studies, described by Meyer, Kay, and French (19), the General Electric Company examined the value of appraisal interviews to the company. The investigators discovered that the supervisor's dual roles of judge and counselor conflicted. In the role of judge the supervisor explained his or her ratings and recommendations for salary action based on the ratings. Typically subordinates reacted defensively to explicit criticisms or to those implied by suggestions for improving performance. As a consequence, the supervisor's advice fell on deaf ears; little improvement in performance ensued.

A different approach was decided upon and named Work Performance and Review (WP&R). The new approach was designed to separate the roles of judge and counselor. Supervisors using WP&R were encouraged to meet more frequently than once or twice each year with each of their subordinates. At the initial meeting the supervisor and subordinate jointly agreed on specific work goals for a specified time period, often quite short. At subsequent meetings the subordinate's accomplishments were reviewed and agreement reached on new goals. Performance ratings and recommended salary actions were not discussed at these meetings.

To evaluate the effects of WP&R, a study was designed to compare the new approach with the traditional appraisal interview. The results of the study showed that whereas subordinates of supervisors using the traditional approach made very few improvements in performance, those of supervisors following WP&R recorded many improvements in performance. In addition, the attitudes of these subordinates toward the appraisal process and their supervisors proved more favorable than did the attitudes of subordinates reporting to supervisors adhering to the traditional approach. Furthermore, supervisors using WP&R reported satisfaction with it because the approach made it possible to counsel subordinates effectively.

Reports of the GE studies and other studies supportive of the findings spurred many organizations to establish programs comparable to WP&R. For that matter, along with the evolution of Management by Objectives (MBO), goal setting as a motivational device has proven generally effective. According to McConkie (20), goal setting accompanied by periodic reviews of accomplishments have become an integral part of MBO. The interested reader is referred to Henderson (17) and McConkie (20) for descriptions and discussions of goal setting and its relationship to the appraisal process.

Improving Appraisals

Psychologists have contributed considerable research on appraisal methods. The studies reported by Meyer et al. (19) exemplify such research, while Landy and Farr (18) review many efforts to improve performance ratings. Their review encompasses reports of studies made since 1950.

Many of the efforts of psychologists have focused on rating methods. The history of performance rating is strewn with innovations. Among the more recent to gain considerable attention and to stimulate many studies is a method named Behaviorally Anchored Rating Scales (BARS). The method, discussed in both Henderson (17) and Landy and Farr (18), is designed to direct the rater to observable behaviors of the person being rated. Supervisors of people performing a job participate in developing the rating scales. They select the behavioral dimensions to be rated and provide input into the content of the scale for each dimension. Consequently, the rating instrument reflects what supervisors judge to be important to successful performance and uses their language to describe it.

BARS has been the object of considerable research. Use of it has been compared to such conventional methods as graphic rating scales. The results of the comparative studies do not generally support the superiority of BARS as a method for rating performance. Because BARS is costly to develop, failure to demonstrate gains over less costly methods raises doubts over the advisability of investing in the people, time, and expertise required for its development.

The history of BARS and of preceding innovations in rating methods does not indicate that methods for appraising performance are of no importance. It does suggest, however, that factors other than the instrumentation used may have greater impact on the output obtained. Unfortunately, research on many factors that may influence performance ratings has not revealed which ones are critical.

One factor that does have some effect on rating output is rater training. The results of studies show that training raters is effective in reducing errors in performance ratings, especially if the training is extensive and provides for practice in making the ratings. As Landy and Farr (18) point out, however, the studies do not provide information on the longer-range effects of training raters nor on the validity of the ratings. Furthermore, the studies provide little information on how to optimally train raters.

Though Landy and Farr (18) remain optimistic over the prospects of improving performance ratings via additional research directed at identifying and controlling for sources of error in rating, it appears reasonable to ask whether some entirely new direction to performance appraisal might be more productive. Though hardly a certainty, MBO may offer such.

MBO provides an organizational approach to performance appraisals. Goals set for an individual are directly related to organizational goals. The focus of the process is on objective performance standards and objective measures of performance. Studies cited by McConkie (20) show that measuring performance generally improves performance and the appraisal process. Furthermore, the attitudes of those appraised and of those making the appraisals toward the process, as was demonstrated by the GE studies previously cited, are positive.

Applying MBO to the appraisal process requires the development of objective measures of performance. Participation by subordinates in goal setting is preferred, though, as shown in the studies reported by Meyer et al. (19), some subordinates prefer having their supervisor set the work goals. Appraisals should be periodic, as often as necessary according to McConkie (20). Though in general the supervisor is expected to do the appraising, both Henderson (17) and McConkie (20) discuss self or group appraisals as possible alternatives or supplements to supervisory appraisals.

Developing objective measures of performance is seen as essential to the MBO appraisal process. Simple methods for so doing, however, are not readily, if at all, available. An approach to developing such measures is exemplified by Sloma (21), who presents a general model for measuring managerial performance based on organizational goals. In addition, guidelines for setting specific goals for 15 major managerial jobs, both line and staff (for example, sales, production, treasurer, personnel), are provided. The guidelines offer much detail, and can serve business organizations, especially manufacturing firms, seeking to develop objective performance measures.

The need for research on the MBO approach to performance appraisal is recognized by McConkie (20), who views much of the available empirical support as weak. I believe that research on developing objective measures of individual performance is crucial. Reliable and valid measures are required to supplant the traditional subjective rating methods.

Appraising Potential

For reasons previously discussed, performance appraisals may not furnish the information necessary to making promotional decisions. Furthermore, assessment centers or other appropriate selection methods may be unavailable and unobtainable. Consequently, having supervisors rate potential as well as performance is receiving consideration.

The notion of appraising potential evolved out of the work of AT&T psychologists with assessment centers. Its application requires that supervisors be trained in assessment center concepts and methods. Practice in rating potential is provided via exercises that permit the supervisor being trained to observe behaviors relevant to the dimensions that are to be rated. If, for example, resistance to stress is a dimension to be rated, video tapes of people reacting in various ways to work situations involving stress are presented. The trainees rate the observed behaviors and receive feedback on the accuracy of their ratings. Rating of writing skills offers another example. The supevisors are presented with samples of writing that vary greatly in quality and are instructed to rate the quality of each sample. Again feedback on the accuracy of rating is provided.

Because a particular job may not offer their subordinates opportunities to perform in ways appropriate to evaluating potential, the supervisors are also trained to make such opportunities available. Many staff jobs, for example, require little or no leadership. To rate leadership potential, the supervisors are instructed to place their subordinates in situations requiring leadership (directing a group discussion, for example) and to observe performance in such situations.

Application of appraising potential is described by Henderson (17) and accompanied by a specific example. Studies evaluating the process are essential, however, because it has not been established that supervisors can distinguish between performance and potential, nor that the kinds of errors made in rating performance won't show up in rating potential. The rather dismal history of performance rating suggests the need for skepticism.

Validation of Appraisals

The need to validate appraisals is comparable to that for selection methods. Organizations assuming that their appraisals are valid may be deluding themselves. The methods used in validating appraisals, described by Henderson (17), are technically complex and require professional expertise. Furthermore, the need is a continuing one; initially valid appraisals may become invalid over time.

In civil rights cases the courts have tended to view appraisals as tests and to apply the same standards in evaluating them as they do for selection methods. Henderson (17) cites a number of such cases. For legal protection, therefore, and as a sound personnel practice, organizations should insure that their appraisal procedures are valid.

Humanizing Appraisals

The traditional approach to performance appraisal is not only subject to considerable error but also tends to be very impersonal. Both the people appraised and their appraisers find the process distasteful. Finding ways for improving the process should focus, therefore, on helping organizations to better achieve their objectives and to make the process more acceptable to their people.

I believe, as previously indicated, that the MBO approach to appraising performance offers the most likely means for accomplishing these goals. MBO requires objective in contrast to subjective measures of performance. Those appraised participate in setting work goals. Furthermore, provision can be made for self appraisals, group appraisals, and even subordinate appraisals. The supervisor can shed his or her judicial robes and direct attention to working with subordinates toward accomplishing organizational objectives. Teamwork in a climate of trust, rather than in one of threat, can become a reality.

Though this point of view may appear utopian, it reflects a growing recognition that building effective organizations can only be accomplished through people. The road ahead may be rocky, but who wants to remain stuck in the mud of ineffective tradition?

CONCLUSION

This brief review of selecting people and appraising their performance offers no panaceas. Developing and applying appropriate methods for selecting and appraising people poses many problems. Organizations seeking to improve their utilization of human resources must expect to invest considerable time and resources in the methods and processes involved in selecting people and appraising job performance.

The objectives are to select people who can perform organizational jobs effectively and to monitor their performance through appraising it. The overall goal is an efficient and a productive organization staffed with highly motivated, satisfied people.

Many methods for selecting and appraising people are available. For neither is there a "one best way" for any organization. The methods available are prone to error and require continuing attention.

The trend today is increasingly toward meeting both organizational and individual needs. Using procedures that take into account the needs of both can result in mutual benefit. Selection and appraisal systems must give consideration to organizational requirements and the desires of people.

Finally, organizations should pay close attention to their policies and practices in selecting and appraising people. The need for improvement is universal. Effective utilization of human resources depends on finding better ways for carrying out these functions.

REFERENCES

1. Schneider, B. *Staffing organizations.* Santa Monica, Calif.: Goodyear Publishing Co., 1976.
2. Wanous, J. P. *Organizational Entry: Recruitment, Selection, and Socialization of Newcomers.* Reading, Mass.: Addison-Wesley Publishing Co., 1980.
3. Schmitt, N. Social and situational determinants of interview decisions: Implications for the employment interview. *Personnel Psychology,* 1976, **29,** 79–101.
4. Ghiselli, E. E. The validity of aptitude tests in personnel selection. *Personnel Psychology,* 1973, **26,** 461–477.
5. Asher, J. J. & Sciarrino, J. A. Realistic work sample tests: A review. *Personnel Psychology,* 1974, **27,** 519–533.
6. Owens, W. A. Background data. In M. D. Dunnette (Ed.). *Handbook of Industrial and Organizational Psychology.* Chicago: Rand-McNally, 1976.
7. Thayer, P. W. Somethings old, somethings new. *Personnel Psychology,* 1977, **30,** 513–524.
8. Dunnette, M. D. & Borman, W. C. Personnel selection and classification systems. In M. R. Rosenzweig and L. W. Porter (Eds.). *Annual Review of Psychology.* Palo Alto, Calif.: Annual Reviews, 1979.
9. Miner, J. B. Motivational potential for upgrading among minority and female managers. *Journal of Applied Psychology,* 1977, **62,** 691–697.
10. Sundberg, N. D. *Assessment of Persons.* Englewood Cliffs, N.J.: Prentice-Hall, 1977.
11. Bray, D. W., Campbell, R. J. & Grant, D. L. *Formative Years in Business: A Long-Term AT&T Study of Managerial Lives.* New York: Wiley, 1974.
12. Moses, J. L. & Byham, W. C. (Eds.). *Applying the Assessment Center Method.* New York: Pergamon Press, 1977.
13. Guion, R. M. Recruiting, selection, and job placement. In M. D. Dunnette (Ed.). *Handbook of Industrial and Organizational Psychology.* Chicago: Rand-McNally, 1976.
14. Miner, M. G. & Miner, J. B. *Employee Selection within the Law.* Washington, D.C.: The Bureau of National Affairs, 1978.
15. Uniform guidelines on employee selection procedures (1978). *Federal Register,* 1978, **43,** 38290–38309.
16. Task Force on Assessment Center Standards. Standards and ethical considerations for assessment center operations. *Personnel Administrator,* 1980, **25** (2), 35–38.

17. Henderson, R. *Performance Appraisal: Theory to Practice.* Reston, Va.: Reston Publishing Co., 1980.

18. Landy, F. J. & Farr, J. L. Performance rating. *Psychological Bulletin,* 1980, **87,** 72–107.

19. Meyer, H. H., Kay, E., & French, J. R. P., Jr. Split roles in performance appraisal. *Harvard Business Review,* 1965, **43** (1), 123–129.

20. McConkie, M. L. A clarification of goal setting and appraisal processes in MBO. *Academy of Management Review,* 1979, **4,** 29–40.

21. Sloma, R. S. *How to Measure Managerial Performance.* New York: Macmillan, 1980.

—2—

Needs Assessment Approaches for Training Development

Irwin L. Goldstein
William H. Macey
Erich P. Prien

This chapter concerns needs assessment issues involving systematic modes of instruction designed to produce environments that mold or shape behavior to satisfy stated objectives. In this sense, training can be defined as the systematic acquisition of skills, rules, concepts, or attitudes that results in improved performance in a work environment.

If an opinion on the relationship of training programs to performance and productivity is entirely based upon the criteria of hours of effort or funds expended, then it would be necessary to agree that training must be an extremely efficient approach. For example, most surveys indicate that over 90 percent of private corporations have some type of systematic training program. A catalogue released by the U. S. Civil Service Commission (4) presenting training programs for use by educationally disadvantaged employees lists over 50 basic reading programs, and an analysis of the program of the Department of Defense for fiscal year 1977 indicates that over 6 billion dollars are allocated for military training efforts (5).

These efforts are expended on training efforts because there is an inherent faith that such instructional efforts provide results in terms of better job performance and increased productivity. Indeed most of these financial awards are for the development of expensive new techniques (e.g., flight simulators), and very little attention is given to needs assessment techniques or evaluation efforts to determine the utility of the approaches. However, there is a growing concern tht training programs do not achieve their potential.

Many persons do not want to attend training programs. That might be a rude shock to persons who design and sell instructional programs. However, many trainees find that training programs are not relevant to their job, or that training emphasizes constructs previously learned, or that what is learned in training is not accepted by the supervisor for on-the-job performance. Further, there are researchers who believe that constraints within the work organization prevent effective training programs from producing changes on the job. All such concerns reflect the lack of emphasis given to the needs assessment aspects of instructional design.

Many of the ideas in this article were liberally borrowed from previous work (see references 1, 2, and 3) by the first author.

THE USE OF NEED ASSESSMENT TECHNIQUES

Training analysts are unique in their treatment of need assessment techniques. For some reason they have tended to focus their attention on instructional techniques rather than a consideration of the needs and a determination of which instructional technique is likely to best fit that need. Thus, as described by Campbell (6), the training field is dominated by a fads approach. Children go from yo-yos to hoola hoops to skate boards, and training directors move from sensitivity training to organizational development to behavioral role modeling. Probably each of these techniques has a place (for the children also), but analysts never seem to find out very much about their approach before they are off examining another type of program. Following fads in this way places a heavy emphasis on the development of techniques without consideration of needs assessment followed by a matching of the technique to the needs. Machinists examine the job they must perform before choosing their tools, and a gardener usually chooses a sprinkling system rather than a bucket to water a half-acre lawn. Yet analysts still have to be warned about selecting tools and finding something they fit by quotes like the following:

> If you don't have a gadget called a teaching machine, don't get one. Don't buy one; don't borrow one; don't steal one. If you have such a gadget, get rid of it. Don't give it away, for someone else might use it. This is a most practical rule, based on empirical facts from considerable observation. If you begin with a device of any kind, you will try to develop the teaching program to fit that device. (7), (p. 478).

Gilbert is not saying that teaching machines or sensitivity training or CAI or any other technique doesn't work. He is saying that the design of change programs cannot begin with instructional media. Instead it is necessary to use need assessment procedures to determine the objectives of instructional programs so that the criteria for evaluation and the employment of programs are based upon sound decisions.

The consequences that occur when need asssessment approaches are not utilized was amply demonstrated in an investigation (8) of 418 hard-core unemployed trainees in a program to train highway construction machinery operators. The authors were able to obtain information from 270 graduates. Of this group, 61 percent of the graduates were employed and 39 percent unemployed at the time of the interview. In addition, more than half of the employed group said they were without jobs more than 60 percent of the time. Some of the reasons for the unemployment situation were inadequacies in training, which included not enough task practice and insufficient training time. The details showed that the program was not based upon a consideration of the job components. One trainee noted that "the contractors laughed when I showed them my training diploma and said, 'come back after you get some schooling buddy' " (pp. 32–33). In a now familiar lament, the authors of the report wonder how a training program could be designed without a thorough analysis of the skills required.

The reason for this state of affairs is probably rather complex. Training analysts appear to have adopted the fads approach based upon a forlorn belief that the next toy they purchase will provide the answers to their training problem. This appears to have resulted in an approach dominated by anecdotal testimonials rather than a research approach. Campbell, Dunnette, Lawler, and Weick (9) expressed this problem especially well.

> First, we must state quite bluntly that there is simply a great need for more research and for a wider variety of research. This may sound trite, but we are frankly surprised by the extremely limited nature of managerial training studies done thus far. (pp. 480.481)

The importance of techniques that focus on analyses of the required person-analysis techniques is emphasized by Bray's studies (10) concerning the use of assessment centers for middle managers. He noted that 45 percent of the persons attending an assessment center were judged not promotable; the areas in which these managers were judged deficient were natural areas on which to focus future training programs. In another person analysis focusing on the knowledge, skills, and abilities necessary to perform the job of missile technician for the U.S. Navy, Panell and Laabs (11) discovered on the basis of performance-oriented tests that critical performance deficiencies existed. Interestingly, this study found that the performance deficiencies existed because the extreme reliability of the equipment resulted in technicians not practicing their skills, and also resulted in the technicians judging the training to be nonessential.

Most of these studies indicate that as far as need assessment is concerned, it is especially important to establish techniques that help to determine the tasks, knowledge, skills, abilities, and behaviors necessary for job performance. Then there is the additional question of determining which of these behaviors should be taught in the training program and which techniques are most likely to impact those skills. This point is well expressed by Campbell et al. (9) for managerial training.

> Taken together, questions related to what techniques are best for what kinds of content and how such combinations are related to managerial behavior show that the need for more and broader research has reached alarming proportions. (p. 481)

In their original text, McGehee and Thayer (12) identified three important components in the needs assessment process. One component is task analysis, which identifies the relevant tasks to be performed in the work organization. A second component is person analysis, which identifies the required knowledge, skills, and abilities to perform these tasks. Another component is organizational analysis, which refers to the identification of the relevant organizational characteristics that affect the design and success of the training program. Unfortunately, since McGehee and Thayer's work, intensive development of needs assessment procedures has not been quickly forthcoming. The remainder of this chapter discusses an approach to the development of needs assessment information as inputs for the training development process, beginning with material related to task and person analysis.

THE USE OF TASK AND PERSON ANALYSIS AS A NEEDS ASSESSMENT TOOL

Macey, Prien, and Goldstein (13) have designed an approach for the development of input information for the training program. These authors discuss three domains (see Table 2.1) by which jobs can be characterized and identified.

The first domain of interest reflects what individuals do in their jobs. These tasks (or job behaviors as they are referred to in the Uniform Guidelines), as they shall be subsequently referred to, are those activities or job operations engaged in by workers that produce an identifiable output (14). The determination of these tasks corresponds to what McGehee and Thayer referred to as "task analysis."

The second domain deals with why individuals vary in their levels of performance in doing a given task. This domain is defined in terms of the knowledge, skills, abilities, and other characteristics (KSAOs or job elements) that individuals bring with them to or acquire in their jobs. This job element domain serves to explain why some individuals perform tasks in a manner contributing to the effectiveness of the organization whereas others do not. The determination of this second domain of person characteristics corresponds to what McGehee and Thayer referred to as person analysis.

The third domain is that which describes or characterizes the variability among individuals in their performance of the tasks that define their jobs. This *performance* domain differs from the *task* domain in that it is in the performance domain that a sense of quality or quantity is attached to a particu-

Table 2.1 Definition of Job Content Domains

Task domain	Activities or processes in which workers engage to produce an identifiable output.
Element domain	Knowledge, skills, and abilities or other characteristics required to perform tasks.
Performance domain	The interaction of the task and element domain, the description of observable worker activity.

lar activity. The type of performance statements collected in this type of analysis are often used in performance appraisal rating scales. These types of scales are useful in analyzing performance both in training and on the job. They also clearly indicate the target behaviors for the training program.

An elaboration of the specific procedures used to collect information related to the three domains discussed above would be beyond the scope of this paper. However, the next several sections present an abbreviated version of the types of procedures that would be utilized. The reader should note that the procedures discussed here are mainly related to the task and person analysis phases of needs assessment. Organizational analysis is discussed in a later section of this paper.

Phase 1

The collection of job information is greatly facilitated by the use of a structure or framework for organizing and describing the content domain data acquired through the application of various data collection procedures. This is achieved through an examination of available training records and materials, and direct observation of the work setting and process by the researcher. The information acquired in this stage provides a general understanding of business operations, terminology, and so on. The outcome of this research phase is a broad framework within which information acquired in later phases of the project could be placed. This phase is also critical for the collection of organizational analysis information as well as task and person analysis.

Phase 2

The second phase of the job analysis involves a series of interviews with individuals who are qualified as job content experts within the organization. The purpose of these interviews is to collect information about the tasks employees perform, and the duty based knowledge, skills, and abilities required to perform those tasks. The result of these interviews is a set of descriptors in the task (task analysis) and element (person analysis) domain.

Examples of task statements for a large national service organization are presented in Table 2.2. The rules in preparing task statements include the following:

1. Use a terse, direct style avoiding long involved sentences that may confuse that organization. Avoid words that do not give necessay information.
2. Begin each task statement with a functional verb that identifies the primary job operation. Make sure that the word specifically describes the work to be accomplished. For example, the worker may "write a report, or may communicate verbally with the next shift supervisor or may perform both tasks." If it is only indicated that the worker "write a report to another supervisor," it is not clear which activities were involved. Also the primary job

Table 2.2 Examples of Tasks and Elements

Tasks	Elements
Assist customers in opening or closing savings and checking accounts.	Ability to organize recorded information in a way which permits evaluation by others.
Take customer credit information and complete loan documentation form.	Knowledge of budget preparation procedures for department or specific area of responsibility.
Interview customers to complete loan application.	Knowledge of principles of finance.
Investigate and resolve customer problems with personal banking services.	Ability to express explanations of qualitative data in narrative form.

operation suggested is writing rather than communicating or informing another supervisor.

3. The statement should describe what the worker does, how the worker does it, and why the worker does it. In the example presented above, it is not clear why the worker communicated with the supervisor. If the statement said "Inform next shift supervisor of department status through written or verbal reports," the reader would know what, how, and why the task was performed.
4. The tasks should be stated completely but they should not be so detailed that the statement becomes a time and motion study. Tasks should include infrequent as well as frequent duties. If different individuals are given the responsibility of the task on a rotating basis, the task statement should be introduced by the word "may."
5. After the task statements are collected based upon the activities specified in phases 1 and 2 above, the statements are then evaluated for ambiguity, clarity, and accuracy by the researchers and training analysts to insure that all of the content domain was represented.

Examples of element statements for a large national service organization are also presented in Table 2.2. These characteristics, which specify the person attributes necessary to perform the tasks, are also developed during phases 1 and 2. The characteristics include the following:

Knowledge (K) An understanding of facts and principles related to a particular subject or subject area.

Skill (S) Ability to perform acts with ease and precision.

Ability (A) The power to perform a function, physical or mental.

Other Characteristics (O) Other characteristics including personality interest factors.

There are several general rules for writing element statements. They are:

1. Maintain a reasonable balance between generality and specificity. Exactly how generally or specifically an element should be stated will depend on its intended use. When the information is being used to design an instruction program, it must be specific enough to suggest what must be learned in training.
2. Avoid simply restating a task or duty statement. Such an approach is redundant and usually provides very little new information about the job. It is necessary to ask what knowledge, skills, or abilities are necessary to perform the task. For example, a task might be to "analyze hiring patterns to determine whether company practices are consistent with fair employment practices guidelines." Clearly one of the knowledge components for this task will involve "knowledge concerning federal, state and local guidelines on fair employment practices." Another component might involve "ability to use statistical procedures appropriate to performing these analyses."
3. Avoid the error of including trivial information when writing the KSAOs. For example, for a supervisor's job "knowledge of how to order personal office supplies" might be trivial. However, because the omission of key job elements is a more serious error than including trivia, include job elements if they are borderline examples.

Phase 3

In this phase of the project, subject matter experts (SMEs) including job incumbents, supervisors, and members of management provide further information about the job content domains. In order to meet the requirements of identifying training needs SMEs provide several judgments of the task and element statement developed in Phase 2. Some of the kinds of judgments that could be obtained include the following:

For Task Statements

1. **Importance.** SMEs rate the criticality of the task for full job performance.
2. **Frequency.** SMEs indicate the relative frequency with which tasks are performed on the job.
3. **Difficulty in acquiring proficiency.** SMEs indicate how difficult it is to acquire proficiency at that task during job operations.

For Element Statements

1. **Difficulty in learning.** SMEs indicate how difficult it is to gain competence with reference to the knowledge, skills, and abilities necessary for full job performance.
2. **Importance.** SMEs rate the criticality of knowledge, skills, and abilities for full job performance.
3. **Opportunity to acquire.** Ratings are collected pertaining to the opportunity to acquire requisite knowledge, skills, and abilities on the job.

Phase 4

The fourth phase of the needs assessment strategy comprises the data analyses necessary to define the content of the job domain relevant for training purposes. Ammerman and Pratzner (15) have suggested that two issues are relevant here. First, which of those tasks that are relevant to a job should be represented in the training curriculum? Second, for those tasks to be represented in the program, what should be emphasized?

Answers to these questions can be obtained through an evaluation of the inventory data. To summarize the inventory responses for decision making purposes, composite indices can be developed to reflect the different judgments provided by the SMEs for the task and element statements. These composite indices can be developed to reflect the logic that the tasks considered most important in the development of training content are those given the highest priority in the job, and those that are difficult to acquire proficiency in. Similarly, the content to be included in the training curriculum can be identified with reference to a composite index identifying the knowledge, skills, and abilities important for full job performance, and for which there is a minimum opportunity to learn on the job. The composite indices are thus evaluated to determine the content and priorities of the training curriculum.

In addition to providing input for the design of new instructional programs, the thoughtful application of job analysis procedures can provide useful input relevant to a variety of training development and evaluation questions. Some of the other potential applications include the following:

1. **Examination of previously designed training programs.** It is possible to compare the emphasis of training programs presently being used with the job analysis information. This type of comparison could determine whether the emphasis in training is being placed on tasks and elements that are important and that are not easily learned on the job.

2. **Design of trainee assessment instruments.** Job analysis information provides valuable information on the capabilities of trainees to perform the job appropriately. As such, the job analysis procedures can provide input to design performance appraisal instruments to assess the capabilities of trainees at the end of training and on the job. It is also possible to design performance appraisal instruments to determine which employees presently occupying jobs might need further training.

3. **Input to the interaction between selection systems and training systems.** The determination of the task and element domains can provide input into the selection system by specifying the KSAOs required to perform the various job tasks. The degree to which the selection system is able to identify and hire persons with various KSAOs affect the design of the training system. For example, training programs should not emphasize those KSAOs already in the repertoire of the trainee. Often this results in a training program that is not only more interesting but also less time consuming.

It is important to emphasize the point that the choice of a particular methodology should be based on an analysis of the particular application requiring job information. Further, even the choice of questions within a particular methodology is dependent upon the application. Thus, in some cases, criticality of performance information is important, while in other cases opportunity to learn or information related to where learning takes place is the key issue. In other instances, a whole variety of questions must be addressed. The critical point is that thoughtful planning that considers the variety of methods and applications must precede any job analysis effort. It is a waste of valuable resources to conduct a job analysis effort only to discover that the wrong questions have been asked or the wrong problem has been solved. It is of course an even more serious waste of valuable resources to design a training program without a careful job analysis. Unfortunately, even when job analysis is performed and the training program is well designed, there appear to be instances when training does not result in learning being transferred onto the job. This problem involves another aspect of needs assessment known as organizational analysis.

THE USE OF ORGANIZATIONAL ANALYSIS AS A NEEDS ASSESSMENT TOOL

While lip service is paid, there is a general failure to understand the implications of the idea that training programs are simply one part of an organization. It is necessary to realize that analyses of training programs force consideration of the fact that something learned in one environment (training) will be performed in another (on the job). Thus the trainee will enter a new environment to be affected by all of the interacting components that represent organizations today. Certainly there are some aspects of the environment that help determine the success or failure of training programs beyond the attributes the trainee must gain as a result of attending the instructional program. Also judgments about the success of a training program involve variables other than the performance of the trainee. For example, training programs are often judged to be failures because of organizational constraints that were not originally intended to be addressed by the instructional program. Salinger (16) reported on disincentives to effective employee training, including supervisors who do not accept the practices taught by the training program and supervisors who cannot meet their required production norms while their employees are in training. In some cases there are implicit organizational goals that the instructional program fails to address because they have never been made explicit. Thus Lynton and Pareek (17) have described a program that successfully results in training foreign-born engineers in American universities. However, failure to specify the organizational objectives and their consequences resulted in a program that did not meet the needs of the original country. In this case an organizational objective was to have the trained engineer return home. Any examination of that objective would have shown the program to be unrealistic because the training qualified individuals for jobs that simply did not exist in their native environment.

As complex as the specification of systemwide organizational objectives appears to be, the determination of the objectives by themselves will not do the job. Unfortunately, many of the situations are also marked by organizational conflicts that are very disruptive. For example, conflicts between government sponsors of the program, the employers, and the training institutions can completely disrupt the program (18). Many of these conflicts are based upon the different parties to the program having different sets of equally unspecified goals and expectations. Thus the community training organizations might see their role as introducing people into the world of work, while the employer is concerned with obtaining and retraining people at a minimum cost. When these conflicts remain unidentified they remain unresolved, and the result is a situation with conflicting goals and objectives that eventually undermines the potential success. These types of problems argue for the establishment of organizational analysis procedures as part of a needs assessment. As a result of this type of analysis, it may be possible to both identify organizational goals and solve potential organizational conflicts. Then the instructional program is more likely to be relevant and produce transfer to the work organization. Researchers and program planners might consider asking themselves the following organizational analysis questions:

Are there unspecified organizational goals that should be translated into training objectives or criteria?

Are the various levels in the organization committed to the training objectives?

Have the various levels or interacting units in the organization participated in the development of the program beginning at the need assessment?

Are key personnel ready to accept the behavior of the trainees as well as serve as models of the appropriate behavior?

Will trainees be rewarded on the job for the appropriate learned behavior?

Is training being utilized as a way of overcoming other organization problems or organizational conflicts that require other types of solutions?

If the responses to these questions leave the reader with an uneasy feeling of uncertainty, perhaps the training program should be reconsidered by performing an organizational analysis first.

CONCLUDING REMARKS

This chapter offers the view that emphasis on the design of new instructional technologies is misplaced. Instead there should be increased concern over the development of appropriate need assessment procedures that consider both job and organizational analyses. Then it should be possible to determine what tasks are performed, what behavior is essential to the performance of those tasks, what type of learning is necessary to acquire such behavior, and what type of training method is best suited to accomplish that type of learning. Finally, further understanding and recognition that training is a process within an organization must be reflected within the study of instructional systems. Thus need assessment should consider the possibility that relevant instructional programs might be consumed by organizational conflicts; evaluation designs must recognize that the training program and the evaluation is an intervention within the structure of the organization.

REFERENCES

1. Goldstein, I. L. *Training: Program Development and Evaluation.* Monterey, Calif.: Brooks/Cole, 1974.
2. Goldstein, I. L. The pursuit of validity in the evaluation of training programs. *Human Factors Journal,* 1978, **20,** 131–144.
3. Goldstein, I. L. Training in work organizations. *Annual Review of Psychology.* Palo Alto, Calif.: Annual Review, 1980.
4. U.S. Civil Service Commission. *Catalog of Basic Education Systems.* Washington, D.C.: U.S. Government Printing Office, 1971.
5. Orlansky, J. *The RDT & E Program of the DoD on Training.* Institute for Defense Analysis (IDA Log No. HQ 77-19304). July 1977.
6. Campbell, J. P. Personnel training and development. *Annual Review of Psychology.* Palo Alto, Calif.: Annual Review, 1971.
7. Gilbert, T. F. On the relevance of laboratory investigation of learning to self-instructional programming. In A. A. Lumsdaine and R. Glaser (Eds.). *Teaching Machines and Programmed Instruction.* Washington, D.C., National Education Association, 1960.
8. Miller, R. W. & Zeller, F. H. *Social Psychological Factors Associated with Responses to Retraining.* Final Report, Office of Research and Development. Appalachian Center, West Virginia University, U.S. Dept. of Labor, 1967.
9. Campbell, J. P., Dunnette, M. P., Lawler, E. E., III, & Weick, K. E., Jr. *Managerial Behavior, Performance, and Effectiveness.* New York: McGraw-Hill, 1970.
10. Bray, D. W. The assessment center method. In R. L. Craig (Ed.). *Training and Development Handbook.* New York: McGraw-Hill, 1976.
11. Panell, R. C. & Laabs, G. J. Construction of a criterion-referenced, diagnostic test for an individualized instructional program. *Journal of Applied Psychology,* 1979, **64,** 255–262.
12. McGehee, W. & Thayer, P. W. *Training in Business and Industry.* New York: Wiley, 1961.
13. Macey, W. H., Prien, E. P., & Goldstein, I. L. *Multi-Method Job Analysis.* Working Paper, 1980.

14. Ash, R. A., Levine, E. L., Sistrunk, F., & Smith, P. L. *The Collection, Analysis and Use of Information about Jobs in the Criminal Justice System: Essential Elements in a Comprehensive Human Resources Program.* Paper presented at the Symposium on Job-Task Analysis, Law Enforcement Assistance Administration, U.S. Dept. of Justice, Dallas, Texas, November 1978.

15. Ammerman, H. L. & Pratzner, F. C. *Performance Content for Job Training.* Vols. 1-5. R & D Series No. 121–125. Columbus, Ohio: Center for Vocational Education, 1977.

16. Salinger, R. D. *Disincentives to Effective Employee Training and Development.* Washington, D.C.: U.S. Civil Service Commission Bureau of Training, 1973.

17. Lynton, R. P. & Pareek, U. *Training for Development.* Homewood, Ill.: Irwin, 1967.

18. Goodman, P. S. Hiring and training the hard core unemployed: A problem in system definition. *Human Organization,* 1969, **28,** 259–269.

—3—

Attitudes and Motivation

Raymond A. Katzell, Ph.D.

INTRODUCTION

A universally accepted psychological law is that performance is a joint product of ability and motivation. This chapter focuses on the last term in that statement, and on its implications for performance, especially as related to work.

Historically, psychology's first applications to industry addressed ability-related issues such as aptitude testing, skill training, motion and fatigue study, and the like. Partly in response to the Hawthorne studies and partly to the democratic ideals of the World War II period, the postwar years witnessed a burgeoning interest reflected in the title of M. S. Viteles' landmark book, *Motivation and Morale in Industry* (1). The theme expressed in that title continues to be important in contemporary industrial and organizational psychology.

There are mainly two reasons for this: (a) motivation and morale are often viewed as impinging on organizational success; and (b) they are also considered important in themselves as ingredients of the well-being of workers and as responsibilities of good corporate citizens. (The term "worker" is used here to refer to all gainfully employed persons, regardless of the type or level of their jobs).

Those two sets of reasons may be categorized respectively as economic and humanistic. They are of course not necessarily unrelated. More recently, attention has focused on the implication of attitudinal and motivational factors in the off-the-job adjustment and happiness of workers and their families (see 2, for example).

Much attention has been given to refining the relevant concepts, instruments, and techniques for studying employee attitudes and motivation; we will soon make reference to examples of that work. We will also cite research on the relationships among them, which is important in understanding their dynamics. The last part of this article will describe programs aimed at improving worker attitudes, motivation, and performance, that is, the practical payoff of the preceding theory, instrumentation, and research.

Adapted with permission from the American Psychological Association from an article by the same author and entitled Work Attitudes, Motivation, and Performance, *Professional Psychology*, 1980, **11**, 409–420. Copyright 1980.

WORK MOTIVATION

Motivation is of course a wide-ranging and central topic that permeates all of psychology, and there are numerous theoretical approaches to it. In part this is because motivation is a multivariate concept, involving properties of a person, of the environment, and of their transactions, and having both cognitive and behavioral aspects. We will confine ourselves here to those approaches that have been most widely applied to explaining work behavior. These approaches will be discussed under two main rubrics: those which emphasize the motivational characteristics or *traits of the workers,* and those which emphasize motivational properties of the *work situation.*

Motivational Traits

Managers, psychologists, and others concerned with predicting work performance have been interested in assessing a person's predisposition to work hard or long or with satisfaction, either in general or under given circumstances. Employment interviews and application forms often are designed in part to get at such qualities. The earliest psychometric approach to this subject was in terms of vocational interests, which gave impetus to the development of questionnaires for the purpose, such as the well-known Strong Vocational Interest Blank (3) and the Kuder Preference Record (4).

Values represent another class of motivational traits that have been employed in studies of workers. They have been defined as "an abstract concept . . . that defines for an individual or for a social unit what ends or means to an end are desirable" (5). Tests for measuring values include some that are concerned with general life values, such as the familiar Allport-Vernon-Lindzey Study of Values (6), and others that are more specifically addressed to values in work settings (e.g., 7). Also of interest has been measuring the degree to which work is valued in and of itself, often called the "work ethic" or "Protestant ethic" (8).

A third group of motivational dispositions have variously been termed needs, wants, desires, and similar terms indicating states or objects that workers say they would like to obtain. Psychometrically, these are sometimes assessed by simple ratings of how much of them a person would like, and sometimes by inventories that infer their strength from responses to a set of questions, such as assessment of Murray's system of needs (9) via the Edwards Personal Preference Schedule (10).

Trait measures have traditionally been employed as predictors of vocational choice, tenure, satisfaction, and effectiveness. More recently they have also been employed as moderators of the relationships between organizational practices and their consequences. For example, it has been found that employees' reactions to supervisor authoritarianism are moderated by the former's need for independence: the more dependent the employee, the more favorable the reaction to authoritarian supervisors. There is also a small but important body of work that concerns changes in traits as a consequence of occupational experience (e.g., 11).

Another strand of interest has been stimulated by Maslow's (12) theory of the hierarchy of motives. The current consensus appears to be that motives do not align themselves neatly into Maslow's five-stage sequence of prepotency, but that there is some substance to the notion of hierarchy. Thus Alderfer's (13) reformulation is that there are three basic sets of needs that are always present (existence, relatedness, growth), that these form a hierarchy based on abstraction from low to high as listed above, that higher-order needs become more salient as other needs are satisfied, and that the less that higher needs are satisfied, the stronger becomes the desire to satisfy the lower-order needs.

Motivating Situations

Our second broad category of approaches is concerned with how different situations or environments motivate differences in work behavior. Probably the oldest of these views derives from Thorndike's law of effect and its consequences for the study of potent rewards and punishments. In contemporary thinking, this general approach is illustrated by the two-factor theory of Herzberg and his associates (14). This theory posits that rewards that people may attain through work comprise two types. Hygiene factors are *extrinsic* to the work itself and include such outcomes as pay, relations with the supervisor, working conditions, and job security. Motivating factors are *intrinsic* to work and its accomplishment, and include achievement, recognition, and responsibility. The presence of the latter group of factors is posited as resulting in job satisfaction and productive effort, whereas the former are supposed merely to avert dissatisfaction and withdrawal. Although the intrinsic-extrinsic distinction has been verified, that is not unequivocally true of the assertion that they correspond respectively to unipolar scales of satisfaction versus dissatisfaction and that only the former are associated with the motivation to produce, whereas the latter only prevent withdrawal.

The notion that work can be intrinsically motivating has sparked research aimed at identifying more precisely just what are the motivating features. Deci presents evidence that intrinsic motivation comes from the job itself and that extrinsic rewards may interfere with the development of intrinsic motivation (15, 16). A particularly well documented answer to that question is given by the research of Hackman and Oldham (17). They report that work is intrinsically motivating when it features skill variety, task identity, significance, autonomy, and feedback.

Also related to rewards and punishments is the approach of modern behaviorists, who emphasize the power that certain stimuli have to evoke or to inhibit the behavior that preceded them. Such stimuli are called, respectively, positive and aversive reinforcers. However, whereas effect theorists are largely concerned with the nature and effects of the particular stimuli that serve as rewards and punishments, behaviorists like B. F. Skinner focus on specifying the desired features of the contingencies that exist between that behavior and the reinforcers, for example, whether the behavior is always or only sometimes reinforced or the time inervals elapsing between behaviors and reinforcements (18, 19). Applications of this approach are today often called behavior modification.

Another approach to defining motivating situations goes back to the aspiration studies of Kurt Lewin and his students, and has been applied to work behavior by Locke (20) and others. Its essence is that clear and difficult but attainable work goals induce stronger motivation and better performance than do their opposites. Satisfaction is seen as related to the extent to which goals that have been set are actually achieved.

The approach of equity theory is to define the motivating situation in terms of the perceived disparity between what a worker puts into a job and what he or she gets out of it, especially as compared to others (21). Since people are viewed as requiring congruity in their experiences, inequity is believed to induce a drive to eliminate or at least reduce it. Among the ways of doing so are changes in amount or quality of production, changes in cognitions, and withdrawal. Such predictions have generally been supported in laboratory research using financial rewards, e.g. "overpaid" workers paid by piece rate have lower productivity than those paid "equitably." Because little of the research has been done in real-life organizations, we will not further discuss this potentially useful approach but rather refer the interested reader to the reviews by Campbell and Pritchard (22) and Katzell, Yankelovich, et al. (23).

We will turn next to a theoretical approach that has probably generated the largest amount of interest in recent years, called expectancy theory. Vroom (24) is generally credited with originating its most explicit application to work behavior. The basic notion in expectancy theory is that effort and hence performance is proportional to the expectancy that effort will lead to a reward, weighted by the valence or attractiveness of the reward. Job satisfaction in turn is said to be equivalent to the valence of a job for a person. Vroom used the concept of instrumentality as a determiner of valence, that is, it is the perceived probability that an outcome (such as having a job) would lead to other valued outcomes. His formulation is often called VIE theory, after its three principal elements: Valence, Instrumentality, and Expectancy.

Partly because the original formulation often failed to predict actual work behavior accurately, various addenda and revisions have been made in recent years. Thus distinctions have been drawn between first and second level outcomes (performance and reward, respectively); different expectancies have been associated with those outcomes, feedback loops were added as well as external and internal pressures for superior effort, etc. These and other elaborations are discussed by Campbell and Pritchard (22), who conclude their discussion by saying, "The available data do not portray the VIE model as a very powerful explainer of behavior" (p. 92), but add that operational and conceptual problems may have done it disservice. There is some evidence that when such problems are mitigated, the expectancy approach does have utility.

WORK ATTITUDES

There are several kinds of attitudes that pertain to work, including job satisfaction, job involvement, and organizational climate. All are one or another verbal expression of a worker's interpretation or evaluation of his or her job or work situation. Because such evaluations imply a disposition to act in certain ways with respect to work, attitudes have a conceptual relationship to motivation. However, as we shall see, the correlations between attitudes and behavior are not consistently strong. This is partly because the action components of some attitudes are not particularly prominent, partly because attitudes tend to be tied to very specific aspects of the total behavioral setting, and partly because some of the ingredients of motivation are not well represented in a person's awareness and hence in his or her attitudes. In short, while attitudes play a part in work motivation, the two concepts are by no means identical. Workers may like their jobs but not work very hard, or they may work hard without especially liking it; however, all things being equal, workers who have positive attitudes toward their work are more likely to work hard, and those who are successful are more likely to have positive attitudes.

Because attitudes are verbal in nature, they are usually measured by questionnaires, or sometimes by interview. These techniques yield scores that quantify the respondent's attitudes regarding one or more aspects of the work sitution. Some of the principal types of work attitudes will next be described.

Job Satisfaction (JS)

JS refers to a worker's evaluation of his or her job, or various facets of it, on some scale of like-dislike. Among the more widely used and better standardized instruments for measuring it are the Job Descriptive Index or JDI (25) and the SRA Attitude Survey (26). Those are multidimensional; for instance, the JDI covers satisfaction with the supervisor, co-workers, pay, promotions, and the work itself. There are other questionnaires that furnish summary assessments of overall job satisfaction. Various JS instruments are described by Robinson, Athanasiou, and Head (27).

Job Involvement (JI)

This attitude represents the degree to which people say that they are wrapped up in their work, that is whether the job is a central life interest (28). The most widely used measure was devised by Lodahl and Kejner (29), and comprises questions by which respondents describe how salient their jobs are to them. A related attitude is that of job or organizational commitment (30), which refers to a worker's attraction or loyalty to a work situation.

Organizational Climate (OC)

This is a concept that has not yet quite achieved consensual definition. Indeed some authors have suggested that OC is essentially the same as JS. By now, however, the concept seems here to stay, although definitions and measures have yet to become standard. Some definitions have included both objective and subjective features of the human context of jobs, but the recent trend is to limit it to subjective impressions. Even here, a useful distinction may be made between passively perceived descriptions of organizational properties versus interpretations or meanings inferred by the individual workers. It may be appropriate to think of the former as denotative descriptions and the latter as connotative meanings, in which case it is only the latter that truly belong under the rubric of attitudinal variables and constructs; the term "psychological climate" is sometimes used for these personal interpretations (31).

One approach to measuring connotative work climates has been by means of adaptations of the semantic differential technique, in which interpretations are reported in terms of bipolar adjective scales, such as "weak-strong" and "good-bad." Factor analyses of such scales seem to yield three rather consistent dimensions, roughly corresponding to the semantic factors of evaluation, potency, and activity. Measures that have featured descriptions more than connotations have yielded such factors as autonomy, structure, reward orientation, and supportiveness. Several of the instruments used to measure climate have been described by Payne and Pugh (32), who also have summarized much of the research literature dealing with the subject.

Quality of Working Life (QWL)

QWL is a still newer concept that is receiving increasing attention. The term is being used in a variety of ways, sometimes no more than synonymously with JS. However, there seems to be a growing consensus that QWL is more comprehensive, that attitudinally it embraces not only JS but JI and OC and possibly some other constructs as well. Other conceptions emphasize desirable features of the work or work environment in addition to the attitudinal aspects. Some would even have the concept transcend the job's impact on the worker alone, and include also consideration of its eventual consequences on others whose welfare the worker affects: co-workers, employers, family, and community. The QWL theme is more comprehensively considered in other chapters in this volume, particularly Hackman and Jenks. For a review of the topic the interested reader is referred to Davis and Cherns (33).

RELATIONSHIPS AMONG ATTITUDINAL VARIABLES

Considerable attention has been given to the interrelationships among the variables described above. The purpose of that work is threefold: (a) better definition of the constructs; (b) understanding of their antecedent or causal factors; (c) determination of their possible effects on each other. Although much research has been addressed to those questions, the answers to the latter two remain obscure, primarily because the vast majority of the work has been correlational and cross-sectional. Thus we know quite a lot about what is related to what, but little about why. It would be neither possible nor appropriate to attempt to review that voluminous literature here. However, for illustrative purposes, some of the typical relationships that have been studied and reported are listed below:

JI is positively correlated with intrinsic JS, but not with extrinsic.

JS is higher when OC is viewed as high in achievement orientation.

JI is higher when OC is viewed as relatively participative.

Attitudinal variables have also been studied in relation to motivational characteristics of workers and work settings; some illustrative findings include:

JS is higher among workers who report that their needs are being met on the job.

Workers who have high JI tend to have stronger "higher-order" needs, for example, for autonomy and growth.

JS is positively correlated with job challenge.

Members of more cohesive work groups perceive OC as more employee-centered.

RELATIONSHIPS WITH JOB PERFORMANCE

Understandably, interest in discovering how attitudinal and motivational variables relate to job behavior and performance has been even stronger than determining their relations with one another. Again it is not feasible to review that extensive work here. However, the overall trends in the research findings will be summarized below, in relation to the two major categories of job behavior that have been studied: membership (including tenure, turnover, absenteeism, and tardiness), and effectiveness (usually quantity of production or performance ratings).

Job Satisfaction

By far the largest amount of attention has been given to the relationship between JS and performance. This is probably historically an outgrowth of the human relations hypothesis that happy workers are good workers. The empirical research lends some support to this belief as it applies to membership behavior, but little as it applies to effectiveness. As regards membership, the results of numerous studies indicate a moderate inverse relationship between overall JS and turnover. Relations with absenteeism and tardiness are usually somewhat weaker, but not insignificant.

Relations between JS and productivity are variable, although generally positive but weak. The relationship is moderated by various factors, being stronger, for example, when production is under workers' control, when rewards are contingent on performance, and when workers are relatively capable and involved with their work. To the extent that a relationship exists, it seems to be due at least as much to productivity being a cause of satisfaction as the reverse. However, the two are apparently often affected by different sets of conditions.

Job Involvement

No consistent relationship has been found between JI and effectiveness, possibly because the effectiveness measures have typically reflected quantity of work rather than quality. JI does appear to have modest inverse relationships with turnover and absenteeism.

Organization Climate

Because of lack of standardization of the concepts and measures of OC, it is difficult to draw a general picture. The best that can be said is that various climate variables have been found to correlate with various aspects of effectiveness. For example, a comparison of a number of organizations indicated that those with more employee-centered climates were usually more cost-effective and profitable. Relations between OC and membership behavior have received little attention.

Motivational Traits

There have been numerous demonstrations of significant relationships between various motivational traits and performance effectiveness under laboratory and other controlled conditions, usually with college students. Examples of such traits include achievement motivation, anxiety, Protestant or work ethic, and self-esteem. But those traits have often not been found to have significant correlations with actual job performance. The principal exceptions to that statement are measures of achievement needs and of power motivation when correlated with effectiveness of people in managerial or in sales positions. Personality and interest inventories have occasionally also been found to correlate with effectiveness in those and some other occupations, especially when special scoring keys have been empirically derived for each job situation. Such inventories have more generally been found to be better predictors of job choice, tenure, and satisfaction than of effectiveness.

Motivating Situations

Innumerable features of working environments, both physical and social, have been studied from the standpoint of their effects on worker attitudes, motivation, and performance. Below are lists of factors that research has indicated to be usually associated with superior effectiveness at work, owing at least in part to their favorable effects on attitudes and motivation. The appearance of an item in this list does not mean that it has universally been shown to have positive results, since the effectiveness of any practice depends on its appropriateness to a total context.

Organization-wide factors

Relatively small size (especially as regards turnover and absenteeism)

Few levels of authority

High influence and communication among levels and divisions

Mutual trust

Workers share organizational earnings

Adequate resources and technology

Flexible work schedules

Flexible packages of incentives, benefits, and opportunities (especially as regards attracting and retaining workers)

Work-group factors

Congruent, clear goals

Shared norms for good performance

High cohesiveness, when coupled with foregoing

Autonomy and self-determination, when coupled with self-contained resources and capability

Interchangeable or flexible jobs among members

Earnings proportional to group productivity

Supervisory behavior

Supervisor initiates and defines structure and tasks

Supervisor is supportive and considerate

Supervisor facilitates work of group members

Supervisor represents groups

Supervisor makes and communicates decisions

Supervisor encourages participation in decisions

(N.B. All of the above have variable effects, depending upon such moderating circumstances as the power of the supervisor's position, the capabilities and personalities of group members, environmental pressures, etc.)

Individual job factors

Clear, difficult, attainable, acceptable goals

Work fully utilizes worker's skills and abilities

Work offers variety and scope

Work provides social contacts

Work provides significance or sense of contribution

Work provides feedback regarding performance

Worker has freedom to carry out responsibilities

Availability of valent rewards

Rewards linked to performance and responsibility

Adequate resources

MOTIVATION PROGRAMS

The pragmatic test of the validity of the motivational principles summarized above lies in the results of applying them in work situations. Of the many such applications, an untold number have been informal, and remain unevaluated and unreported. But an appreciable number have been done systematically, and their experimental results published in the professional literature.

Katzell, Bienstock, and Faerstein (34) surveyed the American literature published in the five-year period of 1971 through 1975 and located 103 such programs, each of which was intended to improve the job performance of workers. The vast majority, but not all, involved efforts to do so by improving some aspect of worker attitudes or motivation, either explicitly or by implication. The 103 experiments were grouped under various rubrics corresponding to different kinds of interventions. We will briefly describe the principal types below. Elaborations of these brief descriptions are contained in other chapters of this book.

Selection and Placement

This type of program aims at improving work motivation by selecting workers whose motivational traits, attitudes, or values are better suited to the nature of the work. We have already alluded to studies of this type when, for example, mention earlier was made of the use of interest and personality inventories in improving the satisfaction and tenure of people selected for managerial and sales occupations. Evaluations of motivational characteristics are also usually a feature of management assessment programs (e.g., 11).

Training

As is also true of selection programs, many training efforts are addressed to improving cognitive or motor abilities, rather than motivational properties.

But programs of the latter type are not uncommon in industry. Sensitivity and human-relations training are familiar examples of this strategy. Newer techniques that have had success include behavior modeling, behavior modification, and achievement motivation acquisition. The common thread woven through all such programs is the objective of having the participants acquire new dispositions toward their work behavior.

Appraisal and Feedback

This category comprises various techniques of appraising the job performance of individual workers, and then furnishing individualized guidance by means of coaching, counseling, or information feedback. In contrast with older policies of providing annual postappraisal reports to employees, the newer approaches are more focused, specific, and frequent. Both performance and attitudes have been improved via such programs, but positive results are not universal.

Management by Objectives (MBO)

Like the preceding, MBO also involves appraisal and feedback. Its central feature is the joint definition by superiors and subordinates of concrete performance objectives for the latter's job. However, often in practice, the definition is not developed as jointly as the theory suggests. Levinson (35) wrote that many firms that employ MBO do not implement it in a way to achieve humanistic objectives and that generally the more powerful have the opportunity to manipulate the less powerful.

Goal-Setting

While related to both of the preceding, goal-setting programs usually focus on a limited number of specific production goals rather than the total job. Also the goals are usually set by management rather than jointly. Productivity improvements have often been reported (36), although effects on attitudes are unclear.

Financial Compensation

This category is of course as old as the institution of gainful employment. Recent studies have been concerned with improving the motivational value of specific features of compensation plans. These have included showing that linking compensation to production in some type of incentive plan can have positive effects on white-collar and service workers as well as factory workers, and that the concept is applicable to the improvement of absenteeism and tardiness as well as production. Evidence has also been found of the value of involving workers in the design of their incentive plan. There is growing interest in plant-wide income-sharing plans, although here too rigorous evaluative studies are scarce.

Job and Group Design

Sparked to a considerable extent by the emphasis on self-actualization and responsibility by people like Maslow and Herzberg, there has developed during the past ten or fifteen years a good deal of attention to the motivating content of the work itself. Accordingly, studies have been conducted of the value of increasing the variety of job duties, called job enlargement, and of their complexity or challenge, called job enrichment. In some cases the jobs of an entire work group have been redesigned with reference to one another and to those of other groups, in programs described by such labels as autonomous groups and job nesting. The current picture appears to support the utility of designing jobs so that they provide optimum levels of autonomy, variety, challenge, significance, and feedback (17, 37). The modifier "optimum" in the foregoing generalization signifies the need to tailor the design features to various aspects of the situation, including the needs and abilities of the workers, the technology, and the total management system. Failure to match the context can defeat the efforts, with the consequence that they eventually fail about as often as they succeed.

Supervisory Methods

It has become a platitude that the key to worker morale is the quality of supervision. This belief is reflected in the fact that the selection and training of supervisors and managers continues to be one of the more active applications of psychology in industry and government. Examples include installing a policy of greater participation by subordinates in decision making, and training supervisors in providing reinforcement, in goal setting, and in being more considerate of subordinates.

Work Schedules

Recent research on the effects of work schedules has focused on the 4/40 plan and on flexitime. The former consists of repatterning the 40-hour work week into four 10-hour days; experience with it, in those organizations where it is feasible, is generally but not always good. Women as a group have less favorable attitudes toward such a plan than do men. Flexitime permits workers freedom to arrive and leave daily at their convenience, as long as they work a fixed number of hours per week and are regularly present during a specified core period. Fairly popular in Europe, that plan is gaining acceptance in the United States; the limited experimental evaluations have generally indicated favorable effects on attitudes and sometimes performance (38).

Organization Structure

Various features of organization structure have been found to be correlated with worker attitudes and performance, especially the structure of authority and control. Experimental studies of restructuring are understandably rare.

Katzell, Yankelovich, et al. (23) have reviewed several that focused on the restructuring of authority and control, and found them generally to have positive effects. Organization development programs, discussed next, often include restructuring as part of the reform.

Sociotechnical Systems and OD

This category refers to programs involving changes of sufficient number and magnitude as to constitute a reformed work system. That kind of program is often called "organization development" (OD), especially if it emphasizes changes in approaches to solving problems and collaborative relationships (39). Katzell, Bienstock, and Faerstein (34) summarized the results of 12 such systems experiments reported during 1971 to 1975, 11 of which had generally favorable consequences. A comparison of various OD techniques in 23 organizations (40) has indicated that attitude survey feedback is a particularly effective way of inducing change. Other major change strategies include action, research, process consultation, training (including laboratory training), team building, and top-down policy change. A thorough reform of a work system typically involves several of such strategies employed in various parts of the organization at different times.

CONCLUDING SUMMARY

This overview has briefly described current thinking and practices relating to worker attitudes and motivation. We have seen that those endeavors can be described as being principally addressed to the conceptualization and measurement of relevant attitudinal and motivational constructs, empirical research intended to define the relations among such variables, integration of the resulting information into theoretical frameworks in order to foster understanding and prediction of important aspects of work behavior, and the application of those concepts, measures, and theories via programs designed to improve how workers feel about and perform their jobs. The empirical evidence is that those programs, more often than not, have at least limited success. Even though the field still has much that it needs to learn about the subjects, we appear to have developed a technology that has utility in serving humankind by making work both more humane and productive.

REFERENCES

1. Viteles, M. S. *Motivation and Morale in Industry.* New York, Norton, 1953.
2. U. S. Department of Health, Education and Welfare. *Work in America.* Cambridge, Mass. MIT Press, 1973.
3. Strong, E. K., Jr. & Campbell, D. P. *Strong-Campbell Interest Inventory.* Palo Alto, Calif. Stanford University Press, 1977.

4. Kuder, G. F. *Kuder Preference Record-Vocational.* Chicago, Science Research Associates, 1976.

5. English, H. B. & English, A. C. *A Comprehensive Dictionary of Psychological and Psychoanalytic Terms.* New York, Longmans, Green, 1958, p. 576.

6. Allport, G. W., Vernon, P. E. & Lindzey, G. *Study of Values.* 3rd ed. Boston, Houghton Mifflin, 1960.

7. Wollack, S., Goodale, J. G., Wijting, J. P. & Smith, P. C. Development of the survey of work values. *Journal of Applied Psychology,* 1971, **55,** 331–338.

8. Blood, M. R. Work values and job satisfaction. *Journal of Applied Psychology,* 1969, **53,** 456–459.

9. Murray, H. A. *Explorations in Personality.* New York, Oxford University Press, 1938.

10. Edwards, A. L. *Edwards Personal Preference Schedule.* New York, The Psychological Corporation, 1959.

11. Bray, D. W., Campbell, R. J., & Grant, D. L. *Formative Years in Business.* New York, Wiley, 1974.

12. Maslow, A. H. *Motivation and Personality.* New York, Harper, 1954.

13. Alderfer, C. P. *Existence, Relatedness, and Growth: Human Needs in Organizational Settings.* New York, Free Press, 1972.

14. Herzberg, F. *Work and the Nature of Man.* Cleveland, World, 1962.

15. Deci, E. L. Effects of externally mediated rewards on intrinsic motivation. *Journal of Personality and Social Psychology,* 1971, **18,** 105–115.

16. Deci, E. L. The effects on the contingent and non-contingent rewards and control on intrinsic motivation. *Organizational Behavior and Human Performance,* 1972, **8,** 217–229.

17. Hackman, J. R., & Oldham, G. R. Development of the Job Diagnostic Survey. *Journal of Applied Psychology,* 1975, **60,** 159–170.

18. Nord, W. R. Beyond the teaching machine: The neglected area of operant conditioning in the theory and practice of management. *Organizational Behavior and Human Performance,* 1969, **4,** 352–377.

19. Hamner, W. C., & Organ, D. W. *Organizational Behavior.* Dallas, Business Publications, 1978. Chaps. 3 and 11.

20. Locke, E. A. Toward a theory of task motivation and incentives. *Organizational Behavior and Human Performance,* 1968, **3,** 157–189.

21. Adams, J. S. Wage inequities, productivity, and work quality. *Industrial Relations,* 1963, **3,** 9–16.

22. Campbell, J. P. & Pritchard, R. D. Motivation theory in industrial and organizational psychology. In M. D. Dunnette (Ed.). *Handbook of Industrial and Organizational Psychology.* Chicago, Rand McNally, 1976.

23. Katzell, R. A., Yankelovich, D., et al. *Work, Productivity, and Job Satisfaction.* New York, The Psychological Corporation, 1975.

24. Vroom, V. H. *Work and Motivation.* New York, Wiley, 1964.

25. Smith, P. C., Kendall, L. M., & Hulin, C. L. *The Measurement of Satisfaction in Work and Retirement.* Chicago, Rand McNally, 1969.
26. Science Research Associates. *SRA Attitude Survey.* Chicago, Author, 1974.
27. Robinson, J. P., Athanasiou, R., & Head, K. B. *Measures of Occupational Attitudes and Occupational Characteristics.* Ann Arbor, Institute of Social Research, University of Michigan, 1969.
28. Rabinowitz, S. & Hall, D. T. Organizational research on job involvement. *Psychological Bulletin,* 1977, **84,** 265–288.
29. Lodahl, T. M. & Kejner, M. The definition and measurement of job involvement. *Journal of Applied Psychology,* 1965, **49** 24–33.
30. Steers, R. M. Antecedents and outcomes of organizational commitment. *Administrative Science Quarterly,* 1977, **22,** 46–56.
31. James, L. R. & Jones, A. P. Organizational climate: A review of theory and research. *Psychological Bulletin,* 1974, **81,** 1096–1112.
32. Payne, R. & Pugh, D. S. Organizational structure and climate. In M. D. Dunnette (Ed.). *Handbook of Industrial and Organizational Psychology.* Chicago, Rand McNally, 1976, pp. 1125–1173.
33. Davis, L. E. & Cherns, A. B. (Eds.). *The Quality of Working Life.* 2 Vols. New York, Free Press, 1975.
34. Katzell, R. A., Bienstock, P., & Faerstein, P. H. *A Guide to Worker Productivity Experiments in the United States,* 1971–75. New York, New York University Press, 1977.
35. Levinson, H. Management by whose objectives. *Harvard Business Review,* 1970, **48,** 125–134.
36. Latham, G. & Yukl, G. A. A review of research on applications of goal-setting in organizations. *Academy of Management Journal,* 1975, **18,** 824–845.
37. Hackman, J. R. Work design. In J. R. Hackman & J. L. Suttle (Eds..) *Improving Life at Work.* Santa Monica, Caif., Goodyear, 1977.
38. Ronen, S. *Flexible Working Hours.* New York, McGraw-Hill, 1980.
39. Huse, E. F. *Organization Development and Change.* St. Paul, Minn. West, 1975.
40. Bowers, D. G. OD techniques and their results in 23 organizations. *Journal of Applied Behavioral Science,* 1973, **9,** 391–409.

—4—

Management and Compensation

John M. Ivancevich

To attract qualified people to join work organizations, to keep them coming regularly to work, and to increase their desire to perform at high levels, organizations offer a combination of rewards and incentives to members. In exchange for these rewards and incentives employees provide their ability, skill, energy, and time. This network of relationships between work organizations and their employees has been described as a "psychological contract" (1). Under such a contract the individual employee and the organization each have expectations of the other.

A part of the employee's expectation set is to receive compensation for the contributions made to the organization. Employees want to know exactly what is expected of them and what level of performance they must achieve. They also want to have some say in the development of the performance standards. Through participation in the development of an organization's compensation system a spirit of trust, cooperation, and mutual respect between employer and employee can evolve. Organizations interested in establishing such a human and productive environment must understand the components of equitable compensation systems.

This chapter focuses on the nontechnical aspects of managing a fair and equitable compensation system. Managers can play a crucial role in compensation systems, especially if they understand how such a system can influence employee behavior. Therefore this chapter is primarily concerned with understanding the manner in which motivation to perform is linked to compensation plans. Because of space limitations the importance of noncompensation programs in motivating behavior will not be discussed. Furthermore, most of the descriptions of compensation theory, methods, and procedures must be purposefully kept brief. More complete discussion can be found in entire books about compensation (2, 3, 4).

THE REWARD SYSTEM

Organizations of any size distribute various rewards to their members regularly. Pay, promotions, transfers, time off, status symbols, and fringe benefits are all forms of reward. Because these rewards are important in different ways to each employee, the way they are distributed has profound effects on employees. If the rewards are to have a positive effect on employee behaviors and performance results, they must have several qualities (5, 6).

First, the rewards must be granted in such quantity so that employees' basic needs are satisfied. Research indicates that when employees receive less than they believe is adequate, they tend to become dissatisfied (3, 6, 26).

Second, the reward amounts received must compare favorably with reward amounts in other organizations. Unless favorable comparisons can be made, employees will be dissatisfied with their rewards. These comparisons with others are inevitable, and meeting the test of comparability is important to employees.

Third, the internal distribution of rewards must be perceived as being equitable by employees. Members compare their own situations and contributions with other co-workers inside the organization. If an employee believes that his or her reward is out of line, dissatisfaction, absenteeism, and turnover can result (7, 8).

Fourth, the reward system must contain some degree of individuality. That is, it should attempt to recognize and reward individual contribution. Unless individual differences among the contributions of employees are recognized, it is unlikely that the exchange of employee ability, skill, and effort for organizationally initiated rewards will be positive or predictable.

In summary, because of the nature of employees' reactions to rewards, a compensation program must be developed and implemented to meet four tests: (a) enough rewards to satisfy basic needs, (b) equity with the external marketplace, (c) equity within the organization, and (d) as much individuality as possible (6).

A reward system that incorporates these four tests can be portrayed in a simple framework. One segment of such a model can be designated the *compensation* portion and the other part is identified as the *noncompensation* portion (9).

Compensation

The monetary portion of a reward system is called *compensation*. The objective of compensation is to attract, retain, and motivate employees (10). There are distinct forms of compensation. For example, one concise classification of types of compensation is as follows:

Salaries or wages. The base pay that an employee receives on a periodic basis. The base pay is based on the job activity, seniority, and merit increases received by the job incumbent.

Bonuses. A lump-sum reward, usually distributed on a quarterly, semiannual, or annual basis.

Benefits. Medical, disability, and life insurance payments made by the organization.

The compensation received by employees enables them to exchange their earned dollars for desired goods and services. The employee's paycheck normally includes the base pay earned for a specified period. Benefits are provided in part or in total by the employer. Today benefits can cost an organization \$.10 to \$.40 of every dollar spent on compensation (11). Whether employees recognize the significance of benefit compensation is a debatable issue. Employee understanding and perceptions of the value of benefits in the compensation package have not always been accurate. In some cases the value of such benefits is taken for granted and assumed to be trivial.

Noncompensation

The noncompensation portion of a firm's reward system covers all nonmonetary factors. Any activity of the organization that has a direct or indirect impact on the cognitive, affective, and physical well-being of the employee and is not specifically monetary is considered a noncompensation reward (9).

Noncompensation rewards can enhance an employee's sense of achievement and personal growth. Some examples of possible noncompensation rewards for some employees that organizations have used are the following:

Redesigning jobs so that employees participate in more job-related decisions (12).

Developing small work teams to solve problems without close managerial control (13).

Allowing subordinates to mutually set goals with superiors on a fully participative basis (14, 15).

Enabling employees to make on-the-spot decisions without checking with a superior (16).

Each of these and other noncompensation rewards are not directly tied into the exchange of something monetary. They are purposefully designed to improve the performance and the quality of work life of employees. That is, hopefully the organization receives higher levels of performance and the employee is more satisfied and is inclined to continue working for the company. Unfortunately, not all employees would view these nonmonetary factors and opportunities as rewards.

The compensation and noncompensation portions are integrated into what is designated as the employee's view of rewards in Figure 4.1. Note that employees' motivation to exert effort is first influenced by personality, economics, health, and other exogenous variables. The performance occurs because abilities, skills, efforts, and experience are put to good use. The results of this use are evaluated by managers (performance appraisal) who then distribute compensation and noncompensation rewards. Each employee interprets the quantity, external equity, internal equity, and individuality of the

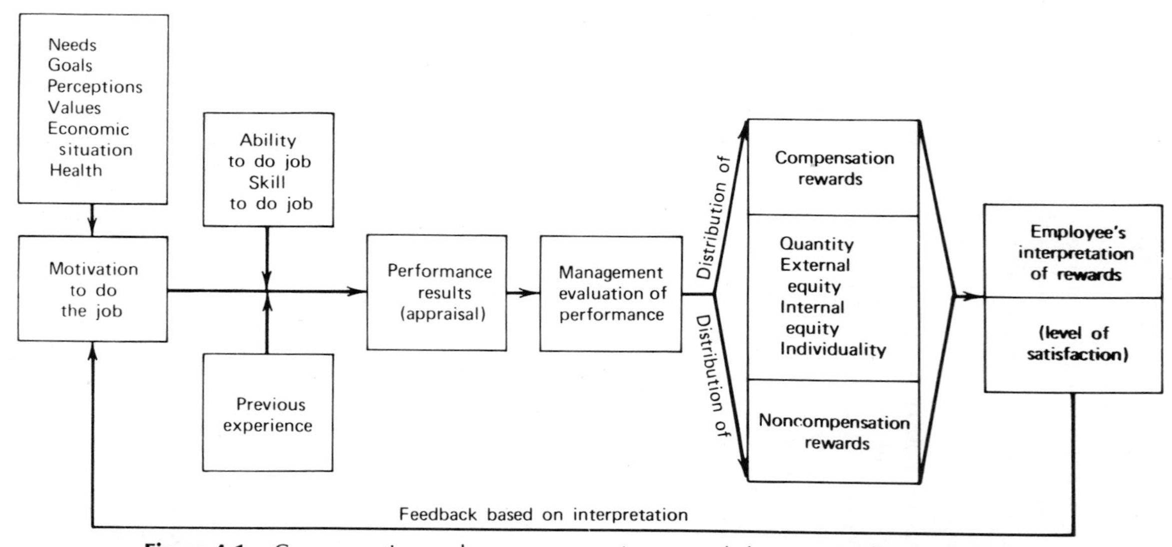

Figure 4.1 Compensation and noncompensation rewards from an employee's perspective.

rewards. To the extent that the rewards meet each employee's expectations, the person achieves a gratifying level of satisfaction.

THE COMPENSATION PLAN: METHODS

If any compensation plan is to attract, retain, and motivate employees it must meet the four tests stated above: quantity, external equity, internal equity, and individuality. To meet these tests and accomplish other organizational goals various methods are employed. For example, organizations use compensation surveys to determine how they match up with competition, performance appraisal to distribute the compensation, and job evaluation to develop internal equity across employees. These are methods that compensation experts and nonexperts have applied systematically on some occasions. Figure 4.2 presents the tests and some of the commonly used methods to accomplish the goals of compensation plans.

Government legislation is a fifth test that is incorporated in Figure 4.2 because of its importance. Such laws as the Davis-Bacon Act of 1931, the Social Security Act of 1935, the Fair-Labor Standards Act of 1938, the Equal Pay Act of 1963, the Civil Rights Act of 1964, and the Economic Stabilization Act of 1970 must be complied with by organizations (18). Thus any compensation plan must be legally correct before it is implemented.

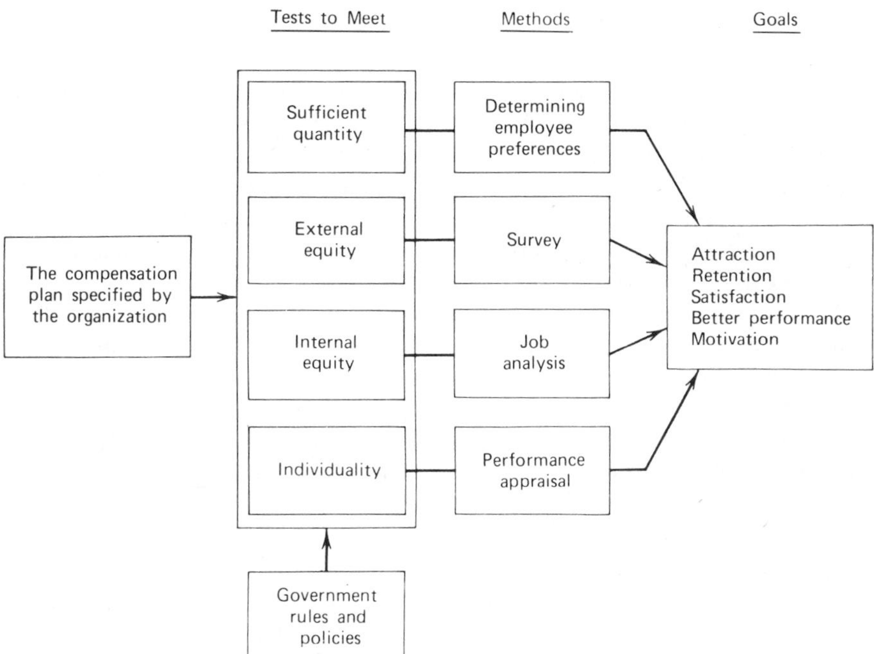

Figure 4.2 Compensation plan: tests, methods, and goals.

Determining Preferences

Employees each have an idea of what constitutes fair, large, and timely compensation. Some people view a $1.00 per hour or a $25 per week increase in pay as significant. Others would view these amounts as small and unimportant. The preferences held by a person are significantly influenced by values, needs, emotions, and goals. Of course, these cognitive and affective facets are not easily identifiable. They are what behavioral scientists aptly refer to as "in the head" variables (19).

Despite the difficulty of teasing out "in the head" preferences about compensation, managers must work at the task. Determining preferences will not occur unless managers observe, counsel, debate, and experiment on a regular basis. They need to *observe* employee behaviors, the linkage of rewards and performance, and their own values, needs, emotions, and goals. They also need to *counsel* with employees asking compensation preference questions, answering employee questions, and listening carefully. Furthermore, they need to *debate* with other managers their feelings about subordinate compensation preferences. This exchange of information can point out oversights and inaccuracies in one's thinking. Finally, they need to *experiment* with varying compensation packages (if within their control) and determine the short and long-term consequences. In essence, the manager must be skilled at observation, interviewing, and behavioral science principles concerning motivation.

Survey

The Bureau of Labor Statistics survey of professional, administrative, and clerical salaries is purchased by many organizations, who use this kind of survey or develop their own to learn about wages, salaries, and benefits. It is generally the rule to collect compensation data from the market area from which the firm draws human resources. For larger firms this may mean a national area must be surveyed; smaller organizations may seek compensation data from a local market.

The job survey is the most popular form of compensation survey (20). This is a survey that attempts to determine how the company matches up with other firms on a job-for-job basis. For example, the median rates paid in survey firms for a keypunch operator are compared with the median rates paid in the organization. Any survey of course attempts to examine the external equity of an organization's compensation plan.

Job Analysis

Job analysis is the systematic study of work requirements (21). In varying degrees every job involves the job holder with data (figures, information, people, and things—such as tools or equipment). Job analysis is used to find out what the employee does in relation to data, people, and things. Determining these job features is done by interviews, questionnaires, direct observation, and the use of job holder diaries.

Researchers at Purdue University have developed a popular questionnaire procedure for conducting job analysis. Their position questionnaire (PAQ) is a structured job analysis oriented set of questions (22, 23). The PAQ is completed by the job analyst, a person who is thoroughly familiar with the job. It has 194 questions, divided into six major divisions:

1. **Information input.** Where and how does the worker get information needed to perform the job?
2. **Mental processes.** What decision making, planning, organizing, and processing activities are needed to perform the job?
3. **Work output.** What physical activities are performed and what tools and equipment are used to do the job?
4. **Relationships with other persons.** What relationships with other people are required to perform the job?
5. **Job context.** Where is the work performed?
6. **Other job characteristics.** What characteristics other than those listed above are important for performing the job?

The completion of the PAQ provides a quantitative score for each job. This enables the manager to divide jobs into different classes and to establish compensation levels for each class.

Performance Appraisal

The majority of employees in organizations have their compensation rewards administered by a merit pay system. This type of system is designed to review and appraise how well each employee performs specific job duties. The merit system is designed to administer individual compensation in an equitable manner. The accomplishment of this worthy goal is more easily stated than accomplished. One reason for the difficulty is that individual contributions are extremely difficult to appraise.

Consider the performance of a major league baseball manager. His record of results is calculated primarily on the basis of wins and losses. These can be assessed on a daily basis throughout the season. On the other hand assessing the record or contributions of a professional engineer, accountant, or personnel manager is much more ambiguous and uncertain. They are ambiguous and uncertain because performance criteria are difficult to establish.

Despite the problems with developing clear and objective performance criteria for many jobs, there are many appraisal systems available (24). They include person-to-person trait comparisons, checklists, essays, behaviorally anchored scales, and management by objectives. Each of the available systems possess some drawbacks including measurement error, lack of clarity, and use of improper implementation procedures (25). However, one of the only hopes of management to meet the individuality test is to develop and implement the best available or developed performance appraisal system.

THE ISSUE OF MOTIVATION: THEORY, FACT, AND MYTH

When certain conditions exist, reward systems have been demonstrated to motivate performance (26). What are these certain conditions? Important rewards must be perceived by employees to be tied to positive performance results. That is, organizations will receive the effort that is believed to lead to rewards employees value. This is a rather exaggerated claim, because it suggests that all that is necessary to achieve desirable behavior is to relate pay and other valued rewards to performance. Relating pay to performance means that valid and reliable measures of performance are needed, individual employee preferences must be known, and managers must be in control of the rewards that employees prefer. Each of these tasks is difficult for any manager to accomplish.

The measurement issue is itself fraught with problems. Determining the performance criteria for many jobs is like searching for a needle in a haystack. The search goes on, the debate continues, and the issue of what constitutes performance still remains largely a mystery (27).

The determination of what the employee's preferences are involves the "in the head" dilemma mentioned earlier. Each employee has his or her own set of preferences. Some are never expressed clearly; others are hidden because of a lack of trust and respect. In some cases there is a lack of communication about preferences because of past superior-subordinate interpersonal experiences.

Finally, managerial control varies across organizations and between levels in the hierarchy. Even if employee reward preferences could be fairly accurately determined, there is the issue of whether managers have the right and power to distribute them to subordinates. In many organizations compensation rewards are not totally controlled by immediate managers, if controlled at all. Economists, personnel directors, executive committees, and other managers in the organization may all be involved in compensation decision making.

Pay for Actual Performance

Although problems of tying rewards to performance continue, there is no shortage of effort to build more effective plans. The effort undoubtely continues because it makes sense that if rewards such as pay can be tied to performance, the entire organization can benefit (28). A number of studies have examined whether employees generally feel they should be paid on the basis of their performance. Almost without exception these studies have shown that employees feel pay should be based on performance (29).

For example, one study measured attitudes of managers about how their pay should be determined. The results showed that managers prefer to have their pay based on performance and that they believe performance should be the most effective determinant of their pay (30). The study also found a difference in how important managers felt performance was in determining pay and how important they felt it should be. This large difference indicates the inability of some organizations to develop compensation plans to fit the needs and preferences of employees.

Managerial Methods for Tying Pay to Performance

There are numerous managerial methods of tying pay to performance. Lawler (6) discusses the mechanics of three types of plans. He classifies the plans as individual, group, or organizational. Next he groups the three plans according to (a) the way performance is measured (measures can vary from a subjective rating to an objective rating such as the number of units actually produced), and (b) the rewards that are distributed for successful performance.

Lawler (6) also provides an effectiveness rating of each plan on the basis of four criteria. Each plan is rated on a 1 (low accomplishment) to 5 (excellent accomplishment) scale for each criteria. The criteria are: the extent to which pay is tied to performance, whether the plan produces negative side effects, the degree to which the plan contributes to teamwork and cooperation, and the acceptability of the plan to employees. Tables 4.1 and 4.2 present the plans and the ratings.

Table 4.1 Lawler's Classification of Pay Incentive Plans

	Reward Offered	
Performance Measure	Salary Increase	Cash Bonus
Individual plans		
Productivity	Merit	Sales commission
Cost effectiveness	rating plan	Piece rate
Superiors' ratings		
Group plans		
Productivity		Group incentive
Cost effectiveness		
Superiors' rating		
Organizationwide plans		
Productivity	Productivity	Kaiser, Scanlon
Cost effectiveness	Bargaining	Profit sharing
Profit		(e.g., American Motors)

Source: Edward E. Lawler, III. *Pay and Organizational Effectiveness. New York: McGraw-Hill, 1971, p. 164.*

Table 4.2 Lawler's Ratings of Various Pay Incentive Plans

	Tie Pay to Performance	Produce Negative Side Effects	Encourage Cooperation	Employee Acceptance
SALARY REWARD				
Individual plan				
Productivity	4	1	1	4
Cost effectiveness	3	1	1	4
Superiors' rating	3	1	1	3
Group				
Productivity	3	1	2	4
Cost effectiveness	3	1	2	4
Superiors' rating	2	1	2	3
Organizationwide				
Productivity	2	1	3	4
Cost effectiveness	2	1	2	4
BONUS REWARD				
Individual plan				
Productivity	5	3	1	2
Cost effectiveness	4	2	1	2
Superiors' rating	4	2	1	2
Group				
Productivity	4	1	3	3
Cost effectiveness	3	1	3	3
Superiors' rating	3	1	3	3
Organizationwide				
Productivity	3	1	3	4
Cost effectiveness	3	1	3	4
Profit	2	1	3	3

Source: Edward E. Lawler, III. "Reward System," p. 195.

The ratings indicate that if pay to performance is an important consideration, then individual plans seem best. This is because in group and organizational plans an employee's pay is not entirely a function of individual effort and contribution. The pay is influenced by economics, market conditions, and co-workers.

Bonus plans are generally rated more effective than pay raise and salary increase (merit) plans. Under bonus plans, an employee's pay may vary sharply from period to period because of changes in performance. This does not usually happen with a merit pay program because organizations work hard at not reducing an employee's compensation. As a result, compensation under a merit plan reflects not only recent performance but also performance over a longer period of time (years). Thus pay as a reward is not considered tied to present performance accomplishments.

IMPROVING THE EFFECTIVENESS OF A COMPENSATION PLAN

Implied throughout this chapter is the idea that no one compensation plan will satisfy the needs of everyone. Organizations differ in their needs and goals and so do employees. A growing body of theory and research suggests that a compensation plan's effectiveness can be improved by managerial action in a number of areas (31, 32).

Assuring External and Internal Equity

If employees believe that their compensation is out of line externally and internally, the plan is doomed to fail. In a practical sense it is necessary to only use plans that are externally competitive and internally fair. Managers need to survey the base pay, fringe benefits, and incentives of competitors. They also need to evaluate and rate jobs so that an internally fair range is established. Special attention should be paid to the incentive portion, since this can be used to reward excellent performance or to discriminate between different levels of performance.

Trust and Objectivity

Since performance criteria for many jobs are difficult to establish, it is necessary to have a high degree of trust between manager and subordinate. A subordinate with little or no trust in the manager will have trouble accepting any compensation plan. Even with the more objectively based plans there is a need to have trust before the plan is acceptable (33). As a minimum managers should clearly portray the compensation plan and inform subordinates about the range and mean of pay received by co-workers at that job level (33). If managers are unable to concisely, correctly, and frequently inform subordinates about pay ranges and mean amounts, there will probably be problems with trust.

Using Pay Correctly

Unfortunately pay is not always tied to performance and negative or unexpected consequences occur. Typically, managers are asked to distribute small pay increases between individuals in the same job, regardless of perceived or actual differences in performance. Everyone receives about the same small increase. Where discriminations are made, they are likely to be based on factors other than performance, such as seniority, future potential, or the need to make up for a past oversight (34).

Unless pay increases can be tied directly to performance increases, their motivational impact will be nonexistent. Thus it makes little sense to use pay to motivate future performance if (a) pay differentials among different levels of performance are small, (b) performance ratings are suspect due to their lack of validity and reliability, and (c) trust between managers and subordinates is low (35).

Managers Should Be Trained in Evaluating Performance and Counseling Techniques

The need to be trained to evaluate performance and provide quality feedback to employees is crucial. One of the obvious weeknesses in many compensation plans is the manager's lack of evaluation and counseling skills. Evaluation of an employee's performance is likely to have some effect on the self-esteem of the individual. Data to verify this contention were revealed in research carried out at General Electric (36). Employees rated themselves on a scale of 0 to 100. If they felt they were poorer performers than all of their peers in a similar job at a similar level they rated themselves at the 0 point. If they felt they were performing better than anyone else at a similar salary level they rated themselves at the 100 point.

The average of self-ratings assigned on the scale was at the seventy-seventh percentile. The managers of these employees were asked to rate the employees on the same scale. The average managerial ratings were at the sixtieth percentile. When individuals' self-ratings were compared to manager ratings, it was found that 85 percent were rated lower by their managers than they rated themselves.

The fact that managerial and employee ratings do not square indicates that somewhere in the process the self-esteem of employees may have become involved. If a person believes that his or her true value is not being recognized, a sense of frustration and dissatisfaction will probably emerge.

If an employee's self-esteem is threatened by an unfair (in the mind of the individual) rating and pay increase, there are a number of possible consequences. Managers would like to see the worker exert more effort to improve performance and receive a higher rating and pay increase in the future. However, a more common sequence of reactions is to first attempt to reduce the managerial standards of performance. If this is not successful, the employee may cope with the threat to self-esteem by downgrading the importance of performing well. Thus if it is indicated by evaluation that *I* am a poor technician, *I* can rationalize this threat by rejecting the importance of being a good technician.

Since self-esteem is a part of any compensation plan, proper training for managers in evaluation and counseling seems almost mandatory (37, 38). Training in the actual use, problems, and errors of performance appaisal seem to be worth examining. Furthermore, training in counseling subordinates on compensation matters also needs to be incorporated. Reliance on personnel-human resource departments to provide compensation information and understanding seems too far removed from the manager and subordinate. The issues of trust, equity, objectivity, and correctness reside primarily between the manager and subordinates. Certainly a personnel-human resources staff function can make valuable contributions to the manager-subordinate interactions about compensation, but the line manager needs to be trained and qualified to conduct the necessary evaluation and counseling activities.

THE FUTURE AND COMPENSATION

The future of compensation will involve many of the same actors in the present cast—managers, employees, union representatives, economists, behavioral scientists, and government officials. In addition, the issues of quantity, equity, and individuality will also remain concerns. There are, however, some trends and recent experiments that suggest that other approaches to pay and legislation will significantly influence compensation plans in the 1980s and 1990s. Some of these trends and experiments seem important enough to briefly introduce.

More Employee Participation: The Cafeteria Approach

Typically, management makes compensation decisions. Recent research in the applied organizational behavior literature has demonstrated that employee participation may be a viable alternative to traditional decision making (6, 39, 40). In the employee participation approach the mix of salary and fringe benefits is decided on partly by individuals. In one study 12,000 employees were allowed to decide what mix of salary and fringe benefits they wanted. More than 80 percent changed their fringe benefit packages. They selected fringe benefits to fit their particular family and life style situations. As a result of this experiment, the employees reported more satisfaction with their compensation package (6).

A few organizations are today experimenting with employee participation in deciding pay rates. Whether increased employee participation in pay rate decisions will increase in popularity depends on a number of factors. If managers are reluctant to allow participation, then problems will immediately surface. It will require top management support from the outset to assure any chance of success. If economic conditions of the organization allow participation, it may be advisable to experiment with some amount of employee involvement.

The wave of employee participation in compensation decisions is not new. It was originated in 1960 with what are now called *cafeteria compensation* plans (39, 40). At this time it was stated that cafeteria compensation exists when employees have the opportunity to determine where, over a wide range of alternatives, their company shall spend their individual and compensation and benefit dollars. One expert claims that "cafeteria compensation has been one of the most overrated concepts ever championed by management theorists" (41). This of course is a debatable statement. It seems more correct to claim that cafeteria compensation has possibilities of improving pay satisfaction, performance, and commitment in some situations. Since it has this potential, more managers will probably continue to experiment with this method of employee compensation participation.

Before any employee participation in compensation decision making is initiated, it must be recognized that three major groups must be involved: (a) the employees, who communicate their preferences and mix of dollars of compensation, (b) top management, who sets the tone and overall objectives, and (c) personnel-human resource specialists, who construct the program and match needs and preferences of the organization and employees. Perhaps failures in the past with many cafeteria style compensation plans resulted from couching them as being under the control and direction solely of employees. Increased employee participation means top management guidance and overall specific economic, legal, and procedural direction being provided by specialists.

All-Salaried Work Force

Most organizations distinguish between their management and nonmanagement employees in terms of wages or salaries paid and the fringe benefit package. Some employees have to punch in and punch out and are "docked" pay for being late or absent. The notion of placing all employees on a salaried basis is growing in popularity (42). It is assumed that an all-salaried work force would reduce administrative costs and increase employee commitment. By treating employees as a salaried part of the team there is supposedly an increase in responsibility and trust, the notion being that the self-esteem of a person will be enhanced. There is little empirical evidence at this date to support these assumptions (6, 38, 42).

Managers from companies like Gillette and Dow Chemical have commented that absenteeism and tardiness decreased when an all-salary plan was implemented (42). Although evidence of improved organizational outcomes is lacking, there are indications that more companies will experiment with all-salary compensation packages (6, 38, 42, 43). If management is sincere about treating employees as responsible and committed members, then the all-salaried plan may be a worthwhile program. However, some unions are openly resisting all-salaried plans, viewing them as another managerial attempt to manipulate employees and prevent unionization.

The Decrease in Individual Pay Plans

Until better and more accurate performance evaluation systems are devised, there is likely to be a decrease in the use of individual incentive compensation plans. Since subjectivity is so interwoven in appraising performance, incentive awards will remain controversial and troublesome. Unfortunately, most compensation experts agree that individual incentive plans are more effective than group or organization plans (6, 26, 43). The fact remains that pinpointing individual performance is extremely difficult. For this reason it appears that individual plans will be replaced in increasing numbers by group incentive plans.

Furthermore, more legislation may make it difficult to pay for individual performance contributions. The employer is being asked more and more by government to prove that no discrimination in compensation has occured. As a result of increased government involvement in compensation decisions, there seems to be more of a propensity to use fewer individually based plans.

COMPENSATION: A FINAL NOTE

The complexities of managing a compensation reward plan have been presented in this chapter. There is every indication that the present complexities along with new problems and issues will continue in the future. Significant managerial resources and time must be allocated to any compensation program. The purpose of this chapter was to provide a picture of why such resources must be allocated. Simply stated: Compensation is an important reality of organizational life that must be properly managed to achieve the objectives of retention, attraction, and motivation. Furthermore, through a fair, equitable, and flexible compensation system an atmosphere of trust, cooperation, and support between employer and employees can be initiated and maintained.

The present chapter was only able to focus on some of the less technical aspects of compensation plans. This emphasis should not lead practitioners to believe that the technical aspects are unimportant. They are, and they usually require qualified specialists to provide advice and support to line managers. Sound management of a compensation plan requires an understanding of statistics, economics, the behavioral sciences, and the law. As compensation planning becomes more complex, these areas of expertise will increase in importance. Thus the practicing manager with the assistance of qualified specialists will have to continually work on using the best compensation plan available for his or her situation. This responsibility means that frequent updating, modifying, and discarding of compensation theories and practices will have to be the rule rather than the exception.

REFERENCES

1. Schein, E.H. *Organizational Psychology*, Englewood Cliffs, N.J.: Prentice-Hall, 1965.
2. Belcher, D.W. *Compensation Administration.* Englewood Cliffs, N.J.: Prentice-Hall, 1974.
3. Bert, J.G. *Managing Compensation,* New York: Amacom, 1976.
4. Rock, M.L. (Ed.). *Handbook of Wage and Salary Administration.* New York: McGraw-Hill, 1972.
5. Coleman, C.J. *Personnel.* Cambridge, Mass. Winthrop Publishers, 1979, pp. 289–290.
6. Lawler, E.E. III, Reward systems. In J.R. Hackman and J.L. Suttle (Eds.), *Improving Life at Work.* Santa Monica, Calif.: Goodyear Publishing, 1977, pp. 163–226.

7. Adams, J.S. Injustice in social exchange. In L. Berkowitz (Ed). *Advances in Experimental Psychology,* New York: Academic Press, 1965, pp. 267–299.

8. Patchen, M. *The Choice of Wage Comparisons.* Englewood Cliffs, N.J.: Prentice-Hall, 1961.

9. Henderson, R.I. *Compensation Management.* Reston, Va.: Reston Publishing, 1979.

10. Flippo, E.B. *Principles of Personnel Management.* New York: McGraw-Hill, 1976, p. 316.

11. Glueck, W.F. *Foundations of Personnel.* Dallas: Business Publications, Inc., 1979, p. 335.

12. Dowling, W.F. Job redesign on the assembly line. Farewell to blue-collar blues? *Organizational Dynamics.* 1973, **4,** 51.

13. Beckhard, R. Optimizing team building efforts. *Journal of Contemporary Business,* 1972, **1,** 24.

14. Latham, G.P. and Yukl, G.A. A review of research on the application of goal setting in organizations. *Academy of Management Journal,* 1975, **18,** 824–845.

15. Locke, E.A. Toward a theory of task performance and incentives. *Organizational Behavior and Performance.* 1968, **3,** 157–189.

16. Meyer, H.H. Kay, E. and French, J.R.P. Jr. Split roles in performance appraisal. *Harvard Business Review,* January-February 1965, **43,** 123–129.

17. White, J.K. Generalizability of individual difference moderators of the participation in decision making-employee response relationship. *Academy of Management Journal,* 1978, **21,** 36–43.

18. *Analysis of Workers Compensation Laws: 1979 Edition.* Washington, D.C.: Chamber of Commerce of the United States, 1979.

19. Rosenberg, M.J. A structural theory of attitudes, *Public Opinion Quarterly,* 1960, 319–340.

20. Engelke, G.L. Conducting surveys. In M.L. Rock (Ed.). *Handbook of Wage and Salary Administration,* New York: McGraw-Hill, 1972, pp. 3–8.

21. U.S. Civil Service Administration, *Job Analysis Key to Better Management,* Washington, D.C.: U.S. Government Printing Office, 1973.

22. McCormick, E.J. and Tiffin, J. *Industrial Psychology,* Englewood Cliffs, N.J.: Prentice-Hall, 1974, pp. 47–63.

23. McCormick, E.J. Jeaneret, P.R. and Mecham, R.C. A study of job characteristics and job dimensions as based on the position analysis questionaire, *Journal of Applied Psychology,* 1972, **57,** 347–368.

24. Henderson, R. *Performance Appraisal,* Reston, Va.: Reston Publishing, 1980.

25. *Ibid.*

26. Lawler, E.E. III, *Pay and Organizational Effectiveness,* New York: McGraw-Hill, 1971.

27. Levinson, H. Appraisal of what performance, *Harvard Business Review,* 1976, **54,** 30–32, 34, 36, 40, 44, 46, 180.

28. Lawler, E.E. III, Managers' attitudes how their pay is and should be determined, *Journal of Applied Psychology*, 1966, **51,** 273–279.

29. *Ibid.*

30. *Ibid.*

31. Hamner, W.C. How to ruin motivation with pay, *Compensation Review*, 1975, **7,** 14–20.

32. Milbourn, G. Jr. The relationship of money and motivation, *Compensation Review*, 1980, **12,** 33–44.

33. Patz, A.L. Performance appraisal: Useful but still resisted, *Harvard Business Review*, 1975, **53,** 74–80.

34. Sibson, R.E. *Compensation*, New York: Amacom, 1974.

35. Hinricks, J. Correlates of employee evaluations of pay increases, *Journal of Applied Psychology*, 1969, **54,** 481–489.

36. Meyer, H.H. The pay-for-performance dilemma, *Organizatinal Dynamics*, Winter 1975, 39–50.

37. Korchin, S.J. *Modern Clinical Psychology*, New York: Basic Books, 1976.

38. Korman, A.K. Hypothesis of work behavior revisited and an extension, *Academy of Management Review*, January 1976, **1,** 50–63.

39. Baytos, L.M. The employee benefit smorgasboard: Its potential and limitation, *Compensation Review*, 1970, **2,** 16–20.

40. Paine, T.H. Flexible compensation can work! *Financial Executive*, February 1974, 56–58, 60.

41. Thomsen, D.J. Introducing cafeteria compensation in your company, *Personnel Journal*, 1977, **56,** 124–131.

42. Hulme, R. and Bevan, R. The blue-collar worker goes on salary, *Harvard Business Review*, 1975, **53,** 104–112.

43. Ellig, B.R. Compensation management: Its past and its future, *Personnel*, 1977, **54,** 30–40.

—5—

Communication and Organizational Dynamics

Douglas T. Hall and Eugene S. Andrews

How does a person talk to an organization? People talk to other people, but does it make any sense to think of communicating with an entity as large, complex, and impersonal as an organization?

The purpose of this paper is to answer this question in the affirmative. Inspite of ample research on interpersonal and group communication, the topic of individual-organization communication has been largely ignored. Yet when we look at failures in person-organization relationships (e.g., resignations, alienation, conflict), we often find associated breakdowns in communication. On the other hand, successful interchanges (e.g., effective career and organization development) usually result from a healthy communication process between person and organization. It will be our purpose to identify the elements in this healthy communication process, as well as ways to enhance it.

THE COMMUNICATION PROCESS

Communication Competence

Terms like "failure to communicate" and "communication gap" are used freely in everyday language, but what exactly do they mean? Or,in a more positive vein, what do we mean by *competence* in communication?

Chris Argyris (1) was one of the first writers to use the term "competence" to describe the quality of a relationship. To Argyris, competence exists under the following conditions:

1. When the parties can communicate so that problems can be solved,
2. In a way that the problems remain solved,
3. Without damaging the relationship.

This defines competence in terms of the process of communication rather than its outcome. If we looked only at the outcome, we could conceive of situations in which parties in conflict arrived at a resolution, but it may have involved threats, legal action, force, or other action that might lead to low commitment by one party to the solution (violating condition 2 above) and a reduced level of trust (violating condition 3). Thus real competence in communication entails both short-term (solving the problem) and long-term (maintaining the relationship) considerations.

Extending this reasoning, higher levels of communication competence exist to the extent to which the parties are able to *strengthen* the relationship while solving mutual problems. This is most likely to occur where creative or "win-win" solutions are found, which enhance both parties' returns.

The Healthy Communicator

Senior-subordinate relations in organizations can be both formal and informal. However, regardless of the formality, the relationship is interpersonal. It is a relationship in which two people express their wants and needs, satisfaction and dissatisfaction. If the relationship between the two individuals is a healthy one, it is probably a reflection of the health of the personalities involved. According to Jourard (2), a healthy personality

> is manifested by the individual who has been able to gratify his basic needs through acceptable behavior such that his own personality is no longer a problem to him. He can take himself more or less for granted and devote his energies and thoughts to socially meaningful interests and problems beyond security or lovability, or status.

On the other hand, the unhealthy personality is one who is self-centered and devotes most of his or her thoughts and energies to satisfying security needs, being accepted by others, and achieving social status. An unhealthy personality is a distracted person, distracted to the point that his or her effectiveness to the organization is impaired. This state of unhealthiness and ineffectiveness is often reflected in the person's competence at communication (3).

The healthy personality is the one who has mastered the skills necessary to communicate fully with another. In contrast, the unhealthy personality, because of self-centeredness, has difficulty expressing his or her thoughts and feelings and difficulty in accurately perceiving the meaning of messages transmitted to him or her. In sum, a healthy personality is synonymous with a healthy communicator.

Effective communication is central to managers' careers and organizational effectiveness. It has been estimated that managers spend some 50 to 90 percent of their time communicating (4). This time is spent in sending communication downward and receiving communication upward from subordinates. The downward communication consists primarily of job instructions, job rationale, organizational procedures and practices, feedback about subordinate performance, and indoctrination of goals (5). The upward communication received from subordinates usually consists of information about the subordinate himself or herself, information about co-workers and their problems, organizational practices and policies, and information about what needs to be done and how it can be done (5). If these messages are to be transmitted and received accurately, it is imperative that the manager be a healthy communicator, and not one who is self-centered and solely concerned with satisfying his or her needs.

In order to be effective, the managers must have healthy communications with not only their subordinates but their superiors as well. In terms of communication with subordinates, Baird and Diebolt (6) discovered that a subordinate's job satisfaction is directly correlated with estimates of communication contact with their superiors. Subordinate's job satisfaction is also a function of the amount of influence their manager has with his or her boss. This notion of upward influence is called the "Pelz effect." (7)

The healthy communicator makes use of open communication with discretion. Because of sensitivity to the needs of other people and the nature of the working environment, a healthy communicator will selectively pick and choose when to be open and when to control the amount of information released to subordinates. In this regard, Willits (8) found open communications to be highly correlated with higher performance. Willits' finding gives us some clues as to the quality of open communication that may be expressed by the manager in resolving his or her dilemma, but there still remains the question of how much? The how much is a matter of judgment involving considerations of how much does the subordinate need to know to (a) effectively carry out his or her task, (b) have an understanding of organizational goals and objectives, and (c) experience job satisfaction and personal growth. Optimum resolution of this dilemma requires the clear thinking and open-mindedness of a healthy communicator. If, however, the manager's thinking is distracted by self-centered concerns, the probability of resolving the dilemma is lessened.

Open communication is a two-way process. Managers need to be concerned with not only how much information they are going to share with their subordinates, but also how much information their subordinates are willing to share with them (upward communication). Very often this is a function of how willing management is to listen to subordinates (9). When it is apparent to subordinates that management will listen and reinforce upward communication, there is apt to be more of it. Managers who genuinely listen to subordinates are not only enhancing the flow of upward communication, they are also sending a message to subordinates that says "we care."

Regardless of the nature of the upward communication, there is bound to be some distortion. The manager can expect that most of the distortion will be in communication that is negative and unfavorable rather than that which is positive and favorable (10).

Communication Cycles

There is a cyclical aspect of communication that either lessens or increases the amount of upward distortion. That is, communication can either be degenerative or regenerative (11). It is degenerative when A does not own up to feelings or ideas vis-à-vis B. Because of this B becomes less open with A. As B becomes less open with A, the trust level between the two parties goes down. The end result of this interactive process is that both A and B perceive an ever-increasing degree of risk associated with attempts at open and healthy communication.

Communication is regenerative when A owns up to feelings and ideas vis-à-vis B. Accordingly, B becomes more open with A. Commensurate with the increases in openness will be a parallel increase in the amount of trust between the two. Unlike degenerative communications, the regenerative communications cycle will enhance the development of healthy communication because the perceived degree of risk of being open with one another is lessened. In sum, the more regenerative the communications cycle within an organization the less the probability of upward distortion. However, when there exists within an organization a degenerative cycle, the probability of upward distortion will be greater. (We will talk later about how to facilitate regenerative cycles).

The healthy communicators contribute to the establishment and maintenance of congruence in communication between themselves and their subordinates. With unhealthy communicators there is apt to be incongruence in senior-subordinate communication. In other words, there will be a gap in the information and understanding between the two. This gap or incongruence may occur when a manager is consumed in his or her self-centeredness and hence is less sensitive to information coming from subordinates. Other unhealthy communications behavior such as dogmatism or close-mindedness might also lead to incongruence. Common results of incongruence in communication are lower morale among subordinates (12) and distortion of interpersonal perceptions.

Let us consider in more detail how degenerative and regenerative cycles operate. Richard Walton (13) has described the operation of cycles in conflict situations. This cycle model can be usefully applied to healthy communication processes. According to Walton, conflict tends to escalate by the following process:

> Two persons who are opposed are only periodically engaged in manifest conflict. At one point in time the issues between them represent only latent conflict. Then, for some reason, their opposition becomes salient, the parties engage in a set of conflict-relevant behaviors, thus experience the consequences of the interchange; and then once again the conflict becomes less salient and less manifest for a time. If the persons remain in interdependence, the manifest conflict will tend to recur at some point. (13, pp. 71,73)

A variety of barriers tend to keep conflict in as latent state (i.e., from becoming manifest). Some of the barriers to the open expression of conflict, a identified by Walton, are task and time requirements, norms against open expressions of feelings, public images (appearing calm and cool), fear of retaliation (physical barriers), and so on. Occasionally, however, these barriers are overcome by some *triggering event,* such as a group meeting in which a critical decision must be made, or an abrupt statement by one party to which the other takes offense and feels the need to respond in kind. Or, if the parties are not normally in contact with each other, a triggering event could simply be an occasion in which they find themselves in the same room.

These triggering events create new issues in the conflict (i.e., there is now a more complex "history" to the conflict), which produce new behaviors and consequences. Then these revised issues may remain latent for a period of time until new triggering events create a new round of issues and conflict behavior.

Although Walton's model focuses on conflict, it is equally useful in understanding communication that is the "flip side" of conflict. These conflict elements have to be dealt with and resolved for the relationship to grow.

Managing conflict in such a way that it leads to improved communication entails analyzing both barriers to conflict and triggering events. Ideally, barriers can be maintained so that the conflict is contained until conditions are right for confronting the conflict issues. At this point, attempts can be made to reduce the barriers or to create triggering events (i.e., a meeting with a third party) to bring conflict into the open.

When the conflict is managed so that it can be worked through in a controlled way, the chances for truly *resolving* it increase, and Argyris's conditions 2 and 3 are met. As the parties experience the success of working through conflict together, this feeling of mutual success can produce more positive feelings about each other. With more positive affect and mutual success experiences, they begin to trust each other more. With a higher level of trust, events that may previously have triggered conflict may now simply pass unnoticed. In everyday terms, the parties are less touchy, less thin skinned, less likely to take things personally.

Therefore it is possible to have *positive communication* cycles as well as conflict cycles. Like conflict, communication and trust can also escalate. As Homans (14) has shown, the more activities people participate in together, the more they interact. The more they interact, the more positive their sentiments about each other become.

How can productive interactions be facilitated? There are seven ingredients for productive confrontation (13):

1. **Mutual positive motivation** Insuring that both parties have more to gain by resolving the conflict than by continuing it.

2. **Balancing the power of both parties** If power is unbalanced, the stronger party may underestimate the positive intent of the other, and the weaker

may feel there is no use in attempting to improve communication. A third party can help equalize power by structuring equal "air time," by insuring that each party is heard by the other, and by including participants who are supportive of the weaker member.

3. **Synchronizing confrontation efforts** Choosing a time and a place that is agreeable to both parties and securing the agreement of both parties to work on the issues at that time. If one is trying to communicate when the other is not, this is perceived as rejection and possibly as a new attack by the party who is putting forth the positive effort. Often one party will make overtures when the other is not receptive, and then they might switch roles at a later date. When their separate efforts are coordinated, success is more likely.

4. **Appropriate pacing of differentiation and integration activities** Conflict resolution requires both the expression of issues and negative feelings that can divide the parties (differentiation) and the expression of similarities, warmth, respect, and common goals that tend to bring people together (integration). If only differentiation and hostility are expressed, the conflict will be confronted but never resolved.
   If only liking and common goals are discussed, the conflict will be avoided. Both activities are required, often in iterative cycles, so that issues are surfaced and resolved successfully.

5. **Facilitating openness** So that opinions, perceptions, and feelings can be expressed, openness must be maintained. This can be aided by building norms for openness, providing emotional reassurance to participants, and using effective interpersonal process skills to facilitate dialogue. Here too a third party is especially useful.

6. **Enhancing the reliability of communicative signs** When parties are in conflict, they often misread each other's communicative acts so that they see and hear more negative content than the sender intended. A third party can increase the validity of mutual perceptions by "translating" and speaking for the respective parties, by structuring in clarifying activities, and by developing a common language for the discussion.

7. **Maintaining optimum tension.** A moderate stress level leads to optimum performance. If there is too little tension, there is no motivation to change; if tension is too high, the parties may be immobilized. A third party can increase stress by bringing the parties together, by focusing on the conflict issues, and by encouraging open communication. The interventionist can moderate stress through emotional support, by focusing on manageable issues, by encouraging descriptive (vs. evaluative) feedback, and by praising the parties for progress made.

In all of these ways the communication process can be managed to convert conflict into trust and positive affect. Trust can escalate in the same manner as conflict, but it is far more fragile. It is easier to break into a communication-and-trust cycle and convert it into a malevolent conflict cycle than it is to go the other way.

Now that we have examined how the basic processes of communication and conflict develop over time, in cycles, let us consider the organizational environment that provides the conditions that feed into these cycles. Our main argument is that the high degree of ambiguity in most organizations provides much leeway in the way events are perceived. Thus whether conflict or communication develops in a relationship will depend greatly upon the predispositions of the parties and the history of their relationship.

THE INFORMATION ENVIRONMENT

Communication entails the exchange of meaningful information. The key word here is "meaningful." The environment of the organization, both internal and external, is rich with information. However, recent developments in organization theory have made it clear that most of this information is not organized in any meaningful way; in fact, it exists in media and in situations that make it extremely difficult to impose or extract meaning. This puts an especially great burden on the manager to be a healthy communicator. Let us examine this information environment in more detail.

In the traditional approach to organization theory, the organization was viewed as having a set of goals, a hierarchy of authority, a division of labor, and a psychological "contract" (a set of mutual expectations) that bound its members to the organization. While rationality was not necessarily assumed, the fact that there was an accepted common purpose or goal(s) meant there could be some common frame of reference that would facilitate the communication process.

In recent years, the writings of March and Olson (15) and Pfeffer and Salancik (16), among others, have indicated that organizations are not nearly as orderly as traditional definitions would indicate. Instead the organization is seen as a "loosely coupled system" of problems needing solutions, of people trying to sell pet ideas (solutions), chance opportunities for actions, sets of resources that could be marshaled, and so on. Problems must be found; they do not simply present themselves for solution. Situations are usually ambiguous, yet facts and information are everywhere. Conflict abounds. When actions are taken, they are less often the result of planned problem solving than the confluence of the right opportunities, available solutions, people who advocate these solutions, resources, and problems. In this sense the internal state of the system is characterized as "organized chaos."

What does organized chaos mean for the manager-communicator? Simply put, it means that the demands for competence and health in the communicator are far higher than they would be with an agreed-upon set of goals and a problem-solving structure. If organizations were more orderly, managers could create stable organization forms to facilitate communication. However, under more turbulent information flows, more flexibility is required. This means the manager must play a more direct, personal role in monitoring the communication process. He or she cannot just set up a mechanism—for example, an interdepartmental task force—and leave it to accomplish its mission; as conditions change, the manager must be prepared to make changes.

Specifically, this ambiguous environment means that the competent manager-communicator must have well developed *skills in exploratory behavior*. This means being sensitive to stray bits of information and being able to piece them together to create meaning. It means being able to diagnose situations, to seek out people who might possess necessary information, to obtain "leads" on where else to look if those people don't have the information needed, and the like. In short, the effective communicator must have the skills of a good researcher or investigative reporter. One cannot transmit valid information effectively until one first learns how to obtain it.

Organizational Versus Individual Communication

As has been pointed out earlier, communication within an organization is both downward and upward. The organization sends messages by way of people on the managerial level to its employees and they send messages to the managers of the organization. However, the manner in which the organization communicates is very often quite different from the communication emanating from its employees. They are different because the perspectives of each are not the same. The essence of this difference is captured in the modern-day slang phrase "Man . . . where are you coming from?" As Argyris (17) pointed out a number of years ago, some of us at one time or another are "coming from" the organization because of our role in the organization; while on other occasions we may be "coming from" our inner selves.

The extent of this difference is illustrated in Table 5.1. As we can see, there are a number of variables that distinguish the individual and organizational communications perspective. The needs of the individual are ego-based and focus on issues that range from pay and benefits and job satisfaction to the fulfillment of status and growth needs. Whatever the individual need is, it will concomitantly influence how the person communicates with the organization. For example, in our discussion of upward distortion, it was pointed out that we can expect some distortion in the upward communication if the individual is interacting with the person who writes his or her "report card." This may be particularly true if the emloyee is overly concerned with upward mobility.

On the other hand, when the organization communicates with the individual employee, it is very often centered on the attainment of organizational goals. Therefore the downward communications will either directly or indirectly focus on issues that impact on productivity. Whether the organization is speaking of meeting deadlines or the annual Christmas party,

Table 5.1 Determinants of Differences in Organizational and Individual Communication

Moderating Variables	Organization	Individual
Focus	Organizational goals	Individual needs
Manner of communication	Objective & rational	Subjective & emotional
Frame of reference	Big picture	Peep hole view
Power associated with communication	Great	Little
Speed of communication	Deliberate & thorough	Urgent

the final impact of the communication is bottom line oriented—attainment of organizational goals, that is, production.

When an organization communicates with its employees the form is usually rational and objective, while the communication emanating from the individual employee is often emotionally based and subjective, particularly when satisfaction of individual needs are being frustrated. In the case of the latter, the once benevolent ABC Company now becomes the infamous "they" coupled with various and sundry expletives that reflect the extent of the employee's frustration. The point is that people have emotions, and in their day to day interaction with supervisors in the organization these emotions will surface and color the nature of their communication with the organization.

However, organizations are certainly different in that unlike people, they do not cry, pout, withdraw, express feelings of anger, or laugh. The collective whole that we refer to as an organization is more apt to address its concerns in a rational and objective manner. It cannot afford to do otherwise. The confidence and trust of its employees depend on communications that are for the most part rational and objective. The point to be made is that these differences influence how the individual may communicate with the organization and how the organization may communicate with the individual. However, that the organization is rational and objective is only an assumption. High level people in the organization are also human beings. Many of them have more frustration tolerance because they are in a position to know the meaning and implications of human events in the setting, but human they are and not immune from expressions of hostility, aggression, and related emotional responses.

Relations between the individual and the organization are formal and relations between individuals within the organization are frequently informal.

Accordingly, communications between individuals are more apt to be spontaneous, direct, and open, whereas communication with the organization is usually deliberate and sent through "channels." For example, information dealing with production schedules would not be something that is casually communicated to the employees, nor would information dealing with employee promotions or terminations be communicated informally. The formality of organizational communications reflects the importance of the event or activity. If an organization takes an informal approach in announcing production schedules, the employees may adopt a casual attitude about conforming to the production schedule.

How the organization communicates with its employees and the way in which employees communicate with the organization is also influenced by each other's frame of reference. The organization's frame of reference is based on having a view of the "big picture." Borrowing from open systems theory, we can say that the organizational communication emanates from a fuller appreciation of its various inputs, transformation process, and outputs than that of the worker. On the other hand, the individual employee's frame of reference in comparison with the organization's is more like a peep-hole view. Concerns of individuals are more apt to be self-oriented or work team or department oriented.

When an organization communicates with individual employees, it communicates from a position of power. The individual represents a cog in the wheel, while the organization will probably have a greater impact and carry more weight than the communication emanating from a single employee. Accordingly, senior managers in an organization need to be careful about how they communicate, because their power, stemming from their positions, is so great that their messages are given extraordinary attention and importance by subordinates. There is also a good chance that because of their organizational distance from many of the employees, such managers may be perceived as having even greater power than they actually have.

This organizational position of power seems to generate systematic distortion. Positive comments are often seen as more meaningful or more positive than was intended; negative comments are often perceived as being more negative than they were intended to be. Even neutral comments may be blown out of proportion. For instance, if the president of a company, while visiting a plant, comments on how much he or she likes the way the grounds are maintained, there are likely to be certain unintended consequences. First, other plant managers may find out about the president's comments and go overboard in landscaping and sprucing up their grounds. Second, the plant manager may overreact to the president's comments, causing undue pressure to be put upon the poor laborer whose job it is to maintain the grounds. Finally, if a powerful person fails to say something or attend to an issue, a host of implications are apt to be read into the gap by subordinates. It is little wonder that so many high-level executives see communication as a major problem.

Another way in which to view how organizations and individuals communicate with one another is to examine the speed of the communications. When individuals are in a state of need there is often a sense of urgency associated with that need—particularly when satisfaction of that need leads to better working conditions, a pay raise, a promotion, or experiencing meaningfulness in one's work. Communications with the organization are apt to reflect this sense of urgency.

However, the reality of organizational life is that requests and other forms of communication must pass through channels. These channels are necessary to preclude conflicting communications that could occur if a link in the chain is bypassed. Because of these organizational realities, organizations through necessity usually do not communicate at a rate commensurate with the sense of urgency expressed in some of the communication of its members.

It should be apparent that because of the dissimilarities between individuals and organizations listed in Table 5.1, the nature of communication between the individual and organization will not always be congruent, and in fact will frequently be in conflict. Fortunately, the degree of conflict need not be inordinate if, in communicating with individual employees, managers recognize that (a) individual needs are often different from organizational goals; (b) it is natural for people to express emotions at work; (c) individual communication tends to be less formal than the organization's; (d) because of their organizational position, their communication may possess more power than they think; and (e) the pace of organizational communication may be so slow as to frustrate some organizational members.

A GUIDE TO HUMANIZING ORGANIZATIONAL COMMUNICATION

Organizational communication is interpersonal to the extent that it involves face to face encounters such as between senior and subordinate. However, when the organization communicates with subordinates it is frequently formal and impersonal. The impersonal communication, although well intended, can have a counterproductive impact on the individual employee. For example, a letter of congratulations can have a less positive impact if the letter was clearly written by a staff member of the scion who signed it, or if the letter contained some misinformation, or if the recipient's name was misspelled. Similarly, a face to face discussion regarding why one is not getting promoted is more meaningful than an impersonal letter with the same information.

The size and structure of many organizations often dictate that much of their communication with employees will be impersonal. Even with this as given, it is incumbent on every manager to personalize communications for the organization whenever the opportunity presents itself. The major dilemma, then, in organization-wide communications is how to provide an effective large-scale information flow and yet humanize or personalize their communication at the same time. Normally the scope of communications and the degree of personalization tend to be inversely related. How can we have both qualities, large scale and the personal touch, simultaneously?

What follows are examples of how some organizations have approached the dilemma of satisfying the organization's need for communications efficiency and the individual's need for personal attention.

United States Army*

An examination of an example of communication in the U.S. Army will demonstrate how prevalent impersonal communications can be and what can be done to offset its possible negative effects. However, singling out the U.S. Army should not be construed to mean that the military is more or less guilty of impersonal communication than other organizations.

For our purposes, let us use the hypothetical experience of an Army lieutenant, a company grade officer whose civilian counterpart would be a new low level manager. At any one time, the U.S. Army may have in its ranks as many as 30,000 second and first lieutenants. At his unit of assignment the lieutenant will usually experience more personal communication than impersonal. However, communications emanating from Headquarters, Department of the Army (DA), or some other high level headquarters will usually be more impersonal than personal. At the unit level the lieutenant is a person whose peers, subordinates, and seniors have a feeling for and know. At DA someone will surely know of the lieutenant, but it is highly unlikely that they will know much about him or her. At the organizational level he or she is more apt to be known as a junior officer with an assigned occupational specialty and a serial number. Granted they would certainly have much additional information but not enough or of the quality to personalize the lieutenant to the extent that he or she is personalized in his unit.

In the Army, as in many other large organizations, numbers are critical to communications with and about subordinates regardless of their position within the organization. There are general order numbers, special order numbers, travel order numbers, promotion order numbers, assignment order numbers, specialty code indicators (numbers), personnel control numbers, voucher numbers, and many other numbers too numerous to list. It is with some accuracy that many soldiers and officers feel that the organization views them as "just another number."

In spite of the plethora of numbers associated with each soldier and officer, there are many who have reason to feel more like a valued member of the organization than just another number. Much of their sentiment can be explained in terms of Schein's three dimensions of the career cycle (18). The

*The views, opinions, and statements expressed herein are solely those of the authors and do not represent the official view of the United States Army.

first is movement along a hierarchical dimension during the course of one's career. The higher an officer moves up the hierarchical ladder, the more visible he or she is to DA. This is particularly true when one attains the rank of general officer. Compared to the lieutenant referred to earlier, DA has a better feel for the general as a person. Accordingly, a greater proportion of the organization communication directed toward him or her will be personal rather than impersonal.

The second of Schein's dimensions is the functional or technical dimension. If an officer has a skill that is a rare commodity, DA will probably keep closer tabs on him or her than the average line officer. The third dimension (centrality) involves movement toward the inner circle of DA headquarters. If the lieutenant happens to know some of the personnel officers at DA who make decisions affecting his or her career, there is better chance that he or she will experience personal rather than impersonal communications with the organization. Very often movement along the inner circle dimension is contingent on movement along one or both of the latter two dimensions.

The benefit of personal communications with someone at DA is particularly salient during reassignment to another post. For a few in the Army the cliché "it's who you know" rings true. Although there are certainly limits on how much a friend can do for you, it is much easier to accept an undesirable assignment knowing that someone at the top did his or her best for you.

In terms of what we discussed earlier in this chapter, knowing someone with influence can also result in more frequent and open communications with the organization. There is less distortion because you can be confident that your contact will "tell it like it is" rather than explain things to you in terms of the "party line." In this kind of personal communication you feel more confident that the emotional component of your message will be listened to and there will be some sensitivity to the urgency of your requests. An organization is fortunate when the "who you know" kind of personal communication with the organization is not its prevalent form of organizational communication.

DA and its subordinate agencies and headquarters do much to personalize the impersonal communications with its officers and soldiers regardless of their rank, specialty, or movement toward the inner circle. When an officer is selected for promotion, he or she is given a sequence number and when the actual promotion occurs, it is in accordance with a particular promotion order number. However, promotions in the Army, whenever possible, are conducted in a rather personal ceremony that recognizes the individual soldier or officer for contributions to his or her unit and the Army in general. Such a ceremony is usually attended by one's family, peers, seniors, and subordinates. Ceremonies of this sort give the organization the opportunity to communicate more than numbers to not only the person being promoted, but also those attending the ceremony. Although the communication from DA is impersonal, it is personalized at lower levels. It is through such a process that DA is able to combine the formal and the personal and lets its people know that the organization cares and that the individual concerned it more than "just another number."

To personalize communication regarding an officer's career development and planning, DA consistently invites officers to go to Washington to visit with and get to know their career manager. Telephone contacts are also encouraged. Since visits are almost impossible for those stationed on the West Coast or overseas, DA will send career managers to the field to visit with officers worldwide. These visits serve two purposes. Through briefings on the Army-wide personnel situation, all officers regardless of ranks are given an appreciation of the big picture. This allows both the career manager and the officer to communicate from the perspective of the big picture instead of the previously held peep-hole view of the concerned officer. The other purpose of the visit is to give the officer the opportunity to meet his or her career manager face to face. The overall effect is to personalize communications dealing with career management and development.

As stated earlier, the Army and other organizations must look for and take advantage of the opportunities to personalize communications required for operational efficiency. Organizations that have a history of consistently trying to personalize their communication stand a better chance of successfully achieving their goals and the goals of their subordinates. Organizations that only give lip service to personal communication soon discover that they have lost the trust and confidence of subordinates. Individual-organizational communication will be locked into a degenerative cycle which will serve to exacerbate the we-they relationship that will surely result.

Current Trends in Personalizing Formal Communications

The U.S. Army information system we have just been examining is one attempt at an integrated individual-organization communication process. There are other, less ambitious mechanisms that organizations can utilize to facilitate large-scale communication. Let us consider a few recent trends.

Person-Initiated Communication

One way to humanize a large-scale information system is to permit interactions to be member-initiated. If the system is under the person's control, it becomes more person-centered (and therefore more personal or humane). In the Army personnel management system described earlier, the individual officer is encouraged to initiate contacts with his or her assignments officer. In this way, the person can control the communication process and can see that the process is available to respond to his or her needs; the system is not there only for the organization's purposes.

Personal relationships with organization representatives are related to person-initiated communication; the information becomes more human if there is a specific person representing the organization with whom the member can communicate and develop a relationship. For example, in the Army personnel system, each officer communicates with a particular assignments officer, not with an office or whoever happens to answer the telephone. In a similar fashion, in a health care setting, most people would prefer to have a particular physician who is their doctor, as opposed to seeing whatever staff member in a clinic happened to be on duty when they came in. Similarly, that particular physician and that particular assignments officer find their work more rewarding when they have specific clients and patients whose unique needs they can come to know and serve.

Mass Media Communications

Although we have seen no relevant statistics, our impression is that increasing numbers of organizations are using mass-media employee communications activities, such as newsletters, daily or weekly bulletins, magazines, and even electronic media such as close-circuit television. Sometimes these are produced informally, perhaps by employee volunteers, and often they are the work of full-time employee relations staff members. Mass media productions are a useful way of communicating personal information (e.g., births, promotions) about employees to other employees, as well as communicating about official policies, new activities, etc., from top management to all employees. These productions can also provide a forum for employees to communicate with top management, through letters to the editor, guest columns, employee surveys, and the like. Our impression is that technological advances in communication can profit from humanizing.

Institutionalized Communication

There are various mechanisms that organizations are using to give formal recognition to the employee-organization communication process. Formal systematic *information systems* are one way to provide rapid communication when needed. *Employee attitude surveys* are frequently used to improve upward communications. Some organizations employ *communications audits* as an attempt to assess periodically the adequacy of an organizations' communication process.

One of the most public indications of organized commitment to communications improvement is the creation of *communication departments,* often including a *vice-president for communications.* Often the vice-president would be responsible for external communications (e.g., public relations, communication with financial analysts) as well as internal communication. With the growing need for business and other types of large organizations to tell their story to their public, the need for a formal communications department and specialized senior executive becomes felt more widely and is humanizing.

Conclusion: Linking Formal and Informal Communication

The key to improving the communications process lies in linking effective formal communication with effective informal communication. It does not accomplish a great deal to have highly effective communication in work teams and good manager-employee relationships if employees feel alienated from the organization as a whole. Similarly, effective mass communication will not totally compensate for poor interpersonal and team communication.

In our opinion, recent communications improvements in many organizations have focused more on informal than on formal communication. Activities such as team building, group process interventions, employee surveys at the local level, and interpersonal skills training have become standard practice in many organizations. What has *not* been done so effectively is work on organization-wide formal communications. This is a high-potential area for improvement, with recent developments in video and computer communications. The critical task is to develop these mass communication instruments to maximize two-way communication between the individual member and the organization. We certainly do *not* need "developments" that are simply more effective means of large-scale employee persuasion. It is also important to remember that linking formal and informal communications entails having healthy communicators as well as healthy information systems. There must be the opportunity for a personal relationship between the individual and the supervisor or other organizational representative. The effective communication between person and organization develops over time, in a series of regenerative trust-building cycles. The climate for this communication is set by high-level managers and administrators. This is necessary to work at both the individual and institutional levels to humanize organization communication.

REFERENCES

1. Argyris, C. *Interpersonal Competence and Organizational Effectiveness.* Homewood, Ill.: Irwin-Dorsey, 1962.
2. Jounard, S. M. *Personal Adjustment.* New York: Macmillan, 1971.
3. Ruesch, J. & Bateson, G. *Communication, the Social Matrix of Psychiatry.* New York: Norton, 1951.
4. Horne, J. H. & Lupton, T. The work activities of middle managers. *Journal of Management Studies,* 1952, **47,** 581–588.
5. Jablin, F. M. Superior-subordinate communication; the state of the art. *Psychological Bulletin,* 1979, **86,** 1201–1222.
6. Baird, J. E. & Diebot, J. C. Role congruence, communication, superior subordinate relations and employee satisfaction in organizational hierarchies. *Western Speech Communication,* 1976, **40,** 260–267.

7. Pelz, D. C. Influence: A key to effective leadership in the first-line supervisor. *Personnel,* 1952, **29,** 3–11.

8. Willits, R. D. Company performance and interpersonal relations. *Industrial Management Review,* 1967, **7,** 91–107.

9. Baird, J. W. Analytical field study of "open communication as perceived by supervisors, subordinates, and peers" (Doctoral dissertation, Purdue University, 1973. *Dissertation Abstracts International,* 1974, 35, 562B. (University Microfilms No, 74–15, 116).

10. O'Reilly, C. A. and Roberts, K. H. Information filtration in organizations: Three experiments. *Organizational Behavior and Human Performance,* 1974, **12,** 253–265.

11. Golembiewski, R. T. Planned organizational change: A major emphasis in behavioral approach to administration. In R. T. Golembiewski and A. Blumberg (Eds.). *Sensitivity Training and the Laboratory Approach.* Itasca, Ill.: F. E. Peacock, 1973.

12. Brown, G. G. and Neitzel, B. J. Communication, supervision, and morale. *Journal of Applied Psychology,* 1952, **36,** 86–91.

13. Walton, R. *Interpersonal Peacemaking.* Reading, Mass.: Addison-Wesley, 1969.

14. Homans, G. *Social Behavior in Its Elementary Forms.* New York: Harcourt, Brace, 1961.

15. March, J. G. & Olson, J. P. *Ambiguity and Choice in Organizations.* Oslo: Univesitets forlaget, 1976.

16. Pfeffer, J. & Salancik, G. R. *The External Control of Organizations.* New York: Harper and Row, 1978.

17. Argyris, C. Personality and organization revisited. *Administrative Science Quarterly,* 1973, **18,** 141–167.

18. Schein, E. H. *Career Dynamics: Matching Individual and Organizational Needs.* Reading, Mass.: Addison-Wesley, 1978.

—6—

Leadership and Stress Management

Harry Levinson

Several years ago, as is my custom, I placed a group of graduate students who were taking my seminar in organizational diagnosis in a small company of about 400 employees. In the initial months of the study, the president of the company treated the students like children. They found his attitude difficult to understand and his behavior somewhat troublesome to cope with.

About midway through the year, an economic recession rocked this small company back on its economic heels. Almost overnight, the previously competent president began to act almost like a child in efforts to become dependent on them. They in turn turned to me. "How do we understand this reversal?" they asked. "What's going on? How is it that a person like this can be head of a successful organization? What shall we tell him? How can we help him?"

Unfortunately, the literature of leadership, or indeed the literature of organizational consultation, doesn't have many good answers to these questions. The work of Vroom (1) might have given some hints as to how much participation one might invite as a leader, but participation assumes that the leader can participate effectively as a leader and can exercise power and authority appropriately. This executive might have discerned from Vroom's model what he ought to do, but whether he could was another matter.

The executive might have made use of Fiedler's (2) work to assess whether he could lead in this situation. But that wouldn't have helped much either. There was little choice but to be the leader, inasmuch as it was his company and there was no one else in it who could have taken his role. He might well have applied Argyris's (3) Model II behavior and shared with his people his thoughts and feelings, his sense of helplessness, and his fear of catastrophe. To do so would have panicked a good many of them who depended on him for stability of leadership. Further, to have done so would have increased his vulnerability to more intense attack from the most aggressive of his three vice presidents. One was already taking advantage of every opportunity to put the president down and to acquire a power base. Yet that person had sales skills that the president needed, particularly at this moment.

This chapter is adapted with permission from the American Psychological Association from Levinson, H. Power, leadership, and the management of Stress. *Professional Psychology*, 1980, **11**, 497–508. Copyright 1980.

I cite this illustration not to deprecate the work of my colleagues but to give substance to the words of Porter (4) about research on leadership. In his introduction to a symposium on which these psychologists appeared, he said, "This pre-eminent work does not deal with leadership as a whole and leaves us with only a limited number of highly circumscribed techniques with which to understand, predict, and guide executive behavior." The limits of what we know from decades of experimental research are most strikingly indicated in Stogdill's (5) exhaustive summary of leadership theories and studies.

LIMITATIONS OF LEADERSHIP THEORIES

Two dominant strains of work in the late 1940s and early 1950s came from the Institute of Social Research of the University of Michigan on the one hand, and the Ohio State leadership studies on the other (5). These efforts eventually declined as it became apparent that a list of characteristics or general qualities such as "consideration" seemed to be of little help either in the selection or training of people for leadership or power roles.

As the group dynamics movement came into being, the emphasis was on interpersonal processes. Aspiration to power, if it existed at all in individuals, was viewed as a negative quality. Exercise of power was viewed as autocratic. Indeed one who unabashedly wielded power was, in Douglas McGregor's (6) terms, by definition expressing Theory X, or in Blake and Mouton's (7) terms, behaving like 9/1.

In such an ethos, a leader was similar to Presbyterian pastors in multipastor churches (and with the same difficulties)—the first among equals. The unfortunate consequences of this kind of thinking became evident in the stress experienced by first-level supervision, reflected in high turnover in the Topeka General Foods dog food plant experiment (8), and by similar problems in other settings in which authority of supervisory power was denied, disclaimed, or emasculated. Metaphorically, the father was destroyed; the fraternal peer group was in. Shades of *Lord of the Flies!* (9).

Then contingency theories began to assume popularity. However, despite discussion about matching the personality of the leader to the situation (10, 2) not much sophisticated thinking about personality is apparent in contingency studies. The result is a continuing flow of low-level correlations that leave most of the variance unaccounted for.

Into this void there came a series of books on power. These varied from Korda's *Power!* (11) and Dubrin's *Winning at Office Politics* (12), essentially modern-day Machiavellis, to Ringer's avowedly self-aggrandizing *Winning Through Intimidation* (13). There was Dyer's self-supporting *Pulling Your Own Strings* (14), the more serious work of McClelland (15) and Winter (16), using experimental techniques to study the power motive, and the Zaleznik and Kets de Vries volume (17), which applied psychoanalytic theory to published information about leaders in business and politics.

The resurgence of books on power (18, 19, 20, 21) compels us to look at a fundamental human fact, heavily rooted in biology and the source of personal power, namely, the management of aggression and its corollary, the management of dependency. The former has been carefully avoided in industrial and organizational psychology despite the work of our colleagues in comparative psychology. We have been content to correlate odds and ends of peripheral behavior. Even McClelland's correlations indicate that while many bits of behavior correlate in minor ways with his definition of power, they do not correlate with each other. Therefore, I suggest, he is dealing with something more fundamental than a power motive, namely, the management of aggression. It is also aggression that underlies the achievement motive, moderated in a different direction for superego and ego defensive reasons.

Aggression in the form of a search for power has long characterized power-oriented organization structures whose hierarchical models have dominated our society. Those same organizations have also provided havens for the less, or less successfully, aggressive. The ancient Chinese philosopher, Yen Chih-T'ui (531–591+) (22), advised those who would succeed as functionaries of the emperors to hide in the hierarchy and to maintain status quo.

In short, the leadership theories prove inadequate unless they deal significantly with power and leadership as the management of aggression.

SELF-ESTEEM AND STRESS MANAGEMENT

Now comes the issue of stress, the current vogue in organizational psychology. There is much talk of stress as precipitated by forces in the organization. Some of this discussion is valid; much of it is simplistic. There is, further, much talk about coping with stress by meditation, biofeedback, progressive relaxation, various forms of imagery, and so on. All of these are palliative. They do not deal with the causes of stress. They cannot therefore deal with anticipating, ameliorating, or significantly alleviating it in organizations.

The core of occupational stress—indeed of all psychological stress—is the increase in the distance between the ego ideal (a picture—only partly conscious—of oneself at one's future best) and the self-image (one's picture of oneself in the present). This relationship may be expressed as

$$\text{self-esteem} = \frac{1}{\text{ego ideal} - \text{self-image}}$$

There are three circumstances in which psychological stress is increased: (a) when feelings of helplessness or inadequacy increase; (b) when people's values and personal rules of behavior are violated; (c) when people feel they are not moving toward their ego ideals. All three lower the self-image.

The importance of a personal goal was one of the core concepts for Adler (23). But personal goal for Adler did not refer to aspiration, but rather the struggle toward resolution of a psychological conflict. Rogers (24) and others have discussed the self-image and the self-concept. However, the ego ideal is something much more positive and refined than Adler's conception—an image of self toward which one strives (much of which is unconscious). And the gap between that image and the present view of self is untouched by those who have discussed self-concept and self-image. Such lack of refinement hinders application. With the specificity of the formula I have proposed, certain kinds of behavior become self-evident.

The greater the gap between the ego ideal and the self-image, the less well one thinks of oneself and the more angry one becomes with oneself (25). Thus feelings of inadequacy are pervasive. We are never as good as we would like to be. Increase in self-directed anger or aggression, a product of feelings of guilt and inadequacy, in turn produces depression. The greater the sense of helplessness and hopelessness, the greater the depression. Suicide is the extreme. Depression is the most pervasive of all emotional illnesses and frequently precipitates physiological symptoms. The depression and physiological symptoms following experiences of loss, and the history of coronaries also following such loss, are both examples.

Loss and consequent lowered self-esteem give psychological weight and importance to the loss of a job, of a family member, or of a familiar community support (26, 27, 28, 29).

Organizational pyramidal structures, with their heavy emphasis on winners and losers, on one track to success, frequently demean people. People in many specialties must shift from those specialties into managerial ranks in order to attain success within the structure, although they may be less competent as managers than as specialists. This problem is compounded by inadequate appraisal systems that do not speak to people's work performance and behavior on the job but to abstractions like promotability (30). When, further, on the basis of inadequate appraisal, people are graded on curves that do not meet the required underlying statistical assumptions, they are arbitrarily defined as unsuccessful when objectively their behavior on the job or their occupational performance is quite acceptable.

Another force that contributes to the lowered self-image in organizations is simply the behavioral consquence of the aging process. Most organizations have no effective or systematic way of describing and defining tasks so that they may place people at different ages or life stages in those roles that most fit where they are physically and psychologically. Still another is discrimination. Females and members of minority groups historically have been demeaned, and only slowly are being given assignments commensurate with their competence and skills.

A major problem in many, if not all, work organizations is the fact that phenomena widely recognized in the family tend to get played out in those organizations. Components of organizations, like members of a family are scapegoated. Frequently the trained observer sees the splitting phenomenon: people or groups are arbitrarily separated into the black hats and the white hats. There is sadistic and overcontrolling behavior, as well as often bitter intraorganizational strife, sometimes chronic, sometimes resulting in the extrusion of some organization members.

Unrelenting pressure for production, managerial inability or unwillingness to solve frustrating problems, or simple inefficiency produce feelings of hostility toward the organization and toward the self for putting up with such conditions.

The inability of organizations to recognize the devastating effects of change, and to build in systematic methods of supporting people through the process of change, further compounds the sense of loss, magnifies the feelings of helplessness, and undermines the self-image. Change takes many forms. A combination of aging and obsolescence may make people less desirable in an occupational marketplace. People who are no longer technically up-to-date feel themselves to be less adequate and more readily threatened. Merger, retirement, transfer, and promotion all disrupt previous relationships and produce losses. People do not easily reestablish ties or adapt to new experiences as they are. Therefore they tend to become increasingly isolated as a function of the aging process, making it likely that they will experience stress and, as a consequence, will focus more intensely on work. Thus they necessarily develop a greater dependency on work as a source of gratification, and are more vulnerable to the effects of whatever decisions are made about them.

In an organizational hierarchy the degree to which a person is valued is related to his or her position in that hierarchy. In the United States, with its great social mobility and competitive economy, there is intense competition for position in the hierarchy, stimulated and fostered by higher management. Thus a population is developed that includes not only winners but also proportionately greater numbers of losers. Those who cannot enter the hierarchy at all in a context that values power and position are the most helpless and therefore, by definition, defeated.

There is a long history of animal studies that indicates that animals lower in the pecking order within a given flock, pack, or other unit have a significantly higher incidence of death and withdrawal than do victors (31). Defeated male mice cling to the corners of their cages for their bodily functions as contrasted to the victors who may extrude body products anywhere in their cages. Defeated male cockroaches die at significantly higher frequencies than those who are victorious (32). Among men, there is an inverse relationship between position in the hierarchy of the organization and the incidence and prevalence of both physical and mental illness (33). In general, the lower the social status, the higher the incidence and prevalence of symptoms (34). The Metropolitan Life Insurance Company reports (35) that top-level executives have fewer illnesses and live longer than line-level people and lower-level managers.

If many people who lose out in the competitive struggle for position or authority experience themselves as defeated, others feel themselves to be engineered into a work process as the equivalent of pieces of machinery. Those who are doing monotonous and repetitive tasks frequently view themselves as being relatively powerless to cope with the factionalism of work and the impersonality of the work organization, which in turn alienates workers from each other and from gratification in the work process and lowers their self-image.

Furthermore, lower-level employees frequently see first-hand the inefficiencies of management. They also suffer from the erratic ups and downs of levels of employment in such highly rationalized industries, a phenomenon over which they have little control. These experiences serve further to exacerbate the widespread sense of inadequacy and passive helplessness, which in turn magnifies and intensifies feelings of self-directed anger. They also precipitate physical and emotional symptoms (36, 37).

When employees rebel against this view of them and against being manipulated by others, they usually do so in the form of strikes, sabotage, resistance, and other forms of hostility. Thus anger and often guilt are mobilized. These, together with economic losses, constitute further strains.

In such a manipulative context it is difficult to evolve an identification with the organization. This inability undermines social relationships at work, depriving people of human support and increasing the sense of helplessness. Group support is a necessary but not sufficient condition for coping with stress (38), though much of the literature seems not to recognize that fact.

Mayo (39) laid heavy emphasis on group membership and thus on the people's needs for the affiliation with their work groups. He recognized that such affiliation and interdependence provided mutual support and group cohesion, which enhanced self-esteem by providing affectionate bolstering of the self-image and simultaneously increased one's power by giving him or her, as a member of a group, greater influence over what went on in the work process.

But if group membership, group cohesion, and interpersonal relationships are primary, there is often great pressure on the individual to sacrifice his or her individuality as the price of getting along. The employee then pays for the degree of cohesion and support he or she gets in the form of being controlled by others. And, except by organized bargaining methods, the employee has little control over his or her own fate.

Under such circumstances, seeking to satisfy employees, managements may undertake morale studies, survey feedback, climate studies, and the like. But employees who feel alienated, alone, powerless, and otherwise inadequate, even as part of a group made cohesive by external pressures, may respond to questionnaires by saying they want higher pay or better facilities, even better supervision. Raising pay, improving facilities, or changing supervision, however, will not deal with their underlying feelings of alienation or being tyrannized by the group. In fact, making such requested changes may confirm their feelings of not being understood at all in the same way that a parent, who substitutes gifts for understanding, may anger the child.

There is much talk of alleviating stress by enabling people to fulfill their own potentials (40). While superficially valid, closer inspection discloses that this simple extrapolation from Goldstein's (41) observation of brain-damaged patients has many shortcomings. As a matter of fact, people do not strive to fulfill their potentials. Many people are quite contented operating at an intellectual or cultural level quite different from that for which they might be ideally competent. There is no clinical or experimental evidence to indicate that failure to achieve self-fulfillment, in the sense of fulfilling potential, precipitates neurosis. I know of no study that delineates what people are fully capable of achieving, then contrasts that with what they have achieved and demonstrates that the gap produces stress.

There are a number of studies that indicate that people are less satisfied with the degree of autonomy they have at work than that which they would like to have. However, we do not know whether the stated wish for autonomy is: (a) the same as self-actualization; (b) a mask for denying underlying dependency needs; (c) a means by which people have rationalized the fact that they have not attained greater autonomy; (d) a reflection of hostility to anybody else who has greater power than they have; or (e) a metaphor that speaks of yearning to escape the constrictions imposed by their own consciences or self-judgments. It is difficult if not impossible to ascertain for any given individual, let alone a group of individuals, what constitutes self-actualization. A person may be actualizing (i.e., moving toward the ego ideal), but that is a process, not a result. Many may be led to frustration in pursuit of a psychological ghost.

When autonomy is equated with self-actualization, and there is a failure to explore the underlying psychology of that wish, one may try to give greater autonomy to work groups that are happily dependent. Then, despite their wish as expressed in words, they may well panic when asked to make their own decisions. Furthermore, the heavy emphasis on autonomy often leads to greater participation in decision making. Naive participatory management efforts often result in emasculating leadership or in abdication of leadership. The absence of leadership leads to greater chaos, lack of direction, lack of cohesion, and to falling back on group defenses and group norms as people try to control the anomalous situations in which they find themselves.

PERSONALITY DYNAMICS IN STRESS SITUATIONS

Violation of values precipitates feelings of guilt. People are then angry with themselves or the organizations in which they work. Violation of personal standards occurs repeatedly and people frequently complain about such violations. Advertising people will write books criticizing their own profession, teachers will complain about schools, and former CIA agents about the activities of their agency. Some people have exposed the dishonesty of their company's actions; others have reported on how they have fudged figures. All respond to internal standards, and the guilt and anger for violations of those standards.

People feel guilty and angry also when they are required to assume responsibilities that they cannot discharge adequately. A significant source of managerial guilt is the appraisal process itself. When managers and supervisors are asked to evaluate or appraise others, they usually feel they are being destructive. This is reflected in the fact that organizations are continuously changing performance appraisal systems because they are unsatisfactory and because, despite much training and pressure, it is difficult to get managers and supervisors to do evaluations. A fundamental reason is that evaluating others touches off unconscious primary process feelings: to think something or to feel it is the same as to do it. Thus to critically evaluate is to be aggressive; unconsciously to be aggressive is to destroy. This problem is exacerbated when younger people are placed in supervisory or managerial roles over older people, as increasingly is the case with higher levels of education and even more youthful management. Carrying out judgmental criticism under these circumstances becomes much like attacking one's own parents, thus reviving ancient childhood anxieties, unconscious guilt, and the fear of retaliation. Fear is already exacerbated in organizations by the intense rivalry for places in the organization hierarchy. It is compounded even further by placing people, unprepared, in supervisory positions over others who were previously rivals or supervisors, thus recapitulating the worst fantasies of early childhood.

Changes in organizations in turn require people to adopt new styles of behavior. Those who are accustomed to administering by not taking charge, as often is the case in management of mental health clinics or art museums or hospitals, are now being compelled to take charge and to become more efficient, to control people rather than merely consult with them. Employees who formerly were encouraged to be dependent now are frequently being required to become more aggressive as more organizations shift from technical or manufacturing orientations to marketing orientations. Thus the long-term pursuit of the ego ideal for such people is undermined, and the fact that they must go off in other occupational directions frequently presents them with a self-image that is anathema to them.

People will be angry with themselves (and therefore depressed) and with their work organizations when they expect, but do not have, a sense of forward movement. The expected movement toward the ego ideal is implicit in those studies that reflect the wish for greater autonomy, opportunity, growth, and challenge.

In addition to negative organizational events, movement toward the ego ideal may be inhibited by social and cultural forces. All cultural units, whether flocks or families, tribes or nations, have pecking orders. Those males who are more dominant in the pecking order, presumably for Darwinian reasons, have greater access to food and females. Thus in male-dominated systems there is a certain inevitability about the way social structures evolve and power is distributed, regardless of economic systems. There is also a certain inevitability about people's willingness to attribute status or "better than" to one kind of work as contrasted with another. The leather workers of India and Japan are drawn only from the lowest castes. In our own country, as well as others in the western world, fewer people are willing to perform personal services, and those who do are now more often immigrants from lesser developed countries. Repeated surveys of the status of occupations indicate that professions are highest ranked. Within given professions there are also well-defined hierarchies. Therefore, even in autonomous professional practices, a sense of hierarchy prevails and people scale themselves, thus significantly, affecting their own self-images.

Although it is true one's position in an organization hierarchy is usually related to one's social position in the community, nevertheless, even if there were no organizations, there probably would still be competition for social position. As noted earlier, social class studies indicate that the lower a person is in the community social structure, the more likely he or she is to have symptoms of mental and physical illness.

In addition there are of course the inevitable socioeconomic forces that go beyond what organizations do of their own accord. When one or another kind of work becomes obsolete or redundant, then its practitioners are compelled to give up their ego ideal pursuits in that particular profession. Then there are problems of racial, ethnic, and educational discrimination, which do permanent damage not only to the self-image but also inhibit the move toward the ego ideal.

Even positive forces can have a negative effect. Sarason (42) notes that frequently even high status professionals are dissatisfied with their work. In an open society, he says, we can do many things well. We promise ourselves we will do those many things. But by devoting ourselves to achievement in our profession, we have no time to move to the other things, and thus we are disappointed in not delivering on our promises to ourselves.

Each of us has a contract with ourself. Many primitive, infantile elements of that contract having to do with the wish to attain perfection and to live forever are inevitably doomed to nonfulfillment. The underlying disappointment in the failure to understand, let alone fulfill, the contract with the self is a significant component of stress. That fundamental disappointment is exacerbated by environmental forces that cause work organizations to violate other elements of that contract (e.g., violations of conscience). It is further magnified by those which become a counterforce or barrier to attain the more conscious expectations of the self. I say exacerbated because I think the fundamental issue for most people, that which Freud (43) called primary narcissism and the wish to endure forever, will not be gratified no matter what happens in the external environment. Therefore there will always be significant elements of stress. From a psychoanalytic viewpoint, unconsciously none of us thinks we will die. Witness all the contemporary focus on relieving the anxiety of dying and the massive denial of death reflected in smoking, overeating, addiction, and other self-destructive behavior. Even those who commit suicide apparently think that psychologically they will live on, as indicated by their notes.

All this is compounded when there is inadequate information from the organization and repetitive change in organization structures. These result in inadequate support from superiors in dealing with both the organization and external reality. Maintaining one's psychological equilibrium in the face of losses and new demands requires simultaneously taxing adaptation (44). In the absence of information and role definition, without an adequately delegated charge and necessary support, people are more likely to be hyper-self-critical, more defensive, more distressed, more overcontrolled, and increasingly at risk of external criticism from superiors.

Thus, while organizations do indeed precipitate stress, one cannot take the position that stress is altogether the fault of the organization. Not only does the culture have an impact but also individuals bring their own ideals and self-images, their own values and expectations to the organizations, and thereby their own vulnerabilities.

THE ROLE OF THE LEADER

If stress is the product of these many kinds of forces and if it is ameliorated by group support and if group support in turn is significantly a product of cohesion around the leadership or, therefore, identification with the leader, it follows that the function of leadership is central to the anticipation, alleviation, and amelioration of stress. The leader, then, is the instrument of fulfillment of the psychological contract (45) with the organization. He or she is the person through whom conscious and unconscious expectations are mediated, and therefore it becomes imperative for leaders at all levels to evolve a sophisticated understanding of the psychology of people, rather than gross generalizations like self-actualization. He or she must use power in an active leadership role to deflect aggression away from self-directed attack in the form of depression and physical symptoms into problem solving.

If all organizations in any culture are essentially recapitulations of the family structure in that culture, then the leader is psychologically in a parent-like role, that is, he or she encounters unconscious expectations that he or she behave in the modal way a parent behaves in this culture. The leader must understand and act upon that role to ensure the perpetuation of the organization.

The leader as a surrogate parental figure in our kind of culture is significantly a teacher (46). It is the task of leaders in a culture that gives extensive support to children to pursue their own ego ideals, to define organizational purpose, and to unite purpose with the people who are involved in that task, that is, to know what are they here for? What do they want to look back on when they have completed these particular tasks and roles? If leaders can understand the need to define the nature of their own ego ideals, which they are trying to pursue in their work, and help subordinates to define and integrate theirs into a statement of purpose, then that gives psychological meaning for people to be together. It is only from such meaning that goals and objectives, long-term steps, and then short-term steps, are derived. Purpose is never attained. Like the ego ideal from which it is derived, it serves as a distant target toward which a cohesive group can move and which gives significance to goals and objectives. The leader may then engage the followers in finding the means and methods by which they will attain those goals and objectives and also the standards by which they will do so. While this may seem very similar to participative management, and in a sense it is participative management, nevertheless, what I mean to imply here is not merely participation but psychologically sophisticated participation in which the leader understands the psychological vicissitudes of followers (and self) as parents must understand those of children, and act accordingly. But the leader unlike the parent, can't abdicate power, for when he or she does, then he or she is no longer in the leadership role.

The leader must understand that he or she must deal with ministration, maturation, and mastery needs. That is, not only do people need to be introduced to jobs and to have appropriate dependency needs met for guidance and supervision, but they must also have the opportunity to increase their competencies and ultimately to have a sense of mastery over task, and indeed, as much as possible over their own fates in the organizations.

This will mean different things for different people, and people who move into leadership roles will have to understand these differences so that their on-the-job behavior can, like the behavior of the knowing parent, be differentiated for each of those who report to them.

It is the task of the leader then to bring the people who report to him or her face-to-face with the realities that they, as organization members, are up against, and to support them in the process of learning to master those realities by which they simultaneously meet their own maturation needs, become increasingly competent, and master a good deal of their working environment—at least as much of it as possible in those specific roles. The leader also serves as a model for how problems can be mastered.

Simultaneously, when the leader acts in these ways, he or she provides affirmation and recognition for individuals and the group as a whole, while at the same time strengthening them by the very process of organizing a group, by differentiated understanding, support for people, and of people by and for each other. That in turn means that it is possible for people to think of how to differentiate themselves in their specific roles, particularly when the organization has a sophisticated performance appraisal system (30) that enables people to get a clear picture of their own consistent and repetitive behavior, both positive and negative, and in turn makes it possible to describe jobs in behavioral terms so that people may be more adequately and accurately fitted to them.

Without minimizing the importance of organization process, policy, structure, and philosophy, nevertheless experience indicates even in the military (47) that given two units of the same numbers for the same task, the significant difference in stress casualties was a product of the kind of leadership those respective units had. The same is no less true of other organizations, particularly those in which people are at work.

REFERENCES

1. Vroom, V.H. & Yetton, P. *Leadership and Decision Making.* Pittsburgh: University of Pittsburgh Press 1973.
2. Fiedler, F.E. *A Theory of Leadership Effectiveness.* New York: McGraw-Hill, 1967.
3. Argyris, C. & Schon, D. *Theory in Practice.* San Francisco: Jossey-Bass, 1974.
4. Porter, L. *Organization Dynamics,* Winter 1976, 2–5.
5. Stogdill, R.M. *Handbook of Leadership.* New York: Free Press, 1974.
6. McGregor, D. *The Human Side of Enterprise.* New York: McGraw-Hill, 1960.
7. Blake, R.R. & Mouton, J.S. *The New Managerial Grid.* Houston: Gulf, 1978.
8. Brimm, I.M. Analytic perspectives in organizational behavior: A study of an organizational innovation. Unpublished doctoral dissertation, Graduate School of Business Administration, Harvard University, 1975.
9. Golding, W. *Lord of the Flies.* New York: Putnam, 1959.
10. Lorsch, J.W. & Morse, J.J. *Organizations and Their Members.* Cambridge: Harvard University Press, 1974.
11. Korda, M. *Power! How to Get It: How to Use It.* New York: Random House, 1975.
12. Durbrin, A.J. *Winning at Office Politics.* New York: Van Nostrand Reinhold, 1978.

13. Ringer, R. *Winning through Intimidation.* New York: Funk and Wagnalls, 1974.

14. Dyer, W. *Pulling Your Own Strings.* New York: Crowell, 1978.

15. McClelland, D.C. *Power: The Inner Experience.* New York: Irvington, 1975.

16. Winter, D.G. *The Power Motive.* New York:Free Press, 1973.

17. Zaleznik, A. & Kets de Vries, M.F.R. *Power and the Corporate Mind.* Boston: Houghton-Mifflin, 1975.

18. Kipnes. D. *Power Holders.* Chicago: University of Chicago Press, 1976.

19. Burns, J.M. *Leadership.* New York: Harper and Row, 1978.

20. Fairlie, H. *The Parties: Republicans and Democrats in This Century.* New York: St. Martin's Press, 1978.

21. Kennedy, E.C. *Himself: The Life and Times of Mayor Richard J. Daley.* New York: Viking Press, 1978.

22. Dien, A.E. in A. Wright (Ed.). *The Confucian Personality.* Stanford, Calif.: University Press, 1962.

23. Adler, A. *Understanding Human Nature.* New York: Greenberg, 1927.

24. Rogers, C. *Counseling and Psychotherapy.* Boston: Houghton-Mifflin, 1973.

25. Levinson, H. *Executive Stress.* New York: Harper and Row, 1972.

26. Slote, A. *Termination: The Closing of the Baker Plant.* Institute for Social Research, Survey Research Center, University of Michigan, Ann Arbor, 1969; and reissued 1977.

27. Janis, I.L. *Stress and Frustration.* New York: Harcourt Brace Jovanovich, 1971.

28. Parkes, C.M. *Bereavement: Studies of Grief in Adult Life.* New York: International Universities, 1972.

29. Weiss, R.S. *Loneliness: The Experience of Emotional and Social Isolation.* Cambridge: Massachusetts Institute of Technology, 1973.

30. Levinson, H. Appraisal of what performance. *Harvard Business Review,* 1976, **54**, 30.

31. Mazur, A. A cross species comparison of status in small established groups. *American Sociological Review,* 1973, **38**, 513–530.

32. Ewing, L. Fighting and death from stress in a cockroach. *Science,* 1976, **155**, 1035–1036.

33. Kornhauser, A. *Mental Health of the Industrial Worker.* New York: Wiley, 1965.

34. Syme, S.L. & Berkman, L.F. Social class, susceptibility and sickness. *American Journal of Epidemiology,* 1976, **104**, 1–8.

35. Cunnick, W. & Smith, N. Occupationally related emotional problems, *New York State Journal of Medicine,* 1977, **77**, 1737–1740.

36. Erikson, K.T. Loss of communality at Buffalo Creek. *American Journal of Psychiatry,* 1976, **133,** 302–305.

37. Foltman, F.F. *White and Blue Collars in a Mill Shutdown: A case Study in Relative Redundancy.* Ithaca, N.Y.: New York State School of Industrial and Labor Relations, Paperback No. 6, 1968.

38. Cobb, S. Social support as a moderator of stress. *Psychosomatic Medicine,* 1976, **38**, 1–8.

39. Mayo, E. *The Human Problems of an Industrial Civilization.* New York: Arno Press, 1977.

40. Maslow, A. *Motivation and Personality,* New York: Harper and Row, 1954.

41. Goldstein, K. *The Organism.* New York: American Book Company, 1939.

42. Sarason, S. *Work, Aging and Social Action.* New York: Free Press, 1977.

43. Freud, S. On narcissism: An introduction. In *Complete Works of Sigmund Freud* (Standard Edition, Vol.14). London: Hogarth Press, 1957.

44. Holmes, T.H. & Rahe, R.H. Social adjustment and rating scale. *Journal of Psychosomatic Research,* 1967, **11**, 213–218.

45. Levinson, H. Price, C.P. Munden, K.J. Mandl, H.J. & Solley, G.M. *Men, Management and Mental Health.* Cambridge: Harvard University Press, 1962.

46. Levinson, H. *The Exceptional Executive.* Cambridge: Harvard University Press, 1968.

47. Menninger, W.C. *Psychiatry in a Troubled World.* New York: Macmillan, 1948.

—7—

Making Supervision Humane and Productive

Herbert H. Meyer

INTRODUCTION

The supervisor undoubtedly has more influence on the productivity and morale of a work group than any other single factor. The differences in results obtained by effective and ineffective supervisors are often astoundingly large. These differences are likely to be reflected in the direct costs associated with quantity and quality of outputs. Equally important, however, are the more indirect costs that result from such morale indicators as employee absenteeism and turnover. Even more indirect are the costs associated with individual state-of-mind variables—the personal well-being of employees in work settings.

Because of the recognized importance of supervision, how to supervise people in work settings has always been a popular topic in business journals. In the early days, articles on supervision tended to be philosophical in nature. The scientific management movement, which started about 100 years ago when many work organizations began to grow very large, focused attention on how employees should be supervised. However, the advice given in such writings was almost always based only on theory or common sense.

Moreover, during the scientific management movement, most of the "experts" on supervisory practices focused primarily on the goal of productivity—on how to maximize the outputs of people at work. They seemed to assume that paying someone to work gave the employer control over that worker's behavior. Therefore much of the advice given about how to supervise dealt with workers in rather mechanical fashion—almost as if their efforts could be programmed like machines. Little emphasis was given to the objective of making work more humane.[1]

In recent years, at least since World War II, a great deal of research has been carried out on the effectiveness of various supervisory practices. Much of this research was carried out in field settings, that is, in actual work organizations. This research has provided more objective and valid information than was previously available about how supervisors can utilize human resources in a work organization to achieve the dual objectives of making workers more productive and making the working climate more humane.

Some of the findings of this research on supervisory practices confirmed the theories and common sense advice given previously by the management scientists. On the other hand, many of the assumptions made by the earlier writers on this topic proved to be false. For example, research proved that human effort could not be programmed and manipulated as if workers were automatons. In fact, such attempts often resulted in decreased rather than increased productivity. On the other hand, when the primary objective of programs introduced experimentally was to make the work situation more humane, such programs often proved also to make the respective work groups more productive.[2]

Most of the early management scientists also seemed to assume that economic motives were all-powerful in work settings. Their writings often emphasized that the key to maximizing human effort lay in finding ways to attach financial rewards very directly to worker output. Here again, the research studies of worker behavior did not bear out this simple assumption. Employees were found to respond to more than just economic motives in work settings. In fact, the attempted use of direct economic incentives often resulted not in increased productivity, but in severe restraints of effort and outputs among workers. The research evidence has shown clearly that the problem of motivating employees is much more complex than it was traditionally thought to be.[3]

A SUMMARY OF RESEARCH FINDINGS

The voluminous research on supervisory practices has shown that certain principles or practices are consistently found to be associated with effective supervision. This research has proved that generally the objectives of making workers both more productive and the work situation more humane are not incompatible. Rather, as was mentioned previously, the research often demonstrated that where the primary objective of a program to change supervisory practices was to make the work situation more humane for workers, it also increased their productivity.

Some of the most significant of the various research-tested principles or practices that have been found to contribute to the achievement of the dual objectives of making supervision both more productive and more humane are:

1. Employees should have a clear understanding of what is expected of them.
2. Goals or work standards should be defined as specifically as possible.
3. Goals or standards should be set at a level of difficulty that will challenge the capacity of the worker, but they must also not be so difficult that they seem to be unattainable.
4. Knowledge of results being achieved on the job should be provided as specifically and frequently as possible. As a corollary to this principle, it is also

desirable to structure the job situation in such a way that the worker can monitor his or her own performance. That is, the job situation should provide feedback information directly to the employee, rather than indirectly through the supervisor or some other source.

5. Praise and recognition are generally much more effective in stimulating improvements in worker behavior than are criticism or punishment.
6. If criticism is used, it should be phrased constructively and in a nonpersonalized manner.
7. If at all possible, employees should have opportunities to participate in the decision making process when plans or programs are developed that will affect them in their jobs.
8. Growth opportunities should be available and visible to employees in the work organization.
9. The considerate supervisor, who combines a humane interest in employees with a strong emphasis on task accomplishment, is likely to be more effective in increasing worker productivity than is the supervisor who emphasizes only task accomplishment.

Each of these principles will be discussed in some detail.

Provide Clear Understanding of What is Expected

This principle may appear to be so obvious and commonsensical that it is hardly worth mentioning. Yet attitude surveys often reveal that employees at all levels, from the assembly line to the executive suite, indicate that they do not have a clear idea of what is expected on the job. Uncertainty of this kind will breed tension, and such tension is not likely to contribute to productivity.

A number of studies have compared empolyees' perceptions of what they thought they were responsible for on the job with their respective supervisors' conceptions of the employees' responsibilities. In many cases the discrepancies in such supervisor-subordinate perceptions were surprisingly large. Moreover, these studies showed that these discrepancies were often associated with the supervisors' appraisals of the subordinates. That is, the more the supervisor and subordinate were in agreement about the subordinate's job responsibilities, the higher were the supervisor's ratings of that subordinate's performance.[4]

How can expectations be made clear? A job description that is revised and updated at least annually can help to define expectations. This need not be a lengthy, detailed, and formalized document. Too often job descriptions are prepared in the form of jargon-filled, legalistic documents that serve primarily to provide formal documentation to justify the salary level attached to the job. They are kept only in personnel department files. They are not used to provide for each employee a clear understanding of what is expected in the job.

A job description that presents in a simple and straightforward manner what the overall purpose or objective of the job is, followed by a list of specific duties or responsibilities, can serve as a useful guide to what is expected of the employee on the job. Such a description can be especially valuable if the employee participates in drafting it. The employee might prepare a first draft, for example, which is then reviewed with the supervisor. The two can then negotiate and reach agreement on just what are the duties or responsibilities of the employee in that job.

Even more effective than job descriptions are frequent discussions between supervisor and employee of performance objectives and results being achieved. This is probably the most effective way to insure that job expections are clear for each employee. Too often a supervisor is so busy solving problems that arise in the course of day-to-day work that the communications needs of employees are neglected. Yet if the supervisor takes the time to discuss with employees the status of their work, many of the problems the supervisor deals with would never arise.

It is easy to take for granted that people know what is expected of them. We may even feel that the employee will resent receiving too much information. However, research has shown that most employees have an insatiable need for information about the job, the work of their department, and how things are going in the company as a whole.

Define Goals Specifically

This principle is obviously related to our first priniciple—to make clear what is expected on the job. This second principle merely adds the provision that expectations be defined in terms of specific and objective standards or goals.

It goes without saying that employees are expected to do their best in carrying out their jobs. Or, to put it in the vernacular, they're expected to give a good day's work for a day's pay. However, the research evidence shows very clearly that performance of tasks of any kind will usually be superior if people strive to achieve specific targets or goals, rather than merely trying to do their best.[5]

By specific goals we mean defining goals or standards in terms that are as objective and definite as possible. For example, instead of asking an employee who is fabricating a product to try to keep rejects to a minimum, the employee might be asked to try to keep rejects to less than 3 percent. Similarly, if quantity of outputs should be increased, it will usually be much more effective to set a specific target, such as a 10 percent increase in outputs, than it will be to merely ask people to do their best to increase production.

This principle applies equally well in jobs at all levels. In the higher level and more complex jobs, the objective or targets set for a project will often be defined in terms of time schedules or deadlines. There is no better way to insure that a project gets accomplished than by setting a hard and fast deadline for completing the task. In fact, if the supervisor wants to make sure that action is taken by an employee on even a relatively small, day-to-day commitment, such as preparing a letter or correcting a machine setup, it is advisable in every such case to set a specific follow-up time or date to check on the results.

Goals Should Be Challenging, but Attainable

Many studies of the goal-setting process have demonstrated that most people will perform best if they are aiming for a difficult goal. Yet it is also important that the goal not be so difficult as to seem unattainable. The individual must be personally committed to attaining the goal. If the goal is set at a level of difficulty that seems to be impossible to attain, the personal commitment will not be there.

In one field experiment, for example, goals were set for foremen in both quantity and quality of production that they were asked to achieve in their work groups.[6] One group of foremen was assigned relatively easy goals in both quantity and quality of outputs. A second group was assigned very difficult goals in both areas. These goals were set at a level of difficulty based on past experience, which had shown that the foremen would be expected to have less than a 50–50 chance of being able to achieve them.

A third group of foremen was given a combination of one easy and one difficult goal. For example, some of the foremen in this third group received an easy goal to achieve in quantity of production, but a difficult goal in quality (e.g., percentage of rejects to be tolerated). Others received an easy goal in the quality area, but a difficult goal in quantity of production expected.

The results of this experiment showed clearly that overall performance was best when just one of the goals was set at a difficult level. Interestingly, performance was poorest when both goals were set at a very difficult level—even poorer than where both goals were easy. Interviews with the foremen revealed that when both of their goals were set at the very difficult level, the assigned task seemed to be impossible. They did not consider the assignment to be realistic. Therefore they were not personally committed to achieving the goals. They more or less gave up without seriously attempting to achieve the two very difficult goals.

Where just one of the two goals was set at a very difficult level, the foremen said that this assignment to improve work group performance was regarded as a realistic challenge. They accepted the commitment and worked very hard to achieve the goals in both areas. Actually there seemed to be some spillover effect of their heightened level of commitment. Most of them performed better even in the area in which the easy goal had been set than they had in the past, or performed better than did those foremen who had been assigned two easy goals.

Provide Knowledge of Results Feedback

Performance in accomplishing goals or standards will also be maximized if workers get continuous feedback as to how they are doing on the job. In other words, try to find a way to "keep score" if you want to see performance improvements. Like the previous principles we discussed, this may seem to be so obvious and commonsensical as to hardly be worth mentioning. Yet experience has shown that all too often workers, and especially those on assembly lines, get very little feedback on the results of their efforts. If they do get any such information, it is likely to be only when performance is unsatisfactory. That is, if they make mistakes they will hear about it. Otherwise they may get few clues as to how they are doing.

Numerous studies of work performance have shown that just finding a way to keep score on the job not only improves performance markedly, but it also makes the worker's job more interesting. In one such study, for example, a shipping department had tried continually to get employees to consolidate packages that were going to the same location. Considerable savings could result if employees took advantage of every such opportunity to consolidate small packages headed for the same destination into one larger box.

Most employees thought that they were doing the best they could to combine small packages in this way when they made their shipments. Yet careful checks of actual results being achieved showed that they were capitalizing on less than 50 percent of the opportunities to consolidate shipments in this way. These results were surprising to the workers themselves. Therefore they designed a scorekeeping system to provide a continuous record of results being achieved in taking advantage of opportunities to consolidate packages.

In a very short time, the records showed that these same employees were capitalizing on over 95 percent of the opportunities to consolidate packages destined for the same location. This was a higher rate of performance than anyone had expected could be achieved. Yet with the scorekeeping system that had been developed, this level of performance was sustained over time. The cost savings that resulted from this improved level of performance amounted to hundreds of thousands of dollars per year.[7]

A similar experiment was conducted in an appliance manufacturing plant. Whenever a model change was introduced, both the overall quantity and quality of production declined badly. Again this problem was attacked by finding better ways to monitor what was happening in the production process during such changeovers.

With the assembly workers' help, scorekeeping procedures were developed whenever possible in the assembly process. Thus it became possible to make immediate corrections or adjustments when quality or quantity of outputs started to decline at any point along the line. The results of this feedback program showed that instead of experiencing declines in quantity and quality of outputs, performance in both areas actually improved during the next model changeover period. Moreover, the workers reported a higher level of interest and enthusiasm for their jobs.[8]

A desirable feature of both this latter study and the previously cited study involving the packaging problem was that they both involved self-monitoring of results by the employees themselves. Where results are measured by an outside source, such as the supervisor or an inspector, the feedback often takes on a punitive quality. That is, the workers feel they are being checked on continuously and may become defensive if their performance is seen as being inadequate in any way. Where the workers keep score for themselves, they have a chance to correct errors or to increase their outputs themselves, before such inadequacies reflect badly on their performance. Moreover, where individuals or work groups monitor their own performance, the incentive to improve comes from within. The commitment to a self-imposed task or goal is almost always stronger than to a goal imposed by someone else.[9]

Use Praise and Recognition Freely

One of the proven principles of motivation that is probably least often applied in work settings is that positive reinforcement is more effective than negative in bringing about improvements in employee performance. Most supervisors must concentrate their attention on keeping things running smoothly. They must be continuously on the alert to spot situations that are getting out of hand. The employee who makes a mistake will usually hear about it immediately. The mistake must be corrected immediately.

Actually, many textbooks on how to manage recommend that supervisors should use the "management by exception" approach in allocating their time and attention to daily tasks. That is, they should attend only to problems or other exceptional situations in which corrective action is needed. Supervisors often admit that if everything always ran smoothly, there would be little need for a supervisor. On the other hand, it also seems obvious that if the supervisor takes this approach to the job, it means that employees who are doing a good job are not likely to get much attention.

This same approach of attending only to those situations in which corrective action is needed is very natural in all circumstances in which we are interested in shaping behavior. In training our children, for example, it is easier to spot and react to deviant behaviors than to give recognition for desirable behavior. Punishment is easy to associate directly with an undesirable behavior. However, the research evidence shows that punishment, such as criticism, ridicule, sarcasm, or disciplinary procedures, will often have undesirable side effects. Frequently such punishment seens to result in an immediate correction of the problem. Unfortunately, this behavior improvement, which seems to result from using punishment, will often be very temporary. Longer-term results are likely to be unpredictable.[10]

A good deal of research has shown that a natural reaction to criticism or punishment is to become defensive. When we become defensive, we are denying responsibility for our behavior. We make excuses at least to ourselves, if not to the supervisor. Moreover, the research has shown that a natural response to criticism or punishment is to develop a dislike for the source.

In one study, for example, employees were asked to rate their supervisors on the degree to which they were helpful to them in getting the job done and in counseling them on job-related problems. They then participated in performance review discussions with their supervisors. In these discussions the supervisors both praised and criticized performance. After the discussions the employees were again asked to rate their supervisors on the same scales. These ratings assigned *after* they had been criticized in the performance review discussions were less favorable, on the average, than they had been in the prediscussion ratings. Moreover, the degree to which they were more negative in these postdiscussion ratings was related to the amount of criticism they had received in their performance review discussions. That is, those who had received more criticism in the discussion were also more negative in their postdiscussion ratings than those who had received relatively little criticism. Obviously these changes in attitude towards the supervisor were not helpful in building good working relationships between supervisor and employee.[11]

Another problem with the use of criticism or punishment is that it is not instructive. It may sometimes be effective in stopping undesirable behavior, but it is usually not very useful in teaching new behavior. This is where the positive approach comes into play. People tend to repeat behavior that is associated with desirable outcomes. Thus, for example, if an employee is praised for improving the quality of his or her output, the chances are strong that he or she will continue to strive to improve. On the other hand, if he or she is criticized when quality slips, the odds are that the employee may only develop negative feelings toward the supervisor and may find reasons to believe that quality isn't actually very important.

The solution to the problem of effecting behavioral changes in others is to ignore undesirable behavior and to watch carefully for opportunities to reinforce desirable behavior. Thus to correct a tardiness problem, it will be much more effective to watch for opportunity to praise the employee for being on time than to criticize or punish the employee for being late. This is hard to do. Yet experience has shown that to punish people who are tardy rarely has any sustained effect in improving tardiness. On the other hand, carefully controlled experiments have shown that a severe tardiness problem in a large office can often be corrected in a few weeks if the supervisors merely ignore employees when they are late but praise them for either being on time or for showing some improvement—that is, they are closer to being on time than they have been. Praising someone for showing improvement in this way is effective in shaping behavior. That is, to give positive reinforcement for improvement will gradually move performance in the right direction—nearer to perfection.[12]

Praise can also be used effectively to sustain performance of the steady, dependable employee. If the supervisor is attending only to situations that need correcting, the steady, adequately performing employees are likely to get little or no attention. Yet these are the very employees the supervisor depends on to get the work out. To make a special effort to compliment such employees will often serve as a tremendous morale booster. It may also help to keep turnover of the most desirable element of the employee population to a minimum. The steady employee who never receives any encouragement may very well lose interest in the job and look elsewhere.

Try to Impersonalize Criticism

Sometimes it may seen necessary to use criticism. When a particular behavior or work habit must be changed or stemmed, criticism may seem to pinpoint the needed change. However, we know that criticism may also have undesirable side effects. The fact that an employee is criticized may threaten the individual's self-esteem, so that a defensive rather than a constructive reaction is elicited. If the employee reacts defensively, the chances are that he or she will not attack the problem constructively.

The solution to this problem is to find a way to phrase the criticism in a constructive and impersonal manner. This can be done by avoiding personal and accusing, blame-placing statements. For example, instead of telling an employee that he or she is producing too many bad parts, the supervisor might say something like, "We have a problem on the line. Our percentage of rejects is getting to be too high. I'd like your help in solving this problem."

The difference in describing the problem in this way rather than directly accusing the employee of producing too many rejects may seem to be slight. But the difference is important. By describing the situation as a general problem, the supervisor does not criticize the employee directly. Moreover, by asking for his or her help in solving the problem, the supervisor builds the employee's self-esteem rather than tearing it down. The individual would have to be rather insensitive to ignore the request for help in solving the problem. Experience in teaching supervisors to use this approach in behavior modeling training programs has shown that it is effective. Almost invariably, the employee who is apprised of a problem in this manner, and asked to help solve the problem, will react constructively.[13]

Allow Employees to Participate in Decision Making

In theory, it seems logical to organize an activity in such a way that each person performs a highly specialized function. In this way we can best capitalize on the specialized knowledge, skills, and abilities that each individual brings to the organization. The management people are usually better educated and more intelligent than others in the organization. Therefore it seems reasonable to expect that they should perform most of the thinking, planning, and decision making functions. The nonmanagement people, who are almost always in the great majority, then merely follow orders in carrying out the functions prescribed by the thinkers and planners. These nonmanagement people are the doers. They actually produce the products or provide the services for the organization.

Almost all organizations of any size, both public and private, are organized in this way. Each person or group is expected to perform a particular, prescribed function. Each employee has little to say about how his or her own job is carried out, since it was designed by someone with a broader perspective and a great deal more knowledge, training, and experience than the job incumbent. The job holder also plays little part in making critical decisions that may affect the job, the work group, or the department or company as a whole.

While this kind of task specialization would seem to be the most efficient way to operate, managers in organizations of all types are learning that it is also very demotivating for the great majority of employees. A highly specialized job will often have little intrinsic interest to the employee. The employee may also experience frustration in not being able to influence what happens on the job or in the organization in general. Task specialization may be especially effective if most employees are very limited in their knowledge, skills, and potential ability to learn. However, with the increasing levels of education of most people in our population today, the differences in the capabilities of management and nonmanagement employees is ever decreasing.

Even more important is the fact that significant changes have taken place in our culture with regard to individual autonomy. Each succeeding generation is being raised in a more democratic and less authoritarian manner. In past generations, for example, children were "to be seen and not heard." Today, in both the home and at school, children are permitted and even encouraged to think for themselves and to express their opinions. Therefore employees who have been raised under this philosophy may find it difficult and discouraging to have to merely do as they are told with little or no opportunity to influence their own job situation.

Recent research and experience has shown that providing opportunities for rank and file employees to participate in the decision making progress—to have more say in how their own jobs are carried out—can result in remarkable improvements in productivity and morale. The increased motivation released in this way often astounds the management people in the organization. While pride in work and conscientious effort to achieve organizational goals are commonly found among people in the management ranks, it is not expected in most rank and file employees. Their motivation is expected to be based primarily on pay and security. Yet in those organizations in which a concerted effort has been made to allow employees at all levels to participate in the decision making process regarding matters that affect their jobs or their work groups, the rank and file employees often exhibit the same kind of attitudes and effort usually seen only in the management ranks.[14]

Greater employee participation can be effected in many ways. The job enrichment movement has demonstrated that jobs that seem basically to be routine and uninteresting can be made meaningful by giving incumbents more responsibility and a feeling of ownership of the function being performed.[15] Too often jobs are structured in such a way that each individual worker has very limited responsibility for performing some highly structured function. Any problems that arise or critical decisions that have to be made are referred to the supervisor. On the other hand, in an enriched job the individual has a more meaningful function to perform, with discretion to solve problems and to make his or her own decisions. Thus on an assembly line, instead of performing some highly fractionated part of the total task of assembling a product, each worker might assemble the entire product, test it, and prepare it to be packed and shipped.

Another approach to achieving higher degrees of employee involvement and commitment has been the use of work teams to perform important functions in the organization. Teams of rank and file workers are given complete responsibility for performing certain operations. Thus, for example, a team of 10 or 12 workers may be given complete responsibility for running a small assembly line. Such teams are not directed by a foreman, supervisor, or other member of management. They organize and direct their own activities.[16]

While this approach to running an organization may seem to be inviting chaos, a great deal of experience has shown that such teams often carry out important functions more effectively and efficiently than had ever been done under the more traditional type of organization in which each job is highly specified and fractionated. The interest and enthusiasm shown by members of such work teams is often unbelievably high. Each team member behaves as if he or she were an important member of management.

There are also simpler and more direct ways of stimulating employee interest and involvement in their work. Just giving employees more information about what is happening in the organization or what factors might influence the business will help to build an identification and feeling of ownership in the job. As was mentioned earlier, attitude surveys have shown that most employees have an almost insatiable need to "be in the know." They desire much more information about what is going on in their work group, their department, or in the company as a whole than they would seem to need in order to carry out their jobs effectively.

Carrying this approach even further, the supervisor can solicit employee opinions and suggestions before making critical decisions that might affect the work. In many cases the supervisor might even allow the work group itself to make decisions relating to the work. A great deal of research and experience has shown that productivity as well as employee morale can be enhanced significantly by allowing employees to make important decisions in this way.[17]

Provide Growth Opportunities

Almost everyone has a desire to improve his or her own lot. Most of us would like to make more money or to have status and respect among our peers. Yet very often we fail to capitalize on this important source of motivation in work settings. Future opportunities may be vaguely defined, and the process of getting ahead may seem to be capricious.

Defining possible career ladders for people in different functions and at different levels in an organization is usually relatively easy to do. Some organizations have used ingenuity in creating hierarchies of status and responsibility that are available to all employees. As employees broaden their knowledge or skill repertoire they can advance to positions entailing higher levels of responsibility and pay. While this might seem to escalate payroll costs, the increased motivation that results will usually yield a handsome return on such investments. The promotions involved do not have to include supervisory responsibilities. Often it is possible to create promotional ladders within a function, which comprise many steps without any of them entailing the supervision of others.[18]

Attitude surveys have shown that people who leave an organization often attribute their leaving more to the lack of any visible opportunities to advance than they do to dissatisfaction with their present lot. This is especially likely to be true for people with special education, such as technical training or a college degree. The fact that such an individual has acquired the advanced training is evidence of motivation to improve his or her own status.[19]

Combine Consideration with Emphasis on Production

A great deal of research has shown that the most effective supervisors combine interest and concern for human problems with a strong emphasis on task accomplishment.[20] The supervisor who emphasizes only task accomplishment at the expense of consideration for people is not likely to get the cooperation needed from the work group to achieve high levels of productivity. On the other hand, the very considerate supervisor who puts little emphasis on production is not only likely to have trouble getting the work out, but may also lose the respect of employees. Most of us like to be on a winning team. High levels of performance will often contribute to high levels of job satisfaction.[21]

The supervisor who is sensitive to the needs and feelings of each employee can contribute to high self-esteem and motivation for task accomplishment by providing opportunities to achieve important goals. This supervisor creates a supportive climate in the work setting, which tends to foster mutual trust and respect. On the other hand, the supervisor who concentrates only on getting the work out, with little or no concern for human reactions and feelings, is likely to develop antagonistic attitudes in employees. Restrictions of outputs are typically found in such an environment. An adversarial rather than a cooperative relationship will usually be found where pressures for production are not accompanied by a consideration for human feelings and values.

SUMMARY AND CONCLUSIONS

The different research-tested principles or practices recommended here are obviously highly interrelated. There is considerable overlapping between many of them. For example, employees will have a clear understanding of what is expected on the job if goals and standards are defined as specifically as possible. Similarly, if goals or standards are well defined and agreed upon, the problem of providing knowledge of results feedback will be simplified. As another example, the supervisor who uses praise freely, allows employees to participate in the decision making process, and makes sure that growth opportunities are available and visible to employees, will certainly be seen as considerate and supportive by his or her employees.

For the most part, the principles or practices presented here may seem to be very simple and commonsensical. Most supervisors would probably feel that they do actually carry out their jobs as recommended here. In actual practice, however, it is not easy to apply the principles we have espoused as would seem to be the case on the surface. To allow employees to participate in making important decisions about their jobs, for example, is not a natural way to manage. The supervisor is usually the most experienced and knowledgeable person in the work group. It seems logical to expect that he or she might be better qualified to make important decisions about the work than are the other members of the group. Moreover, not to make such decisions may be seen as abdicating the leadership role.

Similarly, it is not as easy to use praise and recognition as to use criticism and punishment. As pointed out earlier, the supervisor is usually trying to keep things running smoothly. Therefore he or she is likely to be trying to rectify situations that are getting out of hand. Deviations from desired performance are usually easy to spot. Criticism often seems to be focusing directly on the cause of the deviation. It also seems natural to expect—despite experience to the contrary—that criticism should be effective in getting people to change their behavior. To use praise and recognition to reinforce desirable behavior often seems to take a great deal of extra effort, and it may even seem to be a very indirect way of keeping things running smoothly.

Nevertheless, the research evidence has shown clearly that the extra efforts made to supervise in accordance with the principles recommended here can pay significant dividends, not only in improved employee morale, but in increased productivity as well. The research evidence is clear in indicating that the supervisor who defines expectations clearly, sets specific and challenging goals, provides feedback on results being achieved, uses more positive than negative reinforcement, allows employees to participate in making decisions about their own jobs, provides growth opportunities for employees, and is sensitive to personal feelings and needs while stressing task accomplishment, will achieve results. The payoffs are well worth the effort required to implement these practices.

REFERENCES

1. The classic text on the scientific management movement is undoubtedly Taylor, Frederick W. *The Principles of Scientific Management.* New York: Harper & Row, 1911.
2. A number of books summarize the recent research on motivation of individuals in work settings very well, including Hackman, J.R. & Oldham, G.R. *Work Redesign.* Reading, Mass.: Addison-Wesley, 1980; Nadler, D.A. Hackman, J.R. & Lawler, E.E. III. *Managing Organizational Behavior.* Boston: Little, Brown & Co., 1979; Steers, R.M. & Porter, L.W. *Motivation and Work Behavior.* New York: McGraw-Hill, 1979; and Lawler, Edward E. III. *Motivation in Work Organizations.* Monterey, Calif.: Brooks/Cole, 1973.
3. An excellent summary of the theories, research, and rationale pertaining to the use of money as an incentive, along with a description of case studies in which unpredicted results were encountered, is presented in Whyte, William F. *Money and Motivation: An Analysis of Incentives in Industry.* New York: Harper, 1955.
4. An early study of ambiguity in perceptions of job responsibilities is reported in Meyer, H.H. A comparison of foreman and general foremen conceptions of the foreman's job responsibilities. *Personnel Psychology,* 1959, **12**, 445–452. A more recent study, which also reports considerable individual differences in the way a particular job is perceived, is O'Reilly, C.A. III, Parlette, G.N. & Bloom, J.R. Perceptual measures of task characteristics: The biasing effects of differing frames of reference and job attitudes. *Academy of Management Journal,* 1980, **23**, 118–131.
5. An excellent review of the theory and research relating to the effectiveness of goal setting is presented in Latham, G.P. & Yukl, G.A. A review of research on the application of goal setting in organizations, *Academy of Management Review,* 1975, **1**, 824–845.
6. This study is described in Stedry, A.C. & Kay, E. The effects of goal difficulty on performance. *Behavioral Science,* 1966, **11**, 459–470.
7. This experiment, carried out by George Feeney of Emery Air Freight Corporation, is reported in several places, including: At Emery Air Freight positive reinforcement boosts performance. *Organizational Dynamics,* Winter 1973, 41–50; and in: Where Skinner's theories work. *Business Week,* December 2, 1972, 64–65.

8. This study was carried out in the General Electric Company and described in an internal report that was widely distributed, entitled "The Use of Knowledge of Results in Improving the Performance of Hourly Operators." General Electric Co. Behavioral Research Service, 1965.

9. See Zander, A. Research on self-evaluation, feedback and threats to self-esteem. In *Performance Appraisals: Effects on Employees and Their Performance.* Ann Arbor, Mich.: The Foundation for Research on Human Behavior, 1963.

10. The best known theorist on the negative effects of punishment is probably B.F. Skinner, who has described his theory and research in several books, including *Contingencies of Reinforcement,* New York: Appleton-Century-Crofts, 1969.

11. This was also a study conducted in the General Electric Company and is reported in: Meyer, H.H. Kay, E. & French, J.R.P. Jr. Split roles in performance appraisal. *Harvard Business Review,* 1965, **43**, 123–129.

12. An excellent review of a number of field research projects in which positive reinforcement was used to shape behavior is presented in Hamner, W.C. & Hamner, E.P. Behavior modification and the bottom line. *Organizational Dynamics,* 1976, **4**, 8–21.

13. The "behavior modeling" approach to training supervisors is described in Sorcher, M. & Goldstein, A.P. A behavior modeling approach to training, *Personnel Administration,* 1972, **35**, 35–41. The same two authors have also described this program in greater detail in a book entitled *Changing Supervisor Behavior.* New York: Pergamon Press, 1974.

14. The leading advocate of "participative management" is probably Rensis Likert, who describes his theory of managing and presents much research evidence to support this theory in a book entitled *The Human Organization: Its Management and Value.* New York: McGraw-Hill, 1967. An interesting case example, which demonstrates the impressive results that can be achieved in both productivity and employee morale by managing an entire plant in such a way that employees at all levels can participate in the decision making process, is reported in Marrow, A.J. Bowers, D.G. & Seashore, S.E. *Management by Participation.* New York: Harper & Row, 1967.

15. A leading advocate of job enrichment and a pioneer in the movement is Frederick Herzberg, whose most recent book on the subject is *The Managerial Choice.* Homewood, Ill.: Dow Jones-Irwin, 1976. Two other authors, who were disciples of Herzberg, describe a number of field applications of job enrichment in the A.T.&T. and Texas Instruments Companies in the following books: Ford, R.N. *Motivation through the Work Itself.* New York: American Management Association, 1969; and Myers, M.S. *Every Employee a Manager.* New York: McGraw-Hill, 1970; and experiences of several other companies with job enrichment are described in Rush, H.M.F. *Job Design for Motivation.* New York: National Industrial Conference Board, 1971.

16. An excellent brief review of experiences with the work team concept is presented in Chapter 8, Designing effective work teams. In Nadler, D.A. Hackman, J.R. & Lawler, E.E. III. *Managing Organizational Behavior.* Boston: Little, Brown, 1979. Another good review article on this topic is: Cummings, T.G. Self-regulating work groups: A socio-technical synthesis, *Academy of Management Review,* 1978, **3**, 625–634.

17. Several examples of the effects of employee involvement in the decision making process are described in the book by Rensis Likert (see note 14).
18. The value of good career planning programs for employees at all levels in organizations is highlighted in two recent books by recognized experts on this subject: Hall, D.T. *Careers in Organizations.* Pacific Palisades, Calif.: Goodyear, 1976; and Schein, E. *Career Dynamics.* Reading, Mass.: Addision-Wesley, 1978.
19. The importance of perceived future opportunities in influencing the turnover of highly valued employees was highlighted in a number of studies conducted in the General Electric Company at the time that the author of this chapter directed a corporate staff personnel research function there. Three of such studies that are especially relevant were reported in the following internal reports, which were widely distributed both within and outside the Company: "Determining Causes of Turnover among Exempt Personnel," 1970; "A study of Factors Associated with Turnover of Exempt Personnel," 1967; and "Attitudes Associated with Turnover of Highly Regarded Engineers," 1964. All three of these reports were published by General Electric's Behavioral Research Service.
20. Detailed descriptions of the effects of variations in the degree to which the supervisor places emphasis on human versus task concerns are presented in Blake, R.R. & Mouton, J.S. *The Managerial Grid: Key Orientations for Achieving Production Through People.* Houston: Gulf Publishing Co., 1964. These authors also present detailed and useful description of the value of the supervisor's placing strong emphasis on both human concerns and task accomplishment.
21. While early theorists and researchers usually assumed that high levels of job satisfaction contributed to high levels of job performance, recent research indicates that the direction of causation is often reversed. That is, high levels of performance can often contribute to job satisfaction. This point of view is expounded in: Porter, L.W. & Lawler, E.E. III. *Managerial Attitudes and Performance.* Homewood, Ill.: Dorsey Press, 1968; Locke, E.A. Job satisfaction and job performance: A theoretical analysis. *Organizational Behavior and Human Performance,* 1970, **5**, 484–500; and Siegal, J.P. & Bowen, D. Satisfaction and performance: Causal relationships and moderating effects. *Journal of Vocational Behavior,* 1971, **1**, 263–269.

—8—

Configurations of Organizational Structure

Henry Mintzberg

The "one best way" approach has dominated our thinking about organizational structure since the turn of the century. There is a right way and a wrong way to design an organization. This approach is best captured in Colonel Urwick's famous principle of the 1930s that "no supervisor can supervise directly the work of more than five, or at the most, six subordinates whose work interlocks."* But "one best way" thinking continues to the present day, for example in the activities of consultants who believe that every organization needs MBO, or LRP, or QWL.

A variety of failures, however, has made it clear that organizations differ, that long range planning systems or quality of working life programs are good for some but not others. Just as it would be foolish to restrict a line supervisor to a span of control of six assembly-line workers whose work interlocks, so too is there little sense in forcing formal planning on a firm that must remain highly flexible in an unpredictable market (as many firms discovered during the early days of the energy crisis).

And so recent management theory has moved away from the "one best way" approach, toward an "it all depends " approach, formally known as "contingency theory." Structure should reflect the organization's situation, for example, its age, size, type of production system, the extent to which its environment is complex and dynamic. To cite some of the more established relationships, larger organizations need more formalized structures—more rules, more planning, tighter job descriptions; so do those in stable environments and those in mass production. Organizations in more complex environments need higher degrees of decentralization, while those diversified in many markets need divisionalized instead of functional structures.

I would like to suggest that the "it all depends" approach does not go far enough, that structures are rightfully designed on the basis of a third approach, which might be called the "getting it all together" or "configuration" approach. Spans of control, types of formalization and decentralization, planning systems, and matrix structures should not be picked and chosen

---

*This paper summarizes the main points in the author's book, *The Structuring of Organizations*, published by Prentice-Hall in 1979.

*Reported in Urwick, L. F., The Manager's Span of Control. *Harvard Business Review*, May-June, 1956, 41.

independently, the way a shopper picks vegetables at the market or a diner a meal at a buffet table. Rather these and other parameters of organizational design should logically configure into internally consistent groupings. Like most phenomena—atoms, ants, and stars—characteristics of organizations appear to fall into natural clusters, or configurations.

In fact, I would like to go a step further and include in these configurations not only the design parameters but also the so-called contingency factors. In other words, the organization's type of environment, its production system, even its age and its size, are in some sense "chosen" to achieve consistency with the elements of its structure. The important implication of this conclusion, in sharp contrast to that of contingency theory, is that organizations select their situations in accordance with their structural designs just as much as they select their designs in accordance with their situations. Diversified firms may divisionalize, but there is also evidence that divisionalized firms have a propensity to further diversify.* Stable environments may encourage the formalization (bureaucratization) of structure, but bureaucracies also have a habit of trying to stabilize their environments. And in contrast, entrepreneurial firms, which operate in dynamic environments, need to maintain flexible structures, but such firms also seek out and try to remain in dynamic environments in which they can outmaneuver the bureaucracies. In other words, no one factor—structural, or situational—determines the others; rather all are often logically formed into tightly knit configurations.

When the enormous amount of research that has been done on organizational structuring is looked at in the light of this conclusion, much of its confusion falls away, and a striking convergence appears. Specifically, five clear configurations emerge, configurations that are distinct in their structural designs, in the situations in which they are found, and even in the periods of history in which they first developed. I call them simple structure, machine bureaucracy, professional bureaucracy, divisionalized form, and adhocracy. In this chapter I describe them and seek to show their relevance in the design and functioning of organizations.

To understand the five configurations, we must first understand each of the elements that make them up. After reviewing the various elements briefly, we shall show how all of them cluster together to form our five configurations.

THE ELEMENTS OF THE FIVE CONFIGURATIONS

Organizational structure becomes a problem when more than one individual must coordinate different tasks to get a single job done. That coordination can be effected in five basic ways:

*See Rumelt, R. P. *Strategy, Structure and Economic Performance* (Division of Research, Graduate School of Business Administration, Harvard University, 1974, pp. 76–77), and Fouraker, L. E., and Stopford, J. M. Organizational structure and multinational strategy, *Administrative Science Quarterly* (1968, 47–64).

Direct supervision. One individual gives direct orders to others and so coordinates their work, as when an entrepreneur tells different machine operators to make specific parts of an assembly.

Standardization of work processes. One individual designs the general work procedures of others to insure that these are all coordinated, as when a methods engineer specifies how an assembler should bolt a fender onto an automobile.

Standardization of outputs. One individual specifies the general outputs of the work of another, as when headquarters tells a manager to generate sales growth of 10 percent in a given quarter so that the firm can meet its overall growth goal.

Standardization of skills. An individual is trained in a certain way so that he or she coordinates automatically with others, as when a surgeon and an anesthesiologist perform together in the operating room without having to utter a single word.

Mutual adjustment. Two or more individuals communicate informally among themselves to coordinate their work, as when a team of experts meet together in a space agency to design a new rocket component.

Different parts of the organization play different roles in the accomplishment of work and of these forms of coordination. Our framework introduces five basic parts of the organization, shown in Figure 8.1 and listed below:

The *operating core* is where the basic work of producing the organization's products and services gets done, where the workers assemble automobiles and the surgeons remove appendices.

The *strategic apex* is the home of top management, where the organization is managed from a general perspective.

The *middle line* comprises all those managers who stand in a direct line relationship between the strategic apex and the operating core; among their other tasks, the managers of the middle line (as well as those of the strategic apex) carry out whatever direct supervision is necessary.

The *technostructure* includes the staff analysts who design the systems by which work process and outputs are standardized in the organization.

And the *support staff* comprises all those specialists who provide support to the organization outside of its operating work flow, in the typical manufacturing firm everything from the cafeteria staff and the mail room to the public relations department and the legal counsel.

The division of the labor of the organization into different tasks and the achievement of the various kinds of coordination among these tasks are accomplished through the use of a set of design parameters, which are described in Table 8.1.

These parameters include, (a) for the design of specific positions: the extent to which their tasks are specialized and their procedures formalized (by

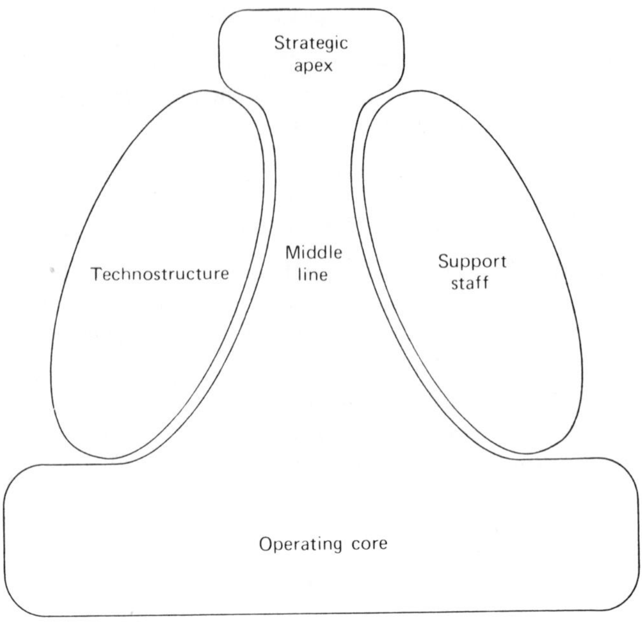

Figure 8.1 The five basic parts of the organization.

Table 8.1 The Design Parameters

Job specialization refers to the number of tasks in a given job and the worker's control over these tasks. A job is *horizontally* specialized to the extent that it encompasses few, narrowly defined tasks, *vertically* specialized to the extent that the worker lacks control of the tasks he or she performs. *Unskilled* jobs are typically highly specialized in both dimensions, while skilled or *professional* jobs are typically specialized horizontally but not vertically. "Job enrichment" refers to the enlargement of jobs in both the vertical and horizontal dimensions.

Behavior formalization refers to the standardization of work processes by the imposition of operating instructions, job descriptions, rules, regulations, and the like. Structures that rely on standardization for coordination are generally referred to as *bureaucratic,* those that do not as *organic*.

Training and indoctrination refers to the use of formal instructional programs to establish and standardize in people the requisite skills, knowledge, and norms to do particular jobs in organizations. Training is a key design parameter in all work we call professional. Training and formalization are basically substitutes for achieving the standardization (in effect, the bureaucratization) of behavior. In one, the standards are internalized in formal training as skills or norms; in the other, they are imposed on the job as rules.

Unit grouping refers to the choice of the bases by which positions are grouped together into units, and these units into higher order units. Grouping encourages coordination by putting different jobs under common supervision, by requiring them to share common resources and achieve common measure of performance, and by facilitating mutual adjustment among them. The various bases for grouping—by work process, product, client, area, etc.—can be reduced to two fundamental ones—by the *function* performed or the *market* served.

Table 8.1 *(continued)*

Unit size refers to the number of positions (or units) contained in a single unit. The equivalent term "span of *control*" is not used here because sometimes units are kept small despite an absence of close supervisory control. For example, when experts coordinate extensively by mutual adjustment, as in an engineering team in a space agency, they will form into small teams. In this case unit size is small and span of control is low despite a relative absence of direct supervision. In contrast, when work is highly standardized—because of either formalization or training—unit size can be very large because there is little need for direct supervision. One line supervisor can oversee dozens of assemblers because they work according to very tight instructions.

Planning and control systems are used to standardize outputs. They may be divided into two types—*action planning* systems, which specify the results of specific actions before they are taken (for example, that holes should be drilled with diameters of three centimeters), and *performance control* systems that specify the results of whole ranges of actions after the fact (for example, that sales of a division should grow by 10 percent in a given year).

Liaison devices refer to a whole set of mechanisms used to encourage mutual adjustment within and between units. They range from *liaison positions,* such as the purchasing engineer who stands between purchasing and engineering, through *task forces* and *standing committees* that bring together members of many departments, and *integrating managers,* such as brand managers, finally to fully developed *matrix structures.*

Vertical decentralization describes the extent to which decision making power is delegated to managers down the middle line, while *horizontal decentralization* describes the extent to which nonmanagers, that is, people in the operating core, technostructure, and support staff, control decision processes. Moreover, decentralization may be *selective*—concerning only specific kinds of decisions—or *parallel*—concerning many kinds of decision altogether. Five types of decentralization may be described: vertical and horizontal centralization, where all power rests at the strategic apex; limited horizontal decentralization (selective), where the strategic apex shares some power with the technostructure that standardizes everybody else's work; limited vertical decentralization (parallel), where managers of market-based units are delegated the power to control most of the decisions concerning their line units; vertical and horizontal decentralization, where most of the power rests in the operating core, at the bottom of the structure; and selective vertical and horizontal decentralization, where the power over different decisions is dispersed widely in the organization, among managers, staff experts, and operators who work in groups at various levels in the hierarchy.

job descriptions, rules, and the like), and the extent to which the positions require formal training and indoctrination; (b) for the design of the hierarchy: the bases on which units are grouped (notably by function performed or market served) and the size of each of the units (that is, the span of control of its managers); (c)for the fleshing out of the hierarchy through lateral relationships: the use of action planning and performance control systems and of "liaison devices" such as task forces, integrating managers, and matrix structure; and (d) for the design of the decision making system: the extent to which power is delegated down the chain of authority (called vertical decentralization) and out from that chain of authority to nonmanagers—operators, analysts, and support staffers (called horizontal decentralization).

A number of contingency or situational factors influence the choice of these design parameters, and vice versa. These include the age and size of the organization, its technical system of production, various characteristics of its environment, such as stability and complexity, and its power system, for example, whether or not it is tightly controlled from the outside. A set of major relationships between these contingency factors and the design parameters are listed in Table 8.2.

CONFIGURING THE ELEMENTS

To this point we have introduced a host of bits and pieces about the structuring of organizations. Lots of trees but still no forests. But a number of forests begin to emerge as we stand back from the specifics and try to perceive the whole picture.

The number five appeared frequently in our discussion. There were five coordinating mechanisms, five parts of the organization, and (in Table 8.1) five types of decentralization. In fact the five configurations bring all of these fives together. Specifically:

> The natural tendency of a *strategic apex* concerned with tight control is to coordinate by *direct supervision*:when that is what the organization needs, *vertical and horizontal centralization* results and the organization tends to use what we call the *simple structure*.
>
> The *technostructure* encourages coordination by *standardization* (especially of *work process*, the tightest form), since it designs the systems of standards; when that is what the organization needs, it accepts limited *horizontal decentralization* to the technostructure and the configuration called *machine bureaucracy* results.
>
> The workers of the *operating core* prefer autonomy above all, which they come closest to achieving when coordination of their work is effected mainly by the *standardization of skills*; organizations that must rely on this form of coordination accept vertical and horizontal decentralization to their highly skilled operators and use the *professional bureaucracy* configuration.
>
> The managers of the *middle line* try to balkanize the structure, to encourage *limited vertical decentralization* to their level so that their units can operate as semiautonomous entities, controlled from above only by performance control systems based on *standardization of outputs*; when this is what the organization needs, the *divisionalized form* results.
>
> And when the *support staff* (and sometimes the operators as well) favor collaboration— the working together in groups whose tasks are coordinated by *mutual*

Table 8.2 The Contingency Factors

The *age and size* of the organization affect particularly the extent to which its behavior is formalized and its administrative structure (technostructure and middle line) is elaborated. As they age and grow, organizations appear to go through distinct structural transitions, much as insects metamorphose, for example from simple organic to elaborated bureaucratic structure, from functional grouping to market-based grouping.

The *technical system* of the organization influences especially the operating core and those staff units most clearly associated with it. When the technical system of the organization regulates the work of the operating core—as it typically does in mass production—it has the effect of bureaucratizing the organization by virtue of the standards it imposes on its lower-level workers. Alternately, when the technical system succeeds in automating the operating work, as in much process production, it reduces the need for rules and regulations, since these are automatically incorporated into the machines, and so enables the structure to be organic. And when the technical system is complex, again, as is often the case in process production, the organization must create a significant professional support staff to deal with it, and then must decentralize selectively to that staff many of the decisions concerned with the technical system.

The *environment* of the organization can vary in its degree of complexity, in how static or dynamic it is, in the diversity of its markets, and in the hostility it contains for the organization. The more complex the environment, the more difficulty the central management has in comprehending it, and so the greater the need for decentralization. The more dynamic is the environment, the greater the difficulty in standardizing work, outputs, or skills, and so the less bureaucratic the structure. These relationships suggest four kinds of structures: two in stable environments, one simple, the other complex, leading, respectively, to a centralized and a decentralized bureaucracy; and two in dynamic environments, again, one simple, the other complex, leading, respectively, to a centralized and a decentralized organic structure. Market diversity, as noted earlier, encourages the organization to set up market-based divisions (instead of functional departments) to deal with each, while extreme hostility in the environment drives the organization to centralize power temporarily, no matter what its normal structure, in order to fight off the threat.

The *power* factors of the organization include external control, personal power needs, and fashion. The more an organization is controlled externally, the more centralized and bureaucratic it tends to become. This can be explained by the fact that the two most effective means to control an organization from the outside are to hold its most powerful decision maker—its chief executive officer—responsible for its actions, and to impose clearly defined standards on it (performance targets or rules and regulations). Moreover, because the externally controlled organization must be especially careful about its actions, often having to justify these to outsiders, it tends to formalize much of its behavior and insist that its chief executive authorize key decisions. A second power factor, individual power needs, especially by the chief executive, tend to generate structures that are excessively centralized. And fashion has been shown to be a factor in organization design, the structure of the day often being favored even by organizations for which it is inappropriate.

adjustment—and this is what the organization needs, *selective vertical and horizontal decentralization* results, and what we call the *adhocracy* results.

Let us now take a closer look at each of these five configurations, whose characteristics are summarized in Table 8.3.

The Simple Structure

The name tells its all. And Figure 8.2 shows it all. The structure is simple, not much more than one large unit consisting of one or a few top managers and a group of operators who do the basic work. Little of the behavior in the organization is formalized and minimal use is made of planning, training, or the liaison devices. The absence of standardization means that the structure is organic and has little need for staff analysts. Likewise there are few middle line managers because so much of the coordination is handled at the top, where all real power is centralized. Even the support staff is minimized, in order to keep the structure lean, the organization flexible.

The organization must be flexible because it operates in a dynamic environment, often by choice since that is the only place where it can outsmart the bureaucracies. But that environment must be simple, as must the production system, or else the chief executive could not for long hold on to the lion's share of the power. The organization is often young, in part because time drives it toward bureaucracy, in part because the vulnerability of simple structures causes many of them to fail. (Often all it takes is one heart attack.) Indeed most organizations seem to start their lives with simple structures, granting their founding chief executives considerable latitude to set them up. And many are often small, since size too drives the structure toward bureaucracy. Not infrequently the chief executive purposely keeps the organization small in order to retain his personal control.

The classic simple structure is of course the entrepreneurial firm, controlled tightly and personally by its owner and usually operating in a competitive niche that is dynamic but not too complex. Sometimes, however, under the control of a very clever autocratic leader who refuses to let go of the reins, a simple structure can grow large, the famous example being the Ford Motor Company in the later years of the first Henry Ford. Extreme hostility in its environment also drives an organization, no matter how large, toward simple structure for a time, as systems and procedures are suspended to give the chief executive a chance to set things right.

The simple structure was probably the only kind of structure known to the people who first organized to coordinate their work. And perhaps its heyday came during the period of the great American trusts of the late nineteenth century. But today it has fallen out of fashion, to many a relic of the days of autocracy in government and in business. And yet it remains widespread and important, a necessary structure for the building up of most new organizations, and the operating of those in simple, dynamic environments and those facing extreme hostility.

	Simple Structure	Machine Bureaucracy	Professional Bureaucracy	Divisionalized Form	Adhocracy
Key coordinating mechanism	Direct supervision	Standardization of work	Standardization of skills	Standardization of outputs	Mutual adjustment
Key part of organization	Strategic apex	Technostructure	Operating core	Middle line	Support staff (with operating core in OP. AD.)
DESIGN PARAMETERS					
Specialization of jobs	Little specialization	*Much horizontal and vertical specialization*	*Much horizontal specialization*	Some horizontal and vertical specialization (between divisions and HQ)	*Much horizontal specialization*
Training and indoctrination	Little training and indoctrination	Little training and indoctrination	*Much training and indoctrination*	Some training and indoctrination (of division managers)	Much training
Formalization of behavior	Little formalization	*Much formalization*	Little formalization	Much formalization (within divisions)	Little formalization
Bureaucratic/organic	*Organic*	*Bureaucratic*	*Bureaucratic*	Bureaucratic	*Organic*
Grouping	Usually functional	*Usually functional*	Functional and market	*Market*	*Functional and market*
Unit size	Wide	Wide at bottom, narrow elsewhere	Wide at bottom, narrow elsewhere	Wide (at top)	*Narrow throughout*
Planning and control systems	Little planning and control	Action planning	Little planning and control	*Much performance control*	Limited action planning (esp. in adm. ad.)
Liaison devices	Few liaison devices	Few liaison devices	Liaison devices in administration	Few liaison devices	*Many liaison devices throughout*
Decentralization	*Centralization*	*Limited horizontal decentralization*	*Horizontal and vertical decentralization*	*Limited vertical decentralization*	*Selective decentralization*
CONTINGENCY FACTORS					
Age and size	Typically young and small	Typically old and large	Varies	Typically old and very large	Typically young (op. ad.)
Technical system	Simple, not regulating	Regulating but not automated, not very complex	Not regulating or complex	Divisible, otherwise typically like machine bureaucracy	Very complex, often automated (in adm. ad.); not regulating or complex (in op. ad.)
Environment	Simple and dynamic; sometimes hostile	Simple and stable	Complex and stable	Relatively simple and stable; diversified markets (especially products and services)	Complex and dynamic; sometimes disparate (in adm. ad.)
Power	Chief executive control; often owner-managed; not fashionable	Technocratic and external control; not fashionable	Professional operator control; fashionable	Middle line control; fashionable (especially in industry)	Expert control; very fashionable

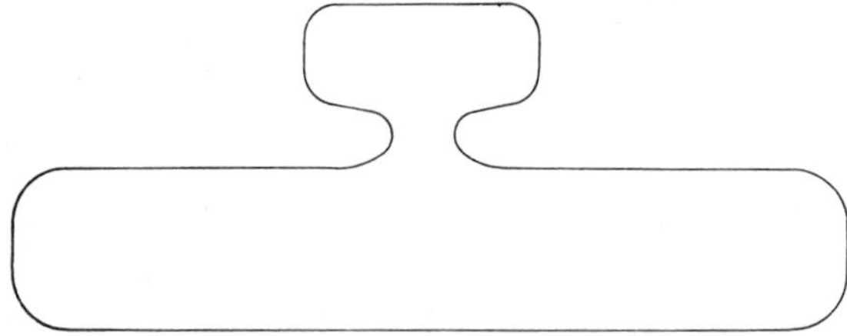

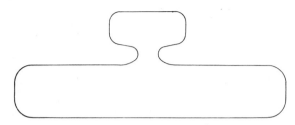

Figure 8.2 The simple structure.

The Machine Bureaucracy

The machine bureaucracy is the offspring of the Industrial Revolution, when jobs become highly specialized and work became highly standardized. As can be seen in Figure 8.3, in contrast to simple structure, the machine bureaucracy elaborates its administration. First, it requires a large technostructure to design and maintain its systems of standardization, notably those that formalize its behaviors and plan its actions. And by virtue of the organization's dependence on these systems, the technostructure gains a good deal of informal power, resulting in a limited amount of horizontal decentralization. A large hierarchy of middle line managers emerges to oversee the highly specialized work of the operating core (that is, to keep the lid on the conflicts that result from rigid departmentalization and the alienation that goes with highly routine, circumscribed jobs). But that middle line hierarchy is usually structured on a functional basis all the way up to the top, where the real power of coordination lies. So the structure tends to be rather centralized in the vertical sense, that is, up the chain of command.

And why the large support staff shown in Figure 8.3? Machine bureaucracies, because they depend on stable environments—dynamic ones interrupt the smooth functioning of the machine—tend to become obsessive about

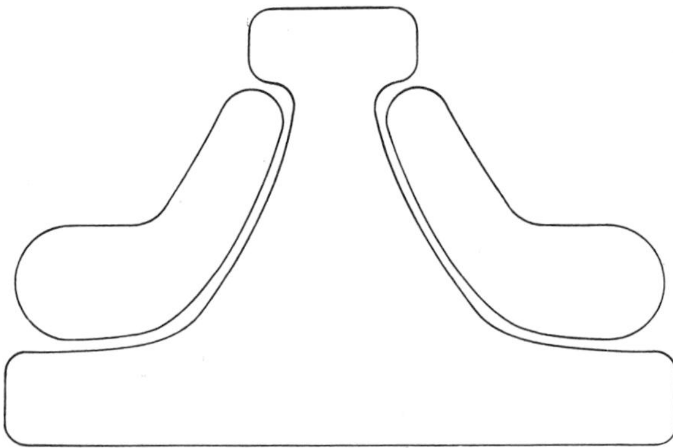

Figure 8.3 The machine bureaucracy.

controlling their environments. In other words they not only seek out stable environments but also seek to stabilize the environments they find themselves in. And one way to do this is to envelop within their structures all of the support services they possibly can, ones that simple structures prefer to buy. For the same reason they also tend to integrate vertically—to become their own suppliers and customers. And that of course causes many machine bureaucracies to grow very large. So we see the two-sided effect of size as a factor in this configuration: size drives the organization to bureaucratize ("we do that every day; let's standardize it"), but bureaucratization (of the machine kind) also encourages the organization to grow large. Aging also drives organizations toward this configuration, the standards being adopted because "we've done that before."

To enable the top managers to maintain centralized control, both the environment and the production system of the machine bureaucracy must be fairly simple, the latter regulating the work of the operators but not itself automated. In fact, machine bureaucracies fit most naturally with mass production, where the products, the processes, and distribution systems are usually simple, or at least highly rationalized and so easy to comprehend, and the production systems highly regulating. And so machine bureaucracy is most common among large, mature, mass production firms, such as the automobile producers, and among the largest of the established providers of mass services, such as the insurance companies and railroads. Indeed it is interesting that this structure is most prevalent in industries that date back to the period from the Industrial Revolution to the early part of this century, just as simple structure is prevalent in pre-Industrial Revolution industries such as agriculture.

The problems of the machine bureaucracy are legendary—its dull repetitive work, its worker alienation, its obsession with control (both internally to keep the lid on conflict and externally to stabilize its environment), its propensity to grow to massive size and to try to monopolize markets, its inflexibility when strategic change is required. For all of these reasons, machine bureaucracy is no longer a fashionable structure. Yet in a society consumed by its appetite for mass produced goods, for a society dependent on consistency in so many spheres (who would fly an airline with an organic structure, where the pilots worked out their emergency landing procedures only when the need arose?), for one unable to automate a great many routine jobs, machine bureaucracy is an indispensable configuration, indeed probably the most prevalent of the five today.

The Professional Bureaucracy

There is another bureaucratic configuration, but because this one relies on the standardization of skills rather than of work processes or outputs for its coordination, it emerges as dramatically different from the machine bureaucracy. Most important, in having to rely on trained professionals—

people highly specialized, but with considerable control over their work—to do its operating tasks, the organization surrenders a good deal of its power not only to the professionals themselves but also to the associations and institutions that select and train them in the first place. So the structure emerges as highly decentralized; power over many decisions, both operating and strategic, flows all the way down the hierarchy, to the professionals of the operating core. For them this is the most democratic structure of all, often too much so for a society that has yet to find ways to correct irresponsible behavior on the part of some professionals.

Because the operating procedures are rather standardized—taking out appendices in the hospital, teaching the American Motors case in the business school, doing an audit in the accounting firm—each professional can work largely independently of his or her colleagues, with the assurance that much of the coordination will be effected automatically, through the standardization of skills. And so the physician treats "his" or "her" patients and the professor teaches "his" or "her" students.

Above the operating core we find a rather unique structure, as can be seen in Figure 8.4. There is little need for a technostructure, since the main standardization occurs as a result of training that takes place outside the organization, not as a result of systems designed internally. Because the professionals work so independently, the size of operating units can be very large, and few first line managers are needed. (I work in a business school where 55 professors report directly to one dean.) Even those few managers, and those above them, do little direct supervision; much of their time is spent linking their units to the broader environment, notably to ensure adequate financing. Thus to become a top manager in a consulting firm is to become a salesman.

The support staff is typically very large, in order to back up the high priced professionals. But there is no democracy for this staff; its work is usually simple and routine, the programmable jobs that the professionals shed. So there emerge parallel hierarchies in the professional bureaucracy, one democratic and bottom-up for the professionals, a second machine bureaucratic and top-down for the support staff.

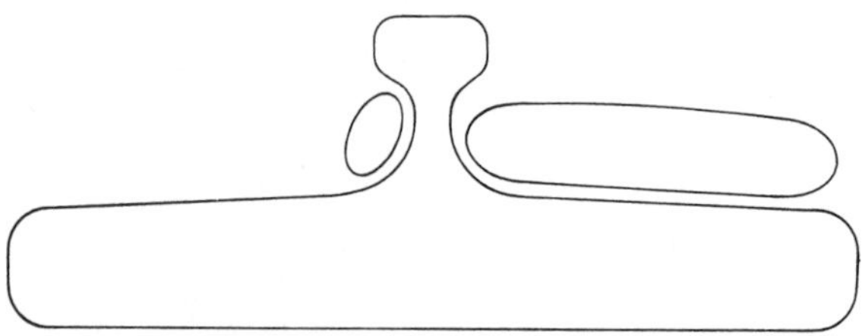

Figure 8.4 The professional bureaucracy.

Professional bureaucracy is called for whenever an organization finds itself in an environment that is stable yet complex. Complexity requires decentralization to highly trained individuals, and stability enables them to apply standardized skills and so to work with a good deal of autonomy. To ensure that autonomy, the production system must be neither highly regulating, complex, nor automated. Thus surgeons use their scalpels and accountants their pencils; both must be sharp, but are otherwise simple instruments that allow their users considerable freedom to perform their complex work.

Professional bureaucracy, a product of this century, especially its middle years, is a highly fashionable structure today for two reasons. First it is very democratic, at least for its professional workers. And second, it provides them with considerable autonomy, freeing them even from the need to coordinate their work closely with their peers. And so many workers seek to have themselves declared "professional," and thereby to free themselves of the close control of administrative hierarchies.

The Divisionalized Form

Like the professional bureaucracy, the divisionalized form is not so much an integrated organization as a set of rather independent entities coupled together by a loose administrative structure. But whereas those entities of the professional bureaucracy are individuals—professionals in the operating core—in the divisionalized form they are units in the middle line, generally called "divisions." The divisionalized form differs from the other four configurations in one central respect: it is not a complete structure, but a partial one superimposed on others. Each division has its own structure. But the point is made below that divisionalization drives that structure to be a machine bureaucracy.

An organization divisionalizes for one reason above all, because its product lines are diversified. And that tends to happen most often in the largest and most mature organizations, the ones that have run out of opportunities—or have become bored—in their traditional markets. Such diversification encourages the organization to replace functional by market-based units, one for each distinct product line (as shown in Figure 8.5), and to grant considerable autonomy to each to run its own business. The result is a limited form of decentralization down the chain of command. It should be made clear, however, that divisionalization is *not* synonomous with decentralization, although the two terms are often confused. Decentralization is a measure of the dispersal of decision making power. Divisionalization refers to a structure of semiautonomous market-based units. In a divisionalized structure, the handful of managers who run these units may retain the lion's share of the power, thereby rendering the structure more centralized than

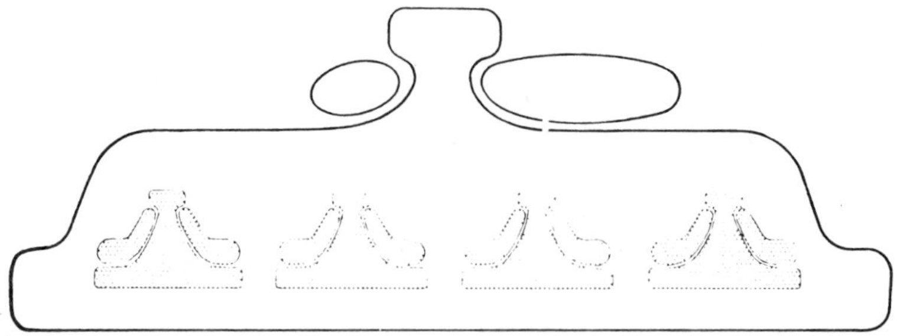

Figure 8.5 The divisionalized form.

many functional structures, where a great many specialists became involved in the making of important decisions.*

But how does the central headquarters maintain a semblance of control over the divisions? Some direct supervision is used—headquarters managers visit the divisions periodically and authorize some of their more important decisions. But too much of that interferes with the necessary divisional autonomy. So the headquarters relies on performance control systems, in other words the standardization of outputs. It leaves the details to the divisions and relies on periodic measures of their performance to assure control. To design these control systems, headquarters creates a small technostructure. This is shown in Figure 8.5, across from the small central support staff that headquarters sets up to provide certain common services to the divisions such as legal counsel and public relations.

The performance control system has an interesting effect on the internal structure of the division. By having its performance controlled by standards, the division is driven to bureaucratize its structure. In effect, each division is assumed to be a single integrated system with a single, consistent, and standardized set of goals, which in turn become diffused as other standards throughout the structure. Moreover, by having these standards imposed through the division manager, who is held responsible by headquarters for the division's performance, the division is also driven to centralize its structure. In other words, divisionalization has the effect of driving the division's structure toward bureaucratization and centralization, that is, toward a machine bureaucratic structure. Or, more to the point, divisionalization works best with divisions that are already machine bureaucracies. Simple structures and adhocracies make poor divisions because they are structured organically and operate in dynamic environments, in which

*In fact, the most famous example of divisionalization was one of centralization. Sloan divisionalized General Motors in order to *reduce* the power of the different units, to integrate the holding company Durant had put together. That kind of centralization appears to have continued to the present day, to the point where the automotive "divisions" seem to be more like functional marketing departments than true divisions. See Wrigley, L. Diversification and divisional autonomy, DBA thesis, Harvard Business School, 1970.

standards of any kind are difficult to establish. And professional bureaucracies are not logically treated as integrated entities, nor can their goals be easily quantified. (How does one measure cure in the hospital or knowledge generated in the university?) This conclusion is of course consistent with an earlier argument, that outside control, in this case headquarters' control, pushes an organization toward machine bureaucracy. The point is invariably illustrated when an entrepreneurial firm, usually with a simple structure, is taken over by a conglomerate and suddenly finds all kinds of bureaucratic systems imposed on it.

The divisionalized form has become very fashionable in the last few decades, a series of studies at the Harvard Business School having documented its spread through most of the Fortune 500 and then over to Europe.* It has also become fashionable in the nonbusiness sector, in the guise of multiversities, large hospital systems and unions, and especially government itself. And yet it seems fundamentally ill-suited to these sectors, for two reasons. First, the success of this structure depends on the presence of goals that lend themselves to quantitative measure. That is the only way the headquarters can allow for divisional autonomy yet maintain a certain basic control at the same time. But outside the business sector, goals are often social in nature, and nonquantifiable.** And second, nonbusiness organizations often require structures other than machine bureaucracy, as in the case of the campus of the multiversity that should be a professional bureaucracy. As a result, divisionalization often gives rise to disruptive tendencies in the design of the structures within the divisions.

The Adhocracy

None of the structures so far discussed suits the industries of our age, industries such as aerospace, petrochemicals, think tank consulting, and film making. These organizations need above all to innovate in very complex ways. The bureaucratic structures are too inflexible, and the simple structure too autocratic. These industries require "project structures," structures that can fuse experts drawn from different specialties into smoothly functioning creative teams. That is the role of our fifth structural configuration, adhocracy.

Adhocracy is an organic structure, without an emphasis on formalization of behavior or planning and control systems to standardize its work or outputs. Rather it relies for coordination on mutual adjustment among its highly trained and highly specialized experts, which it encourages by the ex-

*For a review of these studies, see Scott, B. R., The industrial state: Old myths and new realities. *Harvard Business Review,* March-April 1973, 133–148).

**Indeed a recent study by Robert Ackerman documents how even in the divisionalized business corporation the performance control system drives out social goals in favor of economic ones. Social irresponsiveness can sometimes become irresponsibility. See *The Social Challenge to Business.* Cambridge: Harvard University Press, 1975.

tensive use of the liaison devices—integrating managers, standing committees, and above all task forces and matrix structure. Typically the experts are grouped in functional units for housekeeping purposes but deployed in small market based project teams to do their work. To these teams, located all over the structure in accordance with the decisions to be made, is delegated power over different kinds of decisions. So the structure becomes decentralized selectively in the vertical and horizontal dimensions, that is, power is distributed unevenly, all over the structure, according to expertise and need rather than formal authority or professional status. Managers abound in the adhocracy—functional managers, integrating managers, project managers. This results in narrow "spans of control," by conventional measures. But these measures have nothing to do with control; they merely reflect the large number of managers in the structure and the small size of the project teams. The managers of adhocracy do not spend much time giving orders by direct supervision; rather they become deeply involved in coordinating the work across units by mutual adjustment. Typically they are experts too, who take their place alongside the others in the project teams.

All the distinctions of conventional structure disappear in the adhocracy, as can be seen in Figure 8.6. With power based on expertise instead of authority, the line-staff distinction evaporates. With power distributed throughout the structure, the distinction between the strategic apex and the rest of the structure blurs. In a project structure, strategy is not formulated from above and then implemented lower down; rather it evolves and changes every time a project decision is made. In other words, the adhocracy is continually developing its strategy as it accepts and works out new projects, the creative results of which can never be predicted. And so every-

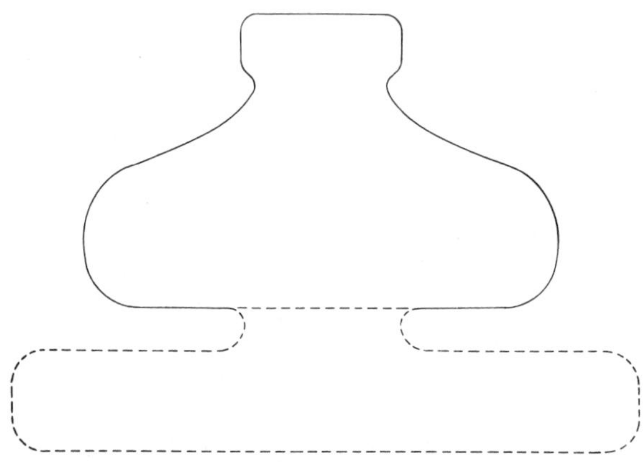

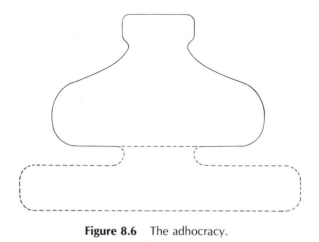

Figure 8.6 The adhocracy.

one who gets involved in the project work—and in the Adhocracy that can mean virtually everyone—becomes a strategy maker.*

To understand what happens to the distinction between operating core and administrative structure, we need to introduce two basic types of adhocracies. The operating adhocracy carries out innovative projects directly on behalf of its clients, usually under contract, as in the case of a creative advertising agency or a manufacturer of engineering prototypes. In fact, for every operating adhocracy there is a corresponding professional bureaucracy, one that does similar work but with a narrower orientation. The operating adhocracy treats each client problem as a unique one and solves it in creative fashion, while the professional bureaucracy pigeon-holes it so that it can apply a standard skill. Thus there are innovative advertising agencies, and ones that base their campaigns on the insecure housewife theme; there are experimental theater companies, and ones that try to perfect their performance of Shakespeare year after year. In one the experts must cooperate with each other in organic structures in order to innovate; in the other, they can apply their standard skills autonomously in bureaucratic structures.

In the operating adhocracy the operating and administrative work blend into a single effort. That is, the organization cannot easily separate the planning and design of the operating work (the projects) from its actual execution. So another classic distinction disappears. The organization emerges as an organic mass (shown above the dotted lines of Figure 8.6) in which line managers and staff and operating experts work together on project teams in ever-shifting relationships.

The *administrative adhocracy* undertakes its project work on its own behalf. And in contrast to the operating adhocracy, it mades a sharp distinction between its administrative component and its operating core, often to the point of truncating the operating core—cutting it off from the administrative component (hence the dotted lines in Figure 8.6). That is because the administrative component must be adhocratic in order to do the project work. Without truncation, it runs the risk of being formalized by an operating core that must be machine bureacratic. Magazines, for example, draw sharp lines between editorial and printing for this reason, in many cases contracting out the printing operations altogether.

The administrative adhocracy also emerges when the operating core of an organization is automated. Automation reduces the need for rules, since they are built right into the machines, with the result that the line-staff distinction loses much of its significance. (What does it mean to supervise a

*This concept of strategy, as an emergent pattern in a stream of decisions rather than a deliberately imposed plan, is developed in Mintzberg, Henry, Patterns in Strategy Formation, *Management Science,* 1978, 934–948.

machine?) The structure becomes less bureaucratic. The job of the administrative component becomes largely one of bringing new automated facilities on line, in other words one of project work requiring the coordination of many kinds of experts, especially those in the support staff.

Both kinds of adhocracies are found in environments that are both complex and dynamic, because those are the ones that require sophisticated innovation, the type of innovation that calls for the cooperative efforts of many different kinds of experts. The administrative adhocracy is often associated with a production system that is very complex and so requires a highly skilled and influential support staff, and it is often automated as well. The operating adhocracy in turn is often young, for the simple reason that age drives it toward bureaucracy. (Often it is the aging of its members that causes this: they tire of the fluid and political nature of the structure and the instability of its environment, and seek ones where they can settle down to an easier life.) The innovative advertising agency settles on a few successful themes and becomes a professional bureaucracy; the manufacturer of prototypes hits on a hot product and becomes a machine bureaucracy to mass produce it. Another reason why operating adhocracies tend to be young on average is that so many of them fail. With no standard products or services, they are highly vulnerable.

Finally there is fashion, a major factor associated with adhocracy. Every characteristic of adhocracy is very much in vogue today—emphasis on expertise, organic structure, project teams, diffused power, matrix structure, sophisticated and often automated production systems, youth, dynamic and complex environments. Adhocracy suits a population growing ever better educated and more specialized, yet under constant exhortation to adopt the "systems" approach—to view the world as an integrated whole instead of a collection of loosely coupled parts. Adhocracy is the only one of the five configurations that combines a certain democracy with an absence of bureaucracy. Yet like all the others, this configuration too has its limitations. It is, for example, inefficient at doing ordinary tasks, tasks that do not require sophisticated innovation.

USING THE CONFIGURATIONS

One message has dominated our story. In general there is no one best structure; in particular, there may be a best structure, so long as that structure is internally consistent and in harmony with its situation.

The theme of this book is "making organizations humane and productive." Our point is that each of these configurations can in its own way be both humane and productive, so long as it is allowed to achieve its own consistency and harmony. Each of course has its own problems, human as well as technical, but these are minimized when "misfit" is avoided, when the organization is not forced to be something it is not.

Simple structure is highly effective in environments that are dynamic yet simple to understand and in organizations that are small and young. When bureaucratic procedures are imposed on organizations under these conditions, as often happens when a conglomerate takes over an entrepreneurial firm, productivity falls and conflict arises. Simple structure, left alone, is a very comfortable place for those who like to work under strong, decisive leaders, in a personalized organization with a sense of direction. Yet to others, who have a greater need for independence, it is anathema, nothing less than autocracy. In other words, while simple structure is certainly human, it is humane only for those who appreciate its strengths.

Machine bureaucracy, and the divisionalized form as well, are most productive in simple, stable environments, typically in organizations that are large and mature, and especially those that mass produce their products or services (and, in the case of the divisionalized form, produce a diversity of these). While machine bureaucracy is the configuration most often accused of abusing its workers—with dull, demeaning jobs—there is also evidence that some people prefer its simple, repetitive work, and the stable relationships that go along with it. Likewise at the administrative level, while some people find the rules and tight divisions of labor terribly restrictive, others appreciate the idea of knowing exactly what is expected of them and where they fit. In other words, for some people this configuration can be humane too, although an increasing segment of the population is turning against the excesses of the machine bureaucracies (and of the divisionalized forms as well, in their case for the excessive concentrations of power and their tendency to ignore social needs, a result of the control systems they use). But what especially reduces productivity and, ironically, even increases the level of conflict in machine bureaucracy, is trying to make it what is is not—to pretend its unskilled operating work can be made professional in nature through ambitious programs of job enlargement, or its rigid administrative structure organic in nature through the use of all those fashionable characteristics of adhocracy. This configuration is meant to be tightly structured; that is how it functions best.

The professional bureaucracy works very effectively in environments that are complex yet stable. Workers who are highly trained and like to work on their own find this a very pleasant place to be, although those who need guidance or prefer collaboration do not. What above all destroys the productivity and morale in this configuration is treating it like a machine, as when government analysts attempt to control school teachers or social workers through technocratic rules and regulations.

Finally, adhocracy is productive when sophisticated innovation is required, in environments that are complex and dynamic and sometimes automated as well. But adhocracy achieves its effectiveness through inefficiency, through remaining loose and encouraging a great deal of communication and experimentation. Trying to make it efficient through tight standards and the like only damages its effectiveness—its ability to innovate. For those who need to be creative above all, for those who like the excitement of never knowing what tomorrow will bring, for those who prefer to work collaboratively with others, adhocracy is humane indeed. For others this is the worst of structures—unstable, insecure, highly politicized. Thus we see that while in some absolute sense, certain configurations appear more humane than others, in a relative sense all can be humane or not, depending on who is involved and how the configuration is used.

But must the organization achieve one of the pure forms of consistency described in this chapter? For some organizations the answer seems to be a rough yes, because so many of their characteristics match the description on one of the configurations. Indeed, as we have seen, a good deal of organizational pathology seems to stem from departures from one of these logical consistencies—public hospitals and universities driven by zealous government administrators to become machine instead of professional bureaucracies; machine bureaucracies that play with techniques of organic structure, such as matrix relationships, in contradiction of their real needs; simple structures and adhocracies whose innovative capabilities dry up when they get inappropriately bureaucratized; and so on. When there is logic in a configuration, change in any of its components must be made with extreme care.

But other organizations are not clearly drawn to one configuration or another. They may be large yet operate in a dynamic environment, and so be drawn toward both organic and bureaucratic structure. Or they may find themselves in a transitional stage, for example, from adhocracy to professional bureaucracy as they settle on certain skills to apply, or from simple structure to machine bureaucracy as they age. Or they may be so complicated that one configuration simply cannot do justice to all of their needs. An IBM can hardly be categorized in terms of a single configuration. These and similar conditions may call for some kind of hybrid of the configurations. The symphony orchestra with its highly trained musicians and dominating conductor finds a natural hybrid of professional bureaucracy and simple structure. The diversified multinational firm copes with a complex, dynamic environment by moving its divisionalized structure toward a matrix one and so emerges with a hybrid of adhocracy and the divisionalized form. Most large complicated organizations find uses for different configurations (or hybrids) in different departments, although one of the configurations may prove dominant.

The point I wish to emphasize in closing is that the five configurations may be of greatest use, not because of any specific prescription they generate, but because they provide a point of view or a theory, a way of looking at the world. These configurations represent five basic tensions that pull on every organization—pulls to centralize at the strategic apex, to standardize by the technostructure, to professionalize in the operating core, to balkanize in the middle line, and to collaborate with the support staff. The designers of organizational structure should bear in mind this set of five pulls as well as the central point of this chapter: that the structures they design as well as the situations they design them for should above all achieve consistency and harmony.

BIBLIOGRAPHIC ESSAY

There is a vast amount of literature—much of it based on empirical research—on the structuring of organizations, most of which falls into a small number of distinct streams.

The early literature focused on formal structure, the documented, official relationships among members of the organization. Two schools of thought dominated the literature until the 1950s, one preoccupied with direct supervision, the other with standardization. The former school was the principal one, fathered by Henri Fayol (1), who first recorded his ideas in 1916, and popularized in the English-speaking world by Luther Gulick and Lyndall Urwick (2). These writers brought into usage terms such as "unity of command" and "span of control." The latter school really includes two groups that, from our point of view, promoted the same issue—the standardization of work. Both groups were established at the turn of the century by outstanding researchers, one on either side of the Atlantic Ocean. In America, Frederick Taylor (3) led the "Scientific Management" movement, whose main preoccupation was the formalizing of the work of the operating core—that of pig iron handlers, coal shovelers, and the like. In Germany, Max Weber (4) wrote of machinelike structures in which activities were formalized throughout by rules, job descriptions, and training. And so for about half this century, organization structure meant a set of official, standardized work relationships built around a tight system of formal authority, in effect, pure machine bureaucracy.

With the publication of Roethlisberger and Dickson's (5) interpretation of a series of experiments carried out on workers at the Western Electric Hawthorne plant came the realization that other things were going on in organizational structures. Specifically, their observations about the presence of informal structure—unofficial relationships within the work group—constituted the simple realization that mutual adjustment was an important mechanism of coordination as well.

More recent research has tended to look at structure more comprehensively, to study, for example, the relationships between the more and less formal, between direct supervision and standardization on the one hand and mutual adjustment on the other. The interesting work of the Tavistock Institute in the early 1950s set the pattern. Trist and Bamforth (6), in a piece of research unsurpassed for detail and insight, studied the effect of technological change on work groups in coal mining and concluded that the technical and social systems of the operating cores of organizations were inextricably intertwined. Most contemporary researchers, working under the title "contingency theory," have concerned themselves with the relationships between parameters of structure and factors of situation. In effect, they oppose the notion of the one best structural form; instead they seek to identify the particular coordinating mechanisms—direct supervision, standardization of one kind or another, or mutual adjustment—that best suit a particular situation. The path-breaking work here was that of Joan Woodward (7), who, in her study of industry in one region of England during the 1950s, concluded that a firm's structure was closely related to its technical system of production. Subsequently, two Harvard researchers, Paul Lawrence and Jay Lorsch (8), concluded in a study of American firms in the container, food, and plastics industries that environmental conditions surrounding the organization significantly affected its choice of structure, while another group, led by Derek Pugh, working out of the University of Aston in England, found tht the size of the organization best explained many of the characteristics of its structure (9, 10, 11, 12, 13).

Most of the literature tends to focus on the elements of structure (often in relations to situation) as opposed to types or configurations of structure. The vast majority of it has studied large numbers of organizations, usually from a distance, for example, through mailed questionnaires. But the most insightful studies, with certain exceptions (notably that of Woodward, 7, who examined many organizations, but firsthand) have concentrated on one or a few organizations, and looked at them in some depth. We have, for example, Jay Galbraith's (14) investigation of the Boeing Company, which first explained clearly the relationship of the various liaison devices to one another and to formal structure. We can read between the lines of some studies to learn about the configurations, and interpret the structures described in others in terms of our five. Simple structure has been little studied per se (perhaps because there is so little to study, although their leaders, about whom there is a lot to study, have been the subjects of a good deal of research). But machine bureaucracy, as one of the oldest, most prevalent, most clearly defined (and therefore researchable) configurations, has been thoroughly investigated, especially as to its dysfunctional consequences, in the literature of management (15, 16) and even more so in that of sociology (17, 18).

Researchers at the Harvard Business School have taken a special interest in the diffusion of the Divisionalized Form among the Fortune 500 (19, 20, 21), although it was a Johns Hopkins professor, now at Harvard (22), who described in rich detail its initial appearance, and a Wharton professor who has presented the strongest justification for it (23). Professional bureaucracy, as a configuration less often found in pure form in the business sector, has had little attention from business school researchers, but much more from sociologists. Adhocracy, as a more recent innovation in structure, has a less developed but more rapidly emerging literature, because of its fashionable nature, although that literature is not identified with this label. In *Managing Large Systems,* Chandler and Sayles (24) look closely at the structure of NASA during the 1960 Apollo years, while a little-known study by the Scandinavian Institutes for Administrative Research (25) describes adhocracy in insightful terms as a proposed alternative to the divisionalized form for UNICEF. And there are the few reports that help put the various configurations in context, notably Woodward's excellent study of unit, mass, and process production, Lawrence and Lorsch's contrast of machine bureaucratic container companies with adhocratic plastics firms (both already cited), Burns and Stalker's (26) comparison of textile firms and electronics companies, each with respectively the same configurations, Segal's (27) contrast of what amounts to machine bureaucracy, professional bureaucracy, and adhocracy in the service sector, and Stinchcombe's (28) article on the construction industry, essentially a comparison of machine and professional bureaucratic forms of organizing.

Finally, special mention should be made of three important books whose basic themes underlie a good deal of contemporary thinking on organizational structuring: James Thompson's (29) *Organizations in Action,* Herbert Simon's *Administrative Behavior* (30), and March and Simon's (15) *Organizations.*

REFERENCES

1. Fayol, H. *General and Industrial Management.* London: Pitman, 1949; first published in French in 1916.
2. Gulick, L. H. & Urwick, L. F. (Eds.). *Papers on the Science of Administration.* New York: Columbia University Press, 1937.
3. Taylor, F. W. *Scientific Management.* New York: Harper and Row, 1947; first published in 1911.
4. Gerth, H. H. & Mills, C. W. (Eds.). *From Max Weber: Essays in Sociology.* New York: Oxford University Press, 1958.
5. Roethlisberger, F. J. & Dickson, W. J. *Management and the Worker: An Account of a Research Program Conducted by the Western Electric Company, Hawthorne Works, Chicago.* Cambridge: Harvard University Press, 1939.
6. Trist, E. L. & Bamforth, K. W. Some social and psychological consequences of the long-wall method of coal-getting. *Human Relations,* 1951, 3–38.
7. Woodward, J. *Industrial Organization: Theory and Practice.* New York: Oxford University Presss, 1965.
8. Lawrence, P. R. & Lorsch, J. W. *Organization and Environment.* Homewood, Ill.: Irwin, 1967.

9. Pugh, D. S. Hickson, D. J. Hinings, C. R. MacDonald, K. M. Turner, D. & Lupton, T. A conceptual scheme for organizational analysis. *Administrative Science Quarterly*, 1963–64, 289–315.

10. Pugh, D. S. Hickson, D. J. Hinings, C. R. & Turner, C. Dimensions of organization structure. ,*Administration Science Quarterly*, 1968, 65–105.

11. Pugh, D. S. Hickson, D. J. & Hinings, C. R. An empirical taxonomy of structures of work organizations. *Administrative Science Quarterly*, 1969a, 115–126.

12. Pugh, D. S. Hickson, D. J. Hinings, C. R. Turner, C. The context of organizational structures. *Administrative Science Quarterly*, 1969b, 91–114.

13. Hickson, D. J. Pugh, D. S. Pheysey, D. C. Operations technology and organization structure: An empirical reappraisal. *Adminstrative Science Quarterly*, 1969, 378–379.

14. Galbraith, J. R. *Designing Complex Organizations*. Reading, Mass.: Addison-Wesley, 1973.

15. March, J. G. & Simon, H. A. *Organizations*. New York: Wiley, 1958.

16. Worthy, J. C. Organizational structure and employee morale. *American Sociological Review*, 1950, 169–179.

17. Crozier, M. *The Bureaucratic Phenomenon*, English translation. Chicago: University of Chicago Press, 1964.

18. Feld, M. D. Information and authority: The structure of military organization. *American Sociological Review*, 1959, 15–22.

19. Scott, B. R. *Stages of Corporate Development*, Part I. Working Paper, Harvard Business School, 14-371-294; BP993, 1971.

20. Rumelt, R. P. *Strategy, Structure, and Economic Performance*. Division of Research, Graduate School of Business Administration, Harvard University, 1974.

21. Wrigley, L. *Diversification and Divisional Autonomy*. DBA thesis, Harvard Business School, 1970.

22. Chandler, A. D. *Strategy and Structure*, Cambridge, Mass.: MIT Press, 1962.

23. Williamson, O. E. *Markets and Hierarchies: Analysis and Antitrust Implications*. New York: Free Press, 1975.

24. Chandler, M. K. & Sayles, L. R. *Managing Large Systems*. New York: Harper and Row, 1971.

25. SIAR, *Management Survey of UNICEF*. Stockholm: Scandinavian Institutes for Administrative Research, 1975.

26. Burns, T. & Stalker, G. M. *The Management of Innovation*, 2nd ed. London: Tavistock, 1966.

27. Segal, M. Organization and environment: A typology of adaptability and structure. *Public Administration Review*, 1974, 212-220.

28. Stinchcombe, A. L. Bureaucratic and craft administration of production: A comparative study, *Administrative Science Quarterly*, 1959–60, 168–187.

29. Thompson, J. D. Organizations in Action. New York: McGraw-Hill, 1967.

30. Simon, H. A. *Administrative Behavior*. 2nd ed. New York: Macmillan, 1957.

—9—

Planning and Decision Making in Managing Organizations

Ronald N. Taylor

> "We do not need new organizations so much as we need new decision processes" (1, p. 276).

We have reached a challenging stage in the development of managerial decision making and planning. The professional literature reports a rapidly expanding knowledge of how decisions are made (i.e., a "descriptive" approach) and prescriptions concerning how they should be made (i.e., a "normative" approach). And there is healthy and at times heated controversy regarding theories, research methods, and techniques. A corresponding need for "good" decisions in organizations is apparent in the complex, interconnected world in which managers and organizations exist, a world whose values increasingly have demanded that good decisions contribute both humaneness and productivity. This chapter attempts to highlight some of the descriptive and normative theories, research conclusions, and techniques that have developed recently in fields related to planning and decision making; are in the process of developing and appear likely to be significant in the next few years; or, in my opinion, are needed to make organizations more humane and productive. A major challenge facing managers is to apply the "new decision processes" drawn from descriptive and normative approaches effectively in solving organizational problems of today.

It is convenient in this presentation to subsume planning under decision making. Ackoff (2) has pointed out the relationship between planning and decision making, stating, "Planning is clearly a decision-making process; but, equally clear, not all decision making is planning" (p. 2). Generally the issues discussed in this chapter apply equally to decision making and planning decisions. Exceptions necessitated by the special features of planning decisions are noted in the discussion.

DESCRIPTIVE AND NORMATIVE APPROACHES TO MANAGERIAL DECISION MAKING

The essential distinction between descriptive and normative theories of managerial decision making is that descriptive theory describes what people *do*, whereas normative theory attempts to specify what they *should do*. The relationship between normative and descriptive decision making theories is important, since normative theories may rest upon assumptions that fail to accurately describe actual behaviors. For example, it is misleading to prescribe that people maximize expected utility if they are unable to process the large amounts of information that confront them in complex decision situations. The importance of recognizing human capability is further evidenced when systems are designed to aid decision making. The basis for human engineering, fitting the job to the person, is knowledge of human capabilities. Human-machine systems that fail to take this into account don't work. Similarly, decision making systems can be improved by considering the attributes of information users in the design of decision systems (3).

Understanding decision making processes can be advanced by considering the interplay among theories (normative or descriptive) and research. Normative theories can be made descriptive by stating their propositions as illustrative of what decision makers actually do and then testing these propositions by empirical research. Descriptive theories can be made normative by using them as bases for prescribing what decision makers should do in various situations. Research is frequently used to test the accuracy with which descriptive theories reflect actual decision behaviors; and at times empirical research can lead to new or refined descriptive theories.

Generally the normative theories of "rational" managerial decision making have been based on assumptions of questionable validity. In describing one major normative approach to managerial decision making, the "economic man," Simon (4) stated the assumptions about human capabilities upon which it rests:

> This man is assumed to have knowledge of the relevant aspects of his environment which, if not absolutely complete, is at least impressively clear and voluminous. He is assumed to have a well-organized and stable system of preferences, and a skill in computation that enables him to calculate for the alternative courses of action that are available to him, which of these will permit him to reach the highest attainable point on his preference scale. (4, p. 99)

Seldom will a manager have available all of the information required by this normative approach to rational decision making, and even if the information could be acquired, the manager would be incapable of processing it. We cannot expect decision makers to have perfect perception, memory, and calculational abilities; therefore the normative models of rational decision making need to be modified to take into account both (a) the limited abilities of actual decision makers, and (b) the features of the organizational context within which their decisions are made. Much recent attention has been devoted to understanding how decisions actually are made in organizations, and the contributions of researchers concerned with the descriptive aspects of mangerial decision making are beginning to influence the normative decision analysts. In this chapter we highlight some of the major contributions derived from normative and descriptive approaches to managerial decision making and suggest implications of the descriptive research findings for modifying the normative models of rational decision making. Finally, we describe techniques drawn from the normative and descriptive approaches that appear useful for making decisions in organizations that consider both humaneness and productivity.

INCORPORATING INDIVIDUAL AND ORGANIZATIONAL FACTORS INTO NORMATIVE MODELS OF MANAGING DECISION MAKING

Descriptive studies of decision making in organizations have yielded many conclusions that have implications for the normative models typically used to prescribe how managerial decisions should be made. In this section research addressed to three aspects of decision making in organizations is discussed: (a) attention to goals in organizational decisions, (b) human cognitive limitations in information processing and decision making; and (c) influence of the organizational context on managerial decision making.

Attention to Goals in Organizational Decisions

Goals figure importantly in problem identification and in establishing criteria for evaluating alternative actions. Normative models of rational decision making assume the prior existence of a set of goals and a well-defined, stable, and consistent preference ordering among goals. In this section recent developments related to three aspects of goals—the nature of goals, problem finding, and multiple objectives—are examined.

Nature of Goals. The preexistence of goals in organizational decision making has been questioned (5, 6). Weick (6), in discussing the nature of "enacted organizations," stated, "An organization can never know what it thinks or wants until it sees what it does" (p. 278). This suggests that outcomes may occur before decisions are made; that is, upon observing a set of events one may attempt to make sense of them by retrospectively positing a decision to account for the events. Similarly, the "garbage can model" of organizational choice (7) challenges both the preexistence of goals to direct choices and the orderliness of the choice process. In this view adequate description of organizational choice is to see a decision as an outcome (or an interpretation) of relationships among our four relatively independent streams of elements: problems, solutions, participants, and choice opportunities. An organizational choice, then, is a "somewhat fortuitous confluence" of these streams. Still, in this model, some order exists since participants tend to find the same types of problems and apply the same solutions as they move about the organization. These thoughts regarding the nature of goals are of course speculative; but they suggest that understanding complex organizational decisions may be advanced by deemphasizing the importance of goals in directing decision making activity.

Other writers recently have challenged the acceptance of goals as given in organizational decisions and have called for more attention to discovering and evaluating goals. Argyris, for example, (8) has charged that goals in the normative model of rational decision making unduly perpetuate the status quo by only identifying problems and choosing solutions that are consistent with the established goals of organizations. Yet this criticism that the rational decision model is dysfunctional seems directed more toward the values underlying the goals held by an organization than toward the purposes served by goals in models of rational decisions. New values would be expected to lead to new goals that would in turn encourage behavior consistent with the new goals. The challenge here seems to be causing organizations to value both humaneness and productivity.

It has been suggested that the discovery of new and better goals should be a conscious effort in organizations to counter the current preoccupation with how good decisions are made. Why not ask how good goals are found? Two approaches have been proposed for discovering new goals—imitation and playfulness (5).

Imitation involves discovering new goals by duplicating the behavior of others. For example, organizations may adopt the behavior of industry leaders and managers may emulate other managers whom they admire, and in so doing discover new goals for themselves. Playfulness can take the form of experimenting with new goals during the decision process, hoping to find new values.

A technique that has been widely used to generate creative decision alternatives, brainstorming, may prove useful in involving many organizational members in the process of discovering creative goals. Brainstorming (9) typically is used by interacting groups, but sometimes group members are asked to work alone for at least part of the exercise. To encourage group members to suggest creative ideas, four "ground rules" are set for the discussion: (a) criticism is ruled out until a later evaluation session; (b) freewheeling is encouraged; (c) as many ideas as possible are suggested; and (d) group members try to build on the ideas of others. The popularity of brainstorming has led to many attempts over the past twenty years to evaluate its effectiveness. There seems to be little doubt that the pooled efforts of individuals working alone to list creative ideas is superior to brainstorming groups (10, 11), but the optimal mix of group members and the conditions of the decision environment that are conducive to creativity have not been clearly specified.

Problem-Finding. Organizational goals would be expected to relate closely to the problems that are found in an organization. Very little, however, is known about the activities that initiate decision making. One of the few studies of problem-finding in organizations classified ways in which problems were brought to the attention of decision makers (12). In the organization studied, apparently many problems either were identified by managers as departures from historical trends (e.g., May sales down 15 percent) or were brought to the attention of decision makers by others (e.g., customers judge product quality, bosses delegate tasks). Relatively few problems were identified by operations planning; these typically consisted of projecting operating variables for the coming year and less detailed projections for the next five years. Considering the likely impact of problem-finding on subsequent managerial decision making activities, it is important that more attention be directed toward understanding problem-finding.

Multiple Objectives. In most practical managerial decision situations it is necessary to cope with a large number of desired objectives (multiple objective decisions) and many characteristics of the decision alternatives (multiple attribute decisions). Choosing a marketing strategy, for example, may require considering the many purposes for which it will be used and the many features of the available strategies. In addition to identifying the desired objectives, frequently it is necessary to determine the relative importance of each objective and to weigh it accordingly in decision making.

Cognitive Limitations in Information Processing and Decision Making

One of the greatest difficulties facing managerial decision makers is their limited ability to process the large amount of information required in most practical decision problems. The normative model that underlies our traditional decision making theories and techniques assumes that rational decision makers are—in the maximizing view of choice— perfectly informed, sensitive, and rational. A complete set of possible courses of action must be developed, all possible results from taking any of these actions must be specified, and the actions must be judged in the light of appropriate criteria. Clearly these requirements would place impossible demands upon a decision maker's cognitive abilities in most managerial decisions.

Simon (13) has distinquished between the narrow economic meaning of rationality implied in the maximizing choice mode and a more general meaning of rationality as being sensible, agreeble to reason, or intelligent. The latter definition of rationality is consistent with the concept of "bounded rationality" in which, since it is impossible to meet the requirements of maximizing, practical decision makers "satisfice." In satisficing a feasible aspiration level is set, alternatives are sought until one is located that is good enough to meet this aspiration level, and this "satisfactory" alternative is chosen. Essentially the satisficing model suggests that decision makers try to compensate for their sharply limited information-processing abilities by using a simplified representation of the decision problem and then behave rationally within the bounds of this simple model of the problem. However, labeling managerial decision making as "satisficing" does nothing to improve its rationality, and the satisficing model can not be tested to determine its validity as a description of actual decision making behavior (14).

A growing body of descriptive research evidence shows that human ability to judge the probabilistic information typically found in managerial decision making (i.e., in highly uncertain decision situations) is subject to a number of serious biases or inaccuracies. Yet the ability to accurately judge the probability of events is assumed in many normative theories of rational decision making. Among the biases found in judging probabilities of events are:

1. **Conservativism.** It has long been held that humans making judgments in the laboratory tend to be conservative in revising the probabilities they assign to events when they are presented with additional information about the events. More recent research has shown that they may also be overly extreme in revising probabilities (15). Although the conditions under which humans are conservative and the conditions under which they are extreme in revising probabilities are not clear, it is generally agreed that they tend to be inaccurate judges of subjective probabilities in the laboratory and that, when judging probabilities or making predictions, people systematically violate the principles of rational decision making underlying the normative model.

2. **Anchoring and Adjustment.** In anchoring and adjustment (16), research has suggested that in judging probabilities of events a natural starting point is set (an anchor), and this first approximation to the judgment is used as a base for adjusting the initial judgment in the face of additional information. This adjustment, however, typically is found to be imprecise and insufficient (17).

3. **Representativeness.** Representativeness (18) appears to explain biases in probability judgments on the basis of a person's opinion about how likely it is that an object belongs to a given class of objects. Apparently the essential features of an object are examined and compared to the features of a general class of objects to see if the object is representative of the class. Yet this simplistic approach frequently leads to errors in assigning objects to classes.

4. **Availability.** Judgmental biases in which an event is judged likely or frequent if it is easy to imagine or to recall relevant instances can be explained by the availability bias (19). For example, frequent events tend to be easier to recall than less frequent events. However, it is possible that events that are not easy for a decision maker to imagine or recall may be very likely to occur.

5. **Overconfidence.** Laboratory studies show that people tend to have greater confidence in their ability to judge probabilities than the evidence warrants. They tend to disregard both the amount of data upon which their

judgment is based (this has been called the "law of small numbers") and the reliability of the data. Moreover, they tend to be inconsistent and inaccurate in making judgments regarding probabilities of events.

In most instances these biases would be expected to distort the judgment of probabilities and hamper managerial decision making. Two cautions regarding the implications of these biases for managerial decisions should be noted. These biases tend to be specific to certain types of problems, and no general theory exists to predict when a given bias will occur. Also, recent studies have found differences on some judgment tasks between assessing probabilities in the laboratory and behavior in the real world (20), raising some concern about generalizing the cognitive biases found in the laboratory to real world decisions. Despite this caution, the implications of information-processing biases for professions such as accountants, geographers, and financial analysts have been discussed in the literature.

Influence of Organizational Context on Managerial Decision Making

In the organizational context in which managerial decisions are made, seldom can the assumptions of the normative model of rational decision making be met. Instead complex organizational problems generally are viewed as single person decisions and much of the organizational context is ignored. Alternative models of decision making have been proposed to represent more adequately the complex social and political processes that are evident in organizations. Two models for resolving conflicts among the members of an organization are discussed in this section: Allison's levels of decision analysis and the political model of disjointed incrementalism.

Models of organizational decisions. Allison (21) described a model of decision making in which the single-person model of rational decision making represents only one of three levels of analysis. This "rational actor" level of analysis views organizations as single agents who perform all stages of decision making. It is consistent with the rational actor analysis to speak of an organization "making a decision." A second level of analysis, the "organizational process" level, expands the rational actor analysis by incorporating other organizational influences that shape decisions. At this level of analysis the organization is no longer viewed as a single agent, nor are the organizational processes rational in the sense described by the rational actor level. Multiple goals and conflict among the goals of subunits are considered and "satisficing" behavior occurs.

Allison further expands the analysis to include the "political process" level. The most significant feature of this level is that actions of an organization are seen as resulting from intricate and subtle maneuvers made by organizational members—alone or in formal or informal groups. Decision processes are analyzed by examining which individuals and groups are involved, what determines their relative degree of power, and how all of the organizational influences combine to produce decisions and actions. The political process analysis therefore deals more adequately with organizational complexities in decision making; and it reflects the fact that frequently the managerial decision maker is not a single person. Rather decisions typically involve many people who interact in a complex social and political environment. This implies that, as a minimum, it is necessary to incorporate group processes into our traditional concept of managerial decision making.*

A model developed to explain political decision making—"disjointed incrementalism" (22)—also appears useful in organizations when decisions are made by groups and conflicting preferences exist. In this approach, decisions involve taking small steps away from the existing state in the direction desired. Few objectives need to be considered; and results, values, and alternatives do not have to be specified completely. Rather than attaining predetermined goals, decision makers attempt to achieve agreement among themselves regarding courses of action. Little research, however, has been directed toward exploring the implications of incrementalizing for decisions in nongovernmental organizations.

In situations in which the political process, incrementalism, or garbage can models apply, it seems wise to abandon the fiction that there is "a managerial decision maker" and to adopt processes that recognize and capitalize upon the social and political nature of decision making. The interactive decision making strategies discussed in a later section of this chapter attempt to do so.

TECHNIQUES FOR BETTER DECISIONS DRAWN FROM THE NORMATIVE AND DESCRIPTIVE APPROACHES

Recent advances in the study of managerial decision making have led to techniques for improving both humaneness and productivity of organizations. The normative approaches to rational decision making generally emphasize the accuracy of decisions in terms of some definition of an "optimal" choice. The developments in decision analysis, multiple-objective decision making, and Multiattribute Utility Analysis (MAU) have been derived from this point of view. In contrast, the descriptive approach has contributed to our understanding of the impact of decisions upon organizational members

*Note that the garbage can model of organizational choice goes even further by suggesting that it gives a false impression of orderliness to describe choice in organizations as involving a sequence of processes ranging from information input to implementation.

and has suggested that decisions may be improved by involving many members of an organization in decision-making activities. The improvements gained by this approach involve: (a) helping decision makers to compensate for cognitive limitations, (b) acceptance of the decision by those who must be trusted to implement it, and (c) developing an egalitarian atmosphere in which decision making is not viewed as a sole right of management. Among the developments derived from descriptive research are techniques for aiding decision makers in coping with excessive informational demands, and strategies for interactive decision making, in which many organizational members work together to reach a decision.

Emergence of Decision Analysis

Decision analysis has emerged as a promising approach to applied decision making primarily due to the efforts of researchers at Stanford Research Instituе, Decisions and Designs, Inc., and Harvard Business School (23, 24, 25). This systematic approach to analyzing complex, dynamic, and uncertain decision situations represents a merger of decision theory and systems analysis in which decision theory provides the philosphy for logical behavior in simple decisions under uncertainty and systems analysis provides the systems and modeling methods for capturing the interactions and dynamics of complex problems. In carrying out a decision analysis, a decision maker typically will decompose and structure the problem, assess the uncertainties and values of the possible outcomes, and attempt to find the optimal course of action. Hence decision analysis attempts to provide a framework in which all available information about a problem is used to deduce which course of action is best in light of a decision maker's stated purposes.* Most textbooks on quantitative methods for business students discuss decision analysis, and books dealing exclusively with decision analysis have recently appeared (24, 26, 27).

Decision analysis has been applied to many problems. Environmental impact, quarantine requirements for interplanetary travel (28), and governmental social and economic policies have been subjected to decision analysis. A particularly well-developed analysis of whether to seed hurricanes to reduce their intensity has been reported (29). Examples of business decisions that have been analyzed include price setting, marketing of new products, and plant modifications.

Despite the apparent potential of decision analysis, two cautions should be noted. Brown (30) observed that often responses to future events are not included in the analysis; this raises concern about effectiveness for planning

*Assessment of probabilities and utilities figures centrally in decision analysis and many techniques from operations research and statistics are used, for example, multiattribute utility analysis (MAU).

decisions. Also the applications need to be evaluated more carefully. Some applications are evaluated by experimental designs, but many are case studies with no controls to permit adequate assessment.

Development of Methods for Dealing with Multiple Objectives

A number of techiques have been developed to assist in making decisions plagued by multiple objectives or multiple attributes. Essentially these strategies attempt to reduce the complexity of the decision problem by aggregating a decision maker's preferences regarding various features of a decision problem. Many decision aids have been developed to help decision makers overcome this difficulty, but one of the most widely used methods is "bootstrapping." When many similar decisions are to be made (e.g., hiring many employees for similar jobs, judges deciding on workers compensation awards), it is possible to build a simple regression model of a decision maker's behavior that can be used routinely in future decisions. Research continues to show that the models frequently perform as well or better than do decision makers (31, 32). MacCrimmon (35) and Keeney and Raiffa (36) provide thorough discussions of techniques for dealing with multiple objectives.*

Use of Multiattribute Utility Analysis (MAU)

Applications of multiattribute utility models (MAU) have increased greatly in the past few years, and MAU analysis is among the more promising techniques for assisting managerial decision makers. MAU attempts to find a single measure of overall utility for a decision alternative that has more than one important attribute and therefore must be judged in the light of more than one criterion. The normative theory underlying MAU prescribes that the weighted utilities for an object be computed and summed across all attributes. For example, in using MAU to help teachers find jobs, jobs were described by the attributes of location, type of position, type of school, community size, and salary (37). MAU models have been used extensively in making decisions concerning budgets, plant locations, student admissions, land use, and personnel assignment. Recent applications include deciding where to build an airport in Mexico City (38) and identifying cultural differences between Japanese and Americans in values concerning peace issues (39).

MAU is based on a normative theory in which axioms specify the models, the methods for measuring utilities, and tests for determining which of the models is applicable (40). There has been disagreement concerning the way

*Kunreuther (33) has discussed when the model should be relied upon in production planning and when it should be contravened. Advances have recently been made in the ability of the model to handle poorly defined or hard to measure variables (34) and in simplifying its computational requirements by demonstrating that unit weights (0 or 1) are acceptable.

in which MAU is carried out, particularly with regard to how lists of attributes should be generated and how weights and utilities should be assessed.* Two approaches frequently used for listing attributes are interviewing, at times extensive interviews with a number of decision makers (41), and use of the nominal group technique. Although omitting important attributes somewhat limits the value of MAU, it has been found that minor omissions do not seriously alter the results (42). A thorough review of methods for assessing utilities has been written by Kneppreth et al. (43).

Techniques for Coping with Informational Demands of Managerial Decisions

Many techniques for aiding decision makers in making the modeling, probability, and utility judgments required by the normative model of rational decision making have been developed by decision analysts and others. These include: (a) decomposition methods, (b) probability judgment methods, and (c) methods for combining information from various sources.

Decomposition. Decomposing the problem into its elements and dealing with each element separately reduces the cognitive demands placed upon a decision maker. Simon (1), believing that the major problems of organizations today are organizing information storage in information processing, has proposed organizational arrangements in which factoring decision making activities, rather than departmentalizing, is emphasized. The reasoning behind this suggestion is that factoring large problems aids decision makers by allowing problems to be solved in parallel by one or more decision makers. For example, when a decision making unit is made up of individuals with different skills, specialization and division of labor can be used effectively.

In techniques for aiding managerial decision making the principle of decomposition has proven to be an extremely useful response to the problem of information overload. Hence, decision makers can simplify complex problems by modeling only important aspects. Two decision aids that operate on the principle of decomposition in modeling problems are "decomposable matrices," which factor problems into the semi-independent components corresponding to their functional parts (44), and "input-output" models" to represent systematically the interrelationships between inputs and outputs of an industry, economy, or other system (45). Research indicates that decomposition aids judgment (46).

Judging Probabilities. A number of techniques for eliciting probability assessments have been developed, but no one technique has emerged as the

*Weights and utilities can be assessed either directly or indirectly. Direct assessement methods (e.g., asking the assessor for the numbers) are much simpler, but are not justified by the theory. Indirect methods are consistent with the theory, but can be very complex, lengthy, and tedious.

best. One difficulty is that no clear understanding of the cognitive processes involved in probability assessment exists. A very promising technique (47) involves the use of a "probability wheel" as a reference point. This wheel has two adjustable sectors, one blue and the other red. One use of the wheel is to ask an individual to bet either on a fixed event (e.g., next year's production will not exceed a given level), or on the blue sector. The amount of blue in the wheel can then be varied until the assessor becomes indifferent between the probability shown on the wheel and the probability of not exceeding the given level of production. The proportion of blue in the wheel then is assigned as the probability of the event. The Decision Analysis Group at Stanford Research Institute has suggested that probabilities should be elicited by several techniques, problems should be carefully structured, personal interviews should be used instead of computer-interactive techniques with new clients, and biases that might distort judgment should be minimized (47).

Combining Information from Different Sources. Techniques that have been used to reduce the cognitive demands placed on a decision maker as he or she attempts to aggregate information include providing information at the appropriate level of aggregation (e.g., regional or individual store sales volume), and helping decision makers to determine the diagnosticity of information. Decision aids have been proposed that effectively aggregate information by partitioning it into the optimal level of aggregation for a decision problem. Also the Probabilistic Information Processing System (PIP) is a human-machine system in which the decision maker estimates likelihood ratios and the computer aggregates these data across hypotheses according to Bayes's theorem to compute the revisions in opinions appropriate to the data (48). Whereas the PIP system generated considerable research attention prior to 1970, little has been reported concerning its use in the past decade.

Although these techniques appear to have great potential, decision makers often show only limited receptivity to decision analysis. Brown (24) reported three difficulties: (a) absence of top-level managers familiar with the technique, (b) bad prior experiences with decision analysis due to attempts to use the techniques without adequate training, and (c) decision makers frequently want the analyst to reduce uncertainty for them, rather than acknowledge and quantify it. Other researchers have reported that decision makers may reject the basic axioms underlying a decision aid or reject the techniques as being divorced from reality, overly complicated, or too difficult to explain intuitively to others (49).

Methods for Using Information to Acquire Power

Information in organizational contexts can be regarded as a "currency." If it has value for organizational members, "inside information" gives both power and prestige to those who possess it. Even in its traditional role as an uncertainty reducer, information in organizations can confer power upon those who have it. Power typically has been linked to dependence. An example drawn from the research literature may serve to illustrate this relationship. Under conditions of task interconnection among subunits, when organizational subunit A can reduce uncertainty for subunit B, then research has indicated that A may possess power over B (50). Although uncertainty reduction can take several forms in this situation, one form involves communicating information needed by a subunit. Similarly, it has been suggested that one of the most effective ways for "lower participants" in organizations to achieve power is by controlling access to information, thus making higher ranking members of the organization dependent upon them (51). Moreover, two ways suggested for increasing power of lower participants in traditional organizational structures—acquiring expertise and attaining centrality in the organizational communication network—involve obtaining information valued by other members in the organization.

Use of Interactive Decision Making

While strategies that focus on individual decision makers have proven extremely useful to managers, it appears that involvement of informed organizational members in interactive decision making—when it is appropriate—has a greater potential to contribute to achieving a humane and productive organization. Involvement of many organizational members tends to diffuse power and may yield both decisions that are of higher quality and people who are more willing to implement the decisions. In addition, interactive decision making seems to more accurately reflect the manner in which a great many decisions in organizations are actually made. Three types of interactive decision making strategies are examined here: informal participation, organizational procedures, and modifications in organizational information systems and structures.

Participation. Participation of subordinates in managerial decisions is a widely used strategy that can be initiated at the discretion of an individual manager and his or her subordinates. Building upon prior research, Vroom and Yetton (52) have developed a procedure by which decision urgency, resources of subordinates, agreement of subordinates with organizational goals, and need for acceptance of a decision are analyzed through a participation tree. The analysis yields strategies that guide a decision maker in the degree to which he or she should consult with his or her subordinates, and the form that the interaction should take. Given sufficient lead time, opening up a decision for subordinates' participation may be advisable when they can be expected to constructively contribute relevant information, or when it is important that the resulting decision be accepted by those people who must implement the decision.

Participation has received a large amount of research, and a critical review of these studies (53) concluded that participation in important decisions sharply increases the acceptance of decisions by those who are actually involved in making decisions. The effects of participation seem to be mediated by personality; those with an authoritarian personality and a low need for independence react positively when little participation is used. However, neither research nor the model proposed by Vroom provide much insight into the manner in which participation should be conducted. This is a serious omission if participation is to take advantage of decision aids in aggregating information and preferences of group members. Research is also needed to examine the impact of participation over time, and to investigate processes such as learning and need satisfaction that may be modified by longer-term exposure to participation.

Organizational Procedures. Other interactive decision making strategies involve change in organizational procedures, and in most techniques require considerable agreement among members of an organization before the strategies can be introduced. Among the strategies of this type are: bargaining, Delphi, Nominal Group Technique, and the use of dialectic. Some of these strategies assume that the group members hold conflicting values or goals; others assume cooperation. Parties to "bargaining" are actively involved and interdependent for information and results, and they are assumed to hold at least some conflicting objectives. Influence attempts frequently involve threats, persuasion, or concessions. The parties try to exploit any advantage they may obtain by gaining information about their own or the other party's position, while concealing or giving false information about their own position. The process frequently involves forming coalitions, a topic that has generated much theorizing and empirical research. Schelling (54) has shown that threats and counterthreats are widely used as bargaining ploys. The effective use of bargaining requires that the parties share sufficient interests to initiate and sustain the bargaining, but it does not require that they completely agree on all desired outcomes at the conclusion of the process. Perhaps the most salient example of bargaining in organizations is in labor-management relations.

The Delphi technique (55) was developed by the RAND Corporation more than thirty years ago for technological forecasting, and has been used in such diverse fields as regional planning, medical forecasting, and corporate planning. It uses interaction among decision makers to integrate the opinions of experts about a particular subject, but attempts to remove the dysfunctional aspects of face-to-face communication (e.g., powerful members dominating the discussion). Although it may be modified to meet the requirements of the decision situation, typically the procedure involves isolating the participants from one another and presenting them with a series of questionnaires in which their opinions and reasons are solicited.

The information is consolidated and circulated anonymously to group members after each round. Despite its long history, the first major Delphi study was published only 15 years ago. Although the types of questionnaires used have been criticized, the anonymous feedback of Delphi has been shown to be superior to conventional discussion groups.

The nominal group technique (NGT) is a group meeting in which members silently and independently list their ideas on the topic being considered, take turns in suggesting ideas to the group, discuss the combined list of ideas, and vote on priorities. The group decision is the pooled outcome of the votes (56). There is some research evidence to indicate that both the NGT and Delphi are more effective than conventional discussion groups. Choosing between NGT and Delphi for solving a fact-finding problem depends upon the urgency of the solution and the feasibility of physically bringing the group members together. When the solution is urgent, use NGT; when group members cannot be assembled at one location, use Delphi.

Other procedures that appear useful in making group decisions are designed to ensure that opposing viewpoints on issues are fairly presented or to protect minority viewpoints in voting. One approach to ensuring that all sides of an issue are considered is the use of dialectic. Derived from the technique used by the philosopher Hegel, this strategy requires that each argument for one side of an issue (thesis) be opposed by an equally reasonable position (antithesis) based upon the same body of data. The greatest difficulty in applying this strategy is that any contradictions in the opposed viewpoints need to be resolved (synthesis). Mason (57) has applied a variation of this strategy to corporate planning in which advocates of positions present their views.

Changing Organizational Information Systems and Structures. Designing information systems to facilitate interactive decision making may take the form of opening or closing communication channels, timing and routing information flows to and from decision units, or expanding or contracting data bases. The design of organizational information systems has occupied the attention of the field of management information systems. The research devoted to communication in organizations also is voluminous. While a thorough review of literature on information systems and communication is clearly beyond the scope of this chapter, it appears evident that effective information processing can be facilitated by accurate and efficient exchange of information among group members.

Shaw (58), in reviewing research done over the past 30 years on the effects of communication networks on group morale and productivity, challenged the standard assumption of organizational planners that communication channels are most effective when arranged as a hierarchy. Evidence from laboratory studies has indicated that the communication network should be suited to the task being performed. For simple tasks (involving only information collection) highly centralized networks are effective. For more complex tasks (in which information must be collected in one place and then processed before the solution is known), decentralized networks are effective. It has been speculated that the greater information load inherent in complex tasks may overload the information-processing ability of any single person in the network. Little is known about the impact of communication networks on morale, but the laboratory results suggest that for the complex tasks found in most organizational decision making the information-processing activities would be performed most effectively when shared among relevant organizational members. Accordingly, those seeking to design communication networks for organizations should be cautious about imposing highly centralized networks.

Many attempts have been made to design organizational structures that facilitate interactive decision making. Galbraith (50) has maintained that the level of task uncertainty is central to the design of production-oriented organizations. Although an important distinction is made in the research literature between objective and perceived uncertainty, uncertainty in this context is defined as the extent to which organizational tasks are made unsure due to the introduction of new products. Decision making represents one response to task uncertainty—for example, decisions to change technology, introduce new products, or adopt new marketing strategies. As uncertainty increases, demands for information become more severe, and appropriate information systems and organizational structures are required. While Galbraith has analyzed production-oriented organizations, the issues he identified appear equally relevant to other organizations.

Organizations facing high levels of uncertainty may attempt to reduce the need for information processing, or to increase their capacity to process information. One strategy for reducing the informatinal demands in highly uncertain situations is "adaptivizing" (2). In adaptivizing, the uncertain aspects of the situation are ignored and an adaptive capacity is built up by creating slack resources to permit a quick response when action is required. A common example of this strategy is for an employer to build up his or her inventory when a labor strike appears imminent. Should the strike occur, the loss suffered by an employer using the adaptivizing strategy will be less severe.

Lateral, self-contained "authority structures" may be adopted to increase capacity to process information (50). This involves decomposing the broad decisions facing an organization and assigning components to self-contained decision units (e.g., product divisions). Although these decision units have a hierarchical arrangement in organizations, the lateral structures are equally important. The advantages of this strategy are: (a) the output diversity required of a single decision unit is reduced since there is less need to share information across decision units; (b) less coordination and scheduling within each decision unit is needed; and (c) the information sources and decision points are brought closer together, thus reducing information distortion or loss produced by long communication chains. Moving decision making down in organizations to a point closer to where the information upon which it is based orginates reduces the extent to which "uncertainty absorption" occurs—a false sense of certainty that information tends to acquire as it is transmitted up an organizational hierarchy. The use of an uncertainty index (59), however, still is advisable when there are several links in the communication chain. The uncertainty index is used to transmit an assessment of the uncertainty with which the information was viewed at its source along with the information.

A major weakness with this approach is that the problems must contain components that are sufficiently independent to make decisions limited to these components feasible. For example, a problem of designing a lighter-weight automobile can be decomposed and assigned to decision units responsible for reducing the weight of certain components. If, on the other hand, the components are highly interconnected and a decision of one unit is highly dependent upon decisions made by other units, this strategy would not be appropriate. Another weakness is that, while less coordination is required within decision making units, coordinating the resources and outputs across decision units may be extremely difficult.

A CONCLUDING NOTE

One major theme runs through this attempt to highlight a few of the current issues in managerial planning and decision making. Sophisticated techniques for aiding decision makers have developed both from normative and descriptive approaches and have given managers useful tools for improved decisions. But it should be kept in mind that these tools will be applied by fallible humans, subject to sharply limited ability to handle information and make judgments, and that the tools will be used in highly complex organizational contexts replete with social and political forces. A major challenge facing those interested in improving the state of the art in decision making is to learn more about the implications of our decision making techniques for developing humane organizations. In preparing this chapter, I was struck by how little attention has been given in the research literature to this issue.

Several suggestions appear to be in order. First, viewing managerial decision making through many lenses is essential if it is to be understood and hopefully improved. A few of the perspectives that may prove useful are touched upon briefly in this paper. Second, the models and assumptions that underlie normative theories of rational decision making should be reexamined before they are applied to decision making in organizations. Finally, there is an urgency in these tasks. In organizations, as well as in societies, rapid changes are occuring in technologies, values, and resources. We can afford neither trial-and-error management decision making nor decisions that ignore the preferences of the people they will affect.

REFERENCES

1. Simon, H.A. Applying information technology to organization design. *Public Administration Review,* May-June 1973, 268–277.
2. Ackoff, R. A concept of corporate planning. *Long Range Planning,* 1970, **3**, 2–8.
3. Mason, R.O. & Mitroff, J.J. A program for research on management information systems. *Management Science,* 1973, **19**, 475–587.
4. Simon, H.A. A behavioral model of rational choice. *Quarterly Journal of Economics,* 1955, **69**, 99–105.
5. March, J.G. *Model bias in social action.* Review of Educational Research, **19** (42), 413–429.
6. Weick, K.E. Enactment processes in organizations. In B.M. Staw and G.R. Salancik (Eds.). *New Directions in Organizational Behavior.* Chicago: St. Clair Press, 1977.
7. Cohen, M.D. March, J.G. & Olsen, J.P. A garbage can model of organizational choice. *Administrative Science Quarterly,* 1972, **17**, 1–25.
8. Argyris, C. Some limits of rational man organizational theory. *Public Administration Review,* May-June, 1973, 253–267.
9. Osborn, A.F. *Applied Imagination.* 3rd ed. New York: Scribners, 1963.
10. Dunnette, M.D. Campbell, J.P. & Jaastad, K. The effect of group participation on brainstorming effectiveness for two industrial samples. *Journal of Applied Psychology,* 1963, **47**, 30–37.
11. Bouchard, T.J. Jr. Personality, problem-solving procedure and performance in small groups. *Journal of Applied Psychology Monograph,* 1969, **53**, 1–29.
12. Pounds, W.F. The process of problem finding. Massachusetts Institute of Technology. *Sloan School working paper no. 145–65.* November, 1965.
13. Simon, H.A. Rationality as processs and as product of thought. *American Economic Review,* 1978, **68**, 1–16.
14. Taylor, R.N. Psychological determinants of bounded rationality; Implications for decision making strategies. *Decision Sciences,* 1975, **6**, 409–429.
15. Funaro, J.F. An empirical analysis of five descriptive models for cascaded inference. *Organizational Behavior and Human Performance,* 1975, **14**, 186–206.
16. Tversky, A. and Kahneman, D. Judgment under uncertainty: Heuristics and biases. *Science,* 1974, **185**, 1124–1131.
17. Slovic, P. From Shakespeare to Simon: Speculations—and some evidence—about man's ability to process information. *Orgeon Research Institute Research Monograph,* 12. Eugene, Ore.: Oregon Research Institute, 1972.
18. Kahneman, D. & Tversky, A. Subjective probability: A judgment of representativeness. *Cognitive Psychology,* 1972, **3**, 430–454.
19. Tversky, A. & Kahneman, D. Availability: A heuristic for judging frequency and probability. *Cognitive Psychology,* 1973, **5**, 207–232.

20. Carroll, J.S. Analyzing decision behavior: The magician's audience. In T.S. Wallsten (Ed.). *Cognitive Processes in Choice and Decision Behavior.* Hillsdale, N.J.: Erlbaum, 1980.

21. Allison, G.T. *Essence of decision: Explaining the Cuban missile crisis.* Boston: Little-Brown, 1971.

22. Braybrooke, D. & Lindblom, C.E. *A Strategy of Decision.* New York: The Free Presss, 1963.

23. Howard, R.A. Matheson, J.E. & Miller, K.E. *Readings in Decision Analysis.* Menlo Park, Calif.: Stanford Research Institute, 1976.

24. Brown, R.V. Kahr, A.S. & Peterson, C. *Decision Analysis for the Manager.* New York: Holt, Rinehart and Winston, 1974.

25. Raiffa, H. *Decision Analysis: Introductory Lectures on Choice under Uncertainty.* Reading, Mass.: Addison Wesley, 1968.

26. Churchman, C.W. Auerbach, L. & Sadan, S. *Thinking for Decisions: Deductive Quantitative Methods.* Chicago: Science Research Associates, 1975.

27. Moore, P.G. & Thomas, H. *The Anatomy of Decisions.* New York: Penguin, 1976.

28. Howard, R.A. North, D.W. & Pezier, J.P. A new methodology to integrate planetary quarantine requirements into mission planning, with application to a Jupiter orbiter. *SRI final report NAS7-100.* Menlo Park, Calif.: Stanford Research Institute, 1975.

29. Howard, R.A. Matheson, J.E. & North, D.W. The decision to seed hurricanes. *Science,* 1972, **176**, 1191–1202.

30. Brown, R.V. Modelling subsequent acts for decision analysis. *D.D.T. Technical Report 75-1.* McLean, Va.: Decisions and Designs, Inc., 1975.

31. Ashton, R.H. User prediction models in accounting: An alternative use. *Accounting Review,* 1975, **50**, 710–722.

32. Dawes, R.M. A case study of graduate admissions: Applications of three principles of human decision making. *American Psychologist,* 1971, **26**, 180–188.

33. Kunreuther, H. Limited knowledge and insurance protection. *Public Policy,* 1976, **24**, 227–261.

34. Einhorn, H.J. Cue definition and residual judgment. *Organizational Behavior and Human Performance,* 1974, **12**, 30–49.

35. MacCrimmon, K.R. An overview of multiple objective decision making. In J.L. Cochrane and M. Zeleny (Eds.). *Multiple Criteria Decision Making.* Columbia, S.C.: University of South Carolina Press, 1973.

36. Keeney, R.L. & Raiffa, H. *Decisions with Multiple Objectives.* New York: Wiley, 1976.

37. Huber, G.P. *Managerial Decision Making.* Glenview, Ill.: Scott, Foresman, 1980.

38. Keeney, R.L. A decision analysis with multiple objectives: The Mexico City Airport. *Bell Journal of Economics and Management Science,* 1973, **4**, 101–117.

39. Guttentag, M. & Sayeki, Y. A decision-theoretical technique for the illumination of cultural differences. *Journal of Cross-Cultural Psychology,* 1975, **6**, 203–217.

40. Slovic, P. Fischhoff, B. & Lichtenstein, S. Behavioral decision theory. In M.R.

Rosenzweig & L.W. Porter (Eds.). *Annual Review of Psychology*. Palo Alto, Calif.: Annual Reviews, Inc., 1977, **28**, 1–39.

41. Beach, L.R. Townes, B.D. Campbell, F.L. & Keating, G.W. Developing and testing a decision aid for birth planning decisions. *Organizational Behavior and Human Performance*, 1976, **15**, 99–116.

42. Aschenbrenner, K.M. & Kasubek, W. Convergence of multiattribute evaluations when different sorts of attributes are used. In H. Jungerman & G. de Zeeuw (Eds.). *Proceedings of the fifth research conference on subjective probability, utility, and decision making*, Rome, Italy, 1976.

43. Kneppreth, N.P. Gustafson, D.H. Leifer, R.P. & Johnson, E.M. Techniques for the assessement of worth. *Technical paper 254*. Arlington, Va.: Army Research Institute, 1974.

44. Simon, H.A. *The Sciences of the Artificial*. Cambridge: M.I.T. Press, 1964.

45. Leontief, W. *Input-Output Economics*. Oxford, England: Oxford University Press, 1966.

46. Armstrong, J.S. Dennision, W.B. Jr. & Gordon, N.M. The use of the decomposition principle in making judgments. *Organizational Behavior and Human Performance*, 1975, **14**, 257–263.

47. Spetzler, C.S. & Stael von Holstein, C.A.S. Probability encoding in decision analysis. *Management Science*, 1975, **22**, 340–358.

48. Edwards, W. Phillips, L.D. Hays, W.L. & Goodman, B.C. *Probabilitic Transactions on Systems, Science and Cybernetics*, 1968, SSC-4, 248–265.

49. Conrath, D.W. From statistical decision theory to practices: Some problems with the transition. *Management Science*, 1973, **19**, 873–883.

50. Galbraith, J.R. *Organization Design*. Reading, Mass.: Addison-Wesley, 1973.

51. Mechanic, D. Sources of power of lower participants in complex organizations. *Administrative Science Quarterly*, 1967, 349–364.

52. Vroom, V.H. Yetton, P.W. *Leadership and Decision Making*. Pittsburgh: University of Pittsburgh Press, 1973.

53. Melcher, A. Participation: A critical review of research findings. *Human Resource Management*, 1976, **15**, 12–21.

54. Schelling, T.C. *The Strategy of Conflict*. Cambridge: Harvard University Press, 1960.

55. Dalkey, N. & Helmer, D. An experimental approach to the Delphi method for use of experts. *Management Science*, 1963, **9**, 458–467.

56. Delbecq, A.L. Van de Ven, A.H. & Gustafson, D.H. *Group Techniques for Program Planning*. Glenview, Ill.: Scott, Foresman, 1975.

57. Mason, R.O. A dialectical approach for strategic planning. *Management Science*, 1969, **15**, B403–414.

58. Shaw, M.E. *Group Dynamics: The Psychology of Small Group Behavior*. New York: McGraw-Hill, 1971.

59. Woods, D.H. Improving estimates that involve uncertainty. *Harvard Business Review*, 1966, **44**, 91–98.

—10—

The Process Perspective on Management

H. Russell Johnston

Management is a process in the sense that it is continuous and follows a course over time with numerous changes, shifts, and nuances. Furthermore, the group or organization being managed represents a process, a human or social process that is also following a course over time. As we look at the state of the art of managing—both how we manage and what we say about how we do or should manage, we find justifications for keeping our notions of management as a process firmly in our awareness. It is particularly valuable to retain this notion as we look at the interface between those who do manage and those who perform research and writing about management. Here recognition of management as a process is important for several reasons:

First of all, neither the situation being managed (the organization or group and its environment)nor the interventions and impact of the manager are static. Both organizational processes and managerial processes are constantly changing and shifting in relation to each other over time. Therefore observations that we make about managing can only be useful for learning to the degree that they capture this crucial quality of managing—the ongoing, evolving nature of management and the organization being managed. Every organization is constantly changing along a variety of important dimensions over time. Examples of positive changes include growth in market share, increased technological capability, and greater understanding and support of corporate objectives by key employees. There are equally important organizational changes that represent decline. The successful manager is able to direct and support the processes that move the organization toward strategic success and reverse or minimize the effects of processes of decline.

However, some very real and pervasive structural problems make the attempt of researchers and writers to capture the ongoing nature of managing very difficult. Our typical opportunities for doing research do not have the continuity and "embeddedness" of contact that allow for observation and understanding of the ongoing processes. Even our consulting arrangements often revolve around a specific event or bounded sequence of events so that the consultant is dealing with a situation in an acontextual way, that is, without the opportunity either to observe the problem or the solution that he or she proposes as part of an evolutionary process with both a history and a future that is both deterministic and uncertain.

This lack of continuity partially accounts for the imbalance within our literature on managing towards solving of problems rather than discovery and exploitation of opportunities arising from the environment and the strengths of the organization as they evolve.

On the other hand, people who are part of and embedded in organizational and managerial processes find it difficult to be accurate observers of and writers about the ongoing phenomena in which they are enmeshed. Oftentimes they are neither trained, nor do they have the disposition or the opportunity to be effective participant observers of the passing scene.

As a consequence, much of what is written about management is based on snapshots of a particular point in an organization's history. The articles may provide interesting anecdotes. They may also stimulate some thinking. However, they often fall short of providing guidance to practicing managers. This point was brought home sharply by a recent comment from a close friend who is the president of a medium-sized company and a graduate of a highly regarded MBA program. This manager commented that he had just about stopped reading articles about managing, including those published in the best known national journal targeted primarily at a management audience. He went on to say that the articles just never seem to contain a sense of reality as he experienced it in his business, and that they were full of jargon, meaning terminology that does not relate to one's own experience. This stimulus from a person whom I knew to be an intelligent and innovative manager—one who had implemented a number of progressive changes in his company—caused me to reflect on the reading habits of other managers with whom I had contact. I decided that my friend's conclusion about articles on management is widely shared. Few managers of my acquaintance in organizations large and small and in organizations in the profit and not-for-profit sectors have journals containing articles about managing in their offices. Few books about management, which look more current than the manager's last academic experience, adorn their bookshelves. Current topics in the management literature seem to be virtually ignored by many if not most practicing managers.

Yet there still remains substantial demand for workshops and seminars where practicing managers have the opportunity to get together and share what they have learned from their own experiences.

While the above comments present a rather bleak picture of the communications and other interactions between practicing managers and those who do research and writing about management, it is both feasible and reasonable to improve these interactions, and some attempts at improvement are already well underway. Improvements would result from the following:

1. Changes in academic rewards and other arrangements to encourage long-term relationships between members of the academic community and pur-

poseful organizations in the public and private sectors. Examples of changes would include broader utilization of modest retainers as a basis for a long-term relationship between an academic and an outside organization. Such an arrangement could involve the academic in consulting and training activities (for instance, organization and management development or consulting in his or her specific functional specialty). For the organization, this type of arrangement would have the advantage of providing an outside process consultant who is able to employ his or her skills to detect both opportunities and problems and participate in responses to them from a perspective of familiarity with the ongoing evolution of organization. A consultant has the opportunity to experience the organization and managing as an ongoing process and to communicate with managers from this perspective. Such arrangements would require joint academic and management evaluation of performance for purposes of determining appropriate career and compensation progression.

2. A second arrangement, which seems to have gradually increasing acceptance and use, is relatively long-term transfers to and from academia. There have been visible examples of this arrangement in the appointment of experienced managers as deans of highly regarded business schools. Far more prevalent, but less visible, are the numbers of businessmen who are given leaves of absence for periods of a year or more to join business school faculties. An even greater number of managers teach a course or two per year at a nearby business school over extended periods of time. Examples of academics moving into managerial situations and back to academia are far less frequent or visible or perhaps both. There are promising signs that the 80s will see a somewhat different climate, in which society comes to value more highly the managerial role and supports a wider variety of efforts to enhance the productive contribution of management.
3. Articles for practitioners need to be oriented around particular management processes as they are experienced by managers, rather than being oriented to the source fields of knowledge as segmented for academic research and teaching. As articles become reoriented toward managment processes, their contents will tend to focus more on the activities in which managers engage—observation of the environment and opportunity finding; organizational diagnoses and problem definition; analysis of the forces that give rise to opportunities or problems; the generation of alternatives for change; planning for implementation; and actions necessary to implement and follow up to see that intended results had been achieved. Such process-oriented material can be augmented by checklists intended to stimulate managerial application of these rather universal processes in their particular organizations. An interesting and promising example of this type of writing is provided by Davis and Luthans (1) in their article about managerial behavior and operating modes. They use social learning theory to analyze and illuminate the experimental and evolutionary nature of managerial development and behavior.

As researchers and writers gain experience with the process orientation toward communication with managers, we shall probably see a dramatic expansion in the market opportunities for journals dealing with the general problems of management and targeted specifically toward a managerial audience. For journals of this type to be successful, editors must be prepared to go beyond normal interactions with authors in order to assist them in gaining and communicating managerial perspectives. In some cases these efforts may well extend to brokering coauthor arrangements between academic researchers and practicing managers so that the strengths of each perspective are brought to bear on the article. Note that such a proposal is not really a radical idea, only a slight variation from what is already being done in this book.

APPLICATION OF THE PROCESS PERSPECTIVE TO MANAGEMENT LITERATURE

Now that we have established the notion of the process perspective for communications between academics and practicing managers, noted some of the barriers to full utilization of the process perspective, and made some observations about how those barriers could be overcome, it will be instructive to look at the preceding chapters in Part I of this book from that perspective. The analysis will proceed in the direction of the traditional ordering of the management process, namely, planning, organizing, directing, and controlling.

We see in Taylor's chapter "Planning and Decision Making in Managing Organizations" a clear and concise review of the academic literature on decision making. For the reader who is both well educated and knowledgeable about the current language of decision making and related disciplines, it is a helpful and well-structured review. From the perspective of this literature, it is an admirable tour de force.

However, the issues around which it is structured (normative and descriptive theories of decision making and conclusions and techniques emerging from research on planning and decision making) do not match directly with the ways in which a manager goes about the process of planning. A more useful structure might be devised around the sequence of strategic planning (what is to be done) and tactical planning (how is it to be done). Under strategic planning, materials dealing with predominantly divergent styles or modes of decision making would be covered. In this mode the manager is attempting to become aware or increase his or her awareness of opportunities and threats in the external environment, develop new and different ways of conceptualizing the capabilities of his or her organization, and determine ways in which those capabilities could be used to greater advantage. This stage utilizes an open system perspective. Taylor's chapter lists a number of decision techniques that are useful in this stage, for example, nominal groups, Delphi process, and dialectic.

As a manager shifts to tactical decision making, the cognitive style employed in decision making also shifts to a more convergent orientation. Here the manager is less concerned with generation of alternatives and somewhat more concerned with intelligent and informed choice among more easily defined alternatives. In this phase of planning, techniques for structuring the alternatives and assessing uncertainties, such as multiattribute utility analysis, come into play.

Just as the alternative generating and decision structuring techniques can be related to the managerial tasks of strategic planning and tactical planning, so also can awareness of human cognitive limitations in information processing and decision making and awareness of the organizational context of managerial decision making be related to planning as it is experienced by the manager. To offset cognitive limitations in strategic planning, managers use a variety of resources such as outside consultants, services that analyze the external environment, and planning models utilizing computers to permit manipulation of key assumptions and estimates to observe the expected strategic impacts. In tactical planning, devices such as temporary organizations (compare project groups) and overcommunication help to offset human and contextual limitations.

What is missing in Taylor's exposition is a sense of flow—planning as an ongoing process of evaluating strategic opportunities and threats and converting this intelligence about the external environment and internal organizational characteristics into an action sequence. Planning and decision making, to be effective in defining and causing organizational action, are meshed with the other management processes (organizing, directing, and controlling) and are also meshed with the actual sequence of actions and reactions as the plan is implemented. Effective planning is not an occasional cerebral activity, it is a continuous, competitive activity, constantly in search of the gaps between what is and what might be and the actions necessary to close those gaps. Planning and the other processes of management are verbs to practitioners, who experience their work as both progressive and aggressive behavior.

Thus Taylor's chapter has a wealth of information about effective decision making in the planning process, and once we begin to look at it from the perspective of that process, it both informs us and provides useful pointers to a wide range of current thinking about decision making.

The chapter on organizing, "Configurations of Organizational Structure," by Mintzberg, provides an intriguing set of concepts for understanding and analyzing organizational structure and processes. His comments about organizations attempting to choose and enact their environments reminds in a haunting way of Toffler's contention (2) that we are experiencing a massive effort by second wave organizations to resist his predicted third wave of civilization. If a manager chooses to reject Toffler's speculations concerning a third wave and instead relies on experience from the past, he or she might still be haunted by Burns and Stalker's account (3) of the plight of the mechanistically structured electrical companies in England as the advent of electronic technology changed their industry. Some of these firms declined precipitously because their structure did not permit them to accommodate effectively to environmental demands for change.

Faced with such concerns, the manager must decide organizational questions such as:

> How do I assess the uncertainties in my organization's environment? Which uncertainties are likely to prove the key to the future of my organization?
>
> How can I segment my environment and my organizational units so that I successfully monitor changes in the external environment in order to devise appropriate responses?
>
> How can I balance my organization in order to meet the competing environmental demands for effectiveness and efficiency?
>
> How do I detect when my organization is getting out of balance in terms of its ability to meet environmental demands?
>
> What do I do when my organization's task calls for a machine bureaucracy, yet my most outspoken and perhaps capable performers prefer and quite forcefully insist on something closer to adhocracy?
>
> Or, as a manager of a young and rapidly growing firm, when and how do I make the transition from a simple structure to a more appropriate form?

Even the practitioner with more than average familiarity with the organizational literature experiences some difficulty in finding clear answers to these types of managerial questions.

Mintzberg's discussion of structural pathologies is interesting and the experienced practitioner will recall organizations that correspond closely with Mintzberg's horror story examples. But if you inherit one of those horror stories, what steps do you take to restore effective and efficient operations?

The chapters entitled "Selecting People and Appraising Their Performance" by Grant and "Needs Assessment Approaches for Training Development"by Goldstein, Macey, and Prien illustrate quite neatly the essentially static quality of much of the writing about management processes. Each of these chapters describes how to perform a critical aspect of the management process. They are instructive, action-oriented in their approach, and thorough in their coverage of their topics. However, each suggested approach implicitly assumes a relatively static organization. In discussing both selection and training, the authors inform the practitioner about how to deal with the task and job structures that he or she finds in the organization at the present time. Use of selection, training, and appraisal as means to implement planned changes over time is alluded to but not given the type of coverage that could be vital to the manager in a dynamic environmental and task situation. In particular, selection, training, and appraisal have high potential leverage for the manager in changing the strategic and tactical potentials of the organization over time, and as such these topics merit a dynamic treatment.

An example of the dynamic properties of a process orientation is available in the chapter titled "Leadership and Stress Management" by Levinson. The aggressive drive and the individual's urge to approach his or her ego ideal in his or her behavior in the organization are posited by Levinson to be the sources of the energy that powers the organization over time. In discussing these forces in the organizational setting, Levinson provides examples of managerial behaviors that frustrate and others that foster the acting out of these basic forces by members of the organization. Levinson's definition of the task of the leader is sufficiently important in this context to merit quoting again here:

> It is the task of the leader then to bring the people who report to him or her face-to-face with the realities that they as organizational members are up against, and to support them in the process of learning to master those realities by which they simultaneously meet their own maturation needs, become increasingly confident, and master a good deal of their working environment—at least as much of it as possible in those specific roles. The leader also serves as a model for how problems can be mastered.

Levinson's descriptions of leadership behavior are embedded in a process notion both of the leadership function itself and of the movement of the organization and its members over time and other dimensions.

The behavioral literature on such topics as motivation, job satisfaction, organizational climate, attitudes, and morale is enormous, and it is growing at a rate that defies the effort of even the most avid readers and students of behavior to keep up to date. Katzell's chapter titled "Attitudes and Motivation" provides the practitioner with a succinct guide to this massive literature. His chapter shows clearly some of the problems that are encountered by the practitioner trying to use the behavioral literature to guide his or her approach to dealing with peers, subordinates, and bosses. Most of the literature is developed based on correlational studies in which the investigator attempts to determine whether relationships exist between variables such as attitudes and performance or indeed even between motivation and performance. These correlational studies are classic examples of the attempt to understand ongoing behavior in organizations utilizing the snapshot approach. They provide the researcher little opportunity to instruct the practitioner in how to achieve improvements in the behavioral aspects in the organization. The existence of a high correlation between two variables leaves open the question of the direction of causation. For example, does high morale cause good performance, or does good performance cause high morale? Another important question related to causation has to do with goal setting. While virtually all writers agree that goal setting tends to be associated with high performance, the literature on goal setting is highly splintered, complex, and inconclusive, as demonstrated by Tolchinsky and King (4). As their article shows, the literature on the effects of goal setting, feedback, and monetary incentives on work performance does not provide clear guidance to managerial practice. Faced with this complexity and indecisiveness on the part of behavioral scientists, many practitioners may understandably ignore the behavioral aspects of managing in favor of concentrating on the less ambiguous areas of planning, organization, and systems design, and development of compensation systems that they hope will prove motivational. Given the indecisiveness of the literature, the practicing manager also may conclude, or at least hope, that if he or she can get the organization winning—in the sense of making substantial and visible progress and meeting the demands of its environment—then the softer behavioral variables will fall in line. That is, if he or she can just get the organization moving, then morale and motivation will increase and the climate within the organization will improve. In this sense the management process instructs the practicing manager how to begin the process of improving organizational performance, whereas behavioral literature oriented around research topics provides no direction as to the appropriate hierarchy of managerial actions.

"Communication and Organizational Dynamics" by Hall and Andrews provides a good deal of useful information about the communication process and the information environment of the organization. However, reorienting this information around the communication and information dissemination roles of the manager would provide a valuable assist in utilizing the information provided. Practicing managers have a number of communications tasks. These communications tasks are defined by the structure of the management process. The practicing manager needs guidance in the appropriate communication skills for developing and disseminating a strategic sense of purpose for organizational members, and in handling the maintenance roles of direction and control.

Both the title of Ivancevich's chapter "Management and Compensation" and its inclusion in the section "Managerial Processes" call attention to several ironies of compensation issues. First of all, managers at many companies do demonstrate by their behavior that they consider compensation to be a vital management process. It is felt to play a central and important role in both the processes of direction and control. Members of top management typically give a high degree of attention, thought, and effort to the design and implementation of various compensation schemes. Yet as Ivancevich shows through the employment of Lawler's ratings of various pay plans, shown in Table 4.2, management's success at achieving a pay system that produces the intended results is not universal. The systems that Lawler studied got generally fair to good marks on the tie between pay and performance and employee acceptance, did not do nearly as well in encouraging cooperation, and were rated as disasters in the production of negative side effects. These results raise interesting questions for practitioners and researchers alike. The first type of question that we should be asking is, "If compensation systems have indeed typically received a substantial amount of top management attention, why are we unable to come up with compensation systems that are more manifestly successful in achieving management's intents and that produce fewer negative side effects?" Questions of this type are questions about means. Given the repeated inability of intelligent and resourceful management practitioners and writers to devise pay systems that achieve management objectives, it also seems appropriate to raise questions about the ends. This type of question suggests an investigation of what management is attempting to accomplish through the mechanism of the compensation system, whether they are appropriate ends, and if so, whether the means are appropriate to the ends.

Observation of practicing managers and perusal of the management literature on compensation suggest that management attempts to use compensation as a tool to achieve the management process steps of providing direction to an organization (emphasizing this objective vs. that objective) and for controlling (rewarding this behavior and not rewarding that behavior in order to shape the behavior of each member of the organization and therefore to shape the behavior of the entire organization). Ivancevich's material suggests some reasons why management may be so generally unsuccessful in employing compensation as a tool, particularly as a control tool. His general theme relates compensation to performance as determined by a system of formal performance appraisal. Yet as Ivancevich says, "The fact remains that pinpointing individual performance is extremely difficult." In practice, this is indeed true.

As a greater proportion of our working population moves into white collar and service jobs with a higher degree of variation, tying compensation to performance promises to become even more difficult. Tying compensation to results achieved may be totally impossible. There are a number of reasons for this. First of all, the usual compensation system attempts to allocate monetary rewards in a way such that actual dollar differences between the increases for worker A and worker B, while they might be on the order of several hundred dollars a year, represent relatively small differences when compared to the total compensation of individuals A and B. In this sense, the system is attempting to make judgments and allocations based on judgments that are simply finer in degree than is possible given the many factors that Ivancevich cites as creating measurement error, particularly rater bias. As a control tool, compensation systems based on inaccurate and perhaps invalid measures of performance through periodic performance appraisals lack most of the basic qualities of effective control systems.

The negative side effects or unintended consequences of compensation systems in all likelihood stem from the negative impact of performance appraisal systems on employee self-esteem. As Ivancevich indicates, employee perceptions of their performance are generally higher than manager perceptions. The lower rating imposed by the boss would be experienced by the subordinate as an actual or attempted lowering of his or her self image. It would operate through the mechanism cited by Levinson in such a way as to lower self-esteem, thereby producing all of the negative emotional results that Levinson describes in the early part of his chapter.

The manager in an organization is frequently under pressure to evaluate his or her employees relative to each other, despite evidence of serious negative side effects of forced ranking. The fundamental source of this pressure is that many compensation plans operate in such a way that the manager is assigned an essentially fixed salary increase budget for the upcoming period. This fixed sum is often not related to unit performance. Unless the salary increase budget exceeds the amount necessary to maintain the labor market rate of all employees in the unit, plus a reasonable amount for actual merit increases, managers find themselves in a zero sum game. In order to increase the relationship of one employee to market rates, he or she must by implication lower the relationship to market rates of another employee. Since the performance appraisal system must justify the pay treatment, the manager must provide a rationale for failing to meet the compensation expectations of employees whose performance is not judged to be as good as others. The manager is thereby encouraged to gather through the performance period sufficient evidence of substandard performance in order to support the compensation decisions deriving from the zero sum game. Psychologically this negative orientation toward the employee is in direct conflict with the supportive coaching role of the manager in helping the subordinate to improve performance over time. The bind that such managers find themselves in becomes particularly excruciating when they have a group of people with a history of high individual performance and yet have a normal salary increase budget. The pay for performance notion saddles them with the necessity of developing a rationale for rating and paying one of their stars as though he or she were a less than average performer.

It may well be that the notion of pay for performance is one of those ideas that is conceptually fine but operationally flawed. A pay system is used for a number of important ends such as maintaining a stable work force, attracting new talent, and maintaining morale through a sense of both internal and external equity. This may well be sufficient burden on a system without also attempting to use it as a device for management control by allocating small differences in compensation increases based on perceived performance.

Perhaps a more realistic approach to differences in compensation could be based on individual growth and performance improvement. Such a system would tend to accent the positive while not forcing quite the glare of periodic publicity on the negative. Given our inability to come up with compensation systems that do not produce the negative side effects cited by Lawler's study, perhaps the best advice for practitioners is that offered by Ivancevich. He suggests that the manager be continually engaged in observation, interviewing, experimentation, and surveying of the employees' perceptions of the behavioral effects of his or her compensation systems. Following Ivancevich's advice would tend to lead to compensation systems that are highly diverse and flexible and that change sometimes rapidly over time.

In summary, the state of the art for both practitioners and theoreticians in compensation systems is in a stage that could be described by its allies as experimentation or by its detractors as groping.

In commenting on the chapters in this section on management processes, I have saved Meyer's chapter "Making Supervision Humane and Productive" until last. The reason for this choice is that it so admirably illustrates the use of a process model to communicate results of research to practicing managers in a way that relates clearly to their experience of their managerial role. His piece provides a clear description of a positive approach to supervision at any level in the organization, which is easily related by the practitioner to the ongoing reality of planning, organizing, directing, and controlling a group of people working together to achieve a task over time.

In his closing comments, Meyer points out that while his prescription "may seem to be very simple and commonsensical," it is not universally applied in daily supervisory practice. As Meyer's references point out (most of the cited work has been published for more than ten years), these ideas are neither new nor unorthodox—at least in the management literature. Yet experience suggests that they certainly are not universally and consistently applied by practitioners. Why should this be so?

There are numerous potential explanations for the perceived lack of widespread and rapid adoption of Meyer's prescription. A central element of Meyer's prescription and perhaps the most basic finding in behavioral science is that positive reinforcement is consistently superior to negative reinforcement in shaping ongoing behavior. This approach is philosophically as well as operationally positive. However, in many organizations the information system is operated in such a way that it tends to focus the attention of both managers and subordinates on negative deviations rather than the pervasiveness of proper performance or even on the occasional performance that exceeds standards. In a sense this is a perversion of the concept of management by exception. As practiced in many organizations, management by exception also tends to focus management attention on problems—negative examples of performance—rather than on the pervasiveness of good performance or the occasional performance that is about standard but not spectacularly so. This can be easily corrected in several ways. One is by reporting performance in terms of percent "right first time" rather than in percent reject rate. A positive reporting orientation leads the manager to coach from a positive perspective to replicate and raise good performance rather than eliminate bad. Another approach employs the quality circles idea of focusing attention on the positive exceptions and finding the causes that account for these unusually positive results in order to continue the extraordinary performance in the future.

It may also be that we have over time become more bureaucratized rather than entrepreneurial in our organizations and have begun to bias our selection of managers more toward those people with a high need for power rather than a need for achievement. This would relate to the problem that Levinson pointed out in which aggression by the boss is not well controlled in the service of the goals of the organization.

It may also be that our pressure for quick results and our focus on the short term has tended to deflect managerial attention away from those practices that make the work situation more humane. The practices that Meyer advocates are generally demanding on managerial time and often do not have an immediate payoff in improved performance. In a sense, the manager following Meyer's prescription is investing in the development of his or her organization and its individuals with the expectation that the investment will pay off in improved performance at later points. One of the side effects of our information revolution is that we now have very timely information on performance that has just occurred. The availability of the information about present performance combined with the ethos of pay for performance may well influence many supervisors to defer investments in future performance in order to maximize current outputs.

Yet another potential explanation is that the manner in which research and reporting of research about management is being done does not inform the practitioner in a way he or she can apply in order to improve managerial performance.

THE PROCESS PERSPECTIVE AT THE TOP

Recent work by Waterman, Peters, and Phillips (5) based on long-term relationships with organizations and their managers provides an interesting focus on the role of management. They describe the role of top management as articulating the central purposes and objectives of the organization and the distinctive characteristics of its strategy in relationship to its environment so that each member shares a broad, metaphorical vision of what the organization of the future should be. Once identity and thrust have been established, the executive must develop structures, processes, and capabilities and then animate the organization through initiation and reinforcement of action consistent with strategy. They point out that this is a constant, never-ending, and extremely time consuming task for the executive, but see it as fundamentally shaping the organization and creating forward motion and growth. Indeed their definition of the role of top management is a very positive response to the failures of leadership cited by Hayes and Abernathy (6), who cite top management focus on short-term market response and efficiency to the detriment of demand and support for entrepreneurial innovation as a major cause of the relatively poor productivity growth in the United States during the decades of the 60s and 70s.

The top management role of defining the central purpose in character of the organization is not merely a planning role. Instead, establishing the basic identity in this way is a fundamental force for establishing integration in the organization. Furthermore, it is integrating device that does not impose the bureaucratic rigidities, the delay for consultation, nor the dilution of the individual accountability that characterize some other methods for achieving integration. By integrating at the level of basic strategic purpose, the organization also avoids the tendency of some integrating efforts to reduce the differentiation so necessary to diversity of response to diverse environmental demands. By focusing on fundamental strategy rather than tactical actions, this style of management creates integration of purpose rather than conformity of behavior. In doing so, it also creates the necessary conditions for the organization to become both more productive and more humane.

REFERENCES

1. Davis, T. R. V. & Luthans, F. Managers in action: A new look at their behavior and operating modes. *Organizational Dynamics*, 1980, **9** (1), 64.
2. Toffler, A. *The Third Wave*. New York: Morrow, 1980.
3. Burns, T. & Stalker, G. M. *The Management of Innovation*. London: Tavistock Publications, 1961.
4. Tolchinksky, P. D. & King, D. C. Do goals mediate the effects of incentives on performance? *Academy of Management Review*, 1980, **5,** 455.
5. Waterman, R. H., Peters, T. J. & Phillips, J. R. Structure is not organization. *Business Horizons*, 1980, **23** (3), 14.
6. Hayes, R. H. & Abernathy W. S. Managing our way to economic decline. *Havard Business Review*, 1980, **58** (4), 67.

—II—

CONTEMPORARY REALITIES

Today managers of organizations are confronted by realities in employment of people that, if not new, are much more complex then they have been in the past. Often these complex realities are experienced as problems, and problems they are. However, thoughtful consideration of each problem leads to an awareness of how organizations can often best serve their survival and growth needs by becoming more humane as well as productive.

Many of the matters treated in this chapter have influenced organizations for a long time. For example, unions and health and safety have been important topics in management literature for some time. Other concerns such as opportunities for minorities, women, handicapped, and aging workers, have only recently received a great deal of attention. The increased attention to these matters does not mean that they are new problems as much as it means that the power of members of these various groups has increased; consequently managers have become more aware of their needs and find it necessary to give higher priorities to their interests. Moreover, affluence from productivity has permitted individual organizations and society as a whole to devote resources to special requirements of these diverse groups. In addition, the expectations that members of society hold for organizations have changed. These changes have been reflected in laws, court rulings, expressions of public opinion, and in the views of professional managers. Thus, while none of the topics dealt with in this chapter are really new, they are far more urgent than before.

As these matters have received greater attention, some discoveries have been made. First, it has become clear that many of the problems can be avoided or resolved by managing well. In other words, if managers do a good job of selection (see Chapter 1 of this book), of training (see Chapter 2), communicating (see Chapter 5), and so on, they are attending to many of the needs of diverse employees in an ongoing way. Second, productivity can often be increased by giving new priority to these humane considerations. The chapters in this part demonstrate these conclusions in a number of ways.

In Chapter 11 Richard Beatty, Madison Holloway, and Craig Schneier describe the evolution of attitudes in the United States towards minorities, particularly towards blacks. They consider the marked changes that have taken place, the barriers to equal opportunity that still exist, and what might help to overcome these obstacles. To date most attention has been given to hiring and training for the first job. Beatty et al. point to the need for greater attention to career decision making and planning.

In the next chapter Tucker focuses on the realities of problems women have in organizations. In the light of her research interest in the problems of eliminating inequities due to sex, she considers the struggle for women and quality in the work place, and indicates that it is gaining momentum. Tucker makes explicit an important theme that runs through several of the chapters in this part: nonhumane treatment and failure of organizations to utilize human resources effectively are due at least as much to established methods of getting things done as by attitudes. In the case of women, established routines for selection, placement, and so on have acted as barriers to their advancement to higher positions.

The chapter on aging realities in managing organizations is based on a series of research studies on workers in two communities, a college town in upstate New York and the city of St. Louis. These studies indicate that stereotypes about older workers by managers, union leaders, and workers produce a false frame of reference for thinking about economic, social, and political reality. Based on the substantial individual differences recorded in these studies, Meltzer shows that general stereotypes about the elderly (e.g., that they are more conservative, less creative, less productive, less mobile, more dependent than the younger workers) are false. Meltzer argues that the retirement issue must be dealt with in terms of the nature of each individual involved, rather than on assumptions about the effects of age in general.

The handicapped, long the hidden minority, are demanding attention to their problems. As expressed by one handicapped person, "Others must begin to see us as people not as crutches, and wheelchairs and canes." In the chapter on opportunities for the handicapped, Raymond Ehrle presents the facts about the present status of education and work of the handicapped and reviews legislation that has been intended to help handicapped workers gain opportunities in the work place. The challenge is for managers of organizations and administrators to demonstrate compassion and sympathy. Ehrle points out that these efforts have both costs and benefits, but that often our humane impulses lead us to overlook the costs.

The chapter on alcoholism and other substance abuse is written by a man whose major professional interest for the last 25 years has been the study of the alcoholism in Western societies. Pittman informs us that the relationship between drugs and human beings is a long one, antedating recorded history. He gives the reader a clear definition of the meaning of such terms as addiction, habituation, dependence, and abuse, all of which are necessary to know in order to think realistically about the problem. He points out the staggering social and economic costs of alcohol abuse. In addition to providing this information, Pittman's attitudes towards the problem provide a valuable orientation for realistically dealing with it.

Job transfers have become a salient feature of modern organizations.

However, the topic of transfer has been very much neglected; in fact frequently in textbooks on career development and personnel management, it is barely mentioned. In his chapter, Pinder considers a number of dimensions of transfers—their extent and nature, their significance, and their implications for productivity and profit. Drawing heavily on his own pioneering research in the area, Pinder examines some of the manifest and latent functions and dysfunctions of transfers and then considers how to make transfers humane and productive.

Most managers have had experience with unions annd out of those experiences have developed attitudes towards them. In his chapter on unions, Dr. Driscoll presents a picture of unions—how they developed, how they work, what their goals are, what their objectives are, and the difficulties they have in attaining them. As with so many other topics treated in this volume, managers often respond to unions on the basis of stereotypes. Driscoll challenges some of these stereotypes by arguing that unions actually help productivity more often than they hurt it; he asserts that union workers are more productive. Of course, there are plenty of differences among unions. Thus it is difficult to develop a list of recommendations on this topic that will apply to all situations. Nevertheless Driscoll develops a set of suggestions for improving union-management relationships that are useful starting points in examining individual cases.

In the final chapter of Part II Gordon and Henifin consider a number of topics that are so basic that discussions of the quality of work life often omit them. In the United States there appear to be movements concerned with improving life in the work place. One emphasizes the quality of work life and humanization. The other is based on a public health perspective and has been concerned primarily with physical and chemical hazards in the work environment. Gordon and Henifin write more from the public health perspective than do our other authors. Consequently they focus on the physical and psychosocial health effects of work and the work place that are so often ignored by conventional treatments of the quality of work life.

All in all, in addition to the knowledge they summarize, the chapters contained in Part II provide perspectives in a number of vital realities that confront management today. The editors hope that this knowledge and these perspectives will help managers to develop creative approaches for coping with these matters as they occur in the context of individual organizations.

Ken Ball, in his review of the contributions in Part II, calls our attention to the fact that the social pressures of the 1960s have crystallized in the 1980s as the goals and strategies of interest groups have become more clearly delineated. Stockholders and owners, lenders and banks, the buying public, consumers, unions and employee groups, governmental agencies, special interest groups, and individual employees—all have pressed their interests. These demands have become important contemporary realities for managers. He advises the readers that functional reality for the practitioner requires attitude changes of business leaders rather than merely a mechanical application of knowledge. The value of the ideas presented in this part is not that they will lead to a panacea, but that they may provide a basis for planned programs. His review emphasizes the top corporate leaders, because that's where effective action for change begins.

—11—

Making Organizations Humane and Productive for Minorities

Richard W. Beatty
Madison W. Holloway
Craig Eric Schneier

The writing of this chapter has been most frustrating, perhaps because in no area of concern related to making organizations humane and productive has there been as much controversy as the employment of minorities in organizations. In fact, when minority employees in organizations are discussed, arguments often follow concerning what is humane and what is productive. Fortunately, this topic is one in which we can test the productivity implications of what is essentially a humane endeavor, although it will be argued that hiring minorities can actually be based purely on economic-productivity grounds alone. There are many common issues and themes in this paper and others in this section such as those by Tucker (Chapter 12) and Ehrle (Chapter 14). Moreover, many of the earlier chapters such as those of Grant on selection (Chapter 1) and Goldstein, Macey, and Prien on training (Chapter 2) underlie many of the ideas in this chapter.

Much has been written during the past 20 years on the increasing participation in the American work force and of minorities who have contributed much to our society. But who are these persons we commonly refer to as "minorities?" They could be called the "hyphenated Americans"—Black-American, Mexican-American, Polish-American, Puerto Rican-American, and so on. Actually the designation "minority" refers to a denial of rights, not ethnic background. Thus the term could refer to women, despite their larger numbers, but women will not be discussed here because their concerns are treated in depth elsewhere in this volume (see Chapter 12).

From a labor market standpoint the hyphenated American becomes very important, because our nation's changing demographics will result in a limited labor supply. During the years 1985 to 2000 there will be a dramatic increase in the age group 45–64, and dramatic reductions in the age group 14–44. An aging work force causes changes in the demands for services and economic support programs, and imposes questions about our capacity to increase productivity, which is currently in decline.

Many minorities are U.S. citizens (primarily blacks and Hispanics), but there is also a large number of illegal aliens, 200,000 of whom were deported by the federal government in 1970. By 1977 this number had climbed to 950,000 and the trend is continuing its upward spiral. But the illegal aliens who have been caught and deported represent only 10 percent of the undocumented aliens in this country. Obviously the need for workers in entry-level jobs continues in agriculture and service occupations. Thus the new waves of hyphenated Americans may be viewed as the latest generation of minorities in America's labor force.

The Boat People represent yet another wave. When the South China Sea was afloat with this tragic human cargo with no legitimate port of destination, President Carter extended a hand to them. Also, in 1980 over 100,000 Cubans fled to join the Cuban community in the United States. Immigration, as reported by the U.S. Immigration and Naturalization Service for 1977, showed Cuba providing 66,000 new immigrants; Mexico, 45,000; the Philippines, 35,000; Korea, 30,000; and the West Indies, 27,000.

Certainly it can be a humane employment effort to review and establish a national policy for this next generation of Americans. In 1977 President Carter proposed regularizing the illegal immigrants' status after seven years. Congress then created a Select Commission on Immigration and Refugee Policy in 1978, which is scheduled to report in 1981. With the report of the Select Commission on Immigration and Refugee Policy comes the opportunity to review our immigration policy and its relevance to our foreign and domestic needs. The need to provide society with an entry-level labor supply is an essential element of a refugee and alien policy. As will be discussed later, the challenge is to provide a cohesive policy that balances traditional humanitarian principles with economic reality.

In addition to being a refuge of a number of homeless and oppressed people, the United States also provides an opportunity for a better life. The available work force, combined with a change in work ethic, creates a shortage of people willing to fill entry-level positions. This latest stock being introduced to the "melting pot" will probably produce the same benefits to our society that we saw in the European immigration a hundred years ago. Fortunately, we should be in a better position to understand the needs of this group and be able to provide it, as well as minorities already in this country, with the social support system that will enable them to be successful in fulfilling their aspirations.

THE CONTEXT OF MINORITY EMPLOYMENT

In approaching this issue the context of minority employment must be clarified. Therefore we must focus upon minorities in their social-developmental environment, in organizations, and as pressure groups that organizations face before we can address humane and productivity issues.

Minorities and Their Environment

The social environment of minorities has changed in recent years. The history of minorities is a cycle of unemployment. This cycle involves not having a job, being on welfare, having no motivation to work, finding no job, receiving no training, developing no self-esteem, and dependency upon society. This is a recurring cycle and one that must be broken if the problem is to be resolved. Obviously it might be broken by simply employing welfare recipients. But requiring society and organizations to merely provide jobs is neither humane nor productive. Furthermore, in order for minorities to be not merely employed but successful often requires training and counseling, to develop the necessary cognitive, behavioral, and attitude changes essential for maintaining a job.

Despite the protestations and the efforts of American industry, the problem of minority employment has not gone away; it has increased! Close to eight million blacks live below the poverty level, while only seven million were below the poverty level over ten years ago. According to a 1979 study by the Department of Housing and Urban Development, most minorities still meet evidence of discrimination 75 percent of the time in attempting to rent a house and 62 percent of the time when attempting to buy a home, and 13 percent of black homes suffer severe physical flaws, such as inadequate plumbing or heat—twice the rate for white homes. Further, blacks are six times as likely to be murdered as whites and according to a report by the National Urban League, nearly 50 percent receive some form of public assistance (1).

Thus the American dream neither has nor is likely to become a reality for minorities in this country, especially when it is recognized that the revised 1981 federal budget has cut 20 billion in funds originally earmarked for domestic programs such as job training and food stamps—while many of the minorities in this country suffer from poor nutrition and rat bites—and fuel bill subsidies. Despite these conditions black self-esteem has increased throughout the 1970s; now it is not lower than whites, but has caused a blaming of the system rather than a blaming of the self, especially among the young (2).

An important element in the cycle of unemployment and poverty appears to be the socialization of minority children. The parents and siblings of minorities are more frequently cited to minority children as models by the mothers of minorities than by nonminority mothers. Certainly it is assumed that minority children have relatively few models for high educational and vocational achievement, but more importantly they often do not have a realistic understanding of what kind of educational program they must follow to attain vocational goals. In fact, job motives of minorities and nonminorities seem to differ significantly. Nonminorities are more interested in securing "a very interesting job" while blacks are more interested in obtaining a job "which you are absolutely sure of keeping" (3).

Finally, two topics stand out as central for the social-economic development of minorities: leadership and education. The leadership must come from minorities themselves; it cannot come primarily from well-intentioned whites. The development of minority leadership is componded by the general distrust of any leadership of any race, and only can be overcome by members of the minority community emerging by working first-hand in these communities. Nonminorities may help the emergence of leadership by providing resources to help minority communities resolve their own problems, but must avoid "puppeteering" change if the minority leadership is to develop. In education there is a parallel. Quality education for minorities must be achieved without destroying self-confidence through competition in desegregated classrooms (4).

Thus there are many problems faced by minorities who are attempting change. But it is extremely difficult to change given that basic needs are unsatisfied and given the hopelessness generated by a history of unrewarded efforts. If minorities are attempting constant gratification of basic needs, or mere survival, it is difficult to expect rapid learning and acquisition of middle class values and norms. When people are hungry they may engage in behavior that is not acceptable to society (and may be punished). Once basic needs are satisfied, perhaps the value changes that society desires may be forthcoming. But this raises a serious ethical question. Should programs attempt value changes, or should they merely attempt to provide opportunities for skill acquisition through incentives whereby minorities become self-sufficient?

Minorities in Organizations

What then do we know about minorities as a work force? Most of the research has focused on blacks (5) and not other ethnic groups, and thus the discussion here will be primarily based on the data available on black populations in organizations, although many of the same problems can be related to other minority cultures.

In the late 1960s and early 1970s there appeared much work related to minorities in organizations, especially the hard-core unemployed (HCU). The impetus for these efforts came primarily from the Civil Rights Act of 1964 and the numerous government programs that were to follow (e.g., Manpower Assistance, Work Incentive, etc.). These programs created a new work force heretofore underutilized in organizations, which often entered the labor market labeled the "hard-core unemployed." This was obviously a new sample for the application of the tools of industrial psychologists who became busy applying psychometric instruments to this new population. Therefore we have learned something of this movement from industrial psychologists who have studied blacks as a poverty culture, and relatively recently from studies concerned with the upward mobility of minorities in organizations. There has been little ressearch on minorities in managerial positions. Consequently most of this chapter will focus on employees below managerial levels, although what is known about the experiences of black managers will be considered towards the end of the chapter. The HCU are a specific group of employees who were primarily characterized by age and lack of employment for a prolonged period of time. This is the group that received federal funds under the Manpower Assistance grants, and the research focused upon variables that were thought to aid in the retention and performance of the HCU.

The HCU employee is in a complex social system. The organization provides the training and job, yet community organizations, government agencies, informal peer groups, and the HCU worker's family are all components of the social system that influence the HCU worker's behavior. In each context there are roles and structures (e.g., job, promotion, and pay opportunities) that influence the HCU worker's behavior. Consideration of these factors is necessary for understanding HCU employees; too often researchers have narrowed the social system to the HCU worker, trainer, and supervisor (6).

Social systems are composed of multiple, interdependent variables. Regrettably, most HCU studies focus primarily on the HCU worker and how to change him or her to fit the organization. On the other hand, a social system model focuses on broader changes at the individual, organizational, or societal level. The following is a brief review of variables included in a social systems analysis of the HCU in entry-level positions.

Age. There have been a few studies related to the age of the HCU and work withdrawal. The general results were that younger workers were more likely to leave the organization whether it meant leaving a training program, regular employment, or higher rates of absenteeism. Only one study was found that demonstrated no relationship between age and work withdrawal (7).

Sex. The data seems to support the finding that women HCUs are retained at a higher rate than men, and in one study the retention rate was higher than that of non-HCU women.

Family Environment. As might be expected, unmarried HCUs have higher turnover rates (7). Main breadwinners are also less likely to drop out, and if they rent or own their own home they are more likely to stay (7) and earn higher wages. The results for family size are mixed. Some researchers found no relationship with HCU behavior, while one study (7) found a relationship between family size and retention. Generally these studies point to the need for organizational rewards for the HCU to aid the family.

Birthplace. The geographical area where the trainee spent formative years seems related to HCU turnover. Higher retention rates were reported for those born in the rural South and the West Indies or Latin America as opposed to those from the urban North. This supports finding on rural-urban differences and suggests that rural-born HCUs might be more compatible with organizations.

Education. Evidence on the relationship between education and various criteria is ambiguous. There have been reports of significant positive relationships between education and job retention. But in one of these studies (8), the finding holds only for the black HCUs. Other studies have shown that scholastic achievement does not affect retention. There have been reports, however, that scholastic achievement has been longitudinally associated with earnings and promotions.

Work History. Usually a predictor of future behavior is past behavior. There are reports that terminations were greater for those with more than two jobs in the last two years as compared with those who held less than two jobs in the same time. Other studies report similar relationships (7), while one refuted this finding.

Personality. The results exploring the role of personality characteristics have not been encouraging. Several studies have obtained few significant results. These studies have involved orientation toward work, personal efficacy, and attitudes about the Protestant Ethic. There was a report (7) that trainees who rated their own ability as high were more likely to be considered highest in performance during a training program. Also individuals who indicated a strong need to be seen as smart by their boss and who perceived themselves as having a high level of energy and activity were less likely to drop out of an orientation program (7).

Supervision. Effective supervision appears to be so important that the *Report of the National Advisory Commission on Civil Disorders* (9) recommended that supervisors be given special training to deal with the hard-core unemployed as one of the basic strategies to reduce urban unemployment rates. This recommendation was not surprising, because supervision has long been mentioned as a critical variable in the performance of most employees, regardless of their employment or cultural histories. Generally supportive supervisors who produce climates characterized by friendliness, encouragement, and courtesies have been found most effective (10). Close supervision has been mentioned as generally dissatisfying to the hard-core unemployed (6) and described as a means of gaining social control over the hard-core unemployed trainess (11), or as an attempt to control the hard-core unemployed due to differing perceptions of job behavior norms (12). A longitudinal study of supervision and the HCU generally supported these findings. The hard-core unemployed's experience with supervisors the first six months on the job appears to be important for initial and future hard-core unemployed job success. The nature of the relationship seems to be that when the HCU perceive a supervisor as considerate or supportive they tend to perform more successfully, whereas when a supervisor is perceived as structuring work activities highly, the HCU tend to perform less successfully. It was further indicated that the concurrent relationship between supervisory consideration and HCU job success does not remain after the HCU's early experience with the company.

Training and Counseling. The content of training has been found critical in retaining HCUs (13, 14). Training has been found to improve the individual's sense of personal efficacy about accomplishment. Also research has indicated that while training can have a positive impact on knowledge acquisition (16), the impact of training on job retention and performance seems negligible. Counseling can also influence retention, but the nature of the counselor seems to play an important role. One study that analyzed the sources of attractivness of counselors and trainers found that the HCU preferred black to white counselors. An analysis of trainees' perceptions indicated that they felt black counselors stressed middle-class values more than white counselors. This finding would seem to indicate that HCU trainees were more willing to accept middle-class socialization attempts from a black than a white counselor. For the most part the effects of counseling methods have gone unresearched.

Peers and Social Self-Esteem. Supportiveness of one's co-workers also appears to be an important factor. In one study HCU workers' perceptions of the supportiveness of their peers and others in the organization to new workers were positively related to supervisory ratings of performance. In general, the more supportive the trainee considered his peers and others in the organization, the more likely he was to be evaluated by his supervisor as competent, congenial, friendly, and conscientious, but not necessarily as more reliable.

Pay. Another organizational characteristic that bears on HCU workers' behavior is pay. A number of studies did examine the effect of pay levels. One found pay was a major predictor among groups (e.g., blacks, young people, and males) that were more likely to terminate and thus served to reduce the propensity to terminate in these groups (8). Other studies (7) indicate a positive relationship between pay and job retention and between pay and completion of training (17).

Minority Supervisors. Another area of concern is the movement to minorities in managerial jobs. Little has been written on this topic except in the popular press, where there are complaints about a lack of promotional opportunities (18). One area in particular that appears to be quite neglected is information on the training and performance of minority first-level supervisors. The little research that has focused on this topic suggested that the performance of black supervisors was evaluated on their social behavior and not their job-related behavior (19).

Part of the paucity of data on minority supervisors is a result of the reporting procedures of the Census Bureau, which combines line supervisors with "craftsmen and other kindred workers" and does not separate them in such a way that a more comprehensive analysis can be conducted. As with other aspects of the experiences of minorities in work organizations, research on minority supervisors is essential if future efforts to develop and promote members of minority groups into managerial positions are to be founded upon an empirical base rather than upon social scientists' perceptions of the needs of minority groups (20).

Pressure Groups and Legislation

Clearly organizations face much pressure to hire, train, retain, promote, and enhance the welfare of minorities. At the same time that minority groups pressure for the "special" treatment, no idea is probably as unpopular with society as a whole as the idea of favoritism of one group over another in these areas. During the last two decades minorities have been successful in obtaining legislation such as the Civil Rights Law of 1964 (as amended in 1973), which has raised the issue of special treatment. Discussions of this problem require understanding of three concepts: affirmative action, adverse impact, and job relatedness.

Affirmative action grew out of Executive Order 11246 (with Order No. 4 and Revised Order No. 4) to assure that federal contractors not only did not discriminate in employment but also assumed the burden for "positive" efforts to seek, hire, train, and otherwise advance the numbers of minorities in the employ of federal contractors. This is quite a different stance from the assurance that the organization would not discriminate (i.e., violate the Civil Rights Law). The Executive Order placed an additional and much greater burden on employers to become responsible for the advancement of minorities or face the loss of federal contracts or debarment from seeking federal contracts. Although this threat certainly existed, the Office of Federal Contract Compliance Programs (OFCCP) debarred few firms. In fact, when the OFCCP was threatened by President Carter's reorganization of the federal agencies concerned with equal employment opportunity and affirmative action, the agency debarred twice as many firms in one year as it had in its entire history. This single flurry of activity may have saved the agency from being folded into one of the remaining agencies responsible for equal employment affirmative action (i.e., the Equal Employment Opportunity Commission, Office of Personnel Management, and the Departments of Labor, Justice, and Treasury).

There is now little question about the effectiveness of minority groups in bringing about legislation, but more importantly they have been effective, despite public outcry, in insuring the necessary federal regulations and administrative capacities to assure that compliance could be pursued. The regulations are in the form of the required procedures, while the administrative capacities are of course the agencies or units within agencies responsible for equal employment opportunity-affirmative action efforts.

The major regulations that exist are affirmative action plans required for federal contractors and "voluntary" plans for all other employers (usually with a labor force of 50 or greater). Essentially these plans are an organization's commitments to affirmative action when the organization is a federal contractor and a sign of "good faith" on the part of "voluntary" employers (i.e., nonfederal contractors). Thus the signing of a contract that included a firm's commitment to hire and advance minorities gave efficacy to the laws. Many organizations then felt the need to have a voluntary Affirmative Action Plan (AAP) despite the lack of a federal contract. Clearly the considerable time and effort required to put together an AAP is evidence of the power of minority group pressure, just as is the statement "an equal employment opportunity employer" on an organization's stationery, recruiting brochures, and so on.

The other aspects of the pressure that minority groups have aided in fostering are the documents developed by the remaining equal employment opportunity agencies, which attempt to set forth the standards against which employers are to monitor the degree of discrimination and fairness of employment procedures. The basic document in this area is the "Uniform Guidelines on Employee Selection Procedures" published in the *Federal Register* on August 25, 1978 (21). These guidelines attempt two major objectives. The first is to show how "adverse impact" may be calculated. That is, how can it be determined if an employer is discriminatory or not? Many methods have been used ranging from simple comparisons with the labor market to sophisticated statistical probability estimates. However, one basic calculation that is now being used is the 4/5 rule. This is a simple measure designed as a trigger to indicate disproportionate minority representation in hiring, training, promotion, termination, and so on.

For example, assume an organization has 100 nonminority applicants and 20 minority applicants for the position of welder. Assume also that there were 40 openings and that 35 nonminorities and five minorities were hired. Would there be adverse impact against minorities in hiring? The calculation would be as follows:

$$\frac{35 \text{ hires}}{100 \text{ applicants}} = 35\% \text{ nonminority hiring rate} \tag{1}$$

$$\frac{5 \text{ hires}}{20 \text{ applicants}} = 25\% \text{ minority hiring rate} \tag{2}$$

$$\frac{25\%}{35\%} = 71\% \tag{3}$$

Since the percent of minority hiring rate is less than 80 percent of the nonminority hiring rate, adverse impact would indeed have been found. The same analysis could be applied to any stage in the hiring process (e.g., interviewing) to discover what step in the hiring process demonstrates adverse impact. It could also be applied to any rate or flow of minorities in organizations such as the rates of admission to training programs, rates of termination, merit pay, and so on.

The second step in assessing discrimination is to discover if there is any defensible reason for this adverse impact. If not, then racial discrimination is assumed. The only reasons that can be used to defend a case, where adverse impact has been shown, are job related. Job related reasons are essentially demonstrating the validity of the decision making process used to determine who was promoted or hired. This is very difficult for most employers, as the guidelines are based upon the Standards for Educational and Psychological Tests (1974), which most employers find difficult to understand and indeed difficult to apply. However, there really is no alternative other than to show that a legitimate rationale was used in making the decisions reached. But many employers balk at spending funds to develop job-related testing procedures that can be shown to predict, to some reasonable degree, future job success.

Thus we find organizations faced with competing pressures to treat minorities favorably or unfavorably. Employers are faced with being taken to court for failure to comply with employment standards that have been cited in court decisions on how minorities are to be scrutinized, standards that seem to have the efficacy to determine what is or is not discrimination. Amid these pressures to hire and develop minorities within the confines of the guidelines and without alienating nonminority employees is where employers find themselves. Despite the level of these pressures a new and potentially stronger pressure is emerging as has been seen in recent Court cases (*Bakke* v. *Regents of the University of California; Weber* v. *Kaiser Aluminum*). This is "reverse discrimination," and it appears as if the Fourteenth Amendment, which provides equal treatment under the law, as well as Title VII, will serve to increase the pressure on organizations to pay closer attention to all decision making pertaining to employees for fear of becoming involved in lengthy litigation, regardless of the race of the plaintiff!

MAKING ORGANIZATIONS HUMANE FOR MINORITIES AND PRODUCTIVE FOR ORGANIZATIONS

Ideally all organizations would be humane to all individuals in the sense of encouraging and helping them to fulfill their potential as employees. With respect to minorities, however, there are specific factors that must be addressed by organizations, because of past deficiencies in their treatment of minorities. Thus we—society as a whole—have now asked, through legislation, moral suasion, and pressure groups, that organizations act in an affirmative and humanitarian way to be more responsive to the needs of minorities in all aspects of employment. That is, the means by which organizations have traditionally treated minorities have been challenged, and in doing so the organizations' treatment of all employees for both humanitarian and productivity objectives has been challenged also. In fact, although the employment of minorities is often questioned in terms of productivity, the humanitarian objectives involved in employing minorities can often be argued from the standpoint of productivity. This is to say that much of what will follow about what organizations must do in the hiring and development of minorities simply makes good business sense and is consistent with the efficiency and effectiveness ethic espoused by American organizations.

Organizations in this country are essentially charged, by their shareholders and society as a whole, with the responsibility of producing quality goods and services through efficient means of production. At the same time they must generate an adequate return on invested capital. If efficient and effective production of goods and services merely means the optimal use of all resources, including human resources, if making organizations humane involves compassion and sympathy for those distressed by economic and racial circumstance, the pursuit of interests is consistent with the long-run financial interests of the organization.

What then can organizations do to become more humane with respect to minorities? There are many efforts that organizations can initiate readily. These are in the areas of hiring, training and counseling, providing feedback and rewards, and promotions and mobility. Generally many of these involve no more than strict adherence to many of the requirements of the *Uniform Guidelines on Employee Selection Procedures*, which in most respects merely articulates good professional practice, and following an affirmative action program.

Hiring

In the area of hiring radical changes are necessary. First an exhaustive review of jobs in terms of their content is necessary. It may seem obvious, but there do exist very real problems in defining the content of jobs. Despite the availability of numerous methods of job analysis, organizations do not seem to devote much attention to understanding the content of jobs (22). This is to say that if more sophisticated methods of job analysis were employed, many of the problems that have caused organizations to exclude minorities would have been overcome long ago. Jobs need to be scrutinized in much more detailed ways in order to understand the specific job content, because the content of a job should dictate the selection procedure used in the hiring process, as shown in Figure 11.1. Jobs must be viewed in a way that first focuses upon "what is to be done," not upon what kind of person is needed. The tasks to be performed must be identified in terms that enable the organization to define precisely what skills a person must have to perform the task.

Skill-based selection begins with job analysis that identifies tasks to be performed. It directs a search for persons who possess the skills to perform the job or who at least have the basic abilities from which the skills can be developed (i.e., training). The focus on skills reduces the use of such artificial criteria such as a high school education and college degrees, which have kept minorities out of many jobs that they would have been able to perform. For example, requiring a high school degree for the job of an assembly line worker in an automobile manufacturing plant would certainly have kept many blacks from being employed and could clearly be in violation of the Guidelines because the selection criteria were not job related. This is not to say that in some jobs educational criteria might not be a good sign of a person's potential for job success, but even in such obvious instances (e.g., graduation from a business college for employment as a secretary) it might be better to sample the level of skill proficiency rather than assume that because the person had provided us with some sign of potential, we actually

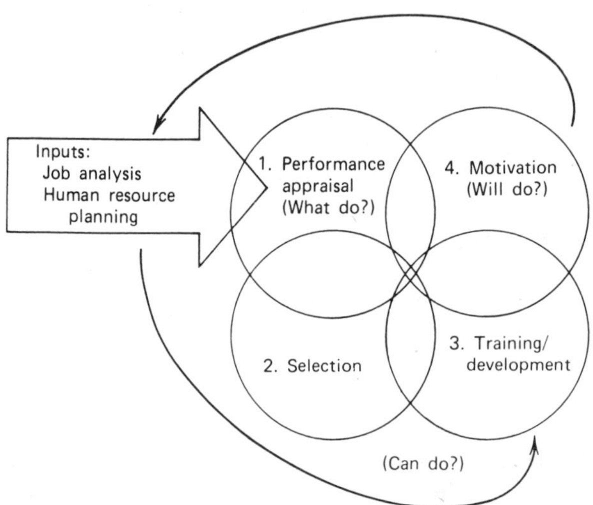

Figure 11.1 The human resource system in organizations.

have a sample of his or her job performance based on items selected from job content (23).

Skill based selection requires measures that closely approximate job content proficiency testing rather than techniques that are self-reports of potential (e.g., resumes and interviews) or that measure levels of verbal skills not really required on the job. Such methods result in creating false negatives (Figure 11.2) and clearly reject minorities who could do a job but were not given the chance to do so because of artificial, non-job-related hiring criteria. Therefore a critical first step in making employment more accessible to minorities is to conduct more sophisticated analyses of jobs whereby the critical tasks are identified and job-related skills are tested through work sampling techniques or simulations. For example, in assembly jobs, instead of seeking application blank and interview data and conducting a plant tour, the time used for these activities could be more efficiently spent in requesting the applicant to perform critical segments of the job in a vestibule setting. The items tested should be developed from a thorough examination of the job and should be determined by management and incumbents to be critical to the successful performance of the job (and should be able to be performed without much training). All applicants would then experience the same work sample and be scored on their performance in the same time frame using a standardized scoring procedure. We would not think of hiring a typist without a work sample test, and we should do the same for welders, machine operators, tree planters, yard laborers, blast furnace helpers, and other workers. Further, such procedures are much easier to defend before EEOC than are unvalidated procedures that make heroic leaps between the actual job and "signs" of future performance such as degrees and tests of mathematical and verbal abilities.

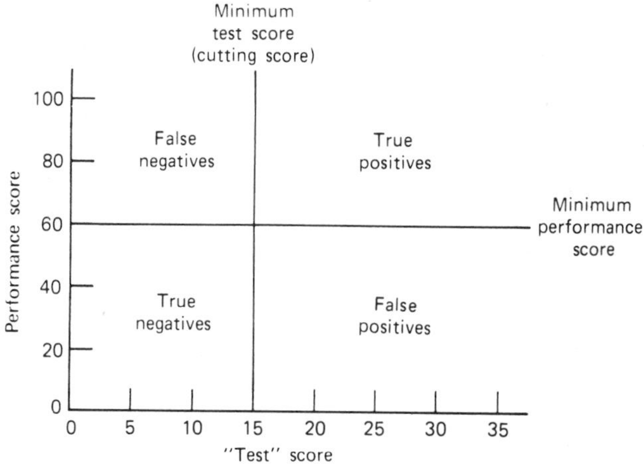

Figure 11.2 An analysis of testing results.

Organizations can also pursue both productivity and humane treatment by better planning of their human resource needs rather than by adding or laying off workers unnecessarily or using overtime only in times of crises or when persuaded to do so by a powerful manager. Human resources are expensive, and organizations must plan for their acquisition based on levels of output required, determine the level of staffing needed to reach varying levels of output, and insure that staff expansion does not lead to dead-end jobs for minorities. The quantitative tools available for such human resource planning are coming into common use to help resolve an area in which more slack in the management of organizations has existed than perhaps any other area. The tools (Markov chains, linear programming, path analysis, structural equations, etc.) enable firms to more precisely predict staffing needs and internal human resource flows (24). For the humane concerns in the treatment of minorities, they also permit special applications for affirmative action planning whereby minority employment goals in all areas of the organization can be established based on internal and external supplies of labor. Other factors, such as training times for full proficiency, can be included in the development of a staffing system that will permit effective planning and help the personnel department to anticipate work force needs and to meet these needs by timely hiring and training.

Training and Counseling

Another area that needs attention for humane reasons is the supportive program often required for the inclusion of minorities in organizations. These training and counseling programs must be maintained to insure that the necessary internal support systems mentioned earlier are available to deal with the special problems of minorities. The training aspects of these programs must be designed around real jobs and the development of real job skills (14). Such programs must provide feedback to not only let minorities know where the stand in terms of job performance but also aid in the building of self-esteem that goes with being successful in learning a new task. The persons training minorities should also be good listeners, have significant social insight, and be supportive of minority efforts; at the same time they should be demanding of performance and willing to supportively confront minorities when the latter fail to perform successfully. Other types of counseling may also need to be provided such as on transportation matters, employee benefits, and current medical problems, and special help in how to successfully interact with other employees. Good orientation programs that candidly tell employees what they may expect of the organization and what the organization expects of them at the outset can go a long way in avoiding serious problems and violations of expectations that may later occur.

The use of feedback and rewards cannot be overemphasized. Feedback that is job specific and stated in behavioral terms can be very instrumental in the successful development of minority employees. This requires well-designed performance appraisal instruments (see Figure 11.1), based on job content. Thus if minority employees are to be employed in counter work at a fast food restaurant and to be evaluated on a dimension of performance such as "customer relations," the specific behaviors required need to be noted. An evaluation on employee customer relations performance that merely says "had bad customer attitude" is not adequate; the behavior required for effective customer relations must be defined. For example, it might be necessary to specify such behavior in terms such as eye contact, smiling, and voice intonation. These may need to be further specified, for example, smiling defined as "corners up, teeth showing." Such detail may sound ridiculous, but if we are to evaluate employees we must do so on a set of unequivocal behaviors and not merely on generalized categories that assess people in the abstract and not their performance as a specific set of observable job-related behaviors. Such specification in orientation can not only be a very valuable training tool, but it also is a very effective retort to plaintiffs' attorneys when questions are raised about the criteria used and feedback given over problems with probation, termination, or promotion decisions. The advantages of using videotape equipment to train minorities on specific behavioral expectations when it comes to public contact or many other aspects of jobs is obvious—and effective.

Promotion

Another important issue is the promotion and mobility of minorities. Every organization needs to perform an analysis of the internal mobility rates of minority employees compared to nonminority employees to determine the rates of progress and time required to move within the organization. Obviously it is not enough merely to hire minorities for entry-level jobs; there must be movement upward into higher-level technical jobs as well as managerial jobs. This requires special developmental programs to prepare minorities for more sophisticated jobs and for the transition from nonmanagerial to managerial jobs. Thus, again, skill based training must be provided, especially if the organization is operating under an affirmative action agreement and wishes to ensure that minorities, especially in managerial jobs, move from the ranks and succeed in higher level positions. Further, the support systems for this transition beyond merely training are helpful. This may be accomplished by forming informal discussion groups of minority managers or technicians, which meet regularly to discuss common job problems and how problems have been confronted and resolved by other minority managers, or "buddy" systems in which experienced minority managers are assigned to new minority managers to aid in the transition by offering support and counsel on resource availability, alternative problem solving methods, and so on.

In some ways the ultimate test of efforts to overcome discrimination in the work place can be measured by the access afforded to minorities to reach the highest levels in organizations. As we shall see below, much remains to be done in this respect.

Entry into Management

There has been little research on blacks in corporate management. One reason for this lack of inquiry is that prior to 1960 few blacks held white collar and professional jobs. However, since then there have been significant changes. As Jones (25) observed, "A new job market for college-educated black Americans was emerging during the 1960s and many black college students were finding previously closed doors to management ajar, and in some companies, actually open" (p. 106).

However, Jones found that black managers have experienced a number of problems. Based on an extensive review of the literature on the reports of black managers, Jones concluded:

> The major problems as perceived by blacks who were hired for management careers in the 1960s related to upward mobility in the management structure. The black managers complained that they were hired as tokens and placed in dead end positions which offered little opportunity for advancement beyond the entry levels of management. The black managers perceived these token placements as "showcase" positions created by corporations for handling public and community relations between the corporations and their special markets, i.e., black markets.
>
> The black managers felt that the social and legal pressures for civil rights and equal opportunity modified the overt discriminatory hiring practices of corporations, but that these practices had been translated into subtle forms of institutional racism which served as a deterrent to black mobility in management. In other words, black managers felt the corporations shifted the point at which they began to apply discriminatory practices against their black management employees. Blacks were no longer excluded altogether from the ranks of management as was the case in the past. Now black managers perceived the corporate employers applying the discriminatory practices to stunt their mobility from entry level positions to middle and upper level managerial jobs. Blacks commonly referred to this corporate development as the "middle-management barrier" to black managers' career progress.

Jones also reported that corporate managers noted the "underrepresentation" of blacks in key managerial positions, but attributed this fact to such causes as cultural differences and a lack of education or training, skills, and appropriate attitudes. Jones concluded:

> White corporate management alleges that the paucity of blacks in management is due primarily to the lack of qualified blacks available for

> hiring and the inability of blacks to fit productively into the organizations. On the other hand, black managers claim that the corporate opportunity structure is "closed" to them and that the legacies of discrimination and institutional racist practices, both subtle and pervasive, impede their upward mobility. Both groups' arguments appear to have some validity, but neither group seems to have relaxed its allegations long enough to offer a sound strategy aimed at resolving the dilemma. (p. 122-123)

Jones also compared the experiences of black MBAs with a matched sample of white MBAs that were 5 to 10 years into their management careers. Among other things, it was found that the black MBAs began their careers in jobs that appeared to be quite similar to their white counterparts but at somewhat higher starting salaries. However, after 5 to 10 years, the annual income of the average white MBA was $5,182 more. (The reasons for this difference are complex and were explored fully. Detailed treatment of these reasons is beyond the scope of this chapter, but Jones reported that 91 percent of the variance in salary could be accounted for by different characteristics of the people in the study rather than by "racial discrimination" as the term is normally used.) Finally, the black MBAs in Jones's survey had attained significantly less authority than had the matched group of whites. Moreover, the increase in authority for the whites was associated with far greater economic returns than it was for blacks. While Jones warns us that his findings are more suggestive than definitive, his research and that of other investigators does indicate that while at entry level position the fight against discrimination appears to have been successful, a great deal remains to be done "to ensure an open road to the top based on job performance" (25, p. 258).

CONCLUSION

By following the above suggestions, the humanitarian objectives of offering meaningful employment to minorities can be accomplished while at the same time the productivity objectives of an organization are met. First, those included are persons who have not had much of an opportunity to hold entry-level positions. If the skills required are normally distributed in both minority and nonminority populations, it is to be expected that in hiring for an entry-level position the probability of selecting an employee with the potential of possessing or acquiring successful job-related skills is higher with a minority population than with a population (nonminority) whose labor supply has been exhausted by prudent selection. Second, if the admonitions above are followed, productivity should be enhanced in two ways. One way is by developing skill-based selection and training methodologies for both minority and nonminority populations by which an organization should be in a position to increase its rates of productivity, especially if performance-based criteria are used for the allocation of organizational rewards. Another outcome should be a reduction in the costs of productivity such as turnover, absenteeism, poor quality work, waste, sabotage, and so on. That is, if organizational support and counseling systems are effective, as well as the training and evaluation systems, we would expect to see a reduction in these costs, especially from a population that has now been given the chance to participate and improve their livelihood, the livelihood of their children, and many others around them. Finally, to the degree that these procedures are followed by most organizations in society, our nation's human resources will be employed most effectively and the overall quality of life for all members of society will be improved.

REFERENCES

1. Kaufman, J. Big city ghettos, life is worse than in the 60s tumult. *Wall Street Journal,* May 23, 1980, 1.
2. Porter, J. R. & Washington, R. E. Black identity and self esteem: A review of studies of black self-concept 1968–1978. *Annual Review of Sociology,* 1979, **55,** 53–74.
3. Singer, S. & Stefflore, B. A note on racial differences in job values and desires. *Journal of Social Psychology,* 1956, **43,** 333–337.
4. Baughman, E. *Black Americans.* New York: Academic Press, 1971.
5. Miller, K. S. & Dreger, R. M. (eds.). *Comparative Studies of Blacks and Whites in the United States.* New York: Seminar Press, 1973.
6. Goodman, P. S. Hiring, training and retaining the hard core. *Industrial Relations,* 1969, **9,** 54–66.
7. Hinrichs, J. R. Implementation of manpower training: The private firm experience. Unpublished paper, IBM Corporation, White Plains, N.Y., 1970.
8. Shlensky, B. *Determinants of Turnover in NAB-JOBS Programs to Employ the Disadvantaged.* Unpublished doctoral dissertation, MIT, Boston, 1970.
9. *Report of the National Advisory Commission on Civil Disorders.* Washington, D.C.: U.S. Government Printing Office, 1968.
10. National Industrial Conference Board. *Managing Programs to Employ the Disadvantaged.* Studies in Personnel Policy No. 219. Author. New York, 1970.
11. Krosney, H. *Beyond Welfare: Poverty in the Supercity.* New York: Holt, Rinehart and Winston, 1966.
12. Triandis, H. & Malpass, R. Studies of black and white interaction in job settings. *Journal of Applied Social Psychology,* 1971, **1,** 101–117.
13. Salipante, P. & Goodman, P. Training, counseling and retention of the hard-core unemployed. *Journal of Applied Psychology,* 1976, **61,** 1–11. See also D. Ford (Ed.). *Reading in Minority Group Relations.* LaJolla, Calif.: University Associates, 1976.

14. Drennan, W. (Ed.). *The Fourth Strike: Hiring and Training the Disadvantaged.* New York: American Management Association, 1970.

15. Purcell, T. & Webster, R. Window on the hard-core world. *Harvard Business Review,* 1969, **47,** 118–129.

16. Beatty, R. W. A two year study of hard-core unemployed clerical workers: Effects of scholastic achievement, clerical skill, and self-esteem on job success. *Personnel Psychology,* 1975, **28,** 165–173.

17. Lipsky, D., Drotning, J. & Fottler, M. Some correlates of trainee success in a complex on-the-job training program. *The Quarterly Review of Economics and Business,* 1971, **11**(2), 42–60.

18. Kaufman, J. Black executives say prejudice still impedes their path to the top. *Wall Street Journal,* February 9, 1980, 1.

19. Beatty, R. Blacks as supervisors: A study of training, job performance, and employers' expectations. *Academy of Management Journal,* 1973, **16**(2).

20. Gordon, J. What shapes poverty programs. *Manpower,* 1971, **3**(4).

21. Uniform Guidelines on Employee Selection Procedures, *Federal Register.* Washington, D.C.: U.S. Government Printing Office, August 25, 1978.

22. Beatty, R. & Schneier, C. *Personnel Administration: An Experimental/Skill Building Approach.* Reading, Mass.: Addison-Wesley, 1977, Exercise 3.

23. Weinmont, P. & Campbell, J. Signs, samples and criteria. *Journal of Applied Psychology,* 1968, **52,** 372–376.

24. Milkovich, G. & Mahoney, T. Human resource planning and PAIR policy. In D. Yoder and H. Heneman Jr., (Eds.). *ASPA Handbook of Personnel and Industrial Relations,* IV. Washington: Bureau of National Affairs, 1976. See also Alvarez, R. Industrial discrimination in organizations. In R. Alvarez, K. Lutterman and Associates, *Discrimination in Organizations.* San Francisco: Jossey-Bass, 1979, & J. Livingston, *Fair Game?* San Francisco: W. H. Freeman and Co., 1979.

25. Jones, W. L. *Determinants of earnings and job authority for black and white MBA managers.* Unpublished doctoral dissertation. Washington University, St. Louis, May 1980.

—12—

Women in Organizations

Sharon Tucker

The struggle for women's equality in the work place has gathered momentum over the last decade until today it is one of the major social issues of our time. Women are in the work force in record numbers, and as they come to work to meet pressing economic need and to satisfy career ambitions, many of them expect more money and better positions than women have had in the past. Organizations, however, are creatures of habit. The coordination of large numbers of people requires establishing routines for getting things done, and these routines get in the way of adaptation to new situations. While many organizations have attempted to integrate women more fully, many have failed to examine and modify their standard operating procedures. Failure to address the root causes of female work segregation and sex bias has resulted in organizations that are less than humane work places and depress the productive potential of women.

ORGANIZATIONAL ROUTINES

Patterns of interaction, from the level of the small group to the level of the total organization, serve useful functions. They make life with other people more predictable by establishing rules and expectations that limit behavior; they reduce conflict by institutionalizing value priorities and hierarchies of power and status; and they reduce the costs of the search for valuable information by limiting the sources of information. These patterns of interaction are necessary for the smooth operation of any organization. But many of the institutionalized patterns that are so useful to organizations and members of organizations perpetuate bias against women and provide stubborn resistance to any attempts at change. A central theme of this chapter is that women are kept out of higher positions in the organization at least as much by established methods of getting things done as by attitudes, sex role stereotypes, and negative beliefs about women's competency.

Organizations strive for predictability (1) and set up routines that both make life predictable and maintain the privileged position of those who control the organization (2, 3). Cyert and March (1) have argued that organizations will go to great lengths to maintain routines that solve short-run problems even when those routines fail to meet adequately long-term problems. Often routines become so strongly associated with a current desired outcome and the future is unpredictable enough that organization members lose the ability to explore new ways of meeting needs that are just around the corner. Of course the quest for predictability is one factor that induces the perpetuation of routines. Perhaps equally important is the quest for control.

Any interruption of routines is likely to upset the power balance achieved with the routine, leading to a period of chaos and conflict. Everyone in management whose work flows more smoothly as a result of routines and whose power is protected by the routine has a vested interest in resisting change and maintaining the status quo. In modern American organizations those in power are nearly always men who have a clear interest in maintaining their positions and therefore support the organizational routines that give them power in the organization. The implication of these power dynamics is that women find it difficult to break into male positions, because those men who may be displaced or passed over for promotion support routines that keep women out. Meyer and Lee (4) found the most resistance to equal opportunity programs from first line supervisors who were likely to be put in competition with women promoted to those positions.

A third factor supportiong established routines is the fact that changing routines is costly. An organization is a system of interrelated components (5). Each time one component changes, ripples are felt throughout the system. New personnel policies for hiring, promotion, and training, if they really make a change in organizational routines, are felt far beyond the personnel department. Policies for integrating women require change at all levels of the organization. The cost for line managers who are suddenly working with women is that they must stop and examine every behavior before taking action. Rather than acting spontaneously and without self-consciousness, they must take the time and energy to consider alternatives to behavior that used to be a matter of course when all of their colleagues were men. A humorous example is the distress that many men and women feel upon approaching a door together: neither is quite sure whether to open it and how the other will react. A major decision is required. At a more serious level, managers will have to analyze such things as whether their gut reactions to a job candidate are colored by the candidate's gender, something that few people considered in the past. New policies also require male and female managers to spend more time coordinating with each other as they try to establish new ground rules for their interaction. Having few established norms for appropriate behavior, men and women must devote energy to hammering out mutually acceptable ways of working together. These costs, as well as concerns over maintaining one's position, set up powerful resistance to integrating women into the higher levels of the organization.

WEAKNESSES OF COMMONLY PRACTICED REMEDIES TO SEX BIAS

The critical requirement for reducing systematic bias against women is changing the organizational routines that make such bias a natural outcome of organizational life. Many and perhaps most organizations have been oriented toward legalities and numbers, however, leaving the routines that are the basis of bias intact.

Legal Remedies

The unique history, mixture of individuals, and problems of an organization result in a unique set of routines for each organization. Legislation, which is probably the most common solution to routines that are biased against women, does not take account of that uniqueness. Laws and regulations provide universal remedies to break the routines and ride roughshod over the particular needs of organizations and individuals. The Equal Pay Act and Title VII of the 1964 Civil Rights Act, including the pregnancy disability amendment, prohibit routines that intentionally discriminate against women, while Executive Order 11246, which is applicable to any organization receiving federal money, requires affirmative action (6). Affirmative action plans can be viewed as mandated counteractions against entrenched and cherished organizational routines. But laws and regulations that affect 222 million people cannot adequately address unique situations. For each new situation that comes to the attention of the federal bureaucracy, federal guidelines become more complex in an attempt to plug every loophole and make universalistic laws binding on particular organizations. As regulations proliferate, organizations begin to groan under the weight of the restrictions put on them and to protest the cost of compliance.

As justified as their claims against federal regulation may be, American organizations are responsible for much of the equal opportunity regulation that has been foisted upon them. While American social values about female equality have been changing, organizational routines that keep women in low-paying, low-authority jobs have changed very little. Research consistently finds clearcut and unambiguous discrimination against women with little evidence to the contrary. Data reported both from the laboratory and the field by male and female researchers indicate discrimination against women in hiring (7–11), in pay (12–14), in promotion (8, 9, 15), particularly in promotion to positions of authority (12), and in access to training (8, 9). The facts are that generally women with education and experience equal to that of their male counterparts continue to be underpaid and blocked from career advancement. Greater awareness of these inequities has led working women to press their demands on the federal government and to become increasingly litigious, spurring the proliferation of complex and expensive regulation.

Organizations tend to react to government regulations and suits by taking a defensive posture—a natural reaction to the proactive position being taken by women and the government. An orientation toward the letter rather than the spirit of the law maintains the adversarial relationship between government and employers. Moreover, as long as sex discrimination exists, the government is likely to push even harder to correct the injustice. The best and least costly long-run solution for organizations, then, is for employers to sharply reduce and possibly eliminate sex bias. While short-run costs will be incurred from such an effort, carefully planned organizational change can greatly reduce the costs of complying with legislation and especially, now that regulations are so extensive, of defending against grievances and suits. To counteract the trend toward further government intervention into personnel policies, firms and agencies must begin to eliminate the inequities that fuel the regulations.

Affirmative Action Goals

While affirmative action plans can serve the very important function of establishing goals and feedback for an organization, they often do not provide a *means* for attaining equity. In time, hiring and promoting larger numbers of women to responsible positions, will gradually change organizational routines that exclude women. However, these changes will be very slow in coming, because current organizational routines greatly reduce the probability of women being hired and promoted into the critical line positions, even though an organization has set goals for integrating women.

Furthermore, the law cannot mandate that women be promoted into powerful jobs critical to the organization, because there are no universal criteria for judging which jobs are considered critical within the organization. Probably the best that the law can do is examine the levels of the hierarchy at which women are placed. As a result, legally mandated affirmative action goals may have the desired effects only after a very long period of time. Until women achieve equity with men, though, government involvement in work organizations can be expected.

ROUTINES THAT INTRODUCE BIAS

A critical examination of organizational routines is a necessary addition to affirmative action goals and legal compliance. Four types of organizational routines are commonly used to reduce the time, money, and anxiety spent on staffing an organization. These routines also reduce the probability that women will achieve the same authority and income as men, and consequently they must be examined in any serious attempt to integrate women.

Hiring and Promoting through Proximity

One of the easiest ways to fill a position is by tapping someone close by. Frequently this is promoting from within. Since in promotion from within the strengths and weaknesses of the candidate are often well-known, the risks associated with filling the position are reduced. Information about the candidate is available at very low cost and is more reliable than information obtained from the candidate's references. In addition, promotion from within may aid in recruiting and serve as a motivator for those who believe they have a reasonable chance for promotion. While promotion from within is attractive for many reasons, it often means women are at a disadvantage, because they tend not to have been hired into positions that prepare them for promotion. Women tend to be segregated into clerical positions, which are not considered for promotion into management. Consequently, the pool of women who are candidates for promotion from within is much smaller than the pool of men, introducing a systematic bias against women when this routine for filling a management position is activated.

Hiring locally is another routine used to fill positions at a lower cost to the organization. Travel expense for the candidate or recruiter and long-distance telephone communication are eliminated. Typically local networks are denser than national networks, providing more points of contact for the organization. In addition, local contacts are more likely to entail face-to-face relationships, implying more responsibility from members of the network to provide accurate and honest information as part of maintaining a proximate ongoing relationship. The closeness and density of the network, in addition to the reduced communication and travel costs, yield more reliable yet inexpensive information about a job candidate than hiring nationally. Requirements for a particularly highly qualified person for a critical position may make the costs of a national search worthwhile and may even be legally required, but for most jobs in the organization, a local search is preferable.

At entry levels, hiring locally generally should have no biasing effect. The exception might be in small, very traditional communities where the number of women in a particular job market may be considerably smaller than the number of men. At higher levels of management, however, hiring locally serves to reduce the size of the pool of women eligible for the job, since women are not found in management positions in any great number in any one location.

Using Networks to Generate a Pool of Job Candidates

The "old boy" network has long been a source of job candidates. It is probably the most common method of recruiting from outside an organization for upper level positions and one that has been attacked by the government through requirements for job posting and newspaper advertising. By hiring an old classmate or colleague, an employer can eliminate the uncertainty of hiring someone unknown. In addition, as with hiring through proximity, the information costs are reduced when the candidate is already known. When an employer cannot hire an old classmate or colleague, then perhaps an old classmate or colleague can refer someone for the job. A trusted person vouches for the candidate, reducing the risk even though the candidate is unknown, and reducing the need to seek extensive information on the potential employee.

The biases against women in the old boy network are obvious. Since most employers are men and most of their associates are men, women infrequently have a chance to enter the system, particularly at the higher levels where network recruiting is so widespread. Women tend to be admitted as candidates for a job only when the network has failed to turn up someone acceptable for the position, though an exceptional woman may occasionally be referred through the old boy network. Even though many companies now comply with federal guidelines by advertising widely, referral through the network can be a critical determinant of who is selected from the pool.

Promoting from Only Certain Jobs to the Exclusion of Others

In nearly all organizations, some jobs have career tracks into management while others do not. Persons in the dead-end jobs, regardless of their skills, are not considered for managerial positions. This routine has an important value for the organization. First, it eliminates the amount of information the organization must process. Not all people have to be considered for a management position that comes open; only those who currently occupy career track positions must be considered. Second, career track jobs often give their incumbents experience and training relevant to the higher level positions—experience and training not available to those in dead-end jobs. Hence those in career track jobs are better prepared for management jobs. The orientation and training costs of promoting them are less than those for anyone coming from a job not on the career track.

Promoting from career tracks can block both men and women, but the systematic bias is against women, because they more frequently hold the dead-end jobs that are not on the career path. This pattern is most obvious in male-dominated businesses and services. However, it is also found at the management level in typically female occupations in which males hold the upper management jobs while females hold the first line and first line supervisors' jobs. Thus female teachers are generally supervised by male principals, female nurses by male doctors, and female social workers by male administrators. In business, Kanter (16) found that secretaries do not get promoted to a better job, they get promoted to a boss higher in the hierarchy. Virtually all secretaries, the vast majority of tellers and clerks, and most retail sales clerks are women (17) who have no place to go in the organization. In each of these cases there are tracks from male jobs to management but usually not from female jobs to management. "Image" problems are likely to be greater for women occupying traditionally female jobs than for women seeking management trainee positions directly out of college, because the woman in the traditional job has difficulty presenting any cues that she should not be treated in sex-biased ways. She is doing a job that women alone have done for many years, and her competence in that job signals business as usual to the organization, rather than suggesting a reevaluation of the appropriateness of a sex-typed job structure.

Clerical workers, particularly secretaries, have an especially severe problem with career tracks. Unlike tellers or sales clerks, there is little or no hierarchy within which secretaries or clerks work and through which they can be promoted. In addition, secretarial and clerical work do not provide experience that is considered to be relevant to line positions. In sum, organizational structures that provide few career paths for female-dominated jobs, and deliberate sex bias that results in men being promoted to the few management positions available, combine to reduce the number of women who can be promoted into management from nonmanagement positions.

Homosocial Reproduction

Homosocial reproduction is a term used to describe the propensity for owners and executives to hire and promote those who are most like themselves. Homosocial reproduction reduces the anxiety of filling a position with someone who may be competent but different and therefore unpredictable. As Kanter (16) argues, men can trust other men because they are alike. They share the same language, discuss sports together, drink together, find humor in the same things. The typical woman does not share this language, does not participate in the football pool, does not drink with her buddies. As a result, communication with opposite-sex colleagues may be awkward and tense. Men, who generally hold the upper management positions and are therefore responsible for hiring, also prefer men because they are more understandable and therefore more predictable. Moreover, it is easier to trust a person who is open and friendly. While men and women *can* interact in a friendly yet nonintimate way, their interests and styles frequently serve as a barrier to such communication. Since they often find it easier to communicate with a man, men frequently give preference to men, assuming that the person who is easy to talk with is best suited for the job.

Lipman-Blumen (18) sees homosocial reproduction as serving another purpose for men, helping them get what they want from work.

> Women are excluded from this world because their lack of resources makes them less useful and interesting both to men and to other women. Men, recognizing the power their male peers have, find one

another stimulating, exciting, productive, attractive, and important, since they can contribute to virtually all aspects of one another's lives (p. 30–31).

Exceptions can certainly be found to the rule of homosocial reproduction. Even before legal pressures to hire and promote women, exceptional women with extraordinary competence could be promoted even though most competent women were made executive secretaries. However, the numbers of women who have been trusted enough by their superiors to be promoted to top jobs have been miniscule. The argument is made that federal regulations have opened more management jobs to women. Whether the increasing numbers of women receiving MBAs (19) are actually resulting in more women in management cannot be ascertained from available statistics, which are somewhat dated. However, informal observation clearly indicates that most women are still being denied access to managerial ranks.

Stereotypes and Expectations. Closely related to the routine of homosocial reproduction are sex-stereotyped perceptions and patterns of interaction that make it difficult for women to be as successful in organizations as men. Negative expectations are likely to interfere with women's performance as well as their ease in relating to others in the organization, reinforcing men's mistrust of women. The expectations for a person's performance held by significant others has a strong impact on his or her behavior, as demonstrated by a number of social psychological studies (20, 21, 22, 23).

Often both men and women have lower expectations of women than of men. These expectations may not be explicit, but they subtly color the value placed on work done by women. In a classic experiment, Goldberg (24) gave two groups of subjects the same essay. The only difference was that one group was told the essay was written by a woman, while the other group was told the essay was written by a man. The group who believed the author was a man rated the essay more highly than the group who thought it was written by a woman. These findings have been replicated in similar studies (25, 26, 27), lending confidence to the conclusion that a woman's performance is frequently undervalued, and she is expected to be less competent.

Moreover, expectations for women conflict with each other. Men resent assertive, unemotional women for acting like men, but they also judge women who are passive and emotional as unsuited to management (16). As a result, women receive conflicting messages about how they ought to behave. This kind of role conflict is linked to job stress (28) and has the potential for immobilizing women who find themselves in "Catch 22." As a result, job performance is likely to suffer.

Women also are frequently expected to perform a sexual role at work (29). Preliminary data from my own research on women with MBAs indicate that even professional managers are not immune to the expectation of performing a symbolic or actual sexual service for men in the organization. While many men express surprise that their remarks are offensive to women, sexually suggestive remarks arouse in many women anxiety and defensiveness, which is likely to reduce optimum performance.

All of these negative or conflicting expectations coming from others must generally have a negative effect on women's self-confidence. They receive the message that their work is not good enough, that their personal traits make them poor managers, and that their sexuality is as important as (sometimes more important than) their job competence. Many women internalize these expectations, building them into their self-images. Schein (30, 31) found that women as well as men defined female traits as very different from good managerial characteristics, while there was a major overlap between perceived male traits and good managerial characteristics. Women tend to believe that they do not come to a job with the requisite characteristics to be good managers.

There is some evidence to indicate that women fear becoming highly successful (32). Recent analysis of the fear of success phenomenon shows that the conclusion that women fear success is faulty, because they become very successful in jobs traditionally held by women. What they fear is success in male jobs, because they dread the social punishment that comes from breaking group norms (33). In work settings this fear of success is manifested in less willingness to strive for the top positions, knowing that the reactions to such ambition may be great hostility. To the company this means less than optimum performance from those women who prefer not to risk punishment by becoming superstars (16).

Finally, women often deny their successes when they do achieve something outstanding. Deaux and Farris (34) found that women attributed their success to others or to events beyond their control, while they attributed their failure to themselves. Men attributed failure to fate, but success to themselves.

The combination of negative expectations from others, usually men in traditionally male jobs, and the negative self-expectations that are fed by others' expectations, can only serve to depress women's accomplishments. These negative expectations are communicated by men to women in the form of expressed doubt about the quality of past work or ability to perform future work, overprotection, assignment to routine jobs, and oversupervision. Women in turn communicate to men self-doubts that arise from negative evaluation of their work and their typically feminine qualities by being hesitant, nonassertive, and deferent. To men, the combination of their sex-biased view of women's competence and women's own self-doubts and depressed aspirations justify the routine of homosocial reproduction.

Job Segregation. Homosocial reproduction is one of the major factors in perpetuating the segregation of men and women into jobs held primarily by members of one sex only. While socialization experiences lead many women to select female occupations (35, 36, 37), homosocial reproduction denies women access to male occupations, segregating them into a small number of female occupations. Blumrosen (38) has caused shock waves among personnel professionals across the country with her argument that job segregation in itself establishes a prima facie case of illegal wage discrimination. If her argument is accepted by the courts, the implication under Title VII of the Civil Rights Act is that the burden of proof that wage discrimination does not exist will be on the employer. Her position is that female and minority jobs, such as secretary, janitor, and seamstress, are underpaid because they are held by socially devalued groups and socially devalued groups are not given access to more valued jobs. She asserts that the lower pay given to women in female jobs accounts for most of the earnings gap between men and women of equal education and experience.

At the same time that Blumrosen has raised the issue of depressed wages in segregated jobs, the Equal Employment Opportunity Commission has contracted with the National Academy of Sciences to study the issue of equal pay for comparable worth. In the past the courts have ruled that employers must pay equal wages for work that is the same or similar enough to be essentially the same. Under this guideline, most organizations have loosely based the pay scale for a particular job on market value. The concept of equal pay for comparable worth bases compensation on the skills and responsibilities required for a job rather than on market value. The argument is that the market value for a welder is higher than the market value for a secretary, because sex bias in the society results in undervaluing the work of females, not because the job of secretary requires less skill or responsibility than the job of welder. Another factor limiting women's wages is that women are squeezed into a very small number of job categories, creating an oversupply of labor for women's job. One of the solutions proposed by advocates of women and minorities is to evaluate jobs in terms of such factors as the skills required and assign wages based on the quality of the job. Such a system would prohibit market value as the major determinant of the wage in order to rectify immediately biases introduced by the operation of the market.

Using a quantitative method of job evaluation that considers the skill, effort, responsibility, and working conditions of a job, Wegener (39) found that the job of industrial nurse rated higher than the job of senior applications programmer. Yet she found the going wage in Los Angeles to be 30 percent higher for the programmer than the nurse. A study conducted by the State of Washington and reported by Wegener showed that for jobs with equal evaluation points (comparable worth), females were earning 80 percent of male wage rates.

The question raised by these arguments is whether the government should impose job evaluation standards on employers as a remedy to wage discrimination that is partially a by-product of homosocial reproduction. The NAS study has not been released as of this writing. The issue is causing a furor among personnel managers, however, because government interventions would require sweeping changes, and reasonable guidelines would be extremely difficult to develop and administer. Jobs from one company to another are likely to be quite different, even when job titles are the same, but a legalistic application of rules is likely to push organizations toward more rigidity and homogeneity in defining jobs. This can be costly for the organization as well as for individuals who might otherwise have more latitude to create their own positions.

The American Society for Personnel Administration is already taking steps to head off government-imposed job evaluation. These steps are not, however, to help organizations find ways to eliminate sex discrimination. Rather ASPA has taken the position that equal pay for comparable worth is not acceptable under the Equal Pay Act and Title VII of the Civil Rights Act of 1964 (40). ASPA's position is that new legislation must be enacted to guarantee equal pay for comparable worth and that the EEOC has no legal mandate to enforce guidelines in this area unless new laws are passed.

Clearly this outcome of homosocial reproduction has the potential for being very costly to employers, probably far more costly than the benefits of trust and comfortable interaction afforded by the routine. By reducing and eventually eliminating job segregation, organizations can eliminate the threat of imposed job evaluation standards.

ESTABLISHING NEW ROUTINES

Diagnosis

The general pattern for establishing new routines is first to diagnose current organizational routines. What are the standard operating procedures for recruiting, hiring, training, and promoting in the organization? Next, these routines should be examined to determine if they introduce systematic bias against women, whether or not the intent is discrimination. This can be done rather simply by assessing the number of women relative to men eligible for hiring or promotion if a given routine is used. If the routine is not generating a reasonably large pool of women eligible for a position, it is probably sex-biased. It may be that for some positions women's job preferences severely limit the size of the pool that can be generated. For example, some blue collar positions are not sought by women (4). However, management and the professions are typically viewed as desirable careers by women (41), so a pool for these kinds of positions should be readily available. The third step in establishing a new routine is assessing the value of the old routines. These old routines cut costs of various types, and it is necessary to know exactly what benefits the routine provides. Finally, those benefits must be incorporated into the new routine. The new routines will usually be costly to initiate but may provide clear long-run benefits at low cost to the organization. For example, hiring and promoting women will nearly double the available pool of candidates, giving the organization more choices for selection among highly qualified candidates. Obviously, eliminating bias against women also reduces the probability of grievances and suits, which can be extremely costly even when the judgment favors the organization. However, the new routines must also provide some of the benefits of the old routines such as reducing information costs and risk. The more of these benefits that can be provided, the less likely will be resistance to change.

Women's Networks

The most significant problem with hiring and promoting through proximity and with using old boy networks is the inadequate pool of women eligible for the job. The organization's task is to find a routine that accomplishes the function of reducing risk and information costs without reducing the probability of hiring and promoting women.

The major benefits from hiring through proximity and through the old boy network are reducing the risk of hiring unknown candidates and reducing the cost of getting information. A reasonable alternative to these two routines is developing a new girl network. A network of women in management can, under the right conditions, likewise reduce risk and information costs while generating a pool of women applicants.

Networks of managerial and professional women already exist all over the country. Women have made a deliberate effort in recent years to make contact with each other in order to have some of the benefits that men receive in an old boy network. Organizations can tap into these existing women's networks as a strong first step in establishing their own women's referral network. The first step is to identify and contact the women already known to the organization. These may be former classmates, former colleagues, women associates from other companies or agencies, or women who currently work in the organization. These women provide a point of entry into existing networks. While they may be unable to refer any job candidates with the appropriate background, they are likely to know someone or know someone who knows someone who can. Consequently, those who ultimately make up the network for a particular organization may not be known directly by the organization.

If the women who form the referral network for the organization are not women who have been previously known to the organization, then the network will not perform the same functions as the old boy network. It will provide a pool of women candidates and, once established, will reduce the search time. But it will not accomplish one of the most important functions of an old boy network: reducing risk by having a trusted friend or associate vouch for the candidate. The referral source from a women's network is likely to be as unknown as the candidate herself. Consequently, an important component of establishing a women's network as a viable alternative to the routine of the old boy network is developing the kinds of relationships with referral sources that will reduce risk in hiring.

Finally, the network should be national in scope to allow recruiting for higher level positions for which only a small number of women are eligible locally. As with men, a national women's network will give the organization hiring choices while counteracting the numerical bias against women introduced by local hiring or promoting from within.

Clearly, implementing a program of developing a women's network is costly, though maintenance costs should drop off considerably. However, in the early stages network development will require a considerable time investment to track down referral sources and establish the kinds of relationships necessary for effective referral. These costs might be shared by a number of organizations cooperating to form a single network (Chapter 23). After the initial investment, though, the network should grow and maintain itself with much less cost, particularly as women with their own contacts are placed in significant positions in the organization. An effective network will result in more women in responsible positions; these women will widen and strengthen the network, making it more effective in recruiting women, until at some point the men's and women's networks will merge or the women's network will cost about the same and provide about the same benefits as the men's network.

Career Tracks For Traditionally Female Jobs

Career tracks serve the purposes of reducing the size of the search necessary to fill positions and of giving employees relevant experiences for a promotion, but jobs that are traditionally held by women have very few, if any, career tracks up. Two different types of remedies for the problem are called for, depending on the organizational structure relevant to the group of women who lack opportunity. The first and easiest change is to include the traditionally female line positions in the career track. This means that efforts should be made to promote supervisors of such groups as tellers and retail sales clerks to the next level of management. But since sex-biased attitudes are part of the dynamics that keep women out of management, a quota system may be necessary as an objective structure for ensuring that the tiny minority of men in these jobs do not disproportionately receive the management positions.

Providing career tracks in traditionally female departments would have the very desirable benefit of allowing hiring by proximity without reducing the size of the pool of women. Information about the performance of these women is available at low cost and their work experience is directly relevant to the next highest position, though the relevance is typically not recognized because the job is not conceptalized as a growth position. Therefore the organization would save in information costs, would reduce hiring risk, and could promote people with job-specific experience. By the economist's definition (42), failure to promote these women into the next highest position constitutes a clear case of sex discrimination, because the employer is willing to incur costs in order to avoid hiring a particular class of people.

Making career paths for secretaries is more difficult. In organizations that use secretarial pools, career tracks can be made in the department that provides administrative support services. However, where secretaries "belong" to particular individuals, there is no natural hierarchy for promotion. One alternative is to move secretaries into pools, although such a move is highly likely to be resisted by managers who have the flexibility of direct control over a secretary. An alternative, particularly for secretaries who work alone, might be to select secretaries for management trainee positions on a regular basis, much as some companies annually recruit new MBAs. The benefits of selecting secretaries for management trainee positions are the same as the benefits of hiring by proximity: a wealth of low-cost information about the candidate is readily available, reducing the risk of hiring. The problem with this alternative is that it does not adequately deal with organizational realities. The cost to the organization is the loss of good secretaries who are scarce. As Kanter (16) points out, many managers are loath to give up a good secretary, blocking opportunities for the employee. In sum, career advancement for secretaries is problematic, because the needs satisfied by current routines are not easily met by alternatives that are beneficial to secretaries. This is an area still in need of creative exploration.

Communication Workshops To Increase Trust

Unlike other organizational routines in which bias is a byproduct of efforts to achieve efficiency and reduce risk, homosocial reproduction is rooted in issues of trust and power. These are qualities of human relationships that require a remedy that addresses the quality of the relationship between men and women in the organization. Communication workshops aimed at reducing mistrust between men and women and at exploring the fear, discomforts, and hostilities men and women have toward each other are a very important step in building relationships. Such workshops can be very valuable, because they provide a place where men and women can try out new behavior appropriate to the collegial relationship that they have so little experience with. An experienced external facilitator can point to patterns of interaction that are barriers to communication and trust and can suggest possible alternatives. Left to their own devices, men and women working together would eventually make some accommodation to each other. However, a deliberate examination of problematic patterns and experimentation with alternative patterns can both speed the time of adjustment and increase the probability of a satisfying solution to the interaction problems between men and women.

There are two critical components of such workshops. One is time. New patterns of interaction do not develop in days or weeks, because the changes are difficult. New behavior is awkward and causes self-consciousness; the old behavior is supported by a web of norms and values shared with other people; and new behavior must ultimately be accompanied by attitude change. For these reasons, workshops for men and women need to occur intermittently over a long period of time, so that motivation for change remains high and social support for change is constant. While sex bias is too institutionalized to be eliminated, it can certainly be reduced by long-term efforts.

The second critical component is the involvement of all levels of management. Lower-level managers should be involved, because they are likely to be faced immediately with day-to-day interaction with women peers. Middle and upper-level managers must be involved, because they hold the power that can make the difference in a woman's success or failure. It is from the upper managers that broad policy decisions affecting women are made. This is the group that will either support or fail to support women subordinates when tension mounts between men and women at lower levels. And perhaps most importantly, this is the group that will either encourage or resist homosocial reproduction at the highest levels. Consequently, every effort should be made to include all levels of management in any attempt to improve trust and communication by altering current interaction patterns.

The impact of communication workshops for men and women is to replace a pattern in which women are defined as an inferior out group with a pattern in which everyone is trusted and respected as a member of the in group. (Minority groups also need to be included in the process of eliminating out groups, but the focus of this chapter is on women.) The payoff for women is twofold. First, if women as a class come to be more trusted and perceived as more competent and valuable, the probability of bias against them in hiring and promotion will diminish. Second, effective communication workshops are likely to begin a process of disentangling perceptions of feminine qualities from perceptions of competence and value. They will help both men and women to understand that being a woman and exhibiting typically female traits and personal styles do not imply incompetence or instability. Finally, helping men and women to find common ground for casual, nonintimate social interaction will improve the ease of relating to each other, allowing women more access to informally transmitted information and to the political channels that are often critical to their careers.

There are four major benefits for the organization. First, the organization can continue to use the time-tested method of hiring and promoting trusted, comprehensible people, but it can add women to the group of trusted people, thereby reducing sex bias. Second, as with other methods of increasing the pool of qualified applicants, including women increases the amount of human resources available to the organization, giving it greater choice in selecting qualified personnel. Third, and perhaps most important for the firm or agency, such workshops can reduce the tension of integrating women and can help to provide the support women need to be effective. Improving communication can circumvent hostility and anxiety so that the work of the firm or agency can proceed smoothly. Finally, human resources are apt to be developed and employed more fully. Developing respect for women workers in the organization will improve women's self-confidence and thereby heighten their level of aspiration. They can then accomplish more and be more effective employees for the organization.

Affirmative Action Officer

Clearly all of the suggested remedies require time and skills in organizational development. Most line managers have neither, and the presence of a specialist who can oversee the change effort is likely to be a critical element in whether significant changes are actually made. Meyer and Lee (4) found that the success of the affirmative action programs they studied was affected in important ways by the presence of a good affirmative action officer. Such a person needs first to have strong organizational support for making changes. As an example, ARCO makes affirmative action performance one of the criteria for executive bonuses. Second, the affirmative action officer needs to make change as easy as possible for line managers. This entails diagnosing the routines, fully understanding the payoffs to management in present routines, and doing the groundwork for establishing new routines. No matter what the affirmative action officer does, change will be difficult and met with some resistance. However, by reducing the time and energy managers must spend on the change, a skilled affirmative action officer can reduce resistance and make change more likely.

Organizational Politics

No plan for organizational change is complete without attention to the organization's internal politics. Unless those who wield power are convinced that they have something to gain from the change, business will go on as usual. Therefore it is critical to design a program that takes account of vested interests.

At top levels, managers are likely to see the change as being disruptive and expensive. In fact it will be both, but the argument can be made that the proposed changes are less expensive over the long run than current policies. The costs of constant documentation of worker behavior, of collecting and analyzing data for defense against grievances and suits, of legal fees and court costs, and of carrying unsatisfactory employees because documentation is inadequate for dismissal are very high, but most of these costs are barely visible because they do not have a line in the budget. Moreover, if job evaluation is required by the government, the costs of compliance over and above the increased wage bill is likely to be astronomical. In comparison, the costs to develop opportunities for women will be moderate. A change agent with access to the budget may actually want to project costs for the two policies over a five-year period, demonstrating the comparative expense of waging a continuing legal battle versus ending sex bias.

If upper-level managers are rewarded in power, status, and income for high profits, then a program to reduce costs should be appealing. Naturally, any internal power struggles among top managers must be considered by the change agent for the impact they could have on the proposed changes. Realistically, many top-level managers will not be persuaded by an argument of reduced costs, because their desire to maintain the status quo obscures their vision in this area. But for forward-looking managers who can tolerate change, the argument may be convincing.

At lower levels, managers and supervisors will be working with women on a regular basis and ultimately will be competing with them for promotion. Because they will bear the brunt of the readjustment, they should be involved in decisions all along the way. It is critical to the success of the project to consider the impact the change will have on these middle and lower-level managers and to plan for the needs and frustrations of this group.

CONCLUSIONS

Social values in the United States, reflected in laws that prohibit employment discrimination against women, have steadily and rather rapidly shifted toward full equality for women in the work force. The short-run orientation of many organizations has left them unprepared to cope with these cultural shifts, however. They continue to fight the government on small legal points rather than making serious efforts to come to terms with the fact that sex discrimination is constantly becoming less acceptable in this society. As a result, these organizations are spending large amounts of money on short-term solutions, but the costs will not abate until the long-run problem is solved. Therefore it is ultimately more cost effective for organizations to set a goal of eliminating sex bias rather than simply complying with the law or disputing the laws in the courts. Women's demands are not likely to subside, so it is in the best interests of organizations to change their routines as quickly and efficiently as possible.

REFERENCES

1. Cyert, R. M. & March, J. G. *A Behavioral Theory of the Firm.* Englewood Cliffs, N.J.: Prentice-Hall, 1963, pp. 114–127.
2. Allison, G. T. *Essence of Decision: Explaining the Cuban Missile Crisis.* Boston: Little, Brown, 1971.
3. Pfeffer, J. *Organization Design.* Arlington Heights, Ill.: AHM,1978.

4. Meyer, H. H. & Lee, M. D. *Moving Women into "Male" Jobs: Successes and Failures in Ten Companies.* New York: Management Resources, Inc., 1978.

5. Katz, D. & Kahn, R. L. *The Social Psychology of Organizations.* 2nd ed. New York: Wiley, 1966, pp. 2–4.

6. Greenman, R. L. & Schmertz, E. J., *Personnel Administration and the Law.* 2nd ed. Washington, D.C.: Bureau of National Affairs, Inc., 1972, pp. 63–128.

7. Shaw, E. A. Differential impact of negative stereotyping in employer selection. *Personnel Psychology,* 1972, **25,** 333–338.

8. Rosen, B. & Jerdee, T. J. Effects of applicant's sex and difficulty of job on evaluations of candidates for managerial positions. *Journal of Applied Psychology,* 1974, **59,** 511–512.

9. Rosen, B. & Jerdee, T. H. Sex stereotyping in the executive suite. *Harvard Business Review,* March-April 1974, 45–58.

10. Dipboye, R. L., Fromkin, H. & Wilbach, L. Relative importance of applicant sex, attractiveness, and scholastic standing in evaluation of job applicant resumes. *Journal of Applied Psychology,* 1975, **60,** 39–43.

11. Haefner, J. E. Race, age, sex, and competence as factors in employee selection of the disadvantaged. *Journal of Applied Psychology,* 1977, **62,** 199–202.

12. Wolf, W. C. & Fligstein, N. D. Sex and authority in the workplace. *American Sociological Review,* 1979, **44,** 235–252.

13. Terborg, J. R. & Ilgen, D. R. A theoretical approach to sex discrimination in traditionally masculine occupations. *Organizational Behavior and Human Performance,* 1975, **13,** 352–376.

14. Taylor, P. A. Income inequality in the federal civilian government. *American Sociological Review,* 1979, **44, 468–479.**

15. Day, D. R. & Stogdill, R. M. Leader behavior of male and female supervisors: A comparative study. *Personnel Psychology,* 1972, **25,** 353–360.

16. Kanter, R. M. *Men and Women of the Corporation.* New York: Basic Books, 1977.

17. *Statistical Abstracts of the United States.* U.S. Bureau of Labor Statistics: Employment and Earnings. October 1973–January 1979, p. 417.

18. Lipman-Blumen, J. Toward a homosocial theory of sex-roles: An explanation of the sex segregation of social institutions. In M. Blaxall and B. Reagan (Eds.). *Women in the Workplace.* Chicago: University of Chicago Press, 1976.

19. Gordon, F & Strober, M. *Bringing Women into Management.* New York: McGraw-Hill, 1975.

20. Rosenthal, R. & Jacobson, L. *Pygmalion in the Classroom: Teacher Expectations and Pupils' Intellectual Development.* New York: Holt, Rinehart, and Winston, 1968.

21. Rosenberg, M. J. When dissonance fails: On eliminating evaluation apprehension from attitude measurement. *Journal of Personality and Social Psychology,* 1965, **1,** 28–42.

22. Orne, M. T. Demand characteristics and the concept of quasi-controls. In R. Rosenthal & R. L. Rosnow (Eds.). *Artifact in Behavioral Research.* New York: Academic Press, 1969.

23. Rosenthal, R. Interpersonal expectations: Effects of the experimenter's hypothesis. In R. Rosenthal & R. L. Rosnow (Eds.). *Artifact in Behavior Research.* New York: Academic Press, 1969.

24. Goldberg, P. H. Are women prejudiced against women? *Transaction,* 1968, **5,** 28–30.

25. Pheterson, G. I. Keisler, S. B. & Goldberg, P. H. Evaluation of the performance of women as a function of their sex, achievement, and personal history. *Journal of Personality and Social Psychology,* 1971, **19,** 114–118.

26. Bem, S. L. & Bem, D. J. Case study of a non-conscious ideology: Training the woman to know her place. In D. J. Bem (Ed.). *Beliefs, Attitudes, and Human Affairs.* Belmont, Calif.: Brooks/Cole, 1970.

27. Linsenmeier, J. A. & Wortman, C. B. Attitudes toward workers and toward their work: More evidence that sex makes a difference. *Journal of Applied Psychology,* 1979, **4,** 326–334.

28. Kahn, R. L. Wolfe, D. M. Quinn, R. P. Snock, J. D. & Rosenthal, R.A. *Organizational Stress: Studies in Role Conflict and Ambiguity.* New York: Wiley, 1964.

29. Farley, L. *Sexual Shakedown: The Sexual Harassment of Women on the Job.* New York: McGraw-Hill, 1978.

30. Schein, V. E. The relationship between sex role stereotypes and requisite management characteristics. *Journal of Applied Psychology,* 1973, **57,** 95–100.

31. Schein, V. E. Relationships between sex role stereotypes and requisite management characteristics among female managers. *Journal of Applied Psychology,* 1975, **60,** 340–344.

32. Horner, M. S. *Sex differences in achievement motivation and performance in competitive and non-competitive situations.* Unpublished doctoral dissertation, University of Michigan, 1968. University Microfilms No. 69-12, 135.

33. Condry, J. & Dyer, S. Fear of success: Attribution of cause to the victim. *Journal of Social Issues,* 1976, **32,** 63–83.

34. Deaux, K. & Farris, L. Attributing causes for one's own performance: The effects of sex, norms, and outcome. *Journal of Research in Personality,* 1977, **11,** 59–72.

35. Penn, J. R. & Gabriel, M. E. Role constraints influences on the lives of women. *School Counselor,* 1976, **23,** 252–254.

36. Esslinger, C. W. *Educational and occupational aspirations and the educational, personal, and family characteristics of selected 12th grade female students.* Unpublished doctoral dissertation. University of Illinois, 1979.

37. Prediger, D. J. Roth, J. D. & Noeth, R. J. *Nationwide Study of Career Development: Summary of Results.* Iowa City, Ia.: Research and Development Division, The American College Testing Program, 1973.

38. Blumrosen, R. G. Wage discrimination, job segregation, and Title VII of the Civil Rights Act of 1964. *University of Michigan Journal of Law Reform,* 1979, **12,** 399–502.

39. Wegener, E. Does competitive pay discriminate? *Personnel Administrator,* 1980, **25,** 38–43, 66.

40. Lorber, L. Z. Job segregation and wage discrimination under Title VII and the Equal Pay Act. *Personnel Administrator,* 1980, **25,** 31–34.

41. Medvene, A. M. & Collins, A. Occupational prestige and its relationship to traditional and non-traditional views of women's roles. *Journal of Counseling Psychology,* 1974, **21,** 139–143.

42. Rees, A. *The Economics of Work and Pay.* New York: Harper and Row, 1973, p. 181.

—13—

Aging Realities in Managing Organizations

H. Meltzer

Today many people, particularly in America, live longer. "But," as pointed out by Glenda Rosenthal (1), "for many of them this extension of life merely means an extension of disease and diminished quality of life." At the beginning of this century, 4 percent of the population in this country was over age 65. At the present time that figure has grown to more than 10 percent, or more than 23 million people. Fifty years from now, one in five Americans will be 65 and older.

In American industry today, the realities are that at the startlingly early age of 40, many individuals find themselves considered too old for employment and promotion. In more dramatic terms, 40 is described as an age in which many find themselves too old to work and too young to die. The self-perception of many older workers is consistent with popular stereotypes about aging workers. The impact of these stereotypes takes on additional significance when they influence the decision making of managers, which they do.

That managers make personnel decisions on the basis of stereotypes of a negative nature, is revealed in the study "Too Old or Not Too Old," by Rosen and Jerdee (2). From a survey of 1500 subscribers to the *Harvard Business Review,* the authors found clear evidence that managers make assumptions about the inability of older workers to perform as well as younger ones in jobs that demand flexibility, creativity, and a high degree of motivation. The managers were asked to react to similar situations of younger and older supervisors. Practically no one favored reassuring or encouraging the older workers who weren't doing well. They favored reassigning the older worker, whereas they favored training or encouraging the younger worker. This, despite the fact that the 1967 Age Discrimination in Employment Act resulted in the United States Department of Labor winning an agreement whereby Standard Oil of California must pay $2 million in back wages to the employees over the age of 40 who claimed that they had been victimized by the discriminatory management practices. The stereotype of the change-resistant older person is responsible for the general practice of not considering older workers for career development or retraining. The result is that fewer older workers are given career options as wide open as the younger.

Harris (3) describes a recurrent stereotype of older people in the following words: "An old population is more conservative, less creative, less productive, less mobile, and more dependent than the younger ones." While this sweeping generalization by Harris is in accord with the stereotypes that many people have about the aged or the problem of aging, it definitely is contradicted by the findings of "Age Differences in Work Attitudes" (4, p. 8).

Contrary to these stereotypes, there are many studies available that present older people in a more favorable light in terms of abilities (Owens, 5; Jones, 6), skillls (McFarland, 7; Shock, 8); learning, motivation, and education (Conrad, 9). While clearly there are some elderly individuals who have lost some of their cognitive or perceptual motor skills, this research reveals that the assumption that ability generally declines with age is a myth.

Moreover, there is evidence that decrements in capabilities are often not totally a function of physiological change. Labouvie-Vief (10) gives possible explanations for the alleged decline in ability. These include the contamination brought about by comparing younger persons of high educational levels with older individuals who dropped out of school early, the increased test anxiety of older workers, and the ritualized habits of not searching for new solutions. Rosenberg (11) recognizes the social isolation of many older workers, which might contribute to the deterioration of cognitive performance through isolation. But Rosenberg also warns that we cannot generalize about the effects of isolation on the worker without taking contextual factors into consideration. Workers who feel economically secure but live among poverty stricken families experienced more isolation than those who are very poor. Conversely, the poor worker living in an area where most are solvent undergoes isolation. While there are age differences in perceptual motor skills and isolation, there are also factors where age as such is not a determining factor, for example, dissatisfaction with work.

Workers of all ages are expressing increased dissatisfaction with their work. Psychologists have long been interested in job dissatisfaction of workers. Their focus has been on the industrial worker who presumably has a boring or unchallenging job. These workers are expected to be dissatisfied, and much of the current interest on the quality of work life and its improvement has been on this segment of the labor force. Sarason (12), in his book *Work, Aging, and Social Change: Professionals and the One Life—One Career Imperative,* makes the disturbing point that there is a high dissatisfaction among professional persons, those whose work is supposed to be "a calling" and who are supposed to find identity, satisfaction, and fulfillment in their jobs. He contends that there are very many highly educated professionals who are alienated from their all too mundane and unrewarding work life. They stick with it because they feel trapped by the one life—one career imperative. What Sarason reveals and emphasizes is that the widespread and rather intense dissatisfaction can be found in professional careers as well as workers. This is in spite of the fact, as Sarason puts it, that the professional "thought he was embarking on a quest in which all of his capacities and curiosities would be exploited, the vibrant sense of challenge, growth, and achievement sustained, and a sense of personal worth and importance strengthened, the material rewards he would obtain would be as icing on a delicious cake. 'Perhaps,' says he, 'expectations like these are absolutely beyond reach and, thus, doomed to failure but what do we substitute for them in midlife?" And Sarason hooks up some of these changes with changes resulting in attitudes and values after World War II, which was often referred to as "The Age of Psychology and Mental Health."

To study the problem of aging realities by focusing attention on the age differences in mental health of workers is the general purpose of this study. The specific purpose of the present study is twofold: to review a series of articles concerning age differences in work attitudes, and to consider the implications of work, leisure, and retirement in the light of the findings of these and related studies. The specific studies reviewed are: (a)"Age Differences in Work and Life Adjustment Attitudes" (4); (b) "Attitudes of Workers Before and After the Age of 40" (13); (c) "Age Differences in Happiness (and Share of Happiness) of Workers" (14, 15); and (d) "Age differences in Positive Mental Health of Workers" (16).

REVIEW OF STUDIES ON AGE DIFFERENCES ON WORK ATTITUDES

Work and Life-Adjustment Attitudes

For the study on work and life-adjustment attitudes (4), 256 subjects were divided into four groups as follows:Group I, composed of 102 workers from 19 to 29; Group II, composed of 98 workers from 30 to 44; Group III, 43 workers from 45 to 59; and Group IV, 13 workers from 60 to 77. All of the subjects were from the parent plant in St. Louis. The results were based on the findings of morale-survey data containing 41 items, 28 of which refer to work attitudes and 13 to life-adjustment attitudes. As a simple expression of the general tendency of an individual toward satisfaction or dissatisfaction, a satisfaction index was used. The formula used is: $S \div T - U \div T$ (where S equals responses indicating above average satisfaction; U indicating responses below average satisfaction; and T indicating the total number of responses). The middle or average choice was not included in the calculations; thus the index is a measure of predominance of satisfaction or dissatisfaction.

The findings of this first study on age differences in work attitudes may be summarized as follows:

1. The emotional climate of an industrial setting, which has distinctive characteristics, influences the nature of work adjustments of employees of all ages and not to the same degree.

2. There are many significant statistical differences in the age groups studied.
3. In considering the company as a place to work and items indicative of identification with management and their policies, there is a tendency for increasingly favorable attitudes with age. Generally workers more frequently identify with democratic organizations rather than autocratic or bureaucratic organizations.
4. Attitudes toward pay become increasingly more favorable with age.
5. In most areas tested, satisfaction increases with age.
6. The differentiating age for attitude toward work conditions is 45.
7. There are individual differences within each age group.

Related to these findings are those of Cherrington. Condie, and England (17) in their study of values of workers. They surveyed 3053 workers from 53 companies throughout the United States. The companies were predominantly involved in manufacturing. The questionnaire used for their study was composed of 191 items regarding attitudes toward one's specific job, towards the company, and towards work in general. The results were similar to those reported in "Age Differences in Work Attitudes," namely, that older workers placed greater importance on the moral importance of work and pride in craftmanship. Younger workers placed greater emphasis on the importance of money, the value of friends over work, and the acceptability of welfare as an alternative to work. Upward striving was not related to age. Older workers held more strongly to those work values traditionally taught and considered important in industrial society. The work values examined included: moral importance of work, pride in craftsmanship, upward striving, importance of money, importance of friends over work, and acceptability of welfare.

Attitudes of Workers before and after the Age of 40

For a study of workers before and after the age of 40 (13), the subjects used were workers in a paper converting company located in a stable college community in upstate New York. The population was composed of 213 workers, of which 120, or 56.3 percent were aged 40 or less, and 93 or 43.66 percent were aged 41 or older. Of the 213 people studied, 65 were classified as doing skilled jobs, 80 were semiskilled, 60 were relatively unskilled, and 13 were clerical.

The questionnaire used for the study was composed of 28 items concerned with work attitudes and 13 items concerned with life adjustments. Of the 28 items concerned with work attitudes, there were 20 statistically significant differences with 19 of these being in favor of the older workers; only one—finding co-workers agreeable and cooperative—was in favor of the younger group. The 19 that favored the older group were: work well planned, supplies on hand, can tell if own work is adequate, on job best qualified for, supervisor friendly and helpful, new employee training, standing with supervisor, supervisory discipline, supevisor's interest in worker, supervisor's competency, confidence in top management, company's pay scale, job rate adequate, rate complaints handled fairly, security felt on job, impression of training program, chance for advancement, supervisory favoritism, company's policies made clear.

Of the items on life adjustment, the most significant differences are that older workers have a more favorable reaction to the neighborhood they live in and to the people they know. They also report greater satisfaction with the amount of time for recreation and more favorable feelings about the effect of work experience on their happiness as well as share of happiness and feel less futile about the national political situation. Of the 41 items, there are 16 with no statistically significant differences between the older and the younger workers. Of these, eight are attitudes towards work items, and eight out of the total 16 are life-adjustment items.

Age Differences in Happiness and Share of Happiness

For the study of happiness and life adjustments (14), the original 257 subjects studied for age differences in work attitudes were used. For the age differences in happiness study, the subjects were 270 workers employed by the same company in three different locations, Northeast, Midwest, and Far West. The general findings concerning age differences in happiness may be summarized as follows:

1. The feeling of the worker that he or she has had his or her share of happiness increases with age.
2. In general, work takes on more significance with age. Spare time decreases in significance with age.
3. With increased age there is increased interest in steady work and decreased interest in advancement. Hope for advancement is low in the youngest group; it decreases with age; and it is practically absent in the oldest group.
4. The correlation of share of happiness with two items indicative of self-concept is relatively consistent, with a coefficient of contingency of .43 for one, and .38 for the other. Thus persons with a better self-image report more happiness.

The most educated group more often picked the 20 to 35 period as the favored age span, and the least educated group picked the 36 to 46 period as the best more often than the other two educational level groups. Wages do make a difference, but it is individually determined rather than by age grouping. Here are some illustrative case studies that portray a relationship of age, situation, developmental history, and other possible variables that can play a role in determing an attitude of a person at a given age, at a given time, in a given place.

The oldest worker in this plant was 75 and had been with the company for more than 30 years. His wife died only a few years ago. He worked because he wanted to. He had a home, which his children and in-laws helped him keep clean, and he had a fair amount of independence. He picked the years after 60 as the second most favored. The most favored were the youngest years, before 20, and the second worst were 20 through 35. This choice was completely based on his background. The worker had nothing to be happy about in his early years; he was reared in a poor family and didn't begin to enjoy life until he was in the 36 to 45 span. His best years started when he began to work in this plant, with continuous security and no layoffs. He was a skilled carpenter in the plant and was self-sufficient in his way of working. His life experiences, in terms of what he had, what he enjoyed, and what he was satisfied with determined his preferences, rather than age as such.

A 48-year-old worker, for example, who had been at the plant for six years came to this company with a history of no layoffs, from a plant where he had experienced three layoff periods in four years of working. He was a high school graduate with an IQ above 100. He was a religious family man and a careful worker; his manner of speaking and thinking were logical. Obtaining a job at his age, in which he had a chance to advance, improve his salary, and have security made him look more comfortably at the 46 to 60 span of years. He picked this span as being relatively happy because "I'm happy with my work and family and have learned to enjoy the better things of life." The period from 20 to 35 was less pleasant for him because he was in the military service and away from the family. It was not especially the wage, which he conceived of as adequate because it was more than he had made before, but the fact that he had security and was not going to make less for the rest of his lifetime (all things considered), which gave him differential pickings.

Age Differences in the Positive Mental Health of Workers

In *Current Concepts of Positive Mental Health*, Jahoda (18) paid little attention to the age factor in mental health, but expressed an awareness of significance of the problem in the following words: "The study of mental health in different age groups is a research problem in its own right" (p. 101). She suggested criteria relevant for considering all age groups in these words: "Perception of reality, meeting the requirements of the situation, and problem solving are the criteria par excellence having meaning for all age groups, even though their empirical study will, of course, have to take age into consideration" (p. 102). Using Jahoda's suggestions, the present investigation studies the relation of age to mental health in an industrial setting. The emphasis is on positive mental health. This is in accord with Mclean's (19) outlook that in the future there will be more concern and greater demonstration of employer responsibility for encouraging mentally healthy behavior in employees and less worry about those with mental illness.

In this investigation (16) an attempt is made to study, by way of the content analysis of life and work stories, the relation of mental health and age of workers with the emphasis not on mental illness, but on positive mental health.

The subjects in this study were 143 workers in a paper converting industry located in a stable college community in upstate New York. This paper mill was the only plant of any size in the community, and obtaining a job there at the time was considered highly desirable by many of the people in the community. The employees were mostly semiskilled and skilled workers ranging from 19 to 78 years of age. The ages were divided into five groups: 20 to 29 ($N = 31$); 30 to 39 years ($N = 36$); 40 to 49 years ($N = 37$); 50 to 59 years ($N = 26$); over 60 years ($N = 13$). The data were collected by tape-recorded interviews. The content was analyzed as follows: the interview was broken down into individual sentences, and the sentences relating to mental health were underlined. About 15 such statements occurred per record. Each of the sentences was then taken individually, given a plus or a minus value, then placed in one of the four categories that was considered indicative of the workers' positive mental health. These categories were adapted and condensed from Jahoda's (1958) six major categories of criteria for total positive mental health. The four categories are self-regard, maturity, personality organization, and relation to environment. The judgments in this assessment were made by a person who was not an interviewer and thus had no knowledge of the optimism or competency scores of the subjects.

After each of the underlined sentences in interviews were scored either positive or negative and placed into one of the four categories, the indices of positive mental health of the worker could be computed. The score for each individual category was determined by subtracting the number of negative statements from the positive ones in that category. The overall total mental health index was determined by adding the four category scores.

A second judge, who was a graduate student in psychology scored 25 of the same protocols, according to the criteria and categories defined above. The same individual sentences were used for both scorings. The interjudge reliability for the total index was found to be .81 for self-regard; .86 for maturity; .71 for personality organization; and .77 for relation to environment.

Results. The findings in the study of age differences in positive mental health as reported in terms of means, standard deviations, and f-ratios may be summarized as follows:

1. The 30 to 39 age group scored significantly higher on all mental health indices than all other age groups. The differences between this age group and the younger (20 to 29) age group and older groups were all significant at the .01 level.

2. The largest difference between the younger and older workers is found in their self-regard. It appears that the younger workers are more idealistic about themselves and are more confident about their abilities than are the older workers, who can look back and see failure in meeting their ideals. The next greatest difference between the two age groups is found in their relations to the environment. Here again the younger workers seem to be able to adapt to the situational demand and be more adaptable to their environment than the older workers, who have apparently become more "set in their ways." There is also some difference in personality organization. The younger workers seem to exhibit a greater resistance to stress and somewhat more reality orientation than do the older workers, who begin to wonder about their future and are contemplating the agonies of retirement and old age. There seems to be little difference in the maturity scale of the two age groups.
3. The general picture of the total mental health index reveals a steep rise in the positive mental health from the 20 to 29 age group to the 30 to 39 age group, with the peak being reached at 39. From there a marked decline occurs to the 40 to 49 age group, with a gradual leveling off from there until the 60-up age group. It would seem that the 20 to 29 age group may be going through the initial rough period of adjustment to marriage and vocation, and thus score lower than the 30 to 39 age group, which has passed through this period and arrived at established lives. This is in accord with the findings in the "Age Differences in Happiness and Life Adjustments of Workers" (14). Workers perceive their own peak age of happiness as arriving later than those of others. The positive outlook and organization decreases drastically from 40 on with the realization of middle-aged decline and the lack of fulfillment of earlier goals and ideals.

Figure 13.1 presents a graphic illustration of the results of the different age groups on the total index. This index shows a significant increase from the 20 to 29 age group to the 30 to 39 age group and then a significant drop to the last three age groups. The latter three age groups did not differ significantly from each other (Figure 13.1).

Work and Personality in the Middle Years

According to Brim and Abeles (20), taking the midlife period as an entry point into the study of various life span processes is a strategy for examining continuity in the midst of change and for locating the missing pieces in the study of individuals over a lifetime. Definitions of middle age differ depending on whether biological, chronological, or self-perceptive criteria are employed. The study of transition between work and nonwork is particularly appropriate in a research program concerned with the middle years because an occupational career was best understood as a relationship to nonwork aspects of life. In terms of time demands, work role increases in young adulthood, either gradually or abruptly, and for men it is generally sustained over the succeeding decades at a culturally decreed 35 to 40 hours

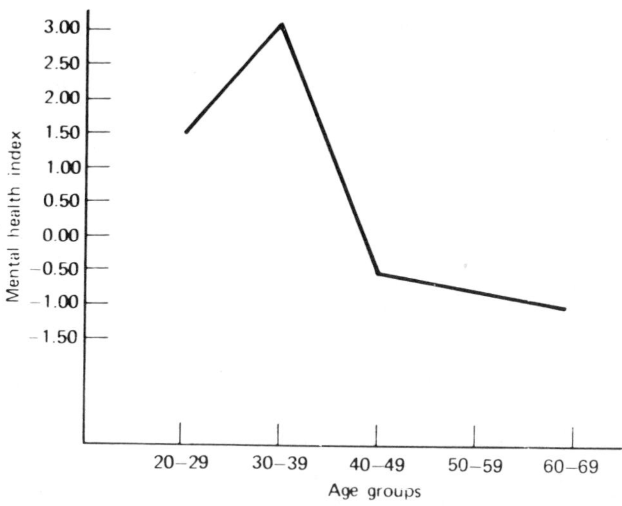

Figure 13.1 Age differences in positive mental health.

per week. For women the pattern is more complex and has probably been more affected by social change. Both men and women, however, are likely to hold numerous jobs, and both have life patterns in which work is likely to show a period of dominance, more or less prolonged, among other major life activities. The statistical, clinical, and anecdotal evidence suggests that the special stresses of the middle years take their toll, as well as produce growth (middle crisis), and that work is significantly involved in this process. In addition to its potential relationship to middle crises, work deserves careful attention as a contributor to personal identity, especially during the midlife period. Such issues as the role of work in self-esteem; the differential impact of work on identity for different social groups, cultures, and historical time periods; individual preferences for the allocation of time between work and leisure; and the consequences of voluntary career changes in the middle years fall within this research domain.

WORK, LEISURE, AND RETIREMENT

An informative picture of what a man from 40 to 45 thinks about midlife development is presented in Levinson's book *The Seasons of a Man's Life* (21). This book grew out of Levinson's longitudinal research on the personality development of 40 middle-aged men, 10 each of biologists, novelists, blue-collar workers, and business executives. The book describes the similarities and differences at this stage of life. After describing various stages of life in the individual studies, common factors given are as follows:

The first phase, beginning with the boy's teens, goes from dependency of adolescence to the independence in the 20s. In this period commitments are tenuous, and changes can easily be made. By 30 the person is settling down, and by 40 he is usually in a stable position in his career. The transition into middle adulthood lasts five years and involved resolving four major polarities: (a) being young or old, (b) being destructive or being creative, (c) being masculine or feminine, and (d) being attached to others or separate from them.

In the World Federation for Mental Health meetings held in 1977, Margaret Mead presented ideas that made the students interested in the problems of aging, leisure, and retirement realize that their sources of information and their thinking were culture-bound. A newspaper caption of some of the things she said was: "Only Westerners Believe Leisure is Wicked" (22). "Recreation is one of the phoniest notions of Western cultures," said Margaret Mead. "Westerners still uphold the Protestant Ethic that 'one should only indulge in pleasure in order to be able to work harder.'" She informed the audience that other societies have no equivalent word for leisure. For the Balinese pleasure means to be able to work very hard at something that is truly enjoyable. Only our peculiar Western culture thinks that leisure is wicked and that to have fun you have to work very, very hard. She gave a number of examples of societies in which recreation plays a natural role in the lives of every citizen from small children to adults and the elderly. She made similar remarks about retirement.

Are the conclusions of Margaret Mead based on observations and anthropological insights in line with empirical evidence? In a study of retirement and satisfaction, Schmitt, White, Coyle, and Rauschenberger (23), the subjects were individuals retired from the Michigan Civil Sevice for a two-year period ending in July 1977. Of the total of 752 retirees, 353 completed the mailed questionnaire package. The findings of the study document the importance of health in satisfaction with one's retirement status and overall life satisfaction. Income does not appear to be nearly as important, though the population studied tended to have reasonably good retirement incomes. The idea that high job involvement means dissatisfaction with retirement was partially supported by the data regarding satisfaction with retirement activities. However, far more important seems to be a general positive attitude concerning job and retirement.

Job satisfaction seems to correlate highly with all four dependent variables. Age is negatively correlated with retirement and life satisfaction, as is the statement that bad health is the major reason for retirement. Internal consistencies for those measures that were scales were all above .70 and were considered satisfactory.

Perceptions that the subjects had concerning their previous jobs were measured by the short form of the Minnesota Satisfaction Questionnaire. Psychological needs or motivation were assessed by three scales presented by Alderfer (24).

These studies of retirement raised the whole question of mandatory retirement. Management and unions often favor it. The young are looking for the jobs that the older workers still have. But the fact is that there are young fogies as well as old fogies, that creativeness often persists and grows with old age. Thomas Hardy and William Butler Yeats wrote their greatest poems in old age. Pablo Picasso and Marc Chagall did not lose their fire when they passed 90. Justices Brandeis and Holmes did some of their best work in their 80s. Older people who are retired from life as well as work are lonely, loveless, helpless, and hopeless. Many turn to drink and become mentally sick. A few of them become depressed and some die at their own hand. The highest rate of suicide in the nation is aong men over 65 years of age.

In the light of the foregoing facts about leisure, training, and retirement, what seems to make sense is to legislate against mandatory retirement and individualize the process of evaluating each person, not on age only but on his or her competency, responsibility, and being generally worthwhile.

CONCLUSION AND RECOMMENDATIONS

The chief purpose of this study was to review the stereotypes that work against elderly workers in American industry, stereotypes that prevail among managers as well as workers themselves, and result in practices which discriminate against older workers. The stereotype is that they are not flexible, they are not creative, they are not readily motivated to work, and it's easier to reassign them if they don't do well on a supervisory level than to train them—that training and development are saved for younger workers. The studies presented here definitely reveal that many older workers are competent throughout their years. Competency is not a matter of age, it's a matter of ability and motiviation. In many respects, for many purposes, older workers have definite advantages over younger ones. It's logical therefore that organizations should face the aging realities in terms of knowledge available, rather than stereotypes due to conditioned practices of the past. Organizations are in position to contribute by knowing the facts, applying facts about aging in industry, and providing programs that are in line with the facts, rather than to keep practicing assumptions based on stereotypes. This implies planning, selecting, training, developing, and evaluating problems of aging, and to consider how to optimize adult development in line with the review of studies by Fozard and Popkin (25). The findings of the studies reported can serve as a knowledge base, and will lead to more individualizing processes in evaluation and practice. It is apparent from the studies reported and from case studies that an aging person has everything in his or her favor if he or she has health, money, work, or some meaningful activities, and a sense of aliveness and realization that life is for living and learning. For considering the aging and retirement problems, the following recommendations are made in the light of the foregoing studies:

1. The problem of who retires at what age should be individualized. All the evidence is that there are plenty of individual differences in how old a person is at a given time, and it is more than merely chronological age that determines it. Also considered should be one's situation, personality, the nature of work, and related factors.
2. Selection should be made on the basis of competency of the individual rather than his or her age or sex.
3. In the selection process, it would be well to keep in mind something like a career dynamics emphasis, namely, whether the individual has needs to be satisfied, which can correlate or integrate with the organizational objectives of the company he or she will be working for.
4. The training process shold be individualized at the outset and at follow-up. At the outset many companies have a set period for learning of a skill, which may take two weeks or a month. Everyone must take it for that time, but some can learn all of it in one week, while some can't learn it even in the allotted time. If it were individualized, it would be more satisfying to the individual, as well as less costly and less wasteful to the organization.
5. Appraisal performance should be in terms of competency and skill and also in attitudes for the use of the skill.
6. Top management is the only one in the position to create an organizational climate that invites openness and shared communication down the line. If human relation programs are introduced anywhere below, all that results is conflict on the part of the people at that level with the people above and below.
7. The introduction of counseling for retirement at least five years before retirement age seems advisable, provided it is done with a relatively clinical approach for understanding the person, helping him or her understand himself or herself in considering the alternatives for life ahead.
8. In evaluating productivity, turnover, absenteeism and tardiness should be included. In most instances the result would favor the older and more experienced people.
9. Unions need to acquire knowledge about the aging of men and women to determine their policies in light of the facts, rather than demand early retirement for everyone.
10. Organizations can profit by paying organized attention to collaboration efforts of workers within a department, as well as for interdependent functioning. It is possible for a department to be composed of responsible individuals and yet not be a cohesive group or have a team approach. The collaboration aspect of communication is deserving of more specialized attention than it usually receives if interdependent functioning is the desired goal.

It would be well for both executives and managers, as well as union leaders, to know and apply the available knowledge considered in terms of the effects described here of age differences in work and life. at the present time, both groups take the road of least resistance and suggest or advise retirement for everybody at the age of 65 or earlier. It managers and union leaders learn to perceive retirement in terms of consequences for all involved, their present resistance could change and make them realize the advisability of moving towards retirement policies that are realistic in nature because they are indivdualized.

REFERENCES

1. Rosenthal, G. Achieving a healthier, more hopeful old age..*Outlook Magazine,* Washington University School of Medicine, April/Spring 1979, **26**(1), 1–9.
2. Rosen, B. & Jerdee, T. H. Too old or not too old. *Harvard Business Review,* November/December 1977, **53**(6), 97–106.
3. Harris, S. E. What to do with 18 million aged? *New York Times Magazine,* July 10, 1949.
4. Meltzer, H. Age differences in work attitudes. *Journal of Gerontology,* January 1958, **13**(1), 74–81.
5. Owens, W. A. Jr. Research on age and mental abilities. In J. E. Anderson (Ed.), *Psychological Aspects of Aging. Proceedings of a Conference on Planning Research of the American Psychological Association.* Washington, D. C.: American Psychological Association, 1956.
6. Jones, H. E. Perceptive and intellective abilities. In J. E. Anderson (Ed.), *Psychological Aspects of Aging. Proceedings of a Conference on Planning Research of the American Psychological Association.* Washington, D. C.: American Psychological Association, 1956.
7. McFarland, R. A. Functional efficiency, skills and employment. In J. E. Anderson (Ed.), *Psychological Aspects of Aging. Proceedings of a Conference on Planning Research of the American Psychological Association.* Washington, D. C.: American Psychological Association, 1956.
8. Shock, N. W. Skill and employment. In J. E. Anderson (Ed.), *Psychological Aspects of Aging. Proceedings of a Conference on Planning Research of the American Psychological Association.* Washington, D. C.: American Psychological Association. 1956.
9. Conrad, H. S. Learning, motivation and education. In J. E. Anderson (Ed.), *Psychological Aspects of Aging. Proceedings of a Conference on Planning Research of the American Psychologocial Association,* Washington, D. C.: American Psychological Association, 1956.
10. Labouvie-Vief, G. Adult cognitive development: In search of alternative interpretation. *Merrill-Palmer Quarterly,* 1977, **23**(4), 227, 263.
11. Rosenberg, G. S. *The Worker Grows Old.* San Francisco: Jossey-Bass, 1970.

12. Sarason, S. B. *Work, Aging and Social Change: Professionals and the One Life—One Career Imperative.* New York: Free Press, 1977.

13. Meltzer, H. Attitudes of workers before and after age 40. *Geriatrics* May 1965, **20,** 425–432.

14. Meltzer, H. Age differences in happiness and life adjustments of workers. *Journal of Gerontology,* January, 1963, **18**(1), 66–70.

15. Meltzer, H. Age and sex differences in workers' perceptions of happiness for self and others. *Journal of Genetic Psychology,* 1964, **105,** 1–11.

16. Meltzer, H. Age differences in positive and mental health of workers. *Journal of Genetic Psychology,* 1971, **119,** 163–173.

17. Cherrington, D. Condie, S. J. & England, J. L. Age and work values. *The Academy of Management Journal,* September 1979, **22**(3), 617–623.

18. Jahoda, M. *Current Concepts of Positive Mental Health.* New York: Basic Books, 1958.

19. McLean, A. *To Work Is Human: Mental Health and the Business Community.* New York: Macmillan, 1967.

20. Brim, O. Jr. & Abeles, R. Work and personality in the middle years. *Social Science Research Council Items,* September 1975, **29**(3), 617–623.

21. Levinson, H. *The Seasons of a Man's Life.* New York: Knopf, 1978, pp. xiv, 363.

22. Mead, M. Only westerners believe leisure is wicked. *The Province,* August 23, 1977, p. 16.

23. Schmitt, N. White, J. K. Coyle, B. W. & Rauschenberger, J. Retirement and life satisfaction. *The Academy of Management Journal,* 1979, **22**(2), 282–291.

24. Alderfer, C. P. *Existence, Relatedness and Growth Needs: Human Needs in Organizational Settings.* New York: The Free Press, 1972.

25. Fozard, J. L. & Popkin, S. J. Optimizing adult development: Ends and means of an applied psychology of aging. *American Psychologist,* November 1978, **33**(11), 975–989.

—14—

Opportunities for the Handicapped

Raymond A. Ehrle

INTRODUCTION: WHO PAYS AND IN WHAT COIN?

In order to understand the problems of providing employment opportunities for the handicapped in organizations of all kinds several things must be understood. It is imperative that: (a) our terms be defined clearly, (b) the problem to be dealt with is conceptualized clearly, (c) unintended second and third order consequences of decision making be understood, (d) we are conscious of what our value systems are, (e) we seek holistic and synergistic win-win solutions as opposed to mechanistic and reductionistic zero sum approaches and (f) we understand there is no "free lunch."

The key terms that need to be defined clearly are "humane," "productive," "organization," and "handicapped." For consistency I shall start with Webster's definition of humane as "marked by compassion, sympathy or consideration for other human beings or animals," and productive as "having the quality or power of producing." Organization is defined as "an administrative and functional structure" (including the personnel of such a structure), and handicap is defined as "disadvantage that makes achievement unusually difficult." Unfortunately, it often seems difficult for organizations to be productive, to employ disadvantaged personnel, and to be compassionate simultaneously.

The central problem I will address is: How can administrative and functional entities established for some purpose, that is having the quality or power of producing (goods, services, or ideas, for example) also demonstrate compassion and sympathy for other human beings, particularly those with disadvantages that make achievement difficult? A corollary question is: Who pays—the individual, third party insurance carrier, the consumer, the organization, stockholders, the government? And in what coin—inflation, taxes, unemployment, reduced capital formation, dollar devaluation?

The answer to these questions involves personal, psychological, economic, social, political, managerial, and ultimately ethical considerations. Three approaches, the doctrine of social responsibility, a political-legal solution, and a problem-solving approach, will be discussed.

SCOPE OF THE PROBLEM: TOWARDS A DEFINITION OF HANDICAPPED

It has been estimated by the federal government that at least 35 million and possibly as many as 60 million Americans are handicapped. This figure includes the blind, the deaf, persons confined to wheelchairs, the mentally ill or retarded, alcoholics, drug addicts, and those with many other disabilities, many of which are not visible. According to this government definition a handicapped person is anyone who: (a) has a physical or mental impairment that substantialy limits one or more of his or her major life activities, (b) has a record of such an impairment, and (c) is regarded as having such an impairment.

Unfortunately, this definition is not precise, it is so broad that it is almost meaningless. Actually most of us are handicaped in one way or another. Moreover, this definition necessitates other definitions. In an attempt to cut a path through this thicket, Nagi (1) defined several related terms as follows:

Impairment indicates a physiologoical, anatomical, or mental loss or other abnormality, or both. Not all impairments are pathological, that is, not all impairments involve the interruption of normal processes and the simultaneous efforts of the organism to restore a normal state of existence.

Functional limitations are the most direct way in which impairments contribute to disability. While altered structure or function of many tissues can exist without limiting the function of the organism as a whole, the reverse is not true. Limitation on functions at higher levels of organization may result from differing impairments and functional limitations at lower levels of organization. The inability to lift a heavy weight may be related to mechanical problems in the lumbrosacral region or be the result of diminished cardiac output.

Disability is defined as a form of inability or limitation in performing roles and tasks expected of an individual in a social environment. These tasks and roles include self care, education, family relations, other interpersonal relations, recreation, economic life or employment, and vocational concerns.

The qualifying phrase "substantially limits" has to do with the degree of disability. A handicapped person having a hard time getting a job or getting ahead on the job because of disability is considered substantially limited. "Major life activities" include such things as communication, self-care, ambulation, education, transportation, and employment (2).

ORGANIZATION TYPOLOGY

Organizations have been classified in a number of ways. Various organizational contextual classifications may be the small business, multinational corporations, or mom and pop stores; or may be more theoretically generated types such as those of Mintzberg (see Chapter 8). Also they have been classified by function: research, manufacturing, or educational; and they have been classified by motive: sheltered workshop, profit making, quasi-governmental, non profit. Given this variety in bases for classification, the typology chosen for any particular study depends on the purposes of the investigator.

Here I shall use Etzioni's typology (3). This typology is useful for the present paper because by relating three kinds of power-authority that an organization may use to the types of involvement that the individual has with the organization, it centers our attention on some central conflicts between humaneness and productivity faced by most work organizations.

Etzioni postulates three types of power-authority and three types of involvement. Typically each type of authority is congruent with one type of involvement. These three combinations result in three basic types of organizations. Some organizations (e.g., prisons, concentration camps, coercive unions, and custodial mental hospitals) are *coercive*. They rely mainly on coercive power; usually individual involvement in these systems is alienative. Others (e.g., the peacetime military, business and industry, and business unions) rely on rational legal authority and economic rewards as mediators. In these organizations that are functional and flexible individuals relate on the basis of pragmatic self-interest. These are *utilitarian* organizations. Etzioni's third class of organizations are primarily *normative* in nature (e.g., religious organizations, professional associations, mutual benefit groups, and certain political organizations). Individuals relate to these systems on a moral basis, that is, what is "right." It would seem that normative-moral organizations are apt to have the most humane individual-organizational relationships and coercive-alienative organizations the least. In this paper attention will be focused on utilitarian organizations in which achieving an acceptable balance between humane and productive objectives is apt to be problematic.

It must be remembered that organizations of whatever type do not function in a vacuum. Many modern theorists (4, 5, 6) conceive of organizations as systems constantly attempting to manage internal stresses and demands, while simultaneously attempting to respond to the pressures and demands of an ever more intrusive and turbulent environment. The term "contingency management" has been coined to describe such situations (7). Moreover, personalities and the history of each individual organization impact its internal dynamics. As a result, Etzioni's typology provides only a general guideline to the quality of relationships we are apt to find in any given system.

PREDICTION OF PERSONNEL PERFORMANCE—KEY TO ORGANIZATIONAL SURVIVAL

No matter what form an organization takes, students of cultural anthropology, biology systems theorists, and practicing bureaucrats generally assume that the primary objective of any organism or organization is to preserve and perpetuate itself in the face of internal changes and external demands, uncertainties, and ambiguities. Clearly all of the traditional management functions—planning, organizing, staffing, directing and controlling—play vital roles in this process. In this paper I will focus primarily on the personnel function of staffing—who shall be recruited, selected, promoted, fired or retired.

In attempting to predict future performance of individuals in organizations, psychologists have devised a variety of assessment procedures, including interviews, paper and pencil tests, vocational evaulation procedures, probationary periods, work history reviews, and hands-on tryouts. (See Chapter 1 for a detailed treatment of these methos.) All of these measures involve a number of practical problems. Interpretations of the information they produce contain a mixture of objective and subjective judgments. Most have only moderate reliability and low validity in predicting job performance. Moreover, particularly in recent years, many of them have become subject to litigation.

Whatever procedure is used, the intent is usually to select the very best people from the pool of eligible candidates to fill specific requirements. This approach is based on the assumption that it will lead to the maximization of group or organization performance. On the other hand, if an organization has an internal work force pool (such as the Army), assessment and prediction may be oriented toward optimizing group performance. In optimizing group performance individual "star" players may be sacrificed to improve overall group productivity. Thus if there is an abundance of lawyers and a shortage of truck drivers, some lawyers may find themselves driving trucks.

Finally, assessment procedures may be used as diagnostic tools, to profile certain individual attributes and then compare that profile to a hypothetical norm. When these two profiles fail to match each other, certain remedial measures may be suggested and prescribed to make up for the deficiencies.

From the perspective of utilitarian organizations, survival in an increasingly turbulent external environment requires as much control as possible over internal resources—personnel, finances, information, and so on. They wish to recruit, select, train, and promote individuals who will enhance the organization now and in the future. The rational-calculative procedures so often found in utilitarian organizations are designed to achieve this control as a means to effective performance. At the same time that the organization wishes to select in order to maximize group performance, societal forces in their environments are demanding that organizations not discriminate against a variety of "minorities." Indeed the full range of protected minorities, including the handicapped, make up well over a majority of the population (8). Often these demands stem from a set of moral beliefs, held by some, that organizations ought to be socially responsible.

THE DOCTRINE OF SOCIAL RESPONSIBILITY AND EMPLOYMENT OF THE HANDICAPPED

Ever since World War II employers have been exhorted to "hire the handicapped" on a voluntary self-interest basis. Placements are routinely made through state Divisions of Vocational Rehabilitation, the state Employment Services, and private rehabilitation agencies. Public consciousness is kept up through efforts of the President's Committee (and 50 state committees) on Employment of the Handicapped as well as efforts of various self-help groups, for example, the Paralyzed Veterans of America, the National Epilepsy Foundation, and so on. And indeed, many thousands of handicapped persons are placed in organizations each year.

Many of these activities take place under the rubric of social responsibility. Social responsibility is a term that seems to have arisen to justify activities of utilitarian organizations that appear to be motivated by moral as opposed to calculative criteria. As Elkins and Callaghan observed (9).

> Firms are surrounded by various constituent or interest groups, each having some call on the firm's resources and energies. Shareholders hold no special status in this doctrine, sharing importance with labor, government at all levels, customers, neighbors, suppliers, minority groups . . . There are calls for the firm to simultaneously strive for lowest prices, well built products, fair wages, attractive and clean plant sites, voluntary pollution control efforts, contributions to charity, training programs for the disadvantaged, and other social and economic actions, while maintaining fair dividends for its shareholders . . . To recognize the supposedly imperfect market structures managerial judgment therefore is called for as a substitute to market mechanisms in many of the relationships between the firm and its surrounding interest groups.

The costs of social responsibility have to be borne by someone. Sometimes these costs are borne primarily by the stockholders. For example, as Burck (10) observed in commenting on the heavy expenditures for social projects by CNA Financial Corporation, "CNA, unlike many less opulent and more price-conscious companies, can absorb the costs—i.e., reduce the profits of its shareholders." However, Friedman (11) argued that most organizations cannot absorb the costs of social responsibility. He observed:

> In a free enterprise private property system, a corporate executive is an employee of the owners of the business. He has direct responsibility to his employers. That responsibility is to conduct the business in accordance with their desires, which generally will be to make as much money as possible while conforming to the basic rules of society, both those embodied in law and those embodied in ethical custom.

It would seem then that opportunities for the handicapped would increase in organizations whose stockholders actively support the concept of social responsibility, whose financial and productive status allow it and whose management is conscious of it. However, for such conditions to exist there must be a long-term educational process, and even then special incentives of a legalistic utilitarian type might be required. For example, Congress has authorized a "targeted jobs tax credit" to encourage business employment for selected minorities including the handicapped and veterans. Using normal utilitarian criteria, it simply does not appear to be good business for an individual firm to engage in actions for moral as opposed to calculative reasons.

Whether it has been good business or not, many opportunities for the handicapped have been developed in many organizations over the years. Organizations have varied in their desires and capacities to absorb handicapped applicants, and the results have certainly not been equitable, either to the individuals or to the organizations. Yet what has been done has been done in the name of enlightened self-interest, undoubtedly for some tasks handicapped workers (who may often be hired at relatively low wages) perform at high levels. Other firms have also acted voluntarily under the doctrine of social responsibility. While not all organizations could or would accept this doctrine, at least some did and in so doing reflected a normative-moral set of humane individual-organizational relationships.

THE POLITICAL SOLUTION

In attempting to open further opportunities for the handicapped in 1977, the admittedly imperfect normative-moral set of individual-organizational relationships was replaced by the prospect of ultimate coercive-alienative relationships. Personal and social responsibility were replaced by the provisions of Title V of the Rehabiltation Act of 1973 (Public Law 93-112) (12). Implementing directives, however, were not published until four years later in 1977–78. Because of the importance of this legislation on contemporary organizations and its potential impact on future policy, practitioners need to be aware of a number of details of the law. Consequently, I will treat the law in considerable depth.

There are four sections of the Rehabilitation Act that have had, and will continue to have, direct effects on the management of organizations.

Section 501 of the Act requires that all agencies of the executive arm of the U.S. government submit annual affirmative action program plans for the hiring, placement, and advancement of handicapped individuals to the Office of Personnel Management. Section 502 established the Architectural and Transportation Barriers Compliance Board made up of the heads of nine U.S. cabinet posts to ensure that all buildings and facilities of the U.S. government be accessible to and usable by people who are physically handicapped. Section 503 of the Act requires every employer doing business with the federal government under a contract (either for the procurement of supplies or services or for the use of real or personal property) for more than $2500 to take "affirmative action" to hire handicapped people. Affirmative action is not limited to hiring but includes job assignments, promotions, training, transfers, working conditions, terminations, and so on. Half of the businesses in America—some three million—are covered. Section 504 states that every institution in the United States receiving financial assistance must take steps to insure that handicapped people are not discriminated against in employment. Included are schools, colleges, hospitals, nursing homes, social service agencies, and so on. Each of these sections and some of their effects will be discussed in more detail below.

Section 501

Obviously the direct effects of Section 501 occurred within the federal government itself. The Office of Selective Placement Programs within the Office of Personnel Management (the former Civil Service Commission) is responsible for the administration of Section 501. It is responsible for reviewing annual agency affirmative action plans. It has also initiated a review of the physical requirements section of the qualification standards for jobs to determine if they are overly restrictive of handicapped individuals. (This study will be completed in 1983.) The Office of Selective Placement Programs has also focused on the modification of architectural barriers. Section 501 regulations create a mechanism for processing complaints of discrimination based on physical or mental handicap. The new regulations extend the coverage of existing procedures for complaints based on race, color, religion, sex, national origin, and age, and are applicable to both handicapped applicants and employees. Finally, federal agencies are now authorized to pay expenses to make training curricula accessible to handicapped employees. In addition they may provide special services such as interpreters for deaf individuals, readers for blind persons, and taping or brailling of materials necessary to provide access to printed materials used in training courses.

Section 502

Section 502 also has its most direct impact on the government itself. This section established the Architectural and Transportation Barriers Compliance Board consisting of the heads of Health, Education and Welfare, Transportation, Housing and Urban Development, Labor, Interior, General Services Administration, U.S. Postal Service, Veterans Administration, and Defense. The Board is charged by Congress to insure compliance with federal laws requiring that all buildings and facilities owned, occupied, or financed by the U.S. government be accessible to and usable by people who are physically handicapped.

Congress also charged the Board with investigating and examining alternative approaches to architectural, transportation, and attitudinal barriers confronting handicapped persons, determining what measures states and localities are using to eliminate barriers, preparing plans and proposals to achieve adequate transportation and housing for handicapped persons, and recommending further legislation.

Section 503

Section 503 has far more pervasive effects. This section is applicable to over 30,000 prime contractors and 250,000 more subcontractors who provide the U.S. government supplies, services, use of property, and construction work, totaling $81 billion per year. Federal contractors and subcontractors include most major businesses and corporations in the country, as well as many small firms. Together they employ more than 31 million people.

When a compliance review team turns up problems that cannot be easily resolved, the Office of Federal Contract Compliance, a part of the U.S. Department of Labor's Employment Standards Administration, attempts to reach a conciliation agreement with the employer. But when conciliation efforts are unsuccessful, OFCCP then turns to its enforcement process. Complaints may also be filed by organizations or other individuals on behalf of the person affected.

This section has a number of very specific provisions. For example, systematic exclusion of specific handicapped groups such as epileptics and diabetics is a clear violation of contractor obligations. However, while an alcoholic or a drug addict may not be disqualified for employment solely because of his or her condition, the behavioral manifestations of the condition may be taken into account in determining whether he or she is qualified. Physical and mental criteria for jobs for which the handicapped person is being considered must be *job related* and consistent with business necessity and safe performance of the job. Preemployment physical examinations cannot be used to screen out the handicapped, and reasonable accommodations must be made to the limitations imposed by the individual's disability.

During Fiscal Year 1978 some 2500 complaints were received (13). Most complaints (on an almost equal basis) were related to hiring and termination; only 10 percent involved upward mobility restrictions.

In addition to these complaints there is clear evidence that the law was frequently being violated. The OFCCP conducted Directed Compliance Reviews of 300 randomly selected contractors and found much public confusion and misunderstanding. Ninety percent of the contractors reviewed were in noncompliance! Frequent violations included:

No affirmative action plan (AAP)	24 percent
Failure to use affirmative action clause	51 percent
Failure to invite handicapped to identify self	57 percent

No posters	29 percent
Failure to review handicapped personnel procedures	53 percent
No review of physical and mental job requirements	50 percent
No review of employment practices	48 percent
No outreach	44 percent
No reasonable accommodation procedure	18 percent
No AAP documentation to employees	53 percent
Inadequate AAP	25 percent

Section 504

Section 504 regulations require that a variety of social, health, and educational programs be accessible to and usable by handicapped persons. Yet compliance has been slow. A 1978 survey (13) revealed that only 19 percent of the nation's schools had toilet facilities accessible to persons in wheelchairs. Only 54 percent had accessible building entrances. Only 5 percent of the schools met all five standards considered: accessible entrance, building levels, toilet stalls, interior doorways, and warning signals.

This section also places some specific demands on public education. It requires that every qualified handicapped person be provided with a free appropriate education. Also it requires that to the maximum extent appropriate to the needs of handicapped persons, they must be educated with persons who are not handicapped. Again compliance has been slow: 55 percent of the 661,170 educable mentally retarded children enrolled were found to spend 100 percent of their time in special education classes, isolated from regular classes.

DEFINITIONS AND INTERPRETATIONS

In addition to these specific provisions, the Act contains four key definitions and interpretations that, while they were written to define the scope of the current law, can be expected to have an impact on future laws and policies as well.

Identification of the Handicapped

The term "handicap" includes a wide range of mental and physical disabilities. Some impairments are obvious, such as paraplegia or blindness. Others such as heart disease, high blood pressure, or diabetes are not always apparent. In other cases people have recovered from their disabilities but have encountered job discrimination because of their past medical records. Cancer and mental or emotional disorders are examples. It is entirely possible that organizations may already have a number of handicapped workers on their payrolls. Consequently they may ask existing employees if they are handicapped, using this definition, but the employee is not required to provide confirmation.

Reasonable Accommodation,to Be Provided by Employer

Reasonable accommodation means that the organization is required to make necessary adaptations to enable a qualified handicapped person to work. It may include making facilities used by all employees accessible (ramps, restroom adaptations, wider aisles) and making modifications to jobs, work schedules, equipment, or work areas, such as simplifying a job so a retarded person might fill it, teaching sign language to the supervisor of a deaf person, or providing a reader to a blind person.

Affirmative Action

Affirmative action does not mean that unqualified persons must be hired or promoted over other employees. It does mean that positive steps are to be taken to provide equal opportunity for those who have been discriminated against on the job and who continue to suffer the effects of that discrimination. Consequently the government demands that employers make special efforts in outreach, recruitment, training, and other areas to help members of selected groups to compete for jobs and promotions on an equal footing with other applicants and employees.

Qualified Worker

Not every handicapped person is eligible for these special programs. A person must be capable of performing a particular job, with reasonable accommodations to the handicapping condition if it is needed. The key concepts are "particular job" and "job related." The underlying assumption is that a job is a property right. In other words, depriving a qualified individual of a job would be tantamount to denying him or her of a livelihod, that is, casting him or her out on the desert to starve.

SECOND ORDER CONSEQUENCES OF THE ACT

The Rehabilitation Act of 1973, as amended, has clearly opened the gates of opportunity for all handicapped, past, present, and future. It has done this by designating them as being in a minority status under special federal protection and by considering the job as a property right. Section V of the Act spells out responsibilities and complaint procedures. In addition, the Act has had will continue to have a number of second order consequences—results that were unanticipated and unintended, but which occur as a byproduct in solving a specific problem.

The desire of all health, education, and welfare activities, educational institutions at all levels, government agencies, government contractors, and subcontractors to be in compliance has generated a rash of specialized consulting and training activities. Private rehabilitation practitioners and psychologists have been called in as consultants to aid in interpreting the intent of the law, to aid in developing "job-related" job descriptions, selection procedures, and performance standards, and to statistically prove that affirmative action is taking place. In addition, other organizations such as the American Coalition of Citizens with Disabilities have generated technical assistance and training programs on topics such as "Reasonable Accommodations and Employment," "Conducting an Accessibility Survey," and "Orientation to Functional Job Analysis" (14). Fountain House in New York City and the Menninger Foundation of Topeka have Projects with Industry, government-funded demonstration projects designed to demonstrate that the mentally ill can enter the competitive labor market (15). The Electronic Industries Association, a trade association of major electronics industries, is using a different approach. Through its Electronics Industries Foundation, training and technical assistance in providing opportunities to the handicapped is provided the 283 member companies so they will be in compliance (16).

While these second order consequences seem to be useful, other second order consequences of the Act are potentially quite troublesome. For example, we might expect resulting shifts as follows:

> Away from a normative-moral view of the problem to one of pragmatic and political utilitarianism with the possibility of ultimate coercion-alienation.
>
> Away from the doctrine of voluntary social responsibility to one of compliance and litigation.
>
> Away from hiring personnel to meet current and future organizational needs to one of hiring to meet specific narrowly defined tasks and functions to be in compliance.
>
> Away from maximizing group or organizational performance to maximizing individual performance (on the part of various minorities) and hopefully optimizing group organizational performance.

The legal philosophy involved is reductionistic and mechanistic in nature, insofar as both the individual handicapped person and the organization are concerned. By focusing on a particular job or collection of duties and tasks at one point in time, that is, the lowest common denominator, in order to meet the "qualified worker" requirement, the handicapped worker is cast in the role of being an interchangeable part rather than a unique human being. It is reminiscent of the Taylor-Gilbreth period of time and motion studies and the "scientific management" of 60 years ago.

And organizations are placed in the position of hiring personnel, not to meet their holistic Gestalt of themselves past, present, and future, but to meet some implied (but vigorously denied) quotas. European countries, on the other hand, openly and consciously use a quota system (17). It is expected that in many instances form will replace substance as managers grapple with reasonable accommodations, affirmative action, and other requirements not very clearly defined.

OTHER LEGAL SOLUTIONS

The Rehabilitation Act of 1973 covers parts of the federal government and recipients of federal funds. However, as Wolkinson and Barton (18) have observed, the rights and protections afforded to disabled employees have also been influenced by provisions of collective bargaining agreements and industrial common law, which has evolved from grievance procedures. Focusing on mental disabilities, Wolkinson and Barton state: "The industrial common law . . . has established definite restraints on management's ability to penalize workers afflicted by mental illness. Furthermore, this industrial common law appears to impose on employers some duty to accommodate the specific needs of affected workers" (p. 41). For example, in some cases arbitrators have indicated that employers "must do everything possible to enable the mentally handicapped employee to adjust to normal work life, including transfer to other jobs" (p. 42). There is a trend among arbitrators to view the routine applications of normal discipline procedures as an inappropriate mechanism and in general to parallel the "reasonable accommodation" procedures of the Rehabilitation Act.

TOWARD A SYNERGISTIC SOLUTION

Maslow defined synergy as (19):

> The resolution of the dichotomy between selfishness and unselfishness or between selfishness and altruism. We normally assume that the more one has the less the other has . . . this need not be so under the correct institutional and social arrangements. It is possible to set up society so that when I am pursuing my own self interest, I automatically benefit everyone else, whether I mean to or not. Under the same arrangement when I try to be altruistic and philanthropic, I cannot help benefiting myself or advancing my own self interest.

The most desirable solution to improving opportunities for the handicapped and maintaining the integrity of organizations would seem to call for a synergistic answer in which each party might achieve its objectives but not at the expense of the other. Consequently the question might be cast as: "How to maintain organizational integrity and productivity while reducing functional limitations of the impaired so that they might better participate in society, including the job market?"

Organizational Integrity and Productivity

The primary task of the organizational manager, chief executive officer, or administrator is to maintain organizational integrity by means of planning, organizing, staffing, directing, and controlling the organization. The manager must be responsive to shifting forces, demands, requests, and requirements emanating from within his or her organization. The manager must also be responsive to external requirements (such as federal, state, local laws, the IRS, SSA, ERISA, ESA, EPA, DOE, and EDA) that impinge upon and limit his or her choices. Finally, the manager must provide "boundary maintenance" at the interface between internal and external forces. These tasks are obviously made easier if the organization lives in a benign environment or is surrounded by supportive rather than coercive forces (20). Ideally the manager is free to employ factors of production in proportion to their optimal contribution to achievement of the organization's purpose(s) and, simultaneously, these decisions contribute to the welfare of society. Indeed this congruence underlies the viability of a free market system. Where this congruence is believed to be lacking, the manager is pressured to respond to political or social concerns rather than economic ones.

In the case of employment opportunities for the handicapped, the easiest synergistic solution would occur in cases in which the provision of meaningful employment opportunities is in the employer's economic interest. Fortunately, this state of affairs often appears to exist.

There is considerable evidence that it is good business to employ the handicapped. Ginzberg (21) has observed that our society offers such a great variety of jobs and so many jobs that require only a limited number of human capacities that even severely handicapped people are physically capable of performing work effectively. Newer (22) found that during World War II, when the economy faced a labor shortage, almost everyone was employable. Gilmer (23) observed that following adequate job analysis, assessment, and training, "the vast majority of handicapped people can be placed in jobs where they can produce as well as nonhandicapped persons" (p. 147). In fact there are some environments where handicapped people actually are better suited than nonhandicapped. (For example, deaf people are better suited to work situations of intense noise.) Handicapped workers often have superior peformance and safety records and tend to stay with an employer. Gilmer reported that a survey of over 100 corporations revealed about 24 percent of handicapped workers produced at a higher rate than their more able-bodied co-workers; two-thirds of the handicapped produced at about the same level.

Clearly there are many situations in which humaneness and productivity can be achieved simultaneously. These possibilities can be realized through sound manpower practices and good human resources management. Manpower policies can provide for effective training and vocational counseling. The potential success of such policies is suggested by Gilmer's (23) observation that one of the reasons handicapped employees are often so successful is that they have been matched more carefully with their job requirements than are typical employees. Investment in these activities is clearly both humane and productive.

In addition, the application of well-established personnel management practices to dealing with handicapped employees is also apt to have both humane and productive consequences. Some of these ideas were presented by Neuschutz in a form directly applicable to the handicapped some time ago (24). Neuschutz advised supervisors: to remember their key role in the success of their employees; to orient their employees appropriately to the organization, their work, and their co-workers; to give prompt and regular feedback, and to be sensitive to the unique needs of the handicapped individual. These thoughts are as relevant today as they were when Neuschutz presented them for contributing to humane and productive employment of the handicapped in a number of cases.

Unfortunately, such synergistic outcomes are often not achieved and may often be impossible. As a result political and social pressures tend to contribute to some dysfunctional actions. Handicapped people are a potent political force. Tax monies are used to create artificial jobs, that is, the government becomes "employer of last resort," while surviving industry is encouraged to hire certain classes of people as part of its social respon sibility, or directed to hire others by law. Since merely being "gainfully employed" does not necessarily mean being productive, one result is institutionalized inefficiency and inflation. There can be no escape from this spiral without a massive increase in real productivity (25).

Opportunities for the handicapped as well as all individuals would be more promising if executives and managers of organizations were represented by human beings who are not only power and profit oriented but have a sense of values more social and comprehensive in nature. For business success in the American scene, there is no denying that power and utilitarianism are necessary values. For sustained effectiveness a sense of social values could be a significant contribution. Social values in the sense of sympathy for the underdog, were personified by such people as Eleanor Roosevelt, Jane Adams, and Pope John XXIII.

The synergistic win-win solution calls for a healthy productive economy, free of inflation, which creates goods, capital, and jobs, and individuals who have been afforded the opportunity to transcend their pathologies and impairments, whose functional limitations have been overcome and whose inability to perform social roles and tasks has been minimized. Actual placement, then, is a function of individual employability (i.e., those who can perform vocational and economic roles and tasks as defined by the real world) and the requirements of the economy at the time.

Potential abilities for productivity they have, and the use of these abilities would be an advantage to them as well as to organizations which employ them. The use of a perspective that included social values in the decision making process would be in line with the demand of the handicapped expressed by one, namely, "that others see us as people, not as crutches and wheelchairs and canes." In short, for organizational effectiveness it would be well for managers to be humane as well as productive.

REFERENCES

1. Nagi, S. *Definitions of Pathology, Impairment, Functional Limitations and Disability.* Mary E. Switzer Memorial Series #1. Washington, D.C.: National Rehabilitation Association, 1975.
2. Rusell, H. *Affirmative Action for Disabled People.* Washington, D.C.: President's Committee on Employment of the Handicapped, 1979. p. 4.
3. Etzioni, A. *A Comparative Analysis of Complex Organizations.* Glencoe, Ill.: Free Press, 1961.
4. Nord, W. R. (Ed.). *Concepts and Controversy in Organizational Behavior.* 2nd ed. Santa Monica, Calif.: Goodyear, 1976.
5. Lippitt, G. L. *Organizational Renewal.* New York: Appleton Century Crofts, 1969.
6. Schein, E. H. *Organizational Psychology.* 2nd ed. Englewood Cliffs, N.J.: Prentice-Hall, 1970.
7. Luthans, F. *Introduction to Management: A Contingency Approach.* New York: McGraw-Hill, 1976.
8. Reid, T. R. Rules to protect minorities rights guard a majority. *The Washington Post,* Washington, D.C. March 18, 1979, p. C1.
9. Elkins, A. & Callaghan, D. W. *A Managerial Odyssey: Problems in Business and its Environment.* Reading, Mass.: Addison-Wesley, 1979. p. 10.
10. Burck, G. The hazards of corporate responsibility. *Fortune Magazine,* June 1973, p. 115.
11. Friedman, M. The social responsibility of business is to increase its profits. *The New York Times Magazine,* September 13, 1970, p. 33, 122–126.
12. Ninety Third Congress. *Public Law 93-112.* September 26, 1973.
13. U.S. Dept. of Health, Education and Welfare. *Annual Report to the President and the Congress, Fiscal Year 1978, on Federal Activities Related to the Administration of the Rehabilitation Act of 1973, as amended.* Washington, D.C.: Office of the Secretary, USDHEW, n.d.
14. American Coalition of Citizens with Disabilities. *Taking Action for Affirmative Action.* Washington, D.C.: Author, n.d.
15. Perlman, L. G. (Ed.). *Rehabilitation of the Mentally Ill in the 1980's: A Report of the Fourth Mary E. Switzer Memorial Seminar.* Washington, D.C.: National Rehabilitation Association, 1980.
16. Electronics Industries Foundation. *Project with Industry.* Washington, D.C.: Author, February 28, 1978.
17. Reubens, B. G. *The Hard to Employ.* New York: Columbia University, 1970.
18. Wolkinson, B. W. & Barton, D. Arbitration and the rights of mentally handicapped workers. *Monthly Labor Review,* April 1980, **103** (4), 41–47.
19. Maslow, A. H. *Eupsychian Management.* Homewood, Ill.: Irwin-Dorsey, 1965, p. 20.

20. Emery, F. R. & Trist, E. G. The causal texture of organizational environments. *Human Relations, 1963,* **18,** p. 20–26.

21. Ginzberg, E. *The Development of Human Resources.* New York: McGraw-Hill, 1966.

22. Newer, B. S. Employment prospects. *Personnel Journal,* 1944, **23,** 135–144.

23. Gilmer, B. H. Special groups in organizations. In B. H. Gilmer & E. L. Deci *Industrial and Organizational Psychology.* 4th ed. New York: McGraw-Hill, 1977, pp. 146–169.

24. Neuschutz, L. M. *Vocational Rehabilitation for the Physically Handicapped.* Springfield, Ill.: Charles C. Thomas, 1959.

25. Ehrle, R. A. Employment—or access to ownership—as a property right? *The Journal of Applied Rehabilitation Counseling, 1979,* **10** (2), 85–88.

—15—

Alcoholism and Other Substance Abuse

David J. Pittman

The relationship of human beings to drugs is a long one, antedating recorded history. Drugs have been used for religious, medicinal, hedonistic, and social purposes. Cultural and legal attitudes towards drugs vary. For example, a drug such as alcohol may be highly exalted by one society (e.g., France) and at the same time prohibited by another (e.g., Libya); or another drug such as cannabis may be widely used by one segment of a community and severely frowned upon by another part of it. Furthermore, over time a community's attitude toward a drug may reverse itself; for example, opiates were legally accepted in the United States prior to World War I and legally prohibited, except under strict regulation, after that time. The current drug problem in the United States and other Western countries is not a new phenomenon, although it is more complex than it was previously.

The increased complexity of the drug problem is related to scientific advances in the field of pharmacology over the last thirty years. Society today has at its disposal drugs that cover the whole spectrum of human behavior. Besides the contraceptive pill, we have others to sedate us when we are nervous, excite us when we are dull, slim us when we are fat, fatten us when we are thin, awaken us when we are sleepy, put us to sleep when we are awake, cure us when we are sick, and make us sick when we are well. Thus, on one hand, drugs can enhance our ability to function more effectively, but on the other side, they can carry our minds out of the realm of reality into loneliness, despair, and hopelessness.

In discussing such an emotionally charged area as drugs, it is imperative to maintain a rational perspective. Miracle drugs of the antibiotic family (such as penicillin), steroids, insulin, and others have brought a revolution to the treatment of many of humankind's illnesses. Thus drugs in a generic sense have achieved widespread acceptance in all countries, whether obtained by prescription or over the counter. The mass media in Western society is filled with advertisements of chemical agents that will remedy many of our problems, whether they be body odor, headache, bad breath, or digestive upset. Yet any drug or chemical agent can be misused with negative consequences to the individual and society. Fortunately, there are few drugs out of the thousands available that are consistently misused by any significant portion of the population (1).

DRUG TERMINOLOGY

Much confusion surrounds the scientific and social terminology used in reference to drugs. The first problem centers on the question, "What is addiction?" Authorities disagree as to what actually constitutes addiction, and as a result, which drugs are addictive.

One reason addiction continues to puzzle scientists is the multifaceted character of the phenomenon. Addiction to drugs (of which alcohol is one) is typically the result of many interacting factors. It is not just the effect of the drug on the person, but the social-psychological state of the individual that is crucial, that is, how he or she reacts to the drug in his or her particular environment.

Since there are many different addictive drugs, and many factors influence a person's becoming addicted, it is difficult to discover any direct cause-effect relationship for addiction. Thus it is not sufficient to state that a reason a person is addicted is that he or she took excessive amounts of a certain drug. One must also consider the drug in question, the laws regarding it, the society's attitude toward the chemical agent (which is not always reflected in the laws), the individual's attitude toward it, and the physical and psychological makeup of the individual. Stated differently, knowledge of the drug per se is necessary for understanding addiction, but it is not sufficient for a full comprehension of the pathology (2, p. 2).

In drug research four terms frequently appear: "addiction," "habituation," "dependence," and "abuse." These terms are not mutually exclusive, and there are frequent disagreements about their precise meaning.

Addiction

There are three properties that a drug must have before it is considered addictive: it must produce tolerance, and abstinence (withdrawal) syndrome, and craving. Tolerance means that the drug must be taken in progressively larger doses in order to achieve the desired result. Simplified, tolerance develops as follows: If a person begins to take daily one grain of drug A, he or she finds that at the end of several weeks the drug no longer affects him or her in the same manner. He or she then increases the dosage to two grains daily. After a month or so, the person again realizes that drug A no longer produces the desired effect. He or she therefore increases the daily dosage to three grains, and so on.

If the person is suddenly prevented from taking any more of drug A, he or she experiences an abstinence syndrome. These symptoms vary from one drug to another and depend on the amount of drugs being taken. The abstinence syndrome is characterized by physical symptoms, such as stomach cramps, diarrhea, and irritability.

The person taking drug A will develop a craving for the drug that is due not only to the physical effects that the drug has on his or her body but also to fear of the abstinence syndrome. Too, he or she may develop a psychological craving that is not fully understood. Typically, many addicts who have been successfully withdrawn from a drug develop a strong desire to begin taking the drug again. This is one of several reasons why the relapse rate after treatment for addicts is extremely high.

Habituation

There are many habit-forming agents that some people use, such as coffee, tea, and tobacco. Also some drugs are habit-forming. Simply stated, all addictive drugs are habit-forming, but not all habit-forming drugs are addictive in the pharmacological sense. Habituation is primarily psychological, as a physical abstinence syndrome does not develop when the agent is suddenly withdrawn from the individual. There are, however, habit forming drugs, such as certain amphetamines, where tolerance does develop, but there is no abstinence syndrome. In short, habituation may consist of tolerance and craving (primarily psychological), but it is never followed by an abstinence syndrome.

Dependence

In 1964 the World Health Organization (3) released a report from its expert committee on drugs which combined the terms "addiction" and "habituation" under one term: "dependence." This committee felt that the scientific literature reflected much confusion between addiction and habituation, and as a result, the classification of a drug as addictive or habit-forming was difficult. The WHO Committee suggested that each drug should be described by its particular type of dependence, for example, "drug dependence of the alcohol type." Thus the substitution of the word "dependence" for both addiction and habituation is an attempt to clarify drug terminology.

Abuse or Misuse

Almost all drugs that have been produced for medical or scientific use as well as beverage alcohol have their consumption controlled by legal statutes. People who use drugs illegally, or for some purpose other than that for which the drug was commonly designed or in a manner other than prescribed by the physician, are said to be abusing the drug. Generally speaking, people who are dependent on drugs are also abusing them. However, there are some people who take drugs but never become dependent upon them. In summary, persons who use drugs for other than the generally accepted reasons or who take them illegally but are not dependent on them are classified as drug abusers or misusers.

PROBLEM DRUGS

The drugs most related to problems in Western society may be divided into seven categories: (a) ethyl alcohol; (b) cannabis; (c) opiates, synthetic opiates; (d) amphetamines; (e) hallucinogens; (f) barbiturates; and (g) cocaine.

In this chapter the major emphasis will be on problems associated with alcohol abuse, since it is the most widely used drug in American society. We shall also discuss cannabis briefly, since it is estimated that 60 percent of high school seniors have used marijuana, and daily use of this drug by some group is reported by 10.3 percent (4).

Ethyl Alcohol

Although there are numerous types of alcohol, ethyl alcohol is the one of concern in this chapter, for it is the type that is consumed by humans. Alcohol is made by small organisms that are found almost everywhere. How these tiny organisms make alcohol has been succinctly stated by Chafetz:

> No grape or grain or other attractive flower makes alcohol. Rather these fruits of the soil are devoured by the yeast, or ferment germ, and the germ then evacuates alcohol as its waste product. (5, p. 37)

Pharmacologically alcohol depresses the central nervous system. It has its most serious effect on the human brain. The intensity of alcohol's effect on the human is directly related to its concentration in the blood and brain tissue. Alcohol begins to impair the brain's ability to function at the 0.05 percent level, that is, 0.05 grams of alcohol per 100 cc. of blood.

Alcohol is the most widely used drug in Western society, and numerically it is the most abused drug by population in the United States, despite the mass media's attention to marijuana or heroin. A study (6) of American drinking habits published in 1969 based on a national probability sample of the population aged 21 or older obtained a wealth of information on drinking practices and attitudes in terms of such sociological variables as age, sex, race, religion, ethnicity, income, and so on. These researchers, by utilizing a Q-F-V index (for quantity, frequency, and variability) of drinking have classified the American population into five groups of drinkers: (a) "abstainers" (32 percent of the sample), who report that they drank less than once a year; (b) "infrequent drinkers" (15 percent), who drank less than once a month; (c) "light drinkers" (28 percent), who drank at least once a month but only in small quantities; (d) "moderate drinkers" (13 percent), who drank several times a month, usually no more than three or four drinks per occasion; and (e) "heavy drinkers" (12 percent), who drank almost every day, frequently consuming five or more drinks per occasion. This latter group probably includes most of the estimated nine million Americans who are considered alcoholics or problem drinkers by health officials. The percentage of individuals in each of the drinking categories does not appear to have appreciably changed in the last decade (7, p. 8).

Cannabis

Marijuana, charas, hemp, hashish, bhang, pot, tea, and weed are just a few of the terms used throughout the world to describe products of the female plant *Cannabis sativa* or Indian hemp (2, pp. 5–7). Cannabis has been used for medicinal, social, and pleasurable purposes for thousands of years, rivaling opium in its history. It was popular with Indian philosophers and was widely used by Arabs at the time of the Crusades.

The plant's popularity has not diminished in the Middle East and India; currently cannabis is enjoying wide acceptance in Western countries despite national and international efforts to suppress its use. Also cannabis' approbation in Western society is based mainly on nonmedical purposes; however it is now used for very specific medical purposes, that is glaucoma and in conjunction with chemotherapy for carcinomas.

Cannabis is commonly called pot, marijuana, hashish or hash, and grass. It is almost always smoked in the form of a cigarette, which is referred to as a joint or reefer. Occasionally cannabis is smoked with opium; this mixture is termed charas. Cannabis varies greatly in its potency, which correlates with the growing conditions to which the plant is subjected. There is regular cannabis, which consists of the pulverized leaves and stems of the plant. Then there is the more powerful type, which is made up largely of dried resin from the flower of the plant; this type of cannabis is hash or hashish.

The effect cannabis has on individuals varies greatly. This variance can partly be explained by the different grades of cannabis. However, it has also been suggested that persons learn what to expect from the drug before they actually take it. (8) Thus if someone is advised that pot will help him or her appreciate the "true" meaning of a painting, the painting will take on new and exciting dimensions for the pot smoker. How much the pharmacology of the drug has to do with the experience is difficult to discern. Still there are several general effects that cannabis appears to have on most persons. Users talk of the drug's euphoric qualities, which give them a sense of well-being, light-headedness, and pleasant experiences in perceiving things.

Cannabis is not physically addictive. Although habituation has been reported in the Middle East, is it not very common to find someone habituated to the drug in Western countries. Users frequently compare it favorably to alcohol, saying it is less dangerous, results in a better form of intoxication, and does not have the unpleasant aftereffects frequently associated with alcohol. Those who advocate legalization of cannabis compare it to a social drug like alcohol, and claim it is less harmful than the latter. Yet cannabis is illegal. It has been accused of leading users to dangerous drugs such as heroin. True, some persons who take cannabis later become dependent upon other drugs; however, many users of cannabis never progress to taking dangerous drugs. In short, it is incorrect to state that there exists a direct causal relationship between cannabis and addictive drugs.

As a result of the illegality of cannabis, persons who use it frequently associate with others illicitly taking other drugs, and vice versa. The cannabis smoker may frequently come into contact with other drug users, and because of this he or she is more likely to become dependent upon some other drug than if there were no such association. This dependence would not be due to any inherent properties of cannabis; rather it would be the result of the social milieu associated with cannabis (which is caused in no small part by its illegality) and the sociopsychological makeup of the individual.

However, it is beyond the scope of this chapter to fully discuss the deleterious effects of heavy and frequent use of marijuana or its effect when used in combination with other drugs such as alcohol or barbiturates. Our major focus will be on problems associated with alcoholism and alcohol abuse.

CONCEPTS OF ALCOHOLISM

Fundamental to any discussion of alcoholism are the orientations held by various researchers and clinicians to this condition. The American Medical Association defines alcoholism as:

> An illness characterized by preoccupation with alcohol and loss of control over its consumption such as to lead usually to intoxication if drinking is begun; by chronicity; by progression; and by tendency toward relapse. It is typically associated with physical disability and impaired emotional, occupational, and/or social adjustments as a direct consequence of persistent and excessive use of alcohol. (9)

The late Professor Jellinek (10) differentiated the species of alcoholism into five major types; namely, alpha, beta, gamma, delta, and epsilon, indicating that the types of alcoholism vary in frequency in reference to the cultural context. However, a major schism in reference to the concept of alcoholism exists in North America.

These two concepts are that alcoholism is a symptom (11) of an underlying mental condition, defect, or pathology (this position is sometimes reflected in the statement that alcoholism is a mental disease); or that alcoholism is a chronic illness. The "symptom" orientation develops from psychoanalytic theory and has permeated the psychiatric and social work professions in particular. A telling critique of this position is found in the article on social workers' attitudes toward alcoholics by Bailey and Fuchs, who state:

> It seems possible that there is a relationship between the pessimism and frustration of these social workers and their tendency to regard alcoholism as a symptom rather than a disease. The helping person's concept of the nature of alcoholism will determine the orientation of his therapeutic efforts. If he regards alcoholism as a symptom, then the treatment program will be designed to resolve the underlying emotional

> problem. This position is entirely logical, but in practice it resembles searching for the causes of a fire while the blaze itself goes unchecked. (12)

There is a further logical extension of the alcoholism as a symptom orientation that is rarely verified clinically. If alcoholism is caused by underlying psychopathology, a resolution of this conflict by the patient in a therapeutic context should allow the individual with his or her revised personality to return to normal or social drinking. This phenomenon, as we know, rarely occurs; therefore we should critically evaluate the merit of this unadulterated psychoanalytic position in reference to our concept of alcoholism.

The competing view is that alcoholism is a chronic disease (13), the etiology of which is not yet established. Hypothesized as possible etiologic factors are biochemical, physiologic, metabolic, or genetic defects in the organism; related to the disease concept of alcoholism is the view of alcoholism as the consequence of prolonged alcohol intake in toxic quantities (14).

The disease concept of alcoholism, however, has implications for the treatment process. When the alcoholic is viewed as suffering from a chronic illness, general practitioners and internists begin to assume more responsibility for the patient's case instead of providing blanket psychiatric referrals. Hospital staffs, because they are prepared for the chronic nature of such illnesses as heart disease, ulcerative colitis, and gastric ulcers, can better accept the relapses of alcoholics. Just as crucial is the fact that the sick role can be assigned to the alcoholic instead of a role that has overtones of moral responsibility.

Despite the pervasiveness of the disease and symptom viewpoints toward alcoholism, we should not overlook the possbility of other orientations toward this condition. For example, alcoholism may be a secondary disorder that results from the convergence of an array of intrapsychic tensions, normative orientations toward drinking, and alternative mechanisms of tension reduction (15).

Unfortunately, the line between alcohol abuse and alcoholism in individuals is sometimes difficult for the clinicians to discern. Almost all diagnosed alcoholics invariably have specific medical, social, and psychological problems. On the other hand, not all individuals who have specific problems as the consequence of drinking beverage alcohol are alcoholic. Perhaps this is most apparent in some individuals who are arrested for driving while intoxicated. Some of these persons are only social drinkers who become intoxicated and are imprudent enough to operate a motor vehicle. Thus all individuals who have problems vis-à-vis the use of alcohol should not be diagnosed as alcoholics. From our point of view the best definition for alcoholism is the one developed by the American Medical Association previously cited. Since the literature on alcoholism frequently lumps alcohol abusers indiscriminately with alcoholics for the purposes of this chapter we will do the same in our discussion of alcoholism, alcohol abuse, and specific medical and social problems.

ALCOHOL ABUSE, ALCOHOLISM, AND SPECIFIC SOCIAL AND MEDICAL PROBLEMS

The abuse of alcohol in American society directly affects almost all sectors of the society—the criminal justice system, highway safety, health programs, given the high incidence of morbidity and mortality rates of chronic alcohol abusers, and industrial productivity with the presence of some alcoholics in executive and assembly line positions. The real cost of alcohol abuse and alcoholism to American society in terms of wasted lines, lost productivity, and human misery and suffering has not yet been adequately measured in monetary terms, and it is doubtful whether it ever can be precisely cost accounted.

Crime and Alcohol Use

Two major research approaches have characterized the investigation of the relationship of crime and alcohol use. First, what is the drinking behavior of the individual when he or she commits a crime? Second, what is the correlation between longstanding alcohol abuse and criminality?

In determining the drinking status of the individual at the commission of the crime, two research techniques have been used. Illustrative of one approach is Marvin E. Wolfgang's (16) study of homicides committed in Philadelphia in 1948 to 1952, composed of 588 victims (cases) and 621 offenders. He reports that "either or both the victim and offender had been drinking immediately prior to the slaying in nearly two-thirds of the cases" (16, p. 322).

A second, more accurate research technique is to analyze the blood or urine of the individual for alcohol content immediately after the commission of the crime. Illustrative of this approach was a research investigation in Columbus, Ohio, where urine analysis for alcohol concentration was completed in a study by Shupe (17) of "882 persons picked up during or immediately after the commission of a felony" (17, p. 661) during the period March 1951 to March 1955. Shupe states:

> The figure show that crimes of physical violence are associated with intoxicated persons. Cuttings (11 to 1 under the influence of alcohol), the carrying of concealed weapons (8 to 1 under the influence of alcohol) are definitely crimes of alcohol influence, even crimes of true intoxication. (17, p. 663)

Thus the closest relationship between intoxication and criminal behavior (except for public intoxication) has been established for criminal categories involving assaultive behavior. This relationship is especially high for lower-lower class Blacks and Whites. More than likely, aggression in these groups is weakly controlled, and the drinking of alcoholic beverages serves as a triggering mechanism for the external release of agression. There are certain types of key situations located in lower-class life in which alcohol is a major factor in assaultive behavior. A frequent locale is the lower-class tavern, which is an important social institution for this class. Assaultive episodes are precipitated during the drinking situation by quarrels that center around defaming personal honor, threats to masculinity, and questions about one's birth legitimacy. Personal quarrels between husband and wife, especially centered on the husband's drinking, frequently results in assaultive episodes in the lower-lower class family.

Shupe's conclusion that 64 percent of his sample of 882 individuals were "under the influence of alcohol to such an extent that their inhibitions were reduced" (17, p.664) is of major significance to Americn criminologists. Excessive drinking of alcoholic beverages is a relevant fact in the commission of some crimes.

Crime Categories and Alcoholism and Alcohol Abuse

There are specific criminal categories that are intimately related to the use of alcoholic beverages. Most clearly involved are violations of public intoxication statutes where it has not been decriminalized, and the closely related charges of disorderly conduct, vagrancy, loitering, and peace disturbance; liquor law violations; and driving under the influence (mainly alcohol but may include other drugs). In terms of magnitude, the most frequent arrests in the United States were for driving under the influence and drunkenness, with over one million estimated arrests for each category in 1978 (18) out of a total of more than ten million estimated arrests in that year (18, p. 186).

The number of arrests for public drunkenness has been declining over the last decade as more jurisdictions have decriminalized this offense, that is, removed it from the criminal code. The first political jurisdiction in the United States to fully implement the decriminalization of this victimless crime was St. Louis in 1967 with the establishment of a detoxification center to treat public drunkenness cases instead of sending those arrested to jail. In short, it was realized that most of those arrested for public drunkenness were chiefly chronic alcoholics or ill individuals who received no aid for their problem by incarceration. Thus jailing was replaced by emergency medical and social care and long-term treatment programs for these individuals.

Unfortunately, despite the endorsement of decriminalization by the major police, correctional, medical, and social organizations, only approximately 30 of the 50 states in 1980 have decriminalized this offense.

Alcohol Abuse and Health

Prolonged heavy drinking, alcohol abuse, and alcoholism are related directly and indirectly to many physical disorders. There is no question that heavy drinkers and alcoholics have a higher incidence of morbidity and mortality rates than those of moderate drinkers or nondrinkers. The mortality rate of alcoholics, based on age-specific data, is approximately two and one-half times higher than that of normal drinkers or abstainers; the life expectancy of alcoholics is reduced by as much as 10 to 12 years (19, p. 45). Alcoholism is intimately related to suicide in that it has been variously reported in the United States that one-fourth to one-third of all completed suicides involve chronic alcoholics.

The host of physical disorders that are highly correlated with alcohol abuse and alcoholism are numerous and the relationships too complex to discuss extensively in this chapter. Alcoholism is frequently associated with nutritional disorders, which are related to diseases of the neurological, digestive, and other body systems. Alcohol abuse and alcoholism are partially implicated in such disorders as liver cirrhosis, alcoholic hepatitis, heart disease, gastritis, esophagitis, carcinoma of the mouth, throat, esophagus, and stomach, and brain disorders such as Wernicke's syndrome and Korsakoff's psychosis. However, some individuals can have these diseases without their having an alcoholism or alcohol abuse problem, for example, liver cirrhosis, heart disease, or gastritis.

Recent evidence (7, p. 55) indicates that heavy ingestion of beverage alcohol by pregnant women can result in a syndrome of abnormalities in the offspring of these women, which has been termed the Fetal Alcohol Syndrome (FAS). The FAS is characterized by such traits in infants as having lower birth weight, facial and cranial abnormalities, and most often impaired intellectual development, placing them in the "borderline or retarded range of intelligence" (7, p. 57). As yet no evidence exists that light or moderate drinking (less than two drinks a day) by the pregnant female relates directly to the FAS.

On the other hand, Klatsky (20) presents evidence from a longitudinal study of 100,000 individuals in the Kaiser-Permanente Medical Group in California that moderate drinkers (two to three drinks daily) compared to abstainers have a 30 percent reduction in the probability of myocardial infarctions (heart attacks). Yano et al. (20) and Stasson et al. (20) present similar results in their studies.

Furthermore, moderate consumption of alcoholic beverages has been an integral part of the social customs in many Western societies, and beverage alcohol has been an integral part in religious, ceremonial, and celebratory occasions by many groups without deleterious effects. In short, moderate drinking may have beneficial effects for some individuals who choose to drink.

What society needs to be concerned about are the consequences of excessive and heavy drinking and intoxication that generally lead to physical and social problems. In conclusion, in dealing with an acute intoxication episode or an alcohol-related disorder in the individual we are confronted with a situation that cries out for the abandonment of the "funny drunk" stereotype that has characterized the mass media in particular and American society in general for decades. When society learns to stop laughing about intoxication, maybe the American health delivery system can focus on the proper treatment of this serious health problem.

Alcohol Abuse and Industry

The relationship between alcohol abuse and alcoholism and decreased industrial productivity is an intimate one. Although statistics are not precise, between 4 and 8 percent of the United States' work force (including military and civilian employees of the government) are alcoholics; they cost business around $10 billion yearly in poor job performance, accidents, absenteeism, inaccurate decisions at all levels of the business command, and related costs. (21)

Alcohol abusers are found at all levels of management and in all positions in the general work force of a company. No industry can make the statement, as some still do, that they have no alcoholic employees or executives. The same fact is true of labor unions, whether it be their heirarchy or mass membership.

Business has a unique ability to mount alcoholism rehabilitation activities, generally under the terms of the "employee assistance" programs or the "troubled" employee programs. These endeavors, which carry the implicit fear of the loss of a job unless the worker or executive does something about his or her alcohol problem, have had recovery rates for the participants of 60 to 80 percent.

The first industrial program to deal with alcoholic workers within the rehabilitation framework was instituted 30 years ago by the Du Pont Corporation as part of company policy, followed later by Eastman Kodak Corporation. But the old company policies of firing alcoholics or denying that they existed, the trade union's position of covering up the indiscretions of the alcoholic, and the military's reluctance to state that alcoholics were in the Armed Forces were slow to wither away. Now these traditions of denial of alcoholism in the work force have begun to collapse at an accelerating rate. In the past few years major "troubled employee" programs, serving mainly alcoholics, have commenced with such activities as the jointly sponsored General Motors-United Automobile Workers program covering 400,000 workers, the Department of Defense's announcement in 1972 of a rehabilitation program for all military personnel, and the United States Congressional mandate in 1970 that the Civil Service Commission establish alcoholism treatment programs for all federal civilian employees.

There has been a significant increase in "employee assistance" alcoholism programs in the last decade. By mid-1977, the number of such programs had increased to around 2400 with about 2000 in organizations in the private sector of the economy and 400 in public sector organizations and agencies (7, p. 110).

The impact of these employee assistance programs will mean that more individuals will obtain help for their alcoholism probably long before they reach the terminal phase of their illness. However, we should not assume that such programs solve the primary problems of the prevention of alcoholism, which are anchored in general cultural and social attitudes toward alcohol use in the society, possible genetic predisposition, and psychological variables.

SOCIAL POLICY RESPONSES TO ALCOHOLISM

The last decade in North America has been marked by a massive social movement to redefine the position of alcoholism and the alcoholic within the health delivery system of the United States. The social movement has been based on the ideology that alcoholism is an illness that is best handled in a sociomedical context instead of as a personal vice or moral weakness. Although the disease orientation to alcoholism has been present in North American society for decades, it was not until the mid-1960s that this ideology was translated into concrete legislative action by the United States Congress and the state legislatures, by specific court rulings, and by a proliferation of both private and public treatment facilities in Canada and the United States.

Specifically, the major developments that have affected social policy vis-à-vis alcoholism were the passage by Congress of PL 91-616, the Comprehensive Alcohol Abuse and Alcoholism Prevention, Treatment, and Rehabilitation Act of 1970, commonly referred to as the Hughes Act, which created the National Institute of Alcohol Abuse and Alcoholism, the primary locus of responsibility for alcoholism activities at the federal level; the extension of this legislation with the passage of PL 93-282 in 1974 by Congress; the enactment by various state legislatures (approximately 26) of the Uniform Alcoholism and Intoxication Treatment Act, which has as its major thrust the removal of simple public intoxication from the criminal justice system to the health delivery system; and the widespread diffusion of health insurance third-party payment plans for the treatment of alcoholics under the primary diagnosis of alcoholism.

Despite these major developments, alcoholism is not fully accepted as an illness that requires the full array of social, psychologic, and medical services. For example, a study on prejudice and disability by Tringo (22) of 455 people composed of high-school students, college students, graduate students, and rehabilitation workers, which asked the sample to rate 21 disabilities from the most acceptable to the least acceptable, ranked alcoholism number 20, only slightly less acceptable than mental illness, which was ranked 21st or last. The most acceptable disabilities were, in descending order, ulcers, arthritis, asthma, diabetes, and heart disease. This study reconfirmed the negative attitudes that still prevail in many sectors of society toward alcoholism and mental illness.

Alcoholism treatment personnel must be cognizant of the general social milieu, in which attitudes of negativism and pessimism exist toward the provision of services for alcoholics. Alcoholics, the reactions of society to them, and organizations working in the field closely resemble the minority group status syndrome. Alcoholics, like many minority group members, know firsthand the segregation procedures. Often they are refused admission to hospitals for treatment or receive only cursory attention in the receiving rooms of municipal and county hospitals; once admitted, they are frequently segregated in a special unit or in the psychiatric ward, because the hospital staff perceive them as different from the usual patient. A stigma is attached to them and their behavior, and frequently this negative evaluation is extended to those who treat them or are advocates on their behalf. Alcoholics of low social status too frequently are thrown into the "drunk tanks" of America for exhibiting the symptoms of their illness, namely, repeated public intoxication. As has been noted by social scientists studying other minority groups, self-hatred occurs among alcoholics, as reflected in their high rates of suicide, depression, and other psychologic ills. Even in communities in which a more enlightened attitude toward alcoholics is relfected by the passage of the Uniform Alcoholism and Intoxication Treatment Act, funding for alcoholism programs to implement this legislation is assigned low priority by politcal divisions, especially the federal government.

Given this background sketch of current societal attitudes and priorities toward alcoholism, a key target group for more information and training in alcoholism becomes the community, especially the sector that may be referred to as the gatekeeper of funds and service allocations.

REFERENCES

1. Pittman, D. J. Drugs, addiction and crime. In D. Glaser (Ed.). *Handbook of Criminology*. Chicago: Rand McNally, 1974, pp. 209–232.
2. Glatt, M. Pittman, D. J. Gillespie, D. G. & Hills, D. R. *The Drug Scene in Great Britain: Journey Into Loneliness*. London: Arnold, 1967.
3. WHO Expert Committee on Addiction Producing Drugs, Technical report series no. 273. Geneva: World Health Organization, 1964.
4. *Marijuana and Health: 1980*. Department of Health, Education, and Welfare's Eighth Annual Report to the U. S. Congress. Rockville, Md.: National Institute on Drug Abuse, 1980.
5. Chafetz, M. E. *Liquor: The Servant of Man*. Boston: Little, Brown, 1965.

6. Cahalan, D. Cisin, I. R. & Crossley, H. M. *American Drinking Practices: A National Study of Drinking Behavior Attitudes.* New Brunswick, N.J.: Rutgers Center on Alcohol Studies, 1969.
7. *Alcohol and Health.* Secretary of Health, Education, and Welfare, Third Special Report to the U. S. Congress, Rockville, Md.: National Institute on Alcohol Abuse and Alcoholism, 1978.
8. Becker, H. Becoming a marijuana user. *American Journal of Sociology,* 1953, **59,** 235–242.
9. *Manual on Alcoholism.* Chicago, Ill.: American Medical Association, 1968.
10. Jellinek, E. M. *The Disease Concept of Alcoholism.* New Haven, Conn.: Hillhouse Press, 1960.
11. Noyes, A. P. & Kolb, L. C. *Modern Clinical Psychiatry.* 5th ed. Philadelphia: W. B. Saunders, 1958.
12. Bailey, M. & Fuchs, E. Alcoholism and the social worker. *Social Work,* 1960, **5,** 14–26.
13. Anonymous, Alcoholism as a medical illness. *Journal of the American Medical Association,* 1957, **164,** 506.
14. Smith, J. A. Psychiatric research in the etiology of alcoholism. In D. J. Pittman (Ed.). *Alcoholism: An Interdisciplinary Approach.* Springfield, Ill.: Charles C. Thomas, 1959, pp. 5–15.
15. Snyder, C. R. A sociological view of the etiology of alcoholism. In D. J. Pittman (Ed.). *Alcoholism: An Interdisciplinary Approach.* Springfield, Ill.: Charles C. Thomas, 1959, pp. 32–39.
16. Wolfgang, M. *Patterns of Criminal Homicide.* Philadelphia: University of Pennsylvania Press, 1958.
17. Shupe, L. Alcohol and crime: A study of urine alcohol concentration found in 882 persons arrested during or immediately after the commission of a felony. *Journal of Criminal Law, Criminology and Police Science,* 1954, **44**, 661–664.
18. U. S. Dept. of Justice. *F. B. I. Uniform Crime Reports: Crime in the United States, 1978.* Washington, D. C.: U. S. Government Printing Office, 1979.
19. *Alcohol and Health,* Secretary of Health, Education, and Welfare, First Special Report to the U. S. Congress, Rockville, Md.: National Institute on Alcohol Abuse and Alcoholism, 1971.
20. *The New York Times,* June 21, 1978.
21. *Business Week,* November 11, 1972.
22. Tringo, J. Prejudice and disability. *Human Behavior,* 1971, prepublication abstract.

—16—

The Role of Transfers and Mobility Experiences in Employee Motivation and Control

Craig C. Pinder

The systematic movement of personnel to meet manpower shortages and other organizational needs has for many years been a common practice of many North American employers. Yet, in spite of the vast number of transfers that take place every year in both the public and the private sectors, there has been a remarkable shortage of research and careful thinking on the part of organizational behavior specialists into the effects of transfers on the people and the organizations involved. Aside from folklore and conventional wisdom, there is little documentation of the role of transfer policies on organizational effectiveness, and only slightly more consideration of the impact of systematized mobility on employees and their families. Recently, however, a growing awareness of employee rights, the quality of life in general, and the quality of working life in particular seems to have precipitated a conscious consideration by many employees of the personal costs and benefits of the reflexive acceptance of organizational transfer requirements, and in many cases conscious decisions to reject requests or directives to move. The uncertainty created for personnel executives by this trend has generated a number of laments in management periodicals (1, 2, 3, 4, 5), but until quite recently, very little has been done to consider employee transfers and their correlates from the perspective of social scientific theories pertaining to organizational behavior or career development. For example, both Hall (6) and Schein (7) make only passing mention of transfers in their recent books on careers. To my knowledge, the work of Edstrom and Galbraith (8) and Brett (9) constitute the first notable attempts to begin construction of a theoretical backdrop for the study of transfers. Accordingly, the purpose of this chapter is to explore the role of transfers in organizational reward and control systems, while trying to construct some preliminary linkage between the growing literature on transfers with the larger general literature pertaining to organizational behavior and careers. Following Brett (9), I will define a transfer in this chapter as any job change within one's present company that entails a geographic relocation.

I will begin with a very brief overview of a two-sample study I began in

The author is grateful to Norman E. Carruthers, Thomas A. Mahoney, and Louis R. Pondy for their helpful comments on an earlier draft of this chapter.

1975 into a number of issues related to job transfers. The purpose of the overview will be to permit me to make reference to a number of findings in that research as they become relevant to various points in the remainder of this chapter. I will then move to a theoretical and empirical examination of the ways in which personnel transfers function to serve the organizational goals of employee motivation and control. Next, I will discuss the recent increase in resistance among many employees to the mobility often required by their employers, from the point of view of a number of larger dynamics in current societal attitudes toward work and commitment to careers. Finally, I will attempt to draw upon the implications of all the preceding analyses to address a question that relates to the central theme of this book: how can we structure personnel transfer policies so as to make organizations both humane and productive?

A STUDY OF TRANSFERRED FAMILIES

My interest in the problem of transfers from the point of view of both the mobile employee and the employing organization began in 1975. After I interviewed several personnel and line managers to gain a number of perspectives on the issue, my research consisted of two mailed questionnaire surveys of a total of 750 Canadian managerial, professional and technical (M-P-T) employees. Four hundred and five (54%) of these employees and their spouses returned usable responses. The samples were drawn from six large corporations in industries where transfers are common (retail, petroleum, and transportation). Included in the samples were people who had been transferred at least once, to and from all parts of Canada and abroad. Married employees were asked to have their spouses independently complete and return a shortened version of the instrument. Further detail about the methodology used in the study, and about the particular results it yielded are reported elsewhere (Pinder, 10; 11; Pinder and Das, 12).

SOME MANIFEST AND LATENT FUNCTIONS OF TRANSFERS

Why do so many organizations rely on transfer programs? What functions and goals are served by transfers that cannot be served by other types of personnel practices? A cursory reading of the sparse managerial literature on job transfers provides the same impression that one receives from asking personnel managers or transferred employees why their organizations practice the policy of moving personnel from location to location. The usual list of reasons includes those identified by Jaffe (13), but normally boils down to two major *ostensible* sets of justifications. The first set includes the need of the organization to adapt to various work force exigencies created by voluntary and involuntary turnover, as well as by organizational changes (such as mergers, acquisitions, and divestitures). The second major set of reasons usually offered to justify the transfer of employees deals with the needs of the organization to train, educate, and socialize managers in preparation for eventual movement into senior executive positions. Many managers discuss this second set of reasons as the most important function of transfers, as if the benefits of this development for the organization are of only secondary importance. In fact, successful employee development is essential for making organizational development possible. But aside from these obvious and well-understood uses of personnel transfers, it can also be argued that policies and programs of deliberate employee relocation can serve a number of other not-so-obvious functions for organizations that have them. Accordingly, in this section I will examine the manifest and latent functions (Merton, 14) of transfers in contributing to the motivation and control of employees.

The Transfer as a Motivational Mechanism

Transfer experiences can be potentially powerful sources of both intrinsic and extrinsic motivation. Intrinsic motivation, as seen by Deci (15) and others can be defined as effort expended for the sake of satisfying what Alderfer (16) calls "growth" needs, or what authors would refer to as the need for competence (17), achievement (18), and self-esteem (19, 20). Transfers can also be instrumental for meeting the more fundamental needs for relatedness and basic existence (Alderfer, 16). To begin, let's look at the potential role of transfers in the satisfaction or frustration of employee growth needs.

Transfers and Growth Needs. The essence of competence motivation is a desire to master one's environment; to seek out and make sense of that which is presently not understood and which is beyond one's control. Relocation to a new job setting generally requires an individual to adapt to (and to conquer) a set of challenges and forms of uncertainty that are new and somewhat unfamiliar. Such opportunities would seem to be especially likely in cases in which the individual is moved into a crisis situation, as often happens when transfers are used to replace employees who have suddenly vacated key managerial positions. Particularly when promotions are involved, the added challenge of the new job (as compared to the former one) can also result in the moderate but attainable levels of difficulty that are essential to arouse maximum achievement motivation (18).

What about the need for self-esteem? Hall (6, 21) has developed a theory of career identity development that features an integration of White's (17) notions of competence motivation with Korman's (19, 20) theory of self-esteem. According to Hall, an individual will experience increased self-esteem and feelings of competence when the attainment of career goals results in feelings of psychological success. Success experiences in turn come from the achievement of challenging goals on the job. Increases in feelings of competence and self-esteem can lead to high levels of involvement in one's career, and the pursuit of even more challenging goals, which in turn may or may not lead to further success experiences, further increases in self-esteem, and strengthened beliefs in one's own competence. The cycle is seen as continuous and self-reinforcing, with successful goal achievement as a key determinant of whether growth, involvement, and higher goal seeking will continue for the employee. The challenges posed by transfers can be critical opportunities for reinforcing or weakening such a cycle for an individual. If the challenges are sufficient and the individual succeeds in meeting them, Hall's theory predicts increases in the person's self-esteem, competence, career involvement, and the setting of higher goals. Alternatively, if the employee fails to master the challenges of transfer experiences, the result could be just the opposite: decreased feelings of competence and self-esteem, reduced career involvement, and a diminished willingness to set and pursue further challenging goals (possibly to refuse further transfer opportunities).

Transfers and Work Enrichment. Recent developments in job redesign by Hackman and his colleagues (22) provide some convergent theoretical insight into the potential of transfers for raising an employee's level of intrinsic motivation. According to this theory, the existence of a number of important "core dimensions" in a job can result in a set of crucial psychological states, which in turn can generate higher levels of intrinsic motivation, job satisfaction and work quality, and reduced levels of individual withdrawal. Transfers, especially when they involve promotions, can potentially lead to an employee's experiencing of at least three of the five critical core factors discussed in the theory: skill variety, task identity, and task significance. In other words, the firsthand experience gained by becoming involved in an organization's operations at several job sites can potentially require the individual to utilize new and different skills, especially when the work performed varies significantly from one location to another. Such experience can also help the individual to better understand how his or her efforts relate to the total operation of the company (task identity), and why the work he or she has done at the organization's various locations and is presently performing is important (task significance). The theory holds that when these three factors are featured in a particular job, the employee is more likely to experience a sense of meaningfulness, which, when combined with two other psychological states (experienced responsibility for one's work outcome and a knowledge of the results of one's work activities), can lead to the favorable motivational outcomes mentioned above.

I recognize that this theory of job design is meant to apply to the design and redesign of single jobs, not to a sequence of jobs in the development of a career. Nevertheless, I submit that a transfer experience can hold great potential for providing the sort of core factors needed for a feeling of meaningfulness from one's work with an organization, even if it is gained as a result of working at several jobs and at several locations. It seems to be a reasonable extension of the theory to predict that such experienced meaningfulness may result in the sort of positive personal and work-related outcomes hypothesized by the theory.

In summary, transfer experiences hold the *potential* for providing for the satisfaction of a set of growth needs that are becoming increasingly more important in motivating and understanding the work behavior of managerial and professional personnel. The association of a promotion with a transfer may increase the likelihood that the move will generate intrinsic work motivation, but formal promotions are not necessarily required. However, if a transfer involves lateral movement in the hierarchy or a demotion, which is sometimes the case, the increment in task difficulty is less likely to be sufficient to arouse significant achievement motivation, although adjustment to the myriad circumstances of a new job site—and generally learning one's way around—does hold potential for arousing the exploratory and inquisitive behavior that is involved in competence motivation, regardless of whether a promotion accompanies the move.

On the other hand, transfers that come too frequently for the employee to effectively master the challenges and uncertainties of a work setting can systematically *prevent* him or her from achieving the satisfaction of these needs, resulting in the sort of withdrawal classically attributed to need frustration (cf Maier, 23) and hypothesized more recently by Hall (6). In short, the proper spacing of transfers seems to be the critical factor.

Transfers and Relatedness Needs. Transfers can also provide opportunities for the satisfaction or the frustration of human relatedness needs, represented by the desires people have to affiliate, form friendships, and develop social networks. As seems to be the case in the role of transfers for meeting or frustrating growth needs, as argued above, transfer experiences may work in either a positive or negative way; and again, the critical factor seems to be the *frequency* of movement. On the positive side, mobility does expose an individual to a greater number of prospective friends and acquaintances than would otherwise be likely. The 46-year-old wife of a manager in my study reflected this perspective: "I believe the benefits far outweigh the cost because it gave us a chance to meet new friends and also a chance to live in different areas of Canada, which is truly a great experience." She and her husband had been moved only four times in 28 years.

By contrast, transfers that come too frequently prevent the establishment of anything but temporary and superficial acquaintanceships. The time needed to develop more meaningful and permanent relationships is often much greater than that which mobile families are permitted at any one location. The tentativeness that results, on a societal level, has been blamed for a host of social ills from rootlessness to the deterioration of the family unit (24). One 30-year-old professional engineer in my sample, who had been transferred three times during his three years with his employer, epitomized the problems experienced by many mobile people:

> The frequency of transfers and another possible transfer within one year make it impossible to become actively associated with voluntary groups or service clubs. We have not had time to develop close friendships at work or in the neighbourhood. I feel that my family is being deprived of close personal relationships outside of the home. The short notice of transfers deeply disrupted our household at the time and put severe emotional strain on our baby due to my coming and going at odd days and times. My wife had to give up her job in order to make the transfer possible. I was not consulted nor asked my opinion of the transfer but was handed a note stating that I was to report for duty at my new location in 14 days. In order to remain with the company I had to accept.

Transfers and Existence Needs. The role of transfers in the arousal and satisfaction of existence needs manifests itself most frequently in discussions of the economic costs and benefits, both short run and long run, that can be associated with mobility, especially when it is frequent. On the positive side, transfers are often accompanied by generous increases in pay and benefits, as well as added security through the movement they involve inward, toward the center of the organization's power structure (7). Additionally, it is often possible for a transferred individual and his or her family to upgrade the physical quality of their lives by moving to a more desirable location and sometimes by moving into superior living accommodations. Many employees who responded to my survey reported that they had managed, often by luck, to repeatedly upgrade the quality of house they could afford with the amount of equity they had accumulated over a sequence of moves through a series of different locations.

More common, however, was the opposite experience. Fully 82 percent of the people in my sample who owned their own homes reported that their most recent move had entailed higher monthly mortgage payments, while 75 percent of these people reported that they had to pay higher rates of interest for their mortgage following their move. Many families indicated that their housing costs had tripled or quadrupled because of their transfers. Sometimes the losses and costs associated with housing and other expenses of relocating can actually offset the financial benefits gained through the salary increments that often accompany transfers. This outcome is most frequent when the employee's spouse loses a job or disrupts a career. Twenty-three percent of the employees responding to my survey reported that their total family income was lower as a result of their most recent transfer, and 16 percent indicated that they had experienced a reduction in their overall standard of living.

Most transferring organizations now provide for the payment of the direct expenses associated with the move itself such as moving vans, and travel, but significantly fewer employers have clauses in their formal transfer policies to deal with other, more long-term risks such as housing differentials. Many senior managers who have themselves experienced many transfers are skeptical about offering such assistance to their younger colleagues, pointing out that transfers sometimes result in net gains on the housing market and arguing therefore that employees should be willing to accept the risk of losses as well as the gains that can accrue over a career that sees several transfers. My personal position is that organizations should be willing to absorb all of the financial costs associated with any transfer it initiates, removing the risk completely from the family involved. Corporate transfer policies can do comparatively less to offset or prevent the human cost related to transfers, so I suggest that permitting possible gain on real-estate exchanges while preventing all potential losses is indicated, especially to the degree that the organization—not the individual—is the ultimate principal beneficiary from the frequent movement of its people.

In summary, the policy and practice of employee transfers and mobility can have important implications for the level of motivation and career involvement of mobile personnel. Depending upon the degree of challenge posed by the new job at the new site and by many off-the-job aspects of settling one's family into a new city, a transfer can be a major source of both intrinsic motivation (through the enrichment of the job) or extrinsic motivation (through the net compensation gains made by the transferee). On the other hand, the intrinsic challenges of the new job may be too slight or too steep to provide any intrinsic reward, and the economic and familial costs of the mobility process may be great enough to preclude any extrinsic satisfaction, resulting in what is tantamount to a punishment experience for both the transferee and his or her family. Timing and frequency are the critical factors.

The Transfer as a Control Mechanism

Transfer policies can legitimately be viewed as one element of the total stock of control devices among those organizations that make use of them (8). Like most control devices, they function to counteract differences between employees and foster homogeneity of thought, opinion, values, and behavior. The higher the overall rates of mobility among a cohort of managers, the more communality is possible in their socialization and training experiences. Transfers help breed informal networks and "old boy" systems that facilitate coordination and understanding among large numbers of managers who, at one time or another, have worked together at common job sites. Yet at the same time transfers forestall the development of cabals that might pose serious threats to the status quo. Effective dissidence requires the sort of cohesiveness, trust, and time in face to face contact that frequent transfers prevent. Like personnel selection strategies that filter out recruits who are too much unlike the present members of a system, and like formal induction and training programs that are designed to inculcate common values and behaviors, active, premeditated transfer programs serve to systematically remove diversity and replace it with regularity and uniformity. On the other hand, the homogeneity of personnel and the standardization of procedures across geographic locations that result from control systems of all varieties contribute to the ease with which transfers can be employed. In other words, transfers seem to contribute to the homogeneity of structures, procedures and values of personnel at diverse locations, and this very homogeneity in turn makes it easier for a given transferee to adjust to his or her new location following any particular move.

Edstrom and Galbraith (8) asserted that one way transfers serve control is through the effect that they can have on the socialization of employees and the building of commitment among transferees to the organization. First, frequent transfers require sacrifice on the part of the employee. Sacrifice before entry to any social system is a powerful means of binding an individual to that system (25, 26). Further, transfers require that individuals constantly make and break social ties at each location, leaving the organization as the only constant source of support available. Frequent moves also make it more difficult for people to commit themselves to alternative attachments and activities that might be distracting. And finally, a policy of frequent movement enables the organization to identify its committed members—they are the ones who continue to accept the sacrifices transfers exact.

While the Edstrom and Galbraith hypothesis has intuitive appeal, results of my study fail to lend it empirical support. Hari Das and I found a significant but very weak relationship between a 12-item measure of company commitment and the number of transfers the individual had experienced with his or her company ($r = .09$); and the individual's average rate of transfers per year ($r = .13$) (Pinder and Das, 12). With the current awareness of the quality of life at work and the changing ethic among many young M-P-T employees regarding careers and work (7, 27), an equally plausible hypothesis, and one that might be more appropriate these days, is that frequent transfers alienate employees from their companies because of the negative impact that high mobility rates often have on the quality of life. Nevertheless, it is plausible to continue to assume that transfers build homogeneity, if not commitment, and homogeneity is absolutely necessary, *in degree,* to make organization possible and efficient. Taken too far, however, uniformity, (as generated by any selection or socialization device, can sow seeds of entropy that can reduce organizational effectiveness in the event of environmental change. Let me explain.

The current ecological perspective on organizational growth and survival (cf Aldrich, 28) holds that organizations, like other living systems, must create, satisfy, and survive in the environmental niches. Moreover, as organizations grow, it becomes necessary that they continue to forsake the policies and structures that have permitted them to survive in the past (Greiner, 29; Kimberley, 30), a necessity that runs counter to basic human nature. Extreme adaptation to one set of environmental circumstances tends to reduce the capacity of the organization to change appropriately to meet new environmental challenges, because high levels of adaptation to present circumstances normally involves ossified structures, bureaucratized policies, and a general smugness justified by the successes of the past. Past and extant strategies and policies tend to be seen as indispensable for the future.

Control mechanisms that homogenize mentalities and behavior repertoires limit the amount of variability that occurs within a system—variability that is vital for change, when it is required, to be possible. (This process is analogous to the "groupthink" phenomenon [Janis, 31] in which informal homogenizing control procedures by participants in small group decision making contexts limit the viability and effectiveness of small social systems.) At the corporate level, the reluctance of the big three automobile manufacturers to produce small cars until energy problems became critical helps explain the difficulties they have experienced in recent years. Reinforced by the strategies of the past when their niche was less hostile and energy was not problematic, North American auto manufacturers have suffered from the ossification of structures and strategies, which have been reinforced by homogenizing control mechanisms (Wright, 32), including the transfer of their personnel. The large and powerful Canadian chartered banks, bastions of homogeneity, internal control, and resistance to change (Newman, 33) provide another example. It is no coincidence that transfers are frequent among Canadian bankers.

I do not wish to overstate the case against transfers using the homogeneity argument. Clearly organizations must have control in order to function, and transfers do contribute to the creation of control by their homogenizing influence. Homogeneity contributes to efficiency of effort and coordination. But efficiency is only one element of organizational effectiveness (Gross, 34) and taken too far, policies oriented too exclusively toward efficiency can hinder policies directed toward the necessary adaptation to change.

WHY DO EMPLOYEES REFUSE TRANSFERS?

Although the specific reasons behind a particular individual's refusal of transfer vary from one case to another, my own research and that of others who have looked into the issue has tended to confirm that the majority of cases can be explained by two general considerations: fear of economic setback and the quality of life. However, many of the ostensibly economic reasons for rejecting job transfers often derive their significance from their probable impact on the quality of life employees plan for themselves and their families as they age and retire. But employees have always been concerned with their own economic and psychological well-being, yet seemed much more compliant in accepting transfer directives than they have been in recent years. Why the change?

Schein (7) has argued that successful management of human resources in the future will require careful observation of broad trends in the values of Western civilization, particularly values concerning work, careers, and commitment to one's employer. Accordingly, he argues that people (he is referring primarily to managers) are placing "less value on traditional concepts of organizational loyalty and acceptance of authority based on a formal position, age, or seniority and are placing more value on individualism, individual rights vis-à-vis the large organization, and 'rational' authority based on expertise and knowledge" (p. 229).

Many M-P-T employees think of their careers as being most effectively advanced through frequent job hopping from organization to organization rather than through the ascension of single hierarchies. In fact Eugene Jennings, in his book *Routes to the Executive Suite* (35) counsels aspirants to upward mobility to leave organizations and employers when it becomes expedient to do so, and to avoid becoming too specialized so as to limit one's options. In a recent study of 85 25-year-old managers, *Fortune* magazine found that young managers are in fact widely adopting such a strategy (Kinkead, 27). These young people confirmed Schein's observations that, compared to previous times, young M-P-T employees are much more loyal to their own careers and chosen life styles than to their employers, and that they are willing to follow whatever strategies seem necessary to develop their careers. Therefore, if transfer requests or opportunities are seen as expedient, they will continue to be accepted. But when they are not seen as desirable from a quality of life perspective or instrumental from a personal career progress point of view, they will be rejected more often. One reason managers of the past were more prone to obediently accept transfers was because, in large measure, more people were prone to accept transfers. Senior executives and personnel managers who directed other employees to pull up stakes and move counted heavily upon not only the loyalty of the individual to the organization, but also upon the realization on the part of the individual employee that to refuse a transfer could detrimentally influence his or her further opportunities for upward movement. So, by a process of divide-and-conquer, the executive giving a transfer order could easily intimidate individuals into acceptance, because each individual realized that if he or she rejected the opportunity, the next person asked would probably not dare to do so. But as more and more employees are willing and able to refuse forced mobility, by virtue of their reduced dependence on particular employers, their increased mobility to other employers, and their realization that not everyone accepts transfers anyway, more of them are in fact rejecting transfer directives. The power of the employer to divide and transfer seems to have been severely curtailed by the new career ethic.

A second major change noted by Schein (7) is the following:

> People are placing less value on work or career as a total life concern and less value on promotion or hierarchical movement within the organization as the sole measure of "success" in life. Instead, more value is being placed on leading a balanced life in which work, career, family, and self-development all receive their fair share of attention, and "success" is increasingly being defined in terms of the full use of one's talents and contributing not only to one's work organization, but to family, community, and self as well.

This change, like the change away from dependence on a single organization for the development of one's career, is attributed to the prolonged period of wealth enjoyed in the Western democracies since the Great Depression of the 1930s, a period of economic hardship and uncertainty that predates the vast majority of M-P-T personnel and lower participants in most of our organizations.

A third major changed noted by Schein (7) is a gradual erosion of the emphasis placed on traditional male and female sex roles with respect to both work and family activities. Dual-career marriages are a fact of life, and may become even more prevalent in the 1980s. The wife of one employee in my study epitomized the feelings of many of the spouses who responded to my survey:

> As a professionally trained person I must commit myself to several years, at least, in one position. Frequent hasty moves make it difficult for me to find, and/or wait for, opportunities in employment which are commensurate with my training and experience. Gaining valuable experience becomes a difficult task and there is no opportunity for advancement. When my husband is transferred he stays with the same company and always knows some of the employees and policies. I always have to seek out a new job with a new employer and prove my capabilities with good references. I only worked for my last employer for 4 months before my husband was unexpectedly transferred. Prospective employers are asking me for guarantees that I will stay in the community for several years. My last (references) have recommended that I have a higher level position which would have been possible in my previous jobs but was not available in the new community when I arrived. (So far our record has been 1½ years at the first location, 9 months at the second and 6 months at the third.) My husband's company does not consider my career at all when deciding where or when to move him.

> If my husband is not guaranteed a minimum length of time of at least 3 years in a community, I expect there will be problems in our home since I will be refusing to *totally* sacrifice my career and children to his company on a long-term basis. When we were married we did not expect so many moves so often on such short notice for such a small increase in financial remuneration . . . . We are presently in our fourth location in 3½ years and have no idea how long we will be here. We don't even know if it is worthwhile making improvements on our home.

It is important to emphasize that not all modern families are dual-career families, and that even among those in which both partners do hold outside jobs, feelings are not always as negative and bitter as those expressed by this woman. But the problem is increasingly more common, and is therefore more frequently related to decisions to refuse transfers.

Brett (9) has provided one of the most thorough and thoughtful analyses of job transfers, particularly emphasizing the effects of transfers on employees and their families. Drawing on recent theory and research pertaining to stress and the processes of coping with stress, she has developed a model that explains how transfer experiences may result in short-term and long-term psychological and physical consequences for mobile people. According to her model, transfers are examples of events that disrupt and threaten learned and valued behavior routines, resulting in feelings of loss, uncertainty, or lack of control. Feelings of loss of control over one's life, particularly when they are chronic or recurring, can lead to a state of experienced helplessness and inefficacy, which in turn may be associated with mental and physical illness. There is some suggestion that even the processes of attempting to cope can contribute to coronary disease. On the other hand, the feelings of loss and of unpredictability of behavior-outcome contingencies may generate coping behavior that can lead to either successful adjustment to the new environment, or to failure. Successful transfer experiences are more likely to contribute to positive attitudes about further mobility. Alternatively, chronic failures to adjust are most likely to be associated with negative reactions to further transfers, contributing to decisions to reject them. Brett's model is entirely inductive, based on the scattered evidence pertaining to job transfers and the growing theory of job stress. But it provides valuable insight into another major reason why many employees refuse to accept job assignments that involve relocation.

In summary, it is probable that high rates of mobility among organizational employees have always held significant economic and quality of life implications. However, the types of social change noted by Schein (7) have only recently resulted in an increased willingness on the part of the prospective transferees to reject opportunities and requests by their superiors to continue moving themselves and their families, at least at the often-high rates of the past. For organizations whose staffing policies have grown to rely on the transfer as a strategy for work force planning, or as a means of compensating for poor work force planning, this trend is naturally seen as a major problem. It is viewed as yet another encroachment on managerial prerogatives and as a critical threat to the effective deployment of human resources. From the perspective of the individual employer who has operations at multiple geographic locations, the perception of threat is understandable. From a more macro perspective this trend could exacerbate the shortage forecasted in both Canada and the United States of competent managerial resources, unless alternatives and supplementary policies and strategies are developed.

MAKING TRANSFERS HUMANE AND PRODUCTIVE

Both my empirical research and the foregoing conceptual analyses suggest a number of implications for the construction of formal policies and the guidance of actual practice to make transfers as humane as possible for the people involved, and as productive as possible for the organizations involved. It is interesting to note that the following prescriptions for the sake of humaneness are for the most part entirely compatible with organizational goals of productivity; these two sets of objectives need not necessarily be in conflict. In fact, by making their transfer policies humane, organizational productivity, efficiency, and effectiveness may all be well served. The reason for this is that more humane transfer policies should reduce some of the hidden organizational costs associated with transfer-related turnover and start-up time (Pinder and Das, 12).

What suggestions are warranted? First, organizations should continue to find ways of reducing the overall number of moves they require of their personnel. The belief that high rates of mobility leads to higher commitment (cf Edstrom and Galbraith, 8) is not supported by my data, so one of the principal latent functions attributed to transfers may in fact not be sufficient justification for their frequent use. To meet work force exigencies and to serve the employee development functions of transfers, Das and I suggested the use of simulations (similar to assessment centers), and a heavier reliance upon manning tables and replacement charts within given locations. I do not deny that transfers can benefit individuals and am not suggesting they be abolished. Rather I am suggesting that they be reduced in frequency in many organizations becasue neither the individual nor the employer truly benefits when transfers are too frequent.

Second, I suggest that employers remove all threats felt by their employees that their careers will be attenuated if transfers are refused. Insofar as more and more employees, "good" employees included, are prone to deny geographic mobility, the employer increasingly runs the risk of losing those individuals who feel confident that they can afford to reject transfers; these are most often the competent ones who are willing and able to leave the organization for positions with other employers. As argued earlier, it is easier for personnel to reject transfers when more of their colleagues are doing the same thing. Competent personnel have employment alternatives and seem increasingly willing to use them. Transfers may alienate the wrong people.

A third factor is time and timing. Related to my first suggestion is the notion that neither the employee nor the employer benefits when moves come too often. But time is crucial in another sense as well. Much of the bitterness toward transfers in my sample was caused by the shortness of time provided by employers for their personnel to relocate. Many respondents reported resentment that insufficient warning had been given before their transfers were required, and that too little time had been allowed them after the move to resettle themselves and their families at their new locations. I recognize that emergencies caused by sudden turnover in key spots can necessitate quick responses, often involving transfers. But I am struck with the lack of planning and simple consideration shown by some employers when they assign staff on short notice to positions in new locations. I believe less resistance to mobility might result in some organizations if more planning and consideration in the form of time were provided.

The most important predictor of posttransfer satisfaction in my research, over and above a large number of personality and economic considerations, was the employee's evaluation of the city to which he or she moved (Pinder, 10). The more the individual preferred his or her new location to the former location, the more happy he or she was with his most recent transfer. Further, the relative size of the two cities was the most crucial variable in determining the employee's reaction to his or her location. When the individual perferred the size of the new location to the size of the former location, his or her net response to his new city was positive. (Many other aspects of cities paled in importance, by comparison to the size factor.) Therefore, to make transfers humane, employers might do what they can to relocate their personnel in cities of the general size they prefer. I recognize that sudden staffing exigencies occur *where* they occur; the size of the city in which they occur is not controllable. But employers might be capable of showing more flexibility in terms of whom they assign to fill the vacancies so created, by keeping the size preferences of prospective transferees in mind.

Another seemingly obvious way to make transfer policies humane is to assure that applicants for jobs in which tranfers are likely to occur realize that mobility will be required of them. Realistic expectations about job requirements are important for tenure and longevity in organizations (Wanous, 36), yet a full 28 percent of my sample of transferees indicated some degree of uncertainty on their part when they began working in their organizations about whether they would be asked to transfer.

Realistic expectations about the nature and quality of life of the city or region to which a family is being asked to move constitute another way to make transfers humane and productive. A number of employers rely on the salesmanship of professinal real-estate firms to handle all of their relocation assignments. These services can be very helpful in expediting transfers. Sometimes, however, the advocacy positon of real-estate personnel can mislead transferees by instilling inflated expectations in the transferred family about what life will (or can) be like elsewhere. To a certain extent, believing is seeing, and positive expectations can contribute to self-fulfilling experiences of satisfaction after a move. On the other hand, false expectations can also result in violations of psychological contracts and resultant reduction in commitment to the organization.

Transfers are more humane the more that transfer policy provisions protect the individual from economic setbacks. In fact, the provisions for covering the long-range, large-scale costs associated with housing cost differentials was the most important correlate in my study of employee satisfaction with their organizations' formal transfer policies (Pinder,11). My position, as outlined above, is that the employee development generated by transfers is, for the organization, not a goal in itself but rather in most cases an instrumental means to other goals. In view of the human costs so often associated with mobility (9, 24, 37), I believe that employers should absolutely assure that the personal setbacks are not compounded by economic ones. These days, this means covering the total housing cost differentials faced by transferees.

Finally, a suggestion that follows from my earlier analysis of transfers as motivation mechanisms is that organizations should seek to maximize the growth need satisfaction, and the motivation provided by growth needs), by attempting to structure transfer experiences so that they pose moderate challenges neither too difficult nor too easy for the employee, and so that the employee has sufficient time between transfers to accomplish the challenges each one involves.

In summary, an analysis of my list of suggestions for the practice of transfers in organizations should indicate that the twin goals of humaneness and productivity can both be served by progressive transfer policies. As long as work values continue to include the quality of life as a major consideration, humaneness in transfers will continue to be instrumental to total organization effectiveness.

REFERENCES

1. The case against executive mobility. *Business Week,* October 28, 1972, 110.
2. Fewer executives are being transferred. *Industry Week,* January 29, 1973, **176**, 26.
3. More executives refusing transfers. *Industry Week,* November 19, 1973, **1179**, 26.

4. Perham, J. Is management mobility obsolete? *Dun's,* July 1970, **96**, 46–48.
5. Why moving day comes less often now for executives. *U.S. News and World Report,* January 13, 1975.
6. Hall, D. T. *Careers in Organizations.* Santa Monica, Calif.: Goodyear, 1976.
7. Schein, E. H. *Career Dynamics.* Reading, Mass.: Addison-Wesley, 1978.
8. Edstrom, A. & Galbraith, J. R. Transfers of managers as a coordination and control strategy in multinational organizations. *Administrative Science Quarterly, 1976,* **22**, 248–263.
9. Brett, J. M. The effect of job transfer on employees and their families. In C. L. Cooper and R. Payne (Eds.). *Current Concerrns in Occupational Stress.* New York: Wiley, 1981.
10. Pinder, C. Multiple predictors of post-transfer satisfaction: The role of urban factors, *Personnel Psychology,* 1977, **30**, 543–556.
11. Pinder, C. Corporate transfer policy: Comparative reactions of managers and their spouses. *Relations Industrielles,* 1979, 272–286.
12. Pinder, C. & Das, H. Hidden costs and benefits of employee transfers. *Human Resource Planning,* 1979, **2**, 135–145.
13. Jaffe, W. A. To move or not to move (employees)? *Industry Week,* 1973, **176**, 26.
14. Merton, R. K. *Social Theory and Social Structure.* 3rd. ed. New York: Free Press, 1968.
15. Deci, E. L. *Intrinsic Motivation.* New York: Plenum, 1975.
16. Alderfer, C. P. *Existence, Relatedness, and Growth.* New York: Free Press, 1972.
17. White, R. W. Motivation reconsidered: The concept of competence, *Psychological Review,* 1959, **66**, 297–333.
18. McClelland, D. C. *The Achieving Society.* Princeton: Van Nostrand Reinhold, 1961.
19. Korman, A. K. *The Psychology of Motivation.* Englewood Cliffs, N. J.: Prentice-Hall, 1974.
20. Korman, A. K. Hypothesis of work behavior revisited and an extension. *Acadeny of Management Review.* 1976, **1**, 50–63.
21. Hall, D. T. A theoretical model of career subidentity development in organizational settings. *Organizational Behavior and Human Performance,* 1971, **6**, 50–76.
22. Hackman, J. R. & Oldham, G. R. *Work Redesign.* Reading Mass.: Addison-Wesley, 1980.
23. Maier, N. R. F. *Psychology in Industry.* 2nd ed. Boston: Houghton-Mifflin, 1955.
24. Packard, V. *A Nation of Strangers.* Richmond Hill, Ontario: Simon and Schuster, 1972.
25. Aronson, E. & Mills, J. The effect of severity of initiation on liking for a group. *Journal of Abnormal and Social Psychology,* 1959, **59**, 177–181.
26. Gerard, H. B. & Mathewson, G. C. The effects of severity of initiation on liking for a group: A replication. *Journal of Experimental Social Psychology,* 1966, **2**, 278–287.

27. Kinkead, G. On a fast track to the good life, *Fortune*, 1980, *101*(4), 74–84.

28. Aldrich, H. E. *Organizations and Environments.* Englewood Cliffs, N. J.: Prentice-Hall, 1979.

29. Greiner, L. Evolution and revolutiion as organizations grow. *Harvard Business Review, 1972,* **50**(4), 37–46.

30. Kimberley, J. R. Issues in the creation of organizations: Initiation, innovation, and institutionalization. *Academy of Management Journal,* 1979, **22**, 437–457.

31. Janis, I. *Victims of Groupthink.* Boston: Houghton-Mifflin, 1972.

32. Wright, J. P. *On a Clear Day You Can See General Motors.* Grosse Pointe, Mich.: Wright Enterprises, 1979.

33. Newman, P. C. *The Canadian Establishment.* Toronto: Seal Books, 1975.

34. Gross, B. What are your organization's objectives? *Human Relations,* 1965, **18**, 195–215.

35. Jennings, E. E. Routes to the Executive Suite. New York: McGraw-Hill, 1971.

36. Wanous, J. P. *Organizational Entry.* Reading Mass.: Addison-Wesley, 1980.

37. Seidenberg, R. *Corporate Wives—Corporate Casualities? New York: AMACOM, 1973.*

—17—

Working with Unions

James W. Driscoll

What do managers think about labor unions in the context of productivity and the humanization of work? I know of no surveys on the subject, but my experience suggests that most managers in the United States view unions as a drag on productivity and a barrier to enlightened managers who attempt to humanize life at work along the lines suggested throughout this book. Evidence for this summary abounds in the growth of union-avoidance consulting into a boom industry and the preference shown by managers for new plant locations in areas of low union activity.

As a student of industrial relations institutions and practices, such negative views of labor unions by managers perplex me. In fact, a broad consensus within my field has reached opposite conclusions. With few exceptions, industrial relations as a discipline has concluded:

1. Unions lead to more productive operations by putting pressure on inefficient management.
2. Unions have contributed far more to the humane treatment of workers in the United States than the sum total of all "quality-of-work-life" projects and enlightened management.

One obvious reason for management opposition to labor unions despite these favorable conclusions is power. Unions constrain managerial discretion and managers don't like it. Another contributing factor is the lack of perspective by managers on the role of labor unions in industrialized societies and on the relatively benign role played by U.S. labor unions by comparison to more militant and political unions in other countries.

Although it is far beyond the scope of this chapter to correct these misconceptions and provide an overview of union history, I shall review briefly the evidence for my controversial assertions and leave the interested reader to pursue my references. The primary purpose of this chapter is to provide an analytical framework for managers who, either by choice or under the press of circumstances, want to work with a labor union to improve productivity and humanize work.

Since most U.S. managers learn little about unions in their training, let me digress for a few pages to provide some background on the U.S. labor movement. For more detail the general reader should read Estey (1), Mills (2), and Kochan (3), summarizing recent empirical research.

INTRODUCTION TO UNIONS

Labor unions in the United States grew most rapidly during the Great Depression when the future of market-based capitalism was in serious jeopardy. Prior to the 1930s, unions represented a small minority of workers in construction, shoe manufacture, and other skilled crafts. The revolt of workers in the great manufacturing industries—automobile, steel, and rubber—culminated not in governmental ownership of factories and other means of production, but in collective bargaining over wages and working conditions. In 1935, Congress, reflecting the conservative orientation of a market economy and private ownership, declared a national policy "to encourage . . . collective bargaining" and, by direct implication, the organization of American workers into labor unions.

Labor unions in this country remain relatively decentralized institutions devoted to collective bargaining. The Washington-based American Federation of Labor-Congress of Industrial Organizations (AFL-CIO), for all its publicity, wields little power over craft and industry-based unions like the Carpenters or the Steelworkers. Indeed the two largest unions, the Teamsters and the Autoworkers, are not members of the Federation. The strength and influence of local unions differs from one unit to the other.

The stability of a pluralistic democracy invites such an institutionalized voice for workers as a group. In any industrialized society such as ours, where almost everyone works for someone else, the likely alternative to labor unions as worker representatives is not what the National Association of Manufacturers calls the "union-free environment," but a labor political party and shop-floor, worker militancy. Kennedy (4) reviews these current alternative forms of worker activity in the Western European democracies.

The structure and philosophy of American unions provide distinct operating advantages to management compared to other industrialized nations. Because the labor movement has never formed a strong political party in the United States, management enjoys remarkable freedom of action. No laws regulate the layoff of workers, plant closings, or regional investment in new operations. Labor contracts in the United States are legally enforceable and generally provide management and labor with two to three years of labor peace. Strong bargaining by decentralized unions does regulate the arbitrary decision making of managers during the life of the contract in personnel policy and pressure them to increase output and revenue in order to pay the increased wages demanded by unions in bargaining. In the 1940s professors at Harvard Business School concluded that labor unions helped create professional managers and increased productivity (5). In 1979 a team of Harvard economists documented the greater productivity of unionized workers (6,7). Table 17.1 describes the labor movement in the United States along with its advantages and disadvantages to U.S. management.

The next two sections consider the direct effects of U.S. unions on the humane treatment of workers and on productivity.

Table 17.1 Labor Relations in the U.S.: A Management Balance Sheet

Distinctive Feature	Assets	Liabilities
1. Exclusive jurisdiction by one union over a set of jobs	Limitation to a single representative in negotiations; one agreement	Strong labor representatives
2. Craft (occupational) organization of many unions	Craft unions do training and provide workers from hiring halls	Multiple representatives and contracts with competition among unions, e.g. construction
3. Single company agreements	Agreements tailored to company conditions and economic strength	Requires local time and personnel to negotiate
4. Complex labor agreements	Reduces settled disputes to writing as precedent	Limits discretion and responsiveness of management
5. Strong grass roots (plant) organization	Some freedom from national union pressure; can build relationship with local leaders	Again politically strong and experienced labor leaders
6. Grievance procedure and arbitration	Regulated conflict (no strikes during contract); no wild cat strikes	Outside judgment by arbitrator with force of law
7. Emphasis on collective bargaining vs. political action	No work stoppages over political issues	High economic settlements
8. Limited governmental influence over wages and other conditions of work	Few costly items imposed despite recent trends, e.g. pension law	Inflationary pressure to follow such settlement in profitable (or strongly unionized) industries
9. Extensive regulation of bargaining procedures	Union power restricted; e.g., no strikes over representation, no sit-down strikes; conflict channeled	Limits ability to resist organization and union demands, e.g., blacklisting union sympathizers

Source: L. G. Reynolds provides the characteristics of the U. S. System. Ken Mericle prepared the commentary for his class at M.I.T., Cambridge, Mass. L. G. Reynolds, *Labor Economics and Labor Relations*, 6th Edition. Englewood-Cliffs, N. J.: Prentice-Hall, 1974, p. 360.

IMPACT OF UNIONS ON HUMANE TREATMENT OF WORKERS

Academic fashion in the 1970s neglected the major contributions of labor unions in the United States to the humane treatment of workers and touted "quality-of-work-projects" based on Scandinavian examples. Fashionable behavioral science professors neglected the context of the Scandinavian experiments. In both Sweden and Norway nearly every worker (more than 90 percent), including managers and professionals, belong to labor unions (see reference 3 for more detail). Labor parties have controlled the government for decades and guarantee each worker a set of benefits by law beyond the demands of the most militant American union. For example, health care, vacations (six weeks after 10 years), sick leave, paternity leave, and livable pensions are provided by government programs. Quality-of-work projects in that context represent two thrusts: first, an effort by labor unions to open a new area of benefits, namely, worker control over the environment; and second, the need of employers to make work attractive to workers who need only call in sick to recieve three paid days off without the need for a doctor's excuse.

Under a government much less favorable to worker interests in the United States, labor unions bargaining over bread and butter issues have made major contributions to humane treatment of workers. An assessment of humane treatment of workers in the United States ought to consider *all* aspects of life at work, not just job enlargement or some other fad. Fortunately, Kochan (3) has recently summarized the empirical research assessing the impact of labor unions on the quality of work life broadly defined. This section relies heavily on his summary. Of course, the section deals only with the direct effect of unions, not on their lobbying efforts to benefit workers indirectly through government action.

Fair and Equitable Compensation

Unionized workers in the United States earn more money than do nonunion workers with the same education and experience. Lewis (8) concluded that unions win higher wages by 15 to 20 percent with even larger effects on women and minorities and during economic downturns. There is some debate in academic circles about whether unions can make *any* employer pay such a differential or whether oligopolistic industries with the ability to pay such wages simply attract unions. On balance, however, the evidence indicated that unions often play a significant role in providing workers with the financial opportunity to share in the good life of the U.S. economy.

Fringe Benefits

Skeptics have long suspected that unionized employers adjusted for higher wage rates by providing fewer fringe benefits such as pensions, health insurance, and life insurance. However, recent evidence suggests the contrary (10). Generally speaking, it is the author's impression that employers who pay higher wages also provide better fringe benefits both in the size of the benefits and the number of benefits provided.

Justice on the Job

Union contracts almost always mandate a formal complaint procedure (the grievance procedure), culminating in binding review by a neutral outsider (an arbitrator) of the reasons for discipline and severity of the punishment.

Nonunion employers almost never agree to allow an employee to bring a complaint to an outsider (11). In addition unions push (with varying degrees of success) for open information and objective standards in the employer's administration of personnel policies. Thus, as a usual practice, unionized employers must post job vacancies and training opportunities; they must follow length of service (seniority) in distributing such benefits as vacations, pensions, promotion, job assignment and protection from transfer and layoff. So unions both establish objective criteria for personnel decisions and provide procedural mechanisms to protect workers rights.

Job Security

Besides the justice mechanisms just described, unions also negotiate a variety of provisions to preserve jobs and protect the incomes of workers who lose their jobs temporarily or permanently. To begin with, work rules often specify who performs the work and how many people are required for each task. Additional rules usually limit the right of employers to subcontract work outside. When work is not available, some unions have negotiated supplementary unemployment benefits and severance pay.

Job Satisfaction

Union workers are more satisfied with their pay, fringe benefits, and job security, reports Kochan (3) in a review of a 1977 national survey. By contrast, union workers were less satisfied than nonunion workers with the adequacy of their resources to get the job done and the content of their jobs. Most quality of work life projects focus narrowly on the last issue, so if humane treatment is defined narrowly as "interesting work," then unions may have little impact. But if the assessment is broadened to include more tangible and fundamental concerns, then unions often significantly improve the quality of work life in the United States. The next section reviews the impact of labor unions on productivity.

IMPACT OF UNIONS ON PRODUCTIVITY

Contrary to popular misconception, unionized workers are *more* produtive than their nonunion counterparts. In a comparison of unionized U.S. manufacturing firms with nonunionized firms, Brown and Medoff (7) concluded that unionized firms were 22 to 33 percent more productive. More recently, Clark (12) conducted a detailed study of the cement industry, including six case studies of recently unionized firms, and found them between 8 and 11 percent more productive. Frantz (13) found similar results in the wooden household furniture industry. I will discuss these results after reviewing several other findings relevant to productivity.

Besides being more productive on average, union workers are much less likely to leave their jobs (14). The voluntary quit rate goes down as the strength of negotiated seniority provisions increases (15). Therefore the costs of training and replacing workers are less.

Finally, there is some evidence that unionized workers, by comparison to the nonunionized, are more loyal and committed to their current employer. They are more likely to agree that they "are unwilling to change jobs under any circumstances" and "would never consider moving to a new job" (14). Thus, while unionized workers may express more dissatisfaction with certain conditions, such as job content or adequancy of resources, they may well be more committed to the employer. Indeed they may feel free to criticize conditions just because of the protection provided by their union. Industrial relations has long recognized the prevalence of dual loyalty to both union and employer (16).

The comparative advantage of unionized workers in terms of productivity and stability does not surprise students of industrial relations. There is no question that unions in some industries and firms have resisted technological change—Bok and Dunlop (17) cite the manufacturer of glass windows and cigars—and imposed costly restrictions on management, for example, firemen on diesel trains. On balance, however, most scholars long ago concluded that the most frequent impact of unions has been positive, in the acceptance of technological change and an increase in productivity. As long ago as 1941, Summer Slichter (18) identified the positive impacts of unions on management. Indeed labor economists have always assumed union workers produced more in order to support the higher wages won by unions in bargaining.

Clearly other factors such as the nature of supervision, style of top management leadership, size of the company, product structure, and the nature of the workers influence productivity. Equally clearly, some nonunion employers are highly productive, have low absenteeism and turnover, and have trusting and favorable relationships with their employees. Indeed the differential may not be union versus nonunion but how humanizing is the organizational climate (19). Nonetheless, an impressive body of evidence suggests that unions, rather than being a drag on productivity, are most frequently associated with *more* productive operations.

The important remaining question for scholars is to discover the role played by unions in improving economic performance. The more conservative explanation cites the shock effect of unions on complacent and inefficient management. By this argument unions first win demands for wages, more comfortable working conditions, and outside review of personal decisions. To compensate for these costs management professionalizes its practices, hires better workers, and purchases less labor-intensive equipment. Indeed, in all of Clark's six case studies following unionization, a new plant manager was appointed and management practices improved, such as staff meetings and production targets. By this explanation, management is the engine for productivity under the goad of pressure from unions.

Furthermore, unions may contribute directly or indirectly to productivity. As outlined above, unions do not spring out of a vacuum. They arise in any organization in reaction to strongly resented management action—low wages, poor conditions, and most frequently, arbitrary supervision. The victory of a union organizing campaign removes some tension from the earlier situation. Specifically, negotiated provisions for the allocation of wage increases and promotion and layoff based on seniority remove sources of worker dissatisfaction and resistance to management. Generally, the grievance venting procedure and the freedom from reprisal provided by the union can help increase the communication of production-related problems upward from the rank-and-file worker. Clark found almost no such communication before the advent of unionization. In some circumstances, unions even cooperate directly with management to generate productivity improvements. For example, under the Scanlon Plan, union leaders encourage workers to suggest ways of improving output (20). Indeed some radicals criticize American unions precisely for contributing *too much* to the discipline of the work-force and the reduction of uncertainty faced by managers. While the evidence is inconclusive, it seems reasonable to assert that unions in the United States both put pressure on management and directly contribute to increased productivity.

How then do managers react to this pressure for humane treatment of workers and increased productivity?

CURRENT MANAGEMENT ATTITUDES TOWARDS UNIONS

Three components must be distinguished within managements' response to unions: the inevitable, the evolutionary, and the current. Inevitably, managers resist any imposition on their discretion, and unions curtail management prerogatives in many ways. Therefore a fair number of my colleagues are under the impression that almost every American manager they have met would like to see unions disappear overnight.

Given that base line of opposition, the tendency in most union-management relationships is a positive evolution over time. An employer's attitude toward the union representing its employees can range from outright aggressive opposition to armed truce to grudging acceptance to cooperation (21). Indeed most local union-management relationships progress through at least the first three stages as time passes. At the outset, the union campaign for recognition rests on criticisms of management that are often personal and sometimes exaggerated. For its part, management may call in consultants to attack the union's credibility and take advantage of existing legislation to delay an election and bargaining until the union's suport has waned. After an initial contract is negotiated, each side will watch the otherwarily for its duration, seizing and exaggerating any possible violation. Since no contract can cover all posible situations, such apparent departures arise most frequently in the early years of the bargaining relationship. Over time, however, as both sides meet to resolve disagreements, both informally and in the formal atmosphere of arbitration and subsequent contract negotiations, the principals on both sides learn to work together and usually develop mutual respect as professionals representing differing interests. Eventually this acceptance and respect sometimes even lead to explicitly cooperative discussions of common problems, such as increasing productivity and the introduction of new technology. In 1981, however, the contemporary management response to unions calls into question the inevitability of this positive evolution.

In work places with long histories of bargaining, managers accept unions and in many cases work with them to solve common problems. For example, the auto industry has sought the cooperation of the auto workers in efforts to improve product quality at Chrysler and the quality of work life at General Motors (22). General Electric and U.S. Steel have developed new procedures to expedite the handling of grievances (23). In newer relationships—for example, in the public sector and in hospital administration—the very warfare is taking place over union recognition and management prerogatives that characterized the early days of the private sector. At the same time, a number of large, long-time unionized firms have opened new operations primarily in the South and fought to keep unions out. Westinghouse, which has gone from nearly complete union representation to less than 50 percent in about 15 years, is the most frequently mentioned example. General Motors opened several plants and sought to keep the UAW out. Similar trends are apparent in construction and retail food where unionized firms have formed new divisions to operate without unions. This is the armed truce stage.

At the national level, too, opposition is apparent. The management community, spearheaded by a virulent antiunion group with the innocuous title the National Right to Work Committee, rejected attempts by the labor movement to modify existing labor law to make union organizing easier (24). While the proposed alterations—mostly technical modifications in the timing of elections and the penalties for noncompliance—had no impact on already-unionized operations, not a single employer in the United States came forward to testify in behalf of unions as institutions, despite union participation in a number of cooperative efforts. Mills (24) has predicted a national chill in union management relations as a consequence of this legislative rebuff to unions. Clearly the national attitude of managers has also shifted toward open warfare. Just as at the local level, national union leaders question why they should cooperate in national programs—whether to reindustrialize the United States or to control inflation—with managers who question their very legitimacy.

The obvious question for a concerned manager is how to stop this local and national drift towards antiunionism and work with unions to achieve the economic and humane benefits described above.

IMPROVING UNION-MANAGEMENT RELATIONS

The oldest law in labor relations is "the management gets the kind of union it deserves." The American economic system and its labor movement guarantees this folk wisdom because management usually initiates action, under our private ownership system, and then the union reacts. Therefore the first step for managers seeking to work with their union is to define their objectives both in terms of human-resource philosophies and working procedures. After these objectives are clearly established, it is possible to offer guidelines on how to create a management-union relationship favorable to its execution.

Human Resource Strategies

Within limits, an employer can set the terms of the psychological contract offered to its employees. Historically, American managers have shifted from seeking to meet only the economic needs of workers to recognizing their social needs and, more recently, their needs for self-expression on the job (25). One of the most fundamental decisions made by an employer concerns the psychological basis on which the manager will appeal to employees.

Economic Strategy

An economic strategy offers low wages, arbitrary supervision, little training or advancement in return for low employee commitment. High turnover, absenteeism, and little employee loyalty are accepted for one of several reasons. The employer may opt for this strategy because he or she has no margin for increased labor costs; the technology may require only limited contributions from employees (ignoring for the purposes of argument employers' role in choosing a technology); or the employer may not believe more substantial commitment is possible from a particular work force (or from workers in general).

Social Strategy

In an organizational climate in which the manager is free to apply social strategy, this strategy may include high wages, but chiefly it emphasizes the social bonds between employees and the firm. Considerate supervision, group recreational activities, and deference to subcultural norms in personnel policies distinguish this strategy. For example, seniority, impartial judges, and majority rule are widely accepted norms in our society, and these are followed closely by the "social" employer. Most union employers follow this strategy, choosing to emphasize predictability in organizational climate at the expense of individual differences in employee preferences.

Humanistic Strategy

Humanistic employers get more attention from the academic community than is warranted by their small numbers. Nevertheless, among consulting firms, research universities, and other professional organizations and in isolated organizational experiments, employers are modifying work demands to suit individual preferences. Flexible working hours, participation in decision making, and opportunities for outside self-development supplement pleasant work conditions.

Clearly the unionized employer may prefer or feel compelled to follow any one of these strategies. Which strategy he or she is likely to apply depends on the organizations's environment, resources, and the personal preferences of its management.

As noted above, most unionized employers currently follow the social human resource strategy. Indeed the union's social functions buttress the employer's offerings and generate simultaneous loyalty to both the union and the employer (16). That strategy needs to be much more carefully examined by behavioral researchers. However, other chapters in this volume and the bulk of behavioral research currently suggests the advantages of the humanistic strategy. Therefore I will confine my discussion here to some techniques for implementing that, perhaps, idealistic strategy. After the selection of an overall strategy the next step is a clear specification of personnel policies.

Specific Personnel Objectives for a Humanistic Strategy

The defining characteristic of unionized work is a formal written contract. Indeed sophisticated nonunion employers now develop employee handbooks to provide the same atmosphere of predictability. To work with a union, then, a humanistic strategy requires the clear public statement of policies.

Individual Treatment. Individual treatment does not violate the purpose of collective bargaining. Critics unfamiliar with life under union contracts may argue that collective bargaining requires identical treatment of similar cases. In fact, no two cases are ever identical, so the question always arises as to how to forge a settlement satisfactory to the individual and the employer. The essential difference under collective bargaining requires a settlement satisfactory not just as to the individual involved but, also to the union as representative of other employees. If such settlements depart from the terms of the contract or tend to give it specific meaning, then the parties can, and often do, agree to settlements *without binding force as precedents*. The humanistic employer might seek the inclusion of contract language to recognize the existence of such non-binding agreements. What is crucial is to express the employer's intent to work with the union to develop solutions satisfactory to every *individual* employee.

Progressive Discipline. A humanistic employer provides illustrative work rules to guide employees, but emphasizes, for each category of offenses, the steps in the process. For example, repeated instances of unexcused absenteeism might warrant, first, an oral warning and counseling with a supervisor, second, a written warning, and counseling with the personnel department, third, a suspension and only fourth a discharge. Some management lawyers caution against listing work rules for fear an arbitrator will consider the list exhaustive. Granted some slight risk in that direction, the humanistic employer attempts to communicate personnel policies as clearly as possible and should post work rules. The discipline process explicitly r equires counseling in an attempt to develop an individualistic solution to the problem. Employee assistance programs should be emphasized.

Equitable Pay. Compensation should emphasize equity and productivity. Some system of job evaluation should govern the relationship between wage rates. Such systems for success require regular consultation with union representatives. There is no reason why innovative pay practices geared to improve productivity cannot find a place in unionized firms. At present unions have agreed to such innovations as having all workers on salary and paying people based on their skill rather than the work performed. To focus attention on productivity, organization-wide bonus systems such as the Scanlon Plan have been agreed to by unions. The Plan uses pay to encourage individual workers to make varying personal contributions.

Encouragement for Technological Change. American unions have often in recent years supported innovation and even favored the introduction of new technology. Unionized employers have learned to nurture that support with policies protecting the job security and financial well-being of current employees. Combining such protection with prior notice and discussion can make the union organization *more* innovative than its non union competitor.

Individual Fringe Benefits. No law of nature requires that all benefits negotiated by a union be uniform. Indeed a few innovative employers have negotiated with their unions to allow individual employees to choose among benefits. For example, in some industries such as the manufacture of agricultural equipment, senior workers can elect to take layoffs before junior workers and make use of negotiated supplemental unemployment benefits. A number of employers have negotiated contracts allowing individual workers to select among flexible working hours. Humanistic employers can seek to extend this area of individual choice to tradeoffs between health insurance (for workers with young families) and pension contributions (for older employees whose family is grown).

Motivational Job Design. Traditionally unions have left the design of the production process to management. There is therefore little reason why a unionized employer could not incorporate recent advantages in designing more interesting jobs and in using partially autonomous work groups. Indeed several employers have involved union leaders and members in the design of the production process and individual jobs (26; also Chapter 21 of this volume).

MATCHING HUMAN RESOURCE AND UNION-MANAGEMENT STRATEGIES

Once the employer has formulated a set of objectives for specific humanistic personnel policies, a vision of the ideal union-management relationship to support those policies is required. In all honesty, an employer who has opted for an economic policy may well decide that the less contact with the union the better. In industries in which such strategies abound (e.g., in retail trade, local delivery, and light manufacture), union corruption and so called "sweetheart" deals are found more frequently than in other industries. However, for employers attempting a humanistic strategy, a more cooperative union relationship is required. Union members and their leaders need a supportive context if they are to accept management's innovative personnel practices described above. Table 17.2 illustrates the relationship between human resource strategies and union-management relationships.

Cooperative Union-Management Relationships

Industrial relations scholars have long sought to identify the components of union-management cooperation because of its inherent advantages. Not only does cooperation imply the absence of strikes, but it holds the promise of optimal solutions to problems such as technological change. For example,

Table 17.2 Fit Between Human-Resource Strategies and Union-Management

	Union-Management Relationship		
Human Resource Strategy	Antagonism	Accommodation	Cooperation
Economic	X		
Social		X	
Humanistic			X

Golden and Parker (27) report a careful investigation of those employers who avoided strikes in the post-World War II period of labor militancy. More recently, Healy (28) reviewed what he called "creative collective bargaining." I have reported on more recent examples of problem-solving behavior in collective bargaining (29). Rutenberg, formerly a union leader and co-author of a book on industrial democracy, now president of a steel company, said that the way to eliminate strikes is to give all workers an annual wage. This is not an idea that has been picked up by many companies.

What is different here is my emphasis on cooperation, not for its instrinsic value as a form of problem-solving between negotiators, but for its importance as a context for humanistic management. Although there is little hard research evidence, I assert that humanistic personnel policies are impossible to implement in a relationship of armed truce or grudging acceptance between the institutions of management and the union.

Fortunately, the body of research on cooperation inspired by other concerns is available to guide the manager seeking to establish a favorable context for the humanistic practices described elsewhere in the volume.

A cooperative union-management relationship has four key components: mutual positive attitudes, frequent and balanced interaction, explicit problem-solving behavior, and a balance of power. Each requires specific management actions.

Mutual Positive Attitudes

The first element is attitudinal. Unless managers accept the legitimacy of the union, respect union leaders, and trust them as well, more sophisticated human resouce strategies are impossible in unionized employers, as will become evident below. While managerial attitudes are shaped by daily interactions with the union (about which more later), a clear orientation from top management is an important foundation. Supervisors, especially at the first level, must harbor no doubts about the positive attitude of the employer toward the union. Additional training in behavioral skills (interpersonal communication and problem-solving) and in specific personnel policies builds on that foundation. Managers should deal with the union with a clear understanding about the legitimate areas of union activity and the areas of common objectives emphasized from top management.

Balanced Pattern of Interaction

The second element,inseparable from attitudes, is interaction—who talks to whom and who goes first. Some years ago Whyte (30) outlined effective interaction patterns between union and management as a balance of initiating and responding, between both organizations, at multiple levels and between levels within each organization. Figure 17.1 illustrates the pattern.

First, stable interaction requires both union and management to *initiate*

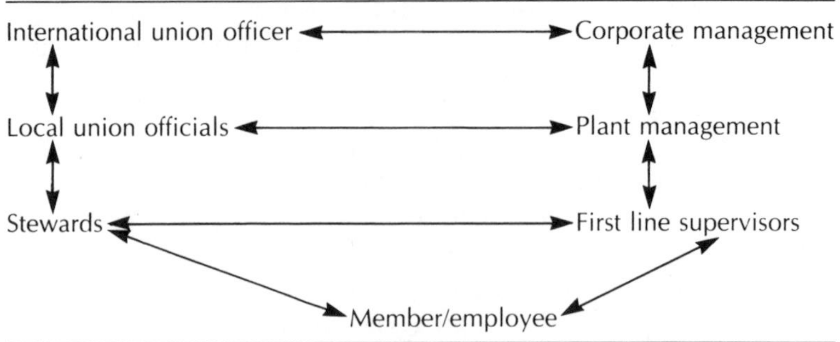

Figure 17.1 Interaction pattern for a cooperative union-management relationship (30).

communication. Too often management denies the union such opportunity outside the grievance procedure and contract negotiations. More enlightened managers provide much more varied and frequent opportunities to union leaders and members, such as monthly plant meetings and weekly departmental meetings and the encouragement of daily discussions between supervisor and steward. In each meeting the respective union leader can raise issues of concern.

Second, the several internal levels of management must be in regular contact over labor issues, with the initiation of topics balanced between the top and the bottom. Two extreme distortions of the internal management balance can undermine relations with the union. Sometimes first-level supervisors are given no power of initiative on labor issues. Instead a corporate labor-relations staff sets policy and resolves the most petty local dispute. Such employers emphasize organization-wide consistency and can never foster the local problem-solving and individualized solutions central in the humanistic strategy. On the other extreme, top operational management, for example in a plant, may delegate labor-relations policy to a staff manager or to first-level supervisors. Such employers cannot engage the union leaders in discussions of the central problems facing the organization because such problems as product-market competition and technological innovation are outside the scope of the labor-relations staff and lower management.

The third and last characteristic of Whyte's ladder is a parallel balance of interaction among the various levels of the union hierarchy. However, influencing union activities poses legal problems for managers. Maintaining that balance is a union matter; managers are forbidden by the National Labor Relations Act from interfering in the union's choice of leadership. Nonetheless, it is in the employer's interest to encourage both discussions and two-way influence within the union hierarchy: among the rank-and-file members, local union leaders, and full-time representatives of the national union. Some managers may prefer personal deals with outside leaders as efficient, but such deals contradict the ideal of responding to individual employee needs. On the other hand, if the rank and file are not influencing national representatives, then the humanistic employer faces problems when the labor contract comes up for renegotiation. No matter how little the national representative knows about local problems, he or she plays a large role in negotiating contracts, in order to pursue national union objectives. An uninformed national representative can unintentionally sabotage the local innovation proposed here.

Problem-Solving Behavior

Besides the balance of interaction summarized by the ladder, humanistic union-management relations also require a certain quality to their discussion. Union and management representatives vary between two extreme styles of interaction (29, 31). Bargaining, on the one hand, relies on the sequential presentation of single proposals, distortion, and the implicit threat of coercion (economic or political). Problem solving, on the other hand, involves the simultaneous definition of common concerns by both parties, sharing of information and exploration of a wide range of possible alternatives. Bargaining is most appropriate to economic issues during contract negotiations, but usually dominates all other interactions between union and management. Problem solving is most appropriate to noneconomic issues such as safety, health, technological change, and productivity improvement. Despite the claims of negotiations to "solve problems", most union-management relationships contain *no* problem solving as an identifiable behavioral pattern.

The ideal union-management relationship for a humanistic employer would emphasize the establishment of problem solving at all levels of interaction and across all possible subjects, both economic and noneconomic. The assumption of the humanistic employer is the existence of some common goals between the employer and employees, including their elected representatives in the union. In an extensive series of studies, I have documented both the possibility of problem solving at all levels—industry-wide, company, and plant-specific—and on all subjects including wages, productivity, and safety (29). The payoffs from problem solving have been substantial and benefited both the union and management. The humanistic employer should settle for no less than occasional problem solving with union representatives on *all* important issues, from wage increases to job design. Based on my personal experience with successful cases, my impression is that problem solving works best under certain conditions summarized in Figure 17.2 (32). However, the specific strategy for achieving this ideal union-management relationship depends on the employer's particular situation.

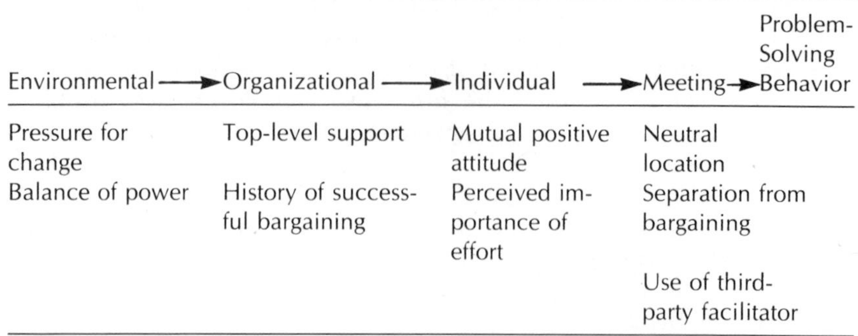

Environmental
Organizational
Individual
Meeting
Problem-Solving Behavior
Pressure for change
Balance of power
Top-level support
History of successful bargaining
Mutual positive attitude
Perceived importance of effort
Neutral location
Separation from bargaining
Use of third-party facilitator

Figure 17.2 Conditions favoring problem-solving between union and management (28).

Balance of Power

The last element in a cooperative union-management relationship is a relative balance of power between the union and management. However, some caution must be taken in defining power. Most labor economists conceive of power in industrial relations as the ability to impose financial costs on the opponent. For example, ATT is considered more powerful than its major union, the Communication Workers of America, because its quarter million supervisors and other nonunion workers can maintain essential telephone service in case of a strike. (The last contract between the parties expired precisely as I wrote this sentence, so I called the information operator and, as my labor-economist friends would predict, the union had settled without a strike). However, such reasoning is foreign to a humanistic employer, since his or her intent is to involve the union as a stake holder in informed discussions concerning employees. The basis of power in the relationship is information, not coercion, and both sides are considered equals in access to information. There may be situations in which the two sides resort to economic sanctions, but the employer's goal is to treat the union as an equal in access to information and to consider its arguments carefully in order to minimize the necessity of strikes.

Both sides will inevitably have different positions on most issues, but by treating the union as an equal much of the *need* for strikes is eliminated. Specifically, the union need not strike to convince the employer of the seriousness of its demands, if such demands are given regular and sympathetic audience during the life of the contract. Likewise the employer must make his or her own demands clear to the union, for example, with respect to competitive costs, technological innovation and the like. With effective information exchange, the employer need not take a strike just to convey commitment to strategies.

The great danger of humanistic strategies to management is their degeneration into concession, giving in to all union positions, no matter how extreme. A humanistic strategy does not ignore differences of opinion between employer and union; it gives priority to other motives rather than overemphasizing economic power.

Effective problem solving *precludes* concession as a way of reaching agreement. The employer's objective is an informed decision about employee interest relative to the employers' other stake holders, such as owners, government, customers, and sources of funds. If a strike is necessary to convince either side of external realities, then a top priority after the strike is the reestablishment of the balanced interaction described above. The Federal Mediation and Conciliation Service offers technical assistance to the parties in such situations through its relationship by objective program (33).

Probably the most important step to the ideal relationship with a union is the explicit formulation of its components in terms of strategy, policies, attitudes, interaction, and power. Certain specific actions fall directly out of such specification such as supervisory training, union-management meetings, and rejection of economic threats as the basis for interaction. However, specific questions remain as to how to reach the ideal relationship.

SELECTING A CHANGE STRATEGY

No strategy for changing a union-management relationship can work in every social setting, no matter what the claims of its proponents. Change strategies must be tailored to meet the specific situation. I have explored the general question of fitting a change strategy to situational differences elsewhere (34). For now let me distinguish two decisions faced by an employer seeking to achieve a cooperative relationship.

Top-Down versus Bottom-Up

In large organizations, an employer can either initiate contact with top union leaders at the company (or goverenment agency) level or begin a series of local experiments in collaboration with local union people. Both approaches have worked well. The General Motors—U.A.W. joint union-management quality-of-work-life program began with the formation of a corporate-level committee. Seven years later, over 50 local plant projects are under way. By contrast, it is possible to start at the bottom. I studied one plant of a multiplant manufacturer where corporate management suported an extensive and successful local effort (29).

The tradeoff is between corporate resources and local commitment. The single plant project I studied ended because of withdrawal of the corporate support, specifically the reassignment of a staff specialist. On the other hand, some of the G.M. projects exist only on paper. Clearly one consideration in the choice is the distribution of power in the employer and union organizations. The top-down strategy fits centralized organizations better.

Structure versus Process

Another decision about change strategy lies in the relative emphasis on structure and process. I have documented the success of the Scanlon Plan for union-management cooperation, a formal structure involving employee committees and a monthly bonus. Such structural initiatives make most organizational development consultants shudder. A *process* for change suits their values better, and several successful prototypes exist for improving union-management relations. Perhaps the best known is the Relationship-by-Objectives Program of the FMCS, cited above. RBO is an intensive series of intergroup-confrontation and information-sharing meetings between union and management leaders to identify current problems and decide on actions to improve the relationship. The Federal Mediation and Conciliation Service conducts such programs, usually after prolonged work stoppages. Similar help is available commercially.

The structural approach, for example, Scanlon, is fast and unambiguous. It provides a clear option for presentation to both sides. However, it may not fit a particular situation. For example, almost all unionized Scanlon Plans are in manufacturing industries, and few are found in process industries. By contrast to the fairly standard Scanlon Plan structure, RBO builds a change program tailored to the needs of the local participants. However, the implementation of such changes is often slow and may attract detractors, especially on the union side. Structural changes such as Scanlon probably warrant more attention in the unionized setting than would be called for by traditional organizational development.

PRACTICAL GUIDELINES

As a way of translating this relatively abstract outline into action, let me begin with suggestion attributed to John Dunlop, former Secretary of Labor and labor-management third party extraordinaire. When asked how he would deal with one employer's tragically muddled union relationship, he is alleged to have replied, "First, I'd take one side out to dinner, then I'd take the other and find out what the problems are." The action steps to reach the ideal union-mangement relationships are that simple (with the minor exception that no one in the labor-relations community would turn down dinner with John Dunlop, while they might require more mortal souls to make more complicated arrangements).

For the manager willing to meet the challenge of working with a labor union to improve productivity and at the same time to treat employees humanely, there are some equally simple steps to follow:

Review Managerial Attitudes Towards Unionism

Unless top management and directors (or key officials in the government sector) are committed to working with the unions, then a humanistic strategy will fail.

Select the Desired Human-Resource Strategies and Formulate Specific Personnel Objectives

Traditional labor-relations departments are the worst source to locate humanistic personnel practices. Begin instead with the guidelines for new plant design developed by behavioral scientists; some examples include autonomous work groups, pay based on qualifications instead of current jobs, and organization-wide productivity bonus. Hackman and Suttle (35) have assembled a smorgasbord of innovative practices. All these practices have been implemented successfully under collective bargaining.

Define the Ideal Union-Management Relationship for the Chosen Human-Resource Strategy

While the humanistic strategy outlined here is most promising and suggests union-management cooperation, circumstances may dictate an economic or social strategy and more antagonistic dealing with unions.

Fit the Change Strategy to the Situation

If the unions and management are centralized, then the strategy must begin at the top. By contrast, if control is decentralized and local operations vary substantially, then action can begin at the local level. If the desired personnel policies are well understood, then a formal structure can be implemented by providing incentives to the union. By contrast, if the desired mode of operation is poorly understood, then the union leadership can be engaged in an open-ended process of goal-setting and problem definition.

Involve Line Management

At whatever level the strategy targets for initial action, the key participants are line managers. Most labor-relations staff managers will reject cooperation as naive and risky. Only managers faced directly with problems of unsatisfactory productivity and increased competition will feel the pressure for change. Although line management exercises formal control over labor relations, most U.S. employers delegate substantial informal control to staff managers with disastrous results.

Enlist the Aid of a Third Party

Special expertise is required to work at the interface of union and management, and a different set of skills is relevant to the implementation of humanistic personnel policies. The ideal mix of skills in the third party depends on the complexity of the union interface. If a past history of hostility or multiple unions complicates discussion with the union leaders, the emphasis must be on labor-relations expertise. One solution is a team of consultants combining labor-relations and organizational-development skills. Some sources of third parties assistance include the regional offices of FMCS and the American Arbitration Association and the institutes of industrial relations at local universities (a list is available from the author).

Initiate Discussions Informally Away From the Bargaining Table

Bargaining sets a climate between people that prevents the open exchange required for a qualitative shift in union-management relations. Do as John Dunlop would do and explore objectives, problems, and alternatives in amenable social settings, at a slow pace, and without the objective of immediate agreement.

Guarantee Some Early Success

The logic of collective bargaining focuses the attention of relevant audiences on both sides of the bargaining table towards visible accomplishments analagous to contract negotiation. Therefore some early success is required to justify continued departures from traditional patterns of discussion between union and management.

SUMMARY

Following these guidelines allows managers to initiate a positive working relationship with their union. For too long managers have blamed unions for low productivity and demeaning personnel practices. The evidence flatly contradicts those complaints. Unionized workers are much more productive than their nonunion equivalents, and labor unions provide a mechanism for human treatment rarely approached by nonunion employers. The challenge facing managers in the United States is to stop scapegoating unions and work with them to maximize on their advantages. This brief review suggests an ideal union-management relationship for a humanistic strategy to improve productivity and humane treatment and lays out some simple guidelines for approaching that ideal.

REFERENCES

1. Estey, M. *The Unions: Structure, Development and Management.* New York: Harcourt, Brace and Jovanovich, 1976.
2. Mills, D. Q. *Labor-Management Relations.* New York: McGraw-Hill, 1978.
3. Kochan, T. A. *Collective Bargaining and Industrial Relations: From Theory to Practice.* Homewood, Ill.: Irwin, 1980.
4. Kennedy, T. *European Labor Relations: Text and Cases.* Lexington, Mass. Lexington/D. C. Heath, 1980.
5. Slichter, S. H., Healy, J. J. & Livernash, E. R. *The Impact of Collective Bargaining on Management.* Washington, D. C.: Brookings Institution, 1960.
6. Freeman, R. B. & Medoff, J. L. The two faces of unionism. *The Public Interest* Fall 1979.

7. Brown, C. & Medoff, J. Trade unions in the production process. *Journal of Political Economy*, June, 1980. **86** (3), 355–378.

8. Lewis, H. G. *Unionism and Relative Wages in the United States*. Chicago: University of Chicago Press, 1962.

9. Stagner, R. *The Psychology of Industrial Conflict*. New York: Wiley, 1956, p. 399.

10. Freeman, R. B. *The Effect of Trade Unionism on Fringe Benefits*. Cambridge, Mass.: National Bureau of Economic Research Working Paper, No. 292. (October 1978)

11. Foulkes, F. *Personnel Policies in Large Non-union Companies*. Englewood Cliffs, N.J.: Prentice Hall, 1980.

12. Clark, K. B. The impact of unionization on productivity: A case study. *Industrial and Labor Relations Review* July 1980, **33** (4), 451–469.

13. Frantz, J. The impact of trade unions in the wood household furniture industry. Honors Thesis, Harvard University (1976). Cited in K. B. Clark, The impact of unionization on productivity: A case study. *Industrial and Labor Relations Review*, July 1980, **86** (3), 451–469.

14. Freeman, R. B. Individual mobility and union voice in the labor market. *American Economic Review*, May 1976, **66,** 361–368.

15. Block, R. N. The impact of seniority provisions on the manufacturing quit rate. *Industrial and Labor Relations Review*, July 1978, **31** 474–481.

16. Purcell, T. V. *Blue Collar Man: Pattern of Dual Allegiance in Industry*. Cambridge, Mass.: Harvard University Press, 1960.

17. Bok, D. C., & Dunlop, J. T. *Labor and the American Community*. New York: Simon and Schuster, 1970.

18. Slichter, S. H. *Union Policies and Industrial Management*. Washington, D. C.: Brookings Institution, 1941.

19. Ball, K. A planned humanizing organization in action. In H. Meltzer and F. R. Wickert (Eds.). *Humanizing Organizational Behavior*. Springfield, Ill.: Charles C. Thomas, 1976, 340–356.

20. Driscoll, J. W. Working creatively with a union: Lessons from the Scanlon Plan. *Organizational Dynamics*, Summer 1979, **8** (1), 61–80.

21. Walton, R. E. & McKersie, R. B. *A Behavioral Theory of Labor Negotiations*. New York: McGraw-Hill, 1965.

22. Guest, R. Quality of work life—learning from Tarrytown. *Harvard Business Review*, July-August 1979, 76–87.

23. Bredhoff, E. New methods of bargaining and dispute settlement. In D. Raff (Ed.). *Proceedings of New York University, 27th Annual Conference on Labor, New York City, June 12–14 1974*. New York: Matthew Bender, 1975.

24. Mills, D. Q. Flawed victory in labor law reform. *Harvard Business Review*, May-June 1979, **57** (3), 92–103.

25. Schein, E. H. *Organizational Psychology*. 3rd Ed. Englewood Cliffs, N.J.: Prentice-Hall, 1980.

26. Hackman, J. R. Work design. In J. R. Hackman and J. L. Suttle (Eds.). *Improving Life at Work: Behavioral Approaches to Organizational Change*. Santa Monica, Calif.: Goodyear. 1977.

27. Golden, C. S. & Parker, V. D. *Causes of Industrial Peace Under Collective Bargaining*. New York: Harper, 1955.

28. Healy, J. J. (Ed.). *Creative Collective Bargaining: Meeting Today's Challenge to Labor-Management Relations*. Englewood Cliffs, N.J.: Prentice-Hall, 1965.

29. Driscoll, J. W. Labor-management panels: Three case studies. *Monthly Labor Review*, June 1980, **103** (6), 41–44.

30. Whyte, W. F. *Pattern for Industrial Peace*. New York: Harper, 1951.

31. Driscoll, J. W. Coping with role conflict: An exploratory field of study of problem-solving in collective bargaining. *International Review of Applied Psychology* (forthcoming).

32. Peterson, R. B. & Tracy, L. N. Testing a behavioral theory model of labor negotiations. *Industrial Relations*, February 1977, **16** (1), 35–50.

33. Popular, J. U. S. mediators try to build common objectives. *World of Work Report*, September 1976, **1** (7), 1–3.

34. Beer, M. & Driscoll, J. W., Strategies for change. In J. R. Hackman and J. L. Suttle (Eds.). *Improving Life at Work: Behavioral Approaches to Organizational Change*. Santa Monica, Calif.: Goodyear, 1977.

35. Hackman, J. R. and Suttle, J. L. (Eds.). *Improving Life at Work: Behavioral Approaches to Organizational Change*. Santa Monica, Calif.: Goodyear, 1977.

—18—

Health and Safety, Job Stress, and Shift Work

Gloria C. Gordon
Mary Sue Henifin

A humane organization is one that provides its employees with a healthy work place. The healthiness of a work environment depends on both its physical and psychosocial conditions. In this chapter we look at the work place from an occupational health standpoint, with the aim of stimulating readers to integrate existing approaches to the health and well-being of workers. Toward this end, we bring together information from a wide range of sources to present the reader with the broad scope of work place health hazards. These include unsafe conditions, physical and chemical agents, job stress, and shift work.

The effects on human health and well-being that result from this broad range of job hazards are only partly understood. It is conservatively estimated that every year nearly 400,000 workers develop a job-related illness, and every year job-related diseases cause over 100,000 deaths. Job accidents annually cause over 14,000 deaths and 4 million injuries, 80,000 of them permanent (1, 2). There are uncounted indirect health effects from exposure to dangerous and toxic environments, psychosocial job-stressors, and shift work. In addition, the reverberations of occupational injury, illness, and death upon the family and significant others in the worker's life must be calculated in estimating the public health impact of the work place.

While some European writers take a broad approach to occupational health (3), in this country the full range of work place hazards is rarely viewed at once. Separate groups of experts from varied professional fields have been concerned with job safety, occupational illness, quality of working life, and work-sleep schedules.

Such compartmentalization is evident in the two essentially separate movements concerned with occupational health and well-being in this country. One group, concerned with quality of working life, work improvement, and humanization (4, 5, 6), promotes intervention projects to improve both quality of work life and productivity. The second group, based on a public health perspective, is concerned primarily with physical and chemical hazards in the work environment (7, 8, 9, 10).

While some authors in the second group also recognize psychosocial stressors, the writers on quality of working life usually ignore exposures to toxic chemicals. For example, in the 1973 landmark report, *Work in America* (4) and a companion volume of background papers (5), produced in response to the then-growing "blue-collar blues," only minor mention is made of physical and chemical hazards on the job.

Enlightened managers attempting to create humanized conditions in the work place often focus upon improving the quality of working life with insufficient awareness of hazardous exposures that may directly affect physical health. These hazards are found in all types of work places, even in places one would least suspect. For example, photocopying machines in offices can emit ozone, creating a health hazard for clerical workers who do extensive copying in poorly ventilated rooms.

OCCUPATIONAL SAFETY AND HEALTH ACT

The Occupational Safety and Health Act (OSHAct), passed by Congress in 1970, represents a major milestone in U.S. history. For the first time the health of American workers was treated as a human attribute to be protected rather than an expendable commodity. The purpose of the OSHAct is to provide "safe and healthful working conditions for working men and women."

The Occupational Safety and Health Administration (OSHA), located in the U.S. Department of Labor, was set up to administer the OSHAct. OSHA's primary responsibility is to promulgate and enforce standards governing the work environment. OSHA also conducts inspections of work places and has the power to issue citations and assess penalties against employers for failure to meet standards. The OSHAct also established the National Institute for Occupational Safety and Health (NIOSH) within the Department of Health, Education and Welfare (now the Department of Health and Human Services), with the responsibility for developing and recommending occupational health and safety standards.

Health and Work

What do we mean by health? While the absence of disease is one way of defining health, a model of positive health proposed in 1946 by the World Health Organization refers to "a state of physical, mental and social well-being" (11). This biopsychosocial definition of health allows for recognition of positive as well as negative changes in health status; it also points to the complex relationships among body, mind and social interaction. To assess the biopsychosocial health of employees, researchers use physical examinations, laboratory analyses, and questionnaires concerning life satisfaction on and off the job, moods, health-related behavior, and social behavior with family, friends, and organizations.

There are two principal facets of work that relate to health as it is defined above. The first is the *physical* job environment. This includes the following: safety factors (such as equipment that permits physical injury); physical factors (such as noise, light, vibration, heat, cold, and radiation); toxic and hazardous substances (such as dusts and cancer-causing chemicals); biomechanical factors (such as the human interface with machines, chairs, and tools); and biological factors (such as bacteria and viruses).

The second facet is the *psychosocial* job environment, including a range of factors usually studied or altered in job satisfaction or quality of working life projects: the work itself, job demands, organizational characteristics, and social relations.

We begin our discussion of work place health hazards by considering the physical environment.

Hazard Prevention

Under OSHA regulations, when employers are found to have violations of standards, they are ordered to institute a program for abatement of the hazard within a given period of time. Three levels of hazard abatement are recognized: *engineering changes* (to control the hazard at its source or along the pathway to the employee); *administrative changes* (to reduce the number of hours each employee is exposed to the hazard); and *personal protection* (protective equipment worn by the worker). Under the OSHAct the preferred method for hazard abatement is to develop alternative methods and materials that eliminate or reduce the hazard at its source. "This policy is based upon the view that the most effective means of controlling employee exposures is to reduce emissions of toxic substances at their source" (12). Administrative changes and personal protection are considered appropriate to use only if engineering changes are not feasible.

In the following descriptions of common work place hazards an underlying concern is how they can be reduced or eliminated. We will briefly discuss acute physical injuries (accidents) and then illustrate the scope of chronic hazardous exposures.

Acute Physical Injury

Prior to the OSHAct, the concept of health danger in the work place focused upon physical injury caused by accidents. Many state workers' compensation laws were written with language like Missouri's statute, which states that only "accidental" injuries are compensated excluding injuries arising from repeated contact with work place hazards. The possibility of a worker developing an irreversible disease from exposure to toxic substances in the work place was not taken into account.

The U.S. accident rate was reduced from 10.9 to 9.4 per 100 employees between 1972 and 1978 (13). While the balance of attention in the health and safety arena in the 1970s was devoted to health rather than safety issues, a new emphasis on occupational safety is now evident.

Early research on accident prevention was based on study of what was called in the early 1900s the "accident proneness" of the worker and today is called the "unsafe act" of the worker. The assumption of such research is that it is the unsafe act of the worker that is to be blamed for accidents rather than unsafe working conditions. However, a study of a sample of accident reports from the State of Wisconsin shows that a reasonable estimate is that one third of all accidents are attributable to "unsafe acts," while the remainder are associated with unsafe conditions in the workers' environment. When accidents are caused by unsafe acts, they are more likely to happen to workers who are young and inexperienced. Another peak in accidents appears to be associated with the aging process (14).

In February of 1980 workers were given the right, without fear of losing their jobs, to refuse work that they believe could threaten serious injury or death, when there is insufficient time to eliminate the danger through normal OSHA channels. This right was articulated by the unanimous Supreme Court decision in the Whirlpool Case.

Chronic Workplace Exposures. The extent of illness and death from physical and chemical hazards is difficult to ascertain. Epidemiologists must learn whether there is an excess of certain kinds of illness or death within specific industries. Many chronic diseases, including cancer, may take 20 to 40 years to develop after initial exposure, and it is hard to demonstrate that the disease was caused by a particular industrial hazard. Workers may change jobs throughout their work lives, and it may be difficult to trace what substances they have been exposed to that might lead to an illness later in life. Some workers do not develop work-related diseases until after they retire.

When a cluster of workers in a single industry develops a rare disease, it is often possible to attribute that disease to an industrial exposure. For example, some workers in the plastics industry who were exposed to vinyl chloride developed an extremely rare form of liver cancer called angiosarcoma. It was not difficult to tie the cancer to a work exposure. But what about more common illnesses? Lung cancer, for example, may be related to an occupational exposure, to smoking, to polluted atmospheric air, or to some combination of these.

Emphasis historically has been on what were considered high-risk occupations employing mostly men, but there is increasing recognition that occupations that have traditionally employed large numbers of women (for example as hospital workers, launderers, and textile workers) also expose workers to serious health hazards (15, 16). Some work environments such as offices and hospitals are only now being evaluated for health hazards. For example, office workers may be exposed to indoor air pollution or may experience eye strain and other problems due to video display terminal use.

Table 18.1 presents a few of the health and safety hazards associated with welding, textile, clerical, and hospital work. These four occupations were chosen to illustrate the diversity of work place hazards and to encourage readers to define the range of health hazards present in their own organizations. The following discussion covers five of the most important occupational health problems: hearing loss, respiratory disease, cancer, dermatoses, and reproductive hazards.

Hearing Loss. Forty percent of all workers in the United States are subjected to hazardous noise (17). The proportion of workers with hearing loss is highest in industries such as product fabrication, product assembly, power generation, and processing, where noise levels may exceed 95 decibels (dB). Decibels are the units used to measure noise intensity. The current OSHA noise standard is 90 dB (as an average level of exposure during an eight-hour work shift), and even the proposed OSHA standard of 85 dB does not completely protect workers' hearing (8). An example of an 80 dB noise level is a diesel truck at 40 miles per hour, measured from a distance of 50 feet.

Researchers now have enough information to tell workers what their chances of hearing loss are after a certain number of years of exposure to a defined noise level. For example, a lumberjack working for five years without ear protection exposed to 120 dB from chain saws for two hours a day stands a 50 percent chance of developing a significant hearing loss. In addition to inducing hearing loss and adding to psychosocial stress, high noise levels are also physiological stressors with potential negative long-term effects on the heart and blood circulation system (8).

Respiratory Diseases. Pneumoconioses, or dust-induced diseases of the lung, may lead to reduction in lung function, heart disease, permanent disability, and death. Many types of microscopic dust particles when inhaled escape the natural cleansing mechanisms of the upper respiratory tract and enter the small airways and air sacs, where they induce a biological response that can lead to scarring of lung tissue (called fibrosis).

Silicosis is lung disease caused by the inhalation of silica or quartz dust. Hard rock, coal, and other miners, granite cutters, makers of china and pottery, roadbuilders, and welders all may contract silicosis. Asbestosis (or white lung) is caused by the inhalation of asbestos fibers over many years.

Respiratory diseases have been classified as the most serious of all occupationally related diseases (18). For example, the death rate from respiratory diseases among coal miners is five times that of the general population of workers. Although coal mining is an industry with a high accident rate, there are four deaths from coal miner's pneumoconiosis for every death from accidents (18).

Organic dusts may also cause lung diseases, for example among farmers and agricultural workers, by inducing immunologically based lung disease. For example, brown lung or byssinosis is a disease caused by exposure to cot-

Table 18.1 Examples of Job Health and Safety Hazards

Occupation	Potential Hazard	Possible Outcome
Textile Workers	Cotton dust	Brown lung or byssinosis (a debilitating lung disease)
	Noise	Temporary or permanent hearing loss
	Chemical exposures	
	Aniline-based dyes	Bladder cancer and liver damage
	Formaldehyde	Dermatitis, allergic lung disease, possibly cancer
	Furfuraldehyde	Dermatitis, respiratory irritation, fatigue, headache, remors, numbness of the tongue
	Moving machine parts without barriers	Loss of fingers or hands
Hospital Workers	Infectious diseases	
	Hepatitis	Liver damage
	Herpes simplex virus	Painful skin lesions
	Chemical exposures	
	Anesthetic gases	Spontaneous abortions
	Metallic mercury	Poisoning of nervous system and kidneys
	Inorganic acids and alkalis	Irritation to respiratory tract and skin
	Physical hazards	
	Ionizing radiation	Burns, birth defects, cancer
	Microwave radiation	Sterility, harm to eyes, possibly increases risk of cataracts
	UV light	Burning or sensitization of skin, skin cancer, cataracts

	Safety hazards	
	Lifting or carrying	Back pain or permanent back injury
	Puncture wounds from syringes	Infections
Welders	Infrared and visible light radiation	Burns, headache, fatigue, eye damage
	UV radiation	Burns, skin tumors, eye damage
	Chemical exposures	
	Carbon monoxide	Cardiovascular disease
	Acetylene	Asphyxiation, fire, explosion
	Metallic oxides	Contact dermatitis, eye irritation, respiratory irritation, metal fume fever (symptoms similar to he flu), posssible kidney damage
	Phosphine	Lethal at even low doses; irritating to eyes, nose, skin; acts as anesthetic
Clerical Workers	Improperly designed chairs and work stations; lack of movement	Backache, aggravation of hemorrhoids, varicose veins, and other blood-circulation conditions, eyestrain
	Noise	Hearing impairment, stress reactions
	Chemical exposures	
	Ozone from copy machines	Irritation of eyes, nose, throat; respiratory damage
	Benzene and toluene in rubber cement and "cleaners"	Benzene is associated with several blood diseases (including leukemia) and toluene may cause intoxication
	Methanol and ammonia in duplicating machine solvents	Irritation to eyes, nose, and throat

ton dust. Approximately 35,000 Americans who have been employed in the textile industries suffer from this disabling disease (19). Acute symptoms include decreased lung function, chest tightness, and shortness of breath or cough. Chronic symptoms are similar to chronic bronchitis or emphysema. Although byssinosis has been recognized as an occupationally induced disease since 1705, it was not until 1978 that OSHA proposed strict standards to govern the levels of cotton dust in the textile industry.

Cancer. The World Health Organization estimates that between 75 and 85 percent of all cancers are environmentally induced. A large number of cancer-causing substances originate in work places and then are discharged into the ambient environment. Cancer strikes about one out of every four Americans. Although no one knows how many cancers are occupationally induced, researchers at the National Institutes of Health estimate that between 23 and 38 percent of the total cancer mortality in the forthcoming decades might be related to occupational exposure to carcinogens (20).

There are approximately 63,000 chemicals in common use; only a few of these have adequately been tested for carcinogenicity. Of the 44,000 substances on NIOSH's toxic substances list, approximately 1500 have shown evidence of carcinogenicity. Workers who manufacture or use these chemicals often become the guinea pigs on which these chemicals are tested.

Workers with especially high risks of cancer include chemical workers, rubber workers, dye workers, and primary metal smelters and refiners, particularly those working with arsenic, nickel, and chromates. An excess of any type of cancer among a group of workers indicates that there may be an occupational exposure to a carcinogen that is shortening workers' lives unnecessarily.

An example is the substance acrylonitrile, thought to be one of the miracle discoveries of the post World War II "chemical age." Acrylonitrile can be linked into a chain or polymer and then spun into "acrylic" fibers and woven into fabric that is used in clothes, carpets, and home furnishings. It was not until 1977 that scientists at a chemical plant producing acrylonitrile discovered that unlinked molecules of this substance were the probable cause of the high rates of cancer of the colon and lung among its textile workers (21).

Asbestos, another widely used substance because of its flexibility and electrical and thermal insulating properties, is now also known to be carcinogenic as well as fibrogenic (discussed above under respiratory diseases). Cancer from exposure to asbestos usually does not show up until 25 or more years after the worker has been exposed. After this latency period there is a greatly increased risk of bronchogenic, pleural, and peritoneal cancer. Only now are many of the workers exposed to asbestos in the large-scale shipbuilding effort during the early years of World War II beginning to evidence cancer. Cases of cancer have been detected in the families of the workers who brought home asbestos in their work clothes. Four cases of mesothelioma, a rare cancer of the membrane lining of the chest or abdomen, have already shown up in the families of 326 asbestos workers from the 1940s (22).

Dermatoses. Dermatoses or injuries to the skin account for the greatest percentage of all reported occupational diseases—over 65 percent. Ranging from mild rashes to severe burns, blisters, and pustules, skin diseases are the greatest in-plant cause of lost time. Every day one out of four employees is exposed to potential skin irritants. Many workers are exposed to a bewildering array of chemicals that may produce skin reactions. For example, construction workers are exposed to such substances as adhesives, cement, creosote, gasoline, pitch, and solvents, all of which may produce dermatoses (23, 24).

The predominant causes of industrial dermatoses are *chemical agents*, particularly acids, alkalies, solvents, essential oils, dye intermediates, petroleum products, and greases. Other causes of dermatoses include friction and pressure, ionizing radiation and electricity, and bacteria, fungi, viruses, and parasites. A particularly serious form of occupational dermatitis is chloracne with its severe acne-like symptoms. Chloracne is caused by contact with certain chlorinated hydrocarbons, oils, tars, and waxes. For example, in a 1971 study of workers making the herbicides 2, 4, −D and 2, 4, 5−T, almost 20 percent of the workers had moderate to severe chloracne, while 66 percent had less severe acne (25).

Reproductive Hazards. Ten percent of the 200,000 children born in the United States each year suffer from serious birth defects. Many other pregnancies end in spontaneous abortions and still births. Dr. Eula Bingham, former Assistant Secretary of Labor for Occupational Health and Safety, connects environmental exposures to certain toxic agents and resulting birth defects: "The more we learn about the effects of environmental toxic exposures on reproduction, the more we suspect that it is a substantial burden" (26).

Reproductive abnormalities due to chemical exposures are on the increase (27). Although most of the attention has focused on hazards to a pregnant woman's fetus, many hazards are known to affect the reproductive abilities of men. For example, many of the male workers exposed to the chemical DBCP (a pesticide) appear to have suffered permanent sterility. Chloroprene (used in the manufacture of rubber) and lead can also reduce the fertility of men.

In 1977 four women chose to be sterilized rather than lose their high-paying jobs in a lead pigment plant operated by American Cyanamid in Willow Island, West Virginia. Although none of these women wanted to have children at the time, the company had a policy of removing women of childbearing age from, or not hiring them for, jobs that could endanger a potential fetus. Other chemical industries are transferring all women of reproductive age out of jobs with exposure to chemicals that may harm the fetus. There is growing concern that such actions constitute sex discrimination in violation of Equal Employment Opportunity Guidelines (28, 29, 30).

Three categories of substances may interfere with workers' reproduction. *Mutagens* change the structure of the genetic material in reproductive cells (either in the male or female) thereby endangering future generations. Examples of mutagens include radiation, anesthetic gases used in operating rooms, vinyl chloride (used in plastic manufacturing), and trichloroethylene (used in dry cleaning). Substances that limit fertility by either reducing or damaging sperm or ova are called *gametotoxics*. Examples are PCBs (used in electrical capacitators and transformers), which reduce fertility in both men and women, and lead, which causes sperm abnormalities. *Teratogens* are substances that act directly on the fetus. Many heavy metals such as lead, mercury, or cadmium have a teratogenic effect. Other substances can cause a loss of sexual libido, such as manganese exposure in male welders, or exposure to estrogen in male workers in drug manufacturing.

Reproductive hazards are an example of a work place hazard that goes beyond the immediate danger to the worker. A child born with a deformity or defect due to parental occupational exposure carries the impact of the hazard beyond the exposed worker. Industries are worried that such children may use their right to sue the company, if the parents and child believe that the occupational exposure is responsible for the defect. In 1979 NIOSH listed 56 mutagens and 471 teratogens. Many more substances that workers may be exposed to remain untested for potential reproductive effects.

Job Stress

A second large category of work place health hazards is found in the *psychosocial* work environment, often encompassed in the term *stress*. When one speaks of job stress, it carries a meaning for everyone from the top to the bottom of a work organization. Yet there is no single accepted scientific definition of the term. Although stress has become a popular topic, these psychosocial work place factors are less well understood than the physical job hazards. As one authority states, stress is "a complex, important, widely-studied but imprecise concept" (31).

It is important to distinguish clearly between the stressful agents in the work place and the stress reaction within the employee. There is confusion because in both scientific and popular writing the word stress is used to refer both to the environmental condition and the biopsychological reaction. Hans Selye, the prominent endocrinologist, first applied the term stress to the biological reaction of the organism when faced with environmental changes (32). Later other researchers, borrowing the stress-and-strain model from engineering, referred to work place conditions as stressors and to biopsychological effects as strains (33). For clarity, we will speak of job factors as *stressors* and of human reactions as health effects or *strains*.

It may be helpful to imagine a conceptual model that includes the various factors involved in job stress. In this model the employee, with his or her individual characteristics, is acted upon by the multiple stressors present in the work setting. In addition the person experiences stressors from the nonwork sphere of life. These interacting stressors can result in physical, mental, or behavioral symptoms or illness.

The main job stressors in this model include the nature of the work itself, the demands or pressures for performance, job insecurity or lack of opportunity, poor interpersonal relations, and lack of participation in decision making. It is important to recognize that a worker's awareness of exposure to a dangerous or toxic environment also serves as a stressor.

For hourly employees, major stressors are found in work that is machine-paced, fragmented, and repetitive, whether on an assembly line or in a modern office (33, 34). Inequitable economic rewards and lack of job ladders constitute stressors for the majority of female clerical workers (35). Compulsory overtime, unpredictable work schedules, and involuntary assignment to shift schedules present problems not only to workers but to their family and friends. Sexual harassment, lack of respect, and "being denied the prerogatives of adulthood as a worker" (36) are frequently cited as stressors by both clerical and blue-collar workers. Fear of losing one's job and becoming unemployed, an anxiety tied to the larger economic picture, may well be the number one underlying job stressor (36).

Stressors tend to interact with one another. In a well-documented example, high job demands or pressures are found to create health strains mainly when workers have low decision latitude or discretion as to how to meet these needs (37). Another example is that workers faced with disturbing situations on the job tend to take less action to protect themselves when there is high unemployment.

The human effects of job stressors are frequently divided into five types. First, the level of job satisfaction or dissatisfaction that the worker reports is an indicator of well-being in and of itself. Second, there are disturbances in mood, such as depression, anxiety, frustation, and anger. These emotional effects may be transient, in response to acute events at work, or chronic, such as the "blue-collar blues" and "white collar woes." In one study, psychological well-being of industrial employees was found to vary with position in the organizational hierachy. People in lower positions showed more psychological disturbance, a trend that could not be accounted for by any nonjob factors (38).

Physiological symptoms are a third type of stressor-produced health effect. These include gastrointestinal symptoms, headaches, extreme fatigue, and difficulty in sleeping. Increased heart rate, elevated blood pressure, and biochemical changes in the blood can accompany job stressors (39). For example, the cholesterol level of accountants has been found to rise just before the income tax deadline (40).

A fourth type of strain is behavioral. This includes behavior detrimental to the worker's health, such as increased use of tobacco, caffein, alcohol, and drugs, all found in relation to job stressors. Less is known about the prevalence of other reactive patterns, such as aggressive, reckless, or dulled behavior, both on and off the job.

Diagnosed illness, both physical and mental, is a fifth category of stressor-induced health effect. The incidence of coronary heart disease and mental ill health is significantly elevated in occupational groups with high levels of job stressors (41, 42, 43).

Given this array of stressors and strains, what steps can be taken to prevent or reduce these negative health effects? Two effective steps can be taken by management. First, it is well-known that taking responsibility for one's self is essential for physical and mental health. In fact, an accepted indicator of mental disturbance is thinking that one is externally controlled. This *is* the case in the dehumanized work place, where the worker is used not as a person but as a pair of hands and eyes, secondary to the machinery. Placing more responsibility in the hands of workers means providing them with a higher level of information and expanded control over their own jobs. This has been done in programs for the rehumanization of work in selected sites in this country and Scandinavia.

Second, it is known that social support at work from supervisors and co-workers can counteract to a degree the health problems resulting from job stress. Social support is defined as "a relationship with . . . relatively frequent interactions, strong and positive feelings, and especially perceived ability and willingness to lend emotional and/or instrumental assistance in times of need" (44). Unsupportive work environments may affect health negatively, as shown in a sample of female clerical workers in which the presence of a nonsupportive boss was a factor in predicting coronary symptoms (42). These scientific findings merely document what every employee knows, that a good boss makes a big difference.

Job design and working conditions should be examined from the standpoint of whether they facilitate or inhibit social support. The substitution of monitoring by a computer for a personal supervisor, high noise levels in factories, and lack of privacy in open-plan offices can all interfere with the development of a supportive work environment.

Employees themselves can take certain steps to reduce the effects of job stress through programs of relaxation, meditation, exercise, and the like. However, it is worthwhile to point out an analogy with industrial noise. It is far preferable from a health standpoint to reduce the noise than to issue ear plugs. Personal solutions to organizationally created job stressors, like ear plugs, do not go to the source of the problem. Expecting a worker to compensate for intense job stressors, whether during the work day or away from work, cannot be considered a permanent solution.

Shift Work. The schedule of job hours is an occupational health hazard that is unique in its breadth of impact on the worker. Roughly 20 percent of the work force in this country performs shift work, defined as any schedule of job hours other than normal, steady daytime working hours starting about 7:00 to 9:00 a.m. (45). Other shifts include the afternoon- evening shift, the midnight shift, and rotating shifts in which the employee changes among two or three shifts in a regular or irregular pattern.

In industrialized countries more workers are being employed on shifts because of increases in continuous-process technology and computerization, both of which lead to around-the-clock staffing for economic reasons. While shift work formerly was found mainly in the worlds of the blue-collar and service worker, it is now on the increase in the white-collar world.

Shift work may cause negative health effects at all three levels—biological, psychological, and social. Physiological effects are related to the disruptions of normal circadian (daily) biological rhythms in temperature, blood pressure, heart rate, and other body functions (46). When a person travels by plane across several time zones these same disruptions take place. For the traveler, it takes three to four weeks to adjust fully to the new schedule of sleeping, eating, and being actively awake in the new location.

Shift workers, in contrast, cannot fully change their biorhythms because they usually try to conform to the normal wake-sleep hours of our daytime world on weekends or other days off work. While many shift workers make a compromise form of physiological adjustment, it is estimated that from 20 to 40 percent of the work force is unable to make the physical accommodation. With increasing age, most shift workers find that their hours of work become more physically stressful.

The main physiological effects of shift work are sleep deprivation, extreme fatigue, and gastrointestinal disturbance. Workers on the steady midnight shift are known to suffer the greatest physiological effects, because the reversal of work-sleep patterns is most extreme for them. To spread the burden of midnight work more evenly in the work force, there is a current trend in Europe to use the rapidly rotating shift, in which employees change every two or three days to a different shift. The rapidity of the rotation does not allow the body enough time to go through a major adjustment process before the shift changes. The solution is implemented at the risk of increased personal and social problems, such as confusion in scheduling one's life and relating to others.

Dissatisfaction with work hours and feelings of depression and irritability are often reported by shift workers. While perhaps 10 percent of day-shift workers in this country are dissatisfied with their work hours, the large majority of rotators and about half of the midnight and afternoon-evening shift workers appear to be dissatisfied with their hours (47, 48, 49). Lack of predictability or control over working hours contributes heavily to the dissatisfaction.

Social interaction with family and friends, as well as involvement in community organizations and activities, can be heavily curtailed for shift workers. Both the afternoon-evening and midnight shifts interfere with sexual relationships with a partner who lives on a normal day schedule. Total family life is altered: shift work parents may be absent from home at times when children are available for contact; when they are at home family members must be quiet when shift workers are sleeping and patient when they are sleep-deprived. The social disruption of shift work is reflected in the term "unsocial attendance" used by the British Post Office to refer to shift work (50).

Social support has been found to moderate the health effects of shift work, just as it helps to reduce symptoms of job stress. The most significant support for a shift worker is likely to come from a supportive partner or other family members.

CONCLUDING REMARKS

A successful society, as judged by humanistic values, is not one in which 200,000 people a year are permanently disabled or die from occupational accidents and disease. How can we move toward work places that are safe, healthy, and humane? Employers and supervisors can play a unique role in improving the health and safety of their organizations:

- Careful evaluation of health and safety problems can be conducted with the help of OSHA, NIOSH, and trained industrial hygienists.
- OSHA requires support for enlightened employers against those forces pressing for its dismantlement, since it provides essential validation for managers and workers who strive for safer jobs.
- Worker health and safety committees can be encouraged and management-worker cooperation can be coordinated through such committees. Worker participation is a key factor in effective health and safety plans.
- Providing physical exams and maintaining careful health records can improve the detection of physical health problems that are work-related.
- Job designs that utilize the skills of employees and provide them with sufficient decision latitude can reduce the health risks from job stressors.
- Shift work schedules that allow workers to volunteer for shifts they prefer can reduce the negative effects of shift work.
- Organizational climate and job designs that permit supportive on-the-job relationships can aid worker well-being.

The benefits of improved working conditions have an impact beyond enhancing the health of the workers immediately affected. Lowered exposure to toxic substances reduces the amount carried home on workers' clothing, preventing exposures to those at home. Prevention of injuries, fatalities, and chronic occupational disease enhances the lives of family members and friends. Reducing the need for physical and emotional recuperation in off-job time allows workers to function more effectively in their roles as parents, family members, intimates and friends.

Some jobs and job environments exert a *positive* effect on health and well-being. The potential for satisfying work to be a health-enhancing activity places the hazards of work in sharp contrast.

Any serious commitment to a value system in which biopsychosocial health is seen as a basic goal of society confronts the primacy of productivity and profit as goals. In a Scandinavian view, the production of goods and services and the provision of income to workers are not viewed as ends in themselves (3). Rather the overriding objectives of working life are to assure optimum physical, mental, and social well-being for as many people as possible and to promote their personal development and self-realization.

REFERENCES

1. Ashford, N.A. *Crisis in the Workplace: Occupational Disease and Injury.* Cambridge, Mass.: MIT Press, 1976, pp. 3–4.
2. American Public Health Association Action Alert, Feb. 1, 1980.
3. Levi, L. Occupational mental health: Its monitoring, protection, and promotion. *Journal of Occupational Medicine,* 1979, **21,** 26.
4. *Work in America.* Report of a special task force to the Secretary of HEW. Cambridge, Mass.: MIT Press, 1973.
5. O'Toole, J. (Ed.). *Work and the Quality of Life.* Cambridge, Mass.: MIT Press, 1974.
6. Walton, R.E. Work innovations in the United States. *Harvard Business Review,* 1979, **57,** 88–98.
7. Wallick, F. *The American Worker: An Endangered Species.* New York: Ballantine, 1972.
8. Stellman, J.M. & Daum, S.M. *Work Is Dangerous to Your Health.* New York: Vintage, 1973.
9. Brodeur, P. *Expendable Americans.* New York: Viking, 1974.
10. Scott, R. *Muscle and Blood.* New York: Dutton, 1974.
11. Constitution of the World Health Organization, 1948. In *Basic Documents.* 15th Ed. Geneva: WHO, 1964.
12. *Federal Register,* 43, 27384, June 23, 1978.
13. *U.S. News and World Report,* February 11, 1980, p. 80.
14. Hagglund, G. Unpublished data reported in Ashford, N.A., *Crisis in the Workplace.* Cambridge, Mass.: MIT Press, 1976, pp. 110–115.
15. Stellman, J.M. *Women's Work, Women's Health: Myths and Realities.* New York: Pantheon Books, 1977.
16. Hricko, A. & Brunt, M. *Working for Your Life: A Woman's Guide to Job Health Hazards.* Labor Occupational Health Program and Public Citizen's Health Research Group, Berkeley, Calif.: 1976.

17. Mass, R.B. Occupational noise exposure and hearing conservation. In C. Zenz. (Ed.) *Occupational Medicine*. Chicago: Yearbook Medical Publishers, 1975.

18. *Enemies in the Dust: Occupational Respiratory Diseases*. Reprinted from the *Bulletin of the American Lung Association,* New York, 1974.

19. *Federal Register,* 43, 27353, June 23, 1978.

20. Bridport, K. et al. *Estimates of the Fraction of Cancer in the United States Related To Occupational Factors*. Report prepared by the National Cancer Institute, National Institute of Environmental Health Sciences, NIOSH, 1978.

21. O'Berg, M.T. *Epidemiological Study of Workers Exposd to Acrylonitrile,* preliminary results, DuPont Chemical Company, May, 1977.

22. Selikoff, I. & Hiatt, H.H. et al. (Eds.). *Origins of Human Cancer,* Vol. 4, Cold Spring Harbor Laboratory, New York, 1977.

23. Pittelkow, T. Occupational dermatoses. In C. Zenz (Ed.). *Occupational Medicine*. Chicago: Year Book Medical Publishers, Inc., 1975.

24. Samitz, M.H. The industrial dermatoses. *American Journal of Nursing,* 1965, **65,** 79–82.

25. Poland, A.P. A health survey of workers in a 2-4-D and 2,4,5-T plant with special attention to chloracne, porphyria cutanea tarda, and psychologic parameters. *Archives of Environmental Health,* 1971, **22,** 316–327.

26. *New York Times,* January 15, 1979, p. D8.

27. Dixon, R.L. Toxic responses of the reproductive system. In J. Doull, D.C. Klassen, and M.O. Amdur (Eds.). *Casarett and Doull's Toxicology*. New York: 1980, pp. 332–354.

28. Protecting women or all workers. *Women's Occupational Health and Resource Center News,* 1979, **1** (1), 6.

29. New U.S. guidelines on reproductive hazards. *Women's Occupational Health and Resource News,* 1980, **2**(1), 4.

30. Robinson, G. The new discrimination. *Environmental Action,* March 1979, 4–9.

31. McGrath, J.E. Stress and behavior in organizations. In M.D. Dunnette (Ed.). *Handbook of Industrial and Organizational Psychology*. Chicago: Rand McNally, 1976.

32. Selye, H. *The Stress of Life*. New York: McGraw-Hill, 1956.

33. Caplan, R.D. et al. *Job Demands and Worker Health*. DHEW(NIOSH) pub. no. 75-160, 1975.

34. *Race Against Time: Automation of the Office*. Working Women, National Association of Office Workers, 1980.

35. Kanter, R.M. *Men and Women of the Corporation*. New York: Basic Books, 1977.

36. Shostak, A.B. Blue-collar stressors. In A. McLean (Ed.). *Reducing Occupational Stress*. DHEW(NIOSH) Pub. No. 78-140, 1978.

37. Karasek, R.A. Job demands, job decision latitude, and mental strain: Implications for job redesign. *Administrative Science Quarterly,* 1979, **24,** 285.

38. Kornhauser, A. *Mental Health of the Industrial Worker*. New York: Wiley, 1965.

39. Rose, R.M., Jenkins, C.D. & Hurst, M.W. *Air Traffic Controller Health Change Study*. Boston: Boston University School of Medicine, 1978.

40. Friedman, M. Rosenman, R.H. & Carroll, V. Change in the serum cholesterol and blood clotting in men subjected to cyclic variations of occupational stress. *Circulation,* 1958, **17,** 852–861.

41. Karasek, R. Baker, B. Marxer, F. & Theorell, T. *Job Decision Latitude, Job Demands, and Coronary Heart Disease and CHD Symptoms.* Paper presented at the annual meeting of the American Public Health Association, 1979.

42. Haynes, S.G. & Feinleib, M. Women, work, and coronary heart disease: Prospective findings from the Framingham heart study. *Journal of American Public Health Association,* 1980, **70,** 133.

43. Cooper, C.L. & Marshall, J. Occupational sources of stress: A review of the literature relating to coronary heart disease and mental ill health. *Journal of Occupational Psychology,* 1976, **49,** 11–28.

44. House, J.S. & Wells, J.A. Occupational stress, social support and health. In McLean, A. (Ed.). *Reducing Occupational Stress.* DHEW (NIOSH) Publication No. 78–140, 1978.

45. Tasto, D.L. & Colligan, M.J. *Shift Work Practices in the United States.* DHEW (NIOSH) Publication No. 77–148, 1977.

46. Luce, G.G. *Body Time.* New York: Pantheon, 1971.

47. Mott, P.E. et al. *Shift Work.* Ann Arbor: University of Michigan Press, 1965.

48. Tasto, D.S. et al. *Health Consequences of Shift Work.* DHEW (NIOSH) Publication No. 78–154, 1978.

49. Gordon, G.C. McGill, W.L. & Maltese, J.W. Home and community life of a sample of shift workers. In L.C. Johnson, D.I. Tepas, W.P. Colquhoun, and M.J. Colligan. (Eds.). *The Twenty-Four Hour Work Day: Proceedings of a Symposium on Work-Sleep Schedules.* Washington, D.C.: HHS (NIOSH), 1981 (in press).

50. Young, M. & Willmott, P. *The Symmetrical Family.* New York: Pantheon, 1973.

—19—

Contemporary Realities as Seen by a Practitioner

Kenneth Ball

CLIMATE, 1980

Concerns over corporate social responsibility reflect both the magnitude of social and human problems and the frequently inadequate attempts to resolve them by community, business, and governmental institutions. In responsibility we must include a manager's willingness and ability to influence and effect corporate change. And all of this must be accomplished within the context of a profitable, productive environment.

In 1972 the social pressures of the 1960s had already come to a head, and it was obvious that the manifestations of these pressures would be felt by industry. In 1980 the goals and strategies of interest groups have become more clearly delineated. The federal government has played an expanding role in defining new responsibilities and value orientations expected from the business community.

"To whom is the corporation responsible?" By 1977 this question was asked by Clark Abt (1) in his book *The Social Audit for Management*. That it had to be asked at all would have been astonishing to the industrial leader of even recent generations. That it must be asked, and in an American Management Association publication, is indicative of the new climate with which the business community must cope.

Past simplistic answers, such as "stockholders, lenders, and owners," created an atmosphere in which the managers could get on with the business of deploying assets for profits. Social responsibilities were, at most, peripheral concerns assigned to public relations-type departments, permitting "line" management to pursue their clearly defined goals.

REALITY 1980 FOR THE PRACTITIONER

Stockholders and owners, lenders and banks, the buying public, and all consumers, unions, and employee groups, all governmental bodies, social institutions, and each individual employee—all have pressed their interests and demands upon business through government and by direct confrontation.

These considerations are set against the backdrop of economic pressures, where stockholders and lenders seldom ameliorate their demands for results in response to the weight of social factors. Even the government strikes conflicting postures as dictated by world trade, military, energy, and fiscal demands. This is the real world for today's industrial manager.

What does this mean to industrial managers in terms of how they perceive their roles and organize their efforts in response to these diverse demands? Clearly they require new behavior patterns and value orientations. Is the manager equipped to function as a responsible corporate agent within the community and toward its institutions? Effectiveness would be epitomized by socially motivated action *not* required by laws or pressure groups.

Guiding their sense of responsibility is the requisite of understanding interrelationships between business and society. Human concerns must encompass people within and outside the company, without ignoring pressures for increased productivity.

The practitioner must bring meaningful order to what might seem like a chaotic situation of conflicting demands. In doing so, he or she will undoubtedly stretch the available resources to their utmost limits. Insights and information as provided in this volume can help in understanding and providing reference points for action. If these efforts fail, his or her future role might become as anachronistic as that of the industrial leader who continues to respond with the same myopic views espoused in the earlier decades of industrialization.

The major challenge confronting the practitioner is to effect change in a broad and in-depth context as the magnitude of the issues seem to warrant. Changes in most of the social areas are already gaining some modicum of acceptance in our industrial society, whether for practical or more ethical reasons. A growing number of corporate annual reports include statements by the chairperson showing the company's responsiveness to the growing number of social issues facing it. This places demands upon managers to provide the mechanism for change and to provide avenues for understanding the conflicting issues in American business.

In order to effectively deal with managers and others throughout the business organization to effect change, it is important to focus on perhaps the greatest conflict for business as seen by the manager: Business seems to have been identifying as its greatest and growing source of conflict the federal government's greater involvement in representing the broad range of interest groups pressuring for responsiveness from industry. This perceived conflict is irrational when one considers that it is only tangential to the real problems. It is, however, a source of conflict with which the practitioner must deal. Rational or not, it is in this context that much of the business community sees its problems in dealing with many external and internal pressures. The primary goal is to bring about change in a real and meaningful way, following legal guidelines, and avoiding the pitfalls of being a party to developing neatly packaged programs for the file and for compliance.

There are enforceable laws governing what organizations must and must not do to achieve a balanced work force representing all minority groups. E.E.O.C. guidelines and laws have recently been enacted extending equal opportunities for women and increasing opportunities for the aged and the handicapped. The active role that government agencies have played in supporting the laws affecting these many groups have created new avenues through which other individuals and groups can seek restitution or at least a hearing for their grievances. Failure to consider someone for a job or for promotion, terminating an employee for refusal of a transfer, or because of suspected drinking, or because he or she has been involved in conflict on either side of union and management, are all grounds for appeal to a government agency. With or without justification, frequently industry finds itself in what it perceives to be a costly defensive role. And, in fact, misusing the law and the agencies on the part of an aggrieved employee does sometimes occur. All of this adds to the already difficult task of changing the attitudes of business leaders.

REAL ISSUES AND EFFECTING CHANGE

Minorities

The successes of the past probably represent the greatest challenge and potentially the greatest failures. Since the 1960s, by comparison with gains made during the first half of this century, blacks and minorities have made significant progress in equal treatment and opportunities in the business world. Looking at the massive problems that still exist against what has been achieved, one must recognize all that remains unresolved. Unfortunately, there is the real risk that having met initial affirmative action plans "in the files" and satisfactory beginnings in the work place, there may be a slowing of the pace for continued progress at least as perceived by minority groups. Perhaps the greatest change needed is in the inherent structure of the organization that permits built-in reasons, excuses, and deterrence to improving rates of progress. Human resource planning as described by Beatty et al. can assure greater success than merely reacting to segmented problems.

Properly, the first and greatest emphasis has been placed on testing. In some circumstances the guidelines, while proven necessary, have caused a retrenchment of scientifically designed selection programs. This overreaction may actually inhibit the professional psychologist or consultant in need of personal data not related validly to job performance but rather to human development and growth. Resolution of this dilemma remains as a major undertaking.

As we move out from the initial phases of making employment opportunities more available to minorities to other barriers, we find, as Beatty, Holloway, and Schneier indicate, a great need to provide reinforcement for all of life's problems confronting the minority individual. Without resolving the problems of everything from transportation to handling personal family situations, job success becomes an almost unattainable goal for too many. The real opportunities should be in smaller companies, where attitude change is frequently more easily achieved.

Perhaps most difficult in reinforcing the broad educational needs of the minority worker is, as pointed out by Beatty et al., the need for selective special treatment. Dealing with the remaining work force and unions is a most significant problem. And, underlying all, is the need to incorporate a change of values and philosophy throughout the organization so opportunities become not just satisfying to E.E.O.C. guidelines, but an honest recognition of industry's social role.

Women

The role of women in our western society derives from the history of the human race. That these roles have become anachronistic is current fact, and sex bias stubbornly lingers at most levels of the business setting and work force. The historical perspective is well presented in Lionel Tiger's *Men in Groups* (2).

The challenge to end sex bias begins with selection and placement and continues through employee development. As the historical role patterning has interfered with role changes for women, so has the historical organizational patterning inhibited their progress. Tucker points out in her paper that "organizations are creatures of habit . . .roles get in the way of adaptation to new situations." Contributions from the social sciences, as in Tucker's chapter, can identify the important variables to consider such as stereotypes, perceptions, self-concepts, and self-perceptions.

Responding to a volatile business and economic environment requires flexibility and effective managerial skills. Women in management can provide a new talent pool for the top. Attitudes and stereotypical perceptions must be changed to reflect this changing environment. For example, there is little if any evidence to indicate that the cost of training women for management jobs is any greater than that which is now being spent for training men.

Business must recognize the fallacy of perpetuating the system by promoting from within. It is necessary to break into the all-male progression system in spite of the negative reaction it may cause. Better understanding of job evaluation and job evaluation methods and improvement in these systems can help define real issues and positive approaches. The object is to attain creative organizational planning. For example, women may be introduced more acceptably into line management roles by utilizing "staff" positions as "quasi-line" functions to demonstrate ability and gain acceptance.

Tucker's consideration of negative homosocial effects as it relates to women has very broad implications for total organizational growth and even for survival. Here the practitioner's work is cut out as a social change agent in the industrial setting. As with any culturally deeprooted stereotype, efforts at attitude change must encompass more than just the job setting.

Career patterning and planning have received increasing attention in recent years. Here is an opportunity to effect planned change, circumscribing the emerging needs of women for a new place in the industrial world. In fact, articles in business magazines seem to report an increase in longrange career planning.

From the most practical point of view, changing attitudes toward women in the work force is fraught with problems of resolving all kinds of basic conflicts. Provisions or considerations must be made for child care; career development may be interrupted for childbearing, although resumed sooner now than years ago. How shall these "noncareer" factors be included in the plan? There will be sexual attractions on the job. Should they be faced and explored, or ignored in the name of equality? Here the affirmative action plan is only a very small part of the real challenge.

Aging

At the most basic level in industry, where all production operations occur, the practitioner is faced with conflicting realities, needs, demands, and prejudices. First-line supervisors must meet budgets and schedules. Federal regulations, as interpreted through the personnel department's pronouncements, and training programs must be considered. Reaction time, judgments, and health and safety needs must be recognized. Stress factors, such as shift work and overtime, seemingly cannot be avoided. Above all, consider the individual!

Demands for problem solving in the whole area of aging seem to rest upon dealing with stereotypes. After stereotypes of minorities and women's roles, there is probably nothing more fraught with stereotypes than attitudes toward the aged. This is a relatively new concern in industry as the average age of the population increases. More recently, it has taken on new and specific meaning, governed by federal law.

As a practical matter, the problems of an aging society are also industry's problems. If one in five people will be over 65 years old in 50 years, planning utilization of productive resources must include considerations of aging. Industry is faced with relating current concepts, such as quality of life, to this large segment of society.

Industry's demonstrated attitudes toward the aged might be reflected all too well in other sectors of society. The misconception of an inverse relationship between aging and production undoubtedly carries through into the other segments. Taking a leadership role in educating individuals and restructuring business to provide new opportunities for the aged could have a significant and positive impact.

Business needs the kinds of explicit studies that Meltzer summarizes on age differences and work attitudes. More than selling panaceas, this can be the real contribution of the social sciences. Meltzer's description of the role of personal experiences in work satisfaction has broad implications for management and its impact on quality of life. His broad analysis of the correlates of worker satisfaction puts worker motivation in a new light for many managers.

And what of life's age cycles'stresses? They require understanding and provisions for professional training and guidance. There are more comprehensive implications of age category stresses for individuals dealing with employee mental health. First is younger-age career planning stress; financial stress; and then later-life family and sex stresses.

Practical implications of retirement satisfaction must be, and are being, more relevantly handled by industry, particularly health concerns, and the need for benefit considerations. Both industry and unions must come to grips with the vested interests that reinforce retirement cutoff dates. Although we cannot ignore the importance of the economics, there is a need for retraining programs and coordinated cooperation among industry, unions, and government.

We have learned that there is not necessarily an inverse relationship between age and creativity. Individuals acquire a creative attitude from experience. Tapping the creative resources of the aged could provide opportunities and productive resources. Meltzer appropriately sums it up: "competency is not a matter of age, it is a matter of ability and motivation." Perhaps we can achieve new gains in industry by teaching the aged how to teach.

Over the past few decades planned vocational growth has received a great deal of attention from counselors from both within and outside the industrial setting. There is now a real need to plan the tail-end of a job career and transfer abilities to jobs that can be handled at later ages. In terms of health and abilities, aging is not always a positive experience, and more planned provisions must be made.

The Handicapped

Perhaps most important in the area of employing the handicapped is that recent findings have revealed jobs to which they are better suited than those not handicapped. Employing the deaf where there can be stress from unusually high noise, or placing mental retardees on repetitive jobs, are examples of how the handicapped can be productive. It is a matter of exploring relevant abilities, rather than focusing on what they cannot do.

Selection, training, and placement are crucial considerations for the handicapped in industry. An overriding and somewhat less obvious need is for understanding within the company, and to change attitudes toward the handicapped as human beings and toward what they really are capable of doing. Perhaps least obvious is that handicapped individuals must be encountered within their context, personally, socially, and on the job, since the three obviously interrelate. The objective should be to become involved in the full range of life adjustment problems.

One area deserves specific mention and that, perhaps unlike other problems in this section, is the need for the company to develop closer ties with outside agencies that are better equipped to assist industry in evaluation and training procedures. The current reality is that most companies are not properly equipped. Except for larger companies, most could not afford to be adequately staffed, and might best turn to the consulting social scientist.

When Ehrle refers to handicapped employees as "substantially limited," it is important to identify the specific areas of limitation. Industry has proven its ability to tackle difficult problems of selection, training, and placement as, for example, during rapid mobilization during World War II. The wherewithal is there to apply for the handicapped. Ehrle questioned how to balance the demand for performance from the work group and yet provide opportunities for the handicapped. Industry has options in hand that it has been applying in recent years to job design and organizational change. Much attention has been paid to using job design as an approach in dealing with work satisfaction problems. The tools are in place to apply to problems of employing the handicapped. In recent years, industry has turned with increasing frequency to the consulting industrial psychologist to solve just about every other organizational "fit" problem. Certainly the problem of "fit" for the handicapped is fertile ground.

The government has taken and played a very visible role. This has become true in almost everything relating to the breaking of old social attitudes and introducing new. The government has also properly taken the lead directly and through its support of private agencies in providing centers for skill identification and training and recently life adjustment training. Additional effort and cooperation are required from the public and private sectors if they are to act in a more concerted and positive manner.

Alcoholism and Drugs

Pittman's chapter goes a long way in helping to understand the basic correlates of alcohol and drug abuse, most often oversimplified by the lay person. Problems of dealing with alcoholism in industry are not new. Problems of dealing with drugs in today's society pose new problems. Today alcoholism and drug usage are seen in a broader perspective. The practitioner or, more likely, the consulting psychologist, must not only solve the problems they engender but also deal with attitudes toward them. Here there is greater complexity, considering the influence of home life, stress, and now the influence of the work place.

Alcoholism was one of the first mental health problems about which industry began to see its causal role. It has become easier to deal with it "down the line" as top management has recognized it as a problem "at the top." The social sciences have been successful in providing the proper focus on the broad problem. It is now more readily recognized as a full social problem, rather than a class problem. However, the bar and cocktail lounge continue to conjure up different images for management and frequently different degrees of tolerance and understanding.

Since there is a long history of handling alcohol problems and the manner in which they affect home life, even at high socioeconomic levels, recognition of drug-related problems has gained relatively fast acceptance in industry. That alcohol and drug problems are related to productivity and must be faced in the business setting is also accepted. That knowledge about them is needed to deal with them effectively is also a fact. Drugs, however, have presented a comparatively new need for knowledge and an assist from the professionals.

While there are probably more in-house programs to deal with these problems today, the need for individual counseling is greater than the availability of psychological facilities in industry. The practitioner must be familiar with agencies to act as an effective referral agent. The greatest cooperative goal is to mount effective preventive and educational programs.

Mobility and Transfer

Perhaps most notable about problems of mobility and transfer is that, comparatively, they have received little attention and are not a focal point of interest within the business setting. The article presented by Pinder should underscore its importance. For the practitioner, in many ways it presents more personal and professional conflict than the others.

Today's multinational or multiplant business must be considered as the organization is patterned. These organizational requirements frequently initiate the transfer of employees in order to place strengths at problem sites. Plans for employee growth often encompass transfer as a part of development. Additionally, the managers must consider all facets of quality of life issues, as well as human and individual rights. These frequently run counter to transfer and organizational needs. There is pressure for managers to participate personally in the larger community. This becomes more difficult when transfers interfere with taking roots in the community and may even bring out feelings of alienation.

Pinder poses the possibility of additional conflict when he suggests that there could be positive value to the old boy networks. Tucker's chapter on women examines problems of rigid continuity created by such systems. For the employee, conflict is frequently the over-riding factor when he or she is confronted with the need (or opportunity) to accept a transfer. Economic differences between the geographical areas become magnified. Reestablishing a home life in a new community setting can create emotional and family pressures. More recently, with women pursuing their own careers, a move can initiate family career conflict.

Here the manager might well call upon the industrial psychologist to mediate the conflicts and to review alternatives. Modern business has undoubtedly faced up to the economic considerations, but not as well to personal need satisfaction. There are, then, multiple opportunities for the practitioner to deal with individuals, the organization, and to seek more in-depth studies of mobility and transfer as provided here.

Unions

Obviously there is more than one power structure impinging upon individual and organizational considerations within the industrial organization. The practitioner must understand the union and its working relationship with the company if all other considerations on behalf of either are to be effective.

Conflict resolution needs are usually greatest during labor negotiations, yet both sides too often turn to legal counsel. Consulting psychologists should be playing a greater role at all phases of conflict, and there is an opportunity for them to preempt it by promoting cooperation if they are called upon as a more vital participant. There may be negative reactions to industrial psychologists, since they are often seen as representatives of management and, much less frequently, functionaries of the union.

Conflicts or opportunities for positive action are perhaps greatest at the juncture of productivity demands and appeals for humane treatment of employees. The whole question of group versus individual concern is embodied here and made even more complex by the involvement of management and unions. The need for interrelatedness between them at all organizational levels creates another dimension in the area of communication when considering the union as the "other" power structure.

Viewing unions from within, one might question some areas of relevance or blind spots. Many have been handicapped by outmoded vested interests in pursuing primarily financial and fringe gains for their employees. It is not the intention here to minimize that need; however, in many instances unions have not adapted as leaders responding to the needs of minorities, the disabled, and other employee social problems. The union organization provides the same challenges to be more reflective of a changing environment as has been the case with business, and needs a similar kind of input from the organizational development specialist. The question can rightfully be asked within the union whether it has updated its perception of the human condition on the job to encompass the full range of life problems rather than only the narrow grievance procedures.

If there is to be continued progress toward productive industrial peace, the opportunities to participate in creatively promoting cooperative planning and problem solving have barely been touched. Driscoll supplies a broad range of alternatives for the reader's consideration.

Health and Safety

Health, safety, and stress management have become almost traditional areas of study in industry. The many important dimensions for managerial understanding are well presented by Gordon and Henifin. On the other hand, in recent years health and safety have become immersed in some of the most heavily publicized conflicts because of O.S.H.A. The arena is emotionally charged! The practitioner must avoid being drawn into corporate arguments that obfuscate the real problems of health and safety. He or she must deal with the corporate attitude, the value of human life, *and* (preferable to versus) corporate goals.

A wide range of studies have explored job factors, personal needs, and job satisfaction as these have related to health and safety. Gordon and Henifin have pointed out that an important goal for the worker is to reach a state of physical, mental, and social well-being through work experiences. Today this must be considered in the context of full life experiences, not just within the narrower confines of the business setting. Priority might well be given to integrate all these, not only conceptually but also for application of programs to effect a more satisfactory life concept that includes productivity and job satisfaction.

In the very real physical sense, all too frequently the potential for work to satisfy human needs is inhibited by job hazards. In the broadest sense, relating work to quality of life must be management's concern, the practitioner's arena, and not governmental demand alone.

Historically, in dealing with matters of health and safety, corporations have recognized the need for more than lip service from the top. Training is one focal point. If on-the-job health and safety are to be brought to worker and supervisory levels, there is a need for programs involving employees. Safety committees date back many years, but authority, responsibility, and controls in the hands of the employees are seldom found. Bridging that gap between management and the worker provides a real opportunity for effective health and safety management.

More recently, emphasis has been placed upon the origins of stress, including shift work, new job, economic demands, and social and family settings (i.e., the work role of women). Perhaps in no area more than health and safety must the practitioner answer a very basic value question: What are the real objectives of work?

CONCLUSION

Functional reality for the practitioner is to relate the accumulation of knowledge, as presented here, for example, and social science theory to action-oriented programs for managers. The practitioner should be the catalyst for changing attitudes and actions within and between institutions, since industry probably sits at the focal point, or at least shares that position with government. The world of the practitioner abounds with applicable theory. The goal is not panacea, but obtaining and providing planned programs, including educating (for attitude change), demonstrating and teaching conflict resolution, helping to develop action programs, and providing meaningful guidance to all levels of management, including, most importantly, the top corporate leaders. That is where effective change begins.

REFERENCES

1. Abt, C. *The Social Audit for Management.* New York: AMACOM, 1977.
2. Tiger, L. *Men in Groups.* New York: Random House, 1969.

—III—

INNOVATION FOR ORGANIZATION DEVELOPMENT AND CHANGE

Innovation for organizational development and change is the theme of Part III. Challenging contributions present knowledge about some of the probable directions of change as well as thoughts about how to succeed in getting there. The focus is on the substance of innovations as well as on how to introduce, sustain, and evaluate ways that are humane as well as productive.

In Chapter 20 Alderfer argues that innovations designed to produce organizations that are both humane and productive must employ diagnostic strategies that are themselves humane and productive. In describing some of the essential ingredients of such a system of organizational diagnosis, Alderfer stresses the central role of theory. He argues persuasively that diagnosis requires the use of theory from three levels of analysis—individuals, groups, and organizations.

For a critically realistic consideration of work redesign, its possibilities and limitations, the reader will find Hackman's chapter on work redesign for organizational development very enlightening. Like Alderfer, Hackman draws on theoretical material several levels of analysis—activation theory, motivation hygiene theory, job characteristic theory, and sociotechnical systems theory. Although Hackman's framework is a broad one, his central theme is clear and direct: Work redesign is far more than a formal intervention technique, it is a core function of management. The potential payoffs of Hackman's analysis for people and organizations are considerable. Moreover, they appear to be receiving serious consideration by important groups in our society today—at labor union headquarters, in executive suites, and in chambers of government.

The process of career development provides some of the most important opportunities for combining goals of productivity with the vital interests of individuals. Unfortunately, all too often these opportunities are missed as organizations follow bureaucratic, routine, and dehumanized procedures in manpower and career planning. In his chapter Dr. Pinto examines changes that some organizations have introduced which appear to hold the potential for taking advantage of these opportunities. Pinto points out a number of new attitudes which these emerging approaches embody and then integrates these thoughts into a 5 stage model for career development. He concludes by observing that humane/productive career development is a burden which requires a fully collaborative effort by organizations and individuals.

As our civilization increases in complexity, the need for effective collaboration—that is, unity for productive organized activity among people who are not in full agreement—is fast becoming a condition for human survival. In her chapter on fostering collaboration among organizations, Gricar considers processes and results of interventions for collaboration among organizations themselves. She extends some of the strategies that have proven useful with organizations to consider them as tools for building cooperation among organizations and to show how change agents can play an important role in facilitating interorganizational cooperation. Gricar conceives of each intervention strategy as being designed to facilitate a particular stage of domain development, and stresses the need for the change agent to tailor any intervention to the stage the system has reached. Like diagnosis as treated elsewhere in this volume, collaboration can be designed, planned, and carried out in a manner that is productive but also humane.

Shulman, in his consideration of humanizing technology, provides a framework for understanding what technology is and describes the technological process in five interdependent phases. He also presents five major themes that characterize positions managers take towards technology during each of these phases: the manager as technologist, elitist, progressive pragmatist, pluralist, and devolutionist. He concludes by considering what it takes to have humanized management and the qualifications of the manager that can confront the realities in humane as well as productive fashion. Throughout the chapter the focus of attention is not on tools or gadgets but on the manner in which managers consider their responsibilities across all five phases of the technological process.

Until recently the physical setting has too often been left to architects. Managers and social scientists have treated it as a hygiene issue that they attend to only when people are dissatisfied. The more complex impact of settings on people and vice versa were overlooked. In his chapter on effective settings for making organizations humane and productive, Stephen Jenks treats many aspects of these "hidden dimensions," as Edward T. Hall called them. Drawing on Jenk's perspective we can see more clearly a number of individual elements that contribute to the creation of the climate of life in an organization. Elements of the physical setting—the ways in which organization members shape and reshape their offices, production areas, and passageways, the presence or the absence of private space, the level of noise, the availability of "public" gathering places (e.g., coffee lounges)—all influence communication processes, feelings of comfort, and the type of behavior that takes place. In short, they influence how people experience the organization and its effectiveness.

Often we learn much about ourselves and what we can do to be better off in the future by studying others. In Chapter 26, Eli Ginzberg draws on recent developments in Europe to help us understand some contemporary

American concerns: the erosion of the work ethic, decline in productivity, and the possible collapse of Western democratic societies. The importance of his analysis goes beyond his optimistic conclusions. Ginzberg provides a perspective for viewing trends in a realistic manner that reflects the complexities of social changes.

Ronald Lippitt, the author of the chapter on humanizing planned change, writes in the light of his vast research on and experience with the introduction of planned change. Lippitt focuses on three basic aspects of humaneness in planning change: goal setting, planning for implementation, and introducing change itself. He has chosen a format that is somewhat different from the other papers in this volume. The result is a concise inventory of concepts and suggestions for the design and implementation of change in a humane and productive fashion.

The diverse ideas in Part III are put to a rather severe test in the practitioner critique by Thomas Standing. Standing employs his experience at Standard Oil of Ohio as perspective for evaluating the degree of applicability of these ideas to everyday practice in *his* organization.

The emphasis on his setting as the basis for evaluation of proposed innovations for organization change makes Standing's chapter a particularly suitable ending for this book. The information presented in this volume supports the view that humane/productive organizations will not be successfully created at abstract levels by social or other scientists. They can be created only by practitioners who are able to employ knowledge in the design and management of their own organizations. While we firmly believe that the knowledge summarized in this book can be an important basis for such practical efforts, the practitioner must evaluate and synthesize this information and translate it into policies and procedures that fit his or her organization. This belief does not mean that the academician has no role or responsibility for facilitating this translation process. However, it does mean that the practitioner who "buys" or "waits to buy" generic programs, theories, and techniques from academicians or consultants is likely to be disappointed with the results.

The practitioner must be an informed user with sufficient knowledge to ask the key questions that will bring out the information for an adequate assessment of a particular approach for the manager's own setting. Similarly, it is the practitioner who must be in a position to insist on the "right" modifications and the "right" timing with right being defined in terms of suitability for his or her particular organization setting.

It is to managers who seek to make their organizations humane and productive that the efforts of the authors and editors of this book have been directed. We hope that this group of managers is larger in size and more aware of the possibilities as a result of these efforts and that they are better able to act as informed users of knowledge currently available in the behavioral sciences.

—20—

The Methodology of Diagnosing Group and Intergroup Relations in Organizations

Clayton P. Alderfer

The development of organizations that are both productive and humane requires diagnostic strategies that are themselves productive and humane. In other words, we need methodologies for understanding living organizations that generate valid data through processes that incorporate human concerns and promote human growth and development. This paper describes some of the essential ingredients for such a system of organizational diagnosis.

It seems to be an exception rather than a rule for behavioral scientists to base their methodological decisions on theories about human behavior. Even more unusual are views that call on professionals to examine their own behavior as a fundamental ingredient in methodological strategy. This chapter assumes that both of these exceptions are essential and provides a theory of method for diagnosing group and intergroup relations in organizations. There are three major sections: In the first section, we define and analyze organizational diagnosis as a clinical methodology for studying organizations. In the second section, we examine the effects on the diagnostic process of dealing with overbounded or underbounded human systems. In the third section, we make use of group and intergroup theory to take account of organizational diagnosis as an intergroup transaction.

THE METHODOLOGY OF ORGANIZATIONAL DIAGNOSIS*

Organizational diagnosis is a process based upon behavioral science theory for publicly entering a human system, collecting valid data about human experiences with that system, and feeding that information back to the system

---

This chapter is adapted from a forthcoming book, *Group Relations and Organizational Diagnosis*, of which L. Dave Brown, Robert E. Kaplan, and Ken K. Smith are co-authors.

*This section makes extensive use of an article by the same title (1).

to promote increased understanding of the system by its members. The purpose of organizational diagnosis is to establish a widely shared understanding of a system and, based upon that understanding, to determine whether change is desirable (2).

Inevitably the organizational diagnosis has a tendency to provoke change in a human system, but the perspective presented here distinguishes the aims of diagnosis from those of planned change. According to the present view, diagnosticians attempt to change an organization only as far as is necessary to accomplish the purpose of diagnosis. Otherwise they do not attempt to promote change, no matter how promising are the opportunities that seem to present themselves. Deriving from the broad class of clinical social science, diagnostic theory and methods may be used for "basic," "applied," and "action" research.

This stance regarding change during diagnosis combines an understanding of organizational behavior with a value position regarding effective professional work in applied behavioral science. The work of organizational diagnosis may require the professional to work with the organization as a whole, including organization-environment relations, groups inside and outside the organization, and individuals whose lives are shaped by the organization and who in turn determine the nature of the organization. As a result, theory relevant to individuals, groups, and the organization as a whole is crucial to the task of diagnosis. Simply to survive, the professional must know how to develop and to maintain working relationships with the system and its major components. To complete the work of understanding a system, the professional must know what data to obtain, how to collect it, and how to feed it back to the system to promote understanding. Because resistance to inquiry is a common human characteristic, diagnosticians are ill-equipped if they cannot identify and work through resistances to their work. Therefore, without skills to effect change, diagnosticians' capacity to complete the diagnostic mission may be blocked by the very processes they are attempting to understand. On the other hand, normally occurring respondent resistance cannot become part of the researcher's justification for acting unilaterally and arbitrarily in the face of that resistance. Researchers who aspire to excellence in their diagnostic work cannot achieve this goal without respondent cooperation. By stating and then maintaining that the initial work with a system is diagnosis, investigators provide respondents with bases against which they can be held accountable. Investigators also provide a means for protecting themselves against excessive and unproductive demands by respondents during diagnosis. This approach sets limits on how researchers will use their skills and knowledge during diagnosis, and in general develops expectations about what investigators and respondents can count on from one another during the diagnostic process.

Organizational diagnosis proceeds in three orderly phases: entry, data collection, and feedback. These phases are well defined because there are a clearly observable beginning and end to each one. But the phases are also overlapping to a degree. The term "recursive" explains the nature of the overlap between each phase and the other two. Each phase has primary objectives, which determine the major thrust of the work in that phase, and secondary objectives, which relate the other two phases to whichever phase is being undertaken. Thus there is some data collection and some feedback during entry, some entry and some feedback in data collection, and some entry and some data collection at feedback.

Entry

The primary objectives of entry are to determine which units of the system (individual, group, and organization) will participate in the diagnosis, and to determine whether the researcher and respondent can reach agreement about their respective roles during data collection and feedback. Entry begins with the first encounter between system and researcher and ends with a decision between the parties stating whether they can work together to complete the diagnosis. Entry is also a time for data collection, as the researcher begins to learn about the system through conversations, observations, and documents. The close of entry, whether the decision is to terminate or to proceed with the next phase, provides respondents with some feedback about how the investigator views the system.

People cannot be investigators in systems in which they are full-fledged members. All individuals have vested interests in their own organizations. Even if individuals did not press their own interests, other members of the system would be unable to accept a researcher relationship from a peer, and the complete insider would be rendered ineffective as a result. Being at least partial outsiders therefore is part of the equipment of the organizational researchers. Without this role, they cannot function effectively. Internal researchers, for example, can work in parts of a larger system in which they have not been or currently are not members. But they cannot study their own groups, and they generally have a great deal of difficulty with parts of the system in which they have recently been members. Being an outsider, while necessary for diagnostic work, is also a problematic feature of the researcher's role. Because researchers are outsiders, they can easily be prevented from understanding crucial elements of the system. Therefore the investigator must establish some type of liaison system to manage the relationship between the researcher and those elements of the system where diagnosis will take place. Depending on the nature of the system, the liaison may be an individual, a series of individuals, or a group.

Whatever the state of an organization's boundaries before the entry process begins, they become more permeable during the time when respondent and researcher are exploring whether a complete diagnosis should take place. Outsiders, at least temporarily, are granted access to the organization, an experience that inevitably generates threat for the organization and its members. Entry is like a natural experiment providing researchers with an opportunity to observe how the system responds when its boundaries become more permeable.

As human beings themselves, researchers also experience the period of entry as a time of anxiety (3). In part this arises because the researchers are dealing with their potential acceptance or rejection by the respondent system. The more self-awareness and experience the researchers have, the less these feelings will interfere with their effectiveness during entry. In addition, the researcher will also experience the effects set off in the system by the stress on the organization's boundaries. As an "authority" on organizational behavior from outside, the researcher is a likely target for feelings that organization members have for authority figures inside their system, via the mechanism of projection (4, 5).

The paradox of entry is that while it provides one of the best opportunities to observe organizational dynamics, it does so under relatively poor conditions. Anxiety and the task of managing the respondent relationship to reach a decision about diagnosis interferes with researchers making the most out of the data available at entry. Nonetheless, entry generally tells the organization's story very well. As a working heuristic, it is useful to assume: "The major dynamics are all observable at entry, if the investigator is able to perceive them."

At the close of entry the researcher should have a reasonably well developed idea of what will be necessary to understand the system, although this knowledge will be incomplete and may require changes in the contract as greater knowledge of the system becomes available. The contract letter should acknowledge the likely limitations of the entry-based knowledge of the system and identify the possibility that either party may want to modify the contract as the diagnostic study unfolds.

Data Collection

The primary objectives of data collection are to gather valid information about the nature of the system systematically and to prepare an analysis of that data for delivery to respondents during feedback. Data collection begins when the investigator prepares a methodology for eliciting information and contacts members of the system to implement the methodology. Data collection ends when the researcher has analyzed the data and is prepared to feed back the results to the respondents. Each data collection episode begins by establishing the bases of the respondent-investigator relationship and, as such, is like entry. These unstructured events provide the researcher with a continuing basis for revising or confirming hypotheses about the organization. In the process of eliciting data from respondents, the researcher becomes increasingly specific about the kinds of data that will be useful. The search for increasingly precise information indirectly tells respondents what the investigator thinks is important and thereby serves as a type of feedback.

From entry to data collection to feedback, researcher actions influence the working relationship with the respondent. Because the investigator's effectiveness depends directly on the quality of that relationship, every action should be taken with reflection upon its likely effects on this intergroup relationship. Data collection methods surely have an impact on the relationship. The selection and ordering of methods therefore should maximize the benefit and minimize the damage to this relationship. As it turns out, the ordering of methods to enhance the relationship also parallels the ordering of methods to verify an investigator's growing precision in understanding the system. Moreover, proceeding from less to more structured methods also tends to produce more valid data (6).

Following from the preceding principles, the preferred ordering of methods during data collection is:

1. Unstructured observations including documents offered by the respondent.
2. Individual interviews.
3. Group interviews, if they are used.
4. Questionnaires, ideally with item content determined organically from the results of steps 1, 2, and 3.
5. Specific documents requested by the investigator, if necessary.

The primary orientation of the present approach to diagnosis is to understand a system on its own terms inductively, rather than to impose preconceived analyses or standardized instruments. In preparing data for feedback, researchers must decide how much emphasis to give to theoretical concepts for understanding the data. Under some circumstances understanding by the system may be enhanced by more extensive presentation of theory, and under other conditions respondent understanding may be aided more by emphasis on concrete elements of the data. Use of theory depends on whether understanding will be aided by increasing or decreasing the number of explanations respondents have for their experience with the system. Introduction of theory by investigators tends to decrease the number of explanations respondents generate, and emphasis on concrete data tends to increase the number of points of view proposed by respondents.

Qualitative and quantitative data have compensating advantages and disadvantages, some of which are similar to the effects of how theory is used. The more that qualitative information is used, the more respondents are encouraged to search for their own explanations; and the more that quantitative data are used, the more the information itself is likely to shape conclusions about the system. Quotations and unstructured observations and richness, complexity, and uniqueness to any feedback presentation. They typically evoke respondent involvement and set off search processes as respondents attempt to determine why anyone would say or do what is reported. Questions about the generality of unique comments arise, and the use of quantitative information often provides answers.

People also have feelings about data concerning human affairs. For some (e.g., English teachers in a New England boarding school) the idea that human experience could be quantified at all might be an anathema. For others (e.g., engineers in a manufacturing plant) quantification might be synonomous with the term "data." In advance of preparing the analysis the researchers will have an opportunity to learn respondent culture about data. This understanding should influence the balance of quantitative and qualitative data used in feedback. Because the purpose of feedback is not to change the respondent culture about data, the balance of quantitative information used in feedback should reflect the respondent culture.

At the close of data collection the consultant has obtained and analyzed systematic data about the respondent system. Prior to the start of feedback there is a period of reduced interaction between respondent and researcher, while the researcher prepares the data for feedback. This period of reduced contact will place some strain on the relationship because the respondent will be anxious to find out what the researcher has learned and may experience the reduced contact with the researcher as a deprivation. The role of the liaison system remains important during this time. Through that entity the researcher can maintain contact with the organization, learn about new developments in the system, and keep the respondent informed about the progress with the data analysis. Perhaps most importantly, the liaison system can be a source of advice about the content and design of feedback. It is frequently desirable to conduct the first feedback with the liaison people, especially if they represent a microcosm of the entire system.

Feedback

The primary objective of feedback is to promote increased understanding of the client system by its members. Effective feedback design relates the *content* of the feedback to the *process* by which the analysis is delivered to the system. The content of feedback is the data analysis prepared at the close of the data collection phase. The process of feedback is the composition of feedback meetings (i.e., who is present with whom), the ordering of the meetings (i.e., which groups receive information first, which second, etc.), the behavior of the system during feedback, and the behavior of the researchers within and between feedback meetings. The overall feedback design should bring together people who are interested in the information presented, and should bring them together in a way that is most likely to promote learning from the experience. Feedback is probably the period of maximum anxiety during the entire diagnosis. All the work that the investigator has done, or has failed to do, to develop effective working relationships with the system will come to fruition (or frustration) during feedback. If this work has been good enough, the system will be able to tolerate the tension of learning about itself.

The oldest and best known feedback design is built around the "family group" of supervisor and immediate subordinates (7). Conventionally structured organizations can be viewed as a series of interlocking family groups from top to bottom. When the content of the feedback pertains to issues found in family groups, then a feedback design should be built around these groups. However, the effectiveness of family group feedback depends heavily on their relationship between supervisor and subordinates. If that relationship is not strong enough to tolerate open disagreement without undermining the leader or punishing subordinates, then an alternative design should be used. The researcher may choose to work with the supervisor alone or to conduct a series of paired interventions with the supervisor and key subordinates in order to establish conditions for a full family group meeting.

If the feedback content pertains more to systemwide issues than to family group issues, if the organization is not conventionally structured, or if there are severely strained authority relations throughout the organization, then the feedback design should depart from the conventional family group model. The alternative design will be some version of the "peer group-intergroup" model (8). According to this design, people meet with members of their own group as peers who have no formal hierarchical differences among members to discuss data relevant to their common concerns, and with members of other peer groups to meet in order to deal with data pertaining to the relationship between the groups. Joint group meetings in the peer-group intergroup process may involve bringing together groups that represent different hierarchical levels (e.g., branch managers and senior vice presidents), different functions (e.g., production and marketing), or different identities (e.g., blacks and whites).

The effectiveness of the peer group-intergroup model depends on managing effectively the tendencies toward ethnocentrism that exist in all groups. Groups exhibiting ethnocentric patterns attribute primarily positive traits to their own group and mainly negative properties to other groups. If ethnocentric dynamics are set off by the feedback process, then the data and analysis will be rejected and little learning will occur. One means to guard against heightening ethnocentrism during feedback is to be sure that the peer groups address their internal conflicts during a first phase of the process, thereby reducing the likelihood that internal conflict will be projected onto outgroups; and to restrict the discussion of external group relations until the intergroup meeting, when both groups will be able to share their perceptions of the relationship between the groups. A second means is to use carefully balanced heterogeneous groups with clear instructions and support for dealing with similarities and differences between groups. A third step in managing these intergroup dynamics is to intervene in the interpersonal relationship between the leaders of the peer groups, whose behavior in the feedback sessions will have a similar impact on the degree of ethnocentrism demonstrated in the joint meeting.

In sum, the methodology of organizational diagnosis calls for the researcher to be competent in the conventional use of social science tools (observation, interviews, questionnaires, and archives) and to possess a sophisticated theory and the related behavioral skills to enter, collect, and feed back information to complex multigroup systems. According to this approach, the investigator uses the techniques and theory of diagnosis to understand a system on its own terms, not to impose preconceived methods or conclusions. Each step in the diagnosis depends upon an effective working relationship between respondents and researchers. Every phase in the process builds upon the work of preceding phases. If properly executed, the methods described here are self-correcting because each phase provides opportunities to discover and to alter limitations of the preceding phases. For systems in which people wish to learn, this methodology provides the opportunity if it is employed by investigators who have been thoroughly and appropriately trained.

DIAGNOSING UNDERBOUNDED AND OVERBOUNDED SYSTEMS

Organizational diagnosis is problematic because of the nature of interacting human systems. Although the method provides a self-correcting, increasingly precise understanding, researchers must nevertheless adjust their methods to the system's dynamics, or they will be unable to develop and maintain a viable working relationship. Thus the sooner investigators correctly determine the basic dynamics of the system, the better their subsequent understanding. A serious error in initial hypothesis formation regarding whether a system is underbounded or overbounded may compromise any future potential for successfully completing the diagnosis.[1] Entry, data collection, and feedback procedures are each in part contingent on the boundary conditions of the system being studied.

Entry

The dynamics of entry differ markedly in underbounded and overbounded systems. The diagnostician may make preliminary observations about any of the 11 variables differentiating system boundary conditions shown in Table

[1]These terms refer to the permeability of an organization's boundaries. As I have written elsewhere (9), "The permeability of organizational boundaries refers to the ease with which resources are passed back and forth between a system and its environment and among the subsystems within an organization. Relatively impermeable boundaries mean that exchanges are difficult, and the organization is in danger of becoming closed off from needed interaction. Excessively permeable boundaries mean that the distinction between organization and environment is nearly obliterated, and the system faces the possibility of being indistinguishable from its environment. Either highly permeable or impermeable boundaries represent a problematic condition for an organization."

Table 20.1 Properties of Overbounded and Underbounded Systems (10)

Overbounded Systems	Variable	Underbounded Systems
Goals clear; priority unequivocal	1. Goals	Goals unclear; priorities equivocal
Monolithic	2. Authority relations	Multiple and competing
Minimal short-term stress	3. Economic conditions	Impending economic crisis
Precise, detailed, restrictive	4. Role definitions	Imprecise, incomplete overlapping
Difficulties with openness when people meet	5. Communication patterns	Difficulties in determining who can and should meet
Constrained, blocked	6. Human energy	Diffuse, exhausting
Positive inside; negative outside	7. Affect distribution	Negative inside; negative outside
Organizational groups dominate	8. Intergroup dynamics	Identity groups dominate
Dependency	9. Unconscious basic assumptions	Flight-fight
Long	10. Time span	Short
Single theory-ideology	11. Cognitive work	Multiple or no theory ideologies

20.1. Entry itself is an "underbounding" transaction because it makes the system more permeable to certain aspects of its environment. Were it not for reactive effects of the system on the diagnostician, this opening of the system would increase the validity of initial observations. But the tendency of the transaction to heighten the diagnostician's anxiety may mean that the initial opportunity is less than fully utilized. Nevertheless, certain variables are especially prominent at entry, and their state may be easier to see if one is looking for them.

Boundary transactions usually heighten authority dynamics. Duff and Hollingshead, for example, note that when patients enter hospitals they must obtain permission from both medical and administrative authorities (11). This event suggests the possibility of conflict between these two major authorities. Should that conflict exist, other phenomena suggesting underbounded dynamics would be anticipated. In general, the process of entering an organization produces rich data relevant to the nature of authority in the system. The nature of this data will vary in underbounded and overbounded systems, and it will have different implications for carrying out the diagnosis.

In overbounded systems formal leaders are able to identify and speak for the system and subsystem under their authority. In underbounded systems the diagnostician may have difficulty determining who the relevant leaders and subsystems are. The table of organization, which is virtually synonymous with the formality of overbounded system, is usually unavailable or notably inaccurate in underbounded organizations. Leaders of overbounded systems, who decide to proceed with a diagnosis, may too readily decide that their subordinates "will" participate, and the investigator may have to take special initiatives to ensure free and informed choice (12, 13). The researcher may advise leaders who speak for their systems that working the decision through with other, presumably lower ranking, members will produce higher commitment and eventually more valid data if the people decide to proceed. Depending on leadership style prevalent in the unit, this may be more or less of an intervention into normally occurring dynamics.

The entry process will take more energy in an underbounded system than in an overbounded system. It will be difficult to establish a communication system that is acceptable to all parties. The goals of the research will probably be hard to integrate with the system and subsystem goals. These dynamics and all others associated with underbounded and overbounded differences will be observable during entry. If diagnosticians are to achieve entry effectively they must adjust their behavior accordingly. It will be easier, for example, to form a liaison group of people representing the various organizational groups in an overbounded system than in an underbounded system. With an overbounded system the investigator may have to establish liaison through a series of interpersonal relationships with individuals representing subsystems, because divergent forces in the larger system are too great to allow for the formation of a liaison group.

Data Collection

This also differs between underbounded and overbounded systems. The basic dynamics of underbounded systems continue to affect the diagnostic process after entry has been completed. Compared to people from overbounded systems, the members of underbounded systems will be more difficult to locate, harder to contact, and less easy to meet. When it is possible to arrange data collection sessions in underbounded systems, the quality of those meetings will also reflect the system dynamics. Respondents are likely to be late or not to arrive at all, even if they have freely and explicitly agreed to participate. The effects of goal structure, role confusion, and energy dispersion will shape the physical and psychological assessibility of underbounded system members to data collection.

When the data collection events do occur in underbounded systems, they are also likely to be influenced by the system dynamics. Respondents may have difficulty understanding the purpose of the work, and their answers, at least superficially, will seem more confusing to researchers. It will be difficult and perhaps impossible to find a common language by which to discuss the nature of the system with all members in the same way. Investigators are likely to feel that it is "impossible to understand" the nature of this organization. Data collection sessions in underbounded systems are likely to be interrupted even after they get underway. The short-term crisis orientation of these organizations is likely to be experienced as well as described during data collection. In one such instance, the manager of a community services center, who initially failed to appear for her interview, eventually had the interview interrupted when her boss called her to an emergency meeting to announce his resignation. Data collection in underbounded systems makes excessive energy demands on researchers just as entry does.

The data collection dynamics of overbounded systems also reflect the broader system conditions. In general, the data collection process is less demanding in overbounded systems than in underbounded systems, and the result is that much more social science knowledge is available from overbounded systems than from underbounded systems. Because data collection difficulties are less apparent in overbounded systems, researchers may be less vigilant about the ways in which conventional methods may mislead them.

Feedback

Feedback dynamics also differ between underbounded and overbounded systems; effects may be observed in both the content and the process of the final phase of diagnosis. The consequences of system properties influence the use of theory, the management of problematic material, and the balance of quantitative versus qualitative information during feedback. System conditions also influence the likely consequences of family group versus peer group-intergroup designs. Preparation for the final sessions may also require different interventions in underbounded and overbounded systems in order to prepare for the stress associated with learning.

For overbounded systems the effect of data should be to increase the amount of divergent thinking by members. If the data collection processes worked, then the diagnostician should be reporting data that raises questions about the adequacy of single monolithic theory of the organization. In this kind of setting the diagnosis provides data to stimulate members to think more complexly about their system. Theory, if it is introduced at all by diagnostician, should be presented later rather than earlier in the feedback process. By comparison, in underbounded systems the respective roles of data and theory reverse. In underbounded systems, confusion rather than clarity predominates, and the role of new data without accompanying theory is probably to add additional complexity. The role of theory in underbounded systems is to promote convergent thinking by members. If no theory at all exists in the system, then feedback should present one. If several theories exist, then feedback should provide a means to translate among them. During feedback with underbounded systems, theory should be presented early in the flow of content.

Underbounded systems differ from overbounded systems in the degree of overt conflict that they manifest. While it is often hard to observe overt conflict in overbounded systems, underbounded systems are usually rife with clearly observable disputes. Feedback will alter the state of conflict in a system. In general, overbounded systems will be aided by increased conflict, while underbounded systems will be aided more if feedback has the effect of resolving conflict or of supportiong the hope that major disputes can be resolved in the foreseeable future. These propositions above suggest that feedback in underbounded systems should diminish conflict, while feedback in overbounded systems should enhance conflict. As a first approximation this deduction is correct, but by itself it is incomplete. The conflict resolution process often requires a period of regression, or heightening intensity, before resolution is posssible (14). This phase assures all parties that their perspectives are expressed. It also indirectly communicates the cost of failing to change to the parties and may serve to motivate them to reduce rather than to escalate the conflict. In underbounded systems the period of regression is more sensitive to manage and may require moment-by-moment judgments by the diagnostician as to whether data that might excessively increase conflict should be introduced into feedback. With overbounded systems diagnostic data may be used more freely as a force to increase observable conflict.

The balance for quantitative and qualitative data during feedback also relates to system properties. For overbounded systems the use of qualitative data serves a similar purpose as delaying theory presentation. The richness may encourage people to expand their thinking and increase the number of alternatives they have for understanding their system. As a result, one can make generous use of qualitative data with overbounded systems, while at the same time taking account of the system's cultural norms about qualitative and quantitative data (see "Data Collection," above). An analogous point applied from quantitative data may serve as a helpful antidote to their characteristic confusion. But again paradox intervenes. To the extent that valid quantitative data is available from underbounded systems, it will probably aid understanding, again subject to the cultural norms about data. But while more quantitative data might help underbounded systems, the likelihood of obtaining such information at feasible costs tends to be lower than in overbounded systems. Once again the centrifugal forces of the underbounded system work against the processes that might alter its basic pathology.

For overbounded systems, however, the choice between the two basic feedback designs turns both on the nature of the issues to be discussed and on the state of the systems. If the primary issues to be discussed pertain to family group problems, family groups are well-defined, and authority relations can tolerate dispute without punishing subordinates or undermining leadership, then the family group design is appropriate for overbounded systems. On the other hand, if the issues are system wide or the authority structure is highly punitive, then the peer group-intergroup design is most appropriate for feedback in overbounded systems.

The final difference between underbounded and overbounded systems pertains to the nature of intervention with key members of the system in advance of the actual feedback. Struggles among conflicting groups in underbounded systems may be so severe that in the judgment of the investigator no feedback design would be immune to uncontrolled disputes.

Third party peacemaking among key leaders therefore may be essential in order to promote constructive response to the feedback sessions (14). In overbounded systems, prefeedback interventions would be with individual leaders, rather than with pairwise relationships. The purpose of these interventions would be to coach people on how to be minimally punitive or defensive in the face of data that is likely to raise questions about the normal way of working.

In sum, the full diagnostic process unfolds quite differently in underbounded and overbounded systems, if the investigator's methodological choices are designed to be responsive to system dynamics.It is generally more time and energy consuming to diagnose underbounded systems than overbounded systems. Often the variables that aid in diagnosing overbounded systems (e.g., a viable and functioning authority system, a list of organization members) are simply not available in underbounded systems. Actions by diagnosticians that aid learning in overbounded systems (e.g., promoting divergent thinking, increasing conflict) will inhibit understanding in underbounded systems. Because the diagnostic process is potentially self-corrective at each phase, diagnosticians have several opportunities to determine the nature of the system they are studying before providing feedback.

INTERGROUP DYNAMICS IN DIAGNOSIS

The intergroup relations of organizational diagnosis pertain to at least three perspectives: (a) the researcher-system relationship, (b) the subsystem-to subsystem relationships within the system being studied, and (c) the subsystem-to-subsystem relationships within the research team (13, 15, 16).

When investigators work with organizations, their role is that of outsiders. The relationship they establish with the system, the data they collect, and the learning that is posible from feedback are all in part shaped by the relationships between the groups represented by the investigators and those by the respondents. In one study the researchers eventually learned that their university affiliation represented a source of severe evaluation for the faculty of a New England boarding school, despite no intention to make such judgments by the investigators (17). In another project the research team was explicitly designed to include a black female, black male, white female, and white male in order to be sure the research team represented the major subgroups being studied (18).

Within the system the intergroup perspective provides a means for identifying the relevant units for study. Entry must be achieved with all groups relevant to the study, and a liaison system for establishing and maintaining relationships with each group must be put in place. To the extent that it is feasible, data collection procedures should match the identity group memberships (i.e., those groups based on family, gender, ethnicity, race, and age) of the researchers with those of respondents. When this is possible, data collection transactions will be minimally shaped by whatever intergroup relationship exists between researcher and respondent. The diagnostic methodology, without taking account of the respective identity group memberships of researchers and respondents, is designed to work through the inside-outside intergroup tensions between the two parties. But when there are well-established historical relationships between the groups represented by investigators and respondents, then all the data that passes between these parties is further shaped by the nature of those historical relationships. Applying intergroup theory to the research transaction thus has implications for staffing research teams. Because it may not be posssible to determine the optimal composition of a research team until after entry has been accomplished, the principle argues generally for a diverse research team, whose members may then be assigned to roles based on the nature of the system being studied.

As time passes and the research team establishes working relationships with system members, they will begin to empathize and identify with the people with whom they have the most sustained contact. This empathy and identification will be intensified, the more that the researchers and respondents share common identity group memberships. But even if research team people do not have group memberships in common with their respondents, they will begin to "represent" their people in research team transactions. As time passes, the research team subgroup dynamics will begin to mirror the intergroup dynamics of the system being studied. Depending on the skill and understanding of the team members, and especially the leadership, these parallel processes may become a major impediment to learning if the team collapses into unresolvable conflicts analogous to those they find in the system, or the forces may become sources of insight unavailable through any other means.

The identity group memberships of the research team become especially important when the focus in diagnosis is on identity group issues in the system and when the organization is underbounded. The history, and therefore the potency, of identity group issues is much greater than that of organization group issues. If the diagnosis is to focus on identity group issues, then the research team should be composed of people who represent the relevant identity groups and whose own personal knowledge and understanding appreciates their own and other groups' history. In an underbounded diagnosis, judgment will be necessary as to the priority given to identity group issues in the diagnosis. But data collection will produce more valid information on both organization and identity group issues, if the research team includes people from the relevant identity groups.

Intergroup theory also provides an interpretation for the standardized questionnaires used in so much of organizational research. These instruments are brought to systems by investigators and are typically administered on the (often unstated) assumption that they reflect universal concerns of people in systems. In this context, universal instruments are vehicles for communication across the insider-outsider boundary. When imposed by outsiders or employed insensitively by others, their use amounts to an ethnocentric act by investigators toward their respondents. Empathic questionnaires, developed after a sustained period of mutual influence between researchers and respondents, eliminates the imposition. In its place the empathic instrument provides a vehicle showing that the researchers are a group who speak to system members on their own terms, and who provide a vehicle that allows them to speak to each other as well.

The liaison system developed between the researcher and the system is the chief mechanism for dealing with the three facets of intergroup dynamics noted at the start of this section. In addition, as noted earlier, the liaison system has a different role to play at each phase of the diagnostic process. While those roles are being executed, the intergroup dynamics of the liaison system also depend upon both the boundary relations of the organization as a whole and the characteristic intergroup patterns found in the respondent system and in the research team.

Whether the parallel intergroup processes of underbounded and overbounded systems simply reproduces characteristic behavior of the system or permit insight and understanding beyond reproduction depends upon the understanding and skill of the research team. The team's capacity both to permit and to reverse parallel dynamics determines whether learning is possible. Understanding the system's dynamics through parallel processes requires that the research team be aware of parallel dynamics when they occur and be able to change their own behavior in order to prevent the organization's dynamics from overwhelming the research task. Such skills take more than intellectual understanding. They require sophisticated training in observation and intervention with group and intergroup dynamics. In fact, we would suggest (and the reader may test for herself or himself) that without this experimental training, the concept of parallel processes and their impact on group and intergroup processes will seem illusive or even imaginary.

CONCLUSION

The purposes of this chapter have been to analyze the process of organizational diagnosis and to relate these understandings to the phenomena of group and intergroup relations in living human systems.

The aim of organizational diagnosis is to produce learning about the system for its members. Diagnosis is a process consisting of three phases: entry, data collection, and feedback. Each phase has its own primary and secondary objectives that contribute to the work of the other phases. As a result, organizational diagnosis is a self-correcting process that permits the activities of subsequent phases to build upon the accomplishments of earlier periods and to correct limitations that arise from the inevitably incomplete work that occur with dynamic living systems.

The process of organizational diagnosis is shaped by the condition of the system being studied. The effects of underbounded and overbounded organizations influence what will happen to diagnosticians as they attempt to proceed with entry, data collection, and feedback. Respondent system dynamics in part determine the consequences of using certain diagnostic techniques. The effect of the intersection between the diagnostic process and an understanding of system dynamics is to establish a series of contingencies that suggest which techniques in what order are most appropriate to particular system conditions.

Organizational diagnosis is an intergroup event when viewed from the perspective of intergroup theory. Thus the process of learning about the group's and dynamics of a system also creates a set of intergroup dynamics, which themselves both aid and impede the diagnostic process. The liaison system established to relate the researchers to the respondent system is the primary vehicle for using and managing the intergroup dynamics of the diagnostic process in the service of the learning objectives. Intergroup theory used normatively to aid learning provides prescriptions for constructing an appropriate liaison system in any given situation and for aiding the diagnostic team in managing its own dynamics (19).

REFERENCES

1. Alderfer, C.P. The methodology of organizational diagnosis. *Professional Psychology,* 1980, **11,** 459–468.
2. Alderfer, C.P. Boundary relations and organizational diagnosis. In H. Meltzer & F.R. Wickert (Eds.). *Humanizing Organizational Behavior.* Springfield, Ill.: Charles C. Thomas, 1976, pp.109–133.
3. Devereau, G. *From Anxiety to Method in the Behavioral Sciences.* Paris: Mouton & Co., 1967.
4. Freud, A. *The Ego and the Mechanism of Defense.* New York: International Universities Press, 1946.
5. Freud, S. *Group Psychology and the Analysis of the Ego.* New York: Liveright, 1922.
6. Alderfer, C.P. Comparison of questionnaire responses with and without preceding interviews. *Journal of Applied Psychology,* 1968, **52,** 335–340; and Alderfer, C.P., and Brown, L.D. Designing and empathic questionnaire for organizational research. *Journal of Applied Psychology,* 1972, **56,** 456–460.
7. Bowers, D.G. & Franklin, J.L. Survey-guided development: Using human resources measurement in organizational change. *Journal of Contemporary Business,* 1972, **1,** 43–55.

8. Alderfer, C.P. & Holbrook, J. A new design for survey feedback. *Education and Urban Society,* 1973, **5,** 437–464.

9. Alderfer, C.P. Boundary relations and organizational diagnosis. In H. Meltzer & F.R. Wickert (Eds.). *Humanizing Organizational Behavior.* Springfield, Ill.: Charles C. Thomas, 1976.

10. Alderfer, C.P. Consulting to underbounded systems. In C.P. Alderfer & C.L. Cooper (Eds.). *Advances in Experiential Social Processes,* II. London: Wiley, 1980, pp.267–295.

11. Duff, R.S. & Hollingshead, A.B. *Sickness and Society.* New York: Harper & Row, 1968.

12. Argyris, C. *Intervention Theory and Method.* Reading, Mass.: Addison-Wesley, 1970.

13. Kahn, R.L. & Mann, F.C. Developing research partnerships. *Journal of Social Issues,* 1952, **8,** 4–10; and Berg, D., Failure at entry. In P. Mirvis & D. Berg (Eds.). *Failures in Organization Development.* New York: Wiley, 1977.

14. Walton, R.E. *Interpersonal Peacemaking: Confrontations and Third-Party Consultation.* Reading, Mass.: Addison-Wesley, 1969.

15. Rice, A.K. Individual, group and intergroup processes. *Human Relations,* 1969, **22,** 562–584.

16. Alderfer, C.P. Groups and intergroups. In J.R. Hackman and J.L. Suttle (Eds.). *Improving Life at Work.* Santa Monica, Calif.: Goodyear, 1977, pp. 227–296.

17. Alderfer, C.P. & Brown, L.D. *Learning from Changing.* Beverly Hills: Sage, 1975.

18. Alderfer, C.P. Alderfer, C.J. Tucker, L. & Tucker, R. Diagnosing race relations in management. *Journal of Applied Behavioral Science,* 1980, **16,** 135–166.

19. Other perspectives on organizational diagnosis may be found in 20, 21, and 22.

20. Levinson, H. *Organizational Diagnosis.* Cambridge, Mass.: Harvard University Press, 1972.

21. Mahler, W.R. *Diagnostic Studies.* Reading, Mass.: Addison-Wesley, 1974.

22. Nadler, D.A. *Feedback and Organization Development.* Reading, Mass.: Addison-Wesley, 1977.

—21—

Work Redesign for Organization Development

J. Richard Hackman

The term "work redesign" refers to activities that involve the alteration of specific jobs (or systems of jobs) with the intent of improving both productivity and the quality of employee work experiences. Although there are no generally accepted criteria for what is a well-designed job, there are some commonalities in work redesign projects. Typically, job specifications are changed to provide employees with additional responsibility for planning, setting up, and checking their own work; for making decisions about work methods and procedures; for establishing their own work pace; and for dealing directly with the clients who receive the results of the work. In many cases, jobs that previously had been simplified and segmented into many small parts in the interest of production efficiency are reassembled and made into larger and more meaningful wholes.

Sometimes work is redesigned to create motivating and satisfying jobs for individual employees, who work more or less on their own. Such activities are usually known as "job enrichment" (1, 2).* Alternatively, work may be designed as a group task, in which case a team of workers is given autonomous responsibility for a large and meaningful module of work. Such teams typically have the authority to manage their own social and performance processes as they see fit, they receive feedback and often rewards as a group, and they may even be charged with the selection, training, and termination of their own members. These teams are variously known as "autonomous work groups" (3), "self-regulating work groups" (4), or "self-managing work groups" (5). A well-known and well-documented example of the design of work for teams is the Topeka pet food plant of General Foods (see reference 6 for a description of the innovation, and reference 7 for a six-year history of the Topeka teams).

This chapter is adapted with permission from the American Psychological Association from Hackman, J. R., Work redesign and motivation. *Professional Psychology*, 1980, **11**, 445–455. Copyright 1980. The contributions of Mary Dean Lee and Greg R. Oldham to the development of the ideas expressed here are gratefully acknowledged.

*Job redesign, job enlargement, and job enrichment are closely related terms and will not be distinguished here. Readers who wish to sort out the connotations of the various terms used to characterize work redesign are referred to Strauss (1974, pp. 38–43).

Both individual and team work redesign can be viewed as responses and alternatives to the principles for designing work that derive from classical organization theory and the discipline of industrial engineering. These principles specify that rationality and efficiency in organizational operations can be obtained through the simplification, standardization, and specialization of jobs in organizations. The assumption is that most employees, if managed well, will work efficiently and effectively on such jobs. That assumption is called into question, however, by research over the last several decades that documents a number of unintended and dysfunctional consequences, for both workers and their employing organizations, of work designed in accord with classical principles (8, 9, 10). Current approaches to work redesign, then, tend to have a behavioral emphasis and attempt to create jobs that enhance work productivity without incurring the human costs that have been shown to be associated with the traditional approaches.

THEORIES OF WORK REDESIGN

Most work redesign activities are guided by one or another of the four theoretical approaches summarized below. We begin with a theory that has a very psychological focus (activation theory), move next to two "mid-range" theories (motivation-hygiene theory and job characteristics theory), and conclude with a more molar and system-focused theory (sociotechnical systems theory).

Activation Theory

As noted above, numerous human problems have been shown to be associated with work on routine, repetitive tasks. Included are diminished alertness, decreased responsiveness to new stimulus inputs, and even impairment of muscular coordination. Employees who work on highly routine jobs are often observed to daydream, to chat with others rather than work on their tasks, to make frequent readjustments of posture and position, and so on.

Activation theory can help account for such behaviors (11). Basically activation theory specifies that a person's level of activation or "arousal" decreases when sensory input is unchanging or repetitive, leading to the kinds of behavior specified above. Varying or unexpected patterns of stimuli, on the other hand, keep an individual activated and more alert, although over time the individual may adapt to even a varied pattern of stimulation.

One approach to work redesign that is based on activation theory is that of job rotation, that is, rotating an individual through a number of different jobs in a given day or week, with the expectation that these varied job experiences will keep the person from suffering the negative consequences of excessively low activation. The problem, it seems, is that people adapt fairly quickly even to new stimulation. If the new tasks are just as boring as the old one, then no long term gains are likely from job rotation.

At present, activation theory seems most useful for understanding the consequences of jobs that are grossly understimulating (or overstimulating). Except for the pioneering work by Scott (11) and more recent theorizing by Schwab and Cummings (12), relatively little progress has been made in applying the tenets of activation theory to the design of jobs so that they foster and maintain high task-oriented motivation.

Motivation-hygiene Theory

By far the most influential theory of work redesign to date has been the Herzberg two-factor theory of satisfaction and motivation (13, 14). This theory proposes that factors intrinsic to the work determine how satisfied people are at work. These factors, called "motivators," include recognition, achievement, responsibility, advancement, and personal growth in competence. Dissatisfaction, on the other hand, is caused by factors extrinsic to the work, termed "hygienes." Examples include company policies, pay plans, working conditions, and supervisory practices. According to the Herzberg theory, a job will enhance work motivation only to the extent that motivators are designed into the work itself; changes that deal solely with hygiene factors will not generate improvements.

Motivation-hygiene theory has prompted a great deal of research, and inspired a number of successful change projects involving the redesign of work (e.g., 15). Especially noteworthy is the series of job enrichment studies done at AT&T (16). These studies document that job enrichment can lead to beneficial results both for individuals and organizations for a variety of different jobs. Moreover, a set of step-by-step procedures for implementing job enrichment were generated as part of the AT&T program (and are detailed in the Ford book, reference 16), and these procedures continue to guide many work redesign activities throughout the country.

The Herzberg theory—specifically, the distinction between motivators and hygiene factors—provides a clear and straightforward way of thinking about employee motivation, and for predicting the likely impact of various planned changes on motivation. The phrases "Yes, but that's really only a hygiene factor," and "But would it change the *work itself?*" have undoubtedly been used to good effect thousands of times as managers consider various strategies for attempting to improve employee work motivation (17).

Because the message of motivation-hygiene theory is simple, persuasive, and directly relevant to the design and evaluation of actual organizational changes, the theory continues to be widely known and generally used by managers of organizations in this country. There is, however, considerable uncertainty and controversy regarding the conceptual and empirical status of motivation-hygiene theory *qua* theory. For a succinct treatment of the theory, see Herzberg (17). For reviews of research assessments of the theory, see King (18) and House and Widgor (19), who are particularly skeptical, and Whitsett and Winslow (20), who are particularly sympathetic.

Job Characteristics Theory

This approach attempts to specify the objective characteristics of jobs that create conditions for high levels of internal work motivation on the part of employees. Based on earlier research by Turner and Lawrence (21), current statements of the theory suggest that individuals will be internally motivated to perform well when (a) they experience the work as meaningful, (b) they feel they have personal responsibility for the work outcomes, and (c) they obtain regular and trustworthy knowledge of the results of their work. Five objective job characteristics are specified as key in creating these conditions: skill variety, task identity, task significance, autonomy, and feedback from the job itself (22, 23).

When a job is redesigned to increase these characteristics, improvements in the motivation, satisfaction, and performance of job incumbents are predicted. However, individual differences in employee knowledge and skill, and in need for personal growth, are posited as influencing the effects of the job characteristics on work behaviors and attitudes. Strongest effects are predicted for individuals with ample job-relevant knowledge and skill and relatively strong growth needs.

A diagnostic instrument, the Job Diagnostic Survey, has been developed to assess employee perceptions of the job characteristics listed above, selected attitudes toward the work and the organization, and individual growth need strength (24). This instrument is intended for use both in diagnosing work systems prior to job redesign and for assessing the consequences of work redesign activities.

For an overview of the theory that emphasizes its practical application to work redesign, see Hackman, Oldham, Janson, and Purdy (25). For the most current statement of the theory, including its application to the design of work for groups as well as individuals, see Hackman and Oldham (26). For a skeptical view of the job characteristics approach, see Salancik and Pfeffer (27).

Sociotechnical Systems Theory

Contrasting the job-focused theories described above, the sociotechnical systems approach emphasizes the importance of designing entire work *systems*, in which the social and technical aspects of the work place are integrated and mutually supportive of one another (28).

This approach emphasizes the fact that organizations are imbedded in, and affected by, an outside environment. Especially important are cultural values that specify how organizations should function, and generally accepted roles that individuals, groups, and organizations are supposed to play in society. Thus there is constant interchange between what goes on in any given work organization and what goes on in its environment. This interchange must be carefully attended to when work systems are designed or altered (29).

When redesigned in accord with the sociotechnical approach, work systems are never changed in piecemeal fashion. Although jobs, rewards, physical equipment, spatial arrangements, work schedules and more may be altered in a sociotechnical intervention, none of these is taken as the primary focus of change activities. Instead organization members, often including rank and file employees and representatives of organized labor as well as managers, examine all aspects of organizational operations that might affect how well the work is done or the quality of organization members' experiences. Changes that emerge from these explorations invariably involve numerous aspects of both the social and technical systems of the organization. Typically, however, such changes do involve the formation of groups of employees who share responsibility for carrying out a significant piece of work—the "autonomous work group" idea mentioned earlier (4). Such groups are becoming an increasingly popular organizational innovation, and now are frequently used even in work redesign projects that are not explicitly guided by sociotechnical theory.

For a summary of sociotechnical systems theory as it applies to work redesign, see Cherns (30), Davis (31), or the now-classic study of coal-mining by Trist, Higgin, Murray, and Pollock (32). For a critique of the theory, see Van der Zwaan (33).

COMPARISON OF THE THEORETICAL APPROACHES

Activation theory, motivation-hygiene theory, job characteristics theory, and sociotechnical systems theory offer different approaches to work redesign. Activation theory specifically addresses the dysfunctional aspects of repetitive work, whereas motivation-hygiene theory and job characteristics theory emphasize ways to create positive motivational features in the work. The Herzberg model differs from job characteristics theory in proposing a more general process for increasing motivation (i.e., identify motivators and increase them), whereas the job characteristics approach provides specific diagnostic procedures to optimize the fit between people and their work. Sociotechnical systems theory contrasts sharply with the other theories in that it emphasizes the design of work for groups rather than individuals.

Another difference among the theories lies in their assumptions about how the redesign of work should be planned and implemented. Activation and motivation-hygiene theories appear to put the burden on management to identify the problematic aspects of the work. Neither approach suggests extensive gathering of information and inputs from employees. At the other end of the continuum, sociotechnical work redesign projects involve a high degree of worker participation. Job characteristics theory emphasizes the importance of understanding workers' perceptions and attitudes toward their jobs, but does not explicitly require their participation in actual planning for work redesign.

OUTCOMES OF WORK REDESIGN

How successful are work redesign activities in achieving their intended objectives? Systematic data about the matter are surprisingly sparse, given the popularity of work redesign as an organizational change technique. My assessment of the state of the evidence is summarized briefly below; more thorough or analytic reviews are provided elsewhere.*

1. Work redesign, when competently executed in appropriate organizational circumstances, generally increases the work satisfaction and motivation of employees whose jobs are enriched. Especially strong effects have been found for employees' satisfaction with opportunities for personal growth and development on the job, as well as for their level of internal work motivation (i.e., motivation to work hard and well because of the internal rewards that good performance brings). There is little evidence that work redesign increases satisfaction with aspects of the organizational context such as pay, job security, co-workers, or supervision. Indeed enrichment of the work sometimes prompts decreases in satisfaction with pay and supervision, especially when these organizational practices are not altered to mesh with the new responsibilities and increased autonomy of the persons whose jobs are redesigned.
2. The quality of the product or service provided generally improves. When a job is well-designed from a motivational point of view, the people who work on that job tend to experience self-rewards when they perform well. And, for most people, performing well means producing high quality work of which they can be proud.
3. The quantity of work done sometimes increases, sometimes is unchanged, and sometimes even decreases. What happens to production quantity when work is redesigned appears to depend mostly on the state of the work system prior to redesign (26). Specifically, productivity gains would be expected under two circumstances: (a) when employees were previously exhibiting markedly low productivity because they were actively "turned off" by highly routine or repetitive work; or (b) when there were hidden inefficiencies in the work system as it was previously structured, for example, redundancies in the work, unnecessary supervisory or inspection activities, and so on. If such problems preexisted in the work unit, then increases in the quantity of work performed are likely to appear after the work is

*See, for example, Davis and Trist (1974), Katzell, Bienstock and Faerstein (1977), Katzell and Yankelovich (1975, Chapter 6), Paul, Robertson and Herzberg (1969), and Pierce and Dunham (1976). For a skeptical view of the evidence, see Fein (1974).

redesigned. If such problems were not present, then quantity increases would not be anticipated; indeed decreases in quantity might even be noted as people worked especially hard on their enriched jobs to produce work of especially high quality.

4. Findings regarding employee attendance at work—absenteeism and turnover—are not clear. The research needed to draw trustworthy conclusions about turnover are not yet available; and it may be that turnover is far more powerfully affected by economic and labor market conditions than by how jobs are designed in any case. Research findings regarding absenteeism, like those for production quantity, are inconsistent: some studies report improvements in attendance when jobs are enriched, some report no change, and some show worse absence problems than before. It may be that *who* is absent is different for routine, simple jobs compared to complex, challenging jobs. More talented employees, for example, may show higher absence rates for routine jobs because of boredom. Less talented employees may be more unhappy (and therefore more frequently absent) for challenging jobs because they find themselves overwhelmed by the same complexity that engages and motivates their more competent peers. This hypothesis awaits research test. If it should be borne out, it would suggest that any overall indicator of absenteeism for total work groups could be misleading because of the differential effects of work redesign on employees who differ in competence.

Although it is now generally recognized that work redesign is not a panacea for all organizational ills, it remains difficult to arrive at a "bottom line" estimate of the costs and benefits of job changes. Simple reports of improvements in job satisfaction are not likely to significantly warm the hearts of cost-conscious line managers; and for reasons outlined above, simple measures of production quantity or labor cost are inappropriate when used as the sole measure of the effects of work redesign.

Other outcomes, including many that may be among the most appropriate indices of work redesign effects, are presently difficult or impossible to measure in terms that are comparable across organizations. What, for example, is the ultimate cost of poor quality work? Or of "extra" supervisory time? Or of redundant inspections? Or of absenteeism, soldiering, or sabotage? Until we become able to assess the effects of work redesign on such outcomes, it will continue to be difficult to determine unambiguously whether or not work redesign pays off in traditional economic coin.

UNANSWERED QUESTIONS AND FUTURE DIRECTIONS

Despite the recent popularity of work design as a research topic and change technique, many unanswered questions remain, especially regarding the application of work design principles in complex, ambiguous organizational situations. In the paragraphs to follow, I briefly highlight several conceptual and practical problems that strike me as among the most currently pressing.

Diagnostic and Evaluation Methodologies

How are we to assess the readiness of work systems for work redesign, to ascertain precisely what changes are called for in those systems, and to measure the consequences of the changes that are made? Heretofore most diagnostic and evaluation methodologies have relied on paper-and-pencil instruments completed by individuals whose jobs are about to be (or have been) redesigned. As Walton (34) notes, there are reasons for caution and skepticism in the use of such methods, even when they are psychometrically adequate (also see reference 35 for a critical analysis of the psychometric properties of existing instruments that measure perceived task characteristics). Yet there also are significant problems in relying on the views of managers and consultants about employees and their jobs when work systems are diagnosed and the effects of job changes are assessed. Research has shown, for example, that both cognitive limitations and social distortions can significantly bias what is seen by observers who have a "stake" in the organization or in contemplated changes (26).

What then is to be done to improve our diagnostic and evaluation capabilities?

Researchers both at the University of Michigan (36) and the University of Pennsylvania (37) recently have developed organizational assessment packages, some parts of which include observational and archival measures as well as paper-and-pencil instruments, that may be of considerable use in diagnosing and evaluating work redesign programs. One especially promising approach to measuring the outcomes of work redesign has been developed by Macy and Mirvis (38) as part of the Michigan project. This methodology involves defining, measuring, and costing certain kinds of behavioral outcomes in economic terms. It offers the potential for more rigorous assessment of the economic effects of work restructuring than has heretofore been possible, and it could help reduce some of the ambiguities noted in the previous section in comparing the results of different work redesign activities.

The Role of Individual Differences

Although only one of the theoretical approaches to work redesign reviewed earlier (job characteristics theory) explicitly incorporates individual differences as a part of the theory itself, literally dozens of studies have tested the general proposition that different people react differently to enriched, challenging work. A great heterogeneity of individual difference measures have been tried, ranging from theory-specified measures of growth need strength, to subcultural background, to relatively esoteric personality measures. In general, results have been inconsistent (i.e., individual difference moderators have sometimes operated as predicted and sometimes not), and of limited magnitude (i.e., the moderating effects, when obtained, have not accounted for major portions of the variation in satisfaction or performance).

Yet when one watches how people react to enriching changes in their jobs it is clear that different individuals do react very differently. Some employees are aggressively eager for the changes ("At last! This is just what I've been waiting and hoping for!"); others resist the changes with equal vigor; and still others seem virtually frozen with anxiety about what the changes may bring. That there are important individual differences in readiness for enriched work and reactions to it seems indisputable; but it also is clear that existing theories and research methods have so far failed to provide satisfactory ways of conceptualizing and measuring whatever it is that accounts for the highly variagated reactions of people to their work. How is this discrepancy to be understood? Some new thinking and some new research methods clearly are called for to resolve this conceptually interesting and practically important question.

Individual versus Team Designs for Work

The theories of work redesign reviewed earlier in this chapter vary in their relative emphasis on the design of work for individuals versus teams (i.e., motivation-hygiene theory is essentially an individual-focued theory; sociotechnical systems theory is oriented primarily to work teams). Presumably an individual design is more appropriate and will be more effective in some organizational circumstances, and a team design will be better in others. Yet whether an individual or a team design is installed in a given work redesign project seems at the moment more dependent on the theoretical orientation of the change agent, or occasionally on the prior preferences of managerial clients, than on any specific attributes of the people, imperatives of the work technology, or properties of the organization itself. When a consultant of the Herzbergian persuasion carries out a project, for example, individual job enrichment is very likely to be installed; when the consultant is of the sociotechnical tradition, a team design is well-nigh inevitable. Except for some untested conjectures about the circumstances under which one or the other design is more appropriate (26), there is little in the way of research and theory to guide decision making about whether an individual or a team design is relatively more appropriate for given organizational circumstances. There should be more.

The Job of the Supervisor

Few research or change programs have focused on the design of lower-level jobs in management. These jobs deserve greater attention, for two reasons. First, supervisory jobs in many organizations are as poorly designed as are rank-and-file jobs selected for enrichment. Especially troublesome are restrictions on the autonomy lower-level managers have to carry out their work and limitations on the amount and the validity of the feedback they receive about their performance. Yet in the rush to attend to the jobs held by supposedly alienated rank and file workers, very real problems in the design of managerial jobs often are overlooked.

Second, the jobs of lower-level managers invariably are affected, often negatively, when their subordinates' jobs are improved. Indeed improvements in employee jobs are sometimes made directly at the expense of managerial jobs: decision making responsibilities and special tasks that traditionally have been reserved for management are given to workers, and the jobs of managers may be denuded to about the same extent that subordinate jobs are improved.

When this happens, supervisors may become justifiably angry at the effects of work redesign on the quality of their own life at work, with predictable effects on their continued cooperation with the work redesign activities. Moreover, constraints on the supervisory job, and limited opportunities for training and practice, may make it difficult for supervisors to learn the new behaviors that they need to effectively manage employees who work on newly enriched jobs.

Walton and Schlesinger (39) have recently completed a detailed analysis of supervisory role difficulties when work is restructured. They offer some provocative ideas about how that role might be redesigned, and how persons might be selected and trained for it, that merit careful attention by both scholars and practitioners of work redesign. Among other things, they suggest: (a) supervisors be selected so as to achieve a broad mix of skills, age, and educational experience; (b) all supervisors be provided with extensive training in human relations skills and group dynamics; (c) each supervisor be educated and rewarded on the basis of his or her team's development, which ultimately leads to the end of the supervisor's position; (d) the development of supervisory support systems; and (e) the development of strategies for utilizing the capacity of supervisors as they become less involved in their traditional supervisory tasks.

Tensions in the Installation Process

Although the hoped-for results of work redesign are generally clear in a given change project, planning about how to get there from here is often a rather murky and uncertain affair. In general, our theories about the *content* of work redesign are much better than our theories about the *process* of making the needed changes.

Among the questions at issue are the following. How responsive should changes be to idiosyncracies of the people, the setting, and the broader environment? How closely should changes be tied to one or another of the theories of work design, as opposed to a more *ad hoc* approach to change? How fully should the employees whose jobs are to be changed participate in the planning and execution of those changes? If one aspires to diffusion beyond the initial site of the change, how should the first site be selected, i.e., should it be an "easy" or a "difficult" change target? How should one manage the expectations of employees and managers about the magnitude of the change and its anticipated benefits? Should expectations be kept low to avoid possible disappointment, or should they be raised to provide a hedge against possible conservatism and retreat when the time comes to actually put planned changes in place? What is the appropriate model for union-management collaboration in carrying out work redesign? How should other persons or groups who have a stake in the results of the changes be dealt with so that their views can be heard and incorporated, and so that the chance of uninformed resistance to change can be minimized? How can evaluation activities be carried out so that data are available for midcourse corrections of the change process, but the risk of premature judgment of the project as either a success or a failure is minimized? How can one determine whether or not existing organizational systems, which have evolved over time to support work on traditionally designed jobs, will so constrain the intervention that it would be foolish to proceed? How can managerial practices, for example, those affecting compensation, training, supervisory style, and career mobility, be adjusted so they support the motivational benefits of enriched work?

There is little research evidence available to help answer questions such as these.* Moreover, each question involves difficult tradeoffs between different kinds of risks and benefits. It appears that installing changes in jobs is much like trying to walk on a slippery log: not only is it easy to fall off, but one can fall in either direction with equally unpleasant consequences.

ALTERNATIVE USES OF WORK DESIGN PRINCIPLES

To redesign work halfheartedly or to use flawed change processes is, in most cases, to assure failure. And it is *hard* to do work redesign well. It requires highly skilled managers and change agents to competently diagnose the work system and implement the changes. It requires a good deal of vision, commitment, and risk taking to make sure that changes large enough to make a real difference are installed. And it requires that existing organizational structures, systems, and practices be sufficiently congruent with the innovations in work structures (or that they themselves be amenable to redesign to make them more congruent with the innovations) so that the changes have a chance to persist over time.

*There has been some theorizing about these questions, however, and a good deal of advice has been offered by practitioners who have experience in dealing with them. See, for example, Cummings and Srivastva (1977), Ford (1969), Oldham and Hackman (1980), Sirota and Wolfson (1972), and Walton (1975).

It appears that only organizations that are already relatively well designed and well managed are likely to meet the conditions required for successful use of work redesign as a strategy for planned organizational change. What we may have, then, is yet another case in organizational life where the rich get richer, and the poor—if they try to make the leap—are likely to fail.

One could conclude that the case for using work redesign as an organization development technique is not a terribly compelling one, given all the problems and difficulties in installing and maintaining changes in jobs that we have been discussing. Yet planned, developmental change is not the only appropriate use of the principles of work redesign. In concluding this essay, let us briefly review three other uses of these principles, uses that in many cases may be more powerful and enduring than more traditional job enrichment interventions.

Designing New Organization Units

As noted earlier, one reason for pessimism about work redesign as an organization development technique is that the changes often are overwhelmed by the interdependent operating systems, organizational structures and management practices that give the organization its stability. When new organizations are designed, or when there is a major reorganization of an existing unit, it often is possible to design organizational systems, structures, and practices from the ground up so that they support rather than undermine innovative designs for the work itself. The result can be a nontraditional design for work that has both powerful and beneficial effects; see, for example, the cases reported by Lawler (40), in his discussion of "the new plant revolution."

Seizing Opportunities

The chance to wholly redesign an organization appears rarely. Yet the principles of work redesign also can be used to good effect on those frequent occasions when the stable organizational systems that make planned change so difficult become temporarily unstable. During such periods of turbulence the defenses of an organization against change are less strong, and it may be possible both to introduce meaningfully large changes in jobs and to develop an appropriate fit betwen those innovations and the surrounding organizational systems before things settle down again.

The opening for introducing changes in jobs may be provided by the advent of a new technology for accomplishing work (e.g., word processing), by a reshuffling of line managers, by the introduction or elimination of a product or service, by rapid growth or shrinkage in the size of the unit where the work is done, or by changes in the market, the economy, the labor market, or the legislative or regulatory context in which the organization operates.

The point is that organizations regularly move back and forth between periods of relative stability and periods of transition and instability. Rather than use work redesign to try to change an organization when things are relatively stable, it may be better to lie in wait for those times when the organization is, for whatever reasons, particularly open to the possibility of alterations in the way jobs are structured. The wait rarely will be a long one.

Local Changes

The principles of work redesign also can be used by individual managers, more or less on their own, to make enriching changes in the ways in which the work of their subordinates is structured and managed. Managers can release some of their own decision making responbilility to subordinates; they can place subordinates in direct contact with the clients of the work; they can encourage sharing and rotation of responsibilities on an informal basis, and so on.

No complex diagnosis of the work system is involved in such undertakings, no planning groups meet to develop the changes, and there is no systematic evaluation of what changes were made with what effects. The manager simply decides that he or she is going to do everything that can be done to create conditions for high motivation and high quality work experiences among his or her subordinates, and then proceeds to do so within existing organizational constraints.

Work redesign, at the core, is really more a way of managing than it is a formal intervention technique, and the potential payoffs for people and for organizations from "local" changes in how jobs are designed should not be underestimated. Indeed there is probably more job enrichment going on today at local initiative than there are seized opportunities and planned work redesign programs combined.

What kind of life do we want to create for the people who do the productive work of this society? How hard are we willing to work for that, and how much are we willing to pay for it? These questions are being debated in executive suites, in labor union headquarters, in the councils of government, and in the minds of individual managers and citizens. The answers that emerge, far more than answers to questions about how much we do or do not know about the theory and strategy of work redesign, will determine how work is actually designed in organizations in this society—now, and in the years to come.

REFERENCES

1. Herzberg, F. The wise old Turk. *Harvard Business Review,* September-October 1974, 70–80.
2. Strauss, G. Job satisfaction, motivation, and job redesign. In G. Strauss, R.E. Miles, C.C. Snow, & A.S. Tannenbaum (Eds.). *Organizational behavior: Research and Issues.* Madison, Wis.: Industrial Relations Research Association, 1974.

3. Gulowsen, J. A measure of work group autonomy. In L.E. Davis & J.C. Taylor (Eds.). *Design of Jobs.* Middlesex, England: Penguin, 1972.

4. Cummings, T.G. Self-regulating work groups: A socio-technical synthesis. *Academy of Management Review,* 1978, **3,** 625–634.

5. Hackman, J.R. The design of self-managing work groups. In B. King, S. Streufert & F.E. Fiedler (Eds.). *Managerial Control and Organizational Democracy.* Washington, D.C.: Winston and Sons, 1978.

6. Walton, R.E. How to counter alienation in the plant. *Harvard Business Review,* November-December 1972, 70–81.

7. Walton, R.E. Work innovations at Topeka: After six years. *Journal of Applied Behavior Science,* 1977, **13,** 422–433.

8. Kornhauser, A. *Mental health of the industrial worker.* New York: Wiley, 1965.

9. Vernon, H.M. On the extent and effects of variety in repetitive work. *Industrial Fatigue Research Board Report No. 26.* London: H. M. Stationery Office, 1924.

10. Walker, C.R. & Guest, R.H. *The Man on the Assembly Line.* Cambridge, Mass.: Harvard University Press, 1952.

11. Scott, W.E. Activation theory and task design. *Organizational Behavior and Human Performance,* 1966, **1,** 3–30.

12. Schwab, D.P. & Cummings, L.L. A theoretical analysis of the impact of task scope on employee performance. *Academy of Management Review,* 1976, **1,** 23–35.

13. Herzberg, F. *The Managerial Choice.* Homewood, Ill.: Dow Jones-Irwin, 1976.

14. Herzberg, F. Mausner, B. & Snyderman, B. *The Motivation to Work.* New York: Wiley, 1959.

15. Paul, W.J. Jr. Robertson, K.B. & Herzberg, F. Job enrichment pays off. *Harvard Business Review,* March-April 1969, 61–78.

16. Ford, R.N. *Motivation through the Work Itself.* New York: American Management Associations, 1969.

17. Herzberg, F. One more time: How do you motivate employees? *Harvard Business Review,* January-February 1968, 53–62.

18. King, N. A clarification and evaluation of the two-factor theory of job satisfaction. *Psychological Bulletin,* 1970, **74,** 18–31.

19. House, R.J. & Wigdor, L. Herzberg's dual-factor theory of job satisfaction and motivation: A review of the evidence and a criticism. *Personnel Psychology,* 1967, **20,** 369–389.

20. Whitsett, D.A. & Winslow, E.K. An analysis of studies critical of the motivator-hygiene theory. *Personnel Psychology,* 1967, **20,** 391–415.

21. Turner, A.N. & Lawrence, P.R. *Industrial Jobs and the Worker.* Boston: Harvard Graduate School of Business Administration, 1965.

22. Hackman, J.R. & Lawler, E.E. III. Employee reactions to job characteristics. *Journal of Applied Psychology Monograph,* 1971, **55,** 259–286.

23. Hackman, J.R. & Oldham, G.R. Motivation through the design of work: Test of a theory. *Organizational Behavior and Human Performance,* 1976, **16,** 250–279.

24. Hackman, J.R. & Oldham, G.R. Development of the Job Diagnostic Survey. *Journal of Applied Psychology,* 1975, **60,** 159–170.

25. Hackman, J.R. Oldham, G. Janson, R. & Purdy, K. A new strategy for job enrichment. *California Management Review,* Summer 1975, 57–71.

26. Hackman, J.R. & Oldham, G.R. *Work Redesign.* Reading, Mass.: Addison-Wesley, 1980.

27. Salancik, G.R. & Pfeffer, J. An examinaation of need satisfaction models of job attitudes. *Administrative Science Quarterly,* 1977, **22,** 427–456.

28. Emery, F.E. & Trist, E.L. Sociotechnical systems. In F.E. Emery (Ed.). *Systems Thinking.* London: Penguin, 1969.

29. Davis, L.E. & Trist, E.L. Improving the quality of work life: Sociotechnical case studies. In J. O'Toole (Ed.). *Work and the Quality of Life.* Cambridge, Mass.: MIT Press, 1974.

30. Cherns, A. The principles of sociotechnical design. *Human Relations,* 1976, **29,** 783–792.

31. Davis, L.E. Developments in job design. In P.B. Warr (Ed.). *Personal Goals and Work Design.* London: Wiley, 1975.

32. Trist, E.L. Higgin, G.W. Murray, H. & Pollock, A.B. *Organizational Choice.* London: Tavistock, 1963.

33. Van der Zwaan, A.H. The sociotechnical systems approach: A critical evaluation. *International Journal of Production Research,* 1975, **13,** 149–163.

34. Walton, R.E. Quality of work life activities: A research agenda. *Professional Psychology,* in press.

35. Barr, S.H. Brief, A.P. & Aldag, R.J. *Measurement of Perceived Task Characteristics.* Working Paper 78-14, College of Business Administration, University of Iowa, 1978.

36. Seashore, S.E. Lawler, E.E. Ill. Mirvis, P.H. & Cammann, C. *Observing and Measuring Organizational Change: A Guide to Field Practice.* New York: Wiley-Interscience, in press.

37. Van de Ven, A.H. & Ferry, D.L. *Measuring and Assessing Organizations.* New York: Wiley-Interscience, 1980.

38. Macy, B.A. & Mirvis, P.H. Measuring the quality of work and organizational effectiveness in behavioral-economic terms. *Administrative Science Quarterly,* 1976, **21,** 212–226.

39. Walton, R.E. & Schlesinger, L.S. Do supervisors thrive in participative work systems? *Organizational Dynamics,* Winter 1979, 24–38.

40. Lawler, E.E. III. The new plant revolution. *Organizational Dynamics,* Winter 1978, 2–12.

—22—

Career Development

Patrick R. Pinto

When futurists identify a change in basic philosophy and underlying social values, they call this movement a "paradigm shift." There is such an emerging trend in career development. I believe there is movement away from organizational dominance over employee careers, toward a situation in which the individual has a growing share of information, resources, and control.

This shift stems from society's general questioning of the pillars of modern business. Our systems of production, and corporations in particular, are based on such foundations as the philosophy of growth, the supremacy of technology, management authority, the profit motive, and the belief that hard work and company loyalty will result in career progress and job fulfillment. These pillars of business have been shaken by external realities such as government intervention, environmental concerns, international events, consumerism, employee "entitlement," and so on.

This shift is also occurring because of subtle changes in employee expectations and values. Quality of life is of prime concern to many of today's workers (1). It is not unusual to find talented employees quitting in midcareer to pursue a small entrepreneurship, where opportunities for independence and personal accomplishment are greater. It is also not unusual for young professionals to turn down advancement opportunities because they do not want to relocate their families (2).

Certainly the emergence of former homemakers as new breed workers has been overwhelming (3). Such persons, conscious of their identity as unpaid houseworkers, want to get out of the kitchen to take any job in which earning money is a badge of membership in the larger society.

One theme underlying these subtle changes in values and expectation is that individuals want freedom of choice. They want a chance to "do their own thing" on the job, exercising autonomy, independence, and need fulfillment. Rather than interpret this as a hedonistic search for gratification, I consider it more a search for meaning and identity, an answer to the question, "Who am I?"

Most answers to the question "Who am I?" are in terms of employment relationships. Since employed persons spend most of their waking hours on the job, it is not unusual to find one's psychological identity defined in terms of work status, work role, and work relationships. Thus career questions are lifetime questions, but the answers begin well before entry into an initial job. How children are raised and socialized by their families and schools will influence later satisfaction, productivity, and adaptability on the job. At the other end of the work spectrum, as retirement approaches, psychologists report increased fantasies regarding death. Medical research shows that there actually is increased mortality within the first year or two of retirement, even controlling for retirement due to the onset of illness. Thus work gives meaning to individuals through their lifetime.

There are further changes in personal values that correspond to career stages. At the entry level, the prime concern is for mobility, developing specialty skills, concern for work assignments, dealing with feelings of competition and rivalry, and ultimately getting ahead.

However, at midcareer there is a drastic shift as one becomes introspective and faces the hard reality of one's accomplishments. Unmet expectations, choices taken, decisions made, all are faced with the realization that one's fulfillment has likely been less than one's earlier ambitions. Even for those who have attained high status and power, there is often the syndrome of career success and personal failure (4). Such "achievers" reflect Oscar Wilde's dictum regarding the two greatest tragedies in life: One tragedy is not getting what you want; the other is getting it.

These shifts in individual beliefs and values regarding one's work identity and the need for freedom of choice are in conflict with traditional models of employment staffing and development. Most models for human resource planning are established without regard to the career planning done by individuals. Every organizational decision has a concomitant or analogous individual decision. As Table 22.1 shows, traditional human resource activities are matched by personal decisions and choices on the part of individuls.

This table suggests what might be called Pinto's Third Law of Career Planning: "For every organizational action, there is an equal and opposite individual reaction."

Table 22.1 Individual Activities Corresponding to Organizational Activities

Organizational	Individual
Establishment of job specifications	Sorting through occupational and locational preferences
Recruitment procedures	Planning where, when, and how to look for a job
Selection decisions	Job choice
Evaluation of performance	Appraisal of the organization and management
Compensation decisions	Analysis of one's own compensation needs
Future placement and promotion	Choices among future opportunities

EMERGING TRENDS

Among those enlightened organizations who recognize the changing context of work in the larger society, we can identify a number of emerging trends in career management. The movement is away from a traditional or classical approach toward a more contemporary one reflecting some of the individual and organizational changes mentioned above.

Movement from Logical Matching of Persons to Jobs toward Exploration of Human Individuality and the Nature of Work

Most systems for initial entry and future placement within organizations assume there is a single best person for a given job. Jobs can be analyzed on the basis of skill, knowledge, and experience requirements. People can be assessed for their abilities and motivation. Incorporating both components, a rational matching system ensues. The trend is moving away from such a fixed system toward one in which the nature of human individuality and the nature of the work context is examined.

Realistic Job Expectations. Several programs support this trend, such as those that provide realistic job previews (5). These programs at the time of recruitment and initial orientation facilitate employee socialization. Atlas Van Lines, Inc. uses realistic information (including sociopolitical factors) on the new locale prior to a transfer to help their managers adjust. College relations brochures found in a typical college placement office now contain more than just slick pictures of smiling young workers. They often contain more specific information about future opportunities, career paths, expected time frames for movement, training programs, and so on.

Career Information Centers. Many organizations, such as Gulf Oil and Xerox, have established career information centers. These are staffed by career specialists and have available resources and information about job clusters, including materials beyond the simple job description, so that employees have a better idea of expected work roles, salary brackets, promotion requirements, and career opportunities available to them.

Career Assessment and Counseling. In recent years the availability of improved career assessment materials has also increased. Besides such vocational assessment instruments as Holland's "Self-Directed Search" and Crites' "Career Maturity Inventory," both of which are commercially available, there are numerous tailored instruments developed for in-company use. Assessment centers that are more extensive and reliable than simple paper-and-pencil instruments have been used for career development rather than solely for selection purposes.

Within organizations there is also a trend toward increased career counseling. Since supervisors are often asked by employees about job openings, the Internal Revenue Service has a programmed text to teach first line supervisors skills in upward mobility career counseling. Professional counselors, psychologists, social workers, and others are now in the employ of firms to provide career guidance to workers. Interestingly, many employee assistance programs (developed originally to aid in personal counseling for chemical dependency, family problems, emotional issues, etc.), are now receiving referrals for career counseling.

Career Planning Materials. In almost any bookstore there is an abundance of career planning materials available to the public. These materials tend to have a personal focus, providing encouragement and motivation to analyze career opportunities and to assess one's own capabilities (6,7,8,9).

Virtually all of these materials and resources attempt to answer similar questions:

> Who am I? (Give ten different answers to this question; choose a character in history that you'd like to be; write your own obituary, etc.).
>
> Where am I now? (Develop a time line showing levels of productivity and achievement at each age level; develop a life inventory of what you do well, what are your peak experiences, what do you want to learn to do better, etc.; write a detailed resume showing not only experience but also accomplishments, rewards and satisfactions, etc.)
>
> Where am I going? (Create a fantasy trip; list your ideal attainments in terms of achievement, compensation, and satisfaction; analyze your avocational projects, etc.)
>
> How do I get there? (Analyze career paths available; prepare a self-audit of your skills; list plans for job enrichment; identify resource people, etc.)
>
> What do I do if . . .? (List potential obstacles, contingencies, resources, alternative plans, etc.)

An AMA survey reported that virtually all responding companies provide certain basic career planning aids to employees, including workbooks, workshops, and special communications (10).

These activities and opportunities attempt to integrate work and career values. Given the complex nature of human learning and growth as well as the changing nature of work in a fragile economy, any system to match people and jobs must be organic and flexible.

Movement from Initial Vocational Choice toward the Process of Ongoing Career Decision Making

The rapid changes in business and society suggest that the environment for career planning is not static. Changing worker attitudes, changes in business conditions, increased international competition, and the lack of security in some organizations means that a static, one-time vocational choice must give way to a dynamic process of continuous decision making.

Adult Stages of Growth. One compelling foundation for this trend is the understanding of predictable changes in individuals as they progress through various life stages. A number of solid research studies report that career stages correspond roughly to chronological age, but more importantly to stages of psychological growth (11, 12, 13). As adults grow from tentative autonomy to a more mature intimacy, from competence to renewal, and from needs for identity to needs for generativity, their career interests will change. Decisions to enter and remain in an occupational field are constantly challenged by these psychological tensions.

Evolution of Jobs. Just as individuals progress through their growth stages, so also do jobs evolve. The unfolding or sequential nature of jobs corresponds to stages of organizational growth (14). This suggests that career development cannot stop with entry into a particular job title or even into a general occupational field.

For example, as industry becomes more sophisticated in the years ahead, we can expect the manager's job in particular to change. The evolving complexities of management suggest that human relations skills, understanding the larger social context of employment, coping with the information explosion, and developing a futures orientation are only some the ways in which managers' jobs will develop.

Interruptions in Job Sequence. Also supportiong this notion of dynamism is the trend toward interruptions in job sequence. Just as academics can take sabbaticals from time to time for reflection and rejuvenation, so too are sabbaticals in industry beginning to appear. A number of firms such as IBM and Xerox have long had social service leaves whereby employees can take time off at full pay to work on some governmental or social service project. There are an increasing number of sabbatical opportunities that go beyond service or education. According to the Conference Board, just under 45 percent of 272 companies polled said they have some sort of formal or informal sabbatical policy.

One company that puts virtually no restrictions on its sabbatical program is Time, Inc. After 15 years of continuous service any Time employee from top executive to secretary is entitled to a six month leave at half salary. Employees are encouraged to travel and write and pursue anything that interests them. The only restriction that Time puts on its on-leave employees is that they do not take a salaried job with another company.

Delayed childbearing by female workers means more requests for time off to rear children. Males have begun to request paternity leaves. Both groups are demanding that no stigma be attached to "blanks" in a job resume when accounted for by family reasons. These trends suggest there will be more interruptions allowed, or even encouraged, in one's work activities.

Movement from Mobility Upward Only toward Mobility in Multiple Directions

It is a peculiar notion of western society that mobility must be upward (15). Equating career growth with promotion to a higher organizatonal level is a myth. It frustrates workers as they realize that organizations are typically structured as pyramids, with a narrowing number of people near the apex.

A more appropriate sense of mobility within a firm is that it may be upward (convergent), diagonal (divergent), lateral, or to a new function (radical). Sometimes the best career move is downward in terms of decreased responsibility and activity. Many midcareer workers have examined the importance of leisure and family compared to rewards (and demands) of higher level jobs, and have opted for a reduced work role. And sometimes mobility is even outward in the form of discharge.

Mobility Outward. In overstressed jobs such as air traffic controller, the Federal Aviation Administration has a liberal policy of retraining so that as controllers "burn out," they are guaranteed up to two years' schooling in almost any legitimate field as a way of retreading them back into less stressful occupations. In that sense mobility for an air traffic controller is outward. Other firms with outplacement programs available can encourage managers to take business risks. Managers know that, should they be asked to leave, they can work at full salary for a specified period of time (usually two to three months) using company office facilities, including secretarial help, to look for a job. Outplacement counseling can help deal with the emotions of separating from the organization, and provide encouragement to look upon the new job as an opportunity for creative career redirection.

Open Mobility. Other organizations use perpetually open job bidding systems whereby anyone, at any time, can bid on any job in the organization. Obviously the requirements for entry or promotion are clearly spelled out. But individuals may seek to leap several levels in such organizations if they feel truly qualified, or may shift laterally or diagonally into nontraditional areas of movement without discouragement.

In-Place Mobility. An emerging characteristic of mobility systems is to use job enrichment as a form of "in place" mobility. The paradox here is that one may still grow in experience, skill, and confidence without changing job title or job level within an organization. The studied history of job enrichment suggests that people can be motivated and challenged through increasing responsibility (with corresponding increases in autonomy, status, and recognition) without changing their position in an organization. For the bulk of workers in a hierarchical organization, this may be the most appropriate form of career development.

Movement from a Narrow, Short-Run Perspective toward a Broader, Long-Range Perspective

If we recognize that careers represent a continuing series of choices and decisions over a lifetime, then career decision making should look beyond the next most immediate job opening.

Steering Committees. Most organizations recognize that since the immediate supervisor is concerned with day-to-day work assignments and controlling current performance, he or she may not be able to deal with future-oriented career issues. There is also the implied threat that any subordinate's most likely next move is the boss's position. Therefore many organizations seek to use other resources for individual career development. ONAN Corporation uses a process called "skip-a-level," whereby career development is a responsibility of the boss's boss, a person more likely to be in an overview position to match the broad needs of the organization with special needs of the individual.

Many organizations such as International Paper, Sun Oil, Northeastern Bell, and Union Carbide use steering committees, or management development panels, to review the career potential of professional and managerial employees. Under the purview of these committees is the entire scope of a person's long-term development, including compensation, benefits, transfers, special assignments, and work relationships. On a regular basis these panels meet and review a dossier filled with data on career history, performance reports, job experiences, bosses' ratings and recommendations, and so on. While the supervisor may be present, the committee is usually chaired by a line manager from another functional area.

One company, Citicorp, uses the label "corporate property" to identify "stars" in each of their divisions (16). These high talent people would likely be hoarded by division managers for use within the division, rather than allowing their talents to be developed in other parts of the business. To avoid this problem of hoarding, "corporate property" managers may be transferred by a steering committee to almost any other corporate division where the individual will have the most opportunity to learn and produce, and where the corporate need is greatest.

Career Pathing. A long-run perspective is also enhanced by using career pathing for increased communication and motivation (17). Traditional career paths are simple retrospective looks at where people have come from and where they have gone. These historical paths reflect narrow and static opportunities within an organization. A more contemporary approach is to do a behavioral analysis of skills, abilities, and experiences needed for each job in the organization, create job families of related positions, and determine relationships among families showing what it takes to move from one to the other as well as movement within families. The basis of behavioral paths is formal analysis of what activities are actually performed on the jobs, and the identification of logical options for each position.

Stress Management. A movement away from a narrow, short-run perspective will also help employees cope with stressful life and work situations. Career issues may be a prime source of individual stress. Goal ambiguity, role conflict, frustration, lack of reinforcement, and lack of direction, are some typical stressors in the work place. As more coping skills are developed in stress management programs, this will facilitate career development.

Life Planning. Most career planning programs are set squarely in the context of life planning (18,19). Careers represent a component of the larger life-space of the individual, and thus any career planning activities may be frustrated unless they are integrated with other interests and plans in the individual's life. Organizations are recognizing this and moving away from their traditional hesitation about "intervening" in the personal lives of individuals.

Notwithstanding that today there is increased need for privacy and protection of individual disclosure, firms are making available resources to deal with the life strains created by the work situation. The book, *Corporate Bigamy* (20) suggests that most managers and professionals are bigamists—married to both their legal spouses and to their organization. Menninger Foundation in Topeka and Dudley House in Duluth present company sponsored programs for spouse of executives and professionals to deal with the family tensions and misunderstandings created by work pressure.

Other firms provide materials such as audiotapes or workshops for spouse and family prior to relocation or at the time of orientation to a new position. These resources encourage dialogue and specific exercises to reduce anxiety as well as provide information on the new employment situation.

These examples point out that firms may be more willing to integrate future psychosocial needs with current corporate plans.

Movement from Boundaries Defined by the Specific Job Field toward Exploratory Job Experiences

The preceding trends also suggest movement away from locking workers into a given occupational setting, toward a setting in which they can try out different career alternatives.

Direct Exposure to Alternatives. One career development tactic is direct exposure to job alternatives through the use of special contracts. High technology organizations often have difficulty transferring scientists and engineers into management. Thus such companies as Bell Labs or General Electric use special contracts whereby an engineer becomes a manager or department head for a specified period with the understanding that, at the end of the period, he or she will go back to the work bench or the laboratory. During this time, usually two to three years, certain perquisites are provided, such as maintaining membership in scientific organizations, journal subscriptions, procurement of equipment and materials, and other resources to prevent technological obsolescence.

Direct exposure may occur via simulation such as that found in an assessment center. For example, presupervisory candidates are exposed over one or two days to most facets of management, including decision making, planning through in-basket exercises, leaderless group discussions, formal presentations, and interviews. At the conclusion of the assessment center the participant has a better idea of what it is like to spend "a day in the life" of a manager.

There are also more complicated simulations, such as "Looking Glass" (21) which recreate the complex reality of a management team in a hypothetical industry.

Vicarious Exposure to Alternatives. Workers may obtain vicarious exposure to jobs. Like many firms, Xerox Corporation has a videotape library of information regarding different career fields. For example, as part of the services of its career information center, an employee interested in the marketing function can play a video cassette that will typically start off with a corporate officer (such as a marketing vice-president) speaking candidly about his or her conception of what marketing is like at Xerox. This presentation may be followed by an informal rap session among Xerox sales representatives, discussing the hardships of living on the road, making "cold calls" on customers, dealing with service complaints, and so on but also sharing their enthusiasm in the challenge and rewards of a marketing career, of working for a progressive company, and selling top quality products. This discussion is then typically followed by a representative from the human resource department describing the experience and abilities required to hire or promote someone into the marketing area. Indirectly this videotape exposes employees to various job experiences available in the company.

Occupational Information. Diverse sources are available for gathering data on jobs, occupations and organizations. For lower level jobs in organizations, the Department of Labor regularly publishes occupational outlook material. Job posting systems, often mandated by affirmative action requirements, provide information and opportunities for all but the highest job levels (22). In some firms, posting and bidding is allowed up to officer positions. Through their career information centers, many firms make available career paths, paper-and-pencil tests, exercises, interest inventories, salary schedules, and promotion requirements. Popular books such as

What Color is Your Parachute? (23) provide a guerrilla guide to infiltrating the organizational and occupational data base to discover critical information about jobs.

The use of sabbaticals also provides an awareness of alternative work and life styles. Media, such as television, movies, and books further expand this awareness. While these media presentations may be exaggerated depictions of organizational life, they at least provide some picture of alternative ways of relating and developing one's career.

Movement from Antagonism and Authority toward Collaboration and Participation

Enlightened organizations are willing to share with individuals some measure of information, resources, and control. Given pressures of organized labor and civil rights activists, organizations are installing internal appeals systems for handling employee complaints or concerns which may include career related issues. A number of firms such as General Electric and Honeywell, Inc. have ombudspersons to handle the special needs of employees regarding their rights to information, fair treatment, and "entitlement" to career opportunities.

Self-Development. Career planning programs today increasingly emphasize self-development and training (24). The operative phrase in most programs seems to be "career development begins with you." Besides the obvious motivational aspects, self-development is grounded in basic learning principles. We learn best by *doing*, actively experiencing within our environment. So too the trend in management and professional training appears to be that the best learning is self-learning. Some companies have moved away from formal management training to a more structured set of tailored job experiences, work assignments, developmental goals, and relationships such as mentoring (25) and coaching. These experiences provide organic development as individuals interact with their work setting rather than through formal classroom instruction.

Career Consciousness Raising. Just as it appeared in the early days of the feminist movement, the phenomenon of consciousness raising is visible in organizations today. Now the consciousness relates to personal career development. Companies are encouraging workers to engage in deliberate reflection about their careers. This is partly to develop an improved talent base for human resource planning, and also to eliminate some of the frustration that comes with perceived career blockage.

This consciousness raising has also led to group sharing of problems (26) whereby people use each other as resources and as support bases in the process of their own career development.

A SPECIFIC MODEL FOR CAREER MANAGEMENT

The foregoing description of emerging trends leads to the conclusion that organizational dominance is slowly giving way toward greater individual initiative and control. The review also suggests five major components that ought to be present in any system for career development: (a) realistic assessment, (b) gathering job and organizational information, (c) goal setting, (d) action planning, and (e) monitoring and evaluation. These activities must exist in the context of principles of adult learning. From adult education studies (27) we know that adults tend to be self-directed, ready to learn immediately useable skills with practical applicability, concerned more about solving problems than learning about theories, and finally, insistent that their personal experience be incorporated in the learning design.

Realistic Assessment

Assessment of individual skills, abilities, and interests should be done by both the person and by the organization. As mentioned, individuals have a variety of self-assessment devices available. The organization may use data from performance evaluations, paper and pencil tests, psychological evaluations, assessment center results, or casual reports.

Gathering Job and Organization Information

Enlightened organizations share a great deal of useful information with their employees. This includes gathering and sharing human resource planning data such as company forecasts of labor demand, career paths, constraints or demands imposed by affirmative action plans, and validated promotion requirements. It also includes organization policies and practices, for example, regarding transfer policies, compensation programs, and retirement practices. Finally, it even includes "softer" data such as organization climate, relationships among departments, performance expectations, principles related to the organization's identity, and organization goals.

Goal Setting

This is best done in the context of a developmental interview between boss, subordinate, and a third party member such as a human resource professional or a counselor. The goals set will depend upon the current performance capabilities of the individual as well as his or her career stage and tenure within the organization.

For the upper 10 percent of individuals who are ready now, mobile and promotable, their short-term career goals are basically to prepare to move to a larger or different job. The organization's objectives in this case are to treat these individuals well, keep them challenged and satisfied, and find a place for them to experience additional career growth as soon as possible.

The next 20 percent or so of performers are on a fast development track, being groomed for future mobility. Having proven their performance in their current job through outstanding quality and quantity of work, they are called to develop specific skills and abilities which are more future oriented.

The majority of workers (50 to 60%) fall into a general growth category in which multiple career opportunities are available, but no specific grooming or fast track development is provided. In terms of current performance these workers are fully satisfactory and typically are developed through a variety of outside classroom experiences, job enrichment techniques, and special work assignments. For each individual, there may be a number of possible career target jobs, but time frames for development are broader.

Finally, for those employees who are clearly below standard, future career development is generally of much less importance than remedial training and direction to overcome performance deficiencies. In this case the short-term performance goals are quite specific, tolerances for error are tighter, time frames shorter, and there is closer supervisory monitoring and control.

Action Planning

Based on long-term goals, an immediate plan containing specific short-term developmental steps should be created for each individual. An action plan should include behavioral statements of what is to be accomplished; specific standards regarding quantity, quality, cost, and time; a listing of resources, anticipated obstacles, and constraints; and a description of special opportunities to be pursued as they occur.

Monitoring and Evaluation

Career development is a continuous process. Therefore evaluation should be done by the organization on an ongoing basis. Using a career advisor or counselor frees the boss from having to monitor progress of each individual in reaching developmental objectives. The organization should also collect information from participants about the effectiveness of the program, as well as obtain cost indicators of the career management system.

CONCLUSION: WHO HAS THE BURDEN?

While the emerging trend appears to be a growing share of individual participation in career development, it will always be true that within the bounds of legal and moral constraints the organization holds the ultimate right to manage employees. It should be obvious that the way to provide both humane and productive management of people is to share the burden of career development between the company and the person.

While the company cannot predict the future, and therefore guarantee its promises, it has far more resources for keeping its commitments to its people. If the organization is willing to reward managers for career development, to share information and resources, and to make career development a major objective in its own survival, then the organization will have begun to fulfill its obligations.

Some individuals tend to be career passive, but the trend today is for people to begin to take charge of their own lives. They are increasingly realistic about their expectations and needs. They are exploring how work fits into their chosen life style, including belief systems, financial concerns, interpersonal commitments, and leisure pursuits. Their input is essential to career management.

Who has the burden in career development? As exemplified by the thesis of this paper, there is one proper answer to this question. The burden must be shared by both the organization and the individual.

REFERENCES

1. Yankelovich, D. The new psychological contracts at work. *Psychology Today*, 1978, **11**(12), 46–50.
2. Pinder, C. Mobility and transfer. In H. Meltzer & W. Nord (Eds.). *Making Organizations Humane and Productive*. New York: Wiley, 1981.
3. Weber, A.R. In the 1980's: A dramatically different labor force. *Across the Board*, December 1979.
4. Korman, A. Career success, personal failure. Paper presented at the annual meeting of The American Psychological Association, Montreal, September 1980.
5. Wanous, J. P. *Organizational Entry*. Reading, Mass.: Addison-Wesley, 1980.
6. Adams, E.L. *Career Advancement Guide*. New York: McGraw-Hill, 1975.
7. Storey, W.D. *Career Dimensions II*. New York: General Electric Company, 1976.
8. Hagburg, J. & Leider, R. *The Inventurers*. Reading, Mass.: Addison-Wesley, 1978.
9. Hall, D.T. *Managing Your Career*. Darien, Conn.: Management Decision Systems, Inc., 1976.
10. Walker, J.W. & Gutteridge, T.G. *Career Planning Practices: An AMA Survey Report*. New York: Amacom, 1979.
11. Levinson, D. *The Seasons of a Man's Life*. New York: Knopf, 1978.
12. Gould, R.L. *Transformations: Growth and Change in Adult Life*. New York: Simon and Schuster, 1978.
13. Vaillant, G.E. *Adaptation to Life*. Boston: Little, Brown, 1977.
14. Leach, J. The career of the organization. *The Personnel Administrator*, 1977, **22**(8), 34–39.
15. Jennings, E.E. Mobicentric man. *Psychology Today*, 1970, **4**(1), 35–40.
16. Saklad, D.A. Manpower planning and career development at Citicorp. In L. Dyer (Ed.). *Careers in Organizations*. Ithaca, New York: New York State School of Industrial and Labor Relations, Cornell University, 1976.

17. Walker, J.W. *Human Resource Planning.* New York: McGraw-Hill, 1980.

18. Crystal, J.C. & Bolles, R.N. *Where Do I Go from Here with My Life?* New York: Seabury Press, 1974.

19. Ford, G.A. & Lippitt, G.L. *Planning Your Future: A Workbook for Personal Goal Setting.* La Jolla, Calif.: University Associates, 1976.

20. Feinberg, M.R. *Corporate Bigamy.* New York: Amacom, 1978.

21. Lombardo, M. & McCall, M. *Manual for Looking Glass, Inc.* Greensboro, N.C.: Center for Creative Leadership, 1980.

22. Pinto, P.R. & Dahl, D. Job posting: An industry survey. *Personnel Journal,* 1977, **56**, 40–42.

23. Bolles, R.N. *What Color Is Your Parachute? A Practical Manual for Job Hunters and Career Changers.* Rev. ed. Berkeley: Ten Speed Press, 1975.

24. Burack, E.H. Self assessment: A strategy of growing importance. *Training and Development Journal,* 1979, **33**, 48–52.

25. Roche, G.R. Much ado about mentors. *Harvard Business Review,* January-February 1979, 14–24.

26. Broussard, W.J. & DeLargey, R.J. The dynamics of the group outplacement workshop. *Personnel Journal,* 1979, **58**, 855–873.

27. Knowles, M. *The Adult Learner: A Neglected Species.* 2nd ed. Houston: Gulf Publishing, 1978.

—23—

Fostering Collaboration among Organizations

Barbara Gray Gricar

INTRODUCTION

Managerial efforts to make organizations more humane and productive have traditionally been focused on internal problems. Managers have sought to improve supervision, career opportunities, quality of working life, motivation and morale, and coordination of work. Organizational development efforts have stressed understanding, shared problem solving, and productive conflict management as vehicles for improving organizational effectiveness. Typically these efforts have fostered collaboration *within* organizations.

Today, however, an increasing number of external pressures influence managerial decision making. These pressures are generated by other organizations whose actions enhance or constrain the activities of the focal organization. For example, managers must contend with energy shortages, emission controls, affirmative action quotas, consumer demands, and advances in electronic media that increase the amount and complexity of information available to them. These pressures have created a fundamental change in the nature of the problems confronting managers. Problems are becoming increasingly more complex and cannot be solved by individual organizations alone. Instead solutions depend upon many organizations working together. This increased interdependence has generated the need for new methods of collaboration *among* organizations.

Collaboration refers to interaction between two or more organizations in which they identify and acknowledge the ways in which they are mutually interdependent with regard to a particular issue or set of issues. Usually collaborative efforts are intended to reduce the uncertainty and feelings of helplessness induced by environmental complexity.

This chapter offers a framework for thinking about collaboration among organizations. Specifically, five strategies to foster collaboration among or-

The author wishes to express special appreciation to Dan Brass, Bob Kaplan, Lynne Markus, and Joe McCann for their critical review of and helpful suggestions on an earlier draft.

ganizations are described: advocacy, diagnosis, networks, search conferences, and referent structures.

Before pursuing these strategies in depth it seems reasonable to describe in more detail why they are needed. It has already been suggested that interdependence among organizations has increased dramatically (1). According to Ashby (2), the environments of organizations are now richly joined. That is, purposeful actions by some organizations affect the ability of others to achieve their goals (3). Corporations, for example, are no longer permitted to construct new facilities without assessing the environmental impact of their plans for the communities in which they operate.

This interdependence is in part the product of a complex technological state that has doubled back on itself. Those achievements that have enabled us to master our environment on the one hand have also generated more complex social, economic, and technological problems in their wake. The nature of this doubling back process is illustrated by the problems associated with the host of chemical dumps across the country. What was once a simple storage problem for chemical manufacturers has created serious housing and health concerns for millions of Americans. A case in point is the genetic damage caused by seeping industrial wastes presumed safely stored 25 years ago in the Love Canal area of New York.

Unfortunately, the problems posed by chemical dumps exemplify a broader class of problems facing managers, which include declining productivity, uncertainty about future energy sources, and conflicting governmental regulations. Knotty problems like these, which Ackoff (4) has so aptly labeled "messes," defy simple solutions and exceed the capability of any single organization to control. In order to cope effectively with problems of this type managers need to shift their organizing perspective to include interorganizational problem solving. Indeed *Business Week* (5) recently called for business, labor, government, minorities, and public interest groups to jointly embark on collaborative efforts to achieve a new social consensus.

The Jamestown Area Labor Management Committee (6) is a good illustration of such collaborative efforts among managers and unions in the face of a complex and uncertain future. Jamestown is a town of about 35,000 located in southwestern New York state. The town was threatened by depressed industrial growth and severe economic decline. In 1973, with the help of some consultants, the Jamestown Area Labor Management Committee was formed. Comprised of upper level managers and union leaders from all the manufacturing facilities in the area, the Committee set as its task reversing the area's economic decline. This unprecedented degree of collaboration among diverse organizations improved labor relations, raised the quality of working life in the plants, and generally stimulated industrial development in the community. This case illustrates a number of concepts that are important to the following discussion.

The first of these is the concept of an interorganizational domain. Interorganizational domain refers to an issue or problem of mutual interest to a set of organizations (1). While organizations may differ radically in their views about a problem, each organization would be affected by actions of the others to cope with it. That is, each group has a stake in how the issue is resolved. In the Jamestown case, the domain, the economic viability of the area, is a concern shared by numerous businesses and many unions. Jamestown's demise or revitalization has serious implications for each of them.

A second important concept is that of stakeholders in the domain. This term originally was used by Ansoff (7) to designate the different groups who have a "stake" in a corporation, including employees, suppliers, customers, and the public. The term has been adopted by interorganizational theorists to refer to groups or individuals who are affected by an issue and claim a right to influence its outcome. Stakeholders in the Jamestown case include the various corporations and the employees (represented by their unions) whose jobs might be affected. (Stakeholders in the domain concerned with storage of chemical wastes include the chemical companies, homeowners who must relocate, families who have suffered genetic damage, and those who must foot the bill for the clean-up efforts.)

A third concept is interorganizational collaboration. Collaboration among organizations refers to interaction between two or more organizations. The critical features of the interaction include the recognition of interdependence and the coalescing of interests among the stakeholders around some common purpose. Collaboration serves to reduce the uncertainty each individual organization experiences and enables the set of organizations to gain some collective control over their domain. Collaboration permits a response of sufficient "requisite variety" (2) to match the complexity induced by the environment (1). More simply put, through collaboration the stakeholders can begin to direct their collective resources toward a common, mutually desirable end.

Now let us turn our attention to strategies and to how they foster collaboration among organizations. Achieving collaboration requires skillful design and careful implementation of a strategy. This process has been referred to as domain development (1). Domain development consists of three phases: problem setting, direction setting, and structuring (8). The five strategies address different phases of the collaborative process. Table 23.1 shows the developmental phase and the anticipated outcomes for each of the five collaborative strategies. In the following sections the theory underlying each strategy is reviewed, the process and its anticipated results are presented, and examples of the strategies are provided. These descriptions are not intended as a "how to" manual, but rather as an introduction to the range of strategies available and to the kinds of results they are designed to achieve. These strategies have been successfully used to address problems

Table 23.1 Developmental Phases and Results of the Strategies

Strategy	Developmental Phase(s)	Anticipated Results
Advocacy	Problem setting	Legitimate status for some new stakeholders Attention directed to previously unrecognized problem
Diagnosis	Problem setting	Mapping of relationships Explication of interdependence
Networks	Problem setting and direction setting	Informal coordination of stakeholders Exchange of resources among stakeholders
Search conferences	Problem setting and direction setting	Discovery of common values Conceptualization of desired future
Referent structures	Problem setting, direction setting, and structuring	Self-regulation of domain

concerned with industrial decline, mortgage lending, health care delivery, neighborhood deterioration, and criminal justice.

ADVOCACY

Assumptions

Advocacy means taking a public stand to affirm a value position on an issue. The advocate actively supports a cause by joining an advocacy organization or by organizing one. Advocacy interventions are designed to achieve voice (9) for a group of stakeholders who are not perceived as legitimate and who do not have access to decisions about an issue that affects them.

Advocacy methods have been well-documented (10, 11, 12, 13) and have been used by activist groups for a wide assortment of causes (13, 14, 15). Moreover, the case for social scientists and practitioners to become advocates has been argued by many writers (16, 17, 18, 19). Managers, on the other hand, may have to contend with public interest groups using advocacy strategies to promote their views. However, even businesses are turning to advocacy strategies (19), although the appropriateness of such activities has generated substantial debate among the business community. Still, as a strategy for stimulating collaborative problem solving among organizations, advocacy remains relatively unexplored. (Notable exceptions include Gricar and Brown, 14, and Tandon, 15.)

The circumstances under which advocacy is an appropriate strategy are substantially different from these conducive to the other strategies discussed in this chapter. The preconditions for advocacy are an unequal resource distribution that leaves some groups deficient and grants other groups control over the process and conditions of exchange (21). Hence definition and control of the domain is not shared, but restricted to formulation of alternatives that are unsatisfactory to some stakeholders. This can lead to conflict among stakeholders over the control of the domain and struggles to obtain legitimacy by those groups who are not recognized as legitimate stakeholders within a domain. Situations in which stakeholders represent sharply contrasting views, or are bitterly antagonistic, may warrant an advocacy strategy to tip the balance of power in the relationship (19). An advocacy strategy presumes that giving voice to the voiceless will improve the rationality of future planning within the domain (18).

Process and Examples

In advocacy situations the primary task is to mobilize a constituency and to help it gain bargaining power as a legitimate stakeholder. Efforts to secure voice for stakeholders are illustrated by the tactics of Saul Alinsky (10, 11). More recently, National Peoples Action (NPA), a housing advocacy group, employed Alinsky-style tactics to garner public attention and to secure agency response to the problems of urban neighborhoods. NPA staged a massive protest at the American Bankers' Association, stormed the home of the President of the Federal Home Loan Bank Board, and crashed a party held by the President of one of Chicago's Savings and Loans to demand state and federal action on the passage of the Federal Home Mortgage Disclosure Act of 1975.

Let me illustrate advocacy as a strategy for intervention by describing a case with which I am personally familiar.

Citizens of an upper middle class residential community adjacent to a large urban center became concerned about financial disinvestment of their community by its lending institutions. Their concerns stemmed from the city's age, racial composition, and proximity to other deteriorated neighborhoods. The city of 60,000 people, built in the 1920s had experienced an influx of black residents from the urban center. White flight and racial "steering," in which realtors directed white buyers out of integrated areas, had contributed to deterioration of the city's housing stock and its commercial strips.

The citizens, members of an activist housing group, suspected that local financial institutions were disinvesting the community by restricting home mortgage loans ("redlining"). To test their suspicions they collected and analyzed data on all mortgages granted in the community over the previous seven years. The data analysis suggested that some lending institutions had in fact begun to disinvest the community. The citizen's group then confronted the lenders with their analysis, first privately and then publicly, but drew from them only categorical denials of redlining.

Unable to influence the lenders, the citizens then presented their findings to the city government and requested that the city exert pressure on the lenders. The city responded by creating a municipal advisory committee on residential lending comprised of representatives from lending institutions, city government and administration, realtors, and citizens.

Through an advocacy process bolstered by the mortgage data, the citizens gained a legitimate public forum (the committee) to air their concerns. Moreover, the committee ultimately became the vehicle for collaboration between all the groups on a revitalization program for the city.

Results

Advocacy is a problem setting intervention for the domain for two reasons. First, advocacy points out and focuses the attention of other stakeholders on an issue of concern to the domain. Hence it sets an agenda for the domain. Second, a desired outcome of advocacy is recognition of the advocacy constituency as a legitimate stakeholder in the domain, one with some power to influence the direction of the domain.

A final point about advocacy is its potential to be system integrative (18). That is, it promotes debate on issues within the domain. The disadvantage of course is that such integration may never occur and that collaborative solutions are never achieved. In extreme cases advocacy can lead to violent confrontation.

From a managerial perspective advocacy may be a strategy used against or in support of their organization. Managers should both anticipate pressure from advocacy groups and consider that one of the other four strategies may be the most appropriate response to such pressure. In addition, organizations have developed advocacy arms of their own, to advance the organization's view on a particular issue in which it is a stakeholder.

DIAGNOSIS

Assumptions

Diagnosis refers to systematic collection and dissemination of data about a subject, in this case, about an interorganizational domain and about those organizations with a stake in it. Alderfer (22) has defined diagnosis as a "process of publicly entering a human system, collecting valid information about human experiences within that system, and feeding information back to the system to promote increased understanding of the system by its members." Kaplan (23) specifically explained diagnosis in an interorganizational setting as "a set of arrangements designed to permit the release of valid information about system dynamics and to assemble relevant members of units of the system to learn about these dynamics." Diagnosis facilitates system learning by first painting a mosaic of the system from the views of individual members and then inviting interpretation of the mosaic by the members. Diagnosis is an "appreciative" intervention in that learning occurs through gaining a different or a deeper appreciation of system dynamics.

Process and Examples

A manager or set of managers within a system may invite a change agent to design and conduct the diagnosis of their system. Typically this involves a number of steps beginning with the change agent's entry into the system. Alternately a single organization or representatives from many organizations within a system may serve as diagnostician(s). In either case, those conducting the diagnosis must negotiate an agreement with the appropriate authorities to conduct the inquiry. In the interorganizational domain these negotiations must occur between the diagnostician(s) and each of the organizations involved. The second step is collecting data through interviews, questionnaires, and observation. This is followed by sharing of the data with those queried. Design of the feedback requires some thought, since aggregate data may be appropriately fed back at the system level, while data about the position of an individual organization within the system may best be shared only with that organization. The final step is interpretation of the feedback by the system itself.

An example of a diagnostic intervention is provided by Kaplan (23). The system was comprised of a network of 11 mental health agencies and a central funding organization. Similar to research on interorganizational networks (24) and loosely organized systems (22), the Kaplan study examined system dimensions such as membership, goal congruity, authority, communication, roles, and resources. The initial focus of the diagnosis was the central organization and the relationships between it and the individual agencies it funded. This diagnosis was conducted as a means of gaining entry to the individual organizations. Data for the system level diagnosis was gathered by a questionnaire to the staffs of all 12 organizations. In the second phase the consultants facilitated a self-assessment by each individual organization. Each organization then shared the results of its self-assessment with the central organization as a part of the diagnosis of the overall system. The significance of this intervention strategy was that individual organizational diagnosis was conducted in the context of the larger organizational system. A secondary consequence of the intervention was the fact that the system as a whole took stock of itself, and relationships among its members were improved.

Of pivotal importance to the success of this intervention were the painstaking entry processes that the consultants undertook to insure that the intervention served the needs of all 12 agencies and was not misconstrued by any as an evaluation of the agencies by the funder. Unlike network *research*, the Kaplan effort truly represents diagnosis as *intervention* for change and stresses the *process* of data gathering and feedback as well as the substance of the inquiry.

Results

The anticipated results of a diagnostic intervention are several. The diagnosis is "appreciative" in that it provides within an organization a shared understanding of its domain. This understanding may include consciousness among system members of a common fate (22). Moreover, diagnosis may be essentially a problem setting strategy that makes explicit members' joint perceptions of system characteristics. It provides a basis upon which other collaborative strategies can be built. More generally, diagnosis can be seen as a precursor to other strategies that explicitly seek to change the existing patterns of interaction between organizations within the domain.

To imply, however, that diagnosis itself does not change a system would be misleading. For example, work reported by Tandon and Brown (25) revealed that diagnostic intervention produced significant changes in the social network within a condominium complex. In the homeowner's association, organized after the condominium diagnosis, those residents who had been interviewed during the diagnosis tended to play more active roles than those who were not interviewed. Moreover, diagnosis can create more explicit organization among members of a domain. In the case of the mental health agencies reported earlier, the diagnosis produced a greater degree of system integration among the agency directors and a spirit of mutuality in the agency-funder relationships (23).

In the earlier example of an advocacy intervention, the citizens conducted a different sort of diagnosis within the domain. Rather than member's perceptions of the domain, they collected and presented an objective measure of the domain—data on mortgage lending patterns. Greater organization of the domain resulted when the city convened the advisory committee to thrash out the differing interpretations of that data.

NETWORKS

Assumptions

A fundamental strategy for facilitating collaboration is constructing a network among organizations. Networks are typically loosely organized structures that create opportunities for the exchange of resources among the participating groups. Network building presumes that stakeholders in a domain have some common interest that binds them together, and that they could benefit from some form of exchange. Networks serve two purposes. First, they make explicit a shared need for exchange of resources—usually information, although it could be goods and services (26); second, they provide some structure by which the exchange can be transacted through informed interaction and personal contact. Networks can be created voluntarily or by mandate from some dominant organization, such as a funding agency or regulatory body.

Structurally, networks are characterized by loose coupling (27). Indeed some members may be unknown to each other and never interact. Member's interactions may vary in intensity from a single exchange to extended interactions (26). Typically coordination of members and activities is handled by a leader or leadership committee. Additional coordination derives largely from member's converging interests, which implicitly regulate their shared domain (28).

Process and Examples

Networks vary in the degree to which they are formalized. The OD Network, a professional group of behavioral science practitioners, represents a formal network with membership dues, rosters, newsletters, and regularly scheduled meetings for exchange. This can be contrasted with a very loosely organized network of lay religious communities (called sodalities), which exist in about ten cities across the United States. The primary glue that holds this network together is periodic visits by members of one community to the homes of members in other cities. In addition, civic organizations like the Chamber of Commerce or Kiwanis offer network opportunities for managers. For example, at a Chamber of Commerce meeting in a midwest town of 60,000, safety directors from 16 industrial firms decided to share confidential information about their OSHA inspection records, types of violations, and fines to gauge the fairness of OSHA enforcement efforts.

Networks often are created by the actions of a single individual or organizational representative who serves as a node for linking many others. Such an individual has been termed a reticulist (1) or leader-coordinator (26). This type of person promotes the exchange of information by initiating and encouraging communication among others with related interests. The reticulist often serves another extremely significant function—as one who recognizes the value of exchange and inspires others to participate in it. Sarason and Lorentz (26) refer to the leader-coordinator as someone with a mission.

As a strategy for improving collaboration between organizations, network-building requires a reticulist of some sort—a central individual or organization with the motivation and energy and need to initiate contacts with others who share the domain. Often the network may exist in a latent form; that is, members already know each other from previous contexts. The job of the reticulist then is simply to activate already existing linkages. For example, after participating in two years of internal organization development work at her agency, the director of a community planning agency recognized that similar efforts were needed to improve planning between social service agencies in the community. With the help of some consultants, she convinced the County Administrator to convene a group of agency directors to begin an exchange of ideas on how to better coordinate their efforts. She was the reticulist in this case, and the consultants assisted her, and later the County Administrator, to organize the network.

Results

Network building is primarily a problem setting process. Formation of a network identifies stakeholders and establishes a mechanism for resource exchange among groups and organizations. To varying degrees, networks make explicit the aspects of a domain that are shared among the members.

To the extent that networks can sustain a sense of common purpose among the organizations within a domain, they are also direction setting. Sarason and Lorentz (26) point out that network members derive a sense of community from mutual satisfaction of their needs for resources. By linking with others through a network, individual organizations can begin to gain control over their environments. The degree to which their members perceive that the network linkages enhance their control over their environment depends in part on whether or not the networks were mandated (29). Networks can also assist organizations to garner resources by gaining public support and legitimacy for organizational activities (30) and to gain control and legitimacy over distribution of resources (31).

THE SEARCH CONFERENCE

Assumptions

Searching is a method of active adaptive planning developed in the 1950s (32). Typically search participants are individuals or organizational representatives with a stake in a common issue, who gather in a workshop setting to explore implications for the future of that particular issue. For example, searches have recently been conducted among prison wardens, half-way house directors, and probation officers to explore the future of the American jail. Other search conferences have focused on the future of the banking industry and development plans for an Australian town.

Based on the idealized search for common values, a search conference's objective is to develop among the participants a shared conception of what the future could be. Unlike forecasting, search eschews prediction. Instead, by drawing on their own knowledge and experience, search participants collectively identify potential future trends and the implications they have for the issue of concern to them (e.g., jails, urban traffic problems, rehabilitation).

Two fundamental assumptions underly search as a strategy for collaboration: (a) Organizations are purposeful systems, that is, they do not merely adapt to but actively shape their external environments; (b) decisions rendered today create the constraints and opportunities demanding a response tomorrow. Search is designed on the premise that planning should not forecast what will happen in the next twenty years, but should identify what people can do now to influence future directions (33).

Process and examples

While the content of a search conference is not prescribed by the facilitators, the process is. Typically the conference is a two or three day workshop with about 30 participants. The conference is designed to minimize barriers to the discovery of common values, such as (a) reliance on others as experts about the future, and (b) using past experience to limit one's view of what is possible.

Structurally the conference proceeds through five phases. Phase 1 focuses on the contextual environment in which the issue is embedded. The participants identify all the possible technical, environmental, social, attitudinal, and demographic trends that influence the issue of concern. From the mass of projections and expectations of what the future may hold, they develop a complex map of the multiple factors bearing upon their domain and of the interdependence among these factors. For example, during a search conference on the jail of the future, participants identified trends such as decline in population, increase in average age, greater concern for leisure time, and concentration of power in multinational corporations in a list of 60 trends comprising the wider environment of the jail. Next the participants examined the positive and negative impacts of these trends on jails. In this way they begin to generate an image of the future rooted in their shared assumptions and values about the desirability of future trends.

Phase 2 focuses on the transactional environment; participants are asked to identify factors in their everyday transactions that pose constraints or create opportunities. In Phase 3 participants are ready to design a model of the desirable future for their issue of concern. In "The Western Search Conference on the Jail of the Future" (33) some participants designed jails without walls. Others developed a model of crisis intervention designed to humanize law enforcement.

In Phase 4 implementation of the idealized designs is considered, with an eye to the underlying tensions implicit in the designs. The designs are criticized by other participants and reality-tested by comparing them with the societal trends projected in Phase 1. Finally, in Phase 5 the participants refocus on the present and explore how they can translate their desired futures into reality.

Results

Search conferences are not intended to produce a concrete plan for action. Nor do they create an ongoing structure within which planning will take place. They produce no specific decisions that are binding on all the stakeholders who attend (34). Instead search conferences have three fundamental results. They open up channels of communication between stakeholders. They promote group identification of a set of ideals that can guide future development of the domain. And they create a basis for control of the domain that emerges from the shared values (34).

Search achieves these results by creating a temporary learning community. The search process unveils the basic patterns of interdependence among the participants. The exhaustive mapping of the context in which the focal issue of the search is embedded legitimizes expressions of multiple value stances on the issue and articulation of those values held in common by the participants. Hence search is primarily an appreciative intervention. It establishes a joint concept of what is possible and a joint conviction that what is possible is attainable.

REFERENT STRUCTURES

Assumptions

Strategies that focus on the appreciative level may not provide sufficient organization among the stakeholders to achieve their collective aims. To do so may require a shift in the structural as well as the appreciative relationships among the stakeholders. Strategies designed to create structures, referred to as referent structures in which stakeholders can engage in extended planning, are being explored (1, 8, 14). Referent structures can evolve gradually over time or can be systematically developed through intervention. I use the term "'referent structures" here loosely to indicate a configuration of stakeholders or their representatives engaged in joint regulation of activities within their shared domain or in developing mechanisms for joint regulation. Warren (35) used the term "referent form" for a single organization with hierarchical control over other stakeholders and distinguished this from a unit that simply provided coordination without any formal control.

Trist (36), on the other hand, refers to referent organizations as collections of stakeholders who democratically manage activities within their shared domain. Referent organizations according to Trist (1) serve three functions: infrastructure support (such as information sharing), appreciation of shared values, and regulation of existing relationships and patterns of activity. It is important to emphasize the developmental character of joint regulation, since it is in the process of developing structure that the basic trust necessary for self-regulation is achieved.

Process and examples

To prescribe a model by which referent structures should be created would belie the very end to which they aspire: self-regulation. McCann (8) has suggested that a variety of structural arrangements are feasible for achieving domain consensus and that one task of the designers is to facilitate agreement among stakeholders about which arrangement is most appropriate to their needs. Still some guidelines for design of referent structures can be offered. Initially convenors of referent organizations need to devote careful consideration to selection of the stakeholders. Deciding who should participate in a referent organization is a part of problem setting for the domain. A preliminary diagnostic effort may be needed merely to identify who the relevant stakeholders are and what their respective status is vis à vis one another.

Following appointment of members, the primary task is creation of a structure within which a shared purpose and plans for domain regulation can emerge. Selection of the appropriate structure to facilitate these objectives is a joint task for the facilitator and the stakeholders.

Emery (37) has devised a referent structure for domains with so many groups of stakeholders that one from each would provide an unwieldy group for problem solving. Instead each constituency nominates a representative to a pool from which 30 to 40 are selected randomly for two year terms on a stakeholders' council. This method is designed to distribute the power to control the agenda among the stakeholders.

The referent organization that emerged in the mortgage lending case was structured differently. It was convened primarily to resolve a conflict. The convening was done by a stakeholder (the city government) who had sufficient power to organize the others. By convening the committee, the city recognized the citizens as legitmate stakeholders in the mortgage lending domain along with lenders, realtors, and appraisers. This structural balancing of power acknowledged the legitmacy of all the stakeholders to participate in decisions about the domain.

While it took the committee a year to shift from an advocacy pattern of interaction to collaborative problem solving, the design of the committee greatly facilitated this process. Subcommittees were a primary feature of the design, for it was within these groups that the real work of appreciation occurred. The subcommittees were purposely comprised of four to five different stakeholderss. They were responsible for researching an issue and recommending action to the committee as a whole. Conflicts in the subcommittees led them to pursue additional data until they reached some joint appreciation about an issue.

In the committee as a whole problem areas were defined, shared goals were acknowledged, and mechanisms for regulating behavior were hammered out. After months of debate on how to monitor lending practices, for example, the committee condoned a review process of all the lending institutions in the city. Representatives from the committee visited each institution to review the data the citizens had gathered on lending patterns and to convey the committee's evaluation of their performance. Evidence that the committee had achieved a level of shared appreciative values was reflected in measures of goals after one and 10 months of work and in statements made during interviews with individual stakeholders. The overriding value in which all committee members shared was preservation of the city as an open, integrated community.

Results

Like search conferences, referent structures represent interventions at the appreciative level. They promote shared values among stakeholders and increased recognition of the interdependencies by which they are linked. Additionally, referent structures undertake the task of domain regulation beginning with "critical value judgements concerning the way in which the domain might best develop" (1, p. 25). The tasks of regulation include setting ground rules, determining membership, sustaining joint values, managing conflict, sanctioning activities, and mobilizing resources (1). Moreover, regulation ultimately implies definition of action steps and assignment of task responsibilities to carry out the jointly determined plans. Referent structures represent a more extensive and more collaborative strategy than the others we have examined in this chapter. The process by which regulation emerges requires extended membership and sustained participation to appreciate, plan, and take the actions necessary to create the stakeholders' desired future.

SELECTING AN INTERVENTION STRATEGY

So far we have examined the need for interorganizational collaboration and five strategies to promote it. Now we turn our attention to the selection of an appropriate strategy, or sequence of strategies, for a domain.

The strategies can be distinguished by the degree of collaboration they achieve. Problem setting, direction setting, and structuring are sequential phases that represent increasing degrees of collaboration. Of the five strategies we have examined, advocacy and diagnosis are primarily problem setting strategies.

Problem setting is concerned with identification of the stakeholders within a domain and mutual acknowledgment of the issue that joins them. "The primary objective of problem-setting is to give the situation an explicit form or identity that allows stakeholders to communicate about it and eventually act upon it" (8, p. 18). The importance of problem setting should not be underestimated. Unless some consensus is reached about who has a legitimate stake in an issue and exactly what that joint issue is, further attempts at collaboration will be thwarted. Advocacy promotes problem setting by focusing the attention of existing members of the domain in a direction they have previously ignored. It is also a vehicle by which previously unrecognized stakeholders achieve recognition as legitimate claimants in the issue. Diagnosis maps the interdependent relationships between organizations and makes these more explicit. Collaboration is achieved through appreciation of the interdependence that exists.

Problem setting also occurs during search conferences and network interventions, but these strategies can accomplish direction setting as well. In direction setting processes stakeholders articulate the values that guide their individual pursuits and begin to identify and appreciate a sense of common purpose. Direction setting gives life to the stakeholders' hopes that their desired ends can in fact be achieved. Networks establish informal coordination among stakeholders and promote an exchange of resources on which they are mutually interdependent. In search conferences participants engage in joint conceptualization of the desired future of the domain. Through this shared value search a collective mission or direction is cultivated.

Finally, the process of structuring is accomplished by referent structures. Through structuring stakeholders generate a system for sustaining their shared values and regulating their domain. Specific goals are set, tasks are elaborated, and roles are assigned to achieve the desired ends. Creation of a referent organization is the most comprehensive and complex of the five strategies, since collaboration is translated into action to create the desired interorganizational relations.

McCann (8) has suggested that these phases comprise a natural developmental sequence for a domain. Still, like any natural process, forces work to impede the cycle. At these points, interventions can stimulate the collaborative process. Since each strategy is designed to facilitate a particular stage of domain development, careful assessment is needed to determine what stage the system has reached before a strategy is selected. Some systems are more ready for collaboration than others. Readiness for collaboration is illustrated by the decision taken recently by a number of international banks to create a "bail out fund" on which any one of them could draw to prevent collapse from unexpected losses (38). Readiness to collaborate may be less evident among a network of social service agencies all vying for a fixed source of funds.

To determine a system's readiness for collaboration, five characteristics of the system need to be examined:

Interdependence Do the organizations share a domain around which they are sufficiently interdependent that intervention is worthwhile?

Legitimacy of the stakeholders To what degree are all the relevant stakeholders in the domain identified and recognized by the others?

Relative parity among the stakeholders To what extent do the stakeholders possess roughly equal capability to influence domain development?

Congruence of values To what extent do the stakeholders already share a common set of values and a similar sense of direction?

Need for regulation To what degree do the stakeholders need to regulate their activities more closely?

These five characteristics can be thought of as preconditions for collaboration. Specific preconditions can be identified for each strategy. (See Table 23.2) For example, if some groups within a domain are not perceived as legitimate, or if parity among stakeholders is not evident or easily achieveable, advocacy is the most appropriate strategy. This assumes of course that there is sufficient interdependence among these groups to warrant intervention in the first place. If all the stakeholders have legitimacy, but some are "more equal" than others, a diagnostic strategy might be useful. It could make more explicit the patterns of interdependence that do exist. Those groups which are more powerful, however, may resist diagnosis in order to preserve their advantage. In that case advocacy may be necessary.

If legitimacy and relative parity already exist, but value congruence

Table 23.2 Preconditions for Selecting a Strategy for Collaboration

Strategy	Interdependence in Shared Domain	Legitimacy of Stakeholders	Parity of Stakeholders	Value Congruence	Need for Regulation
Advocacy	√				
Diagnosis	√	√			
Search conference	√	√	√		
Networks	√	√	√	√	
Referent structures	√	√	√	√	√

is low, diagnosis or search conferences may be appropriate, since they can heighten and make explicit a sense of shared purpose. Once such an appreciation is gained, efforts to sustain it through mutual exchange of resources may be appropriate. At that stage network building would be a reasonable strategy. Finally, the need to more closely regulate the interactions of the domain would call for development of a referent organization.

Moreover, these strategies need not be mutually exclusive. A combination of two or more in sequence may make sense. For example, in the mortgage lending case, a successful advocacy strategy paved the way for the formation of a referent structure. Similarly, diagnosis could logically lead to a search conference, a network initiative, or the development of a referent structure.

The five strategies differ substantially from each other. An appreciation of the distinctions among them is not merely an exercise in logic. Rather judgment about the appropriate strategy for a specific interorganizational setting is a necessary prerequisite to intervention.

I have argued that collaboration is both desirable and necessary to the future of organizations in an increasingly complex technological society. The strategies introduced here for fostering interorganizational collaboration in many ways represent maiden voyages on unchartered waters. Substantial efforts by scholars, managers, and practitioners are needed to understand the circumstances in which such strategies are appropriate and to explore and refine them to encourage collaboration among organizations.

REFERENCES

1. Trist, E. Referent organizations and the development of interorganizational domains. Distinguished lecture to the Academy of Management, 39th Annual Convention, Atlanta, August 9, 1979.
2. Ashby, R. *Design for a Brain.* 2nd edition. London: Chapman and Hall, 1960.
3. McCann, J.E. & Ferry, D. The assessment and management of inter-unit interdependence. *Academy of Management Review,* January 1979, **4**, 113–119.

4. Ackoff, R.L. *Redesigning the Future.* New York: Wiley, 1974.

5. *Business Week,* June 30, 1980, 86–88.

6. Jamestown Area Labor Management Committee. *Commitment at Work.* Jamestown, N.Y., City Hall, 1977.

7. Ansoff, H.I. *Corporate Strategy.* New York: McGraw-Hill, 1965.

8. McCann, J.E. III. Developing interorganizational domains: Concepts and practice. Ph.D. Dissertation. Graduate group in Managerial Science and Applied Economics, University of Pennsylvania, August 1980.

9. Hirschman, A.O. *Exit, Voice and Loyalty: Responses to Decline in Firms, Organizations and States.* Cambridge, Mass.: Harvard University Press, 1970.

10. Alinsky, S. *Reveille for Radicals.* New York: Vintage Books, 1969.

11. Alinsky, S. *Rules for Radicals.* New York: Random House, 1971.

12. Kahn, S. *How People Get Power: Organizing Oppressed Communities for Action.* New York: McGraw-Hill, 1970.

13. Gamson, W.A. *The Strategy of Social Protest.* Homewood, Ill.: Dorsey Press, 1975.

14. Gricar, B.G. & Brown, L.D. Conflict, power and organization in a changing community. *Human Relations.* In press.

15. Tandon, R. Impact of organizational development in under-organized communities. Ph.D. dissertation, Department of Organizational Behavior, Case Western Reserve University, 1979.

16. Lehman, T. & Young, T.R. From conflict theory to conflict methodology: An emerging paradigm for sociology. *Sociological Inquiry,* 1975, **44**(1), 15–28.

17. Laue, J. Advocacy and sociology. In G.M. Weber and G.J. McCall (Eds.). *Social Scientists as Advocates: Views From Applied Disciplines.* Beverly Hills: Sage Publications, 1978.

18. Davidoff, P. Advocacy and pluralism in planning. *Journal of the American Institute for Planners,* 1965, **31**, 331–38.

19. Boje, D.M. The change agent as revolutionary: Activist interventions in interorganizational networks. Paper presented at the Academy of Management Meeting, Atlanta, August 9, 1979.

20. Baxter, J.D., Bennet, K.W., Black, I.G., Post, C.T., Regan R. & Weimer, G.A. Is government having a chilling effect on business' right to speak? *Iron Age,* October 23, 1978, 65–110.

21. Baumgartner, T. Buckley, W. Burns, T.R. & Schuster, P. Meta-power and the structuring of social hierarchies. In T. Burns & W. Buckley (Eds.). *Power and Control: Social Structures and Their Transformation.* Beverly Hills: Sage, 1976.

22. Alderfer, C.D. Boundary relations and organizational diagnosis: A conceptual statement. Paper presented to the District of Columbia Psychological Association, November 15, 1974.

23. Kaplan, R.E. Diagnosis in the interorganizational domain. Greensboro, N. C.: Center for Creative Leadership, 1980.

24. Levine, S. & White, P.E. Exchange as a conceptual framework for the study of interorganizational relationships. *Administrative Science Quarterly*, 1961, **5**, 583–601.

25. Tandon, R. & Brown, L.D. Interviews as catalysts in a community setting. *Journal of Applied Psychology*, 1978, **63**, 197–205.

26. Sarason, S. & Lorentz, E. *The Resource Exchange Network.* San Francisco: Jossey-Bass, 1979.

27. Weick, K.E. Educational organizations as loosely coupled systems. *Administrative Science Quarterly*, 1976, **21**, 1–19.

28. Emery, F.E. *Futures We Are In.* Leiden, The Netherlands: Martinus Nijhoff, 1977.

29. Whetten, D.A. & Leung, T.K. The instrumental value of interorganizational relations: Antecedents and consequences of linkage formation. *Academy of Management Journal*, 1979, **22**, 325–344.

30. Benson, J.K. The interorganizational network as a political economy. *Administrative Science Quarterly,* 1975, **20**, 229–249.

31. Whetten, D.A. & Aldrich, H. Organization set size and diversity: Links between people processing organizations and their environments. *Administration and Society*, 1979.

32. Emery, M. & Emery, F.E. Searching: For new directions, in new ways . . . for new times. *Management Handbook for Public Administrators.* J. Sutherland (Ed.). New York: Van Nostrand Reinhold, 1978.

33. Gilmore, T. Weiss, H. & Williams, T. Western search conference on the jail of the future: A record of the session. Working paper, Management and Behavioral Science Center, The Wharton School, University of Pennsylvania, November 21, 1979.

34. Williams, T.A. The search conference as a methodology of active adaptive planning. Working paper, The University of Western Australia.

35. Warren, R. The interorganizational field as a focus for investigation. *Administrative Science Quarterly*, 1967, **12**, 397–419.

36. Trist, E. A concept of organizational ecology. *The Australian Journal of Management*, 1977, **2**, 171–175.

37. Emery, F.E. *Adaptive systems for our future governance.* National Labor Institute Bulletin, No. 4, New Delhi, India, 1976.

38. *New York Times*, June 9, 1980.

—24—

Humanizing Technology

Arthur D. Shulman

INTRODUCTION

People involved in technological advance have all too often assumed that human improvement followed from it. With the passing of time it has become increasingly clear that technological advance frequently has introduced dehumanizing factors. Given the central role that technology plays, any serious efforts to make organizations humane must find ways to humanize the effects of technology and technological change.

Before considering the humanizing of technology I would like to provide a framework for understanding what technology is and describe the technological process in five interdependent phases. These are:

Phase I The decision to employ a new procedure, device or product.

Phase II The implementation of the new procedure, device or product.

Phase III The development and maintenance of standard operating procedures.

Phase IV Innovations.

Phase V Disengagement.

I then present five major themes that characterize positions managers take towards technology. These positions are: technologist, elitist, progressive pragmatist, pluralist, and devolutionist. Next follows an integration of these positions in terms of what a humanistically oriented manager might take as his or her responsibility. This final section emphasizes the need for managers to consider people in the context of technological as well as societal, legislative, organizational, and individual constraints.

Throughout this chapter I will be drawing most of my examples from computer-based technologies involving the acquisition, collection, and transfer of information. These technologies, like previous ones, increase standardization, but in addition they are creating configurations that are self-controlling. A key feature of these more recent technologies is the sub-

This chapter has benefited from comments made on a prior draft by L. S. Rosenman, A. J. Wearing, and H. Meltzer.

stitution of a machine for the intellectual power of humans. I have chosen these technologies because almost all managers today make decisions in which computerized information is used. Hence for managers, this one field is probably the most widely relevant. Second, the information sector is now the largest growth sector in the major Western societies. Over 50 percent of the Gross National Product of these societies are now being generated by corporations whose major business is information acquisition, processing, and transfer. Third, examples are taken from this area because it is the one most studied by those scientists and humanists who are concerned with technological impact.

What is Technology?

For humanistically minded managers, as well as those working with them, a necessary but not sufficient condition is to know what technology is. Lexical definitions emphasize that technology is *not* an object or device. Technology is the totality of systematic processes and specifications that comprise the which, how, when, where, and who of access to a particular device or product.

The Phases of Technological Processes

Following this definition of technology, Alex Wearing, Craig Lonsdale, and I (1) have developed a framework that portrays technology as the totality of systematic processes. This framework is illustrated in Figure 24.10.

In the first phase, the *decision to change* a procedure or device, I assume that there are technologies in use and for one reason or another (usually related to profit maximization, at least within our society) a decision is made to invest in a new one. The questions on which decisions must be made here are: which ones, when, and where.

The second phase, the *implementation* phase, entails decisions about who will install the new facilities, and how they will be used. For instance, questions that are often raised during this phase include: (a) whether new staff will be brought in from outside or existing staff used; (b) who will operate it; and (c) who will train the operators. Included here are the anticipations of such decisions as well as the decisions themselves (2).

The third phase, the *development and maintenance* phase, occurs after people have been selected and have learned to use the procedure or device for the intended purpose. During this phase a standard operating procedure evolves.

The fourth phase, *innovation,* corresponds to Hiltz and Turoff's (3) insight phase in which the users of the procedure or device, after gaining an understanding of the general concept of the technology, make at least limited use of it for additional purposes other than for what it was originally planned. It becomes a servant rather than a controller of their thinking and action.

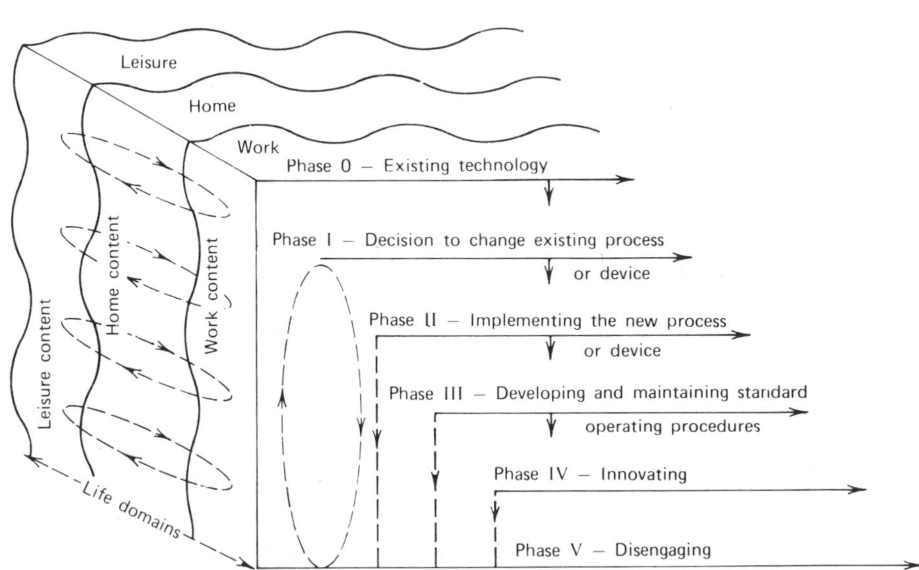

Figure 24.1 Normal progression is from phases 0 to IV. However, disengaging can occur at each phase, and is influenced by direct interaction with experiences with other life domains. Such interaction is documented in the figure by the presence of feedback loops across the life domains for each of the phases.

Normally Phases I through III come into being in order to reach an old goal better. That is, a new technology is brought in as a substitute for an existing one. In the fourth phase, new goals and new applications evolve, sometimes accidentally, sometimes with forethought. There are at least two distinct reasons for the emergence of these innovations. First, intrinsic aspects of the new technology going through the Phases I through III leads to time (which is profit) being saved. This time saved by the new technology can be invested in the pursuit of new goals. Second, the implementation of the new technology from Phases I through III leads the manager to recognize that the capital expenditure involved requires new deployment of the technology. Thus, as Mowshowitz (4) points out, a curious phenomenon is often seen here. Once procedures or devices are selected and brought in to do an existing job through substitution of technologies, then, if not before, more energy is spent in generating a new goal that might justify any capital cost of the procedures or devices. This second rationale is being activated in increasing frequency.

Figure 24.2 illustrates substitution and generation approaches, one being goal driven, the other being technologically driven. These approaches are

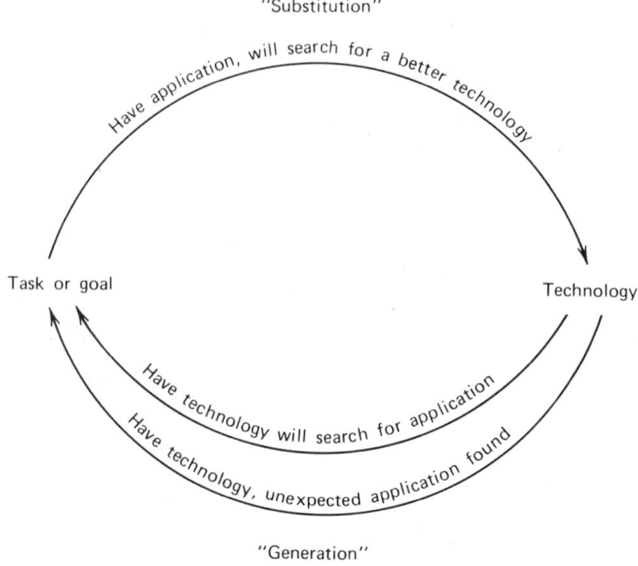

Figure 24.2 Technological input substitution versus generation perspectives.

often presented as being opposite to one another; as explained above they are not. In actuality, they are phase-cycle related.

The last phase is the *disengagement* phase. Unlike the other phases, which normally follow consecutively, this disengagement phase is one that occurs concurrently with all the others. Because of an individual's and an organization's limited capacity for doing X number of things at once, involvement in new processes leads to disengagement from existing ones. The disengagement phase also represents the fact that as we participate in the other four phases, we are at the same time directly affecting our involvement in other technologies. Whether or not managers choose to become aware of the impact of a new technology on workers whose skills were developed for existing technologies, differentiates the humanistically oriented from the purely technical manager.

The technological process phase model also has a third dimension that has been labeled "contextual domain." This third dimension is a spatial dimension and is included to illustrate that what one does on one contextual domain, at work for instance, will also affect what one does in another contextual domain, such as at home.

FIVE MANAGERIAL POSITIONS ON TECHNOLOGY

Mowshowitz (4), in his excellent critique of biases in research on social issues in computing, identified five positions that seem to reflect major streams of contemporary social thought. I use these five positions to illustrate the positions that managers take with regard to their involvement in the five technological process phases that were presented in the previous section. These positions are neither mutually exclusive, nor exhaustive, and I suspect that every manager will see some of their values reflected in more than one of them.

Manager as Technologist

This view holds that technologies are instruments of progress. The success or failure of a particular application of the instrument is defined by the technologist-manager in terms of systems design and implementation. Any changes affecting people, for example, informal networks or changes in tasks or positions, are regarded as organizational changes and external to the technology. The effects on and of workers are treated as independent of the technology. Interestingly, people who take this view towards technology often believe that the goals of the enterprise are best reached if a laissez-faire (5) principle is followed. The assumption is that people will quickly adapt to new opportunity and turn it to their advantage. As pointed out by Mowshowitz (4), people who hold such views mix optimism and the entrepreneurial spirit with the engineering tradition. "The result is a thoroughly positive outlook . . . and boundless confidence in individual initiative." Associated with this commitment to *homo technicus* is a sneaking suspicion that human factors and human-machine interaction research is a less than hardheaded catering to human weakness, to those who lack the right stuff and true grit. When such human factoring does occur under the direction of the technologist, it is often done as a cosmetic in order to prevent costly legal settlements associated with poor design features, such as dials that could not be read easily, or screens that increase the incidence of eye strain.

The Technologists' Position during Each of the Technological Process Phases. During the first phase, that of the decision to choose a particular procedure or device, no attention is usually given by such managers to any effect that technology may have on workers or consumers other than in terms of maximizing profits.

Often managers of this ilk will hold that decisions to bring in new processes are properly made by others. Even less will they consider that those who might be affected by them should be consulted. Rather the choice is regarded as purely technical and belongs to the technical expert or engineer. Throughout this first phase, then, such managers believe the best policy is not to involve the workers in such decisions.

It is during the second implementation phase, however, that technologists regard attention to worker-interface with the new procedure or device as sometimes necessary as a face-saving and profit-making activity. From this position, managers would argue that if productivity and worker satisfaction are related in attitude toward work and the workers' attitudes are influenced by the degree to which they perceive they can control the conditions under which they work, it is in the manager's interest for it to appear that workers are involved in this design and implementation phase. In my experience, I have found managers who take this view, often invoking what may *appear* to be participatory decision making in order to sell to workers a decision already made by management. It is within this second stage, in which the implementation process is being decided upon, that the following technologist position has been recommended (by at least one management journal) to achieve maximum profit. According to this position (6), after you have your computerized hardware chosen and installed, the next step is to program the software. What a manager needs to do is to take the better buyers (for instance) and have them sit down with the computer programmers and tell them what they normally do and what are the detailed steps they normally perform in carrying out their duties. Then the journal suggests that managers should have the various members of the buying force specify as many steps as they can; in that way the programmer can write the necessary program to eliminate, or at least speed up, these activities. One manager of a large retail corporation told me that suddenly he found his best buyers were not cooperating but sabotaging the operation by giving false information. Similar resistance from the work force and from management level staff itself has been noticed when their various duties have been stripped away and replaced by the new technology. Documentation of this occurring during the implementation and learning phase can be found in Zagursky's (7) account of the problems faced by Florida Power and Light Company when implementing their Management Information System. The incidence of such sabotage has been used by some (but not all) technologist managers to further support the reliance on procedures or devices, for replacing unreliable people. For such managers, the downgrading of jobs is separate from the technological progress, but when it does occur, it can facilitate the easy removal of troublesome workers.

During the innovation phase, such managers encourage individual innovation. These managers believe that this is best done by leaving the workers alone. Given time, workers will find new uses for the process, which will lead to more profits and maybe, as a by-product, more jobs. Just as job downgrading is not necessarily part of the technologist's perspective, neither is job creation. Such aspects are regarded as independent of technology.

Disengagements from nonprofitable procedures and devices are desirable and evaluated purely on economic grounds. Disengagement of people and separation of people from practicing their crafts and skills previously learned is normally not an issue for the manager as technologist. While a "pure" technologist would only be driven by the economic imperative, management examples of this are often confounded with other basic drives. The following example of this comes from a conversation overheard by Clark (8), in which a lawyer explains why he is putting in word processing equipment in his firm: "I'll get rid of half of my staff and will keep the prettier ones to run the machines and to perv on." I suspect and hope that this type of degradation is the exception. The fact remains, however, that downgrading and cutting of staff are most prevalent among both clerical and routine computer staff in small service firms that follow an economic determinism principle (9). Though not to the same extent, similar downgrading and underutilization of skills has also been reported of computer personnel who were in large firms (10). Again, such personnel concerns, even if they were positive, would not be associated with technology by the technologist.

The Manager as Technological Elitist

This type of manager has much in common with the technologist. Both believe in the ultimate benefits to all through technological advancement. The ultimate goal is efficient productivity. But unlike the technologist, who believes in a laissez-faire principle and will use subterfuge, the elitist takes the position that strong formal control mechanisms are necessary to have procedures or devices produce in a rational manner. Only the use of hierarchical structures will maintain this control. Without rational design and monitoring, the technology will not be used to maximum utility. Such monitoring needs the cooperation of subordinates, which may best be had through avoiding subterfuge. Managers as technological elitists follow Simon's (11) rational decision making principles. To the elitist, as with the technologist, the task of reaching corporate goals under managerial control is given and nonnegotiable.

The Technological Elitist Position during Each Technological Process Phase. With regard to the five technological process phases, decisions of which procedure or device (phase I), when, to whom, and how the processes (phase II), are to be introduced, are the manager's. Decisions during these phases are intended to maximize what the technology does best and what the human being does best (12). Such decisions should be based on the information available, often sought from experts on the likely problems one might incur in time delay, availability of components, human capability, and so on. New processes themselves must contain procedures with further orderly control and monitoring. Processes using Management Information Systems (M.I.S.), which encourage upward flow of information and quick distribution of managerial commands, are perferred. Usually those technologies that promise to be more efficient at increasing the current upward flow (i.e., substitution) are chosen. A review of such computer based communication technologies under this substitution model is provided in Shulman and Steinman (13).

During Phases II and III, the programming aspect of computer-based technologies is most attractive for the elitist, for it leads to relatively easy control and monitoring of others' work. During Phase IV, the generation of alternative use of the process is welcomed and encouraged by the elitist, as long as it does not interfere with the existing orderliness and leads to more rational design. Similarly, it is becoming more of a common practice for the elitist manager to avoid workers' dissatisfactions (14), which might negatively affect rational planning and increase costs. A prevalent scheme being practiced by such elitists is to allow a work group very limited say in how they will organize their work around the new procedure or device. Often quality circles are given this responsibility. Under the elitist, employees have virtually no say in determining objectives, or what, where, or when technologies are introduced. This power is well confined to inputs on how better to use the procedure or device.

Questions of disengagement of people from other processes are recognized by the elitist as aspects of new technologies that must be planned for in a rational manner. Likewise, workers' dissatisfactions (14) need to be considered in a cost/profit equation.

The Manager as the Progressive Pragmatist

The manager as pragmatist takes a view that the introduction and use of new procedures or devices constrain individual workers' choices of alternatives. This person often acts in a benevolent manner to those beneath him or her. Negative consequences other than those directly bearing on the economic issue are of importance, if not equal importance, to the pragmatist. The economic is not the only imperative; there are other more humanistic ones. Such a manager might request help from one of the new breed of pragmatically oriented ergonomics people as described in Fraser (15), who are indicating their desire to design new technologies so that values other than that of optimizing efficiency and productivity are concerned.

The Progressive Pragmatist Position during Each Technological Process Phase. With regard to the five phases, pragmatists, as those following the two previous positions, believe that it is their obligation and right to have a major say for choosing a proper procedure or device that will not negatively affect profits. However, such people also take into consideration what aspects might negatively affect workers and others. They see it within their responsibility to shelter and protect the worker. This type of manager will therefore choose between technologies that might best achieve all the goals that he or she views as important, and will most likely use the actual introduction of a new procedure, or device (Phase II) to achieve yet other goals including the reorganization of the corporation. The pragmatist believes that during Phase II, it may be necessary to reorganize the organization to smooth out any problems that may have accompanied the introduction of new procedures. One such problem common to firms using M.I.S. and computerized facilities for message transfer is the extension of working hours (16). The reduction of clerical staff and middle management has also been noted by Sullivan et al. (9), Clark (8), and Zagursky (7). The progressive pragmatist holds the optimistic view that he or she will control the technology and its effect through positive action.

During the phase of developing standard operating procedures (Phase III), the pragmatist will be most observant of what he or she believes are potential negative effects. This is in contrast to managers in the previous two categories, in which negative effects were only considered in terms of cost on productivity.

The pragmatist's view during the innovation phase is to encourage at least small innovations, particularly those that may come from the peeople directly involved with the procedures or devices. New goals may also emerge at this stage and be followed under the guidance of the pragmatist.

Usually, but not always, disengagement is accomplished in a manner in which an attempt is made to lessen the discrepancy in power distribution between the haves and have-nots. This is not always perceived in the same way that the workers themselves may see it, since the pragmatist also sees his or her responsibility to determine which values are to be followed.

The Pluralist Manager

This type of management recognizes that technologies may be either good or bad, but believes that they are ultimately controllable and so do not necessarily pose a threat to the individual's well-being. But unlike the pragmatist, the pluralist sees decisions regarding new processes not as management decisions but rather as a product of democratic negotiation of all parties involved. The manager's role is seen within this sociopolitical context as being one of actively coordinating the various interest groups in their negotiations. Government representation, when involved in this configuration, is often concerned with the introduction of controls that are intended to provide open access to information and at the same time protect individuals' privacy and autonomy. Management's adoption of this view was possibly at its highest in North America in the late 1950s and early 1960s, when there was a hope that the new computer based technologies would lead to a more equal distribution of information and thus decision making. Galbraith's (17) vertical information system is but one example of this. Despite the fact that such democratization has been legislated into the organizational structure in some European and Middle Eastern countries, such democratization and accompanying decentralization has not been realized. This is still the case even following the Lordstown strike and the report "Work in America" (18), where this effect was evidenced in experiments attempting to redefine industrial occupations and encourage worker participation in what had been traditionally management tasks (19). Similarly, the introduction of new computerized information systems seems to affect existing power relationships mainly by strengthening them (20, 21). In slightly different contexts Bluestone (22, 23) reports that such attempts at democratizationn most often have ended up in power grabs involving confrontation rather than meaningful negotiation.

The Pluralist Position during the Technological Process Phases. Within the context of the five technological process phases, the pluralist's job during the first two phases (and every other phase) is to bring together the views of all potential interest groups. It is recognized at this stage that resources are scarce and that negotiation is needed to develop consensus. During the third or standard operating phase, the pluralist manager sees as his or her job the reporting to all parties involved on whether or not the various safety procedures and compensatory mechanisms are working as the technology becomes implanted. The pluralist would encourage further development of the technology as long as it did not preclude facilitating democratic involvement. A pluralist manager would have no qualms about negotiating the legal, regulatory, and security safeguards that may be necessary to resolve conflicts between the special interest groups. Such has been the case in the 1960s and 1970s in the United States and elsewhere where freedom of information legislation has been enacted.

Disengagement decisions would also involve negotiations of all parties, with the pluralist manager being the active coordinator of such decisions.

The Manager as Devolutionist

The manager who is a devolutionist takes a more macro approach in identifying factors that are affecting and constraining human potential. These managers take the view that they can have little control of technological processes, not because it should be this way, but because of a strong belief in the technological imperative. Here technology itself is recognized as a dynamic social force. Decisions made by multinationals as to which products are to be developed, where and when they are to be made available, and so on, lock management into being managed by technology. Technology-plant investment decisions made 10 or more years ago are likely to determine the technologies in use today and will continue to do so. Lewis Mumford (24), for one, is an exponent of this position. He suggests that technology has led to the creation of mega-technical systems, whose very size and complexity makes them outside of human control. A manager taking this perspective would look on alleged autonomy of workers as an illusion. In effect, devolutionists assert, as does Mowshowitz (4), that we have become enslaved by our own sociotechnical creations, and that through the action of our prodigious powers of rationalization, we have compromised the ability to see the true nature of our condition.

Thus such managers are faced with the dilemma of recognizing that they are expected to understand a technology that has become so complex that it is not possible to understand how it works, and to control it, knowing that their actions are being dictated more and more by the immediate technological imperatives. These immediate imperatives for the devolutionist are special interest groups. Weizenbaum (25, 26) and Mowshowitz (4) identify such groups as political parties, government agencies, stockholders, trade unions, and so on. The devolutionist, like the pluralist, believes that the act of participation of such groups in the decision making is necessary in order to have equity in the use of technology. But the devolutionists do not believe it is sufficient. Rather there is a need for redistribution of power based on reallocation of social functioning to guarantee socially as well as economically beneficial use of technology.

The Devolutionist Position during the Technological Process Phases. In terms of the five phases, the devolutionist manager would attempt to raise fundamental questions as to the functions actually served by the procedure or device. For instance, Rule (27) suggests that data management systems are mainly used for monitoring the behavior of individuals so that such behavior can be controlled. The cost of such surveillance is individual freedom. Such managers would attempt to have the community of interest bring about alternative social arrangements that place more responsibility on the participating groups, rather than using technical methods. Like the pluralists, they would initially act as catalysts to all parties concerned. But whereas the pluralist would encourage the use of legal, governmental solutions to address the issues raised in either decisions to employ new procedures or devices, or the development of standard operating procedures, the devolutionist as manager would not seek legal or government decisions. This person would argue that such decisions are political and will change with those in power. For instance, such is the case with various safeguards now legislated with regard to consumer access to files on them. The computer based technologies have the continuing built-in potential for *always* providing such confidential information to others. Since the current freedom of information laws are subject to change with a new government, the only way to permanently prevent their misuse is not to collect such data in the first place. For devolutionists as managers, it is their job to continually recognize and inform others of such potential misuse. Such misuse is becoming widely recognized; as a recent survey of 100 individuals in 13 organizations in North America has shown, such potential for misuse of computerized systems is a major concern (28).

It is difficult to pinpoint what the devolutionist's managerial role would be in the remaining four phases as most of the damage is done by just bringing in the new set of procedures or devices. According to this position, attempts at redressing the constraints inherent in the technology through work circles and other such means are illusions. In general, from this perspective, what such managers need is to become aware of: (a) the long-term manner in which the technology constricts human freedom; (b) the fluidity of the sociopolitical context, which may be called upon to control it; and (c) the necessity of making sure all others are also aware.

THE HUMANIST MANAGER'S POSITION ON TECHNOLOGY

What then is the humanist position on technology? First, it is one that explicitly recognizes that technological decisions are value based. The values that humanist managers would espouse openly would be that the decisions and actions on technology must not, in either the short or the long term, seriously restrict the capability of all individuals from achieving self worth through awareness, choice, and intentionality.

Second, it recognizes the necessity of an economic security, but does not follow the economic imperative further, nor does it attempt to equalize economic goals with social value attainment. Rather it recognizes that: (a) an adequate economic base is necessary for maintaining corporate viability; but (b) there is a point at which maximization of profit must yield to the attainment of more highly valued humanistic goals. A similar humanistic view has been voiced by Nord (29) in his exchange with Locke (30), and is congruent with current knowledge about worker motivation. For instance, Inkson (31) has found that from the workers' perspective, an adequate economic base is the main reason people are attracted to a particular position. Their job satisfaction is more a function of the degree to which the technologies facilitate working with others, while maintaining autonomy and responsibility.

Third, this position is constraint based. Like devolutionists, humanistically oriented managers see their responsibility to recognize the social, political, organizational, as well as technologically based constraints that are managing in operating. As Blau, Falbe, McKinley, and Tracey (32) have pointed out, such societal, political, and technological forces are interactive and in a state of flux. It is the understanding and appreciation for continuing monitoring of these interactive forces that is practiced by the humanists. The humanist is not an autonomist but rather a gestaltist in this endeavor.

Fourth, such managers recognize that each person has different abilities. In part because of this, these managers, unlike pluralists, seek and encourage input from others in a selective manner. Furthermore, like devolutionists, these managers explicitly recognize how each person's values (which are not necessarily rational), including their own, underlies differences of opinion among experts from whom this input is sought. Giorgi (33) in a slightly different context has made a similar point. It is only when one's values are explicitly included in decision making that a manager is acting in the humanistic manner. I have labeled this "informed honesty."

Fifth, the humanistically oriented manager in practicing "informed honesty" attempts to see realistically what can and can't be done with a new technology in furthering humanistic values. Awareness of mega-technology constraints are openly shared with others. Such a person recognizes and appreciates that this behavior does not consistently follow that of a rational planner in control of events, and can be better described as that of a frenetic juggler (34). This is not a desired state, but a realistic one.

The Humanistic Position during the Technological Process Phases

With regard to the first phase, that of making decisions to engage in a new procedure or device, the humanistic manager would consider first the ramifications of such a change with regard not only to maintaining an adequate level of economic security, but also to its short and long term potential for constraining the choice, self-esteem, and general well-being of the employees and customers. As pointed out above, such decisions would not necessarily be made in a democratic manner. Most often, though, the power for such decisions by the manager would be arrived at through consensus. As with the elitist, the pragmatist, and devolutionist, informed opinions are selectively sought from those within society having some expertise. Unlike the elitist, however, who would seek such opinions and try to balance economic and social values, the humanist manager would use the experts to become informed about the potential constraints, either good or bad, that a particular technology might have on the quality of life. Values of stockholders, workers, and customers would be openly sought. Where work circles are to be employed, during this first phase, it would be explicitly as advisors and not as decision makers, unless they actually held the power to decide. Throughout this and all other phases, the manager would explicitly state his or her values and act with informed honesty.

During the second phase, the humanistically oriented manager would also take into consideration how procedures or devices can be implemented in such a manner that build upon, rather than replace the skills learned and valued by staff. Job enrichment would not be jeopardized. If for this reason alone, staff representations that utilized their expertise would be actively sought. It is during this phase that all staff would be given a full rationale for change and the benefits to them. This procedure has been found in at least one case to be mandatory for the acceptance of use of a new computerized technology in a clinical setting (35). During this implementation stage, further consideration would be given to results, if any, of prior social audits that had been conducted elsewhere. If no audit was available, a new one would commence immediately. Such social audits would consider what social effects these procedures or devices might have on individuals both on and off the job.

For instance, questions would be raised, and information collected on whether the technology led to increasing stress that might not affect the person on the job, but would be carried into the home environment. Or, would the use of a visual display unit at work lead to eye strain if the person also watched television at home? Another likely question is, does the procedure or device prevent face-to-face contact while on the job, and does this lead to miscommunications among people? What might happen has been demonstrated in one study of crisis management in which a computer conferencing facility was used to hold meetings that had previously been allocated to be held face-to-face. The researcher McKendree (36) found that under the new system, message turn-around coordination that did occur was at the cost of increased misunderstandings, increased passivity on the part of the participants, and rather expensive training and orientation costs. The need to maintain and conduct meaningful relationships, which is embedded in the above example, has been regarded by some humanists as a necessary but not sufficient condition for self actualization. Perhaps as Glass (37) and other humanistically oriented sociologists suggest, the establishment and maintenance of relationships is in itself the acme of human development (see 38 for further discussions on this as an alternative to self-actualization as the highest level of humanistic attainment).

During the standard operating phase, the humanistically oriented manager would probably act in a similar manner to the pragmatist. The people with the most expertise that need to be consulted are probably the workers themselves. The involvement of the workers is important, particularly to insure that they are consciously given as much choice as possible so that they can control the outcomes of their own activities. Without this, people do become alienated. However, this control must be real, and the extent of this control is dependent upon the technology chosen during the first two phases. One of management's responsibilities is to have people themselves monitor potential harmful effects, whether they are direct or indirect (39).

To further this end, work circles may be employed, but with the manager clearly having negotiated and then stated the scope of the group's responsibilities. As Herzberg (29) and others have indicated, it is important to provide within such a scheme a system of rewards and advancements that is necessarily attached to the enactment of the responsibilities assigned to this group. As a practical tool, the systematic use of a job diagnostic survey has been helpful in documenting some of the secondary effects of computerization on personnel (40). My own observations on the use of advanced telecommunication systems and computer conferencing equipment has shown that during this phase, such systems are being used more and more to hold dialogues among staff that used to be held face-to-face. Such systems are extremely good for the exchange of standardized messages. However, with prolonged use and without compensatory face-to-face meetings, the act of holding such interactions leads to stress within the people involved in the now dehumanized contact situation.

During the next phase, innovation is to be encouraged. The criterion employed for evaluating and rewarding such activities is not profit, as the technologist and the elitist would have it. Rather innovation is encouraged as an act of creating or actualizing the potential of people. Though at times difficult, it is the manager's job to help establish the availability of resources (time and the procedures or devices) to those within the organization who might express such creativity. Explicit recognition would be offered by such managers to employees for finding ways in which the processes can be employed for furthering human dignity.

DISENGAGEMENT PHASE

Many of the problems of staff switching over to a new technology have already been covered in previous sections, but little attention has been given to the disengagement of people. The humanistic manager would recognize that at least as much attention as normally goes into personnel selection and then into staff maintenance needs to go into disengagement. As death is taboo as a topic in our society, so it appears is termination of staff by management. As examination of management textbooks reveals that this topic is given little space. In realtiy, a humanist must face the fact that despite the best of intentions, managers have a responsibility of making decisions regarding staff, some of which will require them to eventually dismiss or release some of their employees. More of this will happen with new technologies that cut down staff requirements. The pluralist and the devolutionist might try to rearrange schedules, allow job sharing, shorter work weeks, and so on. So might a humanistically oriented manager. Disengagement is real. As a humanist it needs to be handled with informed honesty and compassion. In this way managers can keep their dignity, and so can the people who they have the responsibility for letting go.

CONCLUDING COMMENTS

The purpose of this chapter was to provide a framework from which managers can clearly see issues of technology as management issues for humanization. The framework described five phases of the technological process and presented the issues that arise during each of these phases from six different managerial viewpoints, only one of which was a consistently humanistic one. While specific tools such as social audits or work circles were mentioned in this context, the focus of this chapter was not on tools or gadgets, but on the manner in which managers consider their responsibilities across all five phases of the technological process.

In examples which I used in this chapter, I have tended to draw more attention to the negative aspects of technology than the positive ones. This is a bias that the reader will find throughout the technological impact literature. Little attention is given to what others do right. Furthermore, no attempt was made to provide a comprehensive list of references that document the societal-organizational and individual impact of new technologies. I avoided this because the few comprehensive studies that do exist until recently have not given much attention to humanistic issues. Most were driven by an economic imperative, and hence do not address most of the issues raised with this chapter (for exceptions see 40). Most importantly, such reviews, while being useful as tools for the manager, are not substitutes for observing and monitoring the effects that a specific technology might have, given the changing organizational and societal constraints operating in and out of a particular corporation.

The moral issue of what is right and what is wrong for the behavior of managers is a major theme throughout this chapter, and for that matter throughout this handbook. Counting the humanistic position, six positions were presented herewith that the reader could identify. It was my purpose and now my hope that by presenting these alternative viewpoints, managers will now constructively question the appropriateness of their decisions regarding the scope and direction of the technologies they employ.

Our awareness of technical impacts is in its infancy, but our knowledge is expanding quickly. While it is a challenge for a manager to keep up with such changes, I believe that there is little choice if one wants a management that is humanistic.

REFERENCES

1. Shulman, A.D. Wearing, A. & Lonsdale, C. Network frames for analysis of social impact of telecommunication systems. Invited address; Kuring-gai College of Advanced Education, Sydney, Australia. June 1980.
2. Billings, R.S. Klimoski, R.J. & Breavgh, J.A. The impact of a change in technology on job characteristics—A quasi-experiment. *Administrative Science Quarterly,* June 1977, **22**, 318–339.
3. Hiltz, S.R. & Turoff, M. Four phases of user development. *The Network Nation.* Reading, Mass.: Addison-Wesley, 1978, pp. 345–346.
4. Mowshowitz, A. On approaches to the study of social issues in computers. *Information Technology and Human Affairs* (in press).
5. McDermott, J. Technology: The opiate of the intellectuals. *New York Review of Books,* July 31, 1969, 13.
6. Introducing a computer with a minimum of fuss. *Rydge's*, February 1980, **53**, 34-36.
7. Zagursky, G.P. Management information system: An engineer's friend or foe. *Joint Engineering Management Conference*, New York: I.E.E.E. Inc., 1978.
8. Clark, A. A sacking chauvinist says "Serve 'em right." *The Age.* Computer Section. March 18, 1980, pp. 37.
9. Sullivan, T.A. & Cornfield, D.B. Downgrading computer workers: Evidence from occupational and industrial redistribution. *Sociology of Work and Occupations,* May 1979, **6**, 184–203.
10. Loeske, D.R. & Sonquist, J.A. The computer worker in the labor force. *Sociology of Work and Occupations*, 1979, **6**, (2), 156–183.
11. Simon, H.A. *The Shape of Automation for Men and Management.* New York: Harper and Row, 1965.
12. Beyond DP: The social implications. *Datamation,* July 1979, 98–102.

13. Shulman, A.D. & Steinman, J.I. Interpersonal tele-conferencing in an organizational context. In M.C.J. Melton, W.A. Lucas, D.W. Conrath (Eds.), *Evaluating New Telecommunications Services.* New York: Plenum Press, 1978.

14. Herzberg, F. *Work and the Nature of Man.* New York: World Publishing, 1966.

15. Fraser, T.M. Job satisfaction and work humanization: Expanding role for ergonomics. *Ergonomics*, 1978, **21**(1), 11-19.

16. Vallee, J. & Gibbs, B. Distributed management of scientific projects: An analysis of two computer-conferencing experiments at NASA. *Telecommunications Policy,* December 1976, 75–85.

17. Galbraith, J.R. *Designing Complex Organizations.* Reading, Mass.: Addison-Wesley, 1973.

18. O'Toole, J. *Work in America: Report of a Special Task Force to the Secretary of Health, Education and Welfare.* Cambridge, Mass.: MIT Press, 1973.

19. Nelson, D. A review of a matter of dignity: Inquiries into the humanization of work. Heisler, W.J. & Houch, J.W. (Eds.). *Technology and Culture,* **20**, 1979, 670–672.

20. Leduc, N.F. Communicating through computers: Impact on a small business group. *Telecommunications Policy,* September 1979, 235–244.

21. Robey, D. Computers and management structure: Some empirical findings reexamined. *Human Relations*, 1977, **30**, (11), 963–976.

22. Heisler, J. & Houck, J.W. *A Matter of Dignity: Inquiries into the Humanization of Work.* South Bend, Inc. University of Notre Dame Press, 1977, pp. x + 214.

23. Herzberg, F. New perspectives on the will to work. *Personnel Administration,* 1979, **24**, 72–76.

24. Mumford, L. *The Myth of the Machine: I. Technics and Human Development.* New York: Harcourt Brace Jovanovich, 1967.

25. Weizenbaum, J. *Computer Power and Human Reason: From Judgment to Calculation.* San Francisco: W.H. Freeman, 1976.

26. Weizenbaum, J. Human choice in the interstices of the megamachine. In A. Mowshowitz (Ed.). *Human Choice and Computers 2.* Amsterdam: North-Holland, 1980.

27. Rule, J.B. Preserving individual privacy in an information-oriented society. In L.J. Hoffman (Ed.). *Computers and Privacy in the Next Decade.* New York: Academic Press, 1980.

28. Edwards, G.C. Organizational impacts of office automation. *Telecommunication Policy,* June 1978, 128–136.

29. Nord, W. Job satisfaction reconsidered. *American Psychologist,* 1978, **33**, 855–856.

30. Locke, E.A. Job satisfaction reconsidered. *American Psychologist,* 1978, **33**, 854–855.

31. Inkson, J.H.K. Worker attitudes: An empirical study of the technology thesis. *Journal of Industrial Relations*, 1977, **19**, 241–254.

32. Blau, P.M. Falbe, C.M. McKenley, W. & Tracy, P.K. Technology and organization in manufacturing. *Administrative Science Quarterly*, 1976, **21**, 20–39.

33. Georgi, A. *Psychology as a Human Science: A Phenomenologically Based Approach.* New York: Harper, 1970.

34. Mintzberg, H. The manager's job: Folklore and fact. *Harvard Business Review*, 1975, **53**(4), 49-61.

35. Johnson, J.H. Williams, T.A. Giannetti, R.A. Klingler, D.E. & Naka shima, S.R. Organizational preparedness for change: Staff acceptance of an on-line computer-assisted assessment system. *Behavior Research Methods and Instrumentation*, 1978, **10**(2), 186–190.

36. McKendree, J.D. Project and crisis management: Application of computerized conferencing. *Bulletin of the American Society for Information Service*, 1978, **4**(5), 13–14.

37. Glass, J.F. The humanistic challenge to sociology. *Journal of Humanistic Psychology*, 1971, **11**(1), 170–183.

38. Nord, W. A Marxist critique of humanistic psychology. *Journal of Transpersonal Psychology*, 1977, **17**(1), 75–83.

39. Ronagone, J. A critical appraisal of technology assessment methodology. In Myers, R.H. (Ed.). *Technological Changes in Australia.* Vol. 4, Canberra: Australian Government Publishing Service, 1980, pp. 405–428.

40. Kling, R. Social analyses of computing: Theoretical perspectives in recent empirical research. *Computing Surveys*, March 1980, **12**,(1).

—25—

Effective Settings for Making Organizations Humane and Productive

Stephen Jenks

In recent years, more and more attention has been paid to the areas of productivity and quality of work life (QWL). In fact, a number of centers for the study of these areas have been established (1), and each year there are more conferences for researchers and managers to exchange ideas (2). It is becoming clear that these are very complex issues that do not have simple solutions. Slogans like "a happy employee is a productive employee" may still have some truth in them, but they no longer can provide guidance to managers. Increases in productivity are achieved by changes in a complex set of conditions, including such things as job design, work flow, automation, worker participation in factors affecting their jobs, organization climate, and teamwork. This chapter will focus on building an effective and humane organizational climate as one important factor that contributes to productivity and the quality of work life.

The subject of organizational climate in general and physical settings in particular has begun to receive increasing attention in recent years for a variety of reasons identified by Steele (3):

1. An expanding interest on the part of behavioral scientists, economists, managers, and public officials in the problems of dehumanization at work.
2. A lower tolerance for regimentation on the part of younger employees in the United States work force.
3. Cross-cultural experiences between countries, between companies, and between different types of organizations fostered by the growth of multinational corporations, which demonstrate that there is generally no single right way to do almost anything.
4. The increasing frequency of organization development programs and other system-wide interventions, which generate both an awareness of process and concrete activities that have a humanizing influence.
5. An expanding interest in the field of environmental psychology, including the interaction between person and environment in the work setting.

As a result of the increased attention, more is known about the factors that make up organizational climate. The major ones are: characteristics of *physical settings*; the *norms* of the work group and of the larger organization; the patterns of *communication*; the dominant *style of management* employed by the system's supervisors and managers. Each factor will be discussed in terms of its role in the process of humanizing the work climate.

WHAT IS ORGANIZATION CLIMATE?

To understand organization climate, it is important to put it in context with other parts of organizational life. Homans' (4) valuable scheme is used here with some modification. Its three major parts; and required system, the emergent system, and the outcomes are seen in Figure 25.1. Organization climate is the major component of the emergent system, the characteristics that provide the day-to-day environment for those who work in the system. It is the social climate in which the work is embedded—what it *feels* like to be at work in the system—pleasures, demands, stresses, opportunities, constraints, and so on.

Another way to think of organization climate is through the metaphor of the weather. As noted in *The Feel of the Work Place* (5):

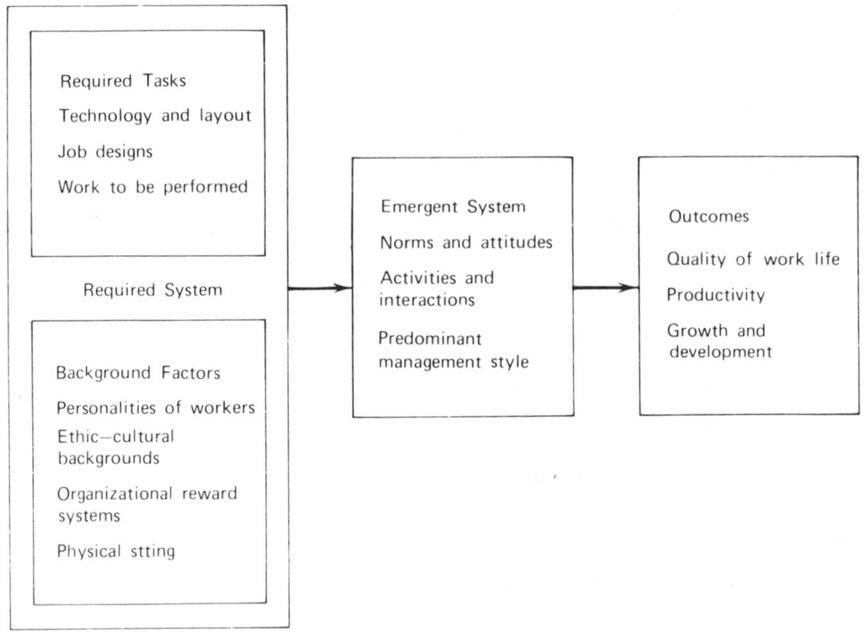

Figure 25.1 Elements of the organization climate.

Organization climate can be thought of in terms of the weather. Some organizations have predictably sunny climates (low demands), while others seem always to encounter storms with lots of precipitation (conflict) and fog (poor communication). Unlike the physical weather system, the organization weather system can be influenced if its pattern is understood. Some storms are natural and merely signal the onset of a new season, while others are potentially dangerous and need to be stopped before damage is done.

Dimensions of Climate

There are four dimensions of organization climate. They can be used to help understand the climate that exists in any organization and whether that climate enhances or inhibits productivity and the quality of work life. The dimensions are total amount of *energy* in the system, *distribution* of the available energy throughout the system, the amount of *pleasure* people experience in the system, the amount of *growth* people in the system can experience. Each of these dimensions is explored briefly.

Energy. As in the physical weather system, some climates have high energy and others have low energy. Work environments can be similarly described. Some places are full of energy. People seem busy; there's lots of movement; few people seem unoccupied. Other places have low energy. Things seem to move slowly; there's not much noise or enthusiasm. Think of places you are familiar with in terms of the amount of energy you can sense there. For example, compare in your mind banks, resturants, factories, libraries, or offices with which you are familiar. Even those in the same category, for example, resturants, can be very different in terms of the overall amount of energy in the system.

Distribution. Within any organization, the energy that is available is not spread evenly throughout the system. Some parts have high energy while other parts have low energy. This is often the case even within an organization as small as a family, in which the children sometimes have much more energy than do the parents. In work organizations energy tends to be distributed unevenly, with some parts of the system more energetic than others. Sometimes the distribution of energy is affected by work flow cycles. Many manufacturing environments become very energetic at the end of the month, quarter, or fiscal year. The same is true in accounting firms whenever there are financial closings, or when tax time rolls around.

Pleasure. This dimension has to do with the amount of fun people have in the system. Some organization climates are very serious. There is little "unnecessary" interchange between people, little humor. In the extreme, such environments are supported by physical settings that make informal contact difficult, norms that oppose having fun ("this is a place to work, not a place to play"), communication patterns that are formal and ritualized, and a management style characterized by formal, structured, and serious interactions. Other organization climates are more lighthearted, and in my opinion often more productive as well as more pleasurable. One important contributor to experiencing pleasure in the work place is the nature of the work itself. Sometimes little can be done about the work itself; it is by nature dull, routine, and boring. Often, however, much can be done to minimize the effects of such jobs. Therefore another important contributor to pleasure is the degree of flexibility in the job itself, and the degree of influence a person has over aspects of the job such as schedule of work, pace of work, scope of work, or hours of work. Cohen and Gadon (6) have explored these notions thoroughly in their book *Alternative Work Schedules.*

Growth. This dimension is a consequence of the other three. If there is sufficient energy, a reasonably even distribution of energy throughout the system, and a fair amount of pleasure, then growth will result. It is hard in the abstract to define what is meant by "sufficient energy," "reasonably even distribution," or a "fair amount of pleasure." As in the physical environment, where there are tropical paradises and barren deserts that enhance or inhibit the growth of crops, organizational environments can enhance or inhibit the growth and development of people. The term "growth" is meant to include increased awareness, knowledge, and skills. For this kind of growth to occur, there needs to be present in the environment at least *some* of each of the three previously mentioned aspects of climate. In addition, growth requires that there be a supportive reward system, one that encourages individuals to try new skills, stretch themselves, and take risks.

FACTORS DETERMINING CLIMATE

As noted in the introduction to this chapter, there are four key factors that determine organization climate: physical settings, norms, communication patterns, and management style. Each factor will be explored in detail in this section, since they are the keys to building humane and productive organizational climates. Figure 25.2 shows the relationship of these four factors to the dimensions of climate already discussed, and placed in the scheme shown in Figure 25.1.

Physical Settings

The physical setting in which work takes place has a major impact on the climate that develops in that work place. Or course, the kind of setting chosen or constructed in the first place may be a reflection of the organization's climate as well. In either case the physical appearance of the work place is a source of information about what the system is like; it gives one the first and

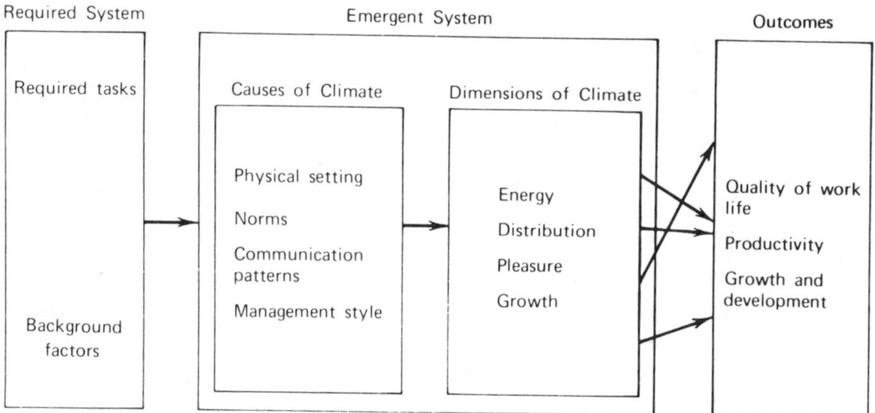

Figure 25.2 Factors determining organization climate.

most tangible "feel" for the place from which one can draw all kinds of inferences. As described in *The Feel of the Work Place* (7):

> The first piece of information we get about an organization is its geographic location. Being in midtown Manhattan (New York City), in downtown Manhattan (Kansas), or in a posh, well groomed industrial park communicates different messages about organization climate, values, and identity than does a location in an older, run-down part of a decaying urban area.
>
> The next impression we receive about a system, after knowing its location is prompted by the actual building, workshop, factory, or whatever that defines and encloses the organization's spaces. The features of external facade play a large role in shaping our initial impression. Many companies today strive to project an image of progressiveness, solidarity, and reliability by building up-to-date solid structures that look like other new office buildings.
>
> For the richest visual picture of the climate of an organization, we must explore the interior spaces of the system. The way in which organization members shape and reshape their offices, production areas, and passageways provides us with most of our data about the social climate in which they operate. . . . An area that has all work benches fixed will encourage continuation of old activities, even when they are no longer particularly profitable or there is a better way to do the same tasks. A setting that allows noise or visual distractions, can promote a climate of excitement and vitality but at the same time be negative for tasks that require concentration and uninterrupted sequences of activity.
>
> On the causal side, settings operate as influences on climate through the activities they allow or inhibit, through the symbolic messages they contain and through the memories and feelings they stimulate in users.

Some characteristics of the physical setting that appear at first to be rather trivial can be very important causes of how humane a work place feels to those who work there. For example, it is very hard for most people to think carefully and analytically in a space that has little or no privacy, much noise, or many interruptions. Yet, often these are the very conditions under which people are asked to do careful or exacting work. If a work place has no natural gathering spots where people can communicate informally, there tends to be less communication of all kinds, and what social contact there is takes place at people's work situations, as interruptions. A gathering spot where people can get coffee, messages, perhaps copies as well, permits the informal communication to take place in a manner that is not interruptive.

Many organizations are moving toward the use of "open offices" made of moveable partitions that define each person's space. If these changes are not planned well, they often make the work place nearly intolerable because of the increase in noise, interruptions, and the decrease in privacy. Open offices can and do work well if they are carefully planned for. It is possible to keep noise down by using a variety of sound absorbing materials on floors, partitions and ceilings, as well as enclosing typewriters and other noise-generating office equipment. In fact, as more offices move to word processing equipment, silent keyboards and video terminals reduce noise even further. Providing a number of enclosed conference rooms of different size allows people additional privacy when needed for telephone calls or face to face meetings. Norms or formal procedures can be put in place concerning interrupting people who are busy in their own work spaces and choose to be left alone for a while. One company gave people small signs to hang at the entrance of their work spaces when they did not wish to be interrupted.

As building costs continue to increase, and the need for flexibility in the use of work space increases, there will be more use of open offices. I have worked in traditional closed office space and a variety of open offices. The control an individual has over privacy, noise, and access is much greater in the traditional arrangement. Poorly planned open office space gives one a sense of violation and unwanted intrusion that makes work very difficult. Morale and productivity both decrease. On the other hand, well-planned open office space can actually be an improvement over closed offices in terms of communication, access, and flexibility to rearrange work spaces as needed. In addition to attention to noise factors in planning open offices, there needs to be explicit involvement of employees in planning how to use the new open space. At a minimum, employees views need to be thoroughly sought, heard, and responded to prior to making such changes. Often they have very creative notions that help to humanize things.

Some of what has been said about office space can also be said about manufacturing space. Obviously there is less freedom for rearranging one's individual work space than there is in any kind of office arrangement, but there still are opportunities to involve employees in planning and laying out their own work spaces. The more people can feel they have some degree of input or control over the physical conditions in which they work, the better. Sometimes merely allowing people to personalize their work space in some way is enough—a chance to paint it (or choose the color), or have a plant or picture on the wall.

Norms

Norms are the unwritten rules of behavior for people in the organization. They are the "shoulds" and "shouldn'ts" people are expected to follow. When new employees are "shown the ropes," "taught the rules of the road," or told "how we do things aroung here," they are being told about the norms of the organization or work group they are joining. Some organizations have more elaborate initiation procedures.

> "The primary function norms play is to lend some stability and predictability to the behavior of group members. Norms limit the range of possible things that can happen at any given instant, and so help provide identity and thrust to the group's actions. Every social system with any connection between members must have some norms to differentiate members from non-members. (8)

Norms can facilitate goals or inhibit them; they can be conscious ones openly determined or unconscious ones that evolve over time.

Some norms are reinforced by statements of policy and procedures; others aren't. The informal norms often are established and reinforced by the behavior of those at the top of the organization, that is, those in power. (If the President eats in expensive resturants on a company expense account, others are very likely to do likewise.) Norms cover all aspects of behavior and set the tone of the organization. For example, few organizations have formal, written dress codes these days. Yet nearly every organization has some norms about dress. Whether it is everyone should wear ties or that no one should wear ties, the norm is the behavior code. Often there are norms about what is acceptable in terms of use of one's physical space. For example, though there may be no policy that says everyone has to have the same type of desk and chair, nevertheless everyone does. The norms that operate in any organizational setting often can be inferred from observing people's behavior.

Organizations that have many norms that constrain people's behavior tend to be less inviting places to work than those with norms that encourage individual expression, risk taking, and experimentation. Norms are the single most important determinant of organization climate. At the two ends of the continuum are a climate of *fear* and a climate of *excitement*. Managers can have a major impact on the kind of climate in their work groups by paying careful attention to the norms that exist, and the ones they reinforce or change through their own behavior. For example, a manager who genuinely seeks information from his or her subordinates and really listens when it comes, even when it's bad news, will set a norm for open disclosure very quickly. On the other hand, a manager who says he or she really wants information but reacts angrily every time it isn't good news will set a norm against open disclosure ("Tell the boss whatever he or she wants to hear"). A climate of excitement is created when those in power are clear and open about their goals, and encourage and reward individual initiative in service of those goals. Norms supportiong such behavior are most easily established through the behavior of those at the top.

Communication Patterns

There are several dimensions to communication patterns. There is the amount or volume of communication; the quality of communication; the vehicle of communication. Communication patterns evolve in organizations along all three dimensions. Effective communication patterns are difficult to establish because there are so many variables involved. In addition to the dimensions mentioned above, there are preferences and relative skills of each person who communicates as a sender and as a receiver. All sorts of organizational problems are blamed on poor communication, so that the subject has become a kind of wastebasket category. Still there are ways to understand and to improve communication patterns. In this section each dimension will be examined, and approaches to establishing effective patterns will be discussed.

Volume. Organizations differ enormously in terms of the sheer volume of communication, just as individuals differ. Like people, some organizations are talkative, some are quiet. Some prefer written communication over oral communication and generate thousands of memos. There is no right amount of communication, and managers who search for it are bound to be frustrated. Some people will complain of communication overload, while others will complain that they don't receive enough information. Finding the right balance between too much communication and not enough communication is dependent on the individual manager's personality and style, the norms or policies of the organization, and the needs of the employees. Some organizations value a great deal of communication, and invest heavily in new technology to aid in the process, for example, teleconferencing, facsimile transmission, or computer networks for data exchange. Other organizations value sparse communication and train employees on how to write memoranda on single sheets of paper and how to keep telephone calls to a minimum. There is no evidence that one approach is any better than another in terms of volume of communication alone.

Quality. There is little argument about the benefits of quality communication. Quality can be measured by asking the receiver to report what he or she heard or read from the sender, and to check with the sender in terms of accuracy as well as other factors such as intent or emotional tone. I once did a research project on downward communication in a large organization, and found that only about 10 percent was received accurately and as it was intended! Quality is the responsibility of both the sender and the receiver, although the heavier burden is on the sender to be clear. Generally the quality of communication is increased when the sender has thought out what is to be communicated, how it could best be communicated, and how the communication should be stated or written most clearly (and concisely). The receiver's responsibility is to check out unclarities with the sender and to provide feedback to the sender on what was actually received.

Vehicle. Often communication breaks down because the message was sent via the wrong vehicle. That is, something is discussed over the telephone when it should have been done on a face to face basis so that nonverbal parts of the communication process such as gestures and facial expressions could be communicated. Similarly, when an interactive form of communication is needed, talking on the telephone is preferable to writing a letter or memo. I once managed a large group of people, most of whom were in remote locations. One technique that helped develop effective communication patterns was listing the kinds of issues and topics that warranted a trip to the remote location so that there could be a face to face interchange, those that warranted a telephone call, those that could be handled by telex, and those for which a letter or memo was appropriate. The list was communicated to those in the remote locations for their input and guidance. Mintzberg (9) has noted that most managers have a preference for the verbal media and for short concise interchanges. These preferences would be fine if all communication could be accomplished effectively by such vehicles. Therefore the content of the intended communication needs to be examined before choosing the vehicle by which to transmit it.

Management Style

Volumes have been written about management style since McGregor (10) wrote about Theory X and Theory Y. There is a growing consensus that no one management or leadership style is correct. In fact, the so-called contingency approach (11) suggests that there are a number of factors that should be considered when determining an appropriate style. These include the nature of the task situation, the expertise of the manager, the attitudes and needs of subordinates, and time pressure. Many people believe that in order to humanize the work setting, the predominant management style should be highly participative. That conclusion is true when the decisions are nonroutine, information is not standardized, there is low time pressure, and subordinates are independent and internally motivated. But how many situations meet those criteria? Perhaps they are met in some places such as engineering design firms or law offices, but certainly not in automobile assembly plants. Appropriate management style is arrived at by matching the situation to the leader and vice versa. In exploring the interactions of factors in the contingency approach, Cohen et al. (12) state a few highlights of effective style:

1. Nature of the task situation:
   If routine, needs control, explicitness and standardization.
   Stressful tasks need high person-concern.
2. Expertise of the leader:
   The greater the expertise, the greater the appropriateness of control.
3. Attitudes and needs of subordinates:
   The greater the subordinate need for independence and ability, the less appropriate is tight control.
   If subordinates' survival is not threatened and work is not unusually challenging, high task and people-concern is appropriate.
4. Time pressure:
   The greater the time pressure, the less shared control is appropriate.

When the management style that is used matches the needs of the situation, the organization climate is much better than when there is a mismatch. Knowing how to create that match is more an art than a science and is usually accomplished by managers who have a relatively wide repertoire of behavioral styles that they can draw upon as necessary. Therefore the single-style manager is less likely to be effective in the complexities of most current work situations than those managers who can adapt their style to the factors mentioned above.

BUILDING EFFECTIVE SETTINGS

From all that has been said, it should be evident that in order to build an effective work setting, a manager must be good at balancing a dizzying array of variables, many of which he or she cannot control directly. Consequently the help of others is required for success, particularly in figuring out where things stand and where they ought to be headed. This task is relatively simple in the area of task requirements, but is very difficult in the area of organization climate.

The primary contributors to effective settings are the causes and dimensions of organization climate contained in the emergent system (see Figure 25.2). In order to begin to develop the emergent system in a planned way, the manager must be a good diagnostician. Just as a doctor must be a good diagnostician if his or her treatment plan is to be effective, the first step in building an effective setting is diagnosis. There must be a thorough analysis of "what is" coupled with a clear vision of "what needs to be." Then work can begin on building bridges between the two. A thorough diagnosis of "what is" requires a degree of objectivity that most managers do not have because they are so completely involved in the situation. Occasionally a newly appointed manager has the objectivity, but often also suffers from needing to learn the operation in detail as quickly as possible. Therefore the diagnostic phase often can benefit from the help of an outsider, either an outside consultant or someone from another part of the organization who can bring both objectivity and a "fresh pair of eyes" to the situation. Managers frequently are so heavily oriented to finding solutions that they do not spend enough time or energy on diagnosis, and end up with a trial and error approach to improving organization climate.

Once a diagnosis has been completed on the present situation, a process must be started to define the desired situation. Information and suggestions from a wide sampling of the organization's members is appropriate in arriving at the vision for the future. The process used must include mechanisms for evaluating and choosing among the alternatives suggested. A logical sequence of steps must be put together, along with some estimate of the cost involved in each step. Finally, there needs to be a feedback mechanism to provide for midcourse corrections as the process moves forward.

Obviously such a formalized procedure is not as necessary when attempting to make changes in norms or individual management style. However, changes in physical settings and in communication patterns usually do require a more formal approach. Changes in all four areas are best accomplished when moving from a clear sense of "where we are" (both good and bad) to a clear sense of "where we'd like to be."

Physical Settings

Changing physical settings is difficult for several reasons. First, decisions about the kind of physical setting itself as well as how to use the spaces within them are often held closely by the person(s) at the top of the organization because they are such visible symbols of executive power. Second, many people do not attempt to influence the decision process around physical settings because they treat them as givens in the environment that are not open to any kind of change.

Norms

Norms may be less difficult to change, but they are much less visible than are physical settings. Because norms are the unwritten rules for acceptable behavior, they often do not come under explicit scrutiny. When they do, through a process called the norm census, they can be fairly easily changed or modified (13). Norms also resist changing because people do not think of them as changeable, and because they usually develop slowly over time, and die out the same way rather than by conscious attention and explicit action to change them.

Communication Patterns

Interestingly, communication patterns, particularly the vehicles of communication, tend to be tinkered with more than most aspects of organization climate. Most positive changes are those toward more open disclosure within the system. These kinds of changes require a change in philosophy toward an assumption that it is good to have few official secrets and that the true facts usually are "friendly," that is, that no one would be hurt by sharing them.

Management Style

Changes in management style are the result of education. First, a manager needs to learn that a single style is not appropriate in many situations. Next, the manager must learn new behavioral skills to expand his or her repertoire. Finally, managers must be able to balance the needs of the situation with their own experience, skills, and preferences to find an appropriate style for any given situation.

Conscious attention to these areas can enable the manager to make positive changes in the emergent system, and thereby contribute directly to the building of more effective work settings as measured by the outcome measures of quality of work life, productivity, and growth and development.

REFERENCES

1. For example, the Work in America Institute and the American Productivity Center.
2. For example, Ecology of work: Improving productivity and the quality of work life. Third Annual Seminar on the Organizational Practice of Behavioral Science, June 1980, St. Louis, Missouri.
3. Steele, F. Humanizing the physical setting at work. In H. Meltzer (Ed.). *Humanizing Organizational Behavior.* Springfield, Ill.: Thomas Publishers, 1976, p. 368.
4. Homans, G.C. *Social Behavior: Its Elementary Forms.* New York: Harcourt, Brace and World, 1961.
5. Steele, F. & Jenks, S. *The Feel of the Work Place.* Reading, Mass.: Addison-Wesley, 1977. p. 26.
6. Cohen, A. & Gadon, H. *Alternative Work Schedules*, Reading, Mass.: Addison-Wesley, 1978.
7. Steele & Jenks, op. cit. pp. 106, 108, 115, 120.
8. Ibid., p. 41.
9. Mintzberg, H. *The Nature of Managerial Work.* New York: Harper and Row, 1973.
10. McGregor, D. *The Human Side of Enterprise.* New York: McGraw-Hill, 1960.

11. Hunt, J. & Larson, L. *Contingency Approaches to Leadership.* Carbondale, Ill.: Southern Illinois University Press, 1974.

12. Cohen, A., Fink, S., Gadon, H. & Willits, R. *Effective Behavior in Organizations.* Rev. ed. Homewood, Ill.: Richard D. Irwin, 1980, p. 290.

13. Steele & Jenks, op. cit. p. 64–66.

—26—

Work and Workers: Some Transatlantic Comparisons

Eli Ginzberg

THE U.S. SCENE

The starting point for this interpretative analysis is a set of three doctrines that have wide currency in the United States at the beginning of the 1980s. The first holds that there has been a serious erosion of the work ethic. The second postulates that a severe decline in productivity has occurred, the causes of which are embedded in the loss of discipline in the work place, largely a reflection of the growing power of trade unions. The third warns about the imminent collapse of western democratic societies because of their responsiveness to the claims of the populace for more and more social services, which is undermining the competitiveness of their economies.

Before taking a closer look at what is happening on the other side of the Atlantic that might illuminate this conventional wisdom, a brief review of recent U.S. developments may sharpen the focus. In these introductory considerations we will raise challenges rather than search for balanced answers.

A few facts about the erosion of the work ethic:

1. During the several decades since the end of World War II there has been a steady rise in the employment-population (E-P) ratio, which reflects the percentage of the total population over 16 that is in the labor force, holding down or looking for a job. In the case of the female population the ratio has increased from roughly one-third to over one-half (1). Even in the case of young people reaching working age whose numbers increased from around two to four million per year, the E-P ratio recently reached an all-time high.
2. While there has been some decline in the hours that employees work over the course of the year as a result of longer vacations and more paid holidays, the basic work week has not been altered except at the fringes: it was 40 hours in manufacturing in 1950 and it is roughly the same today; about 35 hours for office work then and now. The officially reported figures for "moonlighting," that is the proportion of the work force that holds more than one job, has not shown any secular decline, but rather a small increase. A significant minority of workers in industries in which overtime is the pattern work more than the standard number of hours and for the most part are eager to do so. True, younger workers are pressing employers to make

overtime voluntary. They don't want intrusions into their life off the job unless they are consulted.

3. In all analyses of work and workers, it is an error to focus solely on what transpires in the regular economy. Many important shifts are underway in the manner in which people apportion time and energy between household and job. Consider the explosion in "do-it-yourself," from painting the house to paneling the den. More telling are the long hours of work reported by wives who hold down full-time jobs and who at the same time continue to carry most of the reponsibility for running their homes and raising their children. Their behavior surely does not support the argument that the work ethic is weakening.
4. While no reliable data are available, current statistics seriously underestimate the total work that the U.S. population performs because of the sizable and almost certainly growing importance of the "unreported economy." An estimate of 10 percent of the GNP is increasingly used as a first approximation of the size of this unreported sector.

Admittedly the foregoing makes no reference to such countervailing trends as the increasing number of individuals who are able to live without working—those on welfare, unemployment insurance, social security, and private pensions. But except for those on welfare the nonworker has contributed to the system that now helps to support him or her. Some receive more from the system than they put in, some less.

The gross data provide little support for a decline in the work ethic. Of course protagonists can argue that the gross data are beside the point: what they mean by the erosion of the work ethic is not that workers have stopped punching in at 8 a.m. and out at 4 p.m., but that they have stopped doing a day's work for a day's pay. But the protagonists have never come up with data to substantiate their contentions.

What about the second proposition, the decline in productivity that is seen as a result of a loss of discipline in the work place, among other reasons because of the growing power of trade unions? A few questions:

1. How good are the measures of productivity? The answer is, not very. National income accounting in such important sectors as government, banking, and other large service areas uses labor inputs as a proxy for output. But the gross data do point to a marked deceleration of productivity across the economy since the late 1960s. However, if perspective is lengthened one finds that recent developments are more or less on trend, and what really requires explanation are the increases above trend that occurred in the twenty years after World War II. The reason lies ready at hand: absence of international competition that the U.S. economy enjoyed following World War II.
2. If the conventional wisdom about the decline in productivity is suspect, one must be doubly cautious in assessing the correlative claim that a loss of discipline in the work place because of the growing power of the trade unions is

the explanation. As to the power of unions, the truth is that in recent years the proportion of workers belonging to unions has been declining, not increasing, despite the fact that through legislation and administrative action many workers previously excluded have been brought within the purview of the National Labor Relations Act.

3. Union membership aside, the question of work place discipline is worth inspecting. Again the gross data in terms of work stoppages and loss of work time through strikes lend no support. They show no upward drift, rather an erratic pattern. In the early 1960s and again in the mid-1970s, my colleagues and I made two efforts to get beneath the surface to see whether we could discern any significant long-term trends that would support generalizations about discipline in the work place. In both instances the evidence was mixed but served to point in the direction that, union or no union, a management that knew what it was about maintained discipline, and one that was flaccid was likely to be in trouble (2).

The work-satisfaction data tend to support this reading. They show no clear-cut trend in the direction of growing worker dissatisfaction.

This brings us to the third proposition, that the welfare state in the United States and in Europe is threatening the long-term survival of advanced democracies. The neoconservatives support this claim by calling attention to several ominous developments:

1. Voters through the ballot box are forcing governments to provide increasing benefits whose costs so far outpace tax revenues, that the printing presses take over, the prelude to disaster.
2. Special interest groups from farmers to workers facing plant closures have learned how to intimidate politicians into protecting them so that the market can no longer perform its allocative functions, thereby slowing or stopping economic growth.
3. The public's expectations are out of control with the result that in their efforts to protect the environment, the worker, the old and the young, minorities, and many others who are vulnerable, modern democracies are spending too much, investing too little, and thereby jeopardizing their future.

By way of reclaimer, following are some cautionary observations about accepting this dire assessment.

Inflation has been a mounting threat to the long-term viability of the U.S. economy, but it has nonetheless finally been confronted by the federal government as of early 1981.

Special interest groups have a potent influence on legislators, but no persuasive argument has ever been advanced that the United States would have been better off had assistance been denied Penn Central, Lockheed, and most recently Chrysler. One of the overriding responsibilities of democratic governments is to cushion the damage that the market occasionally inflicts on dedicated workers and competent employers. The real challenge to government is to undertake only those interventions that have a prospect of long-term success.

The issue of excessive expectations is complicated. Any society worth its salt should strive to respond to challenges that it has failed to meet adequately in the past, from reducing and eliminating discrimination to protecting its natural and cultural heritage. Admittedly, if the public overestimates the rate at which the economy will continue to grow and underestimates the cost of desirable new programs, it can run into trouble. And that is what happened when the expensive Great Society programs were followed by the costly new environmentalism. But as the recent pressures for tax discipline have come to the fore, both in the states and in Washington, evidence suggests that a democratic society is capable of learning from its errors.

TRANSATLANTIC PERSPECTIVES

The three prongs of the conventional wisdom about work and workers that have just been examined from the U.S. vantage provide a fixed point for looking at the comparable experiences of our friends and allies in Western Europe. There is always something, sometimes a great deal, to be learned by escaping from a narrow parochialism.

The observations offered below on the European scene reflect a half century of activity on my part as resident, visitor, consultant, and researcher. I will comment in turn on the three central themes: the work ethic; productivity and discipline; expectations and the welfare state.

With respect to the work ethic I have been impressed by the following:

> The relatively slow decline in the conventional hours of work in most advanced European economies alongside of quite liberal vacations. Paris empties out in August. The Swedes warn one not to get sick in June or July; most physicians are away. In the Netherlands the welfare grant covers a two weeks' vacation for the recipient. Many European unions continue to press for retirement as early as sixty, largely because of their unease about employment opportunities for the younger age groups.
>
> The German trade unions, worried about rationalization and automation, are pressing for a reduction in the conventional hours of work to 35, not because they place such a high value on leisure but rather because they fear that in the absence of such a reduction there will not be enough work to go around.
>
> The Western European countries, some more and some less, with the Netherlands at the end of the queue, have witnessed the increasing participation of women in the labor force. But since the slowdown in economic growth in the mid-1970s, most of these countries have taken latent or overt actions to impede if not stop the flow of women, particularly married women, into the labor force

(3). But again such action does not reflect a weakening in the work ethic, rather an anxiety of the male leadership in government and in the trade unions about a shortfall in employment opportunities for regularly attached male workers.

In Sweden, some years ago, there were no young native males employed on Volvo's assembly line. Inquiry disclosed that in the face of a booming economy it was harder and harder for management to recruit natives for manufacturing jobs, particularly for work on the assembly line. In France and Germany guest workers had been imported in large numbers and directed to jobs that the natives shunned, such as street cleaning, other unskilled types of employment, and some dirty, heavy blue collar work. Although the French government has belatedly sought to upgrade some of these laboring jobs via wage adjustments and fringe benefits in the hope of reducing the nation's reliance on guest workers, it remains to be seen whether this positive approach will work. If Michael Piore is right, and I suspect that he is, there will always be jobs at the bottom of a nation's structure that are rejected by natives but prove attractive to foreigners who come from a more impoverished environment (4).

Two years ago my wife and I arrived at Heathrow Airport, London, on the evening of the second day of a three day holiday and waited a long time for a taxi. Inquiry disclosed that at the current high marginal tax rates many drivers opted for leisure over working on holidays. This explanation was offered to describe the behavior not only of taxi drivers but the great mass of British workers.

During the course of that visit, I learned that "off the books" employment at every level from unskilled work to the highest professional activity was increasingly common in the United Kingdom, which tends to confirm a recent analysis in *The Economist* suggesting that national income (and hours worked) may be underreported by 7 percent or so.

These perspectives lead one to doubt that the work ethics is eroding. True, natives may avoid low-paying, unpleasant work; they may prefer leisure to overtime when most of their extra earnings go to the government in higher taxes; buy they apparently seek additional work when they can pocket the wages without incurring a tax liability.

The second theme deals with the triad of productivity, work discipline, and trade unions. Here the challenge is more complex both because of the variability among the several countries and my limited knowledge of details. But the following may prove suggestive:

In Sweden, where social democracy in terms of welfare benefits provided by the state has proceeded farther than in any other Western European country, management control over the work place has remained strong, and U.S. automobile workers report that certain lines operate at a higher speed in Stockholm than in Detroit.

But this is only part of the story. The other part relates to the severe financial penalties that Swedish employers face if they discharge older workers; the high wage settlements that they have been forced to accept; and most recently (1980) the collapse of the long-established system of national bargaining, which held to a minimum hours lost through strikes and lockouts.

High labor productivity, good discipline, and labor cost increases that jeoparidize a country's balance of payments are not necessarily mutually exclusive.

The German situation differs markedly from that of its neighbors to the north, west, and south. One hears little about a decline in labor productivity and a weakening of discipline in the work place. In fact, the powerful trade union movement is constantly on the lookout that high investment leading to increasing productivity does not result in displacing workers faster than they can be reabsorbed. Moreover, the unions have been willing to participate with employers and government authorities in keeping the wage bargain within bounds.

What one does hear from conservatively inclined observers of the German scene are the handicaps under which management labors as a result of the political evolution that has placed worker representatives on key management boards. But the continuing strength of German industry suggests that these fears must be exaggerated or their effects must be long delayed.

In the United Kingdom the situation is strikingly different. Here many trade union members at the shop level are engaged in ongoing warfare with their managements, a struggle that has been led by communist or fellow traveler shop stewards. However, I have a different interpretation.

Britain remains, in my opinion, the most elitist of the so-called democratic countries, which is reflected in the wide gap between top and middle management and the still wider gap between management and the work force. Almost forty years ago I warned in *Grass on the Slag Heaps: The Story of the Welsh Miners* that the shabby way in which the nation under Baldwin treated the unemployed and underemployed was a certain invitation to labor strife once the balance of power shifted, as it did after World War II. The evil that men do lives after them. The workers in the shop may feel a little less hostile now and again when the Prime Minister is a member of the Labor Party, but not sufficiently so to lower their fists especially against most managements that have little desire or ability to reach long-term accommodations with them. The remarkable fact is not the decline of Great Britain as an industrial power but the fact that she cannot yet be written off although her revival remains problematic in the face of this unresolved class struggle.

The French situation bears some resemblance to both neighbors, Germany and Great Britain. On the one hand, France became a significant industrial power after World War II, an accomplishment resulting from effective collaboration between the bureaucrats and the captains of industry with labor acquiescing. While the French trade unions are less powerful than the British, a smoldering class conflict persists in France. The glorious revolution of 1789 has not yet been completed. The distribution of income is more uneven in France than in any other developed European country. The large Communist Party may not be growing but neither is it declining.

Italy, the last of the arrivals among the advanced industrial countries, is at once the simplest and the most confused. Since the bloody summer of 1968, the trade unions have become a dominant force. They do not always get their way but without their support, or at least their acquiescence, no management can manage. In public sector enterprises in which unions confront government appointed managers, efficiency is generally very low, since the unions have the muscle to prevent dismissals of surplus workers and reassignments aimed at the improved utilization of the work force. But in typical Italian fashion the economy has demonstrated its continuing vitality and resiliency by the rapid growth of the unrecorded sector, which one cabinet minister estimated a few years ago to constitute at least 20 percent and possibly more.

What about the third theme, the charge that the welfare state has overreached itself and in the process undermined its economy and jeopardized its democracy. The charge can't be dismissed out of hand.

Although economists disagree as to details, they see a close link between the severe inflation that has come to characterize most developed societies and the ambitious goals that the welfare state has been pursuing. When resources fall short of expectations, the printing press is called into service.

Sweden, the Netherlands, France, Italy, and the United Kingdom all suffer from destructive inflationary pressures, which are rooted in government control over half or more of the GNP. However, recent evidence suggests that the public has begun to have second thoughts. There have been significant changes—altered political leadership in Sweden and the United Kingdom, a new economic policy in France, and a partial shift to the right in Italy—all of which suggest that the "overreaching" of the welfare state, long disguised but now on the surface, has forced voters to make some hard choices.

The expansion of the unrecorded economies in each of these countries, with many employers and employees finding ways to beat the high tax and regulatory systems, is also forcing a reassessment of expectations.

But let us be clear: the expectations that led to the rapid growth of the welfare state had much to commend them. They sought to narrow the gap between those lower and higher in the socio-economic-political status system by opening higher education to many people previously excluded, protecting workers from hitherto ignored risks, providing minimum support for older persons, improving access to health care, addressing the special needs of special groups from unmarried mothers to handicapped children. And in all of these developed countries the advance of the welfare state represented an intensified effort to shift the distribution of political power from a small elite to the masses, and to extend the reach of the democratic ethos from the political arena into the work place.

Large-scale enterprises can achieve and maintain a high level of efficiency only in the presence of labor peace. Hence the expansion of social services and the redistribution of political power were not side shows but potent contributors to the high level performance of these modern economies. In the case of Great Britain, where conflict dominated the work place, the economic results were dismal.

The neoconservatives who rail against the welfare state and who predict that the pursuit of equity will retard economic growth and reduce democratic freedoms have missed the point. Unless the mass of the working population believes that the socioeconomic structures are being modified to give them a fair shake, they will prevent the economy from functioning at anything approaching its true potential (7). While the welfare state may have moved too far too fast, it was essential that it move.

SOME UNPRETENTIOUS CONCLUSIONS

Having completed our selective review of three critical dimensions of work and workers where do we come out?

The contention that the work ethic is being rapidly eroded both in the United States and Western Europe has not been substantiated. True, certain groups of workers may opt for nonwork over work because the gains they can achieve from not working exceed those that they can realize from taking a job, increasing their hours of work, or remaining in the labor force. Further, as real per capita and national income have increased, the alternatives to work from extended schooling through early retirement have expanded. But despite this more married women are at work than ever before.

We found little supportiong evidence that productivity is falling because of lack of discipline in the work place, encouraged and supported by the growing power of trade unions. In the United States unions are losing, not gaining power as far as numbers are concerned; discipline in the work place has more to do with the competence of management than with the behavior of trade unions; and reported slowdowns in productivity have been effected by a host of factors, some linked to workers' behavior but others reflecting failures to report activities in the unrecorded economy. One need not deny that the changing climate of industrial relations has any influence on productivity to avoid ascribing undue influence to it.

Finally, we found that the rapid growth of the welfare state reflected the broad-based search for equity. To conclude that expectations advanced more rapidly than resources is not the same as contending, as some have done, that the welfare state was an error and should be dismantled. Unless the developed nations continue to respond to the aspirations of the masses for a more equitable distribution of income, status, and power, they will lack the cooperation required to operate their complex economies efficiently.

History is a grab-bag that debaters dip into to support their contentions. The ominous trends with respect to the weakening of the work ethic, the slowing of productivity, and the expansion of the welfare state are contrasted with an idealized version of the past when workers labored from sunup to sundown, when the employer's word was law, when government was frugal. Conservatives who look back to the good old days, as well as reformers who yearn for the improved society that is still to come, are impatient with the complexities of the human condition. But societies are complex and they are subject to continuing change in which every action or reaction opens still further opportunities for initiatives and responses (7). Only an analysis that is sensitive to this dynamism can contribute constructively to policy.

REFERENCES

1. Most of the data have been drawn from *Statistical Abstract of the United States*, Department of Commerce, Washington, D. C., 1979.
2. Ginzberg, E. & Berg, I. *Democratic Values and the Rights of Management.* New York: Columbia University Press, 1963; Berg, I., Freedman, M., & Freeman, M. *Managers and Work Reform: A Limited Engagement.* New York; The Free Press, 1978.
3. Yohalem, A.M. (Ed.), with a Foreword by E. Ginzberg. *Women Returning to Work: Programs and Progress in Five Countries*, Montclair, N. J.: Allenheld, Osmun and Company, 1980.
4. Piore, M. *Birds of Passage*, New York: Columbia University Press, 1979.
5. Schrank, R. (Ed). *American Workers Abroad.* Cambridge, Mass.: MIT Press, 1979.
6. Ginzberg, E. *Grass on the Slag Heaps: The Story of the Welsh Miners*, New York: Harper and Brothers, 1942, Chapter 8.
7. ___*The Human Economy*, New York: McGraw-Hill, 1976, Chapters 3 and 4.

—27—

Humanizing Planned Changes

Ronald Lippitt, Ph.D.

Some changes that impinge on our lives are nonhuman in origin, such as the eruption of Mount St. Helen, a tornado, a flood, or a heat wave. Other changes are macrohuman and distant in origin from us such as population growth, inflation, and the price of oil. Other changes are more local but nonhumane; for example, the decision of the school board to reduce services to our children, the decision of management to change the hours of the work week without involvement of the workers, and the decision of the parents to restrict the use of TV by the children without discussion and negotiation. Other planned changes of our life spaces meet criteria of *humaneness.* As a working definition of "planned change humaness" let me suggest that the decisions and actions that are involved reflect a concern for benefit-consequences and involvement-process for all the participants involved in the change. The benefit consequences would be reflected in concerns about psychological and physical and economic welfare, the meeting of needs, provision for growth and development, and maximizing utilization of resources. Involvement process concerns would be reflected in sensitivity to psychological involvement, provisions for being influential, providing support, and opportunities for zestful use of energy.

I have divided my analysis of planned change humaneness into three sections: 1. humaneness of planned change decision making and goal setting, 2. humaneness of implementation of planning, 3. humaneness of action-taking for change. In each section I have presented my observations concerning selected aspects of an humane process of planned change and then have offered some observations on the consequences of inhumaneness.

HUMANENESS IN GOAL SETTING FOR CHANGE

The Chance to Hear and Understand the Rationale of Change

Providing a clear rationale for the importance, necessity, and potential positive consequences of a planned change effort represents a minimal level of humaneness. Any leader or manager of a group that wants to achieve a meaningful level of acceptance and commitment to a planned change goal must present the rationale for the contemplated change as clearly as possible and provide opportunities for discussion to clarify implications and consequences for those who will be affected by the change. This is a necessary but usually not an adequate level of involvement to mobilize wholehearted collaboration and energy commitment to the change effort.

Participation in Formulating a Need for Change

A chance for all those who would be involved to participate in an assessment of the way things are and the way things might be is a very important aspect of an humane process of change. With many groups and organizations we have started with what we call a "prouds" and "sorries" brainstorm (3) of the way things are. The discussion and priority setting of the "proudest prouds" and the "sorriest sorries" does a great deal to create a climate of readiness to consider "how we would like things to be different." This is a very different process than the listing of gripes, which tends to generate negative feelings of frustration, depression, and scapegoating.

Participation in Projecting Alternative Scenarios

One of the most sensitive and energizing approaches to a planned change effort is the involvement of those who will be affected in projecting alternative images of potentiality for significant change. Often this involves the presentation for review of future scenarios beyond the experience of the participants. The provision of images of opportunity and possibility beyond what has been experienced is a very important responsibility and contribution of humane leadership, and usually involves drawing on technical resources from outside the group or organization.

Clarification of What We Need to Hold On To

Enthusiastic advocates of a change effort are often insensitive, and therefore inhumane, in avoiding a review and clarification of basic values that represent the carefully developed traditions and identities of the group. Usually change must and can build on respect for, rather than confrontation of, these basic aspects of group or organizational identity. They usually represent strengths to build on rather than impediments to progress. A careful consideration of "who we are" and "where we're coming from" is a crucial aspect of an humane process of change.

A Chance to Openly Articulate Ambivalence

Every effort to initiate change, no matter how humane, activates an internal forcefield of ambivalence about maintenance of the way things are versus the risks and energies involved in a change effort. Insensitive change agents tend to ignore this underground of ambivalence or regard it negatively as "resistance to be coped with." The humane orientation toward the change process regards this ambivalence as a normal and necessary aaspect of considering a commitment to a change effort, and provides opportunities for the open expression of the internal concerns, anxieties, fears, hopes, wishes, and expectations. From this open expression the change agent can derive much helpful information to assist in identifying blind alleys, potential traps, and important unexplored alternatives. In addition, the sharing of ambivalence provides the basis for clarifying issues and developing interpersonal support and objectivity. We have found that providing opportunities to articulate "internal dialogs" between the voices of caution about change and support for change is one of the most important aspects of supportive humaneness.

Some Consequences of Inhumaneness

The quick death, half-hearted implementation, or subversion of many planned change efforts is the result of a separation of the goal setters, the planners, the implementers, and the constituents—those who will be served or affected by the change effort. Our psychological and sociopsychological research literature is full of evidence on the necessity of voluntary involvement in decision making if there is to be a wholehearted commitment to goals for action. Humane change agents have recognized that there are many levels and possibilities for involvement, ranging all the way from participation in information about the rationale and necessity for change to opportunity to be involved in initiating the needs for change and the goals for change.

In all cases significant involvement includes the invitation to be influential, and feedback that the input has been listened to and utilized. The consequences of neglecting such a process are disastrous to various degrees. At the best there will be halfhearted commitment and participation in the change effort, but more frequently there wil be harmful consequences of neglect, irresponsibility, subversion, and alienation from the power structure.

HUMANENESS IN PLANNING TO IMPLEMENT CHANGE

Exploring Alternative Ways

One of the most creative and productive ways of getting the participants involved in a planned change effort is to involve them in brainstorming all the alternative ways they can think of to move toward the defined goals. The wisdom of the planners usually turns out to be relatively limited compared with the great range of alternatives that can be generated by those who will be the implementers. Actually the professional planners themselves are typically released by this opportunity to brainstorm all the possible alternatives before beginning the more disciplined feasibility thinking.

Optionality in Division of Labor

During the planning for action, questions of division of labor arise. Too often these decisions are made by the planners based on who has done what in the past or on the basis of formal structures. The more humane motivation and interest-oriented procedure is to utilize techniques of setting up opportunities for individuals to express their interests and to prove what they can do. Hidden resources are one of the great sources of waste as well as frustration.

Resource Inventory Development

Effective planning for change often neglects the search for the internal resources needed for the new types of responsibilities and actions called for by the planned change effort. Usually there is a serious lack of information on "who would be good at what" as planning for change progresses. The neglect and waste of needed human resources is not only a serious loss for the organization but a serious deprivation for the individuals whose resources are being neglected. Therefore the development of effective resource inventory procedures is an important part of planning for change. The typical paper and pencil procedure tends to fail to identify the needed new types of resources, new types of skills, and competencies. A probing personal interview procedure, often conducted by peers, has proved a more effective tool.

Stepwise Task Development

One of the most depressing and inhumane aspects of much planned change effort is the large gap that exists in everybody's mind between the desired outcome and the "the way things are." This big gap is a continuing source of frustration, depression, and loss of energy. The effective change process involves everyone in clarifying a series of small steps of progress towards the desired goal and the identification of specific criteria or evidences of achievement of each step, so that frequent progress can be experienced rather than the frustrating awareness of a distant goal.

Design for Evaluated Feedback and Replanning

One of the discouraging aspects of much change effort that is moving into new, unexplored territory, is the unclarity about whether we are "on the beam" and whether energy is being wasted in dead-end activity. The effective change program not only has a plan for evaluative data collection on stepwise movement toward the goal, but has a design for involving the participants in review of the data and deriving implications for replanning. Very frequently such a design involves collecting data from the recipients of service to confirm the success of service efforts. In other words, sensitive humaneness involves attention to the implementers and recipients of the change effort.

Consequences of Inhumane Planning

If planning has been a centralized rather than a participative function, the change effort is indeed in serious danger, because people will not be doing what they are best prepared to do. There will be a lack of clarity about direction and progress, a lack of psychological commitment and effort, and a loss of momentum because of a lack of sense of progress toward the desired goals. A very typical subversion in many bureaucracies is a variety of unofficial nonapproved ways of doing things that deviate from "the plan" but that satisfy needs for antiauthority autonomy, and the need to creatively deviate from routines.

HUMANE ACTION-TAKING FOR CHANGE

Rehearsal for Risk-Taking

One of the most inhumane strategies of change is to push persons into new roles and performance requirements for which they are not adequately prepared. There are a variety of methods for providing opportunities for anticipatory preparation for new behavior requirements and tasks. Frequently role playing is used to provide a chance to experience "what it will be like." Skill practice methods provide opportunities to try out, get feedback, and to retry in situations in which one is not playing for keeps. Techniques of simulation provide an opportunity to explore the consequences of alternative ways of coping with new situations. Every initiator of planned change has an ethical responsibility to provide opportunities to rehearse new risk-taking requirements before they must be coped with in reality.

Support for Risk-Taking

Follow-up research on workshops and orientation programs indicates that typically a rather small percentage of the "intentions to try something new" actually are tried out in the reality situation. This is because at the time of genuine risk-taking there is no "at-the-elbow support" available to help cope with the new situation to be faced and the new behaviors to be tried out. The strategists of humane change have utilized a variety of techniques for providing at-the-elbow support, for example, quick debriefing of "how it is going," opportunities for telephone consultation, and the provision of supportive resource materials and tools to reduce the risk-taking.

Peer Teaming as Support System

Many change agents recognize that it is inappropriate to expect individuals by themselves to cope with the requirements and risks of change or innovation. A minimal risk-taking unit of two or three persons is regarded as a critical support unit. For this reason most planned change programs have teams of several peers, or vertical teams of supervisors and supporters as a crucial unit of support for successful planned change efforts.

Ad Hoc Task Forces as Change Units

One of the criteria of humaneness in change effort is attempting to ensure the success of those who are being involved in the change effort, and reducing the resistance to commitment. One of the most effective strategies is to put together as complementary resources the best ad hoc task forces one can mobilize. This means insuring that the combination of skills and resources available to tackle the new challenges are mobilized, and are given a temporary assignment, which reduces the reluctance to commitment because the contract is for a limited time effort.

Achievable Action Expectations

Frequently the eager advocates of a change effort expect and demand too much immediate competency, too much commitment of time and energy, and too rapid results. The first steps of action need to be achievable and finite steps, with opportunites for probable and early success experience.

Celebration and Recognition for Progress

We mentioned earlier that humane change is a zestful experience. There must be reward and fun to ensure the renewal and continuation of energy and commitment to any change effort. We have found one of the most effective ways to ensure this zestful involvement is to help the group identify ways in which they will celebrate each step of progress in the path toward the goal of change. Supervisors and leaders can provide celebrative support by recognizing and rewarding significant efforts. But the group itself needs to be helped to initiate meaningful joint celebration to recognize its own progress.

Some Consequences of Inhumaneness

The consequences of pushing participants into actions they are not prepared for, and not competent to be successful at, are very serious. Individuals are likely to be hurt and the change efforts will be of low quality or a failure. Most successful action-taking requires collaborative teamwork, skilled performance, and maintenance of energy in coping with blocks and difficulties. The typical pattern of criticizing mistakes and expecting rapid success results in a rapid loss of energy and commitment.

A SAMPLE TOOL KIT OF HUMANE CHANGE AGENTRY

The "Prouds" and "Sorries" Brainstorm

We have discovered that focusing on the listing of problems is a very negative, energy-draining, and defense-stimulating way to get involvement in need for change and planning for change. Analysis of tapes of such sessions reveals progressive increase in depression of voices as the list of problems gets longer, and increased mobilization of defensive avoidance of responsibility. This defense development is manifested by increasing comments of attribution of the cause of the problem to forces beyond their influence or possibility of action.

A more balanced and positive procedure of getting a shared diagnosis of "the way things are" is to have a brainstorm of "all the things we can feel proud about" and "all the things we are sorry about" in our situation, or about the way we function, or whatever other focus you may want to use.

If you are working with a small group, for example, 5 to 12, the whole group can brainstorm together and the call-outs are recorded on a pad up front. If you have a larger group, they should be subgrouped by tables of five to eight and each group brainstorm on newsprint sheets on their table. If the group is above 30, half the tables can brainstorm "prouds" and half of them "sorries."

The next step is to set priorities on the most important items on the list. In a small group each person casts three votes for the "proudest proud" and the "sorriest sorry," and the votes are tallied on the list. If several tables have brainstormed, each table votes on their list and they call out their top three on each side for a group master list of priorities. If some tables have done "prouds" and others "sorries," it is fun for the "prouds" to get up, go over and read "sorries" and do their voting, and the "sorry" people reciprocate by reading and voting on the "prouds."

The result is a very nondefensive spirit of developing concensus about the most important needs for change, and the most important values to be maintained.

It is very important to follow vigorously the rules of productive brainstorming. The rules are always listed up front before the activity begins. They are:

1. Say everything that comes to mind.
2. Absolutely no discussion.
3. No evaluative judgment comments.
4. Repititions should be listed without comment.
5. Piggy-backing is encouraged.

The Alternative Scenarios Exercise

Taking a jump into the future and projecting preferred futures, "what we would like to have happen," is a very energizing and involving process of change.

The typical practices of planning and goal setting do not result in such involvement and motivation. These postures are:

1. Getting away from the pain of problems.

2. Adjusting to trends of "the way things are going".
3. Figuring out how to "fit into" the futures that are being predicted.

These are all *reactive* rather than *proactive* postures toward planning and greatly inhibit creativity of planning and motivation to implement.

The procedure of preferred futuring, described in detail in *Choosing the Future You Prefer,* by Lindaman and Lippitt, goes like this:

1. The group decides on or is given the particular time jump, for example, one year, two years, 10 years.
2. They visualize themselves in helicopters, hovering over themselves and their situation (e.g., group, organization, community, self) at that time in the future, making observations with an observation sheet.
3. They are writing down observations of what they see happening, who is doing what, how are things operating that *please them very much* with the way things have developed since back at (present date).
4. Usually each person makes observation notes for a few minutes, then they share and make a call-out list up front, or a subgroup table list—with *no discussion* except questions of clarification to help make the image concrete and clear.
5. Each subgroup posts their images of preferred future on the wall and everyone has 10 votes to cast by reading the items and checking the images of the future they would most like to see achieved.
6. This checking process generates high priority images that become the bases for ad hoc interest groups meeting to focus on "what would need to be done," what blocks coped with and resources mobilized, to move toward the particular preferred future. A planning process flows from this activity.

There are several models of this approach depending on the size of the group, the nature of the task (e.g., organizational versus personal futuring), and the level of knowledge and data resources.

The Internal Dialog Exercise

Opening up underlying ambivalence about participation in a planned change effort is a very important strategy. One procedure we use often is to brainstorm all the assets and liabilities of a proposed change, with task force work on coping with liabilities and maximizing assets.

Another procedure that we use in many variations is the internal dialog of "listening to" and jotting down as dialog the internal pro and con voices. A typical dialog exercise goes like this:

Recording an Internal Dialog. Every time a change is proposed (in goals, regulations, procedures, etc.) that calls for new behavior, energy, and assignments, a pro-con dialog is activated inside each of us, a very normal process of questioning, doubting, and wondering. There are usually, if we listen, some voices that are "anti" the change and others that are "pro." It will help everybody to deal more constructively with this situation if we can tune in on these voices and share some of what we hear. Maybe there are some voices we'll decide are just for us, very personal. In the two columns below, please jot in quotes, as in script, some of the inner dialog you can tune in on:

Voices expressing doubts, concerns about risk, or irritations about the proposed change	Voices expressing acceptance of the idea, support for the change, reasons it's a good idea
______________________________	______________________________

Sharing of these data, legitimizing the feelings and ideas as normal and acceptable, is usually a very important unblocking process. Demonstrating sensitivity to and acceptance of the feelings of others is one of the key characteristics of the humane change agent.

Forcefield Diagnosis

Getting persons involved in alternative strategies of how to achieve a change is one of the most effective types of involvement and use of resources.

One of the techniques for deriving such strategies is the use of the forcefield analysis procedure developed by Kurt Lewin and used widely among organization development practitioners.

Very simply, it is a procedure for identifying the supports and blocks to movement toward a particular goal or desired change, and then assessing weights or priorities to the "forces" to be mobilized and overcome, to get movement toward the desired change. The typical analysis format for this procedure looks like this:

The Change-Goal: Getting New Regulation X Accepted and Implemented

Supports, Resources Facilitation, "Pushes" toward the Change-Goal	**Blocks, Barriers, Restraints against Movement toward the Change-Goal**
Sanction, support of legislature	Antagonism of professional association
Benefit for clients	Mandated deadline
Clarity of steps of action to take in introducing change	Changes in relationship to clients implied

Usually the analysis exercise involves identifying the most crucial blocks and the most important supports. Temporary teams then brainstorm all the ways to reduce, cope with, and overcome a particular block, and ways to mobilize and utilize a particular resource or support.

Often the analysis procedure helps locate needed data that are missing about the nature or strength of a particular support or block, that must be discovered and assessed to plan action.

Developing a Resource Inventory

As we have indicated, one of the inhumane aspects of many planned change efforts is that the wrong people are asked to do the wrong things, and available skills are unidentified and unused. In very few working situations are there available data on "who is good at what," so planners are at a loss to make productive decisions on the best heads to put together for the particular ad hoc task forces needed in every planned change effort.

One of the most simple and satisfying resource inventory procedures is to set up a small task force on development of a resource inventory. Their first job is to try to get help from the leader-planner on all the types of skills and experiences that might be needed, and all the types of tasks that can be anticipated in the changes that are anticipated.

Using their data, the task force develops a resource inventory interview schedule. A questionnaire is much less effective. The staff members are paired to interview each other, with good instructions about probing to get details.

The task force edits the interviews ad gets them reproduced in retrievable form. Often they are computerized. Other times a coding is done of names grouped under different skills and tasks, and some managements have a matrix on the wall of names on one dimension and skill on the other, with the boxes checked for each person.

There is a great morale boost when the staff see it demonstrated that the leadership is making serious use of real data about who has what competencies.

Stepwise Planning, Progress Review, Celebration

Almost as inhumane as being asked to do something one doesn't feel competent at is to be asked to live with a large gap, a discrepancy, between the way things are and the way they are supposed to be, or we want them to be. When the gap is large, there is more often depression and frustration rather than challenge and activation.

So sensitive change agents help everyone to identify small steps of progress toward the change goal. For this purpose a typical planning sheet looks something like this:

Stepwise Planning Sheet

1. What is the eventual outcome image you are moving toward? Be concrete in describing what it would look like if you were there.
2. Brainstorm with your team all the steps of action you can think of that might be steps toward the goal, including coping with the blocks you identified in your forcefield analysis.

3. Now review these possible steps and use what kind of sequence of steps there might be. Some things have to be accomplished before others, or two things need to be done at the same time. Create a possible "path of progress steps" visually for yourself.
4. Now what seems to be desirable, even necessary, as a first step?
5. Who needs to be involved? How? To make this step happen?
6. How will you know you've achieved this step? What specific evidence?
7. When you find you have achieved this step, who will you celebrate with? How might you celebrate?
8. What might be evidence that things are off the beam, or going too slow?
9. Who will you replan with?

Rehearsal, Anticipatory Practice

What we call reality practice is a procedure for trying out alternative ways of coping with anticipated new situations one will need to deal with during the process of planned change. Such rehearsals help one to feel more comfortable and to become more competent in dealing with new situations.

Typically the practicers work in trios. The group has identified kinds of anticipated situations, for example,"Who will do or say what" that one will need to cope with.

Each person, as a practicer in his or her trio, selects the kind of situation they want to practice. They share with the trio colleagues the kinds of behaviors and situations they have the most difficulty with. The colleagues create the needed practice situations, and provide feedback of observations and support re-practice tries.

This is a brief sample of some of the methods change agents have found most helpful in using values of humaneness in managing the process of change. Fuller descriptions of techniques and strategies will be found in the brief bibliography.

CONCLUDING COMMENTS

We have attempted to summarize, in the first three sections, the major dimensions of an humane approach to the strategy of planned change. Humaneness was defined in terms of sensitivity to the process and consequences of a change effort in terms of involvement of participants and impact on recipients.

We recognized that there is frequently a situation of ignorance and limited awareness, that they "may not know what would be good for them." In such situations the strategies of involvement in "images of potential," mind stretching, and sharing of ambivalences about change are even more crucial.

The increasing expectations and demands of all levels of personnel in a system about the "right to have a voice" is reinforcing the importance of the involvement and participative processes we have been referring to as "humane."

The effectively humane leader of change is not passive or soft-headed. The skills of such a leadership role are much more demanding and disciplined than the more simple traditional patterns of authoritarian mandated change, which are less and less successful with each decade.

REFERENCES

1. Bennis, W.G. Benne, F.D. Chin, R. & Corey, K.E. (Eds.). *The Planning of Change.* 3rd ed. New York: Holt, Rinehart & Winston, 1976.
2. Capelle, R.G. *Changing Human Systems.* Toronto, Canada: International Human Systems Institute, 3136 Dundas St., 1979.
3. Herriott, R.E. & Gross, N. (Eds.). *The Dynamics of Planned Educational Change.* Berkeley, Calif.: McCutchan Publ. Corp. 1979.
4. Lindaman, E.B. & Lippitt, R.O. *Choosing the Future You Prefer.* Washington, D. C.: Development Publications, 1979.
5. Lippitt, R. Watson, J. & Westley, B. *The Dynamics of Planned Change.* New York: Harcourt, Brace & World, 1958.
6. Lippitt, G. *Visualizing Change: Model Building and the Change Process.* San Diego, Calif.: Learning Resources Corp., 1973.
7. Schindler-Rainman, E. Lippitt, R. *Taking Your Meetings Out of the Doldrums.* San Diego, Calif.: University Associates, 1975.

—28—

Innovations for Organizational Change as Seen by a Practitioner

Thomas E. Standing

The primary thrust of this chapter is reactive: The chapters of Part III are analyzed from the perspective of an individual "on the firing line." It seems to me important, therefore, that the reader understand the frame of reference of the writer since reaction is based heavily on the prior dispositions of the reactor.

As a practitioner, the writer is by dictionary definition an individual who is engaged in "the doing of something, often as an application of knowledge." The emphasis, it seems to me, is on the application rather than the development of knowledge. This book is useful as a presentation of new knowledge. As a practitioner, therefore, I am faced with the problem of having to determine whether or not I see in that knowledge any opportunity for application in the daily affairs in which I am involved. Of course, the distinction between the development of knowledge and the application of knowledge is an artificial one. Each of the authors in the previous chapters is a practitioner, and there are occasions when each writer is involved in the development of new knowledge based on personal thought and experience. Involvement in the daily affairs of a business organization where the primary role is one of knowledge application, however, often leaves little opportunity for reflective thought on experiences—the process whose distilled product could be called new knowledge.

One of the major problems facing a practitioner is the extent to which his or her personal observations may be generalized. If these observations are unique to the setting in which the observations were made, then, it seems to me, the observations represent knowledge in only a very narrow sense. I hope the knowledge developed by the authors elsewhere in this section is knowledge that transcends the limits of personal experience and can be applied in a variety of ways and settings.

My comments represent one test of the requirement of generalizability in that I examine my own beliefs about whether the ideas stated previously would apply in the setting I know best, that is, my own professional work environment. In so doing, I hope to assist readers in coming to grips with the basic issue involved in a *Handbook for Practitioners*: Will these ideas work in my setting?

My frame of reference is that of an industrial psychologist who has spent a number of years attempting to understand individual differences in the context of work. During my formative educational years, work meant the private sector, oftentimes the manufacturing sector. That was the locale within which most of the controlling ideas in industrial psychology had been developed. The concept of individual differences had its greatest utility in the selection process; therefore, there was a heavy overlay of measurement and statistical inference in my conceptual development.

These basic orientations have been compatible with my own work experience in that I have spent the bulk of my professional life in an integrated petroleum company where engineering orientations are pervasive. As a consequence, the touchstone of much of my "practice" revolves around pragmatism and rationality. As my comments indicate, such an orientation frequently is a disposition that runs counter to the underlying assumptions of many who are engaged in organization development.

Having been so candid in stating my biases, I feel compelled to point out that the process of cognitive development is, as labled by Piaget, one of assimilation and accommodation. Therefore, unless one is confronted by ideas dissimilar to one's own, stagnation is the result. A gain, that means it is even more important that one be exposed to the notions presented in the wide-ranging chapters I comment on.

REACTIONS TO INDIVIDUAL CHAPTERS

While any categorization of these eight chapters is going to be largely arbitrary, I think it is useful to see two basic types of writing in these chapters. I therefore structure my comments on these chapters around two basic clusters: ideas related to broad trends and changes and ideas related to the tools of implementation. In the first category I include the offerings of (in alphabetical order) Hackman, Jenks, and Pinto. In the second category I include Alderfer, Gricar, Lippitt, and Shulman. The alert reader will quickly note that Professor Ginzberg's writing is not included in either of these two categories. This is because his ideas relate less to the topic of organization development and change than to the political milieu within which this change is taking place. Therefore, I feel it would be overly arbitrary to force his chapter into one of the two categories I have identified.

In an effort to proceed from the general to the specific, I will react to the Ginzberg paper first. Ginzberg does have one attribute in his writing that is quite similar to all of the authors: His epistemology is based largely on personal observation and experience. To a large extent, however, his paper is written in a factual vein. This point is raised not to imply a demeaning attitude toward the ideas presented but to put these ideas in perspective. There probably are very few ways in which the scientific method can be brought to bear on the issues Ginzberg discusses, but it is important to remember that he is largely expressing his opinion of these factors. It's somewhat disquieting to review the three factors he emphasizes in his paper (i.e., the work ethic, the productivity of industrial societies, and the economic health of these societies) and see that to a large extent straw men have been set up to be knocked down on each of these points. The explanation for this approach may be found in Professor Ginzberg's statement that he is attempting to debunk what he perceives to be "conventional wisdom" in each of these matters.

There is, I feel, a heavy overlay of political involvement in this particular article. The nature of public policy is, of course, political and, therefore, this overlay should not be surprising upon reflection. I think, however, that a large number of pactitioners still conceive of themselves as working in some sort of a mechanical environment where rational analysis will eventually carry the day. Perhaps the greatest single value in Ginzberg's writing is to remind us that rationality is only one aspect of the world around us at this point. The ebb and flow of public policy debate does have a significant influence on the workplace, and there are occassions when that influence is overwhelming. Examples abound when one considers the influence of U.S. regulatory agencies on the affairs of the private sector. No doubt, one of the major problems in the last 20 years (and probably the next 20) has been management's need to learn to live with those kinds of external constraints—even when they do not mesh with management's economic theories of business practice.

As Ginzberg has stated, some of his comments are based on a limited knowledge of actual events, specifically among trade unions in Europe; therefore, his observations must be taken as "suggestive."I very much agree with that orientation and hope that preconceived notions about the items that Ginzberg discusses would not close the reader's mind to considering his points. Perhaps the most useful reminder in the article relates to the overwhelming need for workforce cooperation in a developing economy. Ginzberg reminds us that unless the workforce believes that their own personal situations will improve as a result of cooperation there will be cessation of cooperative effort.

Cooperation is of central importance in considering what future organizations can be. The underlying theme in many of these papers is that any practice that assumes cooperation and does not examine the specifics may find itself being terribly ineffective. Many of the authors in Part III describe a means by which this cooperation can be developed rather than assumed. As a practitioner, I must say that I am frequently surprised at how often managers forget that basic principal; but, as I will point out further on, organization systems can work effectively despite that particular oversight. One possible sign of increasing sophistication in this particular area of workforce cooperation is the extent to which union-management relations are focusing on the point of mutual survival as they face some of the demands of our current economy. The initial decision of Chrysler's workforce to avoid continuing pay increases epitomizes this awareness.

The three chapters I have grouped into the category of "ideas dealing with broad trends and changes" seem to me to highlight fundamental shifts in our perception of the world of work and of the roles of employees. Hackman's chapter deals with the basic issue of the nature of work and the motivation of individuals to put forth effort in a workplace. His survey of work redesign methodologies and orientations is certainlly a very useful synopsis of knowledge that has developed over the last 30 years. In many ways, Hackman's orientations appear more congruent with my own than any other's in this section. His analysis of work redesign tends to be objective and balanced, and he makes an effort to cite both positive and negative evidence on each issue he raises. Most of his citations are in terms of actual research done on the given topic. Again, I believe that this indicates a desire on his part to look at the scientific method as the basis for discovering what does or doesn't hold true in the world of work. In this sense, Hackman does differ from most of the other authors.

Another aspect of Hackman's description of work redesign that ties to my own preconceptions is the extent to which he tries to identify the pragmatic benefits of redesign efforts. There is continual reference to increased production or improved quality or the elimination of dysfunctional consequences. Again, as a practitioner, I am painfully aware that the inability to make a tie between a recommended program and a specific outcome of value to the decision makers in the organization is a failing that has led many good ideas to go begging within large organizations. Thus, I consider Hackman's approach to the issue helpful for the practitioner, who could use it to sort out the end results he or she would hope to see in implementing a redesign project.

Hackman's emphasis on the role of individual worker differences in work redesign is also a refreshing theme. Other chapters in this section assume a uniformity in the workforce which experience belies. Certainly, it is oftentimes necessary to ignore the multiplicity of responses individual employees might have to a given approach in an effort to make the basic thesis proposed more understandable. Yet each recommended action or orientation must be understood in the context of the workforce existing within an organization and the relative responses that can be expected in different segments of the workforce. Hackman is not the only one who makes reference to this kind of individuality, but he seems to underscore it as a key ingredient in job redesign more than other authors in this section. Having attempted to explain the apparent individuality of worker response (3), I certainly applaud Hackman's reminder of the existence of that phenomenon.

Hackman, at the end of his chapter, indicates his awareness of the fact that the issue of job redesign is embedded in a host of sociocultural changes.

This is an important point; personal values will, even more than the specific evidence of research, have an influence on the nature of work design. In fact, it might be argued that much of the support for job enrichment or job redesign comes as a result of the rapid growth of the service industry in the United States. Much that was thought desirable about job design from the scientific method point of view could not be applied in the context of the service industry. As more and more workers have been employed in non-manufacturing sectors, we have seen the development of work arrangements significantly different from the large labor-intensive manufacturing environment. As managers and other employees move in and out of different organizations (and certainly mobility across organizations is an increasingly frequent phenomenon) there is more and more likelihood that different conceptions of work arrangement will be spread throughout industry.I believe that the effect of this cross-fertilization will be decreasing emphasis on the principles of "classical" work design as it evolved in the manufacturing sector.

Another sociocultural shift—the increasing professionalization of the workforce—is highlighted by Pinto's chapter on career development. While Pinto does not use these terms, he does refer to reflectiions of this kind of development when he cites an increase in desire for individual choice and work identity as the basis for changes in the perception of career development.

The notion of professionalism draws together many of the currents that Pinto identifies and helps, for me at least, to explain some of the pressures currently being felt within large business organizations. Implicit in the professional label is the individual's belief that certain skills and abilities developed through specific educational efforts are transferable across company lines. This gives the individual a sense of supremacy in terms of long-term employment prospects with a proportionate decrease in dependency on a given company to provide upward mobility. In fact, to some extent and in some areas, the notion of upward mobility does not even capture the full meaning of career development. For some specialized professions, the acquisition of in-depth knowledge and the expert use of such knowledge is a more accurate definition of career development. This is one of the many alterations in the concept of career development that Pinto elaborates on.

I think the practitioner should reflect very seriously on some of the themes emerging from Pinto's chapter. In particular, I would hope that there is no general reaction to the effect that Pinto's career planning and development process describes most major corporate programs. To the extent that this reaction takes place, many practitioners feel that they have been left behind in an antiquated world of reactionary management. I believe that Pinto presents a smorgasbord of career development ideas that should be selectively applied in a given organizational context. Again, the effective practitioner must make a case that there are positive consequences to the organization for the use of some of these approaches. As is probably apparent, any institutionalization of major ideas presented by Pinto represents a significant cost to an organization.

Some of the notions Pinto presents bear underscoring. Mention is made of the inadequacy of most immediate supervisors in dealing with the career development issues of their subordinates. This is a significant problem with the way many organizations set up career planning. Very often, the immediate supervisor is expected to also be a career counselor and provide significant feedback and direction (or at least informed conversation) on the question of movement in the organization. More often than not, those individuals who are the key assets in the organization for future movement and whose career development should be the greatest concern to the organization are being asked to seek guidance from individuals who have nowhere near the potential for advancement that they do. This problem argues for the use of the "steering committee" concept that Pinto mentions. The broadest perspective possible on alternate placement and development should be brought to bear on career issues concerning the "fast track" talent in an organization. It has been my experience that narrow definitions of next-step job assignments are counterproductive for maintaining the dynamism and energy of a career development system. Development must always be weighed against organization need and best utilization, and those goals are oftentimes inhibited by specific career path determinations. Pinto is also critical of the idea of a static series of movements leading "to the top." Unfortunately, many new employees come to the workforce from college courses where the notion of a career path is presented as the ultimate proof of career opportunity. Within a growing, vibrant organization, that is far from the true state of affairs.

Pinto, like Hackman, raises the question of individual differences in the context of career development. One aspect of this factor that may not emphasize enough has to do with the skills and abilities of the individuals in the organization. To large extent, the available materials on career exploration topics ignore this very vital factor of personal capacity when seeking to lead an individual to determine career interests and career development. It is a simple fact of human existence that some can and some cannot satisfy the learning and performance demands of increasingly responsible positions by the time they complete their college education and begin working in a business organization. To the extent that a career development system does not bring these differences to bear on the question of personal ambition and choice, I would expect the system to cause more harm that good for the organization and for the people involved in it.

One aspect of career development Pinto mentions several times is the notion of individual choice and personal decision making. As is mentioned in the chapter, the implementation of such choice and decision making requires the organization to "release" some of its power and information. To that extent, career development represents an added burden on the organizational system. More time must be spent communicating and more resources must be devoted to identifying and implementing good career development plans. This cost is fairly significant, even if only a few individuals are identified as being the critical resources in the organization to be monitored for long-range career purposes. The theme of personal control over life decisions is, however, one of the underlying emphases in many of the chapters in this section; and, as that kind of a value system relates to career development, it is probably ignored only with some real loss to the organization in terms of its use of its human assets.

The final chapter in the category of broad trends and changes is that on effective settings. As the reader soon discovers, Jenks' topic is really organization climate, its dimensions and effects. My impression is that in attempting to write for the practitioner, Jenks may have downplayed some complexities. For example, while the four dimensions of organization climate he treats are common ones, it might be well to consider that some writers have suggested other dimensions. Jones and James (1), for example, identified a greater number—and in fact a quite different set—of dimensions. Furthermore, one of the more interesting debates in the professional literature concerns whether organization climate possesses any operational reality at all (Guion, 2).

I applaud Jenks wholeheartedly for raising doubts about the universal utility of the open office environment. As a practitioner who has wrestled with architects on that issue, I certainly am glad to see a willingness on the part of Jenks to acknowledge that the open office approach must be used selectively after studing earlier office experiences. In the remainder of the chapter there are a number of straightforward statements about what is known and not known about organization climate. One that I think is particularly instructive is Jenks' comment on the overuse of "communication problem" as a diagnostic category. On the other hand, I wish Jenks had gone further in specifying what particular steps need to be taken to create climates that are simultaneously humane and productive.

I conceive of the second cluster of chapters as presenting tools for implementing organization change. Gricar, Lippitt, Shulman, and Alderfer are obviously all involved as practitioners themselves. Their contributions all seem to represent efforts to abstract from personal experiences a theoretical model encompassing those experiences and to encourage application of principles to new occurrences.

My reactions to these writings relate to the extent to which I feel valid insights have been communicated by each author. Again, as a practitioner, I consider validity largely a matter of whether their insights are consistent with my own.

Gricar's discussion of interorganizational collaboration is a difficult one to assimilate from my private sector vantage point. Her taxonomy of collaborative strategies relies heavily on public sector examples. Over the last 15 or 20 years, there has developed an increasing reliance on public sector organizations as the settings within which to design, develop, and test strategies for organization change. Previously, business organizations had been the exclusive sites for such activity. The causes for this shift are not as important at this point as is the natural tendency for one to ask whether experiences in one environment are relevant for understanding the other.

A primary example of the differing outlooks between practitioners in the two sectors comes from my reaction to the inclusion of advocacy as a collaborative strategy. As Gricar acknowledges, advocacy may result in polarization rather than integrative, collaborative solutions. Since these dysfunctional consequences seem to predominate when the business sector is drawn into advocacy-based confrontations, it is not likely that such a strategy would be seen as a reasonable for a business entity to initiate. To the extent that Gricar's analysis reminds us that collaboration is often required between the business sector and other stakeholders in order to effectively address broad problems, it is helpful to have advocacy included in the structure.

The four remaining strategies in Gricar's structure are, I believe, recognizable in the private as well as the public sector. The question remains, however, whether the labels and relationships Gricar employs will aid the practitioner in bringing about more effective collaboration. There is a risk that too many esoteric distinctions among naturally occurring events may create a morass of terminology and thereby impede rather than facilitate the development of effective, sustained collaboration. Gricar obviously recognizes this risk, having asserted that the taxonomy is "not merely an exercise in logic." Whether it is or isn't is likely to be left to public sector practitioners to discover.

One underlying theme in Gricar's chapter that is common to each of the writings in Part III is that of individual involvement and participation. The explicitly stated opinion that people are entitled to a say in the decisions that affect them may or may not be found, but it is a value clearly consistent with each of the authors' recommendations. Shulman's chapter, "Humanizing Technology," reminds us how multifaceted the application of that principle may be.

Shulman's thoughts on the subject of computerizations are certainly timely. As real-time, on-line, data-based devices increase their assault on the U.S. workplace, it seems that very few workers will be unaffected by this issue. From the "office of the future" to "industrial robots," decisions about the introduction of computer-based technology abound. Shulman presents some informative distinctions about both the stages of the technological process and the possible management responses to these stages. In so doing, he seems to me to have put the humanistic manager into context.

Shulman's intent, as he describes it, is to bring managers to question "the appropriateness of their decisions regarding the scope and direction of the technologies they employ." Since awareness of value differences seems to be the keystone of the humanistic manager's view of technological change, it is a bit surprising that Shulman would foster the hope that, by simply outlining different approaches to a given problem, for example, technological change, he would be able to alter the behavior of managers who are reading his ideas. It seems to me that the better hope for Shulman would be that managers whose implicit values are consistent with those of Shulman's "humanistic" manager would, after reading and reflecting on Shulman's description of the introduction of technological change, believe and follow the principles espoused by such a manager. In this sense, Shulman has created a management guide the manager can use in attempting to understand how his or her own values should have an impact on approaches to management problems. In other words, it is the developing manager who is most likely going to be "converted" by presentations such as Shulman's.

As with all stereotypes, Shulman's descriptions tend to become bothersome in that the manager's behavior is so consistent with the values they hold. In the "real world," people often behave in a somewhat inconsistent fashion. I think, however, that three of Shulman's stereotypes are instructive in that they help one to better understand how humanism might be applied in work.

The first instructive stereotype is the one that Shulman says is most prevalent in American business. He terms this set of behaviors the "technologist." Indeed, reflecting on my own observation of changes within the refining systems of the United States wherein process control computers have replaced refinery operators as the decision points for these massive capital plants, I certainly have been aware of the engineering point of view, which has held technological sophistication to be the paramount goal of organizational change. I know of at least one plant location where the consequences of such sophisticated hardware have been counterproductive in the long run in that operators, now isolated from the equipment they are meant to monitor, have minimal involvement in the operations of the plant so that even hazardous equipment problems are ignored and "left to the computer." In an effort to reestablish contact with the processing units, management has now introduced video display units that allow the operator to again understand what is happening within the plant system. Even in this heavily capital-intensive industry, the actions of the individual employee can have a traumatic impact on the effectiveness of the operations.

The two contrasting management types Shulman terms "pluralist" and "humanistic" were very instructive to me in terms of their contrasting approaches to technological change. In illustrating how these kinds of different management styles would address the issue of technology, Shulman also helps clarify some of the other underlying themes of the articles that are found in this section. In a sense, Shulman describes the limits of humanism. By acknowledging that "attempts at democratization most often have ended up in power grabs involving confrontation rather than meaningful negotiation," Shulman seems at least to reintroduce the concept of a hierarchy of authority into the workplace. The reassertion that a manager can come to the conclusion that certain employees must be released because of the effects of technological change without compromising on humanism is also reassuring.

Finally, Shulman reintroduces the concept of individual differences as he describes the humanistic manager's outlook on technological change. This distinction allows the humanistic manager to differentiate between various advisory contributions and yet maintain the decision making responsibility within the management sphere. All too often, it appears that those who use the term "humanism" are really talking about the kind of pluralism Shulman describes as being chaotic in implementation. To work constructively toward both economic improvement and the enhancement of worker self-esteem is not, in either Shulman's or my view, equivalent to the democratization of the workplace.

To a large extent, Shulman's description of his managerial types tends to overshadow his outline of the introduction of technological change. His identification of the five phases of this change should not be overlooked by the practitioner. There are many small alterations in the workplace (at least by comparison to massive technological change) which many managers have significant influence over. In particular, word processing will become part of each office in the country at some point. Understanding the kind of sequences Shulman outlines ought to be helpful to any operating manager as he or she approaches the question of introducing this kind of grass roots level change in the workplace. While I am certain that the long-term effects of such changes will be constructive for both the economy and the individuals who work in large organizations, I am certain that there are many who will find the wrong way to introduce such equipment, with consequent dissatisfaction and disruption.

Shulman' framework for understanding how to humanize technology represents a conceptual tool in approaching organizational change. The remaining two articles in this section, those by Lippitt and Alderfer, are even more action-oriented chapters. Each presents a methodology for approaching issues of organizational change and is written from the point of view of a skilled consultant. More than any of the other chapters in this section, these last two are "how-to-do-it" writings.

As a practitioner I have found that the appropriate diagnostic strategy is often shaped by the nature of the problem and the context in which it emerges. In this sense, Alderfer's work on the methodology of diagnosis in organizations seems to pay too little attention to the nature of specific problems. Nowhere in his chapter does Alderfer identify a problem that has caused a desire for diagnosis. In my experience, there has almost always been a set of problematic circumstances leading to the belief that a formal examination of the organization is required. Perhaps it is because my experience with organization diagnosis has been very problem-centered that I find it extremely difficult to maintain a separation between diagnosis and recommendations for change. Clearly, that is the central distinction in Alderfer's thesis and one that is sustained throughout his paper.

Every individual, whether practitioner, academician, or consultant, approaches an organization with preconceived ideas as to how an organization ought to function. Obviously, the nature of theory is to create a tighter, more internally consistent view of organizational functioning than would exist in the absence of the theory. It seems to me important that a potential client of a given organizational consultant should determine the theoretical biases of that consultant before beginning the entry process. The ways in which theoretical biases enter into the relationship are many, but Alderfer gives a very good example when he describes the ways in which the diagnostician should deal with the formal leaders of an organization who predetermine that subordinates "will" participate in data collection. Alderfer suggests that the leaders should be directed to produce greater involvement and participation at lower levels so as to "produce higher commitment and eventually more valid data." The belief that such results will follow greater subordinate involvement is, to my mind, a theoretical bias not borne out by empirical evidence. To introduce such recommendations into an organization is to begin to push in the direction of change well in advance of the diagnostic event's completion.

As I indicated above, it seems to me that most invitations to assist in the process of organizational diagnosis stem from a concern on the part of the formal leaders of the organization that a problem exists which can no longer be dealt with through more routine and traditional methods. Therefore, the pressure to produce constructive recommendations for change following the diagnosis will be great in nearly every case. It is usually possible to anticipate the recommended solution that will stem from the diagnosis by being aware of the diagnostician's prior writings and organizational interventions. I do not believe that there is such a thing as "diagnosis in the abstract." While there may be some who believe that increased understanding of the system is a sufficient goal for organizational diagnosis, I doubt that there are many pragmatic managers who would accept that as a suitable conclusion to a diagnostic effort.

A key concept in Alderfer's chapter is concerned with the distinction between underbounded and overbounded systems. The boundedness of the system does seem to be a useful concept in many of the processes Alderfer describes. In particular, the way in which he suggests data and theory be intertwined in providing feedback seems quite sensible once the differences in the two kinds of systems are understood. Again, with my bias toward problem-centered diagnosis, I am looking for the utility in this concept and do see that a skillful feedback session tailored to the over- or under-boundedness of the system can enhance the follow-up efforts which should flow from such feedback.

I think it is important to understand that organizational diagnosis is not an event that occurs only under contract to an outside consultant. These kinds of efforts take place in most organizations on a continual basis, usually under the supervision of relatively untrained managers. Certainly, the elaborate process Alderfer describes is a relatively rare occurrence for most organizations. The more frequent event is the activity of the internal researcher who works continually to improve the operation of various segments of the organization. While Alderfer sees severe limitations on such an individual's ability to function as a diagnostician, it seems to me that tremendous advantages can be brought to bear in such a process if a person is already within the organization. The challenge will always be to maintain some sense of objectivity, although that is a challenge for both inside and outside researchers.

The final article in this section, by Lippitt, is concerned with humanizing organizational change. Here we have the extreme in specificity. As Lippitt acknowledges, this chapter is a kit-bag of "how-to-do-it" instructions in establishing the circumstances necessary for change. It is useful to fit Lippitt's approaches into the categories established by Shulman. It is fairly apparent that what Lipitt calls humanizing Shulman would call "pluralizing." Shulman has asserted that humane management involves the *selective* encouragement of contribution to the change process. There is an openness and "informed honesty" about planned innovations (changes) coupled with an acute awareness that different values exist within the organization. Lippitt's underlying assumptions seem more inclined toward an equivalency of skill and authority antithetical to effective organizational performance.

Lippitt presents a series of structured exercises intended to produce psychological involvement and commitment to the goals and methods of the change process. He expresses the belief that simply providing a clear rationale for a planned change will not produce an "adequate level of involvement to mobilize wholehearted collaboration and energy commitment to the change effort." This assertion, which runs counter to my own observations, is the foundation for the elaborate sequence of group problem-solving exercises Lippitt then presents as necessary to produce successful, humane change.

It seems to me that several factors would have to be present before an organization would embark upon Lippitt's "regimen." Among these factors are an articulate and dedicated workforce, an uncertain management, and a nearly endless supply of time. While I firmly believe that the effectiveness of a decision is a function of both the quality of the decision and the commitment to implementation, I feel that Lippitt's approach is overly solicitous. While there may be public sector environments that could support the investment his methods call for, I doubt that a private sector management could generate much enthusiasm. If one were operating with a volunteer workforce in a climate of mutual interdependence with minimal expertise in the management ranks, then Lippitt's recommendations might be adopted in order to sustain and direct the effort.

Although I see little in Lippitt's writing that can be uncritically applied to a profit-making environment, I do believe that some of his observations bear noting by practitioners. In particular, his emphasis on the need to attend to the natural inclination to want to keep things the way they are is an admonition that should be referred to frequently in any changing environment. This tendency needs to be at least acknowledged, especially among those who may have performed in a stable environment for a long period of time.

CONCLUDING COMMENTS

Having reacted to each of the chapters in this section, I would like to highlight what I see as some unifying themes in these writings. One that is expressed in various ways is that of individual choice. Most pointedly underscored in Pinto's but also in several other chapters is the desire of the employee to be given an informed choice in the terms and conditions of employment. This expectation does alter the way in which organization change should be planned and implemented. However, even this phenomenon, which seems to me relatively pervasive, must be tempered by an awareness of individual differences. Few of the authors in this section deal explicitly with the individuality of the members of a workforce. The practitioner, however, ignores this factor at his or her own peril. Despite the exhortations of experts and theorists, people will continue to vary in skills, interests, and motivation. The mix of these attributes in a given group of people will have much to do with any effort to improve organizational effectiveness.

A corollary to the influence of individual differences in the workforce is the effect of individual leadership on organizational change. None of the writings in this section includes leadership in its discussion although this is the most important force in inducing significant and lasting changes in the way things are done in organizations. Persuasive and insightful individuals, operating within the traditional framework of hierarchical authority, are likely to continue altering and renewing the organizations within which we live and work. Since the fundamental values that underlie our approaches to the full range of organizational experiences—power, career, productivity, involvement, technology, autonomy—are being transformed by our post-industrial existence, it follows that leaders now espouse more humane policies and practices than those of past eras.

It is not accidental that the Age Discrimination in Employment Act of

1978 did not raise the mandatory retirement age of executives. In the end, retirement will continue to be a factor producing significant organization change.

It is fashionable to suggest that the rate of change is increasing and that future events will therefore be more uncertain and temporary than similar past events. As environments become more uncertain, it is essential that people who are trying to manage those environments develop increasingly complex cognitive structures in order to be effective. I believe a careful reading of the chapters in Part III will aid in that development process.

REFERENCES

1. Jones, A. P. & James, L. R. Psychological climate: Dimensions and relationships of individual and aggregated work environment perceptions. *Organizational Behavior and Human Performance,* 1979, **23,** 201–250.
2. Guion, R. M. A note on organizational climate. *Organizational Behavior and Human Performance,* 1973, **9,** 120–125.
3. Standing, T. E. An application of information theory to individual differences in satisfaction with the work itself. Unpublished dissertation, Bowling Green State University, 1971.

EPILOGUE

This epilogue was written as we were editing the final page proofs. Our basic outlook about the prospects for developing organizations which are both productive and humane has changed little since we began this project two years ago. However, due to some developments since we first outlined the book and our desire to reemphasize a few points, we decided to add this brief epilogue.

For the most part, recent developments have reinforced our basic outlook. As we suggested in our introduction and as many of the authors demonstrated, there is a great deal which managers could do—*right now*—to make their organizations both more productive and humane. However, it is important to note that the achievement of these dual objectives simultaneously is not going to take place as easily or through as rational a process as many academics and consultants have made it appear. Such academics and consultants often have given far too little attention to the context in which managers and organizations exist. The fabric of any given organization and of our social/political/economic system as a whole constrain (although do not necessarily determine) what realistically can be done.

In many cases managers are very fortunate; they can choose *both* improved productivity and increased humanization. Our authors have pointed out many such situations. For example, it is clear that selection, career planning, and training processes can all be designed to produce substantial gains on both dimensions. However, it is also true that sometimes managers must, at least in the shortrun, choose one set of criteria over the other. For example, Kotter and Schlesinger (1979) observed that initiators of change under some conditions (e.g. when strong resistance is anticipated, the resistors have great power relative to the initiators, and the stakes are high) may find it advantageous to employ strategies which ignore the interests of many people who currently are part of the organization. Moreover, as such writers as Pfeffer and Salancik (1977) have reminded us, organizations are composed of actors who have a variety of competing (as well as common) interests. What some people view as productive or humane will be seen as just the opposite by others. Similarly, students of organization effectiveness (e.g. Steers, 1975) have observed that effectiveness is a multidimensional concept. In short, neither productivity nor humanization can be defined unambiguously when the interests of all actors in an organization are included. Consequently, the particular choices between either the general criterion of humanization or of productivity and the specific elements that define these criteria do not lend themselves to simple calculable decisions. Rather, these choices reflect conflicting values and priorities and are influenced by (1) external events over which most individual organizations, at any point in time, exercise little control and (2) the distribution of power within an individual organization.

We believe that many behavioral scientists and management consultants have done a disservice by focusing almost exclusively on how one or a few changes can satisfy the desire of managers for a "quick fix" to achieve both productivity and humanization. The eagerness of sellers to sell and buyers to buy a "quick fix" seems to have contributed to a rather constant flow of fads in the field. What we see as missing in all this is a full recognition of the complexity of the problems and consequently the failure to develop multidimensional approaches.

In this book we have tried to include what we believe are the most important of these dimensions over which individual managers can exercise some degree of control. Despite our attempt to be inclusive, we regret one significant omission.

THE CASE OF JAPAN

At this moment the absence of a chapter on work and management in Japan appears to be an important omission. Although for some time Americans have been interested in learning about Japanese management, in the last year or so American managers have increasingly looked to Japan for ways to increase American productivity. The Japanese seem to be of particular interest because their methods appear to combine many features which Western writers have included in their treatments of humanization with great advances in the levels of productivity and product quality.

We believe that managers and students of management who are interested in finding ways to improve productivity and humanize the workplace at the same time have a great deal to learn from Japan. We will not attempt to summarize this information here, but suggest that the reader consult an article by Ouchi and Johnson (1978), and books by Dore (1973), Pascale and Atlas (1981) for descriptions of the Japanese perspective and an interpretation of the implications of the Japanese experience for the design of Western organization. In addition to what we may learn from the actual substance of the Japanese system, we believe there is another lesson to be learned. Those of us concerned with combining humanization and productivity in American organizations can learn a great deal from attempting to understand the recent response of American management, academicians, and media to the Japanese system.

While parts of the Japanese approach might be modified and transferred into the United States, we feel such possibilities have, like so many other ready-made answers, been considerably oversold.

As Pascale and Athos (1981) observed:

> We may not expect to borrow wholesale and directly from the Japanese . . . . We can't ape the Japanese system. But we can incorporate some of their approach, which will strengthen our areas of weakness (p. 27).

Later they added:

> No quick introduction of uncoordinated parts will address the whole problem. Quality control circles, "Theory Y" reorganizations, team building, two-week organizational development programs, etc., etc.—each has its uses, but unless there is an overall *fit* of all the managerial parts across time, then there will be little sustained leverage and few results (p. 201).

In these two statements, Pascale and Athos have made critical points. First, they tell us that borrowing can be useful, but it can only be done with moderation. Second, they tell us that the congruence among the parts is crucial. Unfortunately these realistic assessments, which we believe apply to most of the ideas contained in this book, seldom seem to guide attempts to apply knowledge to the management of human resources. It is in this vein that we suggest we can learn nearly as much about the prospects for humanizing and improving productivity from considering the response of Americans to the Japanese techniques, as we can from the techniques themselves.

Consider the following scenario which begins with the fact that the United States perceives itself to have a problem with productivity. Japan has become a formidable competitor in such industries as automobiles, where for some time the United States has thought of itself the best in the world. Some obvious differences between Japanese firms and our own are observed and these few differences become highlighted in the popular press. Sensing an opportunity to make careers and profits, writers, teachers, and consultants rush to inform American managers about how these variations can be used to help solve the problems managers perceive.

The result is a classic example of the development of a "quick fix". Unfortunately these efforts omit a great deal of key information. The great complexity of the relationship between the Japanese production system, its cultural heritage, and its political system are seldom conveyed. For example, Dore (1973) observed that, relative to British workers, Japanese workers show greater meekness towards authority and a stronger commitment to the work ethic. Moreover, Dore concluded that among other things, the average Japanese is less of an individualist, less self-confident and ". . . more childishly naive" (p. 298). While these factors may contribute to greater productivity on a variety of tasks, we would not consider these to be consistent with humanization.

In attempting to outline a "quick fix", the realities which constrain the social change process are overlooked. Preliminary steps are bypassed. Managers often find the material interesting and important, but "too abstract" or too far removed from their own organization to be very useful.

Although it is too early to predict exactly what impact the interest in Japanese management will have, it would not surprise us if after many stories in the *Wall Street Journal, Business Week,* etc.; a few specials on TV; and a number of programs for managers on Japan, little will have changed. Some companies will have introduced some things, reported some initial success with them, and then let them die on the vine. Most companies will have changed little, if at all. Undoubtedly by then a new fad or two will have received widespread exposure in the media and management will be busy learning about it. We offer this skeptical prediction despite the fact that we agree with some of the absolute merits of some of the Japanese philosophy and practices as described by Hatvany and Pucik (1981) and Ouchi (1981).

Why will so little have changed? One important set of reasons is likely to be the fact that the media, the educators, and the managers have attempted to introduce new pieces without attending to the "fit" or to the Gestalt. The lure of the "quick fix" will prevent what is really useful from being implemented. We know many things which, in isolation, would have a good chance of producing desired outcomes. However, such interventions are not to be made in isolation. They are made in a complex social context, which involves habits, values, institutionalized procedures, power systems, and so forth. Whether that context be a large society or small business organization, it plays an important part in determining the success of the change. Change either must be gradual enough so as to operate within a narrow latitude which is acceptable and workable within the context, or it must be so revolutionary that the context is changed drastically. Neither approach will be very satisfactory to those searching for easy answers. Unfortunately, there do not seem to be any alternatives.

HUMANIZING AND SELF-HELP

We want to conclude with an observation about the process of humanizing as viewed in the United States. For the most part, treatments of humanization which are familiar to American managers have a common underlying assumption—humanizing is something *management* does. This perspective tells only part of the story and consequently is misleading. Many aspects of humanizing involve the creation of conditions which are "better for" individuals in the organization. In this sense, humanizing is also something that lower level participants do for themselves.

There are many things individuals do at work which humanize their jobs for themselves and their peers. The formation of coalitions or formal groups (e.g. unions) to exercise influence is one obvious example. Others include manipulating the people in organizations who control resources or set the rules, the supervisors, and one's peers and subordinates to make things better for oneself. Donald Roy's (1960) famous study "Banana Time" and the important extension of his work by Burawoy (1980) show how through "games", individuals can improve their conditions and gain autonomy in the workplace. The fact that these "self-help" efforts are often in conflict with productivity and management's other goals does not make them less humanizing. What this conflict does indicate is support for one of our basic contentions—humanization and productivity do not always go together.

However, as our focus in this book indicates, there are many unrealized opportunities to have more of both outcomes than we currently do. In short, while in some cases we will have to make choices, there are great opportunities for optimizing. We believe that contributors to this volume have demonstrated a host of ways which individual managers who want to, can simultaneously make their organization more humane and productive. However, the process will almost always be a long one, requiring persistence, patience, and a tailoring of procedures in a particular work setting if sustenance and continuity are to be provided for. There is no "quick fix"; there are, however, many places where work can begin.

REFERENCES

Burawoy, M. *Manufacturing consent. Changes in the labor process under monopoly capitalism.* Chicago: University of Chicago Press, 1979.

Dore, R. *British factory–Japanese factory. The origins of rational diversity in industrial relations.* London: Allen & Unwin Ltd., 1973.

Hatvany, N. & Pucik, V. Japanese management practices and productivity. *Organizational Dynamics,* 1981, **9** (Spring), 4–21.

Kotter, J. P. & Schlesinger, L. A. Choosing strategies for change. *Harvard Business Review,* 1979, **57** (March-April), 106–113.

Ouchi, W. G. Organizational paradigms: A commentary on Japanese management and theory 2 organizations. *Organizational Dynamics,* 1981, **9** (Spring), 36–43.

Ouchi, W. G. & Johnson, J. B. Types of organizational control and their relationship to emotional well–being. *Administrative Science Quarterly,* 1978, **23,** 293–317.

Pascale, R. T. & Athos, A. G. *The art of Japanese management.* New York: Simon & Schuster, 1981.

Pfeffer, J. & Salancik, G. R. Organization design: the case for a coalitional model of organizations. *Organizational Dynamics,* 1977, **6** (Autumn), 15–29.

Roy, D. F. Banana time—job satisfaction and informal interaction. *Human Organization,* 1960, **18,**158–168.

AUTHOR INDEX

SUBJECT INDEX